The Catholic Church

The Catholic Church

Nature, Reality and Mission

Walter Kasper

Bloomsbury T&T Clark
An imprint of Bloomsbury Publishing Plc

BLOOMSBURY
LONDON • NEW DELHI • NEW YORK • SYDNEY

Bloomsbury T&T Clark
An imprint of Bloomsbury Publishing Plc

Imprint previously known as T&T Clark

50 Bedford Square
London
WC1B 3DP
UK

1385 Broadway
New York
NY 10018
USA

www.bloomsbury.com

First published 2015

British Library Cataloguing-in-Publication Data
A catalogue record for this books is available from the British Library.

ISBN: PB: 978-1-4411-8709-3
ePDF: 978-1-4411-1754-0
ePub: 978-1-4411-4908-4

Library of Congress Cataloging-in-Publication Data
A catalog record for this book is available from the Library of Congress.

Typeset by Fakenham Prepress Solutions, Fakenham, Norfolk NR21 8NN
Printed and bound in Great Britain

To my two sisters Hildegard and Inge and my brother-in-law Roman

CONTENTS

TRANSLATOR'S NOTE

As a rule, quotations from the Bible have been taken from the *New Jerusalem Bible*. In addition, this translation uses the *English Standard Version* where a modification of wording was necessary to highlight the author's emphasis.

The translations of Vatican documents, including the documents of the Second Vatican Council, are taken from the English versions as they are published on the Vatican's own homepage. Likewise, English standard translations have been used for the texts of the Church Fathers.

English translations of books quoted and referred to have been used wherever possible. Where an English quotation has been used, the reference in the footnotes has been adapted accordingly. In all other cases, i.e. where I have translated directly from the German text, the German title has been retained in the footnote and, if there is one, the title of the English translation is given in brackets. Where Cardinal Kasper quoted German translations of books that were originally written in English, the English original has been used.

As the following terms are central to the book, a short note on capitalization:

'Church' (with a capital C) refers to the one Church of faith, 'church' (with a small c) refers to a specific church, a building or denomination.

'Catholic' (with a capital C) is used for Roman Catholic whereas 'catholic' (with a small c) is used with the meaning of universal.

Finally, 'the Council' (with a capital C) is the Second Vatican Council.

Thomas Hoebel

Editor's Note

At a relatively late phase in the development of this important project, the publisher deemed it expedient to borrow an extra pair of editorial eyes for a fresh look at the manuscript. I have checked references both in the original German text and in this English translation, standardized theological terminology throughout to match current academic usages, revised the index according to the updated pagination, and made general remarks concerning English syntax and style. I have not made any changes to the editorial decisions itemized in the Translator's note, above.

R. David Nelson

PREFACE

The present volume, *The Catholic Church: Nature – Reality – Mission*, has a long history. I wanted to write this book after the two monographs *Jesus the Christ* and *The God of Jesus Christ* and towards the end of my academic teaching career. More than twenty years have passed since then. During that time, the project grew and matured because of pastoral, global church and ecumenical experiences. As it could not have been otherwise, some perspectives have evolved and broadened, and many ideas have become more concrete.

My basic commitments – to 'scholarly rigor, ecclesial faithfulness and critical constructive contemporaneousness' – have remained the same. Lacking access to some of the tools standard in academia, I might have missed some things. Nevertheless, in the present ecclesial crisis and beyond, I hope that this book, which aims to combine academic study with pastoral and ecumenical insight, can provide some theological bearings and awaken new joy, both within the Church and for the Church.

I must mention many companions and friends within and outside the Catholic Church to whom I owe thanks. I am particularly indebted to the staff of the institute bearing my name in Vallendar, to its director Prof. Dr George Augustin, and to Dipl. Theol. Stefan Ley for his strong support in the final editing. At Herder I am grateful to Dr Bruno Steimer for his invaluable publishing support.

I dedicate this book to both of my sisters and my brother-in-law, who have accompanied me along the way for ages and with whom, after so many demands and countless journeys, I have always found a good home during those short-lived holiday weeks.

Cardinal Walter Kasper
Rome, Easter week 2011

I

My journey in and with the Church

1. The Church – 'black, but beautiful'

It may seem surprising to begin an examination of the nature, reality and mission of the Catholic Church with a description of my own journey in and with the Church. I have thought long and hard about such a course of inquiry. In the end, the conviction prevailed that I should not write about the Church as a reality detached from me and only of academic interest. Rather, I wanted to write about the very Church in which I have lived now for more than three quarters of a century and in which I feel at home; the Church which I still love despite some of its weaknesses and disappointments, and for which I have worked and have committed my whole life.

Of course, I am aware that ecclesiology, like theology in general, does not derive from subjective experiences which are kept umblemished and lucidly in perspective, but rather from 'objective' sources. Ecclesiology does not emerge out of personal experiences with the Church, whether good or bad, but out of the *common* experience of the Church, both past and present. Precisely so, ecclesiology must proceed from objective sources: from Holy Scripture, the testimony of the liturgy and the Church Fathers, from the great theologians of the past, from the documents of the magisterium, from the testimony of the saints and the whole lived and suffered history of the Church in the past as well as in the present. Such objective sources do not constitute a dead tradition but a living one, a Tradition that is still being lived out by millions of believers. Therefore, if one wishes not to treat the topic of the Church only historically or sociologically, then one must give an account of one's own faith and life in and with the Church. Consequently, ecclesiology always involves personal testimony as well. Ecclesiology has a peculiar set of temporal and historical coordinates and is also inevitably influenced by personal experiences of the Church.

My own personal experience of the Church has a long history.[1] It extends back to my youth, to my time as a student and to my first years as a priest, and includes experiences of ecclesial life during the Third Reich, the Second World War and prior to the Second Vatican Council. It has been influenced by the eventful and moving years during which the Council was in session, and also by developments in the post-conciliar period. Then there was the long period during which time I served as teacher of theology both at home and abroad, my ten years as bishop of a large diocese and as chairman of the *Kommission Weltkirche der Deutschen Bischofskonferenz*, a position for which I was given responsibility over ecclesial charities (Misereor, Adveniat, Caritas International, Renovabis). In addition to all of this are my eleven years of global church experience while in Rome gained from my responsibility for promoting unity among all Christians – a task which required making and maintaining countless contacts with non-Catholic churches and church communities, and, finally, from my participation in the dialogue with Judaism, which, for a German, proved to be a particularly challenging undertaking.

During all of these periods my diverse activities were combined with concrete pastoral duties in parishes as well as in hospitals, as a bishop in incalculable visitations to parishes, with pastoral experiences during stays at universities both at home and abroad, on numerous journeys to the local churches of other continents where I encountered many situations of poverty and misery and, finally, during visits to Catholic and non-Catholic churches and ecclesial communities in all parts of the world. In contrast to what some people may think, in the course of such journeys I never saw myself as a church diplomat. With all due diligence I laboured to be that to which I had been called, namely, a minister. I have always been drawn to the words of Yves Congar: '*Vaste monde, ma paroisse*', 'the wide world, my parish'. Following Ephesians 4:15, my motto as a bishop was '*Veritatem in caritate*' – 'To do the truth in love'.

Throughout all of these years, I have been able to experience the global church in all its diversity, in its great richness and vitality as well as its problems, dramatic changes, difficulties and also crises. These experiences mirror, in personal perspective, something of the way and nature of the Church, its joys and hardships in the twentieth and early twenty-first centuries. My personal history reflects more than five decades' worth of church history and the history of theology.

Especially in recent years and despite all of the positive, joyful and enriching experiences, I have also witnessed the crises which have shaken the Church in Germany and Western Europe, and which have unsettled and worried many Christians. I have not only suffered from the Church but also with the Church. There are the horrible scandals of which we have heard so much in recent years and which one cannot condemn enough, the decreasing numbers of active church members – especially among young people – and the dramatic decline of candidates for the ministry and holy orders. What troubles me most of all is the state of what we might say is the Church's inner soul: the lack of vision and enthusiasm for the Church among its members, the emigration taking place and the even growing chasm between churches, the almost *de facto* schism between the hierarchical view from 'above' and the elements of the Church 'below', the silent exodus of many and, on top of all of that, the spitefulness with which 'left' and 'right' attack each other and the fact that, as a result of such insider myopia, neither side is able to notice that the real problems and challenges facing the Church are, in fact, located elsewhere. It is no wonder that so many are disappointed and are turning away.

I am thus moved by the question of how the Church can continue along this path. I do not have any any remedies to offer, and those of which I am aware seem to me to be mostly too short-sighted. Yet, if one is convinced as a Christian that the Church is more than a sheer human institution and that, rather, it is led and constantly renewed by God's Spirit, then one will understand these crises which are shaking the Church at present as the birth pangs, not of the advent of a new Church, but of the emergence of a new and renewed historical form of the one church for all time.

In this difficult and, in many respects, confusing situation, I would like to propose an ecclesiological reorientation on the basis of the great treasure of Tradition and my first-hand knowledge of numerous ecclesial situations. With this effort I fulfil a long-standing desire. Towards the end of my time in academia, after the publication of the books *Jesus the Christ* and *The God of Jesus Christ*, I intended to write a book about *The Church of Jesus Christ*. My call to the episcopal office and later to Rome rendered this impossible. I did not get beyond many individual articles and a rough draft.[2] Yet, over the course of the last two decades and through various experiences in 'practical ecclesiology', my horizon has expanded and many ideas have become concrete. The basic concerns have remained the same.

What has endured through all of this is my love for the Church. And not just any church, but, specifically, the Catholic Church, in which, for me, the Church of Jesus Christ remains concretely present and which, nonetheless, has to renew itself through purification and sanctification in order to be perceived more clearly as the catholic Church, as the Church of Jesus Christ, and as a Church for the people. As the Church Fathers have already said, it is 'black, but beautiful' (Song 1:5). It is lovely, in spite of all of its imperfections and wrinkles (Eph. 5:27). It is of this beauty that I speak in this book in order to demonstrate how the Church can remain the one and same Church of Jesus Christ and still not have to appear old. It can be new and young and can communicate to future generations what they need more than anything else: the hope that comes from faith.

2. My coming-of-age during the pre-conciliar renewals

In my childhood and youth, and as a student and during my first years as a priest, I encountered in the family, in the seminary and in the parish what today is often called the pre-conciliar *Volkskirche*. The difficult situation during the Nazi period, the Second World War and the immediate post-war years was so different from that of today that it is quite a challenge to help younger people in particular understand what happened in those days and what it was like to live through them.

Church and regular attendance at worship services, as well as praying together daily in the home, were integral parts of our lives. Yet my experiences of the Church at that time were by no means, as some might perhaps think, marked by restriction, lack of freedom or even unenlightened darkness. On the contrary, I experienced the Church as home. It was, despite all external constraints, a vibrant church rooted in its people, a church where I felt at home in the rhythm of the church year. The dissociation from National Socialism through both my parents' education and the attitude of the majority of those within the Catholic milieu further strengthened my sense of identification with the Church. I was proud to belong to the Church and proud of our diocesan bishop, Johannes Baptista Sproll († 1949), who, from the beginning, courageously opposed the Nazis and who, because of his brave speeches, was the only German bishop to be sent into exile. Due to such experiences the idea of becoming a priest had been growing slowly in me since childhood.

In addition to all of this, after the Second World War and in the *Bund Neudeutschland* [a Catholic democratic organisation, T.H.], I experienced the late phase of the German Youth Movement (*Bündische Jugend*). The First World War brought an end to the age of the bourgeois and, later, during the interwar period, Europe witnessed an ecclesial and cultural fresh start. The liturgical and Bible movements paved the way for certain aspects of church renewal that eventually came to full expression through the work of the council. Romano Guardini's famous words, 'The Church awakes in the souls',[3] characterize this trajectory and with it the basic attitude of a whole generation towards the Church. Signs of the dawning of a new era of the Church, an ecclesial spring, were in the air. The motto of the *Bund Neudeutschland*, '*Neue Lebensgestaltung in Christus* (Leading a new life in Christ)', at this point became and has remained decisive for me.

Quite early in my life, the writings of Guardini, in particular *The Spirit of the Liturgy* (1918), *Sacred Signs* (1922) and *The Lord* (1937), had a great influence on me. At grammar school I was enthused by Gertrud von Le Fort's *Hymns to the Church* (1924). As a grammar school pupil, I devoured her narratives as well as those by Werner Bergengruen, Reinhold Schneider, Edzard Schaper and others who were then considered to be representatives of a 'Christian fiction'. A special experience was the first papal audience immediately after my A-Levels in the spring of 1952. About 20 young members of the *Bund Neudeutschland* were received in a private audience by Pope Pius XII, a pope who enjoyed the greatest respect in Germany and worldwide.

In retrospect, of course, I can sense the great distance between that time and the present. After the collapse of the bourgeois era during the First World War, the German Youth Movement searched for a new, Christian form of culture and lifestyle. After the Second World War, we were fascinated by the idea of the European founding fathers, which could only be a Western idea because of the division between the Western and Eastern Blocs. This worldview came to an end with the emancipation movement of the so-called 1968 student revolution and, finally, with the collapse of the Eastern Bloc in 1989. This sea change has led, subsequently, to a crisis in European culture and, at the same time, to a crisis in the Church. We will discuss in detail, below, the totally new challenges that have emerged with these crises.[4]

In between all this there was, for my generation, a new beginning with the Second Vatican Council (1962–5) and the post-conciliar reforms. Because of the preparation I experienced in the context of the ecclesial renewal movements, I did not see the Council as a break, but rather as a further step along the way we had been travelling for a long time and for which, in fact, we had unknowingly been waiting. Although the announcement of the Council on 25 January 1959, by Pope John XXIII was surprising, the Council itself did not come out of the blue. Through the interwar renewal movement, the Council had been in the works and, whether consciously or not, was longed for, both theologically and spiritually, in the hearts and minds of many. My years studying at Tübingen strengthened my own desire for the Council.

3. Theological formation as a student

I received my theological training for the tasks ahead by studying theology from 1952 to 1956 in Tübingen (with the exception of one semester in Munich). After my ordination to the priesthood (1957) and one year as a chaplain in Stuttgart, I was able to deepen my knowledge of theology while working as lecturer at the *Tübinger Theologenkonvikt Wilhelmstift* (1958–61), and, subsequently, as academic assistant in the faculty for Catholic theology (1961–4).

The Tübingen School

One might think that studying theology in Tübingen can hardly have done any good for the ecclesial spirit. At times it has been almost fashionable to quote Vladimir Solovyov's comment that the antichrist will be an honorary doctor of the theological faculty of Tübingen.[5] Yet, those who know only this about Tübingen have never encountered the Tübingen of Hölderlin, Schelling, Hegel, Mörike and Uhland. Romano Guardini and Eduard Spranger taught there after the Second World War. The Catholic Tübingen theology at that time was neither a petrified Neo-Scholasticism nor infected by the spirit of a shallow liberalism. It was characterized by the spirit of the Catholic Tübingen School of the nineteenth century, which was inspired by the Church Fathers as embodied in particular by Johann Sebastian Drey († 1853), Johann Adam Möhler († 1838) and the systematic theologian Johannes Evangelist von Kuhn († 1887). In the nineteenth century, these theologians contributed substantially to the ecclesial renewal that followed the Enlightenment and Secularization. They had an influential effect on those theologians who, in turn, decisively influenced the Second Vatican Council.[6]

The Catholic Tübingen School of the nineteenth century was guided by three principles: scholarly rigour, ecclesial faithfulness, and critical constructive contemporaneousness.[7] It was in this spirit that my teacher Josef Rupert Geiselmann († 1970) taught me the ecclesiologies of Johann Sebastian Drey and Johann Adam Möhler. Geiselmann also taught me Möhler's theological development, which progressed from the Catholic enlightenment to a pneumatological and finally a Christological understanding of the Church. The fundamental theologian Heinrich Fries († 1998), as well as (during my semester in Munich) the fundamental theologian Gottlieb Söhngen († 1971), introduced us to the thinking of John Henry Newman, also one of the great pioneers of twentieth-century theology. Newman's doctrine helped me to arrive at a personal understanding of the faith. His *Apologia pro vita sua* and his teaching on the development of doctrine deepened and served to reify the historical understanding of Church that we had learnt from the Tübingen theologians.

Möhler and Newman are justifiably viewed as the ones who prepared the way for the ecclesiology of the twentieth century which found its universal ecclesial recognition through the Second Vatican Council. In addition, as a student I read with enthusiasm *The Spirit of Catholicism* (1924) by Karl Adam († 1966), a younger representative of the Tübingen School. This book was published in many editions and translations and influenced and enthused an entire generation of priests and laypeople. In contrast, the significance of another important pioneer (and not only for Italy), Antonio Rosmini († 1855), became apparent to me only later.[8]

The nature of the liturgy and the Eucharist, the centre and climax of ecclesial life, was revealed to me during my time as a student through the above-mentioned volumes by Romano Guardini, *The Spirit of the Liturgy* (1918) and *Sacred Signs* (1922), and, in particular, through Josef Andreas Jungmann's *Missarum Solemnia* (1949; *The Mass of the Roman Rite*). This standard textbook on the history of the liturgy introduced me to a deeper understanding of and historical access to the Eucharistic mystery, and also a sense for the liturgical reform in the wake of Vatican II. The Council Fathers did not intend to abolish or destroy the Latin liturgical tradition. Rather, they held that fundamental structures were to be made more transparent so that the people of God would have better access to the liturgy of the Eucharist. Regrettably, this transparency also resulted in superficialities. Yet, neither the Council itself nor the aforementioned forerunners of the reforms can be blamed for this.[9]

Since my time as a student in Tübingen, I have thus been familiar with living historical as well as pneumatological and Christological approaches to the Church. For me, the Church has never been merely an institution, but the body of Christ, kept alive and constantly renewed by the Holy Spirit. I have been committed to this ecclesiological vision of the Tübingen School, especially to the thought of Johann Adam Möhler, ever since.[10]

In my doctoral thesis, *Die Lehre von der Tradition in der Römischen Schule* (1962), I demonstrated that, already in the nineteenth century, there had not only been conflicts between Tübingen and Rome, but also a positive influence of Möhler on the Roman theology of the time (Perrone, Passaglia, Schrader, Franzelin). In addition, I argued that Möhler's view of the Church had an astonishing influence on John Henry Newman in England, and, as I discovered later, in Russia on Aleksey Khomyakov and Vladimir Solovyov, who, in turn, had a great influence on the Orthodox theology of the twentieth century. Above all, through my study of the Roman School I also encountered its most important representative, Matthias Josef Scheeben, and his volume *The Mysteries of Christianity*, then considered a kind of insider tip for those looking for some more demanding theological reading.

This early formation through the Tübingen School also formed the reason behind my dislike of the original topic of my habilitation: the beginnings of an independent ecclesiology in late medieval theologians such as James of Viterbo, John of Ragusa and Juan de Torquemada. During the controversy with late medieval conciliarism, these theologians developed a doctrine of the Church which, in the end, was more of a hierarchiology than an ecclesiology. It was for this reason that I abandoned this topic following an extensive conversation with Yves Congar in Strasbourg.

Schelling and Thomas Aquinas

As the topic for my habilitation, I chose the philosophy and theology of history found in the later philosophical works of Schelling.[11] I am frequently asked why I chose precisely this topic, since it seems to lie far off the beaten track of theology. This topic interested me because of its close connection with the Tübingen theology that was influenced by German Idealism. Johann Sebastian Drey, as well as Anton Staudenmaier († 1848), who belonged to the second generation of the Tübingen School, dealt with

Schelling. Alert Catholic minds of that era, such as Franz Baader († 1841) and Josef Görres († 1848), were inspired by him. In the post-war period, different thinkers ranging from Karl Jaspers to Martin Heidegger, Jürgen Habermas and Paul Tillich occupied themselves with the later Schelling. More recently, bishop Klaus Hemmerle († 1994), who was a pupil of Bernhard Welte († 1983) in Freiburg, dealt with Schelling's later philosophy in his habilitation. Besides that, I must also name the great work by Xavier Tilliette, whom I got to know by chance in Tübingen. I was also inspired by the philosopher Walter Schulz († 2000), then teaching in Tübingen, and his interpretation of Schelling, the central thesis of which is the contention that Schelling's later philosophy is both the completion and crisis of Idealism.[12]

My encounter with the works of Schelling gave me access to modern philosophy: to Kant, Fichte and Hegel, and to the early post-idealistic epoch, in particular, to Kierkegaard, Marx and Nietzsche. Because of these studies, I could never, as many theologians still do today, consider modernity only the history of a decline into an abysmal subjectivism. Modernity, rather, is far more diverse than such stereotypical characterizations can express. Modernity also includes the Renaissance and Baroque periods in Western culture. Alongside Descartes and Kant, we find Pascal, Hamann and Herder; alongside the Enlightenment are Pietism and Romanticism; alongside Idealism, we encounter Materialism and Positivism; alongside Liberalism are conservative and restorative trends. There can be no legitimate talk of a continuous process of de-Hellenization. Platonism and neo-Platonism are quite strongly present in the Renaissance and in Idealism.

Schelling is a particularly interesting figure in the complex history of modernity. In his early natural philosophy, he highlighted the natural conditions of freedom. In his later philosophy, he questioned the limits of the modern philosophy of freedom. In this way there are lines running from Schelling directly to post-idealistic thought, which, in the work of Kierkegaard, profoundly influenced the theology of the twentieth century, and which had, through Marx and Nietzsche, a dubious reception history (*Wirkungsgeschichte*). All of this helped me in due course to find a critical-constructive position in the debates with neo-Marxist trends and the present postmodern or late-modes of thinking.

However, before I occupied myself with modern philosophy and while I was still a student, there was a essay contest over the *Quaestiones disputatae de veritate* by Thomas Aquinas. Through this, I gained an early familiarity with the most important figure of high medieval Scholasticism. In time, Thomas Aquinas would become increasingly important for my theological thinking, and also for my ecclesiology.[13] It was already while engaging with Schelling that my engagement with and appreciation of the metaphysical tradition became important for me. I expressed this again in my farewell lecture in Tübingen in 1989 on the indispensability of metaphysics for theology.[14] Without knowing the great philosophical tradition, theology will run out of breath.

Karl Rahner – Henri de Lubac – Yves Congar – Hans Küng

Additional influences emerged during these theologically formative years. I met Karl Rahner († 1984) when, already a world-famous theologian, he led the annual spiritual exercises for the theology students at the Wilhelmstift in Tübingen. I still remember the day when I bought the first volume of Rahner's *Theological Investigations* (1954). His essay 'The Development of Dogma' gripped my attention so intensely that I began reading it immediately in the street. Much of what I had been looking for as a young student was profoundly deliberated and clearly formulated in this essay. From Rahner I learnt to distinguish the abiding authenticity of church doctrine from that which emerged contingently and historically. Further, I learnt how to make authentic doctrine accessible to modern thought and so to discover in Tradition itself perspectives for the future. Even though his transcendental approach, which ultimately harkens back to Kant and Fichte, has remained alien vis-à-vis my more historically orientated way of theology, like many other theologians of my generation, I owe a great deal to Karl Rahner. He encouraged us to think for ourselves.

In addition, during this time I discovered the literature of French theologians of the then wrongly labelled '*nouvelle théologie*'. It was not, in fact, a new theology but a renewal of the old patristic and high medieval theology. I owe decisive inspirations for my understanding of the Church to, in particular, Henri de Lubac († 1991) and Yves Congar († 1995). I not only learnt from them an astounding historical knowledge of patristic, medieval and modern ecclesiology, but also gained a deeper love for the Church and its mystery.

Hans Küng arrived in Tübingen in 1960, just before the beginning of the Council. For us, his – in some respects – unconventional perspectives and ideas concerning reform had the air of freshness. My time as his assistant in Tübingen opened the door for us to develop a strong personal collaboration. Yet, I soon became wary of his attempts to force his own program of reform single-handedly and, increasingly so, in conflict with the pope and bishops. In addition, it is important to note that I was simultaneously the assistant of Hans Küng and Leo Scheffczyk († 2005). Scheffczyk was a theologian with rare integrity who was also deeply oriented and committed to the Church. During the post-conciliar upheavals, he became a rock – opposed by many, but also a symbol and source of strength and security for numerous others. I was delighted that, on the feast of Cathedra Petri in 2001, we were both received into the College of Cardinals.

A living tradition

In the following way the historical view of the Church and its Tradition, which emerged from the spirit of the Tübingen School and was rooted in the

Church Fathers, became decisive for me. Johann Sebastian Drey had spoken of the 'transmission of the faith to a continuous present'. My teacher Josef Rupert Geiselmann summarized this basic idea in his book with the telling title *Lebendiger Glaube aus geheiligter Überlieferung* (1942; Living Faith out of Sanctified Tradition). The pastoral theological consequences of this view were explained to us by the pastoral theologian Franz Xaver Arnold (1969), who insisted that it is the fundamental task of pastoral work to keep the Church alive into the future.[15] This resonates with what Popes Paul VI, John Paul II and, most recently, Benedict XVI have programmatically called the new evangelization. This pastoral aspect became fundamental for me during my time as bishop (1989–99).

It was because of this basic attitude that the terms 'conservative' and 'progressive', buzzwords both during and after the Council, have never been meaningful alternatives for me. I have always refused both labels. As a result, people from both sides have occasionally distrusted me. Yet, already the early Tübingen theologians considered themselves to be independent thinkers. Thus I have always tried to think with my own head, at times with Swabian stubbornness, and have gone my own way. It was and is my conviction that every theology has to be conservative in the sense that it keeps alive and promotes the apostolic Tradition as it has been handed down through history by the Church. Of course, one cannot preserve Tradition by engraving its formulas onto stone, repeating and inculcating it over and over again. On the contrary, the faith that is handed-down must be passed on alive. It must be translated into new questions and handed down with the future in mind. A differentiated knowledge of modern philosophy will serve to foster a constructive and, at the same time, critical engagement with modernity, and thus obviate unfruitful, stereotypical, and anti-modernisti theses.

In short, I received anything but a liberal heritage and formation, even though some have incorrectly identified me as a theological liberal. In the spirit of the Catholic Tübingen School and its living understanding of Tradition, I have always considered myself to be at home in the centre of Catholic theology.

4. The lasting significance of the Second Vatican Council

Awakening and renewal

The experience of the Second Vatican Council (1962–5) became for me a profound Church experience and a lasting reference point. When Pope John XXIII announced the Council on 25 January 1959, it was a big surprise. Thereafter followed a breathtaking, exciting and interesting time, unimaginable for the young theologians of today. We saw how the old venerable Church displayed youthful life, how it opened doors and windows and entered into inner-ecclesial dialogue as well as dialogue with other churches and religions and with modern culture. It was an awakening Church that did not dispose of or deny its Tradition, but, rather, remained true to its Tradition. Still, it broke open old barriers and so tried to make the Tradition new, alive and fruitful for the future. I am still convinced that the sixteen important documents of the Council are the compass for the way of the Church into the twenty-first century.[16]

The Second Vatican Council has frequently been called the council of the Church *about* the Church. At the Council, the Church, which had been on the streets of history for 2000 years, became more deeply aware of the nature from out of which it had so far lived and acted. In his opening speech on 11 October 1962, Pope John XXIII stated that goal of the Council was to ensure that the sacred deposit of Christian doctrine is guarded unconditionally and without falsehood and taught more efficaciously. Pope Paul VI expressed the same view at the solemn promulgation of the constitution on the Church, *Lumen gentium*, together with the decree on ecumenism, *Unitatis redintegratio*, on 21 November 1964, stating: 'This promulgation really changes nothing of the traditional doctrine of the Church. What Christ willed, we also will. What was, still is. What the Church has taught down through the centuries, we also teach. In simple terms that which was assumed, is now explicit; that which was uncertain, is now clarified; that which was mediated upon us, discussed and sometimes argued over, is now put in one clear formulation.'[17]

One can also say, in the spirit of Hans-Georg Gadamer's hermeneutics, that everything that has been true thus far and has been believed as true is, of course, also true and authoritative in the future. Yet, such truth is put into a new light and into a more comprehensive horizon; it shines anew and so becomes, in a certain sense, newly visible.[18] This new horizon in which the Council received the Tradition was expressed in the opening speech by Pope John XXIII when he defined the goal of the Council as pastoral. This pastoral self-understanding encapsulates the particular spirit of the Council. What exactly is meant by this is, of course, not easy to grasp. What does 'pastoral' in fact mean and how do the pastoral concerns relate to the doctrinal statements which the Council undoubtedly intended and made? Trying to construct an opposition between the two, as some have attempted, is a false approach. There can be no pastoral orientation without a doctrinal basis. Likewise, doctrine is in no way a dead formula carried about like a monstrance. Rather, doctrine must be pastorally translated into life and proclamation.[19]

In the meantime, the sense of fascination and enthusiasm inspired by the Council has disappeared. A time of rational stock-taking is underway, which, in part, entails a critical evaluation of the Council and its aftermath. A new generation has emerged for whom the Council is something in the remote past that belongs to another time to which, unlike my own generation, they have no personal connection. What happened and what was said at that time must be laboriously explained to them so that they might warm to it. This necessitates a rigorous hermeneutics of the Council.

Principles of conciliar hermeneutics

To be sure, we should not turn the Council into a myth onto which everyone can project their own wishes. Rather, the texts of the Council need to be carefully interpreted according to the generally valid rules of theological hermeneutics. In doing so, one should not detach the so-called real or presumed spirit of the Council from the letter of the Council. We must unfold the spirit of the Council from out of its history and texts.

The texts of the Council need to be understood from their contexts and from the occasionally acrimonious debates that took place during the Council. Next, each individual phrase must be interpreted in the light of the entire corpus of conciliar texts. In doing so, one must respect the inner hierarchy of the different documents of the Council (constitutions, decrees, declarations). Not least, one must interpret each conciliar text in view of the sources to which it is bound and from which it extensively drew. The Council viewed itself as heir of Tradition and, on the other hand, as an authentic interpreter of Tradition for a new era of fast and far-reaching change. Finally, for an appropriate hermeneutic of the Council, it is essential to consider the reception of the statements of the Council in the doctrine and life of the Church. Properly understood, reception is not a kind of mechanical acceptance, but, rather, a living, ecclesial process, guided by the Holy Spirit, which occurs in the area of doctrine as well as, moreover, the entire life of the Church.[20]

The experience of councils throughout the history of the Church repeated itself in the post-conciliar period that followed Vatican II. In the wake of the debate concerning definition, there always follows a controversy over reception. The periods after previous councils were fraught with difficulty and controversy – just think of the turbulent time after the first ecumenical council in Nicaea (325), or the period following the fourth ecumenical council in Chalcedon (451). Already during Vatican II there emerged two groups which have often been called 'conservatives' and 'progressives'. Yet, those two terms originally had different meanings from those which they received after the Council. On the one hand, those who were originally called progressives were, in fact, conservatives who promoted anew the great and older Tradition of Holy Scripture and the Church Fathers. On the other, those who were originally called conservatives focused exclusively on the post-Tridentine tradition of the previous handful of centuries. In order to be fair to the legitimate concerns of both sides and, in good conciliar tradition, to reach as broad a consensus as possible, a number of compromises had to be formulated in many cases. Those who are familiar with the history of councils know that this is no new phenomenon.[21]

The controversies that emerged during the Council often carry on, albeit in different forms, in the ongoing debates concerning the interpretation of the Council. Here we have the 'progressive' interpretations that claim the Council for 'neo-modernistic' positions which the Council, because of its rootedness in Tradition, consciously did not adopt. On the other hand, there are traditionalistic positions that question the Council, whether in part or in whole or interpret it in the sense of precisely those pre-conciliar positions of the eighteenth or nineteenth centuries which the Council tried to overcome.[22]

Recently Pope Benedict XVI, himself one of the Council's most significant theologians, has provided an important impulse for a conciliar hermeneutics of the Council. He contrasts the hermeneutic of interruption with a hermeneutic of continuity and reform. He pleads for an interpretation of Vatican II that places the Council within the context of the whole Tradition and as one part in the long chain of Tradition.[23] Indeed, one can understand Vatican II neither as a break nor as the beginning of a new church. This would contradict its self-understanding and its conscious and intended rootedness in Tradition. Still, at just this point there emerges the question: what is the meaning of continuity and reform?

The way the Council itself understood the Tradition in which it stood makes two things clear. First, continuity must not be understood simply as the sheer repetition or purely logical or organically understood explication of previous statements. Second, the hermeneutics of reform are not to be understood as having a simple, practical application. This becomes particularly apparent in the way the old axiom of previous councils, '*extra ecclesiam nulla salus*',[24] received a surprisingly new interpretation by the Council.[25] There is also a straight, logical, organic development from the *Syllabus* (1864), with its rejection of modern ideas including the freedom of religion, to the council documents *Gaudium et spes* and *Dignitatis humanae* (1965), which adopt precisely those ideas in a critical-constructive way. The same is true for the encyclical *Mortalium animos* (1928), with its rejection of the ecumenical movement, in relation to the ecumenism decree *Unitatis redintegratio* (1964), that calls precisely this ecumenical movement an impulse of the Holy Spirit. In all of these cases, we certainly cannot speak of a break, but rather must speak of a creative continuity in renewal.

If we want to comprehend continuity in renewal, then the hermeneutics of Vatican II must proceed from the idea of development as found in the writings of the great teachers of the Tübingen School and of John Henry Newman. This idea assumes that one and the same Church travels through all centuries and is present at all councils. This continuity, however, is a *living* Tradition, and thus by no means an *arbitrary* one. In his famous *Essay on the Development of Christian Doctrine* (1845), John Henry Newman demonstrated, with many examples from the older ecclesial Tradition, that, despite continuity of principles, the past is marked by complicated developments, and that the idea of continuity must include the emergence of new definitions as well as creative receptions and differentiated inculturations.[26] One must distinguish the lasting authoritative and yet always young *Traditio* from the many *traditiones* which express the one *Traditio* in time-conditioned ways that can also darken or distort it (one thinks of anti-Judaist, somatophobic or misogynistic traditions).[27] In this respect, the Council opened time-conditioned *traditiones* on several occasions in order to make the one lasting, authoritative *Traditio* shine again.

Hence, reform does not only mean a return to the origin or to a form of Tradition previously perceived as authentic. It means a renewal, so that the old, original and lastingly valid *Traditio* does not appear old but newly asserts itself in its newness and comes to shine anew. Pope John XXIII indicated this concern in the famous, though difficult to translate and often abused word '*aggiornamento*'. It does not simply mean adapting to today, but the making of Tradition present today in its newness. Such 'renewal' is different from innovation. Renewal, rather, asserts the biblical understanding of 'new' in the sense of gracious, non-derivable, unused and continuously surprising eschatological newness.[28] The Gospel is never just the already well-known, but is also the eternally new. Therefore, we should understand the hermeneutics of reform in terms of renewal and, by consequence, we should speak of a hermeneutics of renewal.

This renewal is not *our* work! It is the work of the Holy Spirit, who brings everything into remembrance (Jn 14.26), and who guides into all the truth (Jn 16.13). His bringing of all things into remembrance does not simply mean repeating the past, but making present the Gospel which occurred once and for all. According to Irenaeus of Lyons, it is the work of the Holy Spirit to keep the Tradition constantly young and fresh.[29] Such pneumatological hermeneutics are in accordance with the intention of Pope John XXIII, who expressed at the convocation of the Council the expectation of a renewed Pentecost.[30]

Post-conciliar reception history (*Wirkungsgeschichte*)

The post-conciliar period witnessed the emergence of many liturgical, pastoral and canonistic reforms which were welcomed by a great majority of the faithful. It also initiated a biblically as well as patristically orientated renewal in pastoral care and theology. Yet, after the Council, there was neither a renewed Pentecost nor the hoped-for spiritual spring. Not only were there controversies concerning the interpretation of the Council.[31] More significantly, the period witnessed a dramatic decline in religious life, with fewer pursuing spiritual vocations and, more generally, faith itself becoming increasingly superficial. The expected new missionary appeal failed to materialize. Instead of new joy in the Church, there was increased criticism of and annoyance with the Church.

In other words, there is light and darkness in the post-conciliar era. This was the differentiated and sober view of the Extraordinary Synod of Bishops in 1985 and on the occasion of the twentieth anniversary of the Council's end.[32] The Synod put a damper on the post-conciliar enthusiasm and, at the same time, rejected prophecies of doom and catastrophic scenarios.

The reasons behind this ambivalent development are manifold. Mono-causal explanations are insufficient, even more so one-sided judgements and condemnations. We cannot say, of course, that everything that has come after the Council has happened as a direct result. Perhaps we could argue in the opposite direction and claim that, against the new wave of secularization that had begun immediately afterwards, the Council provided a cushion of sorts and helpful arguments to be used when facing the new challenge. Yet, this also succeeded only partially. In general, theology and, above all, the ecclesial public were not sufficiently prepared for the opening up towards modern times as it is expressed particularly in the pastoral constitution *Gaudium et spes* and in the declaration on religious freedom *Dignitatis humanae*. Neo-scholasticism and its fundamental philosophical structure had more or less disappeared without a trace. They were often replaced in theology by injudicious modes of historical or salvation-historical thinking. This led to a biblicism and historical positivism that left little room for the dimension of faith.

Through these developments many impulses of the Council were suffocated or abusively instrumentalized in the sense of an 'enlightened' and liberal understanding of Church. On the other hand, there were unedifying fights with forces that, if possible, desired to go back before the Council. All that these controversies and trench warfare in the Church did was to distract from the great challenges and real problems we are faced with today.

The Council did not call for a new 'enlightened' church. Rather, it called for a church that is renewed spiritually in the spirit of the Gospel by way of personal sanctification and reform. At no point did the Council deviate from traditional doctrine. Yet, as will be shown later, it put such doctrine into a pastoral context, that is, into a Trinitarian horizon of understanding. It showed the way from a closed and locked identity towards an open, relational and dialogical definition of Church.[33]

The Council was not only the end of one process but also the point of departure for new developments and new spiritual beginnings which, thank God, have emerged in spite of all breakups and breakdowns. As such, the conciliar impulse has unfolded in unanticipated and unintended directions. And yet, those who have followed such paths have, by and large, sought to maintain and continue the Council's legacy. Insofar as they succeed, the Church remains young and alive.[34] The reception history of the Council will therefore not come to an end for a long time. The potential of the Council for the future has not yet been fully utilized.

5. Post-conciliar controversies

The Council was followed by an extremely difficult period. Towards the end of the Council and afterwards, I found myself as a young professor of dogmatics confronted with often heated controversies, at first in Münster, Westphalia (1964–70) and later at home in Tübingen (1970–89).

My time in Münster

Münster was, in many respects, a great time for me. At the faculty for Catholic theology, I met the then Professor Joseph Ratzinger. He played a significant part in working out the Council's ecclesiology and was publishing influential commentaries on the Council which are still worth reading. Through his widely acclaimed publications, he contributed substantially to the clarification and deeper understanding of the Council's ecclesiology.[35] In Münster I also met Johann Baptist Metz, who, in those years, developed further his anthropological approach (originally orientated towards the thought of Karl Rahner) to political theology, and so partly inspired the theology of liberation. When Joseph Ratzinger left Münster for Tübingen, Karl Rahner arrived from Munich with his assistant, Karl Lehmann. Rahner was one of the great thinkers before, during and after the Council. But he was increasingly dissatisfied with a post-conciliar development that, he argued, was both lagging and backward looking.

In this time immediately after the Council, very different positions collided. The progressives were now no longer the conservatives who stressed the greater and wider Catholic Tradition in opposition to recent narrowings. They were, rather, those who, in recourse to the New Testament or certain historical-critical interpretations of the New Testament, were concerned with engaging the modern world and philosophy concerning a new form of the Church and a new understanding of its doctrine. Inevitably, far-reaching emancipations of Tradition lead to disorientation. This situation called for further reflection upon the nature of Tradition, the development of dogma and its criteria, the methods of dogmatics, as well as serious engagements with the modern history of freedom.[36]

Pastoral issues

The attempt to establish a new orientation immediately ran up against pastoral questions. How can the faith be translated into a language that is comprehensible today? How can the faith be lived today? Such questions loomed directly following after the Council at the Dutch pastoral council (1966–70) and appeared in the *Dutch Catechism*,[37] leading to controversial discussions. At that time I published *Introduction to the Christian*

Faith (1972 in German),[38] which I had presented before in Tübingen and Münster to members of all faculties and which later appeared in many editions and languages and was gratefully received by many as a basic guide to the faith. I gave the same lectures shortly afterwards to missionaries and missionary sisters in Taiwan. Many of those had previously suffered unspeakably for their faith in Maoist prisons. These lectures were a test of endurance for me. However, the grateful support of my listeners convinced me that they actually consisted of more than a bourgeois conformist theology.

The crisis caused by the fierce reaction to the encyclical *Humanae vitae, On the Regulation of Birth* (1968) was followed in Germany by the Würzburg Synod (1971–5), and ten years later in my home diocese by the Rottenburg diocesan synod (1985–6) under my immediate predecessor, the popular and much-liked bishop Georg Moser († 1988). Both were synods in the original sense of the Greek word 'sunodos': the fellowship of the people of God 'on the way' – that is, an expression of a Church that is together along the way. This latter aspect was particularly emphasized in the resolution inspired by Johann Baptist Metz, *Unsere Hoffnung. Ein Bekenntnis zum Glauben in unserer Zeit.*[39]

From today's perspective, one is likely to have a different opinion on the texts that appeared in those days. The Church has not remained in the state of debate that marked that period of time. We have moved well down the road, as important, clarifying and deepening aspects have been added. Nevertheless, we cannot deny that both synods honestly and diligently struggled for responsible pastoral solutions in those turbulent years. They contributed to the perseverance in unity of the church in Germany, in spite of all tensions to the contrary.

Yet, it became apparent that further reflections were necessary. The word 'pastoral', which had a history in the pastoral constitution, *Gaudium et spes*, and then through the Dutch pastoral council, often degenerated into a buzzword. Some have thought that 'acting pastorally' entails ignoring doctrine in doing so. But that was never the view of the Council. To escape this neglect of the truth, I looked for a theological solution which, with the help of the principle of *epikeia*, or in the Eastern Church, *oikonomia*/economy, could facilitate the translation of doctrine into practice adequate for the subject, the people and the situation.

According to Thomas, *epikeia* does not abolish justice, but is rather indicative of a higher justice.[40] It does call into question the basic principles, but takes the singularity of each person and each situation seriously. The individual and the specific situation can never be regarded as merely a 'case' under general law or apart from consideration of the particular situation of life.[41] Pastoral disposition is therefore pastoral prudence which, to follow the logic and virtue of prudence, applies a generally valid law to a specific situation according to the rules of practical reason adequate for the person and the situation.[42] This is not situational ethics, which make the situation the key to the knowledge of truth. It is, rather, a pastoral attitude that, except for actions which are in themselves evil and in no case permitted, comes to a conscientious consideration in the light of an objective complexity.[43] A shining example of this is Alphonsus Maria de Liguori († 1787) who, as a patron saint and moral theologian was, above all, a great pastor and an experienced confessor.[44]

If, instead of such pastoral prudence, a purely pragmatic behaviour or, vice versa, an unrealistic, ultimately merciless and unloving focus on principles dominates, a vertical schism can occur between those principles kept 'at the top' and the praxis that hovers 'down below', which itself often follows its own wild and unordered path. Anyone who realistically observes the present situation of the Church cannot overlook the danger of such a development. It has become the reality in many areas of morals and pastoral care. Such a development does not contribute to the Church's credibility and poses significant dangers to its unity.

The 1968 revolution and the theology of liberation

The controversies mentioned thus far were only a prelude to the more fundamental shake-up that arose in connection with the 1968 movement that affected the whole Western world. This movement was driven by very different forces. What is generally known as a student revolution was, in fact, a cultural revolution that caused a change of mentalities and social values that reached far beyond students and academia. It was the watershed between the immediate, by now unjustly named reactionary post-war period, and a new historical phase that was determined by a new wave of enlightenment, secularization and emancipation from the traditionally general human and Christian values. In the course of this, an extremely individualistic, emancipated and anti-authoritarian understanding of freedom became mixed together with a usually vulgarized neo-Marxist ideology of socialization, fundamental democratization and politicization of all sectors of life, including the Church.

In many student communities there were wild experiments and hardly imaginable excesses. It was necessary to challenge such ideological and sociological reductionism and political functionalization of the Church and the democratization of the Church, then perceived in a mostly one-dimensional manner. Thank God this has now been overcome. By contrast, the political theology as formulated by Johann Baptist Metz,[45] the theology of liberation and feminist theology (as an independent branch of liberation theology) have left lasting marks on theology and on the Church.

I could not, in good conscience, follow any of these directions. In my view, the philosophical and theological foundations were too ambivalent and the modern problem of freedom not really elucidated. Still, despite all justified criticism of some forms of liberation theology, we should not ignore its legitimate concerns.[46] Its proponents have highlighted the public relevance of faith and raised awareness of often outrageous injustice and structural violence. The preferential option for the poor has become the ecclesial standard since the second general conference of Latin American bishops in Medellín (1968). So I have always felt great respect towards Gustavo Gutiérrez, who was the first to speak of the theology of liberation.[47] By contrast, the more radical representatives of liberation theology remained alien to me in their affinity with Marxist social analysis and the class struggle. Their social criticism, often seen as prophetic, was at times in danger of taking on a more ideological character. Consequently, it became essential for me to engage in a critically constructive manner with the modern, emancipatory understanding of freedom in Christology (1974).[48]

Controversies concerning Professor Hans Küng

In Tübingen, these global debates were soon overshadowed by the controversies that began soon after the Council between the Roman Congregation for the Doctrine of Faith and Professor Hans Küng. For many years, I worked well, collegially and amicably with him. After the publication of his book *Infallible? An Inquiry* (1970)[49] and the long debates and exchanges that followed, there came, immediately before Christmas 1979, the publication of the decision of the Congregation for the Doctrine of Faith[50] and then the withdrawal of the *Missio Canonica*. This caused a wave of indignation at the university and among the wider public.[51] By the time the crisis appeared, I had already determined my own positions on the issues surrounding the controversy. Küng and I had reached differing views of the Church as *communio* and of the '*Sentire ecclesiam*'. Nevertheless, having worked cooperatively with him for years at the collegial level, I found this discord to be personally difficult. Tough decisions are necessary whenever ecclesial and collegial solidarity dissolves into an irresolvable conflict.

For just this reason, the turbulent weeks before and after Christmas 1979 were, for me, the most difficult season of my entire academic career. Still, the events of that time forced me to clarify and sharpen my own position.[52] Concerning the issue of the lasting authority of ecclesial doctrine, the discussion raised fundamental questions concerning the meta-critique of modern criticism, theological hermeneutics and the understanding of the Church. As John Henry Newman had done in the nineteenth century, it was necessary to situate the dogmatic principle over against the liberal principle.[53]

'Consolidation'

In this situation, I obtained help from Hans Urs von Balthasar and his writings. He had contributed greatly to the theological groundwork of the Council. I had known his works for many years, in particular his *Apokalypse der deutschen Seele* (1937–9), his famous book on *The Theology of Karl Barth* (1951) and his *Razing the Bastions* (1952). These volumes display a universality of spirit that, though catholic on the basis of the catholicity of its breadth, broadness, overcomes old limitations and points to new ways. Though some wrongly suspected it, Balthasar did not, as some have suggested, intend during the difficult post-conciliar period to construct new bastions to replace the old ones razed during the Council. He certainly showed no restraint in criticizing some theological foolishness (or what he considered to be such). Yet, after all of the controversies that altered the ecclesial landscape, in his great theological trilogy (*The Glory of God – Theo-drama – Theo-logic*, 1961–87) he genially succeeded in making visible once again the Catholic cosmos in all its inner wealth and inner beauty, and in unfolding a vision of catholicity in the original meaning of the word. He did this with an astounding knowledge of the Tradition and modern theology, and also of poetry and philosophy. This appeared as a firm basis upon which one could build.[54]

I offered to make my own contribution to consolidation with two major publications, neither of which deal with ecclesial 'day-to-day politics' but rather with the foundations of faith, faith in Jesus Christ and in the triune God: *Jesus the Christ* (1974) and *The God of Jesus Christ* (1982). Both volumes have appeared in many editions and translations and are used in many places as textbooks for theological education. Faith in Christ and faith in God are the only possible foundations upon which ecclesial renewal and a renewed Catholic ecclesiology can be built. Without this, everything hangs in the air and eventually crumbles. As the person chiefly responsible for the composition of the *Katholische Erwachsenenkatechismus* (1985), I made every attempt to craft my work for a broad audience. Here I attempted a comprehensive exposition of the faith of the Church based upon the creed.

6. Breakthrough to my own ecclesiological approach

The Extraordinary Synod of Bishops, 1985

During the controversies of the 1970s, I needed time to define my own way more precisely (and on the basis of the Tübingen tradition), and to systematically unpack my own ecclesiological approach. In analogy to the Pneuma-Christology explored in *Jesus the Christ*, I first developed an ecclesiology from a pneumatological perspective.[55] In the creed, the confession of the 'one holy Church' stands within the context of the confession of the Holy Spirit. Hence, ecclesiology must not be developed only as a doctrine of an institution, but has to be dealt with in the context of pneumatology and the entire diversity of charisma in the Church.

The Second Vatican Council also clearly emphasized the pneumatological and charismatic dimension of the Church.[56] Inspired by my then Tübingen colleagues Hans Küng, Ernst Käsemann and Jürgen Moltmann, I tried to make the Pauline doctrine of charisma fruitful and to integrate the Church's ministry into this context.[57] This attempt was, in connection with the hopeful charismatic departure and the new spiritual movements that emerged in the 1970s and 1980s, providing ecclesial life with unexpectedly new youthfulness and freshness.[58]

The actual breakthrough came when Pope John Paul II made me the theological secretary of the Extraordinary Synod of Bishops in 1985. Taking place twenty years after the Council, the Synod was to take stock of the developments since the Council.[59] While studying the council documents in preparation for my work, I came to the conclusion that *communio*-ecclesiology was the central concern and the main motif of the conciliar ecclesiology.[60] Together with the relator of the Synod, Cardinal Godfried Daneels von Meecheln, I was able to contribute this aspect to the Synod. It has become fundamental for me ever since.

Communio as guiding principle

The *communio*-ecclesiology had been prepared long before the Council and appeared in several parts of the council documents.[61] At first glance, it is not in the foreground in these texts. In the foreground are the description of the Church as mystery, and images such as people of God, body of Christ, temple of the Holy Spirit, etc. In the time immediately after the Council, it was the metaphor of the people of God that played a dominant role. For a short time, it superseded the image of the body of Christ image that had been dominant since Pope Pius XII's encyclical *Mystici corporis* (1943). Yet, it can be demonstrated that the *communio*-ecclesiology lies behind all of the aforementioned biblical images for the description of the nature of the Church.[62] In this respect, it is legitimate to call *communio* the ecclesiologically guiding principle of the Council.[63] Following the theology of the Church Fathers, the Council grounds its own ecclesiology in the inner-Trinitarian *communio* of Father, Son and Holy Spirit. The Church as *communio* is the image and, so to speak, the icon of the Trinity.[64]

Since the *synod*, the idea of the Church as *communio* has become decisive for me.[65] Later, and in the context of the dialogue with Orthodox theology, I was able to develop this approach into a Eucharistic ecclesiology. Accordingly, Eucharistic ecclesiology means that the Church *is* wherever and whenever the Eucharist is celebrated. In the celebration of the Eucharist, the Church understood as *communio* becomes concrete reality. Moreover, ultimately, the Church lives out of the Eucharist. Since the one

Lord is present in every celebration of the Eucharist, we are, in the event of the celebrating, connected with all the communities also celebrating the Eucharist at the same time. For precisely this reason, I do not see a fundamental contradiction but rather a complementary relation between the Eucharistic ecclesiology which, as we often find it stated in the Eastern Church, proceeds from the local church, and the universal ecclesiology, which, as is formulated in the Western tradition, proceeds from baptism.

In the meantime, the *communio*-ecclesiology has largely become a common feature of good in Catholic,[66] Orthodox[67] and also Protestant[68] theologies. The Congregation for the Doctrine of Faith has taken up important issues in the letter *Communionis notio* (1992). Of course, the broad reception should not obscure the fact that, behind the one term '*communio*', there are widely diverging ideas and concepts, the differences of perspective concerning which point to unresolved ecumenical disputes in the area of ecclesiology.

A new communial and relational way of thinking

Occasionally, *communio* is regarded as a new paradigm, not only for ecclesiology, but also as a kind of new 'world formula'.[69] This makes sense if Jesus' life and sacrifice for many, that is, for all (Mk 10.45 par.), is understood as pro-existence and if one sees in it the revelation of God as self-giving love (1 Jn 4.8.16). God can only be love for the world and for us because God is love in himself, in the inner-Trinitarian communio of Father, Son and Holy Spirit. If God is thus love and communio, then love and *communio* are the essence of all reality. If carried through to the end, the theological understanding of the Trinitarian persons as subsisting relations has far-reaching consequences for our understanding of reality as the whole. In that case, neither the passive substance of ancient philosophy nor modern subjectivity are any longer the point of departure or of reference of thinking. Relation, rather, becomes the all-determining ultimate reality.[70]

For the Church, such relational thinking means that its identity is no longer contained within itself but, rather, is an open and dialogical identity in the Church's communication *ad intra* and *ad extra*. Such a dialogical self-understanding is expressed in many passages and contexts of the council documents. For this reason, it must be regarded as foundational for the Council's understanding of Church.[71] In it, the aforementioned extension of the horizon of the Second Vatican Council finds concrete expression. This does not entail a change of previous doctrine, but a new, extended horizon, so to speak – a new light and a new overall context in which doctrine must be seen. Therefore, this new perspective must not be confused with theological relativism. It does not say that everything is relative, but that everything is relational.[72] Thus, this renewed ecclesial self-understanding stands in the context of a comprehensive perception of the nature of reality.

Consequently, *communio*-ecclesiology does not intend to be an abstract theory detached from reality and the world, and certainly not any kind of ecclesiological ideology. Rather, it must become concrete in the life of the Church. There it must lead to a deeper understanding of the nature of the Church and, in particular, of the liturgy, and to a renewed communicative-dialogical form of Church. This perspective necessitates many steps of ecclesial renewal.[73] At present the Church suffers from an internal and external communication deficit. There is an urgent need to build a communicative culture, a dialogical style and communicative, particularly synodal structures.[74] Hence, *communio*-ecclesiology must be theologically deepened. Then, in a practical way, it must also become the basis for communication within the Church as well as with other churches, with the non-Christian religions, and with modern and postmodern culture.

7. Pastoral and ecumenical expansions of the horizon

Pastoral experiences as a bishop

After twenty-five years of academic work, I was called to become the bishop of a large diocese, which signalled my departure from the much-loved world of academia. The transition to ecclesial responsibilities signified a new phase of my life. I shall never forget my episcopal ordination, with all its significant symbols. Ordination brings one into the worldwide communion of bishops who, together with the pope, have been entrusted with the message of the gospel.

The diocese of Rottenburg-Stuttgart, with approximately 1,000 parishes, is quite diverse. There are urban-industrial as well as rural regions of the diocese. Some parts have a Catholic majority, others are predominantly Protestant. The diocese is, to be sure, a local church in the midst of swift social changes and deep pastoral upheavals. As often as possible, I tried to visit parishes each Sunday and on many weekdays, in order to be in regular conversation with the priests and to encounter the laity, individuals in religious orders, ecclesial associations and new movements, people in leading positions and people at the edge of society – immigrants, disabled people, homeless people, drug addicts, and prisoners, etc. In such encounters, the Church was concretely present as the people of God. As such, it was just here that the *communio*-ecclesiology had to pass the concrete test of experience.

Already by that time the hermeneutics of the Council had become a pressing problem. There were frequent struggles and debates about the proper interpretation of the Council and its *communio*-ecclesiology. In terms of pastoral care, in the parishes, it was necessary to distinguish, time and time again between a legitimate and a misled understanding of *communio*. The debate concerned the indispensible priestly ministry in the parish and for the parish, the place of the post-conciliar councils, cooperative pastoral care, laypeople preaching at the Eucharist, the position of pastoral assistants, etc. All of these issues put *communio*-ecclesiology to the test.

In addition, part of the pastoral experience included recognizing the dignity and relatively independent importance of the local church and its specific problems and, resulting from this, the personal responsibility of a local bishop within the global Church. It forcefully necessitated a new balancing of the universal Church and the local church. What was initially a pastoral concern led, unintentionally, to a controversy with Cardinal Joseph Ratzinger.[75]

Extending the perspective internationally

The experiences of my own diocese were complemented by other unforgettable experiences gained through pastoral visits to the young churches in the so-called Third World – or, as some today prefer to say, the Two-Thirds World. My immediate predecessor, Bishop Carl Joseph Leibprecht († 1981), had already established extensive contacts with the young churches during the Council. These contacts, along with aid for poorer churches, had been a trademark of the diocese ever since. Within the bishops' conference I was put in charge of these relations. On many journeys to the young churches in Africa, Latin America and Asia, I got to know their vitality and also their problems, and I encountered many situations of poverty and destitution.

I returned from each of these journeys a different person, moved and profoundly disturbed by all the misery and injustice I saw in these places. Yet I was also proud of my Church, in which so many courageous women and men worked with all their strength for the poorest of the poor, and lit a warm light of hope in even the darkest situations. These journeys expanded my view of the Church. It strengthened in me the awareness that Germany and Western Europe are not the world but only a small part of it, and that the Catholic Church is more diverse and vibrant than it may seem to us in the 'old Europe'. It is not only we who have something to give to them; they too have a lot of joy of faith to give to us.

In all this, it became apparent that the Church in the 'old Europe', with its great and rich Christian tradition, stands before a deep upheaval and shift of paradigms, the emergence of which was, at that time, still on the distant horizon. The necessity of a new evangelization of our continent became a central concern of mine.[76] In the meantime, the shift of Christianity from North to South has become even more evident. In particular and regarding ecumenism, critical questions from the South to the North have increased significantly. A southerly wind is blowing within the Church.

My ten years as diocesan bishop were followed, from 1999 to 2010, by eleven years' experience of the universal Church on the staff of the pope as the member of the Roman Curia responsible for ecumenical dialogue and religious relations with the Jews. At first I was reluctant to accept such a task in the Roman Curia, as I was ill prepared. I never desired to become a 'typical' member of the Curia, and, in fact, I never became one! My experience serving in local churches proved to be a great asset for my conversations with bishops from all over the world. This experience was extended through countless visits to other churches and ecclesial communities on all continents. These confirmed my previously held impression that the problems and experiences of local churches are not sufficiently represented in Rome. Many of those who work in the Curia have never really seen a parish or diocese from the inside.

My new responsibility in the Curia entailed for me, in the literal sense of the word, a *catholic* extension of perspective. In Rome, one experiences directly and daily the global church in its universal spectrum and vast richness. I wish that everyone, especially my friends at home, had the opportunity to experience such an expansion of horizons. The church in Germany is far too concerned with itself and, also, too self-satisfied. The universal ecclesial aspect is often perceived more as a burden and restriction than as an enrichment. The Church is thus in danger of becoming provincial. It would be good for the German church to look further beyond its own borders. Among other things, this would help to soothe anti-Roman sentiments.

Expanding the horizon ecumenically

I was able to look beyond my own horizons and to gather new experiences, particularly in the course of my encounters with other churches. As I come from the land of the Reformation and had worked at two universities, each of which have a Catholic and a Protestant faculty, the encounter with the churches of the Reformation was nothing new to me. I had previously been involved in international ecumenical dialogues (Faith and Order and the Lutheran-Catholic dialogue).[77]

I did not, however, have much experience with the Eastern churches – that is, with the Oriental-Orthodox churches (Copts, Syrians, Armenians, Ethiopians, Malankarians) as well as the Byzantine and Slavonic Orthodox churches. I quickly became fascinated by their rich spiritual, theological and liturgical traditions. The world of Protestant Christianity also revealed itself to me anew in its great variety and diversity, especially among Anglican, Lutheran and Reformed Christians. In addition, there was the multifaceted world of the free churches and fast-growing new Pentecostal churches and charismatic communities that have substantially changed the ecumenical landscape since the beginning of the twentieth century and have made it more confusing.

I encountered the great diversity and richness of Christianity and came to the comforting realization that God's Spirit is also at work outside the Catholic Church. However, I also saw the tragic fragmentation of Christianity into hundreds of churches and communities. In a world that is threatened by so many conflicts and, despite the trend of globalization, internally rent asunder, it is this fragmentation of the Church that prevents us from convincingly fulfilling the commandment that Christ has given to us and from testifying, with one voice, to the one God and the one mediator Jesus Christ. We have torn to pieces the seamless, undivided garment of Christ (Jn 19.23). The Church, which is the body of Christ, is bleeding from many deep wounds.

We can thus only be grateful for the gift of the Holy Spirit who, in the ecumenical movement of the twentieth century, initiated in all churches repentance for this situation which contradicts the will of Jesus Christ, awakening a deep desire for the unity of all Christians and inspiring the ecumenical movement. The ecumenical dialogue was officially opened by Vatican II with the decree *Unitatis redintegratio*. With *Ut unum sint* (1995), John Paul II wrote the first ecumenical encyclical by a pope. In it he gives essential impulses for ecumenical dialogue and calls the ecumenical opening irreversible. My predecessors Cardinal Augustin Bea († 1968), Cardinal Jan Willebrands († 2006) and Cardinal Edward I. Cassidy had established many contacts on this basis, built mutual trust and achieved understanding and convergence. Upon this foundation I sought to further build a genuinely ecumenical Catholicism.

Some have claimed that ecumenism leads to a loss of Catholic identity. In fact, the opposite is the case. In the encounter with other Christians, one rediscovers the richness and beauty of the Catholic Church. For instance, one experiences the extent to which the Petrine office is a great gift of the Lord to his Church, which provides it with an inner stability absent from and painfully missed by other churches. Moreover, one discovers that the Petrine office offers heretofore unrealized ecumenical possibilities.

One thus learns that the ecumenical dialogue is not a one-way street, but rather a reciprocal give-and-take. For me the definition by Pope John Paul II became central, namely, that ecumenical dialogue is not only an exchange of ideas but also of gifts.[78] In all of this, ecumenism is not a profitless exchange for the Catholic side, but, rather also provides Catholics with opportunities for growth. Ecumenism enriches the unity that is already present in the Catholic Church. It does not make us *less* Catholic, but, in a concrete sense, *more* catholic. Catholicism and ecumemism do not stand in opposition to each other but are two sides of one and the same coin. That is why today I am more than ever convinced that ecumenism is a construction site for the Church of the future.

Taking everything into account, my period serving the Church's ecumenical efforts was a beautiful but challenging time, with many conflicts emerging that required great effort. On the day I left office, 1 July 2010, the canticle of the Morning Prayer read: 'he who scattered Israel will gather him and will keep him as a shepherd keeps his flock' (Jer. 31.10). If that is not an encouraging promise!

Dialogue with the Oriental churches

We often underestimate the importance of dialogue with the Oriental churches. This not only overlooks the fact that these churches are present among us and that, without them, integration between Eastern and Western Europe is unthinkable. What is overlooked in particular is their rich traditions, from which we 'Westerners' have much to learn. Among the non-Catholic churches, they are, in dogmatic terms, the ones closest to us. Pope Benedict XVI has spoken of an *almost* full unity. The first contacts began already during Vatican II. On the penultimate day of the Council, the excommunications of 1054, often regarded as the beginning of the schism, were declared to be erasable from the memory of the Church, and this was accompanied by a long applause from the Council.[79] I dare say that this deserves to be called a prophetic act.

Of course, there are other schisms that are much older, for instance, with the Assyrian Christians in the fifth century after the Council of Ephesus (431), and with the Copts, Syrians, Armenians and others after the Council of Chalcedon (451). Significant steps forward in the ecumanical dialogue, most of which, unfortunately, remain largely unknown, have already been taken; for instance, the agreements reached with the Oriental Orthodox churches on Christology, through which a controversy lasting more than 1,500 years might be brought to an end.[80]

However, when I took office in the Council for Unity, the dialogue with the Oriental Orthodox churches had come to a standstill and needed to be rebuilt with great effort. This was far from an easy task, not least because of the cultural differences between East and West. In my estimation, it was something of a miracle that, after five years, it was possible for the dialogue group to produce a joint document, in which we stated that, in spite of 1500 years of separation, we have retained, except divergent understandings of Rome, the same apostolic Tradition concerning essential aspects of the nature, structure and mission of the Church.

The theological dialogue with the Orthodox churches began in 1980. At first it was necessary for us to clarify the common ground between us in the areas of the doctrines of the Eucharist and of the sacraments, and the understandings of the episcopal and priestly ministries. Yet, at the very emotional dialogue in Emmitsburg/Baltimore (2000), the sensitive issue concerning the status of those Oriental churches in full communion with Rome led to a severe crisis which caused a de facto interruption of five years. In addition, the establishment in 2002 of four dioceses in the territory of the Russian Federation led to a considerable degree of resentment on the part of the Moscow Patriarchate. Many difficult and discreet conversations were required to restart the dialogue. Thus it was possible that, at the funeral rites for Pope John Paul II and the solemn installation of Pope Benedict XVI in April 2005, all Oriental Orthodox churches and all Orthodox churches were represented by high-ranking delegations. It was a situation without precedent in church history that highlighted, despite all existing differences, a new ecumenical situation. The churches are still separated but they have moved closer together.

With the document of Ravenna (2007), the renewed dialogue brought a breakthrough that now allowed for the central controversial issue to be addressed: the primacy of the Bishop of Rome. This dialogue will continue for quite some time and will certainly not be easy. Some Orthodox churches or groups of Orthodox Christians still find this issue to be a source of difficulty because the theological clarifications brought by Vatican II have not yet been addressed on the Orthodox side as a whole. Nevertheless, these days a relaxed and friendly atmosphere marks our ecumenical encounters. A good cooperation has begun in many political, ecological and pastoral questions. We see ourselves as one Church in – though not in full – ecclesial communion.

Dialogue with the churches of the Reformation

During the first year I worked in Rome, the dialogue with the churches of the Reformation was already off to a hopeful start. On 31 October 1999, the *Joint Declaration on the Doctrine of Justification* was signed in Augsburg. In regard to the central controversy of the sixteenth century, the *Joint Declaration* established a consensus in the fundamental question between Catholics and Lutherans. Pope John Paul II called the agreement signed in Augsburg a milestone of ecumenical convergence. In 2006 in Seoul, South Korea, the World Methodist Council also joined the declaration.

And yet, soon after this, the ecumenical situation with the churches of the Reformation became, once again, rather difficult. On 30 June 2000, the Congregation for the Doctrine of Faith published the *Note on the Expression Sister Churches*, and shortly afterwards, on 6 August 2000, the *Declaration on the Unicity and Salvific Universality of Jesus Christ and the Church – Dominus Iesus*. Many Protestant Christians understood the latter as a termination of the ecumenical dialogue. The affirmation of *Dominus Iesus* seven years later, on 29 June 2007, with the document *Responses to Some Questions Regarding Certain Aspects of the Doctrine on the Church*, seemed to confirm their view.

In substance, *Dominus Iesus* was a rejection, not of ecumenism, but of widespread relativism, and, especially, of unchecked religious pluralism. The emphasis on the unicity and salvific universality of Jesus Christ is fully consonant with the Reformation position. For precisely this reason,

Dominus Iesus could have become a joint ecumenical text. Yet, in the fourth chapter the document also speaks against ecclesiological relativism and clarifies that the unicity of the Church subsists in the Catholic Church. This has been and is the traditional Catholic position, and thus does not necessitate the termination of the ecumenical dialogue. The Orthodox churches maintain the same position for themselves no less strongly. Everyone who has read the catechism should know that Catholics and Protestants have different understandings of being the Church and that, when speaking of the Church, they do not mean quite the same thing.[81] For this reason, the problem has never been the content of the declaration. Rather, the true point of contention is the sharpness of several negatively phrased, demarcating formulations, which, in turn, have been perceived by many Protestant Christians as degrading and insulting. And yet, the harsh responses issued from the Protestant side were, in fact, far from ecumenically friendly.[82]

As a result of all of this, the dialogue became emotionally burdened and difficult. It became additionally so due to the fact that most of our Protestant dialogue partners had reached positions regarding the question of women's ordination and, later, concerning ethical questions that are far removed from the traditional joint positions on such matters. This opened up new rifts between us and our conversation partners and even within the churches. The most painful setback occurred in the context of Anglican-Roman Catholic conversations (ARCIC) upon which great hopes had still been placed at the conference in Mississuaga (Toronto, Canada, 2000). At least the joint document *Growing together in Unity and Mission* (2006) had demonstrated what had been achieved and how much practical cooperation is already possible today in many places. On the European level in 2001, the *Charta Oecumenica* could be signed as a joint document of the Conference of European Churches (CEC) and the Council of European Bishops' Conferences (CCEE).

In a collaborative publication with my staff, appearing towards the end of my time in office, I made the case that we cannot truly speak of an ecumenical winter. This book is titled *Harvesting the Fruits*,[83] as it attempts to bring in the harvest of forty years of bilateral dialogues with Anglicans, Lutherans, Reformed and Methodists. This publication showed that substantially more has been achieved in the past forty years than ever could have been dreamed as possible. At the same time, I try to clearly identify the open questions that still separate the churches. It has been gratefully received by our partners. With this publication, I hope to have laid a solid working basis for future conversation in the future.

Dialogue with the free churches

In addition to the dialogues with the historical Protestant churches, in recent years dialogue has also become important with the free churches

(Methodists, Baptists, Mennonites, Disciples of Christ, Brethren, etc.), and with evangelical movements and communities. In Germany, these constitute only small communities. On a global level, these movements consist of millions of members. Evangelicals and Catholics are very close together when it comes to fundamental biblical truths of faith, particularly the confession of Jesus Christ as the Son of God and the salvific significance of the Cross and Resurrection, as well as ethical questions. In addition, the free churches have pre-empted many problems which the traditional churches are also facing today, especially concerning independence from the state, minority status, the responsibility of the laity and missionary awareness.[84] We should not have any reservation over entering into dialogue with them.

Since the beginning of the twentieth century, the ecumenical landscape has changed dramatically through the appearance and exponentially fast growth of evangelical and charismatic communities, Pentecostal churches and similar, partly sectarian, groups. Conversations with bishops from the southern hemisphere quickly turn, not to the traditional Protestant churches, but to the Pentecostals. The Council for Christian Unity has acknowledged the challenge posed by this fact and has organized symposia on the topic for bishops and theologians in Africa, Asia and Latin America, where I have always participated and lectured. This shift in emphasis to the southern hemisphere, often called Global South, has thus become ecumenically important also.

What has been achieved? It is difficult to say. In human terms, the full unity in the faith is apparently further away than we had thought during the early days of the ecumenical movement that followed in the wake of the original impulse at the Council. Yet it is not for us to determine the place and time that our unity will become complete. Still, what has been achieved is more than nothing and by no means insignificant. While we have certainly not achieved the full unity of the Church, we have managed to foster a feeling of fellowship within global Christianity. On the basis of the common baptism and the common 'being in Christ', a nexus of human and Christian relationships has emerged that is hopefully strong enough to resist fundamentalist crossfire and foolish profile neuroses, of which there is no shortage, and which, hopefully, will last.

Yet, towards the end of my time in office, I increasingly realised that ecumenism in its present form has reached an impasse and that new orientations and energies are necessary. The internal differentiation and fragmentation in many churches, the newly re-emerged differences in ecclesiological and especially ethical questions, and the appearance and growth of new ecclesial communities have changed the landscape and the ecumenical climate. To rebuild the full ecclesial community of the Church necessitates, above all, that we agree ecumenically what the Church is and, consequently, what the unity of the Church means. This is to be the main topic for the next phase of dialogue. It will probably be more difficult than easy. For my part, I wish to contribute to this new phase of the dialogue with the present volume.

Religious dialogue with the Jews

After a difficult and complex history of relations, religious dialogue with the Jews has become possible through the declaration *Nostra aetate* of the Second Vatican Council. This historic document condemned all forms of anti-Semitism and highlighted the common roots of Judaism and Christianity. Then in 1974, Pope Paul VI created the Commission for Religious Relations with the Jews and connected it with the Council for Christian Unity.[85] Because of the burden of recent German history, as a German, I at first had reservations about accepting the task. But my Jewish colleagues in the dialogue have never made me feel uncomfortable about my country of origin. This fact has demonstrated to me how much – though certainly not all! – of the heavily-burdened history of Jewish-Christian relations has already been addressed.

Even though the dialogue was not easy and frequently affected by crises, on the whole it was fruitful. Besides all the issues of the past, in particular the Shoah,[86] it was repeatedly overshadowed by complicated situations. This was especially the case with the reformulation of the prayer on Good Friday (2008) and the discussion that ensued concerning the issue of missionizing the Jews – an issue that is very sensitive for Jews[87] – as well as the lifting of the excommunication of four bishops from the Society of Pius X, including one who had gained notoriety for denying the Holocaust (2009). In each case, it took a lot of patience, empathy and good will from both sides. The trusting personal relationships that had developed over the years proved to be of particularly great help in overcoming irritations that had arisen. And so, in spite of a number of difficulties, the Council's declaration *Nostra aetate* succeeded in coming to life. In fact, many of the dialogue partners have become good friends.

In addition to the international dialogue in the context of the International Catholic-Jewish Committee (international encounters in New York, Buenos Aires, Cape Town, Budapest), since 2002 it has been possible to begin an independent dialogue with the Chief Rabbinate of Israel. As the Jewish religion is for us not only something 'external', but also, in some way, belonging to the 'innermost' part of our religion,[88] the encounter with Judaism has opened up essential aspects of our own Church. Biblical research and the study of the Church's early history have profited from this dialogue and, through it, the quest for Jesus has entered a new phase. In some political, social and cultural areas a good cooperation has developed on the basis of the Ten Commandments. By initiating the Jewish-Christian dialogue, Vatican II has helped to usher in a new era in Jewish-Christian relations and in the history of the Christian Church. That I have been able to contribute to this dialogue has been for me, in spite of many resulting tensions and conflicts, a source of deep satisfaction.

8. Present crises and challenges

The present internal crisis

Especially in Europe, recent years have been overshadowed by the experience of an internal crisis of the Church. I have never been one of those prophets of doom who warns that everything is progressively getting worse and that the Church is on the edge of disaster. Rather, I have always considered it my duty to proclaim the Christian message as one of hope. The Church is built upon an unshakable foundation, such that, as the Lord promised, the gates of death and hell shall not prevail against it. Still, we must distinguish such hope from blind optimism which does not face up to harsh and ugly reality and which does not recognize problems and challenges. So I do not suffer *from* the Church but *with* the Church, whose crisis, especially in Europe, has become increasingly apparent in recent years.

By crisis I do not mean the fact that, in some parts of the world today, the Church is also persecuted, oppressed and hindered. Likewise I do not mean the growing, aggressive new atheism, the resentment and criticism directed toward the Church from the outside. All of this is bad, of course. But such difficulties were foretold by Jesus Christ. Struggles are, as it were, ingredients to the Church as it tarries in this world. What is more, the Church has always been strengthened by such controversies. There is, therefore, no reason to be afraid.

The crisis of the Church in the Western world manifests itself in the long-term trend of decreasing church attendance; Germany itself has seen a decrease of more than two-thirds since the Second World War, including a decline in the number of baptisms, confessions, marriages and funerals. This has inevitably contributed to the dramatic decrease in religious vocations and the ever more noticeable lack of priests. Of course, such figures are only the outward sign of a loss of faith or, otherwise, a 'selective Christianity' consisting of only a partial identification with the one faith. Of particular concern is the weakening of the family as the place where faith is transmitted and lived. The shameful cases of abuse have led to a crumbling of trust in the Church. The public exposure of such cases in the months before the writing of the present book have left a foul smell of decay in the ecclesial air. This has ultimately shown that the world (in the Johannine sense) has deeply entered the Church and taken up residence there.

This crisis is far more than an institutional crisis that can be solved with the usual institutional ideas of reform. It is obvious that there are structural deficits in the Church. However, this diagnosis and its respective solution are, on the whole, far too short-sighted. Many Protestant churches without pope and curia have met all respective demands for reform concerning synodal structures, women's ordination, celibacy and remarriage of divorcees. However, they are not really any closer to solving the problem of how they can convincingly live and testify to the Christian faith today. Indeed, they have similar and, in some cases, graver problems than the Catholic Church.

The problems that mark the present crisis demand even more radical, answers than those usually called radical which are, in fact, rather bourgeois-liberal accommodations. If we start at the roots (Lat. *radix*), there is only one possible answer to the crisis: a new enthusiasm for God and for his kingdom, which means a new evangelization, and, concomitantly, a spiritual renewal that reaches far deeper than is possible with external reforms.[89] Institutional reforms absent without inner renewal are soulless and ultimately worthless and without consequence; they only lead to action without reorientation. To the contrary, the renewal of faith and liturgy without consequent reforms is detached from life and is unrealistic. Renewal and reform belong together. New evangelization entails repentance and spiritual renewal as well as necessary reforms.[90] Without the courage for renewal and reform, we will not be able to turn these enormous challenges for the better and to make the crisis a *kairos*.

The end of the Constantinian epoch

To comprehend the present crisis, we must not content ourselves with a snapshot. As the Church shares 'joys and hopes, the grief and anxieties of the men of this age',[91] we must perceive the crisis of the Church in connection with the crises and the fast and far-reaching transformational processes of today's world, which were already emphatically described by the Second Vatican Council.[92] Since then, these processes have accelerated dramatically. In Europe we see thus a crisis of culture and civilization which questions and often intolerantly and militantly fights against both the Christian roots of Europe and the foundational Christian values shared by European societies. There are even attempts to ban the archetypal and basic symbol of Christianity, the cross, from the public sphere. One has to be blind to miss the fact that the Church is heading towards difficult times.

We must see this situation in its larger historical context. The long-lasting Constantinian age (from the fourth to the eighteenth centuries) and its aftermath in the bourgeois era with its traditional *Volkskirche* came to an end with the First and Second World Wars. With this, the 'Christendom epoch' of Europe also ended. The end of the Constantinian epoch meant the end of the *Corpus christianum* and the epoch in which Christianity was practised by the majority of individuals in European society, whereby it could rely on political powers as its secular arm, and determine to a great extent, the social lives of Europeans.

It was an end fraught with horror. In Europe, the twentieth century produced two inhuman totalitarian systems and experienced two world wars that fundamentally changed the world and literally ploughed through the European continent. Auschwitz and the gulags demonstrated in horrific ways the failure of modern ideologies and utopias. Consequently, Western civilization ground to a halt in resignation and desperation of reason. This has led to so-called postmodernism, a term which is just as vague and unclear as the situation it describes.[93] It is characterized by the fact that it questions all great ideas and ideals, not only of Christianity but also of the modern Enlightenment. The consequence of this is nihilism, which Nietzsche predicted as the characterization of the present age. He proclaimed the death of God[94] and defined nihilism as the decline of all previously valid ideals. Such nihilism is marked by the rejection of metaphysics and a belief that there is no truth.[95]

A secular age?

Many have lapsed into despair rather than accepting and facing the challenge for the Church raised by this situation. On the one hand, there is dismay among progressives that the open-minded formulas which appeared after the Council have become banal and are met from the outside with little love. On the other hand, there are those at the other end of the spectrum who are equally horrified by the situation and who, as a reaction, almost desperately attempt to recreate the old certainties and to return to the old practices. And yet, it is impossible to return to self-evident certainties and practices in the wake of the new questions and doubts of post-modernity. Both resignation and restoration require withdrawal into a fortress of sorts in an effort to secure as many of the old certainties as possible. Moreover, they blamed the restorationists, and vice versa. Considering the severity of the problems we are facing, this is an almost pathological situation, and serves to highlight only the Church's present internal crisis, while disregarding the real challenges. But we cannot avoid our Western cultural and intellectual milieu.

There is no way around it. We in the Western world (the Muslim, Buddhist, Confucian and other cultures need to be treated separately) must accept our own current context. Already during the Nazi regime and the Second World War there were two courageous witnesses giving their lives for their faith, Alfred Delp and Dietrich Bonhoeffer, who pointed out that we had entered a secular age which is fundamentally different from the age when religion once permeated private and public life and was taken so much for granted that an atheistic position seemed nearly unthinkable.[96]

Today the religious-transcendent orientation is no longer seen as normal. It is now just one option besides others and not the easiest one.[97] Our world is more or less disenchanted.[98] It has become factually unemotional and often also banal, even though there may be some melancholic, nostalgic and esoteric interests involved. A 'mega-trend religion' can hardly be deduced from this.[99] It is now rather art which, for many, has replaced religion and which keeps a tiny gap open into a reality that transcends the empirical. Where once transcendence pointed towards a different, mysterious, miraculously divine world, this place has been overtaken by a gaping void, and those places where the gods once dwelt are now haunted by new ghosts.[100]

What more or less dominates today in our Western societies is the option of a self-sufficient humanism. It often contains a certain melancholy and nostalgia, the feeling of missing something that is no longer there, perhaps also a certain sadness and joylessness. Yet, this accurately describes the way many people live today. They look for the fulfilment of their lives, not in relation to a transcendent reality, but immanently in a diverse and often absolutely respectable way. One cannot say that they all lead superficial lives, that they are dishonest or even amoral. On the contrary, there are many honest and responsible people among them that we all know, with whom we live together each day and with whom we have to deal with in all areas of life.

Of course, there are also other options, far more radical, yet by no means novel: an intolerant, fundamentalist, ideologically misguided religiosity which we find today not only in Islamism, but in an equally intolerant, new fundamentalist and aggressive, ideological atheism where the much-praised enlightened tolerance has itself become intolerant and thus defames and fights any claim on truth. Both attitudes proceed inversely from the now-obsolete theory of secularization, according to which processes of modernization necessarily entail permeating secularization, such that they either fight modernization because of the danger of secularization or, in order to advance modernization, they militantly repel religion, concrete Christianity, and ban from the public sphere the cross, the symbol which once made Europe great. As always, extremes meet.

In this situation, many in the Church have become discouraged and helpless. Yet, the Church today has reason to be confident. As Jürgen Habermas, who does not come from the Christian tradition, has demonstrated, in the spiritual emptiness that has developed, the Church holds with its message of God's kingdom a resource of meaning that we need more than anything else. In view of the enormous challenges facing our world today it is necessary that this message is rationally decoded and made fruitful.[101] Theodor W. Adorno had already previously written: 'The only philosophy which is justifiable in the face of despair would be the attempt to look at all things as they would present themselves from the point of view of salvation. Knowledge has no light but that shed on the world by salvation: all else is reconstruction and remains mere technique.'[102]

These are voices of qualified observers and objective analysts of the situation. They refer us to the potential that we ourselves have, even to the centre of our very own message – the message of God and his kingdom. In addition there are the qualified voices from among our own ranks. I mention the French philosopher Jean-Luc Marion. One of his books bears the telling title *Le croire pour le voir. Réflexions sur la rationalité et l'irrationalité de quelques croyants* (*Faith to see. Reflections on the Rationality of Revelation and the Irrationality of some Believers*). He sees the future of Catholicism not in questions of structures but in the new current relevance of the question about God.[103]

This shows again that secularization is not a law of nature nor an inevitable destiny to which we simply have to subject ourselves. Contention is possible and not hopeless. However, on the agenda are not primarily questions about the Church but the question about God and issues concerning the Church in the light of the God question.[104]

In this situation, it does not help to look back at the past nostalgically and to think that the old splendour can be rebuilt. Equally, we must not run after utopias thinking we can build a new church in the third millennium. Neither the nostalgic dream of the past nor the utopian dream really help. A realistic conservative attitude does not mean restoring a situation that is past. Rather, it entails the argumentative, critically-constructive recovery of what in the Tradition has been proven to be lasting, precious, and valid for the new situation, and the translation of this anew for the sake of a reality that has changed signifiantly.

The Church as qualitative and creative minority

Some object to this programme because, they contend, the Church lacks the means. Indeed, with the end of the Constantinian era, the time of the old *Volkskirche* Church is behind us as well. Unless we are completely mistaken, the Christians in Europe must prepare themselves – now and even more so in the future – for a situation of diaspora and minority within a culturally and religiously pluralistic society. In addition, they must prepare themselves for the fact that Christianity on a global level will no longer be dominated by Europe, but that it has, in a concrete sense, become a *universal* church.

This is no reason for cultural pessimism as proclaimed by Oswald Spengler in his volume *Untergang des Abendlandes* (*The Decline of the West*, 1918–22). Contrary to Spengler, the historian Arnold J. Toynbee presents in his magnum opus *A Study of History* (1934–61) the theory that cultures survive in crises if they face new challenges creatively. This does not depend on majorities, however, but on creative minorities with distinct identities that face new challenges and find solutions that others can then follow. This thesis that creative minorities can have relevance and influence is confirmed by history. One thinks, for example, of the importance of Judaism for modern Western culture. Therefore, we should not lament about decreasing numbers. It is not quantity that is decisive, but quality and identity.[105]

Obviously, the intention must not be to declare the goal of pastoral care to be a self-seclusion to a so-called holy rest. Rather, we must help, if it is God's will, to accept this development and to derive new missionary energy from it. There is no way for the Church to find identity and strength other than in building on the established apostolic fundament and by making this fruitful in view of the new challenges. The Church can only survive the storms to which it is exposed if it has deep roots. It must be Church in the world of today and tomorrow, but must not be, at the same time, the Church of this world and according to the standards of this world. It is the Church of Jesus Christ and so also the Church under the Cross, the passage to Easter. We may thus assume with confidence that, with some pains, a new shape will emerge from out of the Church that is one and the same throughout all centuries.

What this book seeks to do

It is precisely in this sense that I would like to present in this book an outline of Catholic ecclesiology and to reflect upon the nature, reality and mission of the Church for these precarious times. This book does not seek to present a new, but rather, in the sense of the Second Vatican Council, a *renewed* Catholic ecclesiology. It seeks to expound the question of the Church in light of the question of God and of the message of his kingdom, and to do so in such a way that the Church is properly situated both biblically and existentially. However, the Church can only have relevance for the individual and society if, and only if, it is certain of its own identity. The significance of the Church for us today depends upon its existence as Church of Jesus Christ. From this foundation of the Church in Jesus Christ this book seeks to contribute to the renewal of the Church. More than in other parts of the world, the Church in the 'old Europe' is in need of a new impetus, a refocused vision, and concrete perspectives for the future. These cannot come from an activism which is short of breath. It can only grow out of the recollection of the fundamentals. It is only in this way that, through purification and renewal, the crisis can become kairos, and a renewed Pentecost can become reality.

II

Outlines of Catholic ecclesiology

1. Preliminary considerations from the perspective of fundamental theology

1.1 Introduction

'Church' – an ambiguous word

During my childhood and youth, parish and Church belonged to the normal everyday life in which we grew up and felt at home. For many (though still not most) young people today, this is no longer the case. Martin Luther could still claim that every child of seven years was able to say what the Church is.[1] He would hardly dare to say this today. For many of our contemporaries the Church has become an alien world which might perhaps still deserve due respect for its social services, and yet which is encountered only sporadically, usually through popular forms of the media. Not only for a few people, 'church' has almost become a word without meaning [Unwort, T.H.].

Before we speak about the Church, its self-conception and offices, we must first seek a prior understanding of what we mean when we speak of Church. This becomes even more necessary insofar as 'church' is an ambiguous word which can be understood in numerous and very different ways.

'Church' can mean the building used as a place of assembly for mass and other religious services that also has cultural and artistic value, but can have the effect of turning the Church into a museum piece. If we speak of the present church, what is usually meant is some social entity, a target of apostrophization by critics as an organization with its own institutions, various bodies, and offices. In contrast there is the slogan, 'We are Church'. It does not signify the Church as an institution, but rather sees the Church as a community critical of institutions and with participatory structures.

The aspect of community is also present in a different way in the theological understanding of Church. In the historical symbol shared by all denominational churches we acknowledge the Church as *communio sanctorum*, that is, as communion in the Holy (*sancta*) and therefore also as communion of saints (*sancti*) or believers. Here Church is seen as the communion of faith and worship which then also becomes a serving community.

Yet this does not encompass the entire range of different meanings of 'church'. After all, the idea of the communion of believers can be understood as the local church present in each place as well as the worldwide Church in and out of all peoples and cultures. Finally, since the emergence of the denominations in the wake of the Reformation of the sixteenth century, the Catholic, Orthodox, Anglican, Lutheran and Reformed Church and the free churches call themselves 'church' in a different way, setting themselves apart from each other. We encounter the Church empirically in a confusing multitude of denominational churches. In the ecumenical movement of the twentieth century then, searching for the unity of Christians in the one Church has become urgent.

All this is described with one and the same word: 'church'. No wonder, then, that concerning the Church there are not only many different opinions and attitudes but also manifold misunderstandings, leading to confusion and also incomprehension. So we must ask ourselves: Church, what is this?

Understanding the Church from the inside out

If we want to know what the Church is, then we must not describe the reality of the Church from the outside. To be fair, we must first let the Church itself say what and who it is and then proceed from the self-conception that the Church or the churches have of themselves. Despite all differences, we can depart hereby from a common basic understanding on which all historical churches agree. For the Catholic, Orthodox, Protestant and also largely the free church Christians acknowledge together in the Apostles' Creed the Church as *communio sanctorum*, as the communion of saints or also of believers participating in the Holy. Through the faith in Jesus Christ expressed in this acknowledgement and through one baptism, they belong to the Church. The English word 'church' (German *Kirche*) is derived from the Greek word κυριακός and means the community belonging to and dependent from the Lord (κύριος) Jesus Christ.[2] This fundamental common ground is bigger than all that separates Christians otherwise. This is why the members of all churches today perceive each other more consciously than before as brothers and sisters in the one common Lord Jesus Christ.

This fundamental common ground in the one faith in Jesus Christ and in one baptism sets Christians apart from all others who are not Christians, whether they are adherents to a different religion, whom we treat with respect, or whether they are religiously agnostic, sceptic, indifferent or of an anti-religious disposition, whereby Christians should respect every honest conviction even if they do not share it. In today's pluralistic and largely secular world, we often live as Christians in the diaspora in which being a Christian and actively belonging to a church can no longer be taken for granted and in which we nevertheless should live together tolerantly and respectfully.

Among other things, this new situation of diaspora has brought Christians from all denominations closer together. Yet, this also makes us more painfully aware that concerning the topic 'church', differences arise which lead to separations that often run through families and circles of friends. These differences have been moderated by the ecumenical convergence, but they have by no means been removed. We live in a world that is, increasingly so, globally linked and interwoven, and in which not only members of various denominations but also adherents of different religions live next door to each other; often together under one roof and even in one family. In a world that has become, more and more, a community of fate, there is inevitably the question about the one Church. Ecclesiology as the doctrine of the Church is thus not a purely academic question. In one way or another it touches the life of every Christian.

The basic problem of ecclesiology

It is because of this situation that, for many, differences between denominations have become incomprehensible. If one tries to comprehend such differences, then it becomes apparent that they emerge from the variety of answers given by the denominational churches to the question regarding the reciprocal relation of various meanings of 'church' previously described. Of particular importance is the question of how the Church, understood as the communion of saints which we confess in faith, relates to the Church as social entity. Is the Church purely a reality of faith, or is there an inner correlation to the Church which we perceive as institution? Is it at all possible to grasp and describe it institutionally?

Of course, the Church in all denominations is never only a transcendental reality. It is audible and visible through the proclamation and the word and the administration of the sacraments and thus always connected with social structures. There is no purely charismatic church, no pure church of love that does not display at least a minimum of institutional elements and that also has, to a certain degree, a legal constitution. Yet, this begs the question of the extent of the importance ascribed to this institutional constitution. Must we have to identify with it, practise in it, or is it possible to distance oneself privately or publicly from the constituted church and still belong to the communion of faith which is the Church?

Different denominations have different answers to this question. There are also a substantial number of Catholic Christians for whom the connection between the institutional church and personal faith has been loosened and even dissolved. In many such cases faith is orientated towards a parish community but only marginally rooted in the Church, if not explicitly critical of the Church. Such faith often sees itself in a vague way as ecumenical in a supra-denominational sense.

In this situation which marks both the Catholic Church and present day ecumenism, we must ask how Jesus defined the Church? Did he want a church at all? How did the Early Church understand itself? What do the New Testament and the great witnesses of faith of the past say about the Church? Such questions deserve careful consideration. At this point a preliminary anthropological remark has to suffice. Above all, in a deeply secularized world, it is hardly possible to keep up a purely inner – although perhaps personally deep-rooted – faith. Personal faith is reliant on the social support of a community of faithful. Ultimately, in our highly institutionalized and medially linked world, faith can only be effective in society if it is also institutionally confessed in a binding manner. Again it becomes apparent that this is not only abstract theory, it is about the question of how the Church can be effectively present with its message in the world today and tomorrow. The understanding of Church as advocated in Catholic and Orthodox theology can depart from here. It interprets the visible, institutionally tangible form of the Church as sign and instrument of what the Church essentially is in its spiritual reality.

However, just as there are denominationally different answers regarding the institutional form of the Church, there are different answers to the question of how the one Church, understood as a reality of faith, relates to the many denominational churches. Are the various denominational churches different historical forms and merely parts of the one Church of Jesus Christ, or can one church claim to be the true Church? It is not only the Catholic Church that puts forward such a claim on truth; in one way or another each church must put a claim on truth. If they no longer did so, they would become in the literal sense indifferent, devoid of value. They would give themselves up by doing so.

Therefore, there is not only the question: what is the Church? There is also the question: *where* is the true Church and what gives the true Church its orientation? And how does the true Church relate to other communities that also claim to be the church? Again, different denominations have different and controversial answers to such questions. Despite everything uniting the denominations, ecclesiology is an extremely problematic field of theology with a high potential for conflict.[3]

In this introduction, I can only present a preliminary rough sketch of the differences and controversies, but I will look at them in more detail in the sections that follow. These differences are fundamental for Catholic, Orthodox, Protestant or free church ecclesiologies. They are not just secondary features. This is why there can be no denominationally neutral, ecumenical ecclesiology. There can only be Catholic, Orthodox, Protestant or free church ecclesiologies that, in turn, should – and today also must – engage ecumenically in conversation and exchange. In this ecumenical sense, the following is not about ecclesiology in general but deals consciously and intentionally with Catholic ecclesiology.

1.2 Preliminary methodological considerations

Ecclesiological method – ecclesiology as the science of Faith

Because of the different meanings and dimensions of the word 'church', it is possible to address ecclesiology in a number of divergent ways and with different methods and intentions. The Church can be regarded as a human institution. Accordingly, one can speak of it historically, in cultural and political sciences, and sociologically, and one can research its 'system' and modes of operation.[4] It is possible to discuss what the Church achieved in the past for human progress, art, culture and science and what it still does today; what it presently contributes to the solution of social problems, to the aid of children, the sick, the old and handicapped, to development aid and for peace in the world, as well as for the individual coping with life and finding meaning and sense. It is however also possible to scavenge through church history and collect all the rubbish of human weakness, lust for power, intrigues, failure, stupidity and malice that, in all honesty, have occurred and still exist. These are all questions to which one must give due attention as a theologian; but they are not theology.[5]

Theology proceeds from the creed common to the whole of Christianity: '*credo (in) ecclesiam*' or '*credimus (in) ecclesiam*'. 'I believe (in) the Church' or 'we believe (in) the Church'.[6] For theology the Church is thus an object of faith and theology is science of faith. This, in turn, can be understood in a double sense. On the one hand, the creed says '*credo (in) ecclesiam*' and speaks thus of the subject of faith in the singular. On the other, it also formulates '*credimus (in) ecclesiam*', thus speaking of the faith in the plural, in the 'we-form'.

The wording in the singular 'I believe' was originally a baptismal confession with which the baptized person acknowledged the faith in which he was baptized and received into the Church. In contrast, the confession in the 'we-form' is a liturgical confession of the assembled worshipping community. It expresses the fact that the faith is not purely 'I-faith' but always also a 'we-faith'. The personal faith of the individual means that he or she is joined into common faith of the Church of all times and all places, that is, both synchronically and diachronically. It is participation in the one faith and in the communion in the one faith. One believes as an individual, yet in faith one is never alone, but carried by and connected with the faith of the Church of all times. Thomas Aquinas could thus say: 'The confession of faith is drawn up in a symbol in the person, as it were, of the whole Church, which is united together by faith.'[7]

Ecclesiology is the science of faith in a double sense: it presupposes personal belief and it draws from the faith of the Church. The decisive factor is not personal experiences with the Church, whether bad or good, or pious or impious convictions which the individual theologian might have concerning the subject Church – it is the common confession to the one, holy, catholic and apostolic Church. Theologically understood, ecclesiology as doctrine of the Church is thus no theory about the Church designed from outside. It is, as ecclesial theology, a reflection of the Church about itself and its mission the world.

Ecclesiology as the self-reflection of the Church

It is not only today that the definition of ecclesiology as reflection of the Church about itself and its mission has given rise to some serious ideology-critical questions. Can theology, one may ask, only describe and reinforce what it finds as doctrine of the Church about itself, or is it in fact an ideology with the sole concern of justifying the given ecclesial position or the ruling system, as some claim today? Undoubtedly, there are such forms of ecclesiology which fuel this ideology-critical objection. That is why it must be taken seriously, even though it does not apply to an ecclesiology that understands itself properly.

The ideology-critical objection proceeds from the wrong understanding of faith. Properly understood, faith is not an irrational act, it is not only pure feeling, nor does it spring from a pure decision of the will, and lastly it is not just an acceptance of religious beliefs. On the basis of the ecclesial Tradition, the Second Vatican Council presents us with a totally different and more comprehensive understanding of faith: 'obedience [of faith] by which man commits his whole self freely to God, offering the full submission of intellect and will to God who reveals, and freely assenting to the truth revealed by Him.'[8] Faith is thus a personal act of commitment of man with his whole soul, his intellect and his will (cf. Mk 12.29–33 par). As an act of the whole person it is also an act of reason and needs to be rationally accounted for as such.

Hence, the believer must give a rational account of his faith to himself and others. Paul speaks of a λογικὴ λατρεία, an *obsequium rationale* that is a rational service to God (Rom. 12.1) and 1 Peter asks the Christians to give account (ἀπολογία) of their hope to everyone (1 Pet. 3.15). So, properly understood, faith is always a *fides quaerens intellectum*, faith that asks for comprehension and wants to know what it believes and why.[9] Such explanation is asked of every Christian, especially today. When this happens explicitly and methodologically, then we can speak of theology as a science.

To understand how such accounting is possible without becoming ideological, here particularly in the context of theological reflection upon the Church, it is necessary to pause for a short consideration of the basic structure of human knowledge and human science. In the epistemological and hermeneutical discussion, it has long since become clear that there can be no science without preconditions. In all our cognition we proceed from a preconception.[10] Without this we would not be interested in an 'object' at all. It is only because we think we know something already that we are interested in understanding it better and deeper. In this we are conditioned, more than we are normally aware of, by patterns and habits of thinking decisively impacted by our respective culture, our language and their categories. Such a preconception would be a dogmatic prejudice, in the negative sense, only if it fenced itself off and shielded itself from questions, problems, new experiences and insights, and if it was no longer prepared to reflect upon these experiences with the help of generally recognized rules and to extend and deepen knowledge where necessary.

Such scientific reflection is also possible with regard to the Church. According to Catholic understanding, the Church is one single, complex and, at the same time, concrete reality which grows together from out of a human and divine element.[11] From a theological perspective, these two sides are inseparable. It is not possible to juxtapose a church of law against a church of love or the church as institution against a purely spiritual church. Likewise, both sides are not simply identical; they cannot be separated, but they must be distinguished from each other. Since Vatican II the divine side only accessible to faith has been called the mystery of the Church. This does not mean an ideal church painted in the sky, nor a church as we would like it to be. Rather, we encounter the Church as mystery in a human form. So when we speak of the Church as people of God, body of Christ, temple of the Holy Spirit, we do not make statements of faith about some kind of supernatural church but about the concrete, visible earthly church. In other words, we have the divine dimension always in a visible human form. As Paul says, we have our treasure in jars of clay (2 Cor. 4.7).

Each empirical appearance of the Church is not simply identical with what the nature of the Church is for faith. Hence, no Catholic is expected to identify in faith with everything that he or she encounters concretely in the Church and how he or she encounters it. It is only with God that we can identify totally and undivided; as Jesus says in the central commandment, it is God alone whom we can and shall love with all our heart and all our strength (Mk 12.30 par). Any other reality, including that of the Church, must be considered in faith in its relation to God. This was the great insight of Thomas Aquinas. He made it the central programme of his theology to relate everything to God and to consider it in its orientation towards God.[12] Hence, for the believer, the visible Church is only an object of identification insofar as it is the historical place, sign and instrument of God's presence in Jesus Christ.[13]

The theologian does not face the present church without standard. Yet he or she does not receive criteria from outside, but from faith itself. That is to say, by defining ecclesiology as reflection of the Church about itself, by using methods appropriate to its object, the Church and its self-conception is to be reflected in its relation to God as he revealed himself in the Gospel of Jesus Christ.

Ecclesiology as ecclesial science

We find an, at first sight unexpected, confirmation of what was just said in Holy Scripture. The Gospel in the original sense of the word is not simply identical with the four gospels in the New Testament. The four gospels are not the Gospel but are, rather, authoritative testimony to the Gospel which, as such, is no scripture but the living proclaimed and accepted in faith message of God's salvation in and through Jesus Christ in the Holy Spirit.[14] The Gospel of Jesus Christ is not a dead reality on paper, but a living reality happening in the Holy Spirit, which is believed and lived in the Church. If we take a closer look, we notice that the word of the Gospel of Jesus Christ can be understood in a double way: on the one hand it is the message of Jesus Christ (*genitivus objectivus*) and, on the other, it is the message in which Jesus Christ communicates himself in the Holy Spirit in the proclamation and reveals himself (*genitivus subjectivus*). The Gospel is thus the self-communication of Jesus Christ in the Holy Spirit in and through the proclamation and the faith of the Church.

In this sense, the Apostle Paul writes to the church in Corinth: 'you yourselves are our letter (of commendation), written in our hearts, that everyone can read and understand; and it is plain that you are a letter from Christ, entrusted to our care, written not with ink but with the Spirit of the living God; not on stone tablets but on tablets of human hearts' (2 Cor. 3.2f.). Towards the end of the second century Irenaeus of Lyons says, in the same sense, that many nations of those barbarians have the Tradition written in their hearts by the Spirit, without paper or ink.[15]

It was on this basis, in a situation when the faith was in danger of becoming unclear in the confusion caused by Gnostic voices and of degenerating into speculations, that the early Church Fathers, particularly Irenaeus of Lyons, Tertullian, Clement of Alexandria, Origen and others established the rule of faith (κανών τῆς πίστεως, *regula fidei*) that which, they contended, is authoritative as the apostolic kerygma in the form of its mediation through the Church.[16] By this they did not mean a formal external rule for faith, but the rule which is faith itself proclaimed by and lived in the Church. This point of departure from the Gospel, proclaimed and believed, celebrated in the liturgy and lived in the Church, was intimately known to the Church Fathers, the theologians of High Scholasticism and the Council of Trent.[17] It was also well known among the Reformers and in their understanding of Church as *creatura verbi*.[18]

It was only the Bible criticism of the Enlightenment, specifically Hermann Samuel Reimarus († 1768), that claimed to perceive a break between the proclamation of Jesus and the Church and its teaching.[19] Theology became thereby exegetical and historical bookishness, akin to archaeology. It was thought that faith needed to be historically reconstructed from Scripture and thereby became entangled in hypotheses which often said more about the spirit of their authors than the Spirit of the Bible.

The theologians who led the way out of this morass were, on the Protestant side, Friedrich Schleiermacher († 1834),[20] and, on the Catholic side, the Catholic Tübingen theologians of the nineteenth century in particular. Fundamental were Johann Sebastian Drey with his programmatic treatise *Vom Geist und Wesen des Katholizismus* (*The Spirit and Essence of Catholicism*, 1819)[21] and his volume *Kurze Einleitung in das Studium der Theologie* (*Brief Introduction to the Study of Theology*, 1819),[22] and especially Johann Adam Möhler with his early volume *Unity in the Church or the Principle of Catholicism* (1825)[23] and again in *Symbolism: Exposition of the Doctrinal Differences between Catholics and Protestants as Evidenced in their Symbolical Writings* (1832).[24] For Möhler, concerning the Gospel, 'the living gospel always preceded the written gospel and went along with it'; it is primarily written into the hearts of the faithful.[25] The Church is for him the 'Christian religion become objective, its living representation'.[26]

If one follows this line of thinking, ecclesiology cannot be about laboriously collating a concept of Church out of the vast complex amount – not to say jungle – of disparate exegetical, historical and sociological insights. Ecclesiology is not about artificially reconstructing the nature of the Church from historical sources, even if they are as foundational as the Bible and the testimony of Tradition. Such a reconstruction and a thus-reconstructed church would be a dead, artificially reanimated reality. Even if it was done seriously and respectably, it would remain a hypothesis and would therefore be an insecure and unsound basis for faith. Whoever turns the Bible into a paper pope finds himself confronted with the most diverse and almost incomprehensibly numerous interpretations of the Bible. Even if one can discover a current consensus, it remains a fact that the feet of those carrying away such a reconstruction are already outside the door (cf. Acts 5.9).

Ecclesiology proceeds from the lived, confessed and, often enough, suffered faith of the Church. It begins directly in the life of the Church and aims to reflect faith and life of the Church. For this point of departure one can refer to the famous words of Augustine: 'for my part, I should not believe the gospel except as moved by the authority of the Catholic Church.'[27]

The dogmatic character of ecclesiology

Despite all this common ground as point of departure, it is here that the paths of Catholic and Orthodox ecclesiology, on the one hand, and Protestant ecclesiology, on the other, diverge. Luther still saw himself in line not only with Scripture but also with the Old Church. He did not want to found a new church. Yet, it was already in the disputation with Cardinal Cajetan in Augsburg in 1520 that Luther appealed to his interpretation of Scripture and his personal certainty of faith. Cardinal Cajetan, a perceptive Thomist theologian, immediately realized the consequence of this argument and replied: 'that is what I call building a new Church'.[28] Indeed, despite all that remained in common, Luther's basic decision, which became increasingly clear after the Augsburg disputation, meant a break with the whole Tradition.[29]

Luther still did not advocate a formal Scripture principle. Rather, he wanted to interpret Scripture from and towards its centre or its object, that is, from Jesus Christ. 'That which Christ does not teach is not apostolic.'[30] Lutheran orthodoxy considered Holy Scripture of the Old and New Testament as judge, norm and rule of all knowledge in faith. In contrast, all other symbols were seen not as judge-like Scripture but only as witnesses and expositions of faith.[31] It was in this sense that the symbols of the Old Church (the Apostles' Creed, the Nicene-Constantinopolitan Creed and the so-called Athanasian Creed) were taken into the confessional writings as authoritative interpretations of Scripture. Yet, the Reformation tradition granted these symbols only a relative authority.[32]

Through historical criticism of the Bible and of church history and confessional history in the Enlightenment, the principle of 'sola scriptura' and that of self-interpreting scripture fell into a crisis. That which was considered to be the formal principle of Protestantism became practically unusable.[33] This left for Neo-Protestantism[34] only an undogmatic Christianity. This was impressively demonstrated by Adolf Harnack († 1930) in his own style in the famous lectures *Wesen des Christentums* (*What is Christianity?*, 1900). A public, generally authoritative, objectively dogmatic claim was no longer possible. Basically, it only left the way from the Church to independent free church communities.[35]

In the first half of the twentieth century, the crisis after the First World War saw Lutheran theology searching for a new approach. Departing from the idea of the Church as a creation of God's Word (*creatura verbi*) it came to a Lutheran renaissance that was also of great ecumenical importance.[36] Still, the actual breakthrough came with Karl Barth († 1968), who came from the Reformed tradition. In the preface to his interpretation of the Letter to the Romans (1918) he inaugurates – with a bang, as it were – the theology of the twentieth century: 'Paul spoke as a child of his time to his contemporaries. However, much more important than this truth is the other that he speaks as prophet and apostle of God's kingdom to all men of all times.'[37]

With this a new, basic theological change had been introduced. The Church is perceived as creation of the living, proclaimed, creative and self-asserting Word of God. Therefore, the vast majority of Protestant theologians nowadays no longer advocate in ecumenical discussions the formal Scripture principle in the sense of Protestant orthodoxy or liberal theology.[38] This epochal change in the history of theology found its most profound expression when Barth undertook, as a conscious distancing from Neo-Protestantism, to publish his multi-volume *Church Dogmatics*. In the history of theology this is truly a magnum opus, which, among other things, served to reestablish eccesiology as self-reflection of the Church.

Still, also for Barth, dogma is not the theologically presupposed authoritative doctrine of the Church. Rather, it is the result of the reflection of theology on the proclamation of the Church in regard to its adherence to revelation.[39] Dogma is not the prerequisite but the desired proper content of dogmatic speech.[40] 'Dogmatic calls the teaching Church to a renewed listening to God's Word of the revelation witnessed in Scripture.'[41]

While acknowledging the impressive achievement of Barth's dogmatics, we must observe that this has not solved the problem of the interpretation of Scripture posed by the historical-critical method. The problems of biblical interpretation soon became virulent again, particularly in the dispute between Barth and Rudolf Bultmann († 1976) concerning the latter's attempt to demythologize and interpret Scripture existentially.[42] This virulence can be seen today in the pluralism of differing interpretations and hypotheses in which the canon of Scripture itself is also questioned.[43]

Erik Peterson († 1960) originally drew on Barth and Bultmann. Quite early on, Peterson pointed out that Christianity was not dialectic but, because of God's incarnation in Jesus Christ, essentially dogmatic. In his view, this has nothing to do with the human inclination to dogmatize. On the contrary, the true dogma itself fights all human dogmatizing. Through the incarnation God has become concrete and definitive once and for all; indeed he comes seriously close to us. 'A theology which is not essentially defined by the dogma is thus rather fantasy for in it the revelation in Christ is not concretely expressed.'[44]

This discussion about the significance of the scripture principle also had a Catholic sequel immediately before and during the Second Vatican Council. In the 1950s, Josef Rupert Geiselmann was wrestling with Johann Sebastian Drey's and Johann Adam Möhler's understandings of Tradition. In the course of this he also investigated the understanding of Tradition of the Council of Trent, thereby discovering that the controversial teaching that claimed that the divine revelation was testified to, partly (*partim*) in holy Scripture and partly (*partim*) in oral traditions was not defined by the council at all. With the formula that the revelation was contained in the Holy Scriptures 'and' (*et*) in the non-scriptural traditions,[45] the council had instead left open the precise relation between Scripture and Tradition.[46] For Geiselmann, Scripture and Tradition each contain the whole of revelation, and in this sense they complement and interpret each other. According to Geiselmann, Tradition is thereby the self-tradition of the elevated Lord in the Holy Spirit into continuous presence.[47] This shows for his understanding of Tradition, which was influenced by Drey and Möhler, that a material sufficiency of Scripture in the sense of Lutheran orthodoxy and derived there from an exclusive and final competence of historical exegesis was totally alien to him.[48]

Still, in the public debate, Geiselmann's thesis soon took on a life of its own in the sense of a content-related sufficiency of Scripture. If content-related sufficiency is seen as Scripture understood in the interpretation of the Tradition, then this thesis indeed corresponds to Catholic Tradition. In this sense it is found in Thomas Aquinas[49] and in a very differentiated form in some Roman theologians of the nineteenth century, such as the highly respected Johannes Baptist Franzelin († 1886).[50] However, it becomes erroneous if it leads to the opinion that the historical-critical exegesis emancipated from Tradition was the final authority of theology. Against this thesis, which also contradicts Geiselmann's opinion, Joseph Ratzinger quite rightly put up resistance very early.[51] After long and controversial debates, Vatican II itself left the question of a material sufficiency of Scripture open. Still, it strongly emphasized the close connection between Tradition, Scripture and ecclesial doctrine.[52]

From a Catholic perspective, the point of departure and the basis of theology is Holy Scripture together with – i.e. in the living interpretation of – the ecclesial Tradition and ecclesial doctrine. For this understanding of the dogmatic nature of theology we can refer to the Bible itself, since one of the most important results of the historical-critical exegesis is the thesis that there are fixed formulas of confessions in the New Testament which are older than its oldest writings. It is on the basis of one of those that Paul constructs his argument at a crucial point: the presentation of the message of the resurrection and the meaning of the Eucharist (1 Cor. 11.23-5; 15.3-5).[53] The terms 'dogma' and 'dogmatic theology' are relatively young. Still, what is meant by them is present in Scripture itself and in the theological Tradition through terms such as 'doctrine', 'articles of faith' and others theologically.[54]

The theological objective reason for the dogmatic approach lies in the conviction that God has revealed himself once and for all in Jesus Christ in a historical form and that Jesus Christ, as the elevated kyrios, is present in the Holy Spirit in the Church to remind it of everything he said and did and to lead it into the full truth (Jn 14.26f.; 15.26; 16.13). Catholic theology therefore does not proceed from a dead, laboriously reconstructed image of the Church, but from the interpretation of the testimony of Scripture in confession, liturgy and the whole life of the Church. In this sense it adheres to the dogmatic nature of theology and ecclesiology.

With this procedure, Catholic theology opposes today's dominant trend which despises the retaining of a position, let alone a dogmatic position, as fundamentalist stubbornness and unwillingness to enter the flow of the modern or postmodern world. It opposes a trend which thinks that everything could be chosen according to one's taste, like in a huge department store. But whoever thinks theologically in such a way contradicts the 'once and for all' nature of God's revelation in Jesus Christ and his lasting presence in the Church. He should remember the end of the sermon on the mount, for instead of rock he builds his house upon the sand of time and its fast-changing trends and one must not be surprised that when the storm arrives and rages, nothing but a heap of shards remains (cf. Mt. 7.24-7).[55]

Scripture and Tradition within the self-reflection of the Church

Adhering to the dogmatic character of theology raises the question of what belongs under these circumstances to Scripture and the testimonies of Tradition within the self-reflection of the Church. Right from the start we have to say in answer to this question that they are more than just an arsenal of subsequent proofs. Holy Scripture and the testimonies of Tradition are not a measure applied from the outside to the Church and its doctrine, but rather are an essential part of the testimony of the Church about itself. In other words, they are not instances coming from outside that can be used subsequently as proofs or counter-instances. They are authoritative testimonies of the faith of the Church itself and thus an integrating and constitutive part of the Church's reflection about itself.

In this, Holy Scripture has a special and unique function. The Bible alone is the inspired word of God in and through human words, and this fact elevates it lasting normative apostolic beginning and origin. Johann Adam Möhler speaks of the 'beginning in abundance'. Scripture is therefore the prime message and document of faith by which all proclamation must be nourished and from which it must take its orientation.[56] It was from the testimony of Scripture that, throughout history, renewal movements have proceeded again and again. This cannot be any different today.

We know much better today than in the past that the scriptures of the New Testament emerged from previously living traditions; that they were written for the Church; that they were read and collected in the Church; and finally, after several controversies, that they were put together in the canon by the Church. Thus Church and Bible have belonged together since the origin of the Church as well as the Bible. For this reason, the question of canon has been called the creeping disease of Protestant theology and the Protestant church.[57]

The fact that the canon of Scripture developed in and for the Church does not imply that Scripture was a work of the Church. On the contrary, with the formation of the canon the Church recognized Scripture as the Word of God given to it, as a predetermined canon – in other words, a yardstick. However, this canon cannot be regarded as detached from the previous or subsequent Tradition. Consequently, the interpretation of Holy Scripture cannot be detached from its history of origin and comprehension and its effective history. We cannot omit two – or in the case of the Old Testament, in parts even three – millennia and search for a neutral approach to the Bible. Theologically, the interpretation of Scripture cannot be separated from the living Tradition.

With this thesis the Church does not put itself above Holy Scripture, which is the inspired word of God. The Church does not stand above the Gospel, but it stands above the interpretation of the Gospel by the individual.[58] Holy Scripture does not belong to any individual, neither to the professional exegetes; it belongs to the Church as a whole. It is in this sense that we already find in Scripture itself the admonition not to interpret Scripture independently (2 Pet. 1.20).

If we interpret the Gospel testified in Holy Scripture in the context of the whole history of Tradition, it means we interpret the Gospel in the context not of a dead but a living Tradition. While listening to the testimony of Scripture we must always also hear what others before and beside us heard and understood, what the great witnesses of faith heard and taught and particularly what they lived and often suffered. The Roman theologian Carlo Passaglia († 1887) expressed the relation between Scripture and ecclesial Tradition in a beautiful image: 'Scripture is indeed the light for man but the Church is the lampstand that really lets the light shine for all who are in the house.'[59]

Thus, besides Holy Scripture, the Church's self-consciousness is tangible in the manifold testimonies of the living Tradition. This is particularly true for the liturgy because *lex orandi* is also *lex credendi*;[60] the law of praying is also the law of believing, just as, vice versa, personal and communal faith always translates into personal and especially communal liturgical prayer.[61] Witnesses of the living Tradition are the testimonies of the Church Fathers who, as respected theologians and often as bishops of local churches, are important witnesses of the ecclesial faith, as are also the great respected theologians of the past and the lived testimony of the saints. We need to observe the statements of the ecclesial magisterium, the sense of the faithful (*sensus fidelium*)[62] and also the testimonies of Christian art. This rich Tradition of the Church is not to be compared to an archive or a museum; it is rather to be perceived as an effervescent source (*fons*).[63] It is a reflection of the life-giving presence of the Holy Spirit in the Church, 'through whom the living voice of the Gospel resounds in the Church, and through her, in the world'.[64]

Dogmatics as an open system

The task of understanding the testimonies of Holy Scripture in the context of the manifold testimonies of the theological Tradition confronts us with a huge mountain of testimonies from both Scripture and Tradition. The question is: how are we to deal with this rich material from Scripture, Tradition and present experiences of faith? How can the different testimonies be related to each other?

In its history, theology has gone in numerous directions. Neo-Scholasticism proceeded from the statements of the ecclesiastical magisterium as the nearest rule of faith (*regula fidei proxima*) and subordinated Scripture and Tradition as a more remote rule of faith (*regula fidei remota*) and evidence. Not so the Church Fathers. Their theology is spiritual interpretation of Scripture.[65] During scholasticism the main task of a master of theology was still the interpretation of Holy Scripture. *Sacra doctrina* was synonymous with *sacra pagina*.[66] From a systematic perspective, the theologians of high scholasticism did not write theses but *quaestiones*, whereby they proceeded from the for and against (pro and contra) of different opinions to give their answer (*respondeo dicenum*) and finally to reply to the various objections.

In modern times, the groundbreaking work *Loci theologici* by Melchior Cano († 1560) was fundamental for centuries. In the spirit of humanism he took up the Aristotelian doctrine of the sources of knowledge (τόποι, loci). However, unlike Melanchthon he did not regard them in terms of content as main articles of faith but rather as formal places to find theological arguments and, following Thomas Aquinas, as authoritative instances of theological argumentation.[67] Melchior Cano does not place these manifold instances (*loci theologici*) in a closed hierarchical system. He rather advocated an open system in which the different criteriological instances each have their own specific importance and mutually interpret each other. Also the statements of the magisterium have their own weight, which cannot be suspended by other loci. The different criteriological instances cannot replace or supplant each other. They can and must interpret each other in an open system.[68]

Also belonging to this open form of argumentation is what the Spirit says today to the communities (Rev. 2.7.11.17.29 and others). Therefore, the once and for all handed-down faith (Jude 3) must be interpreted in the here and now for today. This does not mean that today's mentality and everything which is often called 'sign of the times' can be a theological instance beside or even against the faith, but that they have to be the point of reference in the sense that the Christian message must be interpreted for each individual today and constructively engaged with.[69] Thus, there are not only divergences and heresies through neglecting Tradition and accommodating to the spirit of the age; there are also heresies through the narrow-minded refusal to be a theologian in the here and now and to do theology as a living transmission of Tradition and so to miss the respective kairós. Whoever wants to speak for all ages, will ultimately speak for no age.

'Faith seeking understanding' – speculative theology

Even after all that has been said so far, there still remains the objection that ecclesiology was only a conversation of the Church about itself with itself. In other words, it was a purely church-immanent insider theory. Yet, a theology closed up in itself and shutting itself in would be a distortion of theology and ecclesiology. Already the New Testament calls all people to give account (ἀπολογία) of the hope that is in us (1 Pet. 3.15). Paul speaks of a rational worship (λογικὴ λατρεία, Rom. 12.1). So we must come again back to the axiom which was already established by the Church Fathers and which was decisive for high scholasticism, that faith seeks understanding (*fides quaerens intellectum*).

Of course, this axiom also applies to ecclesiology. It demands that we unfold the inner logos of being Church and thereby publicly demonstrate the Church's own rationality before the forum of reason. We must face the questions and criticism of the profane sciences and remain in dialogue with them. Yet, how is this possible without surrendering the nature of theology as science of faith?

From a Catholic perspective there are three ways to elevate faith into understanding.[70]

First, one can regard faith in analogy to natural cognition. This does not mean to prove or deduce faith rationally. If one tried to prove faith rationally, then one would not understand faith. On the contrary, one would abolish faith as faith. According to Thomas Aquinas, theology is in the same position as the first philosophy; as fundamental science it also cannot refer back to a further, supposedly superordinated foundation. It thus argues, as Thomas puts it, against those denying its principles; it tries to solve the objections (*solvere rationes*) presented.[71] It must try to show faith not as irrational but as rationally reasonable and rationally compatible.

Secondly, the individual truths of faith, including those statements of faith about the Church, must be shown in their inner relation to the whole of faith, and the inner logic and structure of faith must be made visible. Individual statements of faith are not to be placed one beside the other, rather they must be presented and made comprehensible as a reasonable whole. In this the hierarchy of truths must be respected.[72] This means that the individual doctrines must be interpreted on the basis and in the light of the fundamental doctrine about God and Jesus Christ.[73] Proceeding from the doctrine of God, Christology and Pneumatology, ecclesiology can thus be understood as a coherent and harmonious whole. If one considers the ecclesiological statements in their relativity – or better, relationality – to God and from God, then it is also possible to fight off a false absolutizing of the Church. Ecclesiology thus always stands under a superior standard against which it must be critically and constructively interpreted.

Thirdly, one can regard faith in view of the purpose and destination of humanity and the world and place ecclesiology in a global context of hope for the world and for humanity. This in turn can highlight the existential importance of ecclesiology. This was the intention of Bonaventura's theology, which was inspired by Augustine. For him, theology is a practical science which originates from the praxis of faith and leads back to the praxis.[74] It is more wisdom (*sapientia*) than science (*scientia*). For *sapientia* is not a theoretical capacity but, saturated in experience, a 'tasting' (*sapere*) of the truth. It is cognition in experience (*cognitio Dei saporatio*) and, as such, almost a tasting (*gustus vel saporatio*) of God.[75] Meister Eckhart likewise describes wisdom as a tasting knowledge (*sapida scientia*).[76] It is therefore no coincidence that we find great theology with those theologians whom we call saints, that is, theologians who have also personally experienced and been touched by the 'object' of which they know to speak very eruditely. Such experience is in the original meaning of the word 'con-vincing'.

Theology as an invitation to faith, not as proof of faith

Faith seeks understanding but, in this, faith is to remain faith and not become a rational truth. That is why the three speculative methodological steps must not be overcharged, just as we must not apologetically expect too much from biblical and historical arguments. Whoever proves too much proves too little. It is simply not possible to prove Christianity as the true religion and the Catholic Church as the true Church. For every argument, even the best, there are counter-arguments possible from different perspectives. This is true of those historical and exegetical questions which today often receive different answers from the separate churches, modern exegetes and historians. The same applies to speculative deliberations.

Finally, this also holds true if we look at the concrete appearance of the Church. The Church may be able to point to the impressive testimony of the martyrs and saints as well as to great cultural and social achievements, yet there are also sinners in its midst; it has sinful structures and, in the past and present, there have sadly also been serious scandals. That is why the Church itself can never be so credible and convincing that it could convince everyone through theological reflection. Individual arguments will always be disputable, just as, of course, the counter-arguments are. In the sense of the Thomist '*solvere rationes*', theology can try to dissolve objections and difficulties, and it can invite to faith; it cannot prove faith and it should not attempt it.

The arguments for faith only become convincing through a synopsis of many individual arguments within a comprehensive overall horizon of purpose and in the light of a fundamental decision. This does not only apply to theology; it applies to all human knowledge and science. The theological Tradition points to Psalm 36.9, 'in your light do we see light', and speaks of the light of faith (*lumen fidei*) which in grace illuminates our human horizon of cognition and lets us discern with the 'eyes of faith' the truth of faith.[77] Similarly the Letter to the Ephesians speaks of the enlightened eyes of the heart (Eph. 1.18). This calls to mind the famous words of Blaise Pascal, 'the heart has its reasons which reason itself does not know'[78] as well as the frequently quoted words of Antoine de Saint-Exupéry, 'it is only with the heart that one can see rightly'.

Finally, the Church can only then be convincing if we encounter the living-present Jesus Christ himself in the concrete church in its word, in the celebration of the liturgy, in its whole life and the person of each individual convincing Christian, if we let ourselves be called to discipleship and if we opt for the community of faithful and the service for the faith. It is not the Church, it is Christ who is the way, the truth and the life (Jn 14.6). He is the faithful and reliable witness (Rev. 1.5; 3.14). The Church can be convincing only from him and towards him.

1.3 Philosophical preconsiderations

Communio and communication

The principle that faith seeks understanding brought theology very early into conversation with philosophy. Similar to theology, philosophy, in its traditional form, dominated by the Greeks, in particular Plato and Aristotle, does not enquire like the other sciences after individual areas of knowledge or reality, but after the whole of reality. This brings it inevitably into conversation with theology, which reflects from God as the all-encompassing reality, as well as the order, destiny and purpose of all reality.[79]

In this conversation, the Catholic Tübingen School was influenced by the mood and thinking of Romanticism and German Idealism. This is no longer our world of today. It was already in Schelling's later philosophy that the idealistic system thinking became aware of its own limitations. Schelling thus prepared the way for Søren Kierkegaard († 1855), who had a lasting impact on the theology of the twentieth century, and also on Friedrich Nietzsche († 1900). The latter's critical questioning of the whole of European philosophical thinking, which was influenced by the Greeks and in particular by Plato, re-emerged in Martin Heidegger († 1976) and is present everywhere in today's postmodern thinking.

In addition, there is a second line of modern thinking which is important for us. It already appeared in Johann Georg Hamann, Johann Gottfried Hegel, Wilhelm von Humboldt and Friedrich Heinrich Jacobi. Then it broke through in Johann Gottlieb Fichte, Friedrich Wilhelm Schelling and Georg Wilhelm Friedrich Hegel, and again in Ludwig Feuerbach. Today this line of thinking is called dialogical philosophy. In other words, the more recent dialogical philosophy of Martin Buber, Ferdinand Ebner, Franz

Rosenzweig and others has older roots. In some respects this approach to philosophy can be traced back to Socrates and Plato. We also find it in quite different thinkers such as Romano Guardini, Gabriel Marcel, Otto Friedrich Bollnow, Hans-Georg Gadamer, Jürgen Habermas, Paul Ricœur, Emmanuel Lévinas and others.[80] Unlike René Descartes, who is often regarded as the father of modern philosophy, the thinkers identified do not proceed from the subjectivity of the individual 'cogito ergo sum'; they each consider subjectivity in different ways as inter-subjectivity. In this the dialogical, inter-subjective communication has become a central philosophical topic and the point of departure for interpreting the world.

Thus, *communio* and communication are not only theological terms but also fundamental, general human phenomena which have already played an important role in ancient philosophy as well as in contemporary philosophical reflection. If we wish to gain a deeper understanding of what Church as *communio* means, we can find help in philosophy. In a first and still preliminary step of reflection, it can make the reality of *communio* accessible to understanding.

The Second Vatican Council and large parts of current Catholic theology were, and still are, also substantially influenced by the dialogical form of thinking.[81] Linked to this philosophical trend himself, John Paul II emphasized the global and existential dimension of dialogue. For him, 'dialogue is an indispensable step along the path *towards human self-realization*, the self-realization both of *each individual* and *of every human community*.' 'It involves the human subject in his or her entirety; dialogue between communities involves in a particular way the subjectivity of each.' 'Dialogue is not simply an exchange of ideas. In some way it is always an "exchange of gifts".'[82]

Already ancient philosophy saw the human person as a rational being equipped with speech (ζῶον λογικόν) and proceeding from this description it saw man defined as ζῶον πολιτικόν, as communal being.[83] The human person as an individual cannot survive, rather, as a being of needs, depends, in many respects, upon living and acting together with others. His linguistic character in particular refers him to others. He can only survive in the polis. When the polis collapsed in late antiquity, the stoic philosophy declared that the human person could only survive in the whole of mankind.[84]

Dialogical thinking assumes that humanity finds itself underivable in the world. The amazement and wonder that something exists and that I exist is therefore the impulse for thinking.[85] In this, humanity does not find itself monological, that is, as a single entity, but rather in monological as a single one but in the ineradicable difference and plurality of being human, especially as man and woman. Human being is essentially encounter and dialogue, not only in the verbal sense but in the integral human global sense of exchange on the material level as well as on the spiritual-ideal level. In this communication there is no absolute point of departure, such as Descartes' 'Cogito ergo sum'. Rather, we have in our respective languages a preset historical and cultural medium of communication. We encounter in and through the symbols of language a world already interpreted in a very specific way.

Our historically predetermined reality and its interpretation are neither a prison nor an inevitable fate or destiny. They are, rather, entrusted to our freedom to be responsibly answered by us in freedom. Humanity cannot only change the external world, but can also modify, extend and deepen the understanding of the world and of life through new insights. Culture and language are alterable dimensions and have often changed in the course of the history of culture. They also change in the present time in a very rapid way, exciting many yet also frightening others. In history, humanity is always exposed to the risk of humanity's own liberty as well as to the liberty of all others and, as such, is always heading towards an open future. Depending upon an ultimately religious basic option, humanity can approach liberty with fear or with trust and hope. The human person can see it as fate, destiny or providence. As different and even contradicting as these interpretations may be, they converge in the view that the intersubjective interrelation in which we find ourselves, regarding its origin and its future, points to a mystery which ultimately cannot be solved rationally. This leads inevitably to the question: from where do we come and whither are we going?

Modern philosophy has developed various utopias of a future ideal state or society. This happened in the belief in progress, which focused on science and technology (a classic example is Auguste Comte). It also occurred in the utopia of a future classless society which would emerge through revolutionary praxis (Karl Marx and Ernst Bloch). Both utopias failed. Today we know about the inner dialectic of enlightenment and progress (Max Horkheimer, Theodor W. Adorno), as well as about the ecological, social and political risks of modern culture (Hans Jonas). Thus, after the collapse of socialism, the utopian energies seem to be exhausted.[86] There is a lack of great guiding perspectives for society and mankind. Hope has become a scarce commodity.

However, no human being and no society can live without hope. As they say, hope dies last. Thus, despite rampant disillusionment and scepticism, there remains the question and search for succeeding *communio* and communication. Immanuel Kant was correct when he identified the question of 'what may I hope' to be the summary of all theoretically unavoidable questions that humanity must ask and which nevertheless cannot be answered theoretically.[87]

Hope for perfect communication

There is hope for successful communication in the macro-context of society and in the private and personal micro-context. Our present time is, on the one hand, characterized by increasingly global economic and technical communication processes and, on the other, by global medial networking. Still this globalization does not necessarily lead to greater unity and general peace in the world. It can also lead to severe collisions and global conflicts (Samuel Phillips Huntington). What is true for the global level manifests itself also on the individual level. We find in each person in the pursuit of a fulfilled life the dream of personal happiness in a successful relationship, family and friends. Yet, the breakdown of many marriages and communities and the social isolation of many people are the benchmark of our time. This demonstrates that the happy life of the individual also depends on peace in the world and the survival of mankind depends on the success or failure of community and communication.

The philosophy of communication (Jürgen Habermas, Karl-Otto Apel and others) places the question of succeeding communication at the centre of its reflections. It demonstrates that in each interpersonal communication we anticipate an ideal communication situation. Yet, it also says that this cannot be achieved within history.[88] This raises the question: is this anticipation a mere postulate, necessary but irredeemable, utopian wishful thinking that only fools us all the time? In this case hope is either the worst of all evils that has escaped from Pandora's Box (Friedrich Nietzsche), or we have to say that Sisyphus who knows about his futility is a happy man (Albert Camus). Yet, is Sisyphus indeed happy? Is the insight into futility the final word? Does this leave in the end only resignation that has become wise or even desperation?

Philosophy usually concludes by calling this anticipation a kind of regulative idea or an *a priori* into an unlimited horizon without clarifying its ontological state any further. Also, it often leaves it at an agnostic point of view. If it is courageously carried through, we cannot deny such an agnostic attitude its due respect. Still the question begs whether, as human, we can resign ourselves to putting aside the hope that has seemingly become wise and let the answer rest. Do we not inwardly rebel against the possibility of world and life becoming a huge question mark? Is there not also the other possibility that we perceive partial experiences of purpose and happiness which exist, though in different ways and intensity, in every life as signs and promise of an ultimate purpose?[89]

In view of the failure of modern utopias, it is reasonable to reflect anew the Bible's message of hope and its promise of fulfilling the desire of humanity for a perfect communication-community in justice, freedom and peace, to decipher its rational nucleus and contribute it as an impulse into the present debate. Jürgen Habermas has recently attempted this, following and continuing Kant.[90] As Adorno indicated, we should at least try to consider the world and life in the light of salvation.[91]

Pre-understanding as an invitation to decision

Demonstrating the structure of anticipation and hope immanent to each communication can mediate a preliminary understanding of what we mean when we speak theologically of *communio*. This does not mean that we can philosophically deduce or prove the theological understanding of *communio*. Proving faith as logically necessary would mean to nullify and abolish it as faith. The relation between philosophy and theology is not a simple relation of question and answer where philosophy asks the questions and theology has the answers prepared. *Communio*, theologically understood, is not simply the answer to the question of humanity and the fulfilment of hope in humanity for succeeding universal communication and community. We can only show that the understanding of *communio* which can be grasped in faith alone can be linked rationally and is, in itself, reasonable. Also, those who do not believe actually do, in their own way, believe something that is, they proceed from unprovable secular conditions of faith. The rational arguments are therefore no proof but an invitation to consider again the message of faith. They cannot replace the decision for faith and they do not relieve anyone from making a decision. Yet, they can demonstrate the decision for faith as a rationally responsible decision.

Theologically understood, *communio* fulfils in a qualitatively new way, which transcends all natural hope, a hope, searching, and longing that is not in anyway self-fulfilling. This is an option for faith for which there are good arguments, yet for which, if faith is to remain a personal, free and human act, there can be no compelling evidence. The individual arguments only become convincing within the overall perspective in the light of faith and with the eyes of faith.

Faith is not simply a ready-made answer for the question of humanity; rather, it is an invitation not to favour scepticism but hope and to risk one's life for hope. Blaise Pascal expressed this idea in a famous fragment of his *Pensées* in the form of a wager: if we win with faith, we win everything; if we lose with it, we lose nothing. It is worth accepting the wager.[92]

The structure of hope pertaining to humanity also applies in a different way to faith. For faith, the successful and perfect *communio* is not an already-present dimension but pertains to eschatological hope. We are redeemed to hope. Yet, hope aims at that which we do not see (Rom. 8.24). In this way, analogous to reason, faith has an anticipatory structure.[93] Thus it cannot be about demonstrating the earthly church as the fulfilment of the hope of humanity. Considering its weaknesses, this would be only little trustworthy and hardly convincing in any case. The earthly church does not understand itself as the fulfilled kingdom of God. It only wants to be sign and instrument, glimpse and, located in real history, often seemingly paradoxical anticipation. Yet, it sees itself in the service of hope and wants to encourage people to hope. Deciding for the Church means being prepared to join this community of hope in the service of hope of all and to place oneself at the service of hope.[94]

We must therefore place ecclesiology in the universal salvation history and eschatological horizon of hope of the Bible and the ecclesial Tradition. We can understand and place the Church only within this overall context. Ecclesiology is thus about the programme of all theology to give account of the hope which is in us (1 Pet. 3.15).

2

The horizons of universal and salvation history

2.1 The mystery of communion

A brief glance at the history of ecclesiology

It is only possible to fully understand the presentation of the Catholic doctrine of the Church, as it officially occurred last through the Second Vatican Council, if we first take a brief look at the history of ecclesiology. For this, there are only a few short comments possible in this context.[1]

The rich ecclesiological passages in the New Testament to which we will often refer are fundamental for the whole further development. However, even insofar as all fundamental aspects are already present, there is no systematic ecclesiology in the books or groups of writings in the New Testament but rather a variety of ecclesiological concepts.[2]

In the period immediately following the composition of the texts of the New Testament, we find already in Ignatius of Antioch († around 115), and then completely in Irenaeus of Lyons († 202), all of the essential elements of the later Catholic ecclesiology, in particular the apostolic succession in the episcopal office. Still, there is also no systematic treatise on the Church in the writings of the Church Fathers.

The Church Fathers speak in the language of the Bible of the Church as mystery, body and bride of Christ, temple of the Holy Spirit, and as *communio*. They liken the Church to the moon which is not light itself but receives it from the sun, or to a ship on the sea of the world, to a vine, and others.[3] Ambrose of Milan († 397) summarizes all in one sentence and describes the Church as bride of Christ, mother of all faithful, body of Christ and people of God.[4] Augustine († 430) in particular became authoritative for Western ecclesiology. As most of the Church Fathers were bishops, they also had to concern themselves with concrete church orders and deal with schisms and heresies. When, after the Constantinian Shift, the Church had become a church of the masses, they fought against superficialities and secularization in the Church.

The Constantinian Shift, which occurred when Emperor Constantine first made Christianity legal in 313 and then Emperor Theodosius declared it a state religion in 380, had a profound impact. Theologically, the Church was still described as mystery; yet, in its external self-representation, it soon adopted civil-service-like structures and imperial traits, and later in the Middle Ages feudal traits. Almost inevitably this led to secular entanglements. The Gregorian Reform and the Investiture Controversy of the eleventh century were a battle for the independence and freedom of the Church. Naturally, it also had to be fought with secular means and turned the Church in its outward appearance into a kind of papal monarchy. Of course, because of Scripture and the Tradition of the Fathers, the theologians of the Early and High Middle Ages had to say deeper and more profound things about the Church. Still, Scholasticism did not know a treatise on just the Church. We find statements on the Church by the great medieval theologians scattered throughout their writings on Christology, grace and the sacraments. Additionally one must study the commentaries on Scripture of the great masters of medieval theology, for the masters of theology considered the interpretation of Scripture as their actual duty. In addition, we must not forget the commentaries on Scripture, the sermons and the more edifying writings by the great saints, especially those by Bernard of Clairvaux († 1153).

During the Middle Ages two profound shifts took place. The first occurred in the wake of the Lord's Supper Controversy in the eleventh century in the dispute with Berengar of Tours († 1088) about the real presence in the Eucharist. Until then the term 'mystic body of Christ' had been commonly used to refer to the Eucharist. In this controversy this term became in a spiritualistic sense ambiguous; it now became free to be applied to the Church. Since, because of this, the focus was no longer on the inner connection between Eucharist and Church, the patristic sacramental-Eucharistic understanding of the Church consequently came to be replaced by a more corporate view of the body of Christ. Nevertheless, for the great theologians of High Scholasticism, such as Thomas Aquinas († 1274), the old church's concept of the Eucharist as the sacrament of the unity of the Church remained alive.[5] On the other hand, a second development of far-reaching consequences generally prevailed. It was, in particularly, the influence of the *Book of Sentences* by Peter Lombard († 1160) that led to a separation between, on the one hand, the ordo, the authority mediated sacramentally through ordination, and an, on the other, jurisdiction. By consequence, the sacramental conception of the Church and the ecclesiastical ministry became obscured. This had far-reaching consequences in particular for the understanding and concrete form and exercise of the episcopal office as well as for the development of the doctrine concerning the jurisdictional primacy of the pope.[6] As a result, developments in church politics as well as in theology, especially in the late Middle Ages, emphasized more explicitly the institutional hierarchical side of the Church.

Against this backdrop, the confrontations with late-medieval Conciliarism and with a spiritualistic view of the Church held by John Wyclif († 1384) and Jan Hus († 1415) resulted in the development of an independent tractate on the Church. The first ecclesiological treatises by James of Viterbo († 1308), John Quidort of Paris († 1306), John of Ragusa († 1443) and Tomás de Torquemada († 1498) were rather a hierarchology than an ecclesiology. In contrast to this were Marsilius of Padua († 1342/1343) and William of Ockham († 1347) with their critical view of the papacy and theories of people's sovereignty applied to the Church.

The absence of a balanced tractate on the Church, the narrowing restrictions as well as theological obscurities, proved fatal in the arguments at the time of the Reformation.[7] It was in Article VII of the *Augsburg Confession* of 1530 that Melanchthon presented, for the first time, a concise theological definition of the Church, according to which it is enough for the unity of the Church (*satis est*) that the Gospel is purely taught and that the sacraments are administered in accordance with the Gospel.[8] Melanchthon put this wording into his *loci communes* (edition of 1535), and Calvin incorporated it in substance into the later editions of his *Institutio christianae religionis* (1559).[9] Since then, this confession has been regarded as the Magna Carta of the Reformation understanding of Church. With it the Reformers did not want to found a new church, but rather wanted to initiate a reform of the Church and the whole of Christianity. That is why they tried in the *Augsburg Confession* to formulate their faith in the greatest possible consistency with the Tradition and the teaching of the 'old church'. That the failure of this attempt to negotiate nevertheless resulted in the creation of an own denomination is not a sign of the success but rather of the failure of their original concern.[10]

The interpretation of Article VII of the *Augsburg Confession* is also disputed within the Reformation tradition. The question is whether this formula can be understood as a comprehensive definition of Church and whether the '*satis est*' is indeed sufficient.[11] The problem results from the fact that the formula does not say anything, at least not explicitly, about the ecclesiastical ministry and its duty of proclamation and in the administration of the sacraments. This occurs in other passages whose interpretation has remained controversial until today.[12] The question concerns the relation between the common priesthood of all believers and the ordained ministry,[13] the understanding of ordination[14] and the episcopal office[15]. Luther's appeal to his own interpretation of Scripture and his subjective certainty of faith[16] led – and still leads – to the basic question of who can, authoritatively, if, for that matter, *anyone* is able to decide authoritatively, where the Gospel is properly proclaimed and the sacraments are administered in accordance with the Gospel.

The questions converge in the Reformation thesis of the hiddenness of the Church.[17] The Catholic controversialist theology opposed this with a concept of the Church the focus of which was on the visible side of the

Church. Especially characteristic is the frequently quoted comment of Robert Bellarmine († 1621), in his *Disputationes de controversiis christianae fidei adversus hujus temporis haereticos*, that the Church was as much visible as the community of the Roman people or the kingdom of France or the republic of Venice.[18] In addition, the Reformation polemic against the papacy produced, as a kind of antithesis within Catholic theology, a shift of emphasis according to which the papacy became, in an unprecedented way, the identifying attribute of the Catholic.[19] The Church was now largely understood and seen as the papal church. At the same time, contact with the rich ecclesiological Tradition of the Eastern Churches was practically lost. The Church became a denominational church, and modern ecclesiology has been determined by this pluralism and the mutual polemic and apologetics of denominational churches.

Of course, one should not simplify things. Even though the emphasis and force in modern theology was on the visible aspect of the Church, the great controversialist theologians, besides Robert Bellarmine, for example Thomas Stapleton († 1598), were well aware of the deeper Christological and Pneumatological dimension of the Church as Christ's body. Controversialist theology does not represent the whole range of ecclesial life of that time. This spiritual dimension of the Church was particularly present in the École française (Vincent de Paul, Jean Eudes, Louis-Marie Grignon de Montfort and others) coming from Cardinal Pierre de Bérulle († 1629). It had a significant influence on modern spirituality. Above all, to do justice to the post-Tridentine period, one has to take into account the testimony of the lives and written testimonies left by the great mystically gifted and pastorally influential modern saints (John of the Cross, Theresa of Avila, Charles Borromeo, Francis of Sales, Philip Neri and others).

The degeneration and watering-down of the concept of Church did not occur until the emergence of Catholic theology that was influenced by the Enlightenment. Such theology typically saw the Church as a moral institution to further human happiness and social prosperity. The Church was understood in categories of natural law and philosophy of law as a society of unequals (*societas inaequalium*) and as a *societas perfecta*, one which contains all of the means necessary to reach its purpose in itself and which is thus independent from the state. This institutional perspective proved to be helpful in the confrontation with modern state absolutism and liberalism where the independence and the freedom of the Church had to be defended. Still, justified as this cause may have been, the categories of natural law and philosophy of law led to a de-sacralized and one-sided sociological view of the Church.

After the Napoleonic wars, the Congress of Vienna (1814–15) brought an upheaval which was, after the Constantinian Shift and the Gregorian Reform, the most important historical break and which led to an ecclesiological turn. In the long run, the end of the old imperial church and the loss of political power turned out to be beneficial for the moral and spiritual authority of the Church. The change in the political situation necessitated a reflection on the nature of the Church and its own place independent of the state.

Theologically, the change came through the renewal inspired by Romanticism and Idealism at the beginning of the nineteenth century. On the Catholic side, one has to name in particular Johann Michael Sailer († 1832), founder of the Tübingen school, Johann Sebastian Drey († 1853), and the best-known representative of the school, Johann Adam Möhler († 1838). Möhler's first pneumatological and then Christological ecclesiology had great influence on the Roman school (Perrone, Passaglia, Franzelin, Scheeben), as well as on French and Russian thinkers (Khomyakov, Solovyov). John Henry Newman († 1890) also knew and esteemed Möhler. Studying the Church Fathers, Newman found his way into the Catholic Church and, together with Möhler, is considered an important forerunner of the renewal movements of the twentieth century.[20]

Among the Tübingen theologians, Johann Sebastian Drey, Johann Baptist Hirscher († 1865) and, in particular, Franz Anton..., highlighted the link between the kingdom of God and the Church. They were inspired in this by the Covenantal theologian Johannes Cocceius († 1669), and by Johann Albrecht Bengel († 1772), the father of Wurttemberg Pietism), as well as by Marian Dobmayer († 1805), influenced by the Catholic enlightenment, and Friedrich Brenner († 1841), who was influenced by Johann Michael Sailer.[21] Even though their perception of God's kingdom was still largely speculative idealistically and less biblical in the modern sense, nevertheless their placing of the Church into the great and all-embracing framework of the idea of God's kingdom and of salvation history as a whole can still be an important impulse for a renewed ecclesiology today. In more recent theology it is, in particular, Wolfhart Pannenberg who has taken up the idea of the kingdom of God and made it seminal for ecclesiology in a horizon of universal history.[22]

After the end of the bourgeois era and in the twentieth century, the First World War was followed in all great churches by an ecclesiological reconsideration. On the Orthodox side, after a more scholastic period, especially among the Orthodox émigré theologians, we see a return to patristic ecclesiology.[23] On the Protestant side, in dialectic theology, especially of Karl Barth,[24] as well as through a renewal of Martin Luther's theology,[25] there was a turn away from neo-Protestantism. On the Catholic side, one has to mention very many names from the biblical, liturgical and patristic renewal movements between the two world wars: for the German-speaking territories Romano Guardini, Hugo and Karl Rahner, Hans Urs von Balthasar, Karl Adam, Erich Przywara, Robert Grosche, Carl Feckes, Dominikus Koster; in French-speaking regions Marie Dominique Chenu, Henri de Lubac, Jean Daniélou, Yves Congar, as well as Charles Journet, Gustave Thils and others; in the USA Gustave Weigel, Avery Dulles and others.

One now tried to overcome the narrowing restrictions of medieval and controversialist theological and to understand the Church as the mystical body of Christ. This view was also adopted by Pius XII in the encyclicals *Mystici corporis* (1943) and *Mediator Dei* (1947), and was then received, developed further and deepened by the Second Vatican Council in the Constitution on the Church, *Lumen Gentium*. Whereas, because of its premature termination, the First Vatican Council could deal conclusively only with the primacy and infallibility of the pope, the Constitution on the Church of Vatican II now presents the first cohesive magisterial treatment of the Church. It has become the starting point of a partly controversial process of reception which is still not complete.[26]

This renewed ecclesiology created new foundations for ecumenical dialogue with the Eastern churches, the Reformation churches and ecclesial communities.[27] Many impasses between the denominations were opened, and the greater commonalities could be emphasized. Nevertheless, to a great extent, the fundamental differences in ecclesiology are still waiting to be addressed. Of late, one notices a new insistence on one's own identity and profile. On the Protestant side, following a period dominated by great names (Gerhard Ebeling, Jürgen Moltmann, Eberhard Jüngel, Wolfhart Pannenberg, etc.), we now witness a return to more denominationally driven ecclesiologies (Wolfgang Huber, Wilfried Härle, Eilert Herms, etc.), and to Neo-Protestantism (Friedrich Wilhelm Gra, etc.). On the Catholic side, in continuation of the approaches by Hans Urs von Balthasar, Joseph Ratzinger and others, a reconsideration of the Catholic trajectory of ecclesiology is occurring. In the long run, properly understood profiling in the sense of finding one's identity can also be beneficial for ecumenical dialogue.

Because of these different and partly opposing tendencies, the situation has become confusing. For me, considering again the Catholic Tübingen School, in particular Johann Adam Möhler, and applying it to the changed problems of today seems to be expedient for Catholic theology. Above all, in the present, largely secularized situation, we must place the idea and reality of the Church into the all-encompassing horizon of the idea of God and the kingdom of God. It is only in this way that we can do justice to the message of Jesus and, at the same time, demonstrate the significance of the Church in the whole of reality and in view of the existential questions of mankind.

The systematic location of ecclesiology

This historical overview shows that ecclesiology is a comparatively young trajectory within theology. There is still no full consensus concerning its systematic place and structure. It was certainly not the task of the Council to clarify this rather inner-theological question. The answer has to be given by theology based on the doctrine of the Council.

The common creed shared by all Christians provides an essential starting point for this discussion.[28] In the creed, the doctrine of the Church has its place in the third article, that is, after the first article which speaks of God the creator of heaven and earth, and after the second article which speaks of Jesus Christ as God's only son, of his cross, resurrection and coming again. In the third article the creed speaks of the Holy Spirit as the Lord and giver of life who is a pledge of the eternal life to come. In this, the first article opens the perspective for the whole of Creation, the second unfolds the universal salvific significance of Jesus Christ, and the third article, which says of the Holy Spirit that he has spoken through the prophets, also points to the whole of God's history with mankind. The Church is thus placed within the context of the whole of salvation history, even the entire history of humanity, which, as a whole, is orientated toward eschatological fulfilment. It is a sign of hope that points ahead to the new heaven and the new earth. Ecclesiology must be dealt with within this overall context. In addition, by placing ecclesiology within pneumatology it becomes obvious that the Church is more than just an organization or institution; it is one form of God's Holy Spirit acting in history.

The Church thus belongs within the comprehensive context of the existential fundamental question of humanity, the question about God, about the origin and goal of history, and about the salvation of humanity. The answer to these questions is not the Church as an institution of salvation, but God's Spirit who uses the Church as medium and instrument to make the work of salvation in Jesus Christ effectively present in history. Hence, the Church must be seen in the horizon of the hope of humanity.[29]

In this we follow the fundamental concern of the theology of Thomas Aquinas. For him, theology primarily deals with God and with man in his relation to God.[30] The formal object from which all truths of faith have to be considered is therefore God as the first truth.[31] Hence, the act of faith does not aim at the statement of faith as such but at the 'object' expressed therein.[32] Thomas quotes the definition of the article of faith by Isidore of Seville, which was widespread during the Scholastic period, as the grasping of the truth which at the same time reaches beyond the intended 'object'.[33] However, as Jesus Christ is for Christians the final revelation of God, Bonaventura comes to the summarizing definition of the object of theology. Accordingly, God is the *subjectum radicale*, Christ is the *subjectum integrale* and the symbolic-sacramental understanding of the world is the *subjectum universale* of theology.[34]

The constitution on the Church of Vatican II follows in the footsteps of this theological tradition.[35] The Council begins the constitution on the Church, *Lumen Gentium*, with the statement: 'Christ is the Light of nations. Because this is so, this Sacred Synod gathered together in the Holy Spirit eagerly desires, by proclaiming the Gospel to every creature, to bring the light of Christ to all men, a light brightly visible on the countenance of the Church.'[36]

This is a surprising opening that is unusual in comparison with traditional textbooks of ecclesiology, for in it the Council stresses that the Church does not exist for itself but for God and humanity and for the salvation and hope of humanity. Hence, ecclesiology must be approached against the horizon of the question concerning God and salvation. Irenaeus of Lyons brought both together and formulates: 'The glory of God is a living man.'[37] The Church is not itself the light of nations. The light of nations is Jesus Christ whose human face reflects the image of the living God. In the old image of the Church Fathers the Church is just like the moon that has no light of its own but which can only reflect back the light borrowed from the sun.[38] The word 'Light of nations' opens the theological and Christological approach towards the universal. Jesus Christ is seen as the way to salvation for all peoples. Through this, the Council's understanding of the Church is Christologically definite as well as universally open. It excludes a blurred and non-committal view of the Church as well as a fundamentalistically narrowed one. The Church is concrete and at the same time universal.

Preliminary considerations for a theological understanding of mystery

Remarkable as the approach of the constitution on the Church may be, it is almost inaccessible for present thinking. Many contemporaries see in the Church anything but the mirror that reflects the face of the merciful father God. Many consider the Church almost an obstacle or stumbling block for faith in God. The problem arises initially with the fact that the word 'mystery', with which the constitution on the Church begins, is not easily understood by many people today. For them it is not only ambiguous but also suspicious. After all, for the average mind today, a secret thing is something that should better not come to light; something that is not and also should not become transparent. For us, something like that is quite rightly suspicious. It is in this sense that we speak of a secret document, secret report, secret archive, secret service. For others, the term 'mystery' suggests that it was an enigmatic, strange, esoteric or even obscure reality.

Traditional theology is not innocent of this misapprehension. This is because it declared truths as mysteries that are inaccessible to natural reason which is accessible to all human beings and that are accessible only in faith. This conception of mystery contains the misconception that the Church was something beside or above the natural sphere accessible to reason, that it was something on the borders of life but beyond the boundaries restricting human thinking, therefore probably an irrational object. Hence, defining the Church as mystery means, for many, the Church as a strange world inaccessible for humans or even an obscure world which is beyond normal life and which is thus, from the outset, in the literal sense 'out'.

The word mystery is also often understood in the sense of a personal, intimate secret of the heart – a secret that have been entrusted with by another, which compels me to silence and which would be a grave breach of trust to tell someone about or even make public. In this sense there are the medical confidentiality, the pastoral secret, and the seal of confession. Such secrets belong to the private sphere and as such are protected by civil and ecclesial law, for without the protection of the private and intimate sphere the coexistence of humans becomes indiscreet and unbearable.

Of course, religion and faith undoubtedly belong to the field of personal decision which touches the individual deeply in his or her heart. Nonetheless, the Church cannot be called a personal secret of the heart. It is a public entity and has to proclaim its message publicly for the entire world. In fact, one should virtually shout the message of the Gospel from the rooftops (Mt. 10.27; Lk. 12.3) and one should rationally bear witness to it (1 Pet. 3.15).[39] In other words, one cannot understand the Church as personal mystery and restrict it to the intimate and private sphere, or at best to the sacristy. This would lead to a secularization of public life which the opponents of the Church want, yet against which the Church always defends itself and against which the Church has always put its universal and public claim.

In consequence, if we want to get closer to the mystery of the Church, we must first aim for an adequate understanding of mystery and demonstrate that it is not something beyond or outside normal life but present right in its midst.[40] In a first, still preliminary step, we can show here that many things in life are contingent and do not follow predictable and understandable rules. This includes unpredictable strokes of fate as well as positive experiences of interpersonal affection, love and mercy. They can be neither planned nor made. In each life there remains an element of irreducible contingency. It is not only a dark edge of life; rather it decides about fortune or misfortune. As the popular saying goes, nobody forges his own destiny. Happiness in life is always a present for which one has to be grateful. Yet grateful to whom?

Does this mean that religion is to be understood as a means of coping with contingency[41] and that faith is the final comfort in disaster or something to solemnize the particularly happy highlights of personal and public life? Dietrich Bonhoeffer rightly rejects this in his letters from prison. God is no stopgap that is introduced as *deus ex machina* when we are at our wits' end. God does not want to be at the borders of life but present in its midst.[42] Religion and faith cannot be reduced to comfort and they do not merely exist to add a special solemn momentum to certain situations of life. All religions, especially Christianity, put forward a universal claim and want to interpret and shape life and reality as a whole.

A deeper philosophical reflection on nature, history and especially on human existence can demonstrate that all three – nature, history and human existence – point to and transcend themselves into a dimension where unavoidable questions appear about their origins and goals, their sense and nonsense. These questions do not touch upon a categorical, empirical or rational accessible segment of reality, but on the whole of reality. In other words, we can discern rationally the 'that' (i.e. the fact, T.H.) of the mystery of nature, man and history, but the 'what' (i.e. its content, T.H.) ultimately escapes rational access.[43]

In terms of the proofs of the existence of God, which, together with Thomas Aquinas, we might better call *ways* to God, theology has identified this mystery as the one who everyone calls 'God'.[44] Today, of course, we no longer dare to claim that everybody calls 'God' all that appears mysterious in life and in the questions of the meaning and sense of the world and of life. There was also already the sceptical answer in the old world that exists more than ever in modern times – the answer according to which the question about the final mystery of existence is to be left unanswered and open. There is the atheistic answer that consciously refuses to call the mystery of life the mystery of God and which instead speaks of nature, matter, evolution, *weltgeist* and so forth. Finally, today there is the nihilistic answer which has become current again. This answer insists that there may be truths, but that there is no one comprehensive, all-embracing truth and, consequently, that there is no metaphysical world and no comprehensive answer to the question of meaning. Our postmodern thinking is characterized by the fact that it doubts the possibility of reason, and also despairs, and by the view that for it there can be no answer to man's ultimate questions of meaning. Are we therefore condemned to live and to cope with our life '*etsi Deus non daretur*'?

In theological terms, this situation has been the hour of negative theology.[45] It is convinced that we can say about God only what he is not, but cannot say what he is. Therefore it makes only negative but no positive statements about God. Such negative statements are: God is invisible, immaterial, infinite and atemporal.[46] We already find such negative theology partly in Plato and then in Neo-Platonism. It is also distinct among the Church Fathers and it is found again among the great masters of scholastic theology, example, in Thomas Aquinas, and later among mystics such as Meister Eckhart, Nicholas of Cusa in his *Docta ignorantia* and, during the late phase of German Idealism, in the later Schelling. For his part, Schelling became influential for Kierkegaard and so for a great part of twentieth-century Protestant theology. In addition, he anticipated much of what we find in Nietzsche and his postmodern descendants.[47]

Still, the religions have never been satisfied with purely negative answers. They have always looked for signals, signs and symbols, and, in this sense, for revelations in which the unspeakable eternal mystery becomes accessible and reveals itself. Revelation in this still very general sense means an indirect experience where something divine makes itself appear 'in, with and through' worldly experiences. Such theophanies can occur in experiences of nature which cause admiration or fears (thunderstorms, lightning, storms, sun, stellar constellations and so forth), in interpersonal experiences such as the fascination between man and woman, or historical events (victory or defeat, founding of cities and states and so forth). They are always revelatory situations where in a particular experience a comprehensive horizon and a light open up in which the whole of reality can be newly interpreted.[48] Religions thus have a narrative character. In each case they tell a story in which a comprehensive sense reveals itself.

Revelation in this general religious sense is not a categorical term but a transcendental one, in other words trans-categorical, in which the whole of reality reveals itself in a salutary or unwholesome and threatening way. Revelation is no given but an 'itself-giving', not a fact but an event. The religious faith which is still generally understood in this sense lets itself in for such a revelation or epiphany story. It does not mean holding individual categorical truths to be true, rather it means letting oneself in for the revealing truth. It is neither a mere act of reason or will nor a mere irrational emotion, but a fundamental option of all humanity regarding the comprehensive sense of existence and reality which is *a posteriori* theologically reflected on and systematized by all world religions.

The biblical revelation does not totally exclude such revelations outside the Jewish-Christian history of salvation. In several passages, the Bible speaks of 'holy heathens' who are witnesses to the living God: Abel, Enoch, Melchizedek, Job and others. The Church regards with esteem non-Christian religions and perceives in them a ray of the Truth which enlightens all men (Jn 1.9).[49] The Church certainly knows that the image of God in the religions is ambiguous and that, besides great insights, it often also shows the grimace of the demonic. The Church is convinced that God, who already revealed himself in the Old Testament through historical words and deeds, finally, fully and unsurpassably revealed himself in Jesus Christ (Heb. 1.1); that God has ultimately shown his divine countenance on the human face of Jesus (2 Cor. 3.18; Col. 1.15; Heb. 1.3); and that God revealed himself as the good and at the same time omnipotent Father. Anyone who sees him sees the Father (Jn 14.9).

Therefore we cannot think of revelation in the Christian sense along the lines of information and instruction. It does not mediate extra secret knowledge. It follows the model of communication, not in the sense of communicating individual secrets but rather in the sense that God reveals and communicates himself.[50] Revelation is, therefore, the self-revelation and self-communication of God.[51] It does not remove the mystery of God. It is ultimately the revelation of God's mystery: the revelation of his, for humans, incomprehensible mercy and his inner-worldly totally underivable, itself communicating and itself giving love (1 Jn 4.8.16). If God as the all-embracing mystery of reality reveals himself as love, then love is revealed as the ultimate meaning and basis of all reality.[52]

While in philosophy the dimension of mystery opens itself from the world, history and man, so to speak from below, and while, like negative theology, it ultimately fails, in the biblical revelation this relation turns itself round. There is a reversal of thinking.[53] It is not man who is the being open towards the mystery. On the contrary, man is locked up in unrighteousness and suppresses the truth (Rom. 1.18) and often makes an image of God in his own image (Rom. 1.22ff.). It is therefore God himself who reveals his mystery and he does it by making foolish the wisdom of the world and by revealing himself in the paradoxical shape of the crucified one (1 Cor. 1.20–31).

So we can say: the undefined open mystery of humanity, the world and history becomes concretely defined in Jesus Christ.[54] Mystery understood in the Christian and theological sense is therefore not a vague and undefined mystery which points towards the void and unspeakable that one can ultimately only revere in silence. In the Christian sense, this is a historically defined mystery, giving itself concretely in history, that, in Jesus Christ, has become historically and concretely incarnate. In him there is the universal sense of all reality; he is the *universale concretum*.[55] As it reveals itself in human finitude, historicity and lowliness, the Christian mystery has an incarnational and kenotic sense. It is part of the Christian paradox that in Jesus Christ the incomprehensible, inscrutable and invisible God has become tangible, comprehensible and visible.[56]

The self-revelation of God does not remove the mystery but enhances and intensifies it. It is connected with the ban on iconographic imagery and the commandment not to use the Lord's name in vain (Exod. 20.4.7; Deut. 5.8.11). God reveals himself as the concealed God (Isa. 45.15) who lives in inaccessible light (1 Tim 1.17). Thus, the revelation is indeed not self-projection and objectification of the mystery that reveals itself in man. On the contrary, it claims that man cannot give this answer himself and that man himself is not this answer. The revelation of the definitive mystery of God is also the definitive answer to the mystery of man and the world. Only the one who knows God also knows man (Romano Guardini).

All these fundamental considerations can only be sketched out here. However, they are of importance in order to understand properly what we mean when we speak of the mystery of the Church. Applied to the Church, the term mystery is not a categorical but a transcendental term. It does not mean that there is 'something' mysterious in and about the Church; rather, in it there shines and is reflected the all-embracing, all-permeating and all-present mystery which we as Christians call God and which is concretely revealed in Jesus Christ. Yet, just as the moon has no light of its own but only reflects the light of the sun, so it is the case with the Church. The Church is sign and instrument of God's mystery revealed in Jesus Christ.

Consequently, the theology of the Church can err in two ways. One can err by saying too little and reducing it to an ethical, sociological or cultural meaning (*per defectum*). Yet, one can also err by saying too much of the Church (*per excessum*), be it that one believes to know too much of it and its mystery or avoids its lowliness and ideologically exalts it. When we speak of the mystery of the Church, we do not speak of some distant, desirable and ideal church, but rather of 'this' concrete Church, of which one has to show how the countenance of God shines in it and how it ought to shine invitingly and convincingly. Yet, how can this be?

The biblical meaning of mystery

When the Second Vatican Council speaks of the Church as mystery, this is not done against the general religious-philosophical background of which we have mainly been speaking so far. Rather, it adopts the biblical understanding of mystery (μυστήριον), which God himself reveals.

This biblical understanding of mystery comes from the apocalyptic texts of Judaism.[57] It has its foundations in the prophet Daniel. The time of Daniel and the period that followed was a difficult time in the history of Judaism, a time full of crises and questions. The Jews felt deserted by their leaders, who had sympathized and cooperated with the pagan occupiers. Nowhere was a prophet to be found who could proclaim a decisive word or show direction. It seemed that God had deserted his people and was far away. Thus, the apocalyptics turned their view to the mystery of God's hidden plan of salvation and its historical realization. In answer to the fearful question of what God planned for his people, Daniel speaks of a coming eschatological kingdom which will be brought about after the fall of all of the previous empires by God's sovereign action and which will last forever (Dan. 2.28f.44.47).

So the apocalyptic understanding of mystery proclaimed by the prophet Daniel expresses again all the eschatological hope of Israel, especially of the normal people in Israel, for a world of law, justice and peace. In this apocalyptic understanding of mystery, the awareness also emerges that we human beings have the ability to do good within our possibilities and that, however, the fundamental change cannot be initiated by us nor can it be achieved by force. Such a change is possible through God alone; it is consequently in him alone that we must trust.

In his proclamation of the kingdom of God, Jesus picks up the apocalyptic sense of mystery and thus the hope that with his coming and appearance the vision of Daniel is fulfilled (Mk 4.11 par.). 'The mystery of the kingdom of God which has been revealed to the disciples is therefore Jesus himself as the messiah.'[58] He remains unnoticed by 'those outside' who are not his disciples, yet he reveals himself to those who have eyes for the beginning of the messianic end time that has come with him (Mt. 13.16).

Paul also takes up apocalyptic language and the apocalyptic hope articulated therein (Rom. 16.25; 1 Cor. 2.7). He unfolds his understanding extensively in his letters during his imprisonment (Eph. 1.9f.; 3.9f.; 6.19; Col. 1.26f.; 4.3). In his usage, mystery signifies the eternal saving design hidden to previous generations and the eternal saving mystery of God which, now in the fullness of time, has been revealed in Jesus Christ, and concretely in the cross of Jesus Christ. Through his kenosis up to his death on the cross, the crucified has become the *kyrios* of the world before whom all in heaven and on earth bend their knees (Phil. 2.6–11).[59] The cross thus becomes the revelation and the occurrence of the universal and final horizon of sense for all reality. As such, the cross is proclaimed through the preaching of the Apostle and through the Church in the world. Thus, for Paul, the mystery is not a gnostic secret teaching nor a doctrine as the wise of this would proclaim it. It is the message of Jesus Christ as the crucified one (1 Cor. 1.23; 2.2). He is the mystery of God's hidden Wisdom (1 Cor. 2.7).

In Col. 1.27 the mystery is described with the formula: 'it is Christ among you, your hope of glory.' It is to this universal-cosmic view that the Apostle adheres, in and despite all present sufferings (Eph. 3.13; Col. 1.24f). Through his apostolic ministry, God's salvation mystery is now also to be proclaimed to the gentiles. They are also to participate in it. In this way the proclamation of the mystery aims to bring about that fullness of time which had already been predestined in God's saving design before the creation of the world. This occurs through the summarizing and heading (ἀναχεφαλαίωσις) of the cosmos in Christ (Eph. 1.10). The Church is the space already fulfilled by Christ through which he now wants to fulfil the cosmos (Eph. 1.22f.).[60]

When dealing in the constitution on the Church *Lumen Gentium* with '*De Ecclesiae Mysterio*', the mystery of the Church, the Second Vatican Council continued in this understanding of mystery as the eternal, saving design of God revealed in time through Jesus Christ and in the Holy Spirit. It proceeds from the Father who, in his eternal plan, has called all human beings to participate in the divine life, who through the Son has redeemed the fallen world and inaugurated the kingdom of heaven on earth, and who in the Holy Spirit continually sanctifies and governs the Church.[61]

In this way, the Council starts with a large-scale view of universal history and integrates the Church into this universal and cosmic perspective. It picks up the expectations and hopes not only of Israel but of all humanity, and it wants to proclaim Jesus Christ as the light of nations and to present the testimony of the Church about Jesus Christ as the answer to the questions and hopes of all human beings. This, of course, is no easy answer. With it, the Church points to the cross that is a scandal to the normal rational human mind and which thus provokes disagreement.

The Church must not avoid this contradiction and scandal. The two beams of the Cross intersect each other and cannot be harmonized into a synthesis. One has to accept the Cross in its total paradoxality and rational offensiveness. We must not, as Hegel did, turn it into a speculative Good Friday by interpreting it as necessary process of the self-alienation of God or by understanding it in the modern sense as the death of God and thereby as justification for a supposedly Christian atheism.[62]

Yet, it is precisely in its paradoxality that the Cross is '*id quo maius cogitari nequit*' (that beyond which nothing greater can be conceived). It is indeed the most extreme of the unfathomable love of God which for us enters even the opposite of itself, the scandalous death at the cross, in order to proclaim him as God who is with us and among us even in the darkness of suffering and in the night of death. By facing death himself, the immortal God could kill death and, through the resurrection, establish life and hope anew.[63] As we read in the Easter preface, 'by dying he destroyed our death and by rising he restored our life.' So the kingdom of life, announced by Daniel, paradoxically begins with the Cross. The Cross is the fulfilment and summary of God's mystery and his eternal saving design for humanity and for the world.

This paradoxical fulfilling of Daniel's promise finds its dramatic expression in the interrogation of Jesus by Pilate. A sharper contrast is inconceivable. Jesus is standing as the powerless accused in front of the mighty representative of the last great empire and replies to his question regarding his kingdom: 'yes, I am a king.' However, he immediately adds: 'my kingdom is not of this world.' His kingdom is the kingdom of truth for he is come into this world 'to bear witness to the truth'. To this, the power-seeker Pilate can only reply with scorn: 'what is truth?' (Jn 18.33–8). Finally the scorn is brought to its climax: wearing the purple coat and the crown of thorns on his head, Jesus is presented to the howling mob: 'this is your king.' It is in this situation that the crowd prefers the ruler of this world, the emperor, to their king and they demand: 'crucify him!' (Jn 19). Yet, he dies on the cross with the word which expresses the fulfilment of his saving work and the eschatological victory of life: 'it is fulfilled!' (Jn 19.30).

One cannot express the mystery of God and the world which is ultimately revealed in the Cross more beautifully than in the sixth-century hymn *Vexilla regis prodeunt* by Venantius Fortunatus: 'The royal banners forward go, the Cross shines forth in mystic glow, where Life himself our death endured and by His death our life procured.' 'The Cross is our saviour's throne, down from cross does rule God's Son.' 'O cross through which hopes comes to us, in your victory we greet you thus.'

The Church in light of the mystery of the Trinity

Thinking the biblical understanding of the mystery of God through to its end, then, we must, with Vatican II, go one step further. The biblical message of God's mystery, which shines in Jesus Christ and is reflected in the Church, must be considered from a Trinitarian perspective, and the Church must be seen as an image of the Trinity. It is, in this sense, that the Council quotes Cyprian of Carthage: 'Thus, the Church has been seen as "a people made one with the unity of the Father, the Son and the Holy Spirit."'[64] Similarly we read in the decree on ecumenism, *Unitatis redintegratio*: 'It is a mystery that finds its highest exemplar and source in the unity of the Persons of the Trinity.'[65] This Trinitarian interpretation of the mystery of God and, from God, that of the Church is of fundamental importance, particularly in Orthodox theology;[66] it has also become decisive for post-conciliar Catholic theology.[67]

For the average reader today, such statements may well sound beautiful and grand, yet they are still not easily accessible. The doctrine of the Trinity very much resembles a book with seven seals. Obviously, the doctrine of the Trinity is not a kind of advanced mathematics designed to explain that one is three and simultaneously three is one. Likewise, it is not meant as a challenge to biblical monotheism, the doctrine of the one and only God, in order to establish some kind of polytheism, as Christianity is accused of by Islam. The belief in the Trinity claims, rather, that the one and only God for all eternity is not a lonely god but the event of eternal self-communication in love. When worked out in just this sense, doctrine of the Trinity is the most precise interpretation of the sentence in which the first Letter of John sums up the whole message of the New Testament: 'God is love' (1 Jn 4.8.16).[68] It is only because God is, in himself, loving revelation that he can reveal himself as self-revelation in history. Hence, the confession of the Trinity does not abolish faith in the one and only God, but rather strives to determine it more precisely. It sees itself as a more precise Christian definition of monotheism, and just so as concrete monotheism.[69]

Therefore the view of the Church as the image of the Trinitarian communion (χοινωνία) is reversion to Platonism and thus far from the Bible. On the contrary, such language is supported by the New Testament. The first Letter of John states that we share in the communion (χοινωνία) with the Father and the Son and that this is the perfect joy (1 Jn 1.3f.). Here, this letter thus takes up other biblical statements which speak of God being in us and of our being in him, of remaining in God and of God remaining in us, or the Father and the Son dwelling in us (Jn 14.23). It is important that the first Letter of John does not speak in the I-form but he writes 'we'. It is not concerned with our individual and personal relation to God, but rather with the 'we' of the community or the Church.[70] We find the same idea in the Johannine parable of the vine and the branches (Jn 15). All such statements go far beyond the stoic popular philosophy which resonates, for example, in Acts 17.28. They also have nothing in common with a purely enthusiastic piety. They want to express a real communion of being and of life.[71]

From this perspective, one can understand the Church as the present-making icon of the Trinity. In its communion it does not only mirror the inner-Trinitarian *communio*, but, moreover, this *communio* becomes present in the Church. The whole life of the Church is permeated by it, particularly in the Eucharist, so that we participate in the Trinitarian life.

This finds its most explicit expression in 2 Peter, which speaks of our participation in the divine nature (2 Pet. 1.4). There have been several attempts to interpret and discount this statement as a Hellenization of the biblical message. Yet, by now we know that there are corresponding parallels to be found in contemporaneous Jewish literature.[72] This language of divinization (θέωσις) has gained importance, especially in Eastern theology. Still, these statements have also found their way into Western liturgy. We find the most explicit expression in the Roman liturgy (nowadays the extraordinary rite) at the mixing of wine and water: 'By the mystery of this water and wine may we come to share in the divinity of Christ who humbled himself to share in our humanity.' This idea has been retained in the post-conciliar missal. It is found in the third preface for Christmas, in the second preface for Christ's ascension, as well as in several offering prayers of Christmas and Easter time (the first and second mass on Christmas day; Wednesday in the second Easter week and so forth). In summary, we can say that the concept of our participation in the divine nature has not remained an abstract theological statement; it has entered the treasure of the Church's prayers.

These are not abstract statements that have no consequences. For if God, the all-embracing, all-founding and, at the same time, all-transcending reality is love, then this statement has consequences for the understanding of reality in total. It says, then, that love is the ultimate purpose of all reality. This means a revolution of thinking. To define love as the meaning of being means that the resting-in-itself substance is not the ultimate reality, such as was thought by antique and then scholastic metaphysics. Likewise, it also means that neither the subject nor the subjectivity of human beings are the starting point or fundament of all certainty, as Descartes and subsequently the modern age thought. Ultimate reality is rather relation.[73] This is because in the doctrine of the Trinity the Trinitarian persons are understood as subsisting relations. Thinking of the Church after the prime image and model of the Trinity therefore means thinking of it as relational and communial reality. The Church does not live out of itself but from the self-revealing love of the triune God, and it does not live for itself but in the inward and outward communication of love.

Erik Peterson has shown that the doctrine of the Trinity signifies an overcoming of an inflexible monotheism and, in consequence, the end of the antique political theology of one god – one emperor – one empire.[74] This imperial concept of unity in which the emperor who rules the one empire represents the one god ended with the doctrine of the Trinity. Now, unity no longer means uniformity but unity in plurality and plurality in unity. To understand the Church as an icon of the Trinity thereby creates a guiding principle of its unity in its plurality and its plurality in its unity.

One has to understand this statement correctly. It does not mean that the imperial and patriarchal understanding of unity and authority has now been replaced by a democratic fraternity in the sense the Enlightenment saw it. Such a misunderstanding is occasionally caused when, by speaking of the Church as an image of the Trinity, one wants to have a pluralism of churches and to replace the imperial or patriarchal understanding of unity with a purely fraternal view. Behind such an interpretation there is an understanding of Trinity which leads to a tritheism (doctrine of three gods).

The Church's doctrine of the Trinity excludes such tritheism categorically. It does not assume three divine persons who unite together into unity; the doctrine rather begins with the Father as the origin and source (ἀρχὴ καὶ πηγή) of the Trinitarian unity. The Father is the origin and source of the Son, and together with the Son that of the Holy Spirit, not in a way that the Son thus would become a divine person subordinate to the Father and that the Spirit would become a servant of the Father and the Son (subordinationism). The Father is origin and source in such a way that he is the basis for the consubstantial dignity of the Son and the Spirit. Thus, there exists an inner-Trinitarian order (τάξις) which is, nevertheless, no subordination. Similarly, there should be a paternal authority in the Church (cf. 1 Cor. 4.15), which is not domination but from which fraternity proceeds. This ideal has often been emphasized in monastic spirituality.[75] In the chapters on the abbot of his Rule, the father of monasticism, St Benedict, has impressively described the character of such paternal authority. He established thus a model of ecclesial authority that combines paternal authority with the fraternity of all. In fact, it is such authority that ultimately enables true fraternity with mutual respect and appreciation.[76] For, in contrast to the enlightenment idea of fraternal equality, paternal authority does not presuppose unity and equality as a given. It is aware of natural egoism, self-assertiveness and conflict among brothers. Neither does it imagine that unity in the fraternal dialogue can be constantly reground and recreated. Paternal authority is predetermined as the starting point and source of unity. It grounds and furthers the unity of equals, and it does this by measuring itself against the one Father in Heaven who is the foundation for the equal dignity of all (Mt. 23.9).

Hence, speaking of the Church as the image of the mystery of the Trinity is anything but pure speculation with which, as Immanuel Kant put it, practically nothing can be done.[77] It contains possibilities for understanding, behaviour and acting that deserve to become fully recognized and exploited in order to completely correspond with the Trinitarian *mysterium communionis* which the Church is.

The Church as the universal sacrament of salvation

In the post-biblical language of the Church since Tertullian, the Greek word for mystery (μυστήριον) was translated as *sacramentum*.[78] Some Church Fathers, such as Cyprian of Carthage,[79] could thus describe the Church as sacrament. Yet, it was not until the nineteenth century that this term was taken up again by Johann Adam Möhler, Johannes Heinrich Oswald and Matthias Joseph Scheeben. At the Second Vatican Council the term could only prevail against considerable opposition.[80] On the other hand, in theology this manner of speaking was generally accepted. Nevertheless, it is still quite alien for the average Catholic perception of the Church and has remained the language only of academic theologians. As such, it requires detailed and not entirely easy explanation.[81]

Vatican II was also rather prudent in its description of the Church as sacrament. It says that the Church was 'in Christ like a sacrament or as a sign and instrument both of a very closely knit union with God and of the unity of the whole human race'.[82] The Council presupposes this careful definition in other places and describes there the Church without any further specification as the universal sacrament of salvation.[83]

The careful way in which the Council speaks of the Church as sacrament contains, in fact, several restrictions which need to be clearly observed when interpreting this statement. The Council says that the Church was 'in Christ like (veluti)' a sacrament. This 'like' indicates that the Church is not an eighth sacrament in addition to the other seven sacraments. More important is a second restriction. The Council says that the Church was 'in Christ like a sacrament'. With this the claim is made that the Church has no independent sacramental significance besides Christ, but only 'in Christ', for Jesus Christ is the only mediator between God and human beings (1 Tim. 2.5). The primal sacrament of salvation in its actual meaning, also according to Augustine, is only Jesus Christ himself.[84] According to the Church Fathers, the whole mystery of the Church emerged out of the side of Christ who died on the cross.[85] The primal sacrament is and remains Jesus Christ himself. For this reason one has abandoned the formula of the Church as original sacrament which had in parts become commonplace in theology. Instead we prefer to speak of the Church as basic or radical (in the literal sense) sacrament. As basic or radical sacrament the Church is, so to speak, the sacrament *in* the other sacraments. It is like the one hand with which God reaches out to us through the other seven sacraments and draws us towards him.

All of this is important to be able to respond appropriately to some criticism which the concept of the sacramentality of Church has found within Protestant theology.[86] We can also point to another statement of the Council where it speaks of a 'no weak analogy' between Christ's theanthropic constitution and the Church as 'one complex reality which coalesces from a divine and a human element'.[87] Again this is to highlight the difference that remains despite all inner connectedness between Christ and the Church.

A properly understood basic sacramental structure of the Church has its foundation in the whole sacramental order of salvation. God reveals himself and effects salvation through historical words and actions, culminating in his Son's incarnation in Jesus Christ. He is true God and true man; in him the invisible God has become visible. Thus, despite all inner connectedness, the differentiation between Christ and the Church is preserved and the Church is seen as divine-human mystery only by analogically applicable logic.[88] Thomas Aquinas called Christ's humanity the instrument of salvation which is united with his divinity. What was visible in Jesus Christ has now passed into the sacraments.[89] Yet, for Thomas, the sacraments are not instruments in Christ united with divinity but instruments of salvation different from the divinity.[90] They and, together with them, the Church understood as sacrament are not the 'thing' itself, they are only sign and instrument. For Thomas, the Church is instrument by being sign.[91] Expressed in the language of modern theology, the Church is a real symbol which also contains and communicates that which it symbolizes.[92]

So the view that the Church was, as it were, a sacrament does not lead to the Church becoming divinized. On the contrary, it becomes in an appropriately understood sense relativized. It does not give rise to an ecclesial triumphalism, but rather aims to overcome it. For, as a quasi-sacramental sign, the Church points to Jesus Christ and his Cross. The Church shaped in the image of Christ is Church under the Cross and in the shadow of the Cross. As Vatican II writes, quoting Augustine, the Church 'presses forward amid the persecutions of the world and the consolations of God'. It embraces in its bosom sinners and is therefore always in need of penance and purification.[93] On the other hand, the earthly Church which 'has the appearance of this world which is passing' points as eschatological sign of salvation towards the future unity of the human race.[94] It stands between the 'already' and the 'not yet'. The eschatological heavenly reality is already present in an anticipatory way, particularly in the liturgy. Yet the Eucharist is at the same time provision for the Church which lives in history and still moves towards its eschatological goal.[95]

With such a double orientation, the Church, as the symbol and instrument of unity with God, is simultaneously the sign and instrument of unity among the human race and thus the sacrament of the world. The one must not be separated from the other. It is only through unity with God and in God that unity and fraternity among human beings become possible. Therefore, the salvific sacramentality of the Church must not be politically instrumentalized. There can be no doubt that the Church has to make every effort to work for peace and reconciliation. Yet, the Church can only be the sacrament of reconciliation and peace in the world as the sacrament of reconciliation with God through and in Jesus Christ.[96]

Such a view of the Church as sacrament places it in an important context of salvation history. As for the sacraments,[97] we can differentiate for the Church between three dimensions: the dimension of the external sign that is the social-institutional dimension (*signum seu sacramentum tantum*); the intermediate dimension of the reality of the Church – already realized but hidden among signs – in communion with God and in the communion of faith, hope and love (*res et sacramentum*); and finally, the fulfilled eschatological reality of the universal kingdom of God towards which the Church moves and which is already present in the mystery (*res sacramenti*).[98]

Understanding the Church as sacrament therefore expresses the great wealth of theological reflection about the Church. A great stream of salvation and universal history moves through this perspective. Nonetheless, it must be said that this wealth is buried under many academic-theological restrictions, explanations and boundaries which make it difficult to communicate the view of the Church as sacrament to the minds of the faithful. So it is to be expected that, in the future, such language will remain basically that of academic theologians. Fortunately there are also other ways of speaking in the theological Tradition which express what is intended here in a far more accessible way. It is this language to which we must now finally turn.

The Church as a work of art – the beauty of the Church

To better understand the great stream that is expressed in the view of the Church as 'like a sacrament', it is worth studying again the theologians of the nineteenth century. What we arduously say with the help of the term 'sacrament', they expressed with far more pleasing aesthetic categories by speaking of the Church as a work of art and of the beauty of the Church. It was nothing new to speak of the beauty of the Church; it is already to be found in the theological Tradition.[99] Yet, after all the rational criticism and superficiality of the Enlightenment, the humiliation of the Church during the French Revolution and Secularization, the discovery and language of the beauty of the Church was taken up enthusiastically.

It began with the epochal volume *Génie du Christianisme, ou Beautés de la Religion chrétienne* (*The Genius of Christianity: or, the Spirit and Beauty of the Christian Religion*, New York: H. Fertig 1976) by René Chateaubriand. It was published in 1802 and soon translated into German and English. It was intended to be a cultural aesthetic justification of Catholicism and was enthusiastically received. With it, Chateaubriand initiated a Catholic renaissance after the Enlightenment and the French Revolution. Apparently, this idea was somewhat in the air at that time. A number of romantic writers such as Wilhelm Schlegel adopted the idea immediately. In the same year Chateaubriand's volume appeared, Schelling published his *Philosophie der Kunst* (1802; *The Philosophy of Art*) in which he calls the Church a work of art which expresses the mediation and reconciliation of the divine with the humane in a real-symbolic way.[100]

Johann Michael Sailer, the great inspirer of Catholic renewal in Germany, also took up the idea and called the Church the greatest work of art.[101] Influenced by him, Johann Sebastian Drey unfolded the idea on a large scale in his programmatic *Vom Geist und Wesen des Katholizismus* (1819),[102] as did Johann Adam Möhler in *Symbolism* (1832).[103] However, the twentieth century had to wait until Hans Urs von Balthasar and the several volumes of his theological aesthetics *Herrlichkeit* (*The Glory of God: A Theological Aesthetics*) for aesthetic categories to be used once again, this time in a historical and systematic way, for a deeper understanding of the Church.[104]

It would be wrong to suspect a pure aestheticism in the idea of the beauty of the Church. There is also no intention to palliate the Church. Viewing the Church aesthetically as a work of art has a much deeper and more central foundation. It points to the beauty which belongs to the Church as it is transparent towards *the* work of art, or in biblical words, towards *the* image of God in Jesus Christ (2 Cor. 4.4; Col. 1.15; cf. Heb. 1.3). It is a paradoxical beauty, for he who suffered and was crucified had neither form nor beauty (Isa. 53.2). And yet, the figure of Jesus Christ is, to this day, both attractive and fascinating, not only for Christians, but also for very many people who do not identify as Christians.

The Church becomes particularly transparent towards Jesus Christ in the medium of the liturgy and the realm of its symbols and rites. Wherever the liturgy is celebrated, whether quite simply or in its most elaborate form, it radiates something of the dignity, beauty and glory (δόξα) of God. Within a frequently heavy reality shrouded in clouds, the liturgy gives us a glimpse of the other, heavenly world and its glory. In this context one might think of the French poet Paul Claudel († 1955). Until the age of eighteen he was a non-believer. When he entered the cathedral of Notre Dame on Christmas day during vespers he had an experience of religious awakening and immediately afterwards he became a faithful Catholic.

The beauty of the Church also permeates those who follow Christ and are moulded in the likeness of him, first sacramentally in Baptism and later in life (Rom. 6.3–6; 8.29), and who in the course of life reflect something of Christ's light and glory (δόξα, 2 Cor. 4.4). We call them saints. Finally, it becomes apparent, as Möhler in particular emphasized, in the inner order of the Church and the interplay in the unity within the diversity of the manifold charismas, services and ministries. In this sense, with all its human weaknesses and in all afflictions which belong to this world, the Church is a real foretaste of the eschatological glory when at the end God will be all in all (1 Cor. 15.28).

The well-known German hymn 'Ein Haus voll Glorie schauet' may sound for some of us today too triumphalist in parts; yet what it says in a later verse remains valid: 'the Church is built alone on Jesus Christ. If it looks to him, it will be in peace.' 'The Lord wants to lead his wandering people on earth through time. At the end of time he has his house prepared for his people.'[105] In this respect, the Church is *sacramentum futuri* and a sign of hope for the world.

2.2 The kingdom of God and the Church

God's saving design – the gathering together and establishment of peace among the nations

The hope for justice and peace pervades the whole history of humanity. It is a fundamental yearning of humanity that also resonates in the Old and New Testaments. As immediately becomes apparent on the first page of the first book of the Bible, the universal human hope is founded upon biblical monotheism. According to the first book of the Bible, Genesis, God creates Adam. That means that God creates Man independently of his belonging to a specific people, tribe or gender in his image and likeness (Gen. 1.28). Consequently all human beings, regardless of their race, skin colour, culture, language, nation, sex or religion are, in the same way, children of the one Father in heaven. All form one human family, all share in the one and same human dignity. This was a revolutionary view in the world at that time, since, in a sense, it democratized the idea that the king alone was the image of God. At the same time it took away the religious grounds for all ethnic and nationalistic hostilities.

The Bible adds a further aspect to this: God creates humanity as a being intended for communion and communication. This is particularly expressed by the fact that both creation narratives state that God created humanity as male and female and as two beings that correspond with each other. God commissioned both of them to multiply and fill the earth (Gen. 1.26f. 2.18–25). The communicative character of humanity is also expressed in the fact that, in biblical understanding, humans are distinguished through language from animals, which are silent (Ps. 49.21; beasts – Hebrew 'behemah' – literally means 'the silent one'). In contrast, humanity is a being with language intended for communication.

Communication was disturbed through sin. Sin brought alienation, separation and dispute into the world. We can see this already in the relationship between man and woman, who, after the fall, realize their nakedness, feel ashamed before each other and become estranged from each other (Gen. 3.20). The history of estrangement continues with the fratricide of Cain and Able (Gen. 4). The alienation finds its most explicit expression in the story of the Tower of Babel. In this narrative, God confuses the language of the peoples addicted to hubris so that they can no longer understand the language of the others (Gen. 11.6–9). As Origen put it: '*ubi peccata, ibi multitudo.*' 'Where there are sins, there is multiplicity, divisions, erroneous teachings and discord.'[106]

Yet, in his faithfulness God did not desert mankind. He did not leave Man alone in this difficult and desperate situation nor cast mankind into the destruction of the Babylonian confusion of tongues. He made a new beginning with Abraham. Though God calls Abraham as an individual and he calls him out of all the others, yet Abraham is called to be a blessing for all peoples (Gen. 12.2; 18.18; 22.17f.). Hence, the history of salvation, beginning with Abraham, aims right from the start – beyond the direct descendants of Abraham and beyond the people of Israel – at the whole of mankind. It is in this sense that the prophets predicted the eschatological gathering of all peoples and a universal peace (shalom; Isa. 2.2–5; 49.9–13; Mic. 4.1–3; Ezek. 37.16–28 and others).

Already the prophet Nathan promised an eternal kingship (2 Sam. 7). The Psalms (Ps. 2.7f.; 47.9; 89; 110; 145.13 and others) and the prophets (Isa. 32.1; 40.10; 52.7; Jer. 23.5 and others) speak of the messianic hope that dawns from God's kingdom, and with it justice and peace (Ps. 72; Isa. 32.1), security and quiet (Ezek. 34). The point thereby is the proclamation that YHWH himself is king (Melech; Ps. 93.1; 96.10; 99.1).[107]

The prophet Daniel then first speaks of the kingdom of God (malkut). It is the final empire that replaces all previous empires (Dan. 2.36–44). With this, history has entered its final stage. Daniel combines this perspective with the expectation of the Son of Man who will come on the clouds of heaven, upon whom rule, honour and kingship will be conferred; his kingship will have no end (Dan. 7.13f.27). The Son of Man represents God's people of saints of the end time.

The book of Daniel marks the beginning of early Jewish apocalyptic writings. They assume a dualistic world view. They see the hopelessness of the present situation and they know that salvation cannot be the result of inner worldly developments or plans, but only the result of God's works. They anticipate an initiative of God which will end the present time of this world and bring about the kingdom of God.

Jesus' message of the kingdom of God

Jesus' appearance and ministry can only be understood in the context of this universal eschatological promise. His central message is the coming of the kingdom of God. Mark condenses it in a summary: 'The time is fulfilled, and the kingdom of God is close at hand. Repent, and believe in the gospel' (Mk 1.14f. par.).[108]

With this message, Jesus takes up the hope of the Old Testament. With his proclamation of the coming kingdom of God, Jesus heralds in the eschatological gathering of the people of God; he gathers the dispersed sheep of Israel (Mt. 9.36; 12.30; 14.27; Jn 10.11–16; 11.52). He is the good shepherd who follows the lost ones and brings them back into the community with God and the others (Lk. 15; 19.10). He envisages that many will come from the East and the West to sit down with Abraham, Isaac and Jacob at the feast in the kingdom of heaven (Mt. 8.11). At the end, the angels will be sent out to gather his elect from the four winds (Mk 13.27). The fourth gospel again magnificently unpacks the image of the good shepherd (Jn 10.1–39) and speaks of the gathering of the scattered children of God (Jn 11.51f.).[109]

With his teaching of the kingdom of God, Jesus adopts apocalyptic language without himself being an apocalyptic prophet. He rejects apocalyptic speculations (Mt. 24.36; Mk 13.32). It is not possible to calculate or determine with external signs the coming of the kingdom of God (Lk. 17.20f.; cf. Acts 1.6f.). The how, when and where of its coming rests exclusively with God. Nobody knows it, not even the Son (Mt. 24.36).

In relation to apocalyptic, his eschatological message is in this respect a novelty, inasmuch as Jesus identifies the coming of God's kingdom with his coming. In him and through him, God himself is coming. He is the Son of Man, predicted by Daniel as the representative of the eschatological people of God. His message of God's kingdom is intrinsically tied to his awareness of and the claim that he, as the Son, is in a unique intimate relationship with God as his father (abba; Mt. 11.27; Mk 14.36). Origen encapsulated it by calling Jesus the Kingdom of God in person (αὐτοβασιλεία).[110]

God's kingdom comes by being proclaimed; his word is a performative proclamation which effects what it says. The kingdom comes through his preaching and through his works (Mk 1.23–6; Lk. 4.33–5; 11.20; 17.21), and finally becomes a real occurrence in his behaviour towards sinners and the lost. After all, Jesus came to call sinners, not the upright (Mk 2.17). Similarly, he calls 'blessed' the poor, those who mourn, the gentle, the hungry, the peacemakers and those persecuted in the cause of uprightness (Mt. 5.3–11; Lk. 6.20–6). He promises God's kingdom to, in particular, the poor, imprisoned, sick, oppressed (Lk. 4.18f.), the children and the little ones (Mt. 10.14 par.). It is already anticipatorily celebrated in the meals that Jesus also celebrates with the sinners who repent (Mk 2.19 and others). In other words, the coming of God's kingdom is quite different from what the people expect it to be. Therefore, 'blessed is anyone who does not find me a cause of falling' (Mt. 11.6; Lk. 7.23).

The coming of God's kingdom demands from the listeners repentance and faith. It means a total new orientation of one's life (Mk 1.15) which comes close to a rebirth (Jn 3.3). We should not make ourselves, our interests or our will the centre of our attention, but God. We should love God and him above anything else and we should make our neighbour the central focus of our conduct. For such a mountain-moving faith everything is possible; in it we participate in the omni-possibility (omnipotence) of God (Mk 9.23; Mt. 17, 20). Yet, we cannot bring about God's kingdom. We can only pray for it: 'your kingdom come' (Mt. 6.10; Lk. 11.2).

The parables of the kingdom of God give us some indication of the 'how' of the coming of God's kingdom. They speak of the growing seed, of the mustard seed that becomes a huge tree and of the yeast that leavens through the whole trough of flour (Mt. 13 par.). These are paradoxical images. They all claim that the kingdom of God is already present in insignificantly small beginnings and in a hidden manner, yet it still has to grow and ripen until the harvest that will occur at the end of time. In other words, the kingdom of God is a dynamic entity. Like a small amount of yeast placed within flour, it leavens and transforms the whole of reality.

Did Jesus want a church?

Neither the preaching nor the public ministry of Jesus speaks explicitly of the founding of a church. Nevertheless, the origin of the Church in Jesus was taken for granted by the whole Tradition. Only since the Enlightenment has the question of the foundation of a church by Jesus become a problem. It began with the Protestant theologian, philologist, orientalist and philosopher Hermann Samuel Reimarus († 1769). After his death, Gotthold Ephraim Lessing published *Fragmente eines Ungenannten*, thereby causing a fierce controversy. Reimarus noticed a radical break between Jesus' preaching of an earthly messianic kingdom and the kingdom of heaven preached by the apostles. According to Reimarus, Jesus' preaching had failed with his death on the cross. The message of the resurrection was a fraud by the apostles only with which the Church and its metaphysical message became possible. In other words, the Church was nothing but a makeshift solution and misunderstanding of Jesus' message of God's kingdom. Like a thunderbolt, this launched the modern quest for the historical Jesus.[111]

There is no space here to outline the development of the quest for the historical Jesus. It reached its end in liberal Protestant theology (Albrecht Ritschl, Adolf von Harnack, etc.). In 1900, Harnack († 1930) gave a public lecture in Berlin on 'Das Wesen des Christentum (What is Christianity)' in which he unpacks his view of Jesus' kingdom of God as a moral ideal: 'Everything dramatic in the superficial sense of secular history has disappeared here, gone is also all secular hope for the future.' All that counts is 'God and the soul, the soul and its God.'[112] The Catholic Church, the sacraments and the idea of the divinization of man are a Hellenization of Christianity. They lack any connection with the Gospel; they are a complete perversion.[113] For Harnack, the dogma is 'the work of a Greek mind based on the Gospel.'[114]

A new situation arose when the Eschatological School (Johannes Weiß and Albert Schweitzer) highlighted again the unworldly and trans-worldly apocalyptic character of Jesus' message of God's kingdom and thus shook the foundations of the liberal position. Alfred Loisy mockingly observed: 'Jesus proclaimed the Kingdom of God, and what came was the Church.'[115] Erik Peterson († 1965) rightly countered polemically that 'what came was humanism.'[116] Thus, what remained for Albert Schweitzer was reverence for life. This rightly earned him great respect personally, though he himself viewed the eschatological message of Jesus as an irretrievable past.

The rediscovery of eschatology raised again the question of de-eschatologization and, in consequence, the problem of the emergence of the Church.

The question was now: how could the apocalyptic charismatic preaching of Jesus become a sacramental-institutionally constituted church? Was it a break or continuity?

Rudolf Bultmann distinguished between the public life and preaching of Jesus and the kerygma after Easter. For Bultmann, Jesus belonged to the antecedent history of the kerygma. His existential interpretation of the New Testament was not interested in the historical Jesus. Rather, his focus was the kerygma, which was current for each age, and the Christ of faith.[117] Bultmann's latent Docetism became a problem in the theology which came after him. Several of Bultmann's students, therefore, raised again the question concerning the historical Jesus and sought to explicate the Christology clearly implicit in the public ministry and preaching of the earthly Jesus.[118] Along the same lines, a group of other researchers (Karl Ludwig Schmidt, Joachim Jeremias, Werner Georg Kümmel, Anton Vögtle, Rudolf Schnackenburg, Franz Musssner, Wolfgang Trilling, etc.) succeeded in demonstrating a kind of implicit ecclesiology for Jesus.[119]

The Jesuanic and Christological foundations of the Church

Through his teaching and miracles, Jesus sought to gather the people of God. Like a shepherd, he wanted to gather the scattered sheep of Israel (Mt. 9.36). The mission of his disciples (Mk 3.13–19; 6.6–13 par.) is aimed only at the lost sheep of the House of Israel (Mt. 10.6). Jesus did not intend to found a separate community besides Israel. That is why we have no explicit word from Jesus concerning the institution of the Church.[120]

The calling of the Twelve, who only after Easter came to be called apostles, belongs in this context of the eschatological gathering and re-establishing of God's People. The number twelve is of symbolic importance; the Twelve are to be the representatives of the eschatological people of God, who will be divided into twelve tribes. The narrative of their appointment and mission, however, also shows the novelty that is happening here. Their appointment is a sovereign, creative act by Jesus. It says: 'he called those he had chosen', 'he made them (that is: he created them) the Twelve'. It is important that the text continues: he chose them 'so that they were with him and that he would send them'. The gathering is centred around Jesus, who is the new centre of God's people which is to be gathered together. Communion with Jesus is the basis and the starting point.[121]

What led to the break was the claim by Jesus, perceived as a scandal, articulated in his interpretation of the Mosaic Law, his treatment of the Sabbath, his eating with sinners and his forgiving of sins. After initial enthusiasm among the crowd, there emerged a division of opinion. In particular, the leaders of the people became opposed to him. The cross soon cast its shadow. Jesus interpreted his mission in the sense of the vicarious suffering of Isaiah's fourth Servant Song (Isa. 53; Mk 10.45 par.). He now intercedes 'for the many' by taking the place of all. His death decides the salvation of many. Whoever wishes to be his disciple must follow him in this vicarious service and take up his cross to find life (Mk 8.34f. par.). A new community of disciples begins to emerge.

Yet, most surprisingly, Jesus finds faith among individual heathens. Examples are his encounters with the Syro-Phoenician woman and with the centurion of Capernaum (Mk 7.24–30; Mt. 8.5–13). Here Jesus takes up the prophecy of the coming of the gentiles and threatens his Jewish listeners: 'many will come from east and west and sit down with Abraham and Isaac and Jacob at the feast in the kingdom of Heaven; but the children of the kingdom will be thrown out into the darkness outside, where there will be weeping and grinding of teeth' (Mt. 8.11f.). We find a similar episode in John's gospel. It is in Jesus' encounter with the Greeks that the fourth gospel perceives the beginning of the eschatological hour (ὥρα, Jn 12.20–3). So, already during Jesus' earthly life, this indicates the beginning fulfilment of the promise of the universal eschatological gathering.

This universal claim is particularly clear in the material unique to Luke who, in addition to the appointment and mission of the Twelve, also narrates the mission of the 70 or 72 disciples (Lk. 10.1–16). This number has also a symbolic significance; in the Old Testament it stands for the common Jewish theory that there are 70 or 72 peoples on earth (Gen. 10; Exod. 1.5; Deut. 32.8). Luke wants thus to express Jesus' universal claim addressed to all humanity and his mission to all nations.[122] Hence, Luke anticipates what is indicated in the ministry of the Jesus which, however, became full reality only after Easter.

The decisive step that led to the constitution of the Church occurs at the Last Supper, during which Jesus ate with his disciples before his suffering and death. There are many questions concerning the transmission history of the accounts of Matthew, Mark, Luke and Paul, which cannot be discussed here in detail.[123] Yet, one word of Jesus is undisputed: Jesus says that he will not drink from the fruit of the vine until the day he will drink the new wine in the kingdom of God (Mk 14.25 par.). In this logia, Jesus once again summarizes the centre of his message: the coming of the kingdom of God. Yet, in view of his approaching death, Jesus looks beyond it. He does not consider his death a failure of the eschatological message, but rather the final dawn of the coming of God's eschatological kingdom. The Last Supper of Jesus is thus anticipation of the eschatological feast in the kingdom of God. Portentous quotations from the Old Testament are spoken over the bread and the cup (Exod. 12 new Passover; Exod. 24 blood of the covenant; Jer. 31 new covenant; Isa. 53 Jesus as God's servant). They all highlight in different ways that, with the death of Jesus, the prophetic promises are fulfilled and that his death is to be understood as vicariously giving up his life 'for the many'.

The Last Supper of Jesus was not a Church establishing act in the juridical sense of the word. It is far more. It lays the foundation for that which from the beginning after Easter was, has been and is the centre of the Church. In this comprehensive sense it is the founding event of the Church. Admittedly, it is contested among exegetes whether Jesus did indeed exactly use the words 'do this in remembrance of me' (Lk. 22.19; 1 Cor. 11.24f.). However, there can be no doubt that the early Church celebrated the commemoration of Jesus' death with eschatological rejoicing (ἀγαλλίασις; Acts 2.46) and that, with the acclamation 'maranatha' (1 Cor. 16.22; *Didache* 10.6), they thereby longingly looked forward to the final eschatological coming. In this respect, the Last Supper of Jesus was the foundation of what became the sensual centre of the Church after Easter: the present-making celebration of death and resurrection and the anticipating preliminary celebration of the final kingdom of God.

Such a development becomes understandable if we realize that Jesus' resurrection from the dead was, for the disciples, the decisive eschatological moment. According to the contemporaneous apocalyptic imagination, the resurrection of the dead was expected for the eschaton at the end of time. Thus, saying Jesus was resurrected from the dead meant a pre-occurring of the eschaton in the middle of this world's time.[124] This contains a fundamental correction of the apocalyptic concept.[125] Through the resurrection, God demonstrated his faithfulness to Jesus and his message. The logic of the story of the coming of God's kingdom therefore entailed that the Resurrected gathered his scattered disciples after Easter and sent them to all nations. This definitively introduced the eschatological gathering among all the peoples (Mt. 28.19; Mk 16.15; Lk. 24.47; Acts 1.8).

According to Acts, the outpouring of the Spirit fulfilled the vision of the prophet Joel that God would pour out his Spirit on all humanity at the end of time (Joel 3.1–5; Acts 2.17–22). At the Tower of Babel, the attempt to create unity among the civilizations of the earth on the basis of their own effort and power failed. Now the Babylonian confusion of languages has come to an end through God's Spirit. At Pentecost all hear and understand the teaching of the apostles, who proclaim the marvels of God, in their own language. A new communication and a new understanding across all ethnic and cultural boundaries is now possible (Acts 2.6.12). The eschatological gathering of God's people from out of all the peoples has thus irrevocably begun. At the same time, Pentecost calls to memory the covenant at Sinai, the giving of the Ten Commandments and the Torah. Hence, the idea of the New Covenant underlies the miracle of Pentecost, a covenant not written on tablets of stone but through the Spirit on human hearts (2 Cor. 3.3). Through the miracle of Pentecost, therefore, the Church appears for the first time publicly in its global and – as it was understood at that time – ecumenical universality.[126]

If we realize that with the death and resurrection of Jesus, as well as through the outpouring of the Spirit, the eschaton has already begun and that we are through baptism in Jesus Christ a new creation (Gal. 6.15), then we understand why the so-called delay of the parousia did not become a significant problem for the early church. After all, Jesus saw himself as God's kingdom in person, and now this kingdom has been initiated through the resurrection and the outpouring of the Spirit. The turning point and the saving victory have already occurred (Rev. 12.10f.), so that we can now say: 'The old order is gone and a new being is there to see' (2 Cor. 5.17). Therefore, it is incorrect to make the so-called delay of the parousia the master key of all exegetical problems, as has repeatedly happened since Johannes Weiß, Albert Schweitzer and Alfred Loisy.[127] The actual foundation of the Church is Jesus himself resurrected and present in the Spirit. Ultimately, the foundation of the Church is given and established in the being of Jesus Christ in baptism (1 Cor. 12.13; Gal. 3.27f.). Through participation in the Eucharistic body, as Paul puts it, the Church is the body of Christ (1 Cor. 10.16f.).[128]

The post-Easter Church is therefore no makeshift solution. Rather it has to be seen in the context of the total dynamics of the kingdom of God which is coming with Jesus and which has once and for all began with the resurrection. In this sense it is implicitly present in the teaching and ministry of Jesus. It entered life in the course of the history of God with his people that reached its final phase with Jesus. Therefore it is a moot point to discuss whether the earthly Jesus, the cross of Jesus, Easter or Pentecost is the origin of the Church. The Church emerged out of the overall dynamics of the coming of God's kingdom and appeared publicly for the first time at Pentecost. Hence, ecclesiology results from the dynamic of the impending eschatology.

To sum it up, together with the Second Vatican Council we can speak of a gradual emergence of the Church as part of the eschatological gathering[129] and we can say that the Church is the kingdom of God now present in mystery.[130] Yet, the Church has the appearance of this world.[131] It is the still-incomplete kingdom of God. The Church is an intermediate reality, a sign and instrument of the coming kingdom. 'Missionary activity is nothing else and nothing less than an epiphany, or a manifesting of God's decree, and its fulfilment in the world and in world history.'[132]

What is the meaning of 'ecclesia' – 'Church'?

Let us now ask ourselves: what do we actually mean when we say 'Church'? To answer this question, we can start with the name that became the most important self-description of the Church in the New Testament: ἐκκλησία.[133] The word 'ecclesia' serves as a translation of the Hebrew word 'qahal'. This is used for the people of the covenant gathered at Sinai (Deut. 4.10; 31.30 et seq.). Such gatherings happened repeatedly (Josh. 24.1–28), later, after the building of the temple, at the important religious festivals during the year. The ecclesia of the New Testament is, in this respect, the renewal and fulfilment of the covenant gathering of the Old Testament.

The understanding of ecclesia is often derived from this use in the Old Testament. Recent research, however, necessitates that we take a different look at the direct derivation from the Old Testament. In the Hellenistic-Roman imperial period, ecclesia was also often widely used as a political term. During this late era, it no longer had the meaning of 'people's assembly' it had during the golden age of Athenian democracy. The ecclesia of the imperial period was officially structured. The people's assembly that had to be duly summoned by the responsible authorities and was led by civil servants. It did not have any decision-making power but only an acclamation right and, in addition, some cultic functions. Therefore, in contrast to societies under private law or the rules for associations such as the mystery cults, the term 'ecclesia' belongs to the field of public law.[134]

The Hellenistically influenced meaning of ecclesia is behind a number of passages in the New Testament. The account of the 'Apostolic Council' (Acts 15) is of particular importance. Like the pagan gatherings, there the ecclesia meets under the leadership of the apostles and together with them a decree is decided which is fundamental for the future of the young Church: 'it has been decided by the Holy Spirit and by ourselves' (Acts 15.28). Also the only two passages where the synoptics use the term 'ecclesia' speak of legally binding acts of 'binding and loosening' (Mt. 16.18; 18.17f.; cf. also 1 Cor. 5f.). This means the power to make doctrinal decisions, to exclude from the community (banning), and also to revoke a ban.[135]

To understand how such Hellenistic language could also play a role in the early church, one has to know that, at the time of Herod the Great († 4 BC), Jerusalem was a metropolis that was distinctly Hellenistic in character. Correspondingly, the Hellenistic Jewish Christians in the group around Stephen (Acts 6.1) played an essential role in the early church. It is also quite telling that the group name 'Christians' appears for the first time in Hellenistic Antioch (Acts 11.26).[136]

So, we may interpret the term 'ecclesia' not only (and not directly) against the background of the Old Testament, but, concerning its public and official meaning, we have to understand it in the context of the contemporary Hellenistic use of language. From the biblical use of language it follows thus that the ecclesia of the New Testament was never a purely charismatic or in some way democratic entity, but from the beginning it was legally structured.[137] It was not an association of believers for the practice and support of their private piety; it was a public-legal entity.

In opposition to the political ecclesia, the novelty of the New Testament ecclesia was that it did not see itself as political. It was founded not by political citizenship but by being called out of (ἐκ-κλησία) all peoples and by a new being one in Jesus Christ founded in baptism. This highlights the fundamental difference of the determination as 'ecclesia of God' (ἐκκλησία τοῦ Θεοῦ; 1 Cor. 1.1; 15.9; 2 Cor. 1.1; Gal. 1.1.13 and others) and even more so as 'ecclesia of God in Jesus Christ' (1 Thess. 1.1; 2.12; 2 Thess. 1.1; Gal. 1.22). Also Jesus speaks in Matthew 16.18 of 'my' ecclesia. This emphasizes again the Old Testament background. The Church is the people chosen and called out by God that has to proclaim the great deeds of God (1 Pet. 2.9). The people of God of the New Covenant is the people of God but only in Christ and only as the body of Christ.[138]

This novelty relativizes all natural and political affiliations and distinctions which were important for the political ecclesia. Now there was neither Jew nor Greek, neither slave nor freeman, neither male nor female; all are 'one' in Christ (Gal. 3.28; Col. 3.11). It was new for the world of that time that not only men but also women and children belonged to the New Testament ecclesia. The novelty in opposition to the Old Testament qahal was that, through the decision of the Apostolic Council (Acts 15), the New Testament ecclesia was a church of Jews and gentiles (Eph. 2.11–22) which lives in this world as aliens (παροικία) and in the diaspora (διασπορά; 1 Pet. 1.1; 2.11; cf. Heb. 11.13).

Therefore, the New Testament ecclesia is no longer bound to a geographical political ecclesia. It is in every place where Christians are gathered in Jesus Christ. It is present in each local ecclesia. Yet, as it is the one Lord Jesus Christ who is present in each local ecclesia, is not only a part, a province or section of the one ecclesia in Christ; rather the one ecclesia is present in it. The local church represents the Church and the Church is present in the local church. Paul expresses this very precisely when he speaks of the Church that is present in Corinth (τῇ ἐκκλησίᾳ τοῦ Θεοῦ τῇ οὔσῃ ἐν Κορίνθῳ; 1 Cor. 1.2; 2 Cor. 1.1). Thus, the New Testament can use ecclesia to mean each local church as well as the worldwide Church. As it is always the one Lord who is present in all churches, the universal Church is not the sum or summary of the individual churches. It is always the one Church that is present in many places.[139]

Against the Old Testament as well as, in particular, the Hellenistic political order of that time, the Christological novelty poses the problem of how the New Testament ecclesia is organized in the unity and diversity of the *ekklesiai*. Is it organized at all? Is it an institution or an event happening each time respectively?

The Church – institution and/or event?

All languages derived from Latin have kept the Greek loan word 'ecclesia': French *église*, Italian *chiesa*, Spanish *iglesia*, Portuguese *igreja*. The Germanic languages go back to the Greek κυριακόν, the gathering belonging to the Lord. So we have in German *Kirche*, in English *church*, in Dutch *kerk*, in Swedish *kyrka*. It is similar in the Slavonic languages: old-Slavonic *crk'ky*, Russian *cerkev*, Ukrainian *cervka*, Polish *cerkiew*. The general view is that they are also derived from the Greek *kyriakón*.

Luther was the first one to deviate from this common view. He spoke of the 'blind and unclear word "Church"'.[140] His translation of the Bible does not use the word 'church' at all. Instead he always uses community (*Gemeinde*). In the *Large Catechism* he specifically translates the word 'church' with 'a Christian congregation or assembly (eine christliche Gemeinde oder Sammlung), or, best of all and most clearly, holy Christian people (eine heilige Christenheit)',[141] and in the *Smalcald Articles*, 'the holy believers and lambs who hear the voice of their Shepherd'.[142] It is similarly expressed in the *Small Catechism*.[143]

The translation of ecclesia as assembly is in line with Luther's basic tendency of distinguishing himself from the contemporary, institutional church. Yet, compared with the dominant use of language in the Bible as well as in the whole Tradition, this results in a significant shift of meaning which had considerable theological consequences, for now the community/assembly became 'the pivotal idea of the Reformation knowledge and patterns of thought'.[144] With this terminology, liberal theology later intended to set itself apart from the early Catholic view of the Church as a legal-sacramental institution of salvation, and from the, as it was conceived, subsequent juridification of the original biblical understanding of ecclesia. The Church was to be seen as a spiritual entity and a spiritual event in the proclamation of the Word and the administration of the sacraments.[145] By consequence, 'church' became more or less a negative term.

Emil Brunner spoke of the misunderstanding of Church.[146] For him, the community founded by Jesus in the Holy Spirit has nothing of the character of an institution and cannot be identified with any historically institutional church. Karl Barth rightly said that Brunner's statement is itself a misunderstanding. He warned against an ecclesial docetism that creates his own image of church which exists only as wishful thinking. For him, the Church is 'Jesus Christ's own form of worldly-historical existence'. He describes it as fraternal Christocracy.[147] Yet, for him, God's acting runs vertically; it touches – so to speak – our world only at a point, like a tangent touches a circle, yet it does not permeate the world from inside. For him, too, the Church is event but not institution.

On several occasions, the relation between the content and the form of the Church has been the topic of conversation with Protestant ecclesiology.[148] Meanwhile, such a theological definition of the Church as event is also criticized by some on the Protestant side.[149] A legal form has belonged to the Church since its very beginning. According to the New Testament, the exalted Lord builds up his Church from heaven by appointing apostles, prophets, evangelists and pastors (Eph. 4.8-11). It is he who knits everything together and holds all things together (Eph. 2.21; 4.16). Hence, the Church does not itself establish its own ecclesial being. Rather. It is built up from heaven by the exalted Lord and lives from him and out of his Spirit. Built as it is by and from Christ, the Church is, however, not only event, it is also, as it were, a building. It has a structure in which the apostles, prophets, evangelists and pastors each have a clear place and a specific task. They are, like Paul himself, God's co-workers (1 Cor. 3.9).

Categories such as Hellenization and juridification are insufficient to do justice to the theological problem. The New Testament language rather shows that, not only in the sense of its ancient profane usage but also according to its self-understanding, ecclesia entails a legal order. The Church on earth also lives in its institutions from the exalted Lord and out of his Spirit. Institution and event, the content and the form of the Church, can be distinguished but not separated. The Church as institution is at the same time always more than institution. As an institutional event it is an eschatological, spiritual event; as an eschatological event it is simultaneously institutional.

Where institutions are concerned, the problems are never solely theoretical; rather the respective theoretical positions have concrete institutional consequences. Thus, because of their self-understanding, the Reformation churches first organized themselves on the level of local communities, but soon thereafter, out of political necessity, territorially, both in a regional sense (Germany) and nationally (Sweden, England, etc.). In the course of this reorganization, the awareness of a universal Church was, to a large extent, lost, at least initially. In Pietism and the newer, fast-growing Pentecostal communities, the communal element remained dominant. The historical Protestant churches have come to see the danger of particularism and nationalism, leading to the formation, in the nineteenth and twentieth centuries, of denominational church federations (Lutheran World Federation, World Alliance of Reformed Churches, Anglican Communion, World Evangelical Alliance, etc.).[150] Yet, these do not see themselves as churches but as federations or alliances of churches. It is only recently that there are tendencies to just develop the concept of federation towards an understanding of communion in the theological sense. Even so, at present, the Community of Protestant Churches in Europe (CPCE) based on the *Leuenberg Agreement* is not a church.[151] Neither does the Protestant Church of Germany (EKD) define itself as a church, but as a community of member churches and as part of the one Church of Jesus Christ.[152]

In the *Leuenberg Agreement* (1973), which emerged out of the consensus between Lutheran, Reformed and other Reformation traditions, the underlying concept of the Church remained initially undetermined. It was not until the document *The Church of Jesus Christ* (1994) that it became specified more precisely. In line with CA VII and the questions 54–5 of the *Heidelberg Catechism*, for a community of churches this self-conception considers essential a fundamental consensus concerning the Gospel and its proclamation in word and sacrament. By contrast, the respective form of the Church accepts different models of church order; for example, episcopal-synodal as well as synodal-presbyterial orders. So far, the Leuenberg Community of Churches does not know a common synodal, let alone episcopal, structure. In it, all denominations that have these attributes can be accepted as part of the one, holy, catholic and apostolic Church.

In this concept of Church, the one Church (singular) of faith is present in the differently shaped churches (plural). The one Church (singular) itself, however, does not have one visible place and no fixed form; it exists as a hidden Church, as it were, floating freely above the churches (plural) and becomes an event occurring in Word and Sacrament there 'where and when it pleases God'. The difference between this Protestant view of Church as event and the sacramental understanding of the Catholic and Orthodox Church where content and form belong together is obvious. For the Catholic observer, this Protestant view of the Church reeks of ecclesiological docetism.

The problems converge in the question of the Petrine office. Still, the resulting questions certainly do not present a particular, isolated problem, but rather express a different basic conception of Church. We will return to this later.[153] For the time being, we mention this only in order to illustrate that the Catholic basic understanding of ecclesia/Church is neither a de-eschatologizing Hellenization nor a juridification of Christianity. Because of a Christologically informed eschatology, it has incorporated the Hellenistic understanding of ecclesia, and, at the same time, has changed this view from the inside. Therefore, the understanding of ecclesia in the New Testament and the Old Church is a novelty that has taken shape from the Christological centre of the Gospel. This means that, while we can distinguish between the content and form of the Church, these cannot be separated, just as the earthly Jesus cannot be separated from the exalted Christ or the humanity from the divinity of Jesus Christ. The Church has its content in concrete form. Another way to put this is to say that this is the nature of the Catholic understanding of Church.

The earthly church and the heavenly church

The Catholic understanding of the Church is directly related to the great context of the gathering of all nations and the bringing together of the cosmos (Eph. 1.10), where at the end God will be all in all (1 Cor. 15.28). The New Testament concept of ecclesia so leads to a further eschatological, yet unfortunately often overlooked aspect.[154]

The place of the ancient ecclesia is the polis; for the New Testament Church it holds true: 'Our city (πολίτευμα) is in heaven.' (Phil. 3.20) This statement does not stand isolated in the New Testament. In another passage Paul speaks of an everlasting house in heaven (2 Cor. 5.1). In Gal. 4.26 he speaks of the heavenly Jerusalem as our mother. In Ephesians we hear of the gentiles, who were at the beginning excluded from the citizenship (πολιτεία) of Israel (Eph. 2.12), and who are now fellow-citizens (συμπολῖται) with the saints (i.e. the angels) and part of God's household, built upon the foundation of the apostles and prophets with Christ being the cornerstone (Eph. 2.19f.). Accordingly he speaks of our place in heaven (Eph. 2.6) and of the hope which is prepared for us in heaven (Col. 1.5). The ecclesia is thus not only the earthly church gathered on earth. As such it is always simultaneously the heavenly Church.

In this, the Church reaches beyond the ecclesia that is gathered on earth. The angels and saints belong to it, too. It is the domain of the kyrios who is exalted above heaven and earth, over powers and might. In its liturgy the earthly church already participates in the heavenly liturgy; it already has a share in the eschaton. Yet, it is under the eschatological reserve; it is not identical with the heavenly city or the kingdom of God. It still lives as strangers (παροικία; 1 Pet. 1.17; cf. 1.1; 2.11). This will only come to an end when the kingdom of God will be finally revealed and God will be all in all (1 Cor. 15.28).

The clearest eschatological reference is in Hebrews.[155] It says that we are only strangers on earth and that God has prepared for us a heavenly homeland and city (Heb. 11.13–16; cf. 13.14). Still, it is already now that we participate in the heavenly liturgy together with all the angels and all the righteous ones already made perfect. 'But what you have come to is Mount Zion and the city (πόλις) of the living God, the heavenly Jerusalem where millions of angels have gathered for the festival (ἐκκλησία), with the whole Church of first-born sons, enrolled as citizens of heaven. You have come to God himself, the supreme Judge, and to the spirits of the upright who have been made perfect; and to Jesus the mediator of a new covenant, and to purifying blood which pleads more insistently than Abel's' (Heb. 12.22–4). This prepares us for what the Revelation to John explains in many passages and with great images. This speaks of the city of the new Jerusalem which descends from heaven and has the names of the Twelve Apostles written on its twelve foundation stones (Rev. 3.12; 17.18; 21.2.10.14–23; 21.14; 22.14.19).

The Church Fathers frequently expressed the concept of the Church as anticipation of the universal eschatological kingdom of God – the kingdom of peace which includes all peoples and cultures. Already the *Didache* writes: 'let your ecclesia be gathered together from the ends of the earth into your basileia' (*Didache* 9.4). 'Remember, Lord, your Church, to deliver it from all evil and to make it perfect in your love, and gather it from the four winds, sanctified for your kingdom which you have prepared for it' (*Didache* 10.5; cf. 1 Clement 29.1–3). The Church, according to Irenaeus of Lyons, gathers the whole of mankind with all their goods under the one head Christ in the unity of his Spirit.[156] All peoples have become one choir through the Pentecostal Spirit to offer, in the wake of the end of all discord, as the first fruit hymns of praise to God in the harmony of all languages.[157] In the same spirit Hrabanus Maurus says: 'Each people sings psalms to the Creator in its respective country.'[158]

The Church is a *congregatio populorum* gathered from all peoples.[159] They have been made one body in the Holy Spirit so that 'the dweller in Rome deems the Indians a member of himself'.[160] According to Hilary of Poitiers, we will be the city of God, the holy Jerusalem, for 'Jerusalem is built as a city of which all parts gather towards unity'.[161] Finally, Augustine lets the Church say: 'My language is Greek. Syriac is mine. Hebrew is mine.

Mine is the tongue of every nation, because I am within the unity that embraces all nations.'[162] It is in the Church that out of all peoples and out of all languages one single kingdom of peace prepares itself in the one faith.[163]

The Church as eschatological sign

The relation between the earthly and the heavenly Church takes us back once again to the question which became a big problem at the beginning of the twentieth century with the rediscovery of eschatology: the relation between the kingdom of God and Church, eschatology and history.

The New Testament does not provide us with a single answer to this question. Mark and Matthew assume that the interim period between the coming of Jesus and the coming of God's kingdom will only be a short span of time (Mk 9.1; Mt. 10.23). Initially Paul also expected the coming of the Lord during his lifetime (1 Thess. 4.15; 3.13. 5.23; Phil. 3.11; 4.4). The Revelation of John also anticipates an early coming (Rev. 1.1.3; 22.7.12.20). 'The time has become limited' (1 Cor. 7.29). Other writings of the New Testament, however, already speak of a longer delay (Mt. 25.5.19; Lk. 12.35–46) and reflect upon what has been called the delay of the parousia. In the synoptic, eschatological discourses (Mk 13 par.) the beginning of the eschaton already becomes the eschata, the last things only to happen at the end of time of this world. It is particularly in the Lucan writings that the originally short time until the parousia becomes the historical, lengthy time of the Church.[164] In John's writings it is the presentist statements that dominate (Jn 3.18f.; 5.25; 11.25f.), whereas the futuristic ones are left aside (Jn 5.28f.; 11.24). Occasionally there seem to have been concerns about the delay of the parousia (2 Thess. 2.1–8); there were mockers who ask: 'What has happened to the promise of his coming?' (2 Pet. 3.3; cf. 8–13). Yet, this did not cause a fundamental concern or even a crisis in the New Testament time.

That there was no crisis lies in the nature of the New Testament eschatology itself. For Jesus and the New Testament proclaim the kingdom of God in apocalyptic language, yet this is newly interpreted from the perspective of Christology. The kingdom of God is a person, Jesus Christ himself. In him the kingdom of God has already appeared. The eschatological message of Jesus and the New Testament is therefore a novelty. The eschaton has already occurred in the resurrection and exaltation of Jesus. Jesus is as the resurrected and exalted Lord in the proclamation, in the sacraments, especially the Eucharist permanently present in the Church, and through the Spirit he lets us already now share in the new life. Thus, there is basically no delay of the parousia, and the non-appearance of the apocalyptic near-expectation could not lead to a crisis.

God's kingdom, which has already begun, is justice, peace and joy in the Holy Spirit (Rom. 14.17). That is why it is decisive that we should live as new people in this old world (Rom. 6.4; Eph. 4.24; Col. 3.10). We should throw out the old yeast and become new dough (1 Cor. 5.7). Such eschatological existence remains existence under the normal conditions of this world. Still, it also contains a certain otherness towards 'this world'. We should be involved in it as if we were not engrossed in it (1 Cor. 7.29–31). Yet, we should also strive to leaven this like yeast in the dough. We should have a helping and healing effect upon this world so that something of the justice, peace and joy of the coming kingdom of God becomes visible already in the here and now.[165] According to John, we live in this world but we are not from this world (Jn 17). That is why the world hates us as it hated Jesus. Conflicts and persecutions are part of the Christian existence in this world; they are, so to speak, foundationally intrinsic to the Church (Jn 15.20). It is particularly the Book of Revelation that, with the first persecutions of Christians in mind, highlights this element in the vivid images of the conflict between the heavenly Jerusalem and the great whore of Babylon. This conflict continues in different forms throughout the whole history of the Church. Christians have no permanent home in this world; they remain strangers and pilgrims (Heb. 11.14–16); their home is in heaven (Phil. 3.20).

The eschatological understanding of the kingdom of God and its paradoxical presence in the Church is of fundamental importance not only for the individual Christian but also in order to understand the Church and its place in history. This question has been given quite different answers and has also led to serious political conflicts. Whole libraries of books have been written on this topic; our context here allows only a very brief sketch.[166]

On the one hand, there have always been mystical interpretations of God's kingdom. According to Meister Eckhart († 1327/1328) and Johannes Tauler († 1361), the kingdom of God dwells in the innermost, deepest and most hidden core of the soul. We find similar explanations in today's existential interpretations of the eschatological existence. In this view each moment is eschatological; the meaning of history lies in its respective present.[167] On the other hand, there has always been the danger of identifying the kingdom of God with earthly kingdoms. This was the case with Eusebius of Caesarea († 339/340) who saw the kingdom of God realized in the Roman Empire, having become Christian. In the Middle Ages there was a danger that God's kingdom would be identified either secularly with the empire or clerically with the church of the clergy.[168] Against such secularization of Christianity, the monasticism of the old church was a kind of counter and protest movement.[169] In medieval times there were apostolic movements which criticized the church that had become powerful and which wanted to return to the original, apostolic Church with its poverty and simplicity. Francis of Assisi and the mendicant orders took up this cause in an ecclesial way.[170]

The question is how to get through between Scylla and Charybdis. It was Augustine who, until today, presented the most impressive and historically powerful concept with his doctrine of the two kingdoms, the *civitas*

Dei and the *civitas terrena*. Augustine's view of the Church is complex and has seen quite different interpretations. The basic lines of his argument, however, are clear. Augustine has to defend himself against the accusation that Christianity, by deposing the old gods, has caused the fall of the empire of the *pax romana*, and denies downright that the Roman Empire was, or indeed is, 'the' empire of peace.[171] He does not equate the *civitas Dei* and the *civitas terrena* with State and Church. For him, *civitas Dei* and *civitas terrena* are not two external kingdoms but two forms of love: self-love and the love of God.[172] Both have been in conflict with each other since the beginning of the world.

For Augustine, the Church is a reality which has a share in both kingdoms. It is, in this interim, a *societas permixta*.[173] It anticipates the end and yet it is only at the end that the perfect kingdom of God will be revealed.[174] During this interim period it will go its way between God's comfort and the persecutions of this world.[175] It will only be at the end that 'true peace shall be there where no one shall suffer opposition either from himself or any other.' 'There we shall rest and see, see and love, love and praise – for this is to be in the end without end.'[176] With this conception, Augustine overcame the political theology of antiquity.[177] He separated the idea of peace from political peace in the *pax romana*. At the same time he also excluded an ecclesification of the kingdom of God. While the kingdom of God already reaches into history in the Church, it still remains a transcendent-eschatological reality, which is only fulfilled in the eternal contemplation of God.

Augustine wrote his work *de civitate Dei* at the end of antiquity and in view of the collapse of the Roman Empire. A Christian Holy Roman Empire as it emerged out of the collapse of the Roman Empire during the Early and High Middle Ages was, in this situation, in no way imaginable or predictable. It is for this reason that the political interpretation which was bestowed upon it in this new situation cannot be attributed to itself. So it is even more interesting to get to know the conception of history that Thomas Aquinas developed in the High Middle Ages at the peak of this new situation.[178]

Thomas basically goes back to an archaic scheme that became fundamental in Platonism which thinks in the pattern of emanation (*exitus*) and return (*reditus*) of all reality into the origin. The end and final perfection is the return into the origin. Thomas implements into this cyclical thinking the biblical thinking often described as linear. The circular movement, as it were, is not left empty-handed; it is not meaningless. Rather all reality emanates from God in order to return again through Jesus Christ as the turning point (*vertex*), axis and centre of human history back to God. In Jesus Christ the decisive novelty has occurred. He is the absolute event and point of unity, the *universale concretum*. For this reason there cannot be a new development of salvation history beyond Jesus Christ. With Jesus Christ the definitively new has occurred.

For Thomas, the Church is not yet the kingdom of God. Rather, the Church is the community of those who are on the way towards the transcendent kingdom of God. As the earthly Jesus Christ once and for all and through his humanity effected the salvation of the world, so now does he, as the exalted Lord, act in the Church through faith and the sacraments.[179] Just so, the present time is end time, but it is such by opening a new way. It is the way of the *lex evangelica* as the new law. While it is mediated through visible sacramental signs and also has an effect upon visible human acts, it is nonetheless not an external but an internal law that is given in faith through the Holy Spirit.[180] In this way, one is to expect neither a new salvation history nor a new church, but the constant renewal of the Church out of Christ's Spirit. When Joachim of Fiore († 1202) expected that the age of the laypeople and the age of the clerical church would be replaced by the age of the monastic church, Thomas Aquinas described these speculations about a third kingdom with, for him, exceptional acrimony as *stultissimum*.[181] For Thomas, progress in salvation history beyond Jesus Christ was inconceivable.[182]

The crucial new aspect in Joachim of Fiore's view was that the kingdom of God as a transcendent entity became a future historical entity. Thus, his actual influence was not in theology but in philosophy. There the historification of eschatology became the starting point of the modern utopias (from Rinaldo, Thomas More, Campanella, to the later Schelling and to Ernst Bloch and others).[183] The Social-Gospel-Movement, the new political theology and the theology of liberation tried to build on such utopian ideas.[184] With this, the message of the coming kingdom of God was in danger of being turned into a programme for shaping and changing the world in order to serve justice and peace.

It is self-evident that Augustine and Thomas Aquinas cannot give direct answers to the challenges of our present situation. However, there is one thing we can learn from these two great theologians: the line of conflict does not lie between the Church and the world (society, culture, state) rather, the line often runs right through the Church. Unfortunately, the Church often contains more world than it can really want. Hence, one should be careful when calling the Church a counter-society.[185] The Church lives between the times and is not itself the kingdom of God on earth; even after completing all seemingly necessary ecclesial reforms, it will never be the kingdom.

The Church is an eschatological sign. As such it rejects all tendencies that seek to achieve the accomplishment of the world on the basis of human efforts. Additionally, the Church itself will always remain imperfect in this world. This realistic view liberates the Church from over-exertion which thinks it possible to build and create the new world. It liberates the Church from arrogant pride as well as fanaticism. It makes one humble and able to acknowledge that there are signs of the coming and materializing kingdom of God, not only in it but also beyond its institutional borders.[186]

On the other hand, the kingdom of God is already present as mystery in the Church.[187] Yet, it can be an eschatological sign in the midst of the world only if it retains its identity and independence and does not allow itself to be exploited for some inner-worldly, cultural, social or other purpose. The Church can only be the thorn in the side of the world if indeed it lives itself the opposition that it claims against a self-sufficient world intending to perfect itself. Still, preservation of identity does not mean that the Church can or should withdraw from this world. The Church has its identity in the existence for God and for the world. Dissociation and solidarity are two sides of one coin.

The Church is to be the salt of the earth. It can be this only if the salt does not lose its own power. It should be the city on the hill and the light of the world. This is only possible if the Church does not hide its light under a bushel (Mt. 5.13–16). If the Church wants to be salt and light, then it must have, without giving up its otherness, a healing and helping, stimulating and also provoking presence in the world. As yeast it must try to leaven through the world from inside (Mt. 13.33). It can help the world to live in the provisional and still maintain the hope for the final coming of God's kingdom and his justice. The Church can help a world that has often become devoid of perspective in its actionism. It can help, beyond enthusiastic excitement and apocalyptical fears, to do in inner serenity what is possible here and now.[188] The Church will comfort in view of inexpugnable pain and suffering, but it will also encourage, inspire and motivate to work for justice, peace and freedom. The Church can do this because it stands fast in the hope that in the end all will pass, but love alone will remain (1 Cor. 13.8.13). Only the deeds of love will count in the eschatological judgement (Mt. 25.31–46). They endure permanently and they are, ultimately, foundationally inscribed into the existence of reality in a way that they cannot be quantified individually. It is also with this message that the Church is eschatological sign of the hope in this world.

2.3 The Church as the house of wisdom and temple of God

The Church as the house of wisdom

Ultimately, the eschatological orientation of the Church would be a nice but empty dream that would be nothing more than pie in the sky if it did not have a fundament in reality itself and also a creational basis. Eschatology without protology would be utopia, as the Church would be an ideological addition, addendum and superstructure to reality which would have nothing to do with real life. Yet, according to the testimony of Scripture this is not the case. Just as Jesus Christ himself was before all creation (Jn 1.1–3), as he is the firstborn of all creation in whom and through whom everything was created (Col. 1.15f.) and as we were elected in him before the creation of the world (Eph. 1.4), so also, according to the Church Fathers, the Church has a protological foundation in creation. According to some Church Fathers, it exists already before all creation.[189]

These speculations are not remote from the world and the Bible. On the contrary, they take up what is already laid down in the wisdom theology of the Old Testament. The Old Testament wisdom is one of life and experience; it takes up the experience of life, seeks to order its reality and orientate its praxis towards this order. According to the wisdom texts of the Old Testament, wisdom is ultimately the first principle and principle of order of the created world.[190] Wisdom was before all creation and underlies all creation (Prov. 8.22–31; Sir. 24.3–12). This wisdom teaching of Israel stands in the tradition of the old Orient, especially of Mesopotamia and Egypt. However, it is the distinguishing awareness of Israel that wisdom has found a dwelling nowhere in the world and nowhere among the peoples. It is only in Israel, the people of God, in Zion and in the Law that it has found a resting place (Sir. 24.4–19). Therefore, for the pious Jew, the Law was not a heavy burden placed upon the individual, but a gift, a joy. It was light and lamp on the way of life (especially Ps. 119).

The New Testament took up and expanded this idea. It recognizes in Jesus Christ the place where God's wisdom appeared in the fullness of time in the world and took its place. Everything is created in him, the eternal logos. He is light and life in all reality (Jn 1.3f.14). The eternal logos in which all was created is the light that gives light to every man coming into this world. Yet the people did not accept him (Jn 1.3–5.10f.); they loved darkness more than the light (Jn 1.3.10). Yet God desired that we humans would not lack the light of life. So the logos himself became man and lived among us (Jn 1.14). He appeared as the light of the world (Jn 1.8.12).

Paul focused and sharpened this idea. Humans suppress the truth of God which can be discovered with reason since the beginning of the world (Rom. 1.18–20). The law of God is also written on the hearts of the heathens (Rom. 2.15), but they exchange God's truth with a lie (Rom. 1.25). So God's Wisdom appeared in the Cross of Jesus in a paradoxical form; through the Cross, a folly for the gentiles, God has made foolish the wisdom of the world (1 Cor. 1.24.30). Now the Wisdom, which orders the whole world and gives it meaning and which appeared to the world hidden in Christ, is proclaimed by the Church (1 Cor. 2.6–9). Through the Church, the whole world should come to know the 'manifold wisdom of God' (Eph. 3.10), which appeared in Jesus Christ. The Church is to proclaim the Wisdom which appeared in Jesus Christ as the true wisdom and to juxtapose it as God's Wisdom against the worldly wisdom which shuts itself against God.

The early Christian apologists described this idea with the help of terms from the stoic logos doctrine. In this teaching, the logos permeates all reality; in all reality there are seeds and fragments of the logos (λόγοι σπερματικοί).[191] So the apologists could say that the universal logos, which permeates everything, lives in everyone.[192] It is in Socrates as well as in the barbarians.[193] Yet, it is in Jesus Christ that the logos appeared in its fullness. By consequence, all that live according to the logos are actually Christians.[194] We find similar considerations in Clemens of Alexandria, who speaks of a divine pedagogy.[195] Eusebius of Caesarea composed a fifteen-volume *Praeparatio evangelicirca*. In modern times it was Nicholas of Cusa († 1464) in particular who took up again such ideas in his tractate *De pace fidei*.[196] Vatican II made this theory its own in many places.[197]

One can also express this idea in the following way: the universal Wisdom of God has become concrete in Jesus Christ. He is the *concretum universale*. This concreteness was already a scandal for his contemporaries (Mt. 11.5; Lk. 7.23) and has lasted as such. As one might wish to ask: how should my salvation and the salvation of the whole world depend on this single one who lived in that remote corner of the world at that time? Why this one and not someone else, why not Buddha, or Mohammed, or one of the many who have appeared as saviours and messiahs or that have been presented as such? Why not one of those who still appear today and are considered as such? The Bible counters: God has not become man – God has become *this* man.

This scandal is also transferred to the Church. It is the revelation of God's Wisdom and the unveiling of the true wisdom of the world. Through its message of Jesus Christ it is to bring light into the darkness of the world (Jn 1.4.9; 8.12). *Cum grano salis*: the messengers of the Gospel are not men and women of darkness. Engaging with godless, worldly wisdom, they are the harbingers of true enlightenment. They unlock the deep and ultimate meaning of reality and life and thus shed light upon and give orientation to the way of life.

It is through the light that enlightens every person that the one people of God lives in all nations. Jesus Christ has come to gather it out of all peoples and cultures. The 'Church or people of God in establishing that kingdom takes nothing away from the temporal welfare of any people. On the contrary it fosters and takes to itself, insofar as they are good, the ability, riches and customs in which the genius of each people expresses itself. Taking them to itself it purifies, strengthens, elevates and ennobles them.'[198] In this, the Council highlights a threefold relation: recognizing and keeping – purifying – fulfilling. Following Hegel, one could also speak of a threefold meaning of the German term '*Aufhebung*': in the sense of keeping and retaining – in the sense of abolishing – in the sense of lifting up unto a higher level. All this is the task of the Church in the proclamation of God's Wisdom in Jesus Christ.

The public mandate of the Church

This threefold relation has consequences for the relation of the Church to the secular order. Jesus' disciples are to be the light of the world and the city on the hill (Mt. 5.14). This means the Church does not function as a convent or monastery to which one can withdraw from the world in order to find a private piety or edification, nor can it withdraw into the sacristy. The Church is to mediate the light and strength of the Gospel in the secular and public realm also.

In this, the Church has a mandate for the world and thus a *public* mandate, yet not a political mission in the sense of concrete policy-making. It is measured against the person and message of Jesus Christ. He refused to be the judge in inheritance disputes (Lk. 12.14) and admonished his followers to render to the emperor the things that are the emperor's, but to render to God the things that are God's (Mk 12.17 par.). Jesus therefore recognizes the authority of the emperor, but he also shows the limits of this respect, for we must obey God more than the leaders of this world (Acts 5.29).[199] The kingdom of Jesus Christ is not of this world (Jn 18.36), so the Church has no mandate in purely secular issues. It is to encourage everything that is in the spirit of the Gospel honourable, pure, loveable and commendable (Phil. 4.8). The Church must also dare to object where the truth and Wisdom of God are perverted by utopias and ideologies and where the secular order suppresses, perverts and resists God's order. Where this happens, objection is called for.[200]

The debate about the correct relation between the secular and spiritual spheres runs through the whole of church history. The concrete relation of both spheres can be historically determined by various theological, philosophical, political and cultural influences and trends. The churches in the East and the West, and later the churches of the Reformation, have gone different ways in this. After the end of the old order of the imperial church at the turn of the nineteenth century and the experience of totalitarian systems in the twentieth century, a new situation in free democratic orders emerged for all churches in Europe and the Western-orientated world. At Vatican II the Catholic Church gave up the idea of a Catholic state and recognized the principle of freedom of religion and the legitimate autonomy of secular areas (culture, science, economy, politics and others).[201] It demands no secular powers or privileges. Still it claims the right to judge secular fields in the light of its message and the right to criticize everything that is against God's order and the dignity of man. In this sense the Church wants to further everything that is in accordance with God's order and the wellbeing of man and thus contribute to the common good and to a just and permanent order of peace.[202]

It would indeed be an illusion to think that this was the end of the conflict between the secular and spiritual spheres. This conflict also continues in a different form under democratic conditions. In Western societies, a secularized mentality which disregards transcendent orientation has become dominant. At times it can become intolerant against religious views which are made public and contradict the prevailing public opinion. Mostly the conflict no longer concerns the public power of the State, but public opinion which is determined to a large extent by modern media. In a free society they are a substantial element. The secular attitude of many media, however, repeatedly leads to public controversies and conflicts – for example, concerning the protection of life, the order of marriage and family, education, social justice, international peace, order and so forth. In such controversial debates it is essential for the faithful to find standards and orientation in the Church as the house of Wisdom that are neither guided by the interest of individual groups nor by self-interest, but by the order of things given by God.

The Church as temple and house of God

Apart from the image of the Church as the house of Wisdom, the Bible uses another image to illustrate the universal creational basis of the Church. It speaks of the Church as temple and house of God. With this image the New Testament takes up an old and, in the history of religion, important image.[203] In the old world the temple was considered as a holy area (τέμενος) demarcated and separated from the profane environment and as dwelling place of the godhead, in many religions as the symbolic centre and image of the whole cosmos.

The Old Testament expresses similar ideas. According to the text in Exodus, Moses was to build for God a tabernacle with a blueprint that God himself gave to Moses on Sinai (Exod. 25.9.40). Consecrating the temple, Solomon is aware that God does not dwell on earth. Even heaven and the highest heaven cannot contain him; how much less a house built by humans (1 Kgs 8.27; 2 Chron. 6.18). Hence, Solomon emphasizes in his prayer of dedication again and again: God's dwelling place is heaven, yet the temple is the place where his name lives and which is filled with his glory (kabod; 2 Chron. 7.1.16; cf. Sir. 36.19). We encounter a similar image in the inaugural vision of the prophet Isaiah: the temple is filled with the hem of the robe of the inapproachable three-times-holy God (Isa. 6.1). In this respect the temple is also, for the Old Testament, the intersection between the heavenly and the secular world and also the hub of the world. According to wisdom theology, Wisdom has built itself a house (Prov. 9.1; cf. 14.1; 24.3). According to later Jewish ideas, the temple was erected by cosmic measures and as centre of the cosmos.

In the Psalms we encounter an explicit temple piety. The pious one goes to the temple to see God's countenance (Ps. 42.2–4; cf. 5.8; 27.4); in fact the heart is consumed with longing for the temple of the Lord (Ps. 84.3). Therefore the prophetic criticism in Jeremiah's temple sermon attacking a false and deceptive trust in the temple which is paired with injustice, oppression, bloodshed and idolatry is all the more severe (Jer. 7.1–15). For the pious Jesus, the final horror occurred when the temple, which is a holy place, was defiled and desecrated by heathens (Ps. 79.1; 1 Mac. 3f: 2 Mac. 1f.; Acts 21.27–30).

It is necessary to have this in mind in order to understand what it means when the New Testament calls the Church temple and house of God (1 Cor. 3.16f.; 6.19; 2 Cor. 6.16; Eph. 1.19–22). Jesus himself acts and teaches in the temple. The early Christian community naturally participated in the temple worship (Acts 5.42). Yet already, a distance and something new became apparent in Jesus himself. Jesus' cleansing of the temple signifies more than moral indignation that the building has become a market hall. It is a prophetic symbolic act and stands in prophetic tradition. Jesus is concerned about the holiness of God and the temple which is to be a house of prayer, and as such for all nations (Mk 11.15–19 par; Jn 2.13–22). Just like the prophets before him, Jesus relativizes and criticizes the purely external temple cult. 'God is spirit, and those who worship him must worship in spirit and truth' (Jn 4.21–4). Like the early Jewish apocalypses, Jesus speaks of the destruction and the reconstruction of the temple. Yet, the Christological novelty is that, by this, he means the temple of his body (Jn 2.21; cf. Mk 14.58; 15.29 par.). In this Christological interpretation of the temple we encounter the novelty of the New Testament. Jesus himself is God's temple in his person. He is the place where God has irrevocably and totally made his dwelling, where God's glory has finally appeared (Jn 1.14). In him God wanted to dwell in his whole fullness (Col. 1.19).

In Christ also, the community is the house of God. Already the Old Testament speaks of the house of Israel and says that Yahweh lives and walks with his people (Lev. 26.11f.; Ezek. 37.26f.). In the New Testament we find a Christological rereading of the Old Testament. Where two or three are gathered in the name of Jesus, there he is among them (Mt. 18.20). So the Church is temple in Christ and in the Holy Spirit, a house not built from dead stones but from living stones and as a spiritual house (1 Pet. 2.5). This temple must not be desecrated. 'If anyone destroys God's temple, God will destroy him. For God's temple is holy, and you are that temple' (1 Cor. 3.17; cf. Heb. 3.6; 1 Pet. 4.17; 1 Tim. 3.15). The temple of God is not compatible with idolatry (1 Cor. 6.16) nor with immorality (1 Cor. 6.18f.). It is a holy area separated from the world. If not, then there will be the judgement for it, which begins with the house of God (1 Pet. 4.17).[204]

In the New Testament, the images of the house and temple of God do not refer to a building of stone, but serve as symbols for the living community. It also belongs to this interpersonal ecclesial understanding of Church as house of God that all enjoy civic rights in the house. In it there are no strangers; all are members of the household (Eph. 2.19). Again this statement contains something of the contemporary understanding of house as (οἶκος) as household, extended family, tribe, also a familial and relational structure which included servants and slaves and where everybody had their fixed place, found protection and recognition. Similarly we hear from the early Christian community in Jerusalem that they were all together one heart and soul and had all things in common (Acts 2.44). Hence, the Church should be a house open for all, like a big family. It must not ossify to become solely an institution or bureaucratic organization; rather it should be living interaction and fraternal *communio*.

As such an open and familial house, the Church is not yet the final reality. Rather it points ahead towards the temple and the liturgy of the heavenly Jerusalem (Rev. 7.15; 11.19; 15.5–8). Shaped according to the eternal plan, the Church is simultaneously pre-image and anticipation of the eschatological heavenly Jerusalem which comes not from below but from above, from God. It is here that God will finally dwell among his people. There will no longer be a temple, for the temple of the New Jerusalem is God and the Lamb. They are the light that enlightens all, and all nations will walk in this light. All peoples will contribute their riches. Yet nothing unclean will enter, nobody who commits abominations and tells lies (Rev. 21.2–4.22–7).

In this way, the Church is, in the time of this world, the intersection between time and eternity. Already in this interim period it is a house that offers safe protection and is built solidly, not on sand but on a foundation of stone (cf. Mt. 7.24–7). It is the location of salvation in this unholy world and it is already now the place of the experience of God's nearness.[205] In it we are able to live and weather the storms without becoming too restricted, for it is constructed according to the measures of eternity – that is, in universal dimensions. It does not lead a negligible existence at the edge of the world. Even if numbers decrease in our cultural sphere, or if it gathers as a small poor community at the end of the big world, it is no marginal reality. Even under such circumstances it still retains a universal human and cosmic dimension.

Current significance

The image of the Church as a house can be misunderstood as signifying a fortress, castle, or fortification against an evil world. It can be understood as the regressive and restorative dream of a lost home. Yet it can also be understood as the longing of modern humanity for a space of security, quiet and homeliness in an unsettled, fast-changing, homeless and often chaotic world.[206] If the house metaphor is understood in the latter sense, then it is not in contradiction to the biblical path and exodus metaphor. On the contrary, it means going out of the pure, fast-evaporating timeliness which is perhaps becoming outdated into the eternal home, to that which remains valid in all changes of time. In this, it applies also to modern man: 'one thing I ask of the Lord that I seek after: that I may dwell in the house of the Lord all the days of my life, to behold the beauty of the Lord and to meditate in his temple' (Ps. 27.4).

I was fascinated very early on by the idea of the Church as the house of Wisdom. It was so important for me that I based my episcopal coat of arms on it. The crest depicts the Church as a house resting on seven pillars which

Wisdom has built for itself (Prov. 9.1). This expresses the bishop's task of proclamation. He is to witness God's Wisdom to the world which is in danger of forgetting it because of daily worries and the flood of information and which is thus in danger of losing sight of the eternally valid standards. The bishop is to build up the Church as a house in which all can live and find their spiritual home, in which there are no strangers but where all in the one faith speak the same language and so are able to understand anew each other and the world. The grapes in the crest refer to Saint Martin, the patron saint of the diocese Rottenburg-Stuttgart and patron of winemakers. On a deeper level they refer to the centre of the Church and the central task of the episcopal ministry: the celebration of the Eucharist, the sacrament of unity. So this episcopal crest contains in heraldic language a whole ecclesiology in a nutshell.

2.4 The Church as *congregatio fidelium* and *communio sanctorum*

The Church is the eschatological gathering movement of God which reaches its destination in Jesus Christ. Yet, the Church still lives between the times. It is institution and an event. It must bear witness to the deepest sense and purpose of all reality and of man and it already anticipates the heavenly glory to come. The question we now have to ask is: how is all this to happen?

The answer from Scripture and Tradition is that this happens through the proclamation of the Word and the celebration of the sacraments, particularly the Eucharist. Thomas Aquinas summarizes both together in a statement he frequently repeats: the Church is sanctified by faith and the sacraments.[207] Following again an old tradition, it lives from the table of the Word and the table of the sacraments, particularly of the Eucharist.[208] This leads to two fundamental statements about the nature of the Church: the Church is *congregatio fidelium* and *communio sanctorum*, i.e. *sacramentorum*.

The Church as *congregatio fidelium*

If we proceed from the literal meaning of the Greek word for 'church' (ἐκκλησία), then the Church is the eschatological vanguard called by God from out of (ἐκ-καλεῖν) all nations. The God of the Old and New Testament is a god who speaks. This fundamentally distinguishes him from the idols that are dumb and cannot speak (Ps. 115.4f.; 135.15–18; Jer. 10.5 and others). The God testified by the Bible and in whom Christians believe is therefore a living God (Deut. 5.26; Josh. 3.10; Jer. 10.10; Dan. 6.26; Mt. 16.16 and others). He is no otiose god (*Deus otiosus*), existing somewhere far from the world and detached from what happens there. Above all, he is not a dead god, as Friedrich Nietzsche and others in modern times thought they could proclaim. He is the living God of Abraham, Isaac and Jacob, a God of the living and not of the dead (Exod. 3.6; Mk 12.26f.; Acts 3.13; 7.32). He turns to humans, speaks to them, promises himself to them. God does not only communicate something; he communicates himself to us and is thus, through his word, present in the midst of his people (Exod. 3.14). Hence, the Word of God is not only information but, above all, personal communication in which God addresses us in overflowing love as friends.[209]

God calls his people together through his Word. So already Israel perceives itself as *qahal Yahweh*, as God's gathering (cf. Deut. 23.2ff.; 1 Chron. 28.8; Neh. 13.1; Mic. 2.5; Ps. 74.2, etc.). The New Testament adopted this name as self-description and understood it as God's Church, i.e. the people called and gathered by God.[210] When the gathered people heard the word of Peter, it cut them to the heart. So the Church began through the outpouring of the Spirit and the preaching of Peter at the first Pentecost (Acts 2.37). According to Paul, the Gospel took effect in the congregation (1 Thess. 1.5). In fact, Paul can say 'it was I who fathered you by the Gospel' (1 Cor. 4.15). For Paul, the Church is, as it were, created through the Word; it is *creatura verbi*.[211]

In the Tradition this became the name of the Church as congregation of the faithful (*congregatio fidelium*). This is often seen as a specifically Reformation label. However, it is very often found literally or in terms of content in the Catholic Tradition.[212] It cannot therefore serve as a distinctive feature between denominations. The distinction between a church of the word and one of the sacrament is obsolete – if it ever was valid at all. *Congregatio fidelium* can be considered ecumenically joint self-description of the Church.

Obviously, this description must be properly understood. *Congregatio fidelium* does not mean that the Church is the subsequent association of individual believers. Individual believers do not gather together to form the Church, rather it is God who calls the Church together through his word as his people and unites them in the one faith. Martin Luther expressed this in the concise formula: 'God's word cannot be without God's people and God's people cannot be without God's word.'[213]

The Second Vatican Council expressed this nature of the Church in the opening of the constitution on the revelation *Dei Verbum* with the genial formula: '*Verbum Dei religiose audiens et fideliter proclamans*', 'hearing the word of God with reverence and proclaiming it with faith'.[214] The Church exists in the double gesture of hearing the Word of God and witnessing the heard Word of God. Thus, the Church cannot and must not pass on its own wisdom; it can only pass on what it has itself received beforehand. Only as hearing Church can it also be teaching Church. In this case it cannot keep to itself what it has heard but must pass it on. Through witnessing the

Word of God the Church is to gather God's people. Therefore the Church is essentially missionary;[215] evangelizing is the true identity of the Church.[216]

The Church as *communio sacramentorum*

The second aspect, the Church as *communio sacramentorum*, ensues from the first one. The Word of God is not hollow; it is a living word which also effects and creates what it says (Heb. 4.12; cf. Isa. 55.10; Wis. 18.15f.). We read in the account of the Creation: 'he spoke and it was' (Gen. 1.3.9). The Creation itself is the realization of the word of God and speaks of God's greatness: 'The heavens declare the glory of God, the vault of heaven proclaims his handiwork' (Ps. 19.2; cf. 50.6). Throughout the history of salvation the word of God realizes itself in the great and miraculous deeds of God (*mirabilia Dei*). A central event is the redemption out of Egypt 'with his outstretched arm' (Exod. 6.6; Deut. 6.22; 7.19). Such signs and miracles then become the object of proclamation and lasting memory (Ps. 9.2; 26.7; 89.6; 111.4 and others). In the fullness of time, the Word became flesh and dwelt among us (Jn 1.14). God's self-communication in Jesus Christ is the unsurpassable peak and summary of God's self-revelation. Jesus Christ is the Word of God in person. He is the *verbum abbreviatum*.[217] Theologically, all other events of revelation must be understood and interpreted towards him and from him.

Insofar as the Word of God is efficacious – the creative and eschatological word of God which, in the fullness of time, became flesh – the proclaimed word cannot be the end. Rather, the proclamation of the Word of God means, so to speak, that the Word becomes flesh in the sacraments and is liturgically celebrated. Just so, Jesus Christ is present in the Church through his word and, in analogy to the incarnation, also in sacramental signs.[218] In this sense we can say: 'that which was till then was visible of our Redeemer was changed into a sacramental presence.'[219] The sacraments are signs and instruments of the salvific presence of Christ in the Church.

So, from the beginning, we encounter in the Church baptism and the celebration of the Eucharist. This already becomes apparent in the Lucan depiction of the early Christian community in Jerusalem. Those who came to believe through Peter's preaching let themselves be baptized and the whole community participates in the breaking of bread and in prayers (Acts 2.37–42). Paul perceives baptism as the basis of the Church. Through it we are incorporated into the body of Christ (1 Cor. 12.13; Gal. 3.28). Through baptism we are in death and resurrection more and more formed into Jesus (Rom. 6.3–11). We become not only united with Christ, but we become even one (εἷς) in Christ: Jews and Greeks, slaves and free, men and women (Gal. 3.26–9; Col. 3.11). This holds true similarly for the Eucharist. The New Testament accounts of the Last Supper are not only historical reports; they already show clear signs of liturgical design – in other words, they are also liturgical texts which bear witness to the active liturgical life of the early Church.[220] For Paul, through the participation in the one Eucharistic body of Christ we become the one body of Christ which is the Church (1 Cor. 10.16f.). In other words, the Eucharistic *communio* founds the *communio ecclesialis*. Cyril of Jerusalem[221] and Cyril of Alexandria[222] say that through the Eucharist we become one body (σύσσωμοι) with Christ.

From the beginning the Church is perceived as a worshipping assembly that has its centre of life in the Eucharistic worship. The understanding of the Church as worshipping community is also expressed in the fact that, in the New Testament, the word from Joel 3.5 'those who call on the Lord' has become a fixed self-description of the Church (Acts 2.39; Rom. 10.12f.; 1 Cor. 1.2; 2 Tim. 2.22; Heb. 11.16; 1 Pet. 1.17; Jer. 2.7).[223] So the Church is not only perceived as *congregatio fidelium*, but also as *communio sanctorum*, i.e. as *communio sacramentorum*.

The formula '*communio sanctorum*' has been much discussed, especially regarding its origin and meaning.[224] The original meaning of κοινωνία/*communio* is not the communion among Christians but the common participation of Christians (μέθεξις/*participatio*) in Jesus Christ, the Holy Spirit, the Gospel, and particularly the Eucharist. The beginning of 1 John speaks of the fellowship through which we participate in the communion that exists between Father and Son (1 Jn 1.2f.).[225] Therefore, *communio sanctorum* probably does not originally mean the community of the saints (*sancti*), i.e. of the faithful and community with the saints in heavens, but community in the holy (*sancta*), that is, the joint participation in the goods of salvation: Jesus Christ, the Holy Spirit, the Gospel, and above all the Eucharist. The *communio* in the *sancta* then founds the communio of the *sancti* among themselves. *Communio* of the saints thus means, in the language of Paul, the community of the sanctified.

This insight led Augustine to the famous formula that the Eucharist is 'sign of love and bond of unity' (*signum caritatis et vinculum unitatis*).[226] This word made history; it continues to have an effect throughout the whole of Tradition[227] up to Vatican II.[228] In the scholastic theology of the Middle Ages Bonaventura[229] and Thomas Aquinas[230] are important witnesses of this tradition. Therefore the title of Pope John Paul II's last encyclical *Ecclesia de Eucharistia* (*The Church of the Eucharist*, 2003) and the post-synodal exhortation by Pope Benedict XVI *Sacramentum Caritatis* (2006)[231] rightly emphasize the fact that the Church does not live out of itself but out of the Eucharist. On its way through history it is nourished and strengthened by the Eucharist, it grows through the Eucharist and is again and again built up by it.[232]

It is in this way that the sacraments, particularly the two main sacraments baptism and Eucharist, build up the Church as *communio sacramentorum*. This tradition of the church-constituting significance of the altar sacrament is found also in the early Luther.[233] Just like the self-description of the Church as *congregatio fidelium*, the self-description of the Church as *communio sanctorum* clearly shows a basic ecumenical ecclesiological common ground. The Protestant and the Catholic Church cannot be juxtaposed as a church of the word against a church of the sacrament. According to modern understanding, word and sacrament are constitutive for both traditions.[234]

Like the formula of the Church as *congregatio fidelium*, the formula of the *communio sanctorum* must not be understood as a subsequent association of individual believers. Such an individualistic understanding would be totally alien to Scripture and patristic Tradition. It is the believing Church and the Church celebrating faith in the sacraments that receives the faithful into its fold through word and sacrament. This has also led to the idea of the Church as mother. It has a biblical foundation and is well documented in the Church Fathers. Paul can say that he, as it were, goes through the pain of giving birth for the faithful as his children; in the same context he can also call the heavenly Jerusalem our mother (Gal. 4.19.26).[235] In the famous words of Cyprian: 'he can no longer have God for his father, who has not the Church for his mother.'[236]

The 'belonging together' and eschatological dimension of word and sacrament

The two self-descriptions of the Church, *congregatio fidelium* and *communio sacramentorum*, do not stand isolated next to each other; they are intrinsically connected. The Word of God is concentrated and realized in the sacraments. Baptism administered in the name of the Father, Son and Holy Spirit is *sacramentum fidei*.[237] Similarly Paul says of the celebration of the Eucharist: 'whenever you do this, you are proclaiming the Lord's death' (1 Cor. 11.26). The action in the Eucharistic celebration has therefore a proclaiming nature. Augustine summarizes this in the formula '*accedit verbum ad elementum et fit sacramentum* – the word is added to the element, and there results the Sacrament'. For Augustine the sacrament is visible word (*visible verbum*).[238]

Scholastic theology considers the word of consecration or administration as the *forma sacramenti*, the embossing form and soul of the sacrament.[239] Martin Luther also emphasized that word and sacrament belong together. For him, baptism is 'water comprehended in God's Word and Commandment' and the Eucharist is 'bread and wine comprehended in God's Word and connected with it'.[240]

This belonging-together of word and sacrament is liturgically demonstrated in each sacramental celebration. Each sacramental celebration takes place within a liturgy of the word. In the celebration of the Eucharist the liturgy of the word and of the sacrament (in the narrow sense) form a unity,[241] and also in the sacramental part (in the narrow sense) of the Eucharist the words of institution are constitutive. In this the Eucharistic celebration is the celebrated word of God in both its parts. It is also because of this close unity and mutual permeation that the celebration of the Eucharist is the climax of ecclesial life.[242] Conversely, the word of God must be understood in and from its liturgical-sacramental context. The word of God is interpreted in and through the liturgical celebration. As the Church prays and liturgically celebrates, so it believes. The prayed and liturgically celebrated word of God is thus itself the yardstick of faith; the *lex orandi* is *lex credendi*.[243]

From the belonging-together of word and sacrament it follows that both, word and sacrament, have a similar structure. Like the proclaimed word of God, so the sacraments also have an anamnetic dimension. They are remembrance (ἀνάμνησις, *memoria*) of God's saving acts in the past, especially of the death and resurrection of Jesus. As anamnesis they are at the same time symbolic real realization of the once-and-for-all saving event. Finally, the sacraments point beyond themselves to eschatological fulfilment and are as such a real anticipation of the eschata. So the sacraments, in particular the Eucharist, are always also a pre-celebrating of eschatological fulfilment. Thomas Aquinas explicitly stressed this threefold dimension of the sacraments[244] and expressed it poetically in the Magnificat antiphon for Corpus Christi: 'Remembrance of his suffering, fullness of grace, pledge of the coming glory.'

In the celebration of the Eucharist the eschatological gathering of God's people already happens now; through it we are integrated into the great communion of saints spanning heaven and earth. We celebrate worship in a great community to which the saints of heaven and the angels also belong (Heb. 12.22f.).[245] This again points to the eschatological dimension of the Church and the gathering of the eschatological people of God which begins in it. At the Last Supper, Jesus himself looked ahead to the coming kingdom of God (Mk 14.25 par). Paul speaks of proclaiming the Lord's death 'until he comes' (1 Cor. 11.26). The first Christians celebrated the Eucharist in eschatological joyful anticipation (Acts 2.46). Their eschatological expectation is expressed in the acclamation 'Maranatha', 'our Lord is coming' (1 Cor. 16.22; Rev. 22.20; *Didache* 10.6). So the Eucharist, as real symbol, anticipates the eschatological fulfilment; it is pre-celebrated and experienced as a foretaste of the coming kingdom.

The Greek Church Fathers Origen, Cyril of Jerusalem, Dionysius the Areopagite and, in particular, Maximus the Confessor, took up these statements of Scripture and, influenced by neo-platonic thinking, mystagogically understood the Church and its sacraments as image and symbol of the heavenly Jerusalem.[246] This eschatological view of the Church is not to conceal or deny the inadequacies of the Church which also includes sinners in this world. There will be more on that in detail below.[247] It suffices in this context to show principally that in the Eucharist, so to speak, the curtain into the coming heavenly Jerusalem opens slightly. In it the grey daily routine is interrupted and a piece of heaven on earth can be experienced. This purpose is also served with vestments, music and art. If used in an appropriate manner, they are not external pomp but in their own way they are an expression that the liturgical celebration is anticipating sign and foretaste of the glory and beauty of the eschatologically transfigured reality.

2.5 No salvation outside the Church?

Massa damnata or universal salvation?

This universal historical, human and cosmic view of the Church raises, particularly today, a crucial question: what about the salvation of those not belonging to the visible church? This question was by no means as pressing in the Middle Ages as it has become in modern times. In those days one could assume that the message of the Gospel had been spread to the borders of the known world and everyone who wanted to be a Christian could be one. Since the beginning of the modern era, this situation has changed radically. The discovery of other continents extended the view beyond the European sphere to the ancient cultures of America, Asia, Africa and Oceania. This begged the question: what is the state of salvation of those many generations before and after Jesus Christ; the many to whom, even today, the Gospel has never been proclaimed and who therefore, through no fault of their own, have never had the possibility of turning to the Christian message of salvation?

This question is even more pressing today in the context of the dialogue with other religions and cultures, and for some Christians also in relation to the non-Catholic churches. How can we understand today the often-misunderstood axiom '*extram ecclesiam nulla salus*' (no salvation outside the Church) and the word of the Church which alone saves, without appearing intolerant, arrogant or simply narrow-minded?

One often refers to the statement that God wants the salvation of all people (1 Tim. 2.4). From this statement, some conclude that indeed all will be redeemed. Following Acts 3.21 the doctrine of universal salvation is called the doctrine of *apocatastasis*, the restoration of all things. This *apocatastasis* doctrine has often unjustly been attributed to Origen († 254), one of the greatest theologians of the Early Church.[248] In any case, we must not overlook that, in addition to the statements on universal salvation, there are in the Old and New Testament also many, often drastic, threats and statements of judgement that speak of damnation and hell. They must also be taken seriously. Thus we have, on the one hand, the doctrine of *apocatastasis*. On the other hand – its counterpart, so to speak – is Augustine's later teaching of the double predestination and of the *massa damnata* of a large part of mankind. Yet, how can this doctrine be reconciled with the justice and mercy of God and our human and Christian solidarity with these people?

The question is therefore: without giving up any essential part of the conviction that baptism is necessary for salvation and without falling prey to the doctrine of universal salvation or that of *massa damnata*, what can we say to the question, so pressing today, concerning the salvation of the non-evangelized?[249]

Biblical foundations and developments in the history of theology

First of all, we must say that the New Testament does not contain the axiom '*extram ecclesiam nulla salus*', but that there are factually certain indications. So the New Testament says of Jesus Christ that man can find salvation under no other name than his and that there is no other name given to us under heaven by which we are saved (Acts 4.12). Jesus Christ is the one and only mediator of salvation (1 Tim. 2.4–7). He is the way, the truth and life (Jn 14.6). The added final chapter of Mark says: 'whoever believes and is baptised will be saved; whoever does not believe will be condemned' (Mk 16.16). Jesus also says in the fourth gospel that whoever is not reborn of water and spirit cannot enter the kingdom of God (Jn 3.3–5).

In the theology of the Church Fathers, the Ark with which Noah is saved from the flood is seen as type of the Church by which we are rescued as with a saving ark out of the flood of this world.[250] The axiom '*extram ecclesiam nulla salus*' is explicitly mentioned for the first time in the Joshua homilies by Origen[251] and by Cyprian of Carthage.[252] Yet, in both cases it is not a general theory about non-Christians or an admonition to join the Church, but a warning addressed to those who have been proclaimed the message and are baptized and who are now in danger of leaving again the faith and unity of the Church.

Of course, the doctrine proved fatal in the later Augustine, who spoke of a double predestination to salvation or damnation. Along this line, the axiom '*extram ecclesiam nulla salus*' was understood by Augustine's pupil Fulgentius of Ruspe († 532) as a theory about the salvation or non-salvation of non-believers or the non-baptized. It was also used in this sense by the fourth Lateran council (1215).[253] In the bull *Unam sanctam* (1302), Pope Boniface VIII even applied it to all who did not subject themselves to the Roman pope.[254] Finally, in 1442 the council of Florence stated explicitly that no heathen, unbeliever or one separated from the unity could attain eternal life but was condemned to the eternal fire. 'No one can be saved, no matter how much alms one has given, even if shedding one's blood for the name of Christ, unless one remains within the bosom and unity of the Catholic Church.'[255]

Such a sentence horrifies us today. Are we to think that many millions of people of goodwill who have never heard of the Gospel are just one *massa damanta*? How could we reconcile such a supposition with the Christian view of the boundless mercy of God and with Christian solidarity with all people? The statement of the council of Florence becomes only somewhat understandable if it is read against the background of the limited ancient and medieval world view that presumed that the Gospel had, in fact, reached everyone and if one considers the context of the council. It was then not about non-Christians, but about efforts for unity within the split Christianity between the Latin and Eastern Church. That is why we must not detach these statements from their context and turn them, in our completely different context, into a general principle.

The Church reacted soon to the changed situation of the modern era. Already in opposition to Jansenius († 1638), who presented in his posthumously published work *Augustine* a rigorist ultra-Augustinian doctrine of grace, the Church made it clear that Jesus Christ had died for all people.[256] Later it rejected the sentence by Pasquier Quesnel († 1719), who was influenced by Jansenius, that there was no grace outside the Church.[257] In justification of this turn, one fell back to an older tradition which had already been developed by the famous bishop of Milan and Church Father Ambrose († 397), the baptism of desire. This doctrine is also found in Thomas Aquinas,[258] and was also adopted by the Council of Trent.[259] It was then developed further by the most famous of all controversial theologians, Robert Bellarmine († 1621), to the theory of a membership in the Church by desire (*desiderio*).[260] Pope Pius XII adopted this teaching in his encyclical *Mystici corporis* (1943) and spoke of those who are orientated towards the mystical body of Christ because of an unconscious desire and *votum* (*inscio desiderio ac voto*).[261] That the pope was serious in this can be seen from the fact that, in 1949, he defended the teaching of the encyclical against a renewed rigoristic interpretation of the sentence '*extram ecclesiam nulla salus*' and explicitly rejected the opposing rigorist opinion.[262]

The teaching of Vatican II

The Second Vatican Council consolidated the modern development of doctrine. It explicitly states: 'Those also can attain to salvation who through no fault of their own do not know the Gospel of Christ or His Church, yet sincerely seek God and moved by grace strive by their deeds to do His will as it is known to them through the dictates of conscience. Nor does Divine Providence deny the help necessary for salvation to those who, without blame on their part, have not yet arrived at an explicit knowledge of God and with His grace strive to live a good life.'[263]

What is new in the teaching of the Council is that, in contrast to the encyclical *Mystici corporis* for the teaching of possible salvation of non-baptized, it no longer invokes an ultimately fictional, unconscious, subjective desire and longing. Rather, it orientates itself to God's universal will to salvation (1 Tim. 2.4) and to the universal history of salvation. In this sense, one can point out that the Bible knows so-called holy heathens such as Noah, Melchizedek, Enoch and Job. The Church Fathers extended the line and considered the good and truth outside the Church as preparation for the Gospel (*praeparatio evangelii*).[264] According to Athanasius, through the incarnation of the Logos all men are one body in Christ (σύσσωμοι).[265] Augustine speaks of the *ecclesia ab Abel*, the Church existing since the just Abel.[266] This idea entered medieval theology.[267] In Thomas Aquinas, we even find the audacious thesis that Jesus Christ was not only the head of the Church but the head of all people. Also for Thomas Aquinas, the Church is made up of men from the beginning of the world until its end.[268] For this reason he can also say that God is not tied to the sacraments.[269]

Vatican II did not create a new teaching but took up a wide, older line of Tradition. It based its teaching on the view that everything was created towards and in Christ and that in him everything was reconciled (Col. 1.15–20; cf. 1 Cor. 8.6; Jn 1.3–5; Heb. 1.3). He is the key, centre and final goal of the whole history of the human race.[270] In this way the Council took up the early apologist's idea of the scattered seeds of truth[271] and said that in his incarnation the Son of God in a way united himself with every man:[272] 'Christ, who died and was raised up for all, can through His Spirit offer man the light and the strength to measure up to his supreme destiny.'[273] Pope John Paul II continued this idea from a pneumatological perspective and said that the Holy Spirit was, as the spirit of Jesus Christ, at work everywhere, even in other cultures; he moves the hearts of the people towards the good and true.[274]

Concerning the efficacy of Jesus Christ's spirit outside the boundaries of the visible Church and concerning people who do not explicitly know Jesus Christ, it is debatable if we should speak, as Karl Rahner does, of anonymous Christians. Much depends on the interpretation of this erroneous term, which in fact caused misunderstandings in its reception.[275] To understand the Council correctly, it is necessary to see that it does not start from a subjective desire for salvation, but from the objective salvation order which is fulfilled in Jesus Christ, from whom and towards whom and in whom everything has its existence and through whom everything is reconciled (Col. 1.17.20). The Council thus retains the universal salvific significance of Jesus Christ and does not regard the other religions as parallel or alternative ways of salvation. Also, the salvation of the heathens is salvation through and in Christ. Neither does the Council teach a universal salvation. While God desires the salvation of all people, whether a specific person finds salvation is decided by whether or not he indeed follows God's merciful offer as the person perceives it in their conscience in their situation. The teaching of the Council therefore has nothing to do with relativism of salvation or with religious indifference or universal salvation.[276]

Still, the teaching of Vatican II on the possibility of salvation outside the Church presents a formidable dogmatic-hermeneutical problem. After all, on the literal surface the Council of Florence and Vatican II seem to contradict each other. This contradiction can only be resolved if the older statements are understood in the context of their times and, equally, if they are read together with all other statements that are already found in the older Tradition. In this case, the doctrine of the last council does not simply suspend the axiom '*extra ecclesiam nulla salus*'. Rather, it gives it a Christologically and pneumatologically based universal historical interpretation. The teaching does this in recourse to patristic and scholastic theology by seeing the Church as a reality that has been present and efficacious in the world 'since the righteous Abel' and by understanding the visible Church as eschatological sign established among the nations and as instrument of the universal history of salvation.

Why then still mission?

The assertion that salvation is at least possible for all people begs the question of the Church must still engage in mission. Should not each individual be encouraged to become holy in their own way? Does it not suffice that the Hindu becomes a better Hindu, the Buddhist a better Buddhist and the Muslim a better Muslim?

That would be a grave misconception of the universal-salvific view of the Church. It misses the teaching of the Second Vatican Council, which gave up neither the salvific necessity of the Church nor the vocation to mission. The contrary is true![277] Yet, it misses also the reality of the other religions as the Bible and Tradition see them. They see in the other religions and cultures not only darkness but also some of the light shining which is Jesus Christ and which enlightens every person who comes into this world (Jn 1.9). They see lights but not the light which is Jesus Christ. The prophets of the Old Testament leave no doubt that all truth that is found there is often darkened, mixed with error and inhumanely distorted, and that true worship has been replaced with idolatry. Paul says that the heathens keep down the truth which shines up in creation (Rom. 1.18; cf. 2.15).

The missionary proclamation should therefore recognize what is good and noble. It should take up what it finds to be positive in other religions and learn from this in order to understand its own message more deeply.[278] It is also to purify it prophetically and it should help the people with the message of Jesus Christ to live no longer in shadows and images but in the full light of truth and to participate in the whole fullness of truth. It is to invite and gather all to the one people of God to join together in the praise of the one God and to become themselves witnesses for God's truth. In this way it is to contribute to the realization of universal peace (shalom) which God wants to bring about for all mankind.

The Church is a sign of hope among the nations. However, the hope it witnesses is not a utopian one, i.e. one without place. In it the eschatological reality is already coming. The kingdom of Jesus Christ is already present in the Church in a mysterious way. Let us thus ask: how are we to understand this? How can we interpret the nature of the Church? How does the Church understand itself and what is its nature?

3

Defining the nature of the Church

3.1 The Church as 'people of God' – the theocentric and doxological architecture of the church

The meaning of the term 'people of God'

The Church is a multifaceted reality. It has many aspects that cannot easily be brought together in one term or summarized in one definition. The New Testament therefore does not use abstract terms but images to describe the nature of the Church. Indeed, it uses quite different images. Yet, instead of images it would be better to speak of symbols, for the symbol is more than a metaphor; it contains, as it were, what it expresses and signifies. The Second Vatican Council listed these images/symbols: people of God, sheepfold, land to be cultivated, tillage of God, vine, building, family of God, temple of God, body of Christ and bride of Christ.[1] It would be futile to argue which of these images/symbols is the fundamental description of the Church's nature, as none of them can express the mystery of the Church completely. These images/symbols are not in opposition to each other, they are not interchangeable and they cannot replace each other. They complement and mutually interpret each other. In the following we can only look at the most important of these images – those which have become in a special way historically efficacious.

In the post-conciliar period, the term 'people of God' was particularly emphasized and often presented as the conciliar definition of the Church's nature. It was even called a conciliar novelty and a step beyond the encyclical *Mystici corporis* and ecclesiology of the body of Christ. Attempts to promote the image of the people of God over against that of the Church as body of Christ had already existed in the pre-conciliar time.[2] Yet, after the Council, the people of God ecclesiology was often mixed with socio-political agendas or one-sided emphases or congregationally oriented ecclesiological concerns. Against this one-sidedness and concomitant interpretations, Hans Urs von Balthasar and then, in particular, Joseph Ratzinger called for clarity and correction.[3]

It is indeed impossible to say that the Council emphasized, in a one sided way, the definition of the Church as people of God and thereby ignored or classified as marginal the definition of the Church as body of Christ and as the house of the Holy Spirit. As will be shown below, the ecclesiology of the people of God cannot be understood at all without or apart from the ecclesiology of the body of Christ. In addition, the description of the Church as people of God was by no means a novelty and originally it had nothing to do with a socio-political view of the Church. There is a broad and ancient tradition behind this symbol. The descriptions of the Church as *populus* and as *familia Dei* are well accounted for and widespread in the liturgy and in medieval theology.[4] The ecclesiology of the people of God is neither a novelty nor a marginal description of the Church. It is central and stands firmly on the ground of ecclesial Tradition.

The significance of 'people of God' in the history of salvation

A sociological and national definition of the term 'people of God' is impossible alone due to a simple linguistic observation. The Bible speaks of the Church not simply as a people; it speaks of the people of God. The Greek Bible for this does not use the sociological-national term δῆμος which is found in language regarding democracy. Instead, the Bible uses the salvation-historical term λαός in the sense of the people chosen by God and set apart from all other nations, or more precisely from the heathen nations (ἔθνοι).

Therefore, the term 'people of God' must be biblically, salvation-historically defined. The Church must be understood as God's people called together by God.[5] This self-description goes back, in fact, to the beginnings of salvation history in the narrative of Abraham. Abraham is called by God: 'Go from your country and your kindred and your father's house to the land that I will show you. And I will make of you a great nation, and I will bless you and make your name great, so that you will be a blessing ... [I]n you all the families of the earth shall be blessed' (Gen. 12.1–3). Already this passage makes it clear that the calling of Abraham is not aimed at his person, his tribe or a specific people, but that it has a universal meaning and dynamism that is significant for all nations. (cf. Gen. 18.18; 22.18; 26.4; 28.14).

In the event of God's self-revelation to Moses at the burning bush, God refers to the promise made to the fathers Abraham, Isaac and Jacob (Exod. 3.15). When Moses asks about his name, God answers 'I am he who is here' (Exod. 3.14) – that means: I am the God who is here and who is with you in all of your ways.[6] This name is a promise and a pledge: 'I shall take you as my people and I shall be your God' (Exod. 6.7; cf. Lev. 26.12; Jer. 32.38;

Ezek. 11.20; Ps. 95.7). Corresponding to this pledge, Israel regards itself as God's people (λαός τοῦ θεοῦ), as God's own people chosen by God and set apart from all other nations (Exod. 19.4–7; Deut. 4; 7.6–12; 32.8–15; Ps. 135). God guards it like the apple of his eye and like the eagle that protects its nest and flies above its young (Deut. 32.10f.).

Yet, the course of history between God and his people is, as described in the Old Testament, dramatic. Because of the unfaithfulness of the people, the relation between God and his people experiences again and again severe crises and deep breaks, but God's faithfulness is immutable. The words of the prophet Hosea are moving. Here the covenant between God and his people seems to be finally broken. We read 'not my people' not the 'I am here' (Hos. 1.9). Then God's mercy wins against his wrath (Hos. 2.1.25). God has pulled his people towards him with human ropes and chains of love (Hos. 11.4). 'How can I give you up, O Ephraim? How can I hand you over, O Israel? [...] My heart recoils within me; my compassion grows warm and tender' (Hos. 11.8). Israel is so not rejected as a whole; the hope remains that a rest will repent (Isa. 10.21f.).

In the prophets this present tense becomes a future tense of promise: 'you will be my people' (Jer. 7.23; 24.7; 31.3; 32.36ff.; Ezek. 11.20; 14.11). As with Abraham, this promise again transcends the framework of a merely national expectation. Already Isa. 11.10 says of the messiah that the nations are waiting for him. The universal extension becomes most explicit in the prophet Zechariah: 'Sing, rejoice, daughter Zion, for now I am coming to live among you – declares the Lord. And on that day many nations will be converted to the Lord and I will live in the midst of you' (Zech. 2.10f.). Hence, the people of God message of the Old Testament is a story of the loving election by God, his mercy, his guidance and his immutable faithfulness. Yet, ultimately it remains open for a greater and more comprehensive fulfilment.

The New Testament applies the term 'people of God' in Old Testament quotes to the Church (Acts 15.14; 18.10; Rom. 9.25f.; 2 Cor. 6.16, etc.). Still, the Old Testament term 'people of God' is mostly not translated by the word 'λαός' but by the term 'ἐκκλησία' or 'ἐκκλησία τοῦ θεοῦ' (Church of God, Acts 20.28; 1 Cor. 1.2; 10.32; 11.22; 15.9; Gal. 1.13; 1 Tim. 3.5.15, etc.), God's Church in Jesus Christ (1 Thess. 2.14; cf. 2 Thess. 1.1). The most important passage in the New Testament speaking of λαός is found in 1 Peter 2.9f.: 'You are a chosen race, a royal priesthood, a holy nation, a people to be a personal possession to sing the praises of God who called you out of darkness into his wonderful light. Once you were a non-people and now you are the people of God; once you were outside his pity; now you have received pity.'

This fundamental text ecclesiology of the people of God can only be correctly understood in its context. It is addressed to Gentile Christians and is a baptismal admonition. That is why it goes beyond the Old Testament and presupposes the novelty of the Christian salvation history and the saving act of Jesus Christ. Through it, gentiles who let themselves be baptized also become God's people. By stating that gentiles that have come to believe also belong to the people of God, the text takes up the universal promise given to Abraham. Paul gives the explanation for this in the letter to the Galatians. He points out that the promise to Abraham does not speak of heirs in the plural but of the one heir of the promise (Gen. 22.17) who is Jesus Christ (Gal. 3.16). For Christians, being people of God thus has a Christological basis. We are people of God in and through Jesus Christ. Through the baptism in Jesus Christ (1 Cor. 12.13; Gal. 3.26–9) we are taken into the death and resurrection of Christ (Rom. 6.3–5).

So there can be no question of whether the ecclesiology of the people of God includes or excludes the eccelsiology of the body of Christ. On the contrary, it presupposes it. Yet, the ecclesiology of the people of God places the ecclesiology of the body of Christ more clearly into an eschatological context. For now we are still between the cross and full participation in the resurrection. So, in the New Testament the people of God are on the way along the dusty roads of history towards the eternal destination, the eternal Sabbath (Heb. 4). The people of God have no permanent city here, but looks for the city which is to come (Heb. 13.14).

The language of the people of God thus expresses the historical nature of the Church. This is the specific difference of this image in comparison with others which are all taken from the agricultural and organologic sphere (plantation, vine, body), or from architecture (house, temple). In contrast, the term people of God expresses the being-on-the-way in history of God's people and, at the same time, God's being with us and among us on this way.

Medieval theology and the *Catechismus Romanus*[7] retained and kept alive the biblical use of language. In modern ecclesiology the term is not as often used. A reason for this might have been anti-Reformation tendencies, for Luther defined the 'blind and unclear word "Church"' often as congregation and gathered assembly.[8] For Luther this was not the only definition of the Church; he obviously knew about the deeper dimension of the Church or the congregation as body of Christ. Yet, the pronounced rejection of the word 'church' and its definition as people, assembly, gathering has become negatively efficacious on the Catholic side. The rediscovery of the term people of God by the Second Vatican Council is therefore also of ecumenical importance.

The Second Vatican Council

After appropriate theological preparation, Vatican II broke open the anti-Reformation narrowness and took up again the biblical, old church and liturgical term 'people of God'.[9] In this, several motives played an important role. This term allowed the Council to place the Church in the whole of salvation and human history. Also, the question concerning the salvation of non-Christians could be brought closer to a solution.[10] It was thus possible to explain the Church not solely from one founding act at a specific point in history, but to understand it within the whole context of salvation history. At the same time, it allowed the novelty of the New Testament covenant people, which is based not on biological descent but on the covenant founded in Jesus Christ and written into the heart by the Holy Spirit, to be retained. Against tendencies of individual salvation it could emphasize that God does not save the people individually, independent of a reciprocal relation. Instead he calls and sanctifies them as a community.

In addition, the term 'people of God' helped the Council to say that all baptized participate in the priestly, prophetic and royal dignity of God's people.[11] From this perspective it was the crucial decision of the Council, against the original draft of the constitution on the Church, not to begin with the hierarchical constitution of the Church, but to place before it the chapter on the people of God which embraces and includes the hierarchy as well as the laity. Finally, the constitution on the Church leads to the chapter on the eschatological nature of the Church and its unity with the Church in heaven. It describes with this term the historical character of the people of God which is on its way along the dusty roads of history towards its eternal home.

Universal significance

Ecclesiology of the people of God is fundamental for placing the Church within the whole of human history. It helps in particular to define properly the relationship between Jews and Christians. Despite their deep differences, Jews and Christians together are the one people of God, for 'in Christ' the differences between Jews and heathens no longer count (1 Cor. 12.13; Gal. 3.26–9f.; Col. 3.11).[12] The heathens who have come to believe are planted into the root of Israel (Rom. 11.16–20). It is for this reason that the Church in the New Testament is never called the new people of God. On the contrary, the New Testament maintains that God's faithfulness to Israel is immutable (Rom. 11.2.9). The term 'new people of God' is not found anywhere in the New Testament; it is found for the first time in the *Epistle of Barnabas*,[13] where it has led to the so-called theory of substitution, according to which the Church has taken the place of non-believing Israel. This theory already presupposes a later development not yet found in the New Testament. Consequentially, it has led to a history of mostly bad relations between Jews and Christians. The New Testament itself speaks of the one people of God made up of Jews and heathens having come to believe (Eph. 2.14). This being God's people by Jews and gentiles has its basis therein that in Jesus all promises for Israel and the gentiles have become 'yes' (2 Cor. 1.20).

The Council goes even further. It begins by stating that, at all times and in every nation, God's pleasure rests on everyone who fears him and acts justly (cf. Acts 10.35). Hence, besides the particular history of salvation beginning with Abraham, there is a universal history of salvation. Augustine classically expresses this by speaking of the *ecclesia ab Abel iusto*,[14] a statement explicitly quoted by Vatican II.[15]

Within the universal history of salvation, the Council describes the Church as messianic people of God. Although itself a small flock, the Church is to maintain hope in the world. 'So it is that that messianic people, although it does not actually include all men, and at times may look like a small flock, is nonetheless a lasting and sure seed of unity, hope and salvation for the whole human race. Established by Christ as a communion of life, charity and truth, it is also used by Him as an instrument for the redemption of all, and is sent forth into the whole world as the light of the world and the salt of the earth.'[16]

The Church Fathers expressed the historical nature of the Church by likening the Church to a ship in the stormy sea of the world. According to the metaphor, the Church steers on the rough sea of this world towards the eschatological destination.[17] The Church lives between the 'already' and the 'not yet'. It shares Jesus Christ's earthly form of a servant. It is pilgrim church on its way along the dusty roads of history, and it goes its way between persecutions by the world and God's comfort.[18] On the one hand, the Church is the holy Church coming, as the heavenly Jerusalem, 'from above' (Gal. 4.26; Rev. 21.2), and on the other, lives 'in the below' of history and carries its treasure in earthen vessels (2 Cor. 4.7). Because of this, it is the Church under the Cross constantly in need of forgiveness. Also – and only in this way – it is the Church of Jesus Christ.

Unfortunately, it was not only since the Council but already in antiquity that ecclesiology of the people of God was misunderstood. It was always a case of 'people' being understood not theologically, in the sense of God's people, but sociologically, politically or nationally. This happened already with Eusebius of Caesarea († 339/340). He wanted to identify God's people with the Constantinian, Roman-Byzantine Empire. The Bible forbids such an interpretation, just like the national meaning that the term acquired from the Slavophiles under the influence of the romantic idea of national spirit by Aleksey Khomyakov († 1860). According to this, the Russian people perceived itself as the God-bearer people and keeper of the right faith.[19] What is absolutely excluded is ultimately the ideological use of the term 'God's people' as was the case with National Socialism, identifying it with the supposedly specially chosen German people. Excluded is also a democratic understanding which does not want to understand the term 'people' in the biblical sense of λαός but in the profane sense of δῆμος and which tries to deduce from that some kind of democratization of the Church. Finally, people of God cannot be equated with people in the sense of ordinary people, the poor and oppressed, as happened partly in liberation theology. Let us therefore ask again about the genuine theological understanding of the term.

Theocentric and doxological aspects of 'people of God'

In opposition to the socio-political misconception regarding the people of God as constituted through a common history, culture or socio-political roots, we must emphasize the theocentric nature of the term. Other than a political nation, the people of God is called and gathered from out of all nations and classes. It does not come together to decide what is to be done but to listen to and to celebrate what God has decided and done. In the passage in which the New Testament speaks most explicitly about the Church as people of God, it describes it as a holy priestly people of God destined to 'to offer spiritual sacrifices acceptable to God through Jesus Christ' and to proclaim God's excellencies (1 Pet. 2.5.9).

What makes ecclesiology of the people of God specific is its theocentric and doxological structure. The Church is not any people; it is God's people destined to proclaim and to praise God's mighty works. With such doxology it is to reflect something of God's glory (δόξα) and therefore has a doxological structure.[20]

This doxological aspect of the theology of the people of God serves to liberate us from a false ecclesiocentrism and a new fixation on the community. We are far too concerned with ourselves and assume that people are particularly interested in this. This is a great self-deception. If they are religiously interested, people ask first of all not about the Church, but about God. They ask about the Church insofar as something of God's reality shines in it and the Church has to tell them something of this. We should take the hymn to heart: 'Our office is to praise God.'[21]

Thomas Aquinas emphatically highlighted the theocentric nature of the act of faith.[22] For him, the act of faith does not refer to the article of faith but to the 'object' testified in the article.[23] According to the definition of Isidore of Seville, the article of faith is, in fact, a real grasping of God's truth, but in such a way that it aims and points beyond the article to the truth itself.[24] Ultimately, faith is hopeful knowledge which will only come to fulfilment in the eternal vision of God.[25]

The insight into the theocentric structure of ecclesial faith is essential to comprehend what is meant in Catholic ecclesiology when it speaks of the ecclesial mediation of faith. This is often considered a contradiction to the immediate experience of God available to every Christian and is used to pinpoint an apparently specific difference from Protestant ecclesiology.[26] This can easily lead to a misconception, for, from a Catholic and especially Thomistic point of view, the act of faith is not directed toward the Church but immediately to God. The ecclesial mediation of faith serves and leads to this immediacy of the Christian to God. In Catholic understanding, the immediacy to God of each Christian is a *mediated* immediacy.

In the context of modern subjectivity, the idea is of crucial importance. Cardinal John Henry Newman expressed it classically in his episcopal motto '*cor ad cor loquitur*', 'heart speaks unto heart'. According to Newman, the Catholic Church allows nothing to come between the soul and its Creator. It is face to face, '*solus cum solo*', in all matters between man and God. He alone creates; He alone has redeemed; before his awful eyes we go into death; in vision of Him is our eternal beatitude.[27] It is from this that Newman derives his plea for the dignity of the conscience. Conscience is for him 'the aboriginal Vicar of Christ'. 'So indeed it is; should the Pope speak against Conscience in the true sense of the word, he would be committing a suicidal act. He would be cutting the ground from under his feet.' This is followed by Newman's famous words: 'Certainly, if I am obliged to bring religion into after-dinner toasts, [...] I shall drink – to the Pope, if you please – still to conscience first and to the Pope afterwards.'[28]

We could also formulate that each Christian stands in immediacy to God, but never stands before God alone. Personal faith is made possible, carried and supported by the 'we' of faith, by the Church as the one people of God embracing synchronically and diachronically all time and space. Our personal faith is always catholic faith which participates in the one path of faith of the Church of all times and spaces. As the one people of God we are a pilgrim community that is in faith and in the praise of God on the way to the heavenly Jerusalem.

3.2 The Church as body and bride of Christ – the Christocentrism of the Church

Biblical foundations

Looking at the Church as people of God, we must notice that we are God's people only in and through Jesus Christ. This foundational aspect of being God's people will now be unpack in detail with the description of the Church as body and bride of Christ.[29]

In order to understand the image and reality of the Church as the body of Christ, appeal is often made to the ancient theory of the state. Here, the idea of the state refers to a body of many parts whereby the community is only alive if all parts collaborate and fulfil the tasks pertaining to them.[30] Yet Paul only appears to adopt this metaphor when he speaks of the Church as body of Christ. For he does not say in 1 Cor. 12.12: just as the body has many parts, so it is also with the Church. Paul says instead: 'so it is with Christ'. Paul does not write against the background of a Hellenistic idea and metaphor. He follows the Hebrew idea of the corporate personality, a communal 'big I' that unites the individual subjects synchronically and diachronically to a community without deleting their individuality.

Speaking of the body of Christ is thus, for Paul, not a comparison but a reality.[31]

Paul considered neither the socio-political metaphor nor the comparison with a biological organism with many parts as decisive; he ultimately thinks sacramentally. The source for the Pauline body-of-Christ ecclesiology is found in his perception of baptism and the Eucharist. Paul sees in Jesus a descendant from Abraham (Gal. 3.16). As we are in Christ through faith and baptism, we are descendants from Abraham and thereby people of God. Through baptism we form in the one spirit of Jesus Christ the one body of Christ (Rom. 12.4f.; 1 Cor. 12.12.27; Gal. 3.28). 1 Cor. 10.17 is even more explicit: through the participation in the one Eucharistic body of Christ we become the one ecclesial body of Christ. We, the many, are one body in Christ. So for Paul, the body of Christ is a sacramental – or, more precisely, a sacramentally mediated – pneumatological reality.

This sacramental perspective also has, on a secondary level, ethical consequences for Paul. As the Christians are parts of Christ, they cannot at the same time be clients of a prostitute and become one flesh with her (1 Cor. 6.15f.). As all are parts of the one body, they have to behave as parts of one body, care for each other with one soul and show solidarity with each other (Rom. 12.4–8; 1 Cor. 12.12–27). 'If one part is hurt, all parts share its pain. And if one part is honoured, all the parts share its joy' (1 Cor. 12.26). 'Carry each other's burdens; that is how to keep the law of Christ' (Gal. 6.2).[32]

Whereas the main Pauline letters concerning the 'body of Christ' idea focus more on the individual community, the letters from captivity focus more on the universal Church aspect. This contains a noticeable shift in emphasis. The captivity letters do not simply speak of the Church as body of Christ but of Christ as the head (κεφαλή) of his body which is the Church (Eph. 1.22f.; 5.23; Col. 1.18). So the primacy in all pertains to Jesus Christ (Col. 1.18). He is the Lord superordinated to the Church and he is devoted to it in caring love. He is the origin (ἀρχή), the Church has its origin in him and the Church is nourished by him. Again the image of the corporative personality and sacramental understanding shine through.[33]

What the captivity letters mainly express is the superordination of Jesus Christ as head over the Church. Therefore the Church cannot be identified with Jesus Christ and it cannot *tout court* be called the Christ living-on. It depends on what is respectively subject in such a statement and what is the predicate object: not the Church is Christ, but Christ is present in the Church as his body; he lives and works in it. The Church is the space filled by Christ, his fullness (πλήρωμα). Through it and in it Christ fulfils all in all (Eph. 1.22f.). This demonstrates that the ecclesiology of the body of Christ has a universal, cosmic dimension. Through the Church and in it, God includes in Christ the universe into his pleroma.[34]

The Johannine writings contain statements which are factually in accord with the Pauline body of Christ idea. The words of the new birth out of water and Spirit (Jn 3.5), as well as the statement in the great bread discourse according to which Jesus is the bread of life which he gives us to eat that we have life (Jn 6.48–50), both correspond to the sacramental understanding of Paul. The Pauline body idea is most clearly in the discourse of the vine and the branches: 'Whoever remains in me, with me in him, bears fruit in plenty; for cut off from me you can do nothing' (Jn 15.5). Finally, the fourth evangelist reports at the end of the gospel that blood and water flowed from the pierced side of the Lord. In the symbolic language of the fourth gospel, this signifies the two sacraments, baptism and Eucharist, which build up the Church (Jn 19.34). In this Jesus has fulfilled his promise that streams of living water shall flow from his heart (Jn 7.38).[35] So John also says that the Church lives totally from Jesus, it lives out of him and in him; it is nourished and quickened by him through the two sacraments of baptism and Eucharist; the Church is in him and he is in it.

An eventful historical development

The sacramental view of the Church as body of Christ is largely echoed among the Church Fathers. According to Origen, the Church is born at the moment of Christ's death out of his heart's blood.[36] Augustine and other Church Fathers compare the emergence of the Church to the creation of the first woman out of the side of the sleeping Adam. They say that the Church emerged in a similar fashion out of the side of the new Adam who died on the cross. According to Augustine, Christ's weakness at the cross is thus the strength of the Church.[37]

For Augustine, the idea of the Church as the body of Christ, and in particular the idea of the '*totus Christus, caput et membra*',[38] is the central idea of his theology.[39] '*Caput et corpus unus est Christus*';[40] '*totus Christus et caput et corpus.*'[41] '*Christus enim totus cum membris suis est propter ecclesiam, quae est corpus eius, plenitude eius.*'[42] '*Non ille unus et nos multi, sed et nos multi in illo uno unum.*'[43] Both head and body are '*una quaedam persona*'.[44] '*Et nos ipse est*';[45] '*et nos ipse sumus.*'[46] Through this unity with Christ, the suffering of the Church is also Christ's suffering. 'Brothers, observe the loving affection of this head of ours. He is already in heaven and he is still suffering here, as long as the Church is suffering here; Christ is hungry here, thirsty here; he is naked, is a stranger, he is sick, he is in prison; for he said whatever his body suffers, he suffers too.'[47] Augustine can determine the relation also as a reciprocal one: '*In Christo loquitur ecclesia et in ecclesia loquitur Christus et corpus in capite et caput in corpore.*'[48] He also knows that the relation is one-sided and irreversible: '*Sine illo nos nihil, in illo autem et ipse Christus et nos; simul omnes cum capite nostro Christo, sine capite nostro nihil valentes.*'[49]

Augustine sees this view of the Church founded in the mysteries of baptism and Eucharist. It is particularly the Eucharist that he considers as being central to the life of the Church.[50] It is the sacrament of the baptized. The Eucharist is the '*sacramentum unitatis et vinculum caritatis*'.[51] In it, not only the earthly Jesus is present but the '*totus Christus, caput et membra*'.[52] The Eucharist thus connects us not only with the head but also with the mystical body: '*Efficimini panis, quod est corpus Christi*'.[53] '*Ergo vos estis corpus Christi et membra. Mysterium vestrum in mensa dominica positum est: Mysterium vestrum accipitis ... Estote quod videtis at accipite quod estis*'.[54] In this sense Augustine always connects '*unus panis, unus corpus multi sumus*' (1 Cor. 10.17) with the words of institution.[55]

This sacramental-eucharistic interpretation of the image of the body of Christ, which was fundamental for the Fathers and especially for Augustine, became largely lost in the wake of the second Lord's Supper Controversy in the eleventh century. In this debate about the symbolic understanding of the Eucharist ascribed to Berengar of Tours, the then-common term for the Eucharist as mystical (mysterious, sacramental) body of Christ became misleading.[56] To emphasize the real presence of Christ in the Eucharist, it became standard to speak of the Eucharist not as the mystical but as the true body of Christ. The term 'mystical body' was thus set free as a term for the Church. Yet, mystical was now no longer understood in the sacramental sense of mystery but in the sense of an inward-religious reality. The consequence was the loss of the sacramental-mysterious dimension of the Church. It was now understood as body according to the ancient political science in the corporate-institutional sense and was more or less identified with the religio-socio-political entity of medieval Christendom.

The Reformation went back behind the juridical idea to Paul, but it understood the word 'mystical' as a symbolic expression for the inner community of grace between Christ and the individual Christian and as a term for the hidden church in contrast to the juridically constituted form of the church represented by the pope and bishops. This in turn had fatal consequences for the Catholic perspective, as it made the word of the mystical body of Christ sound, to Catholic ears, a statement suspected of Protestantism. This suspicion and this misunderstanding were still alive among a number of the council fathers during the discussion at the First Vatican Council, which is why they called the idea of the mystical body of Christ vague and enthusiastic.

However, the concept of the Church as sacramental entity was never totally lost, either in the Middle Ages or in modern times. Thomas Aquinas extensively reverts to the Augustinian idea of *signum unitatis* and *vinculum caritatis*.[57] For him, the real presence of Christ in the Eucharist is only an intermediate reality (*res et sacramentum*) which points to the actual 'object' (*res*) of the Eucharist, the unity of the Church.[58] In modern times the body of Christ concept was also well known to controversial theologians such as Robert Bellarmine († 1621) and Thomas Stapleton († 1598). The French School, going back to Cardinal Pierre de Bérulle († 1629), unfolded it in the context of its Christocentric spirituality. However, in the apologetics of the eighteenth century, a sociological view of the Church as *societas perfecta* prevailed.

This sociological view of the Church was successfully opposed by the Tübingen School, especially by Johann Adam Möhler, whose pneumatological and Christological understanding in *Unity in the Church* (1825) and in *Symbolism* (1832) also influenced the Roman School (Perrone, Passaglia, Schrader, Franzelin, Scheeben).[59] Also important were John Henry Newman († 1890) and Antonio Rosmini († 1855) with his reform treatise *Cinque Piaghe della Santa Chiesa* (1832–3). In the twentieth century, in the wake of the inner-ecclesial reform movements between both world wars, the reality of the body of Christ was rediscovered. It was often interpreted in the sense of an organic concept, particularly by Karl Adam in *The Spirit of Catholicism* (1940). In contrast, Jacques Maritain presented a more personal interpretation.

The encyclical by Pope Pius XII, *Mystici corporis* (1943), took up the cause of ecclesial renewal and once again gave the description of the Church as body of Christ magisterial recognition. Yet, the encyclical also warned against the danger of misinterpretation, not only against a one-sidedly juridical view of the Church, but also against an organic or biological view and a mystical-quietist understanding which ignores the hierarchical view. The sacramental view of the body of Christ as emphasized by Henri de Lubac and Yves Congar[60] had not yet entered the encyclical. Nevertheless, the encyclical was an important preparation for the Second Vatican Council.

The Second Vatican Council

The development before and after the encyclical *Mystici corporis* prepared the ground for the treating the ecclesiology of the body of Christ at Second Vatican Council.[61] However, after a lengthy debate, the Council avoided the expression 'mystical body of Christ' at this point, as it seemed as if the phrase could easily be misunderstood. Indeed, three times the Council emphasized a pneumatological approach over against the idea of mystery. According to the Council, it is Christ's Spirit who joins the many parts into the one body and who unites them with Christ and each other. The Council also stressed the sacramental foundation and referred to baptism and Eucharist and, in another place, to the other sacraments.[62]

The post-conciliar ecclesiology developed these approaches further in the direction of a Eucharistic ecclesiology and an ecclesiology of the local church. It could thereby refer to Henri de Lubac and, at the same time take up aspects of the Orthodox churches. According to the Eucharistic ecclesiology, the Church is in every place where the Eucharist is celebrated. Yet, as it is always the one Lord and the one Eucharist, in each celebration of the Eucharist not only each respective, congregated individual church becomes present but also the one Church. Every celebration of the Eucharist contains the communion with all the individual churches celebrating the Eucharist and with the whole Church.[63] In this way the term 'body of Christ' expresses the synchronic and diachronic unity of the Church at all places and times.

Finally, the Council emphatically stresses that Jesus Christ himself is the head of the Church's body. It refrains therefore from speaking of the continuation of the incarnation in the Church and the identification of the Church as Christ's body with Christ himself. It says, rather, that the Church, which is a complex reality growing together out of a divine and human element, is 'by no weak analogy, [...] compared to the mystery of the incarnate Word. As the assumed nature, inseparably united to Him, serves the divine Word as a living organ of salvation, so also, in a similar way, does the visible social structure of the Church serve the Spirit of Christ, who vivifies it in the building up of the body.'[64]

If these specifications are taken seriously, then we cannot say that the Church was the present and continuously effective Christ and the continuation of the incarnation. It is more correct to state that Christ is efficaciously present in the Church. One must take care that Jesus Christ remains the subject of the statement, and that the subject Jesus Christ must not be replaced by the subject Church. 'In Christ' we are simultaneously under Christ. That is why we call in the liturgy Jesus Christ our Lord and worship him: 'you alone are the holy one, you alone the Lord, you alone the highest: Jesus Christ' (Glory). This makes clear that there is not only a Protestant but also a Catholic '*solus Christus*'! However, the Catholic *solus Christus* always includes the Church and means the *totus Christus* with head and members.

The Church as bride and prostitute

In the New Testament, the word of the Church as the body of Christ is closely connected with the image of the Church as bride of Christ. Both statements complement each other and act complementarily. The bride image is also found in the Constitution on the Church of Vatican II.[65] In post-conciliar theology it became important to highlight the feminine dimension of the Church. Pope John Paul II himself called in the apostolic exhortation *Mulieres dignitatem* (1988) to reflect on the role of women in the Church and how the feminine dimension of the Church can be realized more.[66] This is undoubtedly an important question. Yet the bride symbol is about far more. It is about the basic understanding of the relation between Christ and the Church which has far-reaching consequences for the understanding of the sacraments, particularly the Eucharist, the sacrament of orders and, of course, the sacrament of marriage.[67] Ultimately it is to highlight spousal love as the soul of the Church effected and permeated by the Spirit and holiness as the set purpose of the Church.[68]

To understand the image of the Church as Christ's bride, one has to go back to creation. According to Genesis, God created humans as man and woman, both equal as his image and likeness (Gen. 1.27). Adam articulates the equality: 'this one at last is bone of my bones and flesh of my flesh' (Gen. 2.23); both are equal and at the same time created for each other. This is why a man leaves his father and mother and becomes attached to his wife and they become one flesh (Gen. 2.24), which means, in the language of the Bible, that they become, as it were, one person. So the relation between man and woman expresses at the same time equality, reciprocity and unity. It is similar when we consider the relation between Christ and the Church mirrored in that between bride and bridegroom. This image expresses the mystery of the love between Christ and the Church as communion, which is a unity in differentness. In this respect, complementary to the image of the body of Christ, the image of the Church as bride expresses more clearly the lasting juxtaposition of Christ and the Church.

Already the Old Testament knows that one must not romanticize the image of the bride. It knows about the nature of tension conditioned by sin in the relation between man and woman which is marked by fidelity, infidelity and continually new forgiveness. It is in this sense of drama and tension that the Old Testament also speaks of Israel as the bride chosen by Yahweh.[69] The time of the exodus out of Egypt and of the covenant at Sinai is considered the betrothal of Israel (Jer. 2.2). Then, with the prophet Hosea, the drama of this relation becomes obvious. Israel the pure bride has become a prostitute. Yet, in his immeasurable mercy, God holds back his just wrath and does not give her up (Hos. 2.16–24; cf. Isa. 54.4–8). This dramatic tension is also found in Ezekiel (Ezek. 16). Matthew's ancestry of Jesus mentions women's names such as Tamar, Rahab, Ruth, Bathsheba, the wife of Uriah, and does not hide the fact that God has repeatedly effected the history of salvation through matrimonial infidelity (Mt. 1.1–17). In the Bible the image of the bride is always interwoven with the motif of the unfaithful prostitute.

It is only against this Old Testament background that we can comprehend what it means when Jesus calls himself bridegroom (Mk 2.19f. par.; cf. Jn 3.29), when the wedding motif plays an important role in the kingdom of God parables (Mt. 22.2–14; Lk. 12.36), and when the coming of God's kingdom is described with the image of the bridegroom's coming to the wedding (Mt. 25.1–13). The seriousness of these parables is expressed in the parable of the wise and foolish virgins waiting for the bridegroom. It is an eschatological judgement parable that warns us that we must be vigilant so as not to oversleep and miss the arrival of the bridegroom, so that when the final catastrophe comes unexpectedly upon unprepared mankind we are prepared, like the wise virgins, and have oil burning in our lamps to meet the bridegroom, i.e. with hearts burning with love (Mt. 25.13). Finally, it is significant that, according to the fourth gospel, Jesus begins his public ministry with a sign at the wedding of Cana (ἀρχὴ τῶν σημείων) and that with this messianic-prophetic symbolic act he reveals his glory (δόξα) (Jn 2.1–12).[70]

Paul stands in the same tradition which was, incidentally, also common with the rabbis. He writes that he loves the church of Corinth with the jealousy of God and he gave them 'all in marriage to a single husband, a virgin pure for the presentation to Christ' (2 Cor. 11.2; cf. Gal. 4.24–31). He describes the relation between husband and wife in view of Christ and the Church and speaks of a great mystery (Eph. 5.32). Still, also according to this text, the Church is not simply the pure and shining virgin. Rather, he speaks of the Church's faults and wrinkles. Yet, Christ nevertheless loves the Church and gave himself for it to cleanse it through the baptismal bath and to sanctify it so that it be glorious and faultless (Eph. 5.25–7).

It is impressive how the seer of Patmos sees the Church in the image of the bride who has prepared herself and made herself beautiful for the wedding (Rev. 19.7f.). The seer views the heavenly Jerusalem coming down like a bride who has dressed herself for her husband (Rev. 21.2.9). In the end she calls to her husband full of joy, longing and hope. 'The Spirit and the bride say "Come!"' (Rev. 22.17).

The Syrian church fathers in particular praise the Church because of its beauty as the beloved bride of Christ.[71] The biblical bride motif appears very often in the history of Christian piety. Especially since Bernard of Clairvaux († 1153), the Song of Songs, originally a profane love song, has become effective in mysticism through symbolic interpretation.[72] We encounter this tradition particularly in the woman and bride mysticism of the high and late medieval period with Mechthild of Magdeburg († 1299), Angela of Foligno († 1309) and others.[73] The love between Christ and the Church becomes here internalized; when she is in intimate conversation with Christ as her husband, the mystic is, as it were, the representative of the *anima ecclesiastica* Similar things could be said of Thérèse de Lisieux († 1897); like all the above-mentioned female mystics, she did not write any ecclesiology, but lived the Church up to the end in the drama of the experience of God-forsakenness. The mysticism of the bride remains restricted to Catholicism. Johann Sebastian Bach († 1750), who knew this mysticism through the Lutheran theologian Johann Arndt († 1621), was also deeply moved by it. In the setting of the famous song 'Wie schön leucht uns der Morgenstern' (How lovely shines the morning star) by Philipp Nikolai († 1608) he gave this mysticism genial expression and, at the same time, made it accessible for the normal piety of the congregation.

Obviously it would be wrong to perceive, in the image of the Church as bride, only the lovingly intimate and harmonious features which it undoubtedly contains. Like in the Old Testament and with Paul, many other passages in the New Testament express the dark side and also, even more clearly, the unheard willingness of God to forgive. This is especially highlighted in the relation of Jesus to women. Jesus did not refrain from encountering prostitutes and forgiving them (Lk. 7.36–50; Jn 8.1–11). For Mark and Matthew these encounters pertain to the Gospel. Following the encounter of Jesus with the sinful woman, they report the word of Jesus: 'in truth I tell you, wherever throughout the world the gospel is proclaimed, what she has done will be told as well.' Her many sins have been forgiven because she has shown great love (Mk 14.9; Mt. 26.13). Here the Gospel takes on the shape of a deeply loving woman willing to repent, who has experienced great forgiveness.[74]

The drama is even more intensified in the Revelation of John. Here the Church as messianic bridal community of the last days is juxtaposed against the whore Babylon (Rev. 17.5; cf. 14.8; 16.19; 18.10). This was pointed against the pagan Rome from which the persecution of the young Church came at that time. This juxtaposition was later often also applied to the Roman church.[75] While he was certainly not the first to apply the image of the whore of Babylon to the Roman church, Martin Luther did so in an effective way, which remains influential to this day, in *The Babylonian Captivity of the Church*.[76] Also a mystic like Hildegard of Bingen († 1179), who instructed her nuns to dress bride-like adorned for worship, sees in a vision the Church covered with dirt and with its dress torn; she laments its devastation through priests committing fornication and thieving who have defiled the one chosen in the blood of the Son of Man as the spotless bride.[77] Less visionary, but likewise realistically, Thomas Aquinas knew that the Church will be the totally spotless one only at the end of time.[78]

In summary, let us ask: what is the point of determining the relation between Christ and the Church in the image of bride and bridegroom? Obviously – and one can notice this first of all – it is about expressing the deep and heartfelt love of Jesus for his Church and the unbreakable faithfulness which attaches him to it. Determining the relation in such a way is intended to spark heartfelt and reciprocal bridal love, represented especially by the great holy women as the destined purpose of the Church. This love is the beating heart of the Church. It also holds true from Christ, even if the Church becomes, in any number of ways, unfaithful and even, as it were, plays the harlot. Yet, just like the sinful woman in the gospel, the Church may know that, no matter how many may mockingly accuse me, Christ will never give me up and he will never let me irrevocably fall. That is why we should love the Church as Christ has loved it. We do not need to ignore or idealize the often-unattractive ecclesial reality. Also concerning the Church, true love is no dreaming enthusiasm; yet it is also not self-righteous or hard-hearted. It is realistic through and through and must stand the test in realism, faithful perseverance and constantly new forgiving.

In addition, there is a second aspect: already in the Old Testament the bride motif served to call to mind the days of old, the pure betrothal, and with this to present the ideal, which is to uphold us and give us orientation again and again. It is to illustrate the necessity of repentance, cleansing and penance and to instruct us to be vigilant and prepared and beautifully dressed for the bridegroom coming to the wedding, so that when he comes we can meet him with burning lamps of love.

Finally, the Church as bride is an eschatological image. It is to make us look longingly and hopefully towards the eschatological wedding. At the same time we may anticipate the celebration of the eschatological wedding feast each time we celebrate the Eucharist. The Eucharist is the sacrament of the bridegroom and the bride. It is to be a bridal feast celebrated in deep bridal love and expectation.

3.3 The Church as the temple of the Holy Spirit – the pneumatological dimension

The Pneumatological dimension of the Church

Jesus Christ did not only live on earth for a short time, establish the Church, institute its offices and then think that, with this, more than enough care had been taken for the Church.[79] As the exalted Lord, Jesus Christ poured out the Holy Spirit and in him remains present in the Church and in the world. Accordingly, in the creed, the '*credo (in) ecclesiam*' is found in the third part, which begins with the statement '*credo in Spiritum sanctum*'.[80] With this, ecclesiology, just as it stands in the context of theology and Christology, has its closest connection with pneumatology. The doctrine of the Church can only be dealt with within the doctrine of the Holy Spirit.[81]

This accords with the testimony of the New Testament. According to the account of the Acts of the Apostles, the Church appeared at Pentecost for the first time publicly as the creation of the Holy Spirit (Acts 2.1–13). He causes the first Christians to be one heart and one soul (Acts 4.32). It was also the Spirit who urged them to mission and who repeatedly showed the young Church unexpected and surprising ways and opened doors (Acts 4.31; 6.5.10; 10.19; 11.12; 13.2; 14.27; 15.28). The Holy Spirit proved himself and still does so again today as protagonist of the mission.

The apostle Paul expresses the lasting efficaciousness of the exalted Lord in the Holy Spirit in the concise formula: 'the Lord is the Spirit' (2 Cor. 3.17). It is in the Holy Spirit that the process happens of turning the world into the kingdom of God which is justice, peace and joy in the Holy Spirit (Rom. 14.17). The transformation begins in the Church and happens through the Church. Hence, Paul describes the Church as building, house and temple of the Spirit (1 Cor. 3.16f.; cf. 2 Cor. 6.16; Eph. 2.21f.; 1 Pet. 2.5). It is the Spirit who unites the Church and holds it together (1 Cor. 12.4–6.11; Rom. 12.6–8; Eph. 4.3f.). All statements about the Church – people of God and body of Christ – are only possible in the Holy Spirit. Through the Spirit we are in Christ heirs of Abraham and so God's people (Gal. 3.14); we are through him in Christ and thus body of Christ (1 Cor. 12.13; Eph. 4.4). Finally, the Church is *communio* as the communion of the Holy Spirit (κοινωνία τοῦ ἁγίου πνεύματος, 2 Cor. 13.13).

According to John's gospel, the Spirit as the Paraclete, i.e. the intercessor, advocate and comforter, reminds the Church of all that Jesus said and did (Jn 14.26), and leads it always dynamically into all truth (Jn 16.13). He makes sure that the Church remains faithful to its origin and so keeps its identity and he leads it at the same time prophetically deeper and deeper into the once-and-for-all revealed truth of Jesus Christ.

Irenaeus of Lyons classically expressed the relation of Spirit and Church: 'Where the Church is, there is also the Spirit of God and where God's Spirit is, there is the Church and all the grace; yet the Spirit is truth'[82]. According to the church order ascribed to Hippolytus, '*festinet autem et ad ecclesiam, ubi floret spiritus*', 'they shall be zealous to go to the church, where the Spirit flourishes'.[83] We find a similar statement with John Chrysostom.[84] Finally, Augustine could say that as much as a person loves the Church, so much he has the Holy Spirit.[85] He coined the word of the Holy Spirit as soul of the Church.[86] Calling the Holy Spirit the soul of the Church is to say that it is he who builds up the Church, maintains it, quickens and animates it, lets it grow, orders and leads it.

Patristic exegesis considered the word of Jesus to be particularly important on the occasion of the ceremony of drawing water during the Feast of tabernacles: 'Let anyone who is thirsty come to me and drink. Whoever believes in me (for him holds true), as scripture says, "From his heart shall flow streams of living water"' (Jn 7.37f.).[87] Jesus himself gives the interpretation of the water, and with it he means the Spirit that all receive who believe in him (Jn 7.39). This passage thereby takes up the prophetic promise that in the time of salvation the desert will be watered and bodily and spiritual thirst will be quenched (Isa. 12.3; 43.20; 44.3; 55.1 et seq.). Jesus calls himself the true source of living water (cf. Isa. 4.10.14). He is the life-giving rock from which Israel could drink in the wandering through the desert (1 Cor. 10.4). One can quote Irenaeus of Lyons: 'He made copious streams to spring forth, disseminating over the earth the Holy Spirit; even as it had been promised through the prophets, that in the end of the days He should pour out the Spirit upon the face of the earth.'[88]

Does the West forget the Spirit?

The biblical and patristic testimonies on the connection between God's Spirit and the Church are overwhelming. Therefore the accusation of forgetting the Spirit, which is often made by Orthodox theology towards the Latin-Western tradition, may seem even more astonishing at first glance. This accusation is in most cases combined with that of a christomonism, an exclusively Christological view of the Church based solely on the incarnation.[89] The Church then appears one-sidedly as an institution and as a rigid and hardened legal structure. There have also been accusations from the side of the free churches and from liberal Christianity that the Catholic

Church would identify itself so much with Jesus Christ that it ultimately took his place and thus had become ideological, immoveable and resistant to criticism. Both critical reproaches boil down to the point that the Roman Catholic Church represented a one-sided institutional view of the Church that left no space for the freedom and dynamic of the Spirit.

The Catholic Church should learn from this criticism of a one-sidedly Christologically orientated ecclesiology. Yet, one must also proceed with caution. Yves Congar explored this criticism in detail, coming to the conclusion that the criticism indeed applies to some advocates of the post-Tridentine theology. Still, it cannot serve as a universal description of the state of Catholic ecclesiology.[90] It was Johann Adam Möhler in particular who, in his early work *Unity in the Church* (1825), broke open an inflexible, purely institutional understanding of the Church and developed a decidedly pneumatocentric ecclesiology. Also pneumatology is still given broad space in the christocentric conception of ecclesiology of the mature Möhler in *Symbolism* (1832).[91] Augustine's formula of the Spirit as the soul of the Church was adopted by Leo XIII in the encyclical *Divinum illud* (1897), by Pius XII in the encyclical *Mystici corporis* (1943), as well as by the Second Vatican Council.[92]

In many passages, Vatican II gave considerable space to the testimony of Scripture and Tradition and emphasized that, in all the Church does, it is a sacrament, i.e. an instrument of the Holy Spirit.[93] The proclamation of the Gospel and the celebration of the sacraments happen in the Holy Spirit. The significance of the Holy Spirit for the sacraments was especially stressed by reviving the *epiclesis*, the prayer to and invocation of the Holy Spirit at the celebration of the Eucharist and the other sacraments. So the Church as a whole has an epicletic structure. Its authority is not high-handed ruling over God's word and grace. On the contrary, the Church must listen time and again to what the Spirit tells the communities (Rev. 2.7.11.17.29 et seq.). At the celebration of the sacraments the Church can only authoritatively pray for the coming of the Spirit. The Church lives out of the constant prayer: '*Veni Sancte Spiritus!*'

After the Council, Pope John Paul II dedicated an entire encyclical, *Dominum et Vivificantem* (1986), to the doctrine of the Holy Spirit. In his apostolic letter on the preparation for the jubilee of the year 2000, *Tertio millennio adveniente* (1994), he again addressed extensively the pneumatological dimension of the Church.[94]

The pneumatological dimension must prevent the Church from becoming a purely, almost bureaucratic institution and keep ecclesiology from being only hierarchology. Paul says that the Gospel of Christ is not written on tablets of stone but through the Spirit of the living God it is written in hearts of flesh (2 Cor. 3.3). This word inspired a long and important effective history. According to Irenaeus of Lyons, the Spirit keeps the apostolic heritage always young and fresh.[95] He prevents bureaucratically administering the Gospel like a dead property. Thomas Aquinas could therefore say that the *lex evangelica* was not an external but an internal law, namely the '*gratia Spiritus Sancti, quae datur per fidem Christi*',[96] and adds that the *lex evangelica* was for this reason a *lex libertatis*.[97]

In the creed it says 'I believe in the holy Spirit, the Lord, the giver of Life' ('*Dominum et vivificantem*'). In other words, the Spirit is a sovereign, lordly, life-giving spirit that is always good for surprises. Time and again he shakes the Church, calls charismatically gifted people who help to keep the apostolic heritage free from encrustations and to make it young and fresh again. Time and again he inspires renewal movements,[98] which renew good and tried forms and open up new forms of piety and spiritual life and which, in times of crisis, open for the Church a new way into the future.

The charismatic dimension of the Church

The conciliar renewal concerning the understanding of the Church in the power and dynamism of the Holy Spirit and as an organism built up and inspired by the Spirit led to the rediscovery of the charismatic dimension of the Church. The Second Vatican Council spoke in many places of the importance of the charismata in the Church.[99] This is also significant as, according to the traditional doctrine, these charismata were only a phenomenon of the time of the beginning of the Church.[100] This position becomes problematic if we consider that the New Testament teaching on charismata is to be read in the context of the accounts of Jesus' miracles and the miracles of the apostles (Mk 6.7; 16.17f.20; Acts 2.22.43; 4.30; 5.12 et seq.; Heb. 2.4). The charismata are signs of the beginning kingdom of God and therefore they belong permanently to the Church.

After the Council, the rediscovery of the charismatic dimension became the point of departure for various renewal movements[101] and led in theology to quite different concepts, ranging from a theology of spiritual renewal of the Church to new concepts for church order and also to criticism of the Church as institution and its so-called structures of domination.[102] Hence it is first necessary to clarify the multifaceted notion of charisma.

Since Max Weber, the sociology of religion has understood charisma as a not-everyday quality and appearance of a person. In this sense one then speaks of charismatic authority and rule.[103] This has to be distinguished from the biblical usage. It is essentially only found with Paul. Yet even within the Pauline writings one can notice different accentuations.[104] One has to proceed from the term 'charis' (χάρις), which originally meant grace, favour, and then becomes the expression and term for the grace of salvation. The charisma (χάρισμα) is then the effect of the charis, God's gift of grace or God's Spirit. In this sense Paul speaks of the gracious gift (Rom. 5.15f.) and the gift of eternal life in Christ (Rom. 6.23). So when speaking of charisma we must not proceed one-sidedly from exceptional and spectacular gifts of the Spirit. The point of departure must be Pentecost, where the Spirit was poured out on all as the fulfilment of the prophetic promise (Joel 3.1–5; Acts 2.17–21). In this way Paul can say that everyone has his charisma, each just so as the Spirit has given it to him (1 Cor. 7.7; 12.6; 1 Pet. 4.10).

If this view of charisma is taken seriously, one can no longer simply speak of the ceasing of the charismatic dimension in the post-apostolic Church. The Spirit gives the charismata as he wills (1 Cor. 12.11); as it were, they are contextual and accord with each historical situation and each respective necessity of the Church. The charismata have continued to live in the history of the Church, especially in the history of the saints and in mystical phenomena. One can also think of great charismatic persons such as Bernard of Clairvaux, Hildegard of Bingen, Catherine of Siena, Francis of Assisi and many others. They all roused the church of their time and have continued to have an effect until today.

The general gift of grace becomes thus effective in very different gifts of grace. Paul lists them in the Letter to the Romans (Rom. 12.3–8) and above all in the first Letter to the Corinthians (1 Cor. 12.4–30; especially 28f.). Paul does not only name exceptional gifts such as miracle healings and speaking in tongues, but also gracious gifts that have a fixed position in the community, such as apostles, prophets, and teachers. He also mentions unspectacular gifts that operate quitely, such as wisdom and knowledge, strength in faith, helping and leading, comforting and exhorting. Yet, all gifts of grace come from the one Spirit who gives them for the benefit and edification of all (1 Cor. 12.8; 14.3.12; 1 Pet. 4.10). For this reason, Paul is no friend of a charismatic and enthusiastic disorder, but rather insists that everything in the Church should take place in decency and order (1 Cor. 14.40). Paul says about prophesy that it has to happen in analogy to faith (κατὰ τὴν ἀναλογίαν τῆς πίστεως, Rom. 12.6), which means in accordance with the faith of the community or the Church; in other words, in spite of the great diversity of charismata in unity.[105]

This view, which dominates the major Pauline letters, becomes somewhat modified in the letters from captivity. Now that Jesus Christ appears more clearly as the head of the Church, the exceptional spiritual gifts noticeably withdraw into the background in favour of the apostles, prophets, evangelists, shepherds and teachers. They have the task to equip the saints, the Christians, for fulfilling their service (Eph. 4.10–12). This indicates already in the New Testament a consolidation of ecclesiastical structures. It is unfolded further in the pastoral letters. They only speak of the charisma which has been given to Timothy by laying-on of hands (1 Tim. 4.14; 2 Tim. 1.6). According to this, the ministries in the Church are spiritual gifts in a special way.

As the history of the great saints shows, ministry and charisma can exist in considerable tension. One thinks, for example, of Hildegard of Bingen, who refused to obey an order of the archbishop of Mainz and who accepted for herself and her nunnery the interdict; or Francis of Assisi, who fought for a long time against founding a religious order; Ignatius of

Loyola († 1556), who was for some time caught up with the inquisition; Joan of Arc († 1431), who was burnt at the stake for alleged heresy. The greatness of all these saints, however, is that they did not rebel against the ecclesiastical ministry or the ecclesiastical institution. These witnesses of the charisma are therefore also witnesses that official and charismatic structures of the Church cannot be played against each other or brought into fundamental opposition.

Charisma and institution – the Church as sacrament of the Spirit

We must still attempt to clarify further the relation between charisma and institution. This is possible if we look at the controversies which we find throughout history between the Church and enthusiastic movements. These often commenced with criticisms of institutional encrustations and petrifications as well as with the charge that the Church has become much too profane and associated with the rich and powerful. Nowadays one might think of the criticism concerning forms of a bureaucratization of the Church detached from life in the parishes.

We encounter such movements quite early in Montanism, in various underground and people's movements of the Middle Ages such as the Valdensians, in the 'left wing' of the Reformation such as the Anabaptists (Thomas Münzer, Andreas Karlstadt, et seq.). A significant example was the movement which Joachim of Fiore began in the twelfth and thirteenth centuries. The Calabrian monk predicted that, after the ages of the Father (Old Testament) and of the Son (time of the hierarchical church), a third age of the Holy Spirit, i.e. of the mots, would emerge. Thomas Aquinas sharply refuted this theory on the basis that, after the fullness of time in Jesus Christ, there can be no more progress in salvation history.[106] The actual effective history of Joachim took place beyond the ecclesial Tradition in the context of the modern, profane utopias (Thomas More, Tommasco Campanella, Francis Bacon, up to Schelling, Hegel, Marx).[107] We find a different echo of it in some free church communities (Quakers, radical pietism et seq.).[108] For the present time we can mention the fast growing neo-Pentecostal which are a challenge not only for the Catholic Church, but also for all other traditional churches.[109]

Against the enthusiastic spiritual movements one has to say that, according to the New Testament, the Holy Spirit is no spirit of enthusiasm. He is the Spirit of Christ (Rom. 8.9; Phil. 1.1) or the Spirit of the Son (Gal. 4.6). In consequence he works through the audible word and the visible sacraments. He institutes ministries in the Church that are assigned in service to the word and the sacraments and who are shepherds of the faithful (Acts 20.28; 1 Cor. 12.28; Eph. 4.11; 1 Tim. 4.13; 2 Tim. 1.6). The description of the Church as house (οἶκος) and the idea of the word of edification (οἰκοδομή) in the Church also highlight the fact that it has a structure and is an ordered fabric. Paul clearly makes an effort to bring order into the enthusiastic exuberance of the church in Corinth (1 Cor. 12; 14).

Ignatius of Antioch unmistakably expresses the necessary submission under the bishop and the presbytery as well as unity with the bishop.[110] Cyprian of Carthage almost defines the Church as 'the people united to the bishop, and the flock which adheres to its pastor.'[111] Basil extensively describes the unity and diversity of the spiritual gifts and their order through the Holy Spirit; also the official order of the Church is a work of the Holy Spirit.[112] In other words, there has never been the pure Church of the Spirit or of love, as Rudolf Sohm wrongly presented it.[113] The Spirit works rather through the Church, its word, its sacraments and the offices of the Church. This is also solid Lutheran doctrine. In his Invocabit sermons of 1522, Luther turned sharply against the enthusiasts. According to Karl Barth, the Church is the earthly-historical form of existence of the Spirit.[114]

In Catholic terminology, the Church can be called sacrament – in other words, the place and instrument of the Spirit. Determining the Church in this way as sacrament of the Holy Spirit excludes both extremes: the extreme of enthusiasm that excludes the sacramental and ministerial mediation as well as the extreme of a purely hierarchical-institutional view of the Church which identifies the Church with the ecclesiastical establishment and thereby overlooks the mere sign and service nature of the institution. Worded scholastically, the institution is sign and instrument (*sacramentum tantum*); the charisma of ministry is in its serving character, so to speak, an intermediate reality (*res et sacramentum*) for the actual object and the life of the Church (*res sacramenti*). It must therefore leave space and freedom and it even has to care actively for the life of the Church in the Spirit-led interaction of spiritual gifts.

So the *communio* structure of the Church is realized in an ordered interaction of different ministries and charismata. The Church is an organism of manifold charismas whose unity realizes itself in a mutually complementing and supporting dynamic interaction. They all have their own specific task and cannot replace, displace or exclude each other. They can fulfil their respective service only in the spirit of *communio* and of listening to each other, in showing mutual consideration, in complementing each other, in tolerating and correcting each other and in the cooperation of all. The Church is not an integralistic or even totalitarian system. Rather, we do well to call it an open system that cannot be directed or even manipulated from one point or by one instance. In this openness it is possible for the underivable new of the Spirit to show itself in each respective situation of history.[115]

Johann Adam Möhler perceived in this interaction of the charismata the beauty of the Church. 'No more beautiful object presents itself to the imagination of the Catholic – none more agreeably captivates his feelings, than the image of the harmonious inter-workings of countless spirits, who, though scattered over the whole globe, endowed with freedom, and possessing the power to strike off into every deviation to the right or to the left; yet, preserving still their various peculiarities, constitute one great brotherhood for the advancement of each other's spiritual existence, – representing one idea, that of the reconciliation of men with God, who on that account have been reconciled with one another.' The Church is beautiful as the appearing and embodying truth which is Christ.[116]

This is an idealizing description and the ideal does not always accord with the everyday reality of the Church. However, this ideal is not just wishful thinking, it has its foundation in the deeper pneumatological reality of the Church and is therefore normatively prescribed for the Church. In an address to spiritual movements and communities during the Pentecost vigil 1998 Pope John Paul II said: 'The institutional and charismatic aspects are co-essential as it were to the Church's constitution.' In his programmatic apostolic letter on the occasion of the start of the third millennium *Novo millennio ineunte* (2001) he saw in them a spring of the Spirit; he repeated the warnings: 'Do not quench the Spirit, do not despise prophesying, but test everything and hold fast what is good' (1 Thess. 5.19–21).[117]

If one tries to comprehend more deeply the interaction of the charismata in the Church, especially between ministry and charisma, then this can happen in analogy to the inner-Trinitarian order. Augustine called the Spirit the love and the gift between Father and Son.[118] He is God as self-giving, as overflowing love, as ecstasy and at the same time as kenosis because he takes himself back in the love, as it were, and gives the other persons space. He is love that unites and binds together and that, like any true love, does not take over but makes free and gives free. In this way, as spiritual gifts, ministries and charismata should be totally themselves by giving themselves and particularly by spreading love they are to keep their own freedom and that of others. In their interaction the relational nature of the Church becomes again visible.[119] They realize the basic law in the kingdom of God which Jesus puts like this: 'Anyone who wants to save his life will lose it; but anyone who loses his life for my sake, and the sake of the gospel, will save it' (Mk 8.35 par).

The universal efficacy of the Spirit

The pneumatological perspective places ecclesiology from a new point of view into a universal horizon, for as *Spiritus creator* the Spirit is the one who gives life to everything that lives and who, similar to Wisdom, permeates all, affects all and holds everything together. 'When you send forth your Spirit, they are all created, and you renew the face of the earth' (Ps. 104.30; cf. Job 34.14f.). 'For the spirit of the Lord fills the world, and that which holds everything together knows every word said' (Wis. 1.7; 7.22–8.1).

As in creation, so the Spirit is also at work in history. He spoke through the prophets; in the fullness of time he rests permanently on Jesus (Mk 1.9–11; Lk. 4.18). Jesus is almost creation of the Spirit (Mt. 12.31f.; Lk. 1.35), all his ministry happens in the power of the Spirit (Mt. 12.18; Lk. 4.14.18; 10.21 et seq.). In the Spirit he gives his life at the cross (Heb. 9.14), in the power of the Spirit he is resurrected from the dead (Rom. 1.3f.). From heaven he sends the Holy Spirit. Thus at Pentecost the eschatological promise of the prophet Joel (Joel 3.1–5) is fulfilled that at the end of time the Spirit will be poured out on all (Acts 2.17–21). Hence at Pentecost with the history of the Church the process begins whereby with groaning and labour pains the Spirit leads all reality towards the eschatological perfection (Rom. 8.22–7). The Spirit, which is at work everywhere, is efficaciously present especially where life and the question about the fullness of life move; he has a universal human and cosmic dimension.

The Second Vatican Council highlighted this universal and cosmic dimension of the Spirit who was already efficacious in the world before Christ.[120] The Spirit is at work in the hearts of all people of good will and offers them the possibility of grace.[121] In the encyclical *Redemptoris mission* (1990)[122] Pope John Paul II emphasized this universal efficacy of the Spirit and applied it to the encounter with other cultures and religions. 'The Spirit's presence and activity affect not only the individuals but also society and history, peoples, cultures and religions. Indeed, the Spirit is at the origin of the noble ideals and undertakings which benefit humanity on its journey through history: "The Spirit of God with marvellous foresight directs the course of the ages and renews the face of the earth".'[123] 'The Church's relationship with other religions is dictated by a twofold respect: "Respect for man in his quest for answers to the deepest questions of his life, and respect for the action of the Spirit in man".'[124]

So the Spirit as the soul of the Church widens the perspective beyond its visible borders. He who is totally in the Church at the same time points beyond himself so that the Catholic Church rejects nothing that is true and holy in other religions.[125] It can also appreciate what the Spirit effects in other churches and ecclesial communities.[126] So it is the Spirit that leads the Church to dialogue internally and externally.[127]

Discerning the spirits

The universal efficacy of the Spirit in other religions and their cultures, on the one hand, and enthusiastic trends in the Church, as well the appearance of false prophets, on the other, were the reason why criteria for discerning the spirits were already developed in the New Testament and then in the spiritual theology since the Church Fathers. Johannes Cassian and, in modern times, Ignatius of Loyola have been historically of particular importance and influence on monasticism.[128] Today these criteria are relevant and urgent anew because of more recent esoteric trends, charismatic movements and, above all, with respect to encounters with other religions and cultures as well as developments within our own culture. For this reason, Vatican II called for an interpretation of the signs of the time in the light of the Gospel.[129]

Paul gives us a double warning. First he encourages openness and open-mindedness. 'Do not quench the Spirit, do not despise prophesying!' At the same time he also calls to vigilance: 'Test everything and hold fast what is good' (1 Thess. 5.19–21). Likewise the first letter of John admonishes: 'not every spirit is to be trusted, but test the spirits to see whether they are from God, for many false prophets are at large in the world' (1 Jn 4.1). Both admonitions result in an openness that does not lead to an all-encompassing syncretism, to a loss of profile and to arbitrariness.

For Paul, discerning the spirits is in itself a charisma (1 Cor. 12.10), because one can judge spiritual issues only in the Spirit (1 Cor. 2.10–15). The Spirit gives for it insight, knowledge and wisdom (Phil. 1.9; Eph. 1.17f.; Col. 1.9), which is no longer blown around by every little wind but leads to an adult maturity in the faith (Eph. 4.14). In this context, the theological Tradition speaks of the sense of faith given to the whole people of God by the Spirit.[130] It is an instinct for faith resulting from concrete experience and an eye of the heart given by the Spirit (Eph. 1.18).[131]

The first rule for discerning the spirits is Christological in nature: 'no one who says "A curse on Jesus" can be speaking in the Spirit of God, and nobody is able to say, "Jesus is Lord" except in the Holy Spirit' (1 Cor. 12.3). The Holy Spirit is thus no enthusiastic everyday spirit; he is Christ's Spirit, the Spirit of the Lord and Son. The decisive criterion for the discernment of the spirits is hence the question of whether these spirits confess to Jesus Christ as the Lord and whether they can last according to the standard of Jesus Christ. This is why Paul warns so passionately against any other gospel than that of Jesus Christ (Gal. 1.6–9; 5.10; 2 Cor. 11.4). The first letter of John is no less explicit, with its warning against the spirit of the antichrist (1 Jn 2.18.22f.; 4.3; cf. 2 Jn 7): 'this is the proof of the spirit of God: any spirit which acknowledges Jesus Christ, come in human nature, is from God, and no spirit is from God which fails to acknowledge Jesus is from God' (1 Jn 4.2f.).

The second rule is of an ecclesiological kind: the spirit is a spirit of unity; it does not divide but brings together and integrates into the one Church in all its great variety of charismata (1 Cor. 12.4–30; Rom. 12.4–8). Therefore, the apostle admonishes that nobody should strive beyond the measure which he deserves but each according to the measure of faith God has given to him. Prophesying is to occur in accord with the analogy of faith (κατὰ τὴν ἀναλογίαν τῆς πίστεως, Rom. 12.6), that is, according to the faith of the community or the Church. It is to serve the edification of the community (1 Cor. 14.3.12; 1 Pet. 4.10), for God is not a god of disorder but of peace (1 Cor. 14.33). Paul counters the slogan of his Corinthian opponents 'all is permitted' with 'but not everything is useful' (1 Cor. 6.12). Paul sees freedom as socially and ecclesially bound. This also includes that prophecies are interpreted with understanding. According to Paul, one should not only pray in spirit but also with the mind (1 Cor. 14.15). Following Eusebius, the Church Fathers often speak of a ἐκκλησιαστκὸν φρόνημα,[132] a *sensus ecclesiasticus*. Origen speaks of the '*anima ecclesiastica*',[133] Ignatius of Loyola of '*sentire cum ecclesia*',[134] and Möhler of '(general) ecclesiastical consciousness'.[135]

The third rule, finally, is of a practical nature. For Paul, more important than extraordinary and noticeable charismas; more important than speaking in languages, miracle healings, enthusiastic ecstasies; more important than superficial excitement and drunkenness; is love. Without love everything else is worthless. Love, therefore, is the high calling of the Christian. If I had all charismata, but I was without love, I would be nothing (1 Cor. 13.2). The charismata are to be discerned therefore if those who claim to have them live according to the Spirit or the sinful flesh (Rom. 8.5–15; Gal. 5.16f.). It is the spirit of prayer that pertains to living after the Spirit, it is the spirit of prayer in which we can call 'Abba, Father' (Rom. 8.15; Gal. 4.6). This also includes the fruits of the Spirit: 'love, joy, peace, patience, kindness, goodness, trustfulness, gentleness and self-control' (Gal. 5.22f.). For Ignatius of Loyola, an important criterion was the experience of comfort or desolation.[136] The Spirit's desire is life and peace (Rom. 8.6). The Spirit must therefore not be confused with one's own excitement; the Spirit rather effects inner composure, inner calm and inner peace.

3.4 Mary – archetype of the Church

Despite their helpfulness and concreteness, the respective images/symbols and determinations of the nature of the Church as people of God, body and bride of Christ and temple of the Holy Spirit, ultimately they remain abstract. Yet, the Christian faith strives for concretion. Thus, already suggestively in Holy Scripture and later explicitly in the Tradition of the Church, these images are put into a concrete and personal image by presenting Mary as archetype of the Church.[137] In this way we are shown again that the Church is not a bureaucratic apparatus, nor an organization nor just an institution dominated by men, but is expressed decisively and most clearly in a person – to be more precise, in a woman.

To speak of the Marian dimension of the Church seems alien nowadays, not only for Protestant Christians, but also for many Catholics. It sparks both incomprehension and rejection. For many this language seems hardly ecumenical. Yet they overlook that Mary appears also in the gospel. Mary is therefore not only Catholic, she is also Protestant. The gospel of Jesus Christ is not at all 'to be had' without Mary, mother of the Lord. It was her 'yes' that made the coming of the Saviour possible at all and under the cross it is again Mary representing the Church. She embodies in a perfect way the nature of the Church as community of faith. Because of this, Vatican II calls her the archetype (typos) of the Church.

The human-earthly person of Mary

More recent Mariology strives to highlight the human-earthly person of Mary as the figure of the perfect disciple and our sister in faith. It has distanced itself from a superelevation of the person of Mary which is often encountered in Marian piety, which has detached Mary from life and from the faith of the faithful rather than bringing her closer to them. As a certain hymn says, Mary is the woman from the people. She, too, had to go the pilgrim way of faith.[138]

Modern exegesis has even gone one step further and has shown the Old Testament rootedness of the New Testament texts about Mary. At the annunciation the angel calls her the 'daughter Zion' mentioned by the prophet Zephaniah (Zeph. 3.14–17); in other words, she is addressed as representative of Israel (Lk. 1.28–31). In the Magnificat (Lk. 1.46–55) Mary adopts the song of thanksgiving of Hannah, mother of Samuel, from the Old Testament (1 Sam. 2.1–10); she anticipates the beatifications of the Sermon on the Mount (Mt. 5.3–11; Lk. 6.20–6). She herself belongs to the anawin, Yahweh's little ones, meek ones and poor whom Jesus calls blessed. Thus she is the representative of the Old and New Testament people of God. As such, in the Magnificat she praises God who helps the low, powerless and meek and who has regarded the lowliness of his handmaiden. With this she stands in the tradition of the great women in the Old Testament. At the same time she is Jesus' first disciple and, as such, the primordial cell of the Church. Therefore Mary must be perceived from the Old and New Testament people of God theology, just as, vice versa, this cannot be understood without Mary.

Mother of God and mother of the Church

The significance of Mary in salvation history becomes apparent when one considers the fundamental Marian title of Mother of God. Already the New Testament regards Mary not only as mother of Jesus. Rather, the New Testament identifies her with the sovereign title of mother of our Lord (κύριος, Lk. 1.43). Already at his conception he is foretold to her as son of the Highest (Lk. 1.31f.35). The council of Ephesus finally confirmed the title and veneration of Mary as God-bearer (Θεοτόκος).[139] The remarkable thing about this first and fundamental Marian symbol is that it was formulated in the context of the controversy with Nestorius. At that time the dispute was not about a Mariological but a Christological question. Thus, the title 'Mother of God' is primarily a Christological confession to Jesus Christ as the true, incarnate Son of God.

Just as Mary is ascribed a central role as Jesus' mother and mother of the Lord at the beginning of Matthew and Luke, so does John's gospel at the end. From the cross, Jesus entrusts Mary to John, the disciple whom he loved and who represents the Johannine ideal of discipleship, just as he entrusts John and thereby all his disciples to Mary: 'Woman, this is your son', and to John: 'this is your mother' (Jn 19.25–7). This passage has quite rightly been called Jesus' testament for the Church.[140] Mary, the mother of Jesus and the mother of God, thus becomes the mother of the people of God; the mother of Christ becomes the mother of all who belong to the body of Christ which is the Church. At the same time the evangelist highlights the eschatological significance of this position when he says that from this hour (ὥρα) the disciple took her into his house (literally, into his very own). With this he refers back to the beginning of Jesus' public ministry at the wedding at Cana when the eschatological hour of Jesus' death on the cross had not yet come (Jn 2.4). Yet, now Mary is taken ultimately into the Gospel of Jesus' death and resurrection.

The Church as discipleship of Jesus is thereby entrusted to the motherly care of Mary who represents most perfectly the nature of the Church and is, as it were, the primordial cell of the Church by her yes which she carried through until under the cross. In this sense she is addressed and called in prayer the mother of the Church.[141] Many Christians in all centuries who entrusted themselves to her motherly intercession and received her help have experienced that this is not only a pious phrase. This goes to show that Marian devotion does not spring from some speculations but from the biblical testimony of Mary, read and interpreted in the light of concrete experience of faith.

Sola gratia – sola fide

The objections against the veneration of Mary which are presented by many Protestant Christians are well known. One can best reply to them by reading the interpretation of the Magnificat which Luther himself left us in the year 1521. In it Luther showed that Mary is the best interpretation of what is regarded the centre of Reformation teaching, the *sola gratia* and *sola fide*, all alone out of grace, all because of faith.[142]

Mary does nothing of herself and she is nothing by herself. She is totally and exclusively open to receive God's word; she is hearer of God's word (Lk. 1.38). Even before she conceives God's eternal word in her womb, she has received it in her heart. She receives him, overshadowed by the Holy Spirit and in the power of the Most High (Lk. 1.35). Against all human possibilities and only because of the working of the Holy Spirit, she thus becomes the mother of Jesus.

As especially the Eastern tradition says, Mary is the 'totally holy' (Παναγία), i.e. the one full grace of the Holy Spirit. The Western tradition factually expresses the same when it says that from the first moment of her existence she was kept free from all sin.[143] She is nothing out of herself, but all out of grace. Where all human possibilities were at an end and the world had lost itself in the remoteness from God, she gave to the world the saviour and Lord (Lk. 2.11) and thus the light of the world and a new beginning.

Therefore, both her virginity and motherhood must not be understood only biologically. They include a bodily dimension, but they understand this as sign of the miraculous, graceful working of God which creates a new beginning totally underivable within this world.[144] The actual miracle and mystery is therefore not the virgin birth but the incarnation of God. The virgin birth is 'the sign which accompanies and indicates the mystery of the incarnation of the Son, marking it off as a mystery from all the beginnings of other human beings.'[145]

Of course, God never treats humanity as a dead instrument; he does not instrumentalize us but recognizes us in our creational dignity as his image and likeness (Gen. 1.27). His grace liberates and enables us to our freedom. So God also never used Mary simply passively, either at the annunciation or at the end under the cross. Mary rather let herself be taken into service as the one chosen and graced by God in free obedience and faith.[146]

The Second Vatican Council avoids any kind of parallelism between Christ and Mary. We can say that Mary participates in the work of salvation only insofar as, aided by grace, she spoke her yes to God's salvation work in Jesus Christ and maintained this yes to the end. Thereby in no way does she obscure Christ as the sole mediator;[147] she takes nothing away from it and adds nothing to it.[148] She herself, even from the first moment of her existence, is redeemed. As Mary cannot have participated in her own salvation, one should avoid the mistakable word of Mary's co-redemption. She says her yes in the power of redemption; only by participating in this way does she cooperate in the redemption.

The Second Vatican Council solves the question of cooperation in the sense of the relation between primary and secondary cause. According to this teaching, the secondary cause can only effect insofar as it participates in the primary cause and effects in its power. What Mary does, she does alone because of the faith that has been given to her out of pure grace. She does not obscure Jesus Christ as the sole mediator and takes nothing away from his position and importance. On the contrary, Mary is totally deferent to Jesus Christ. She tells us: 'Do whatever he tells you' (Jn 2.5). John of Damascus († 754), the last universally orientated theologian of the old Greek church, can tell us: the veneration which one shows to Mary refers to her son Jesus Christ himself.[149]

Mary as type of the Church, new Eve and seat of Wisdom

In summary, we can say that Mary represents in the most perfect way the people of God of the Old and New Testament. She represents the people of God as humble handmaiden who is unconditionally open to God's call and puts herself totally at his service. She is the obedient hearer of the word. For this reason Vatican II calls Mary 'a pre-eminent and singular member of the Church'. She is given to us as 'type and excellent exemplar in faith'.[150] Following the Church Father Ambrose, the Council could call Mary type of the Church.[151] With this it says that the nature of the Church is preformed in Mary and articulated in her most purely.[152]

This entails that neither the apostolic ministry nor the hierarchy is the most perfect articulation of the Church, but Mary as woman and bearer of a unique personal charisma. A more explicit relativization of the hierarchy than that which happens through Catholic Mariology is actually unthinkable. In Mary the Church was already present, even before the apostles as men were called and appointed to their office.[153]

Like the Church, Mary also stands in a perspective of salvation and human history. The Council takes up the tradition of the Church Fathers and contrasts Mary and Eve with each other. Through her obedience, Mary untied the calamitous knot which Eve had tied in her disobedience and Mary gave to mankind the saviour.[154] The Virgin's consent was given in lieu of that of the entire human nature.[155] That God kept her free from all sin from the beginning is a sign that God's original saving design with mankind was not thwarted by sin and that it did not come to nothing. Thus, Mary is the image and sign of God's irrefutable faithfulness to the world and mankind. As the new Eve, she is the dimension of the world and the history of mankind that remained whole. In her assumption into the heavenly glory with body and soul[156] she shines for the people of God on its way through time. She is the eschatological sign that, according to God's plan, at the end all reality – the material and the spiritual – is to enter into the transfiguration of God's glory. The transfiguration is the goal of God's ways.

Thus Mary radiates the splendour and beauty of the original as well as of the new creation.[157] As it were, she is the morning star of the new creation that shows us in the night of the world the new morning and lets shine the whole splendour of God's Wisdom revealed in Jesus Christ. In her the Church as the house of Wisdom is preformed in the most perfect way. She absorbed God's Wisdom totally into her heart, carried it in her womb and gave it in the person of the divine child to the world. So it is only just that we call her in the *Laurentian Litany* seat of Wisdom (*sedes sapientiae*). In this sense the liturgy refers texts speaking of the pre-worldly Wisdom (Prov. 8.22–36; Sir. 24.3–22) to Mary.

Hence Catholic ecclesiology finds in Mariology its archetypal expression. Therefore, without diminishing in the least the primacy of Jesus Christ, Catholic Church piety always articulates itself also in Marian devotion. Where this becomes weak or principally suspicious, in most cases the church piety has also become weak, just as, vice versa, the love of the Church goes together with the veneration of Mary, mother of God. Today this becomes apparent in spiritual renewal movements which are often characterized by a distinct Marian trait. A true renewal of the Church is not possible without a renewed Mariology and veneration of Mary. Thus, Mary can be also today helper and archetype for a renewal of the Church's life in faith, hope and love.

4

The marks of the Church of Jesus Christ

The creed of the Church speaks of the Church not only in general terms. It says more specifically what it means by Church and therefore specifies its confession by naming four properties through which it becomes recognizable. So the Nicene-Constantinopolitan creed professes: 'we believe in the one, holy, catholic and apostolic Church'.[1] These four properties are basically identical with the nature of the Church. They concretely express the nature of the Church under four different aspects. Because of this, they cannot be separated from each other, for together they form a single whole and they include each other.

The four properties of the Church are maintained by all traditional churches. However, because of their different understanding of the Church, the Protestant churches interpret them differently from the Catholic and Orthodox churches. Thus, the four properties highlight again the substantial common ground as well as the specific denominational differences. According to Protestant understanding, the four properties are to be seen as properties of the hidden Church that can be grasped only in faith. That is why Luther complemented the four properties with so-called '*notae externae*' of the visible church: first of all, the pure preaching of the Gospel and the administration of the sacraments in harmony with the Gospel; in addition, the ecclesial ministries, prayer, Cross and suffering.[2] Calvin is different, as he also names, in addition to preaching and administration of the sacraments, the church order.[3]

In the debate with the Protestants and then with the Enlightenment, the apologetically orientated, post-Tridentine theology tried to prove, with the aid of the four properties, the Catholic Church as the true Church. Hereby it understood the properties (*proprietates*) as characteristics (*notae*) of the Church. This apologetic attempt was not successful. As the four properties did not suffice as certain criteria, it was attempted to introduce further criteria. The four properties have often been summarized in the *Romanitas*. This emphasized the Petrine principle as essential for Catholic ecclesiology.[4] In addition there was a great emphasis on the witness of the saints, the testimony of the personal life, the love, the apostolic zeal and the strength to persevere in persecutions. On top of that there came the argument of the inner coherence of the Catholic doctrine as well as the faithfulness and constancy of the Catholic Church in the keeping of the apostolic inheritance. Cardinal Victor Auguste Deschamps († 1883) tried to take up such suggestions and, by applying the 'method of providence', to present the Church as a moral miracle. In this sense the first Vatican Council spoke of the Church as '*signum levatum in nationibus*'.[5]

This line of argument has not always been free from triumphalism that ignores or glosses over the weaknesses and errors of the Church as pointed out by its opponents. Also, the fact that other churches and ecclesial communities are able to present impressive witnesses, too – even martyrs – and that, by departing from their different principles, they are also able to present their doctrine as coherent in themselves has often not been noted. Hence, an extension of the criteria did not provide a strict line of argument beyond any doubt.

In contrast, the perspective the Second Vatican Council took as the basis for its view on the Church, the Church as sign and instrument, leads further. The aforementioned properties also participate in this sign and service nature of the Church. In them the nature of the Church appears only symbolically and historically diversely fragmented. They point to the deeper nature of the Church and express it. Yet, they also demand a repeatedly new, trustworthy and convincing practical realization. Like the Christian faith in general, they become trustworthy only for the person who, in the light of a global experience of purpose and a basic decision, theologically put in the light of faith (*lumen fidei*), makes them the basis of his or her decision of faith.[6]

4.1 The one Church of Jesus Christ and the many churches

The confession '*credo in unam ecclesiam*', which stands in first place among the properties of the Church in the creed, became generally accepted only gradually in the Early Church,[7] until it moved to first place in the Nicene-Constantinopolitan Creed.[8] The confession of the one Church can mean different things. It can mean that there is only the one Church and that there cannot be several churches. Unity can also mean inner unity, that is, being undivided, and thus the identity of the Church with itself and the unanimity in the Church.

Unity as the unicity of the Church

To begin with, let us look at unity in its first sense as the unicity of the Church.[9] The biblical confession to the one and only Church has its place in the overall framework of the Old and New Testament salvation history. It is in accordance with the confession of the one, only and totally unique God (Deut. 4.35; 6.4f.; Isa. 45.6.18.21; Mk 12.29.32; 1 Cor. 8.6; Gal. 3.20) with which the Bible sets itself apart, probably as a result of a long process, from the polytheism of its contemporary religious environment. It is in accordance with the confession to the one Lord, mediator and saviour (Acts 4.12; Eph. 4.5; 1 Tim. 2.5) through which we are baptized in the one Spirit into the one body of Christ (1 Cor. 12.12f.; Gal. 3.28). According to the fourth gospel, Jesus wants to round up the scattered sheep that there is one flock and one shepherd (Jn 10.16; cf. 11.52).

The unity of the Church does not result therefore from the free association of its members of several churches. The principle of unity and the prime basis for unity and unicity is the one God who gathers his people and unites them in Jesus Christ in the Holy Spirit.[10] Ultimately, the Church is one in the unity of the Father, and of the Son, and of the Holy Spirit.[11]

The unity and unicity of the Church follows also from calling the Church 'ecclesia'. In the only two passages in which the Synoptics speak of the Church, the word is always used in the singular (Mt. 16.18; 18.17). When Paul speaks of churches in the plural, he means, as will be shown, individual churches which each represent and make present the one Church of Jesus Christ. Each of them is not only a part but wholly the Church, although as individual churches they are not the whole Church.[12]

From the fact that within the New Testament there was a variability and development of community structures, it cannot be deduced that there can be several churches. It would be an anachronism to read into the New Testament the situation of today, which history produced, of separated denominational churches existing side by side.[13] In the eyes of Paul, such a coexistence and pluralism of different denominational churches would be a totally unbearable idea. The Church brought the different New Testament types of communities together in the New Testament canon. In so doing, the Church has given us a clear interpretative norm to read and take seriously the canon as a whole and to regard the different types of community not as a contradicting pluralism but as a complementary *communio*-unity of sister churches which are all the one Church. The thesis of the pluralism of church forms is only right insofar as unity does not mean a rigid uniformity but has to be understood as *communio*-unity.

In this sense we can note, from the overall context and the inner logic of salvation history as well as according to the will of Jesus, that there can be neither many churches nor pluralism but a plurality of churches in the one and only Church in which the many individual churches are united in *communio* through the one Lord and in the one Spirit.

Inner unity and diversity of the Church

The inner unity of the Church already follows from the foundation of the unity as unicity. Even on the evening before his suffering and death, Jesus himself prayed that all should be one (Jn 17.21). We read about the early community in Jerusalem: 'they remained faithful to the teaching of the apostles, to the brotherhood, to the breaking of the bread and to the prayers' (Acts 2.42). They were 'united in heart and soul' (Acts 4.32). Paul reacts forcefully against divisions in the Church: 'has Christ been split up?' (1 Cor. 1.13). For him, divisions are an eschatological trial.[14]

This inner unity must not be understood as purely external. Jesus Christ did not command the Church to unity; he united it in one faith and one Spirit, and formed it in one Spirit into one body of many parts.[15] The inner unity has its foundation in one Holy Spirit through one baptism (1 Cor. 12.13) and participation in the one Eucharistic bread (1 Cor. 10.17). Paul can even say we are 'one' in Jesus Christ (Gal. 3.28; Col. 3.11). Again and again Paul calls for unity and unanimity in the Church. He believes: 'there is one body, one Spirit, just as one hope is the goal of your calling by God. There is one Lord, one faith, one baptism, and one God and Father of all' (Eph. 4.4f.).

Particularly since Robert Bellarmine, a threefold unity has been deduced from these statements: unity in the one Holy Spirit through unity in one faith (*vinculum symbolicum*), unity in the sacraments (*vinculum liturgicum*) and unity in communal life under one apostolically founded ministry (*vinculum sociale seu hierarchicum*).[16] Vatican II adopted this teaching of the threefold unity.[17]

This inner unity does not mean uniformity. From a purely academic, intellectual perspective, unity is not a number but the measure of number and thus multiplicity.[18] Analogous to God's kingdom, the Church can be compared to a tree in whose ramified branches the birds of heaven, i.e. all peoples and cultures, have their place (Mk 4.31). Since the first Pentecost, there has been in the Church a diversity of nations and languages (Acts 2.1–13) and of charismas, but still only the one Spirit (Rom. 12.4–8; 1 Cor. 12; Eph. 4.7–12). Jesus speaks of a unity just as he and the Father are one (Jn 10.30; 17.11.21f.); in other words, of a unity of reciprocal being in each other. Accordingly, Trinitarian doctrine conceives the unity in God as the unity of the one God in three persons and as their reciprocal existing in each other. The relational unity in love should be the paradigm of unity in the Church. Just as three persons subsist in the one God, so the unity of the Church does not exclude but includes diversity. Hence, Vatican II spoke of a unity as *communio* after the prime image of the Trinitarian unity.[19]

The Church Fathers considered this diversity not as an impairment but as an expression of true catholicity. According to Irenaeus of Lyons, it is the diversity of customs which 'strengthens the unanimity in faith'.[20] In the dispute with the Donatists during his time as bishop of Hippo, for

Augustine the issue of unity and the worry about the restoration of unity became virtually the core issue of his life. He explicated unity in diversity in great detail, using the image of the dove in which the Holy Spirit descended upon Jesus at his baptism (Mk 1.10 par.): while the tongues at the descent of the Spirit at Pentecost are divided (Acts 1.3), they are united in the dove. 'There the tongues are divided, here the dove unites ... In the dove is the unity, in the tongues the community of nations.'[21] The one Spirit effects as the Spirit of love in the Church a unity in love and a bond of love (*unitatis caritatis, vinculum caritatis*).[22]

The Second Vatican Council adopted and unpacked in detail the biblical message of unity in diversity and diversity within unity. The one Church exists in and consists of many individual churches, and the bishop of Rome is to be the visible principle and fundament for unity of the diversity of the bishops.[23] Thus, notwithstanding the primacy of the see of Saint Peter, there are within the ecclesial community individual churches that rightly rejoice in their own tradition.[24] Also the one Gospel has been given to us in four gospels and from the beginning the one apostolic heritage has been received in East and West in different forms and in different ways.[25] Hence, for the sake of unity one should not place unnecessary burdens on the Church (Acts 15.28).

The Catholic Church considers this unity in legitimate diversity of cultures, spiritualities, theologies, individual churches, monastic orders, associations and groups as its strength. It contributes to the Church's trustworthiness and is a valuable good which every member of the Church should help to keep. Each member of the Church is thus called to live and act in the spirit of the *communio* as part of a greater whole (*sese ut partem gerere*), to keep the unity of the Spirit (Eph. 4.3) and to do the truth in love (Eph. 4.15).

Unity of the Church – unity of humanity

The issue of unity is a primal question of humanity. It is addressed in ancient philosophy from Heraclitus and Parmenides to Plotinus.[26] For Augustine also, unity is the principle of being; if unity is taken from a thing, it falls back into nothingness. Humanity's biggest enemy is, therefore, the *dissensio*; *concordia* is the basis for all national coexistence. Peace is a cosmic power which permeates and rules all being.[27] Thomas Aquinas, too, thought that '*ens et unum convertuntur*' (being and one are convertible).[28]

The unity and unicity of God, the one and only redeemer and mediator, and, in the context of this divine unity, the unity of the Church, bears enormous implications for the unity of humanity. After all, for the Bible the confession to the one God, the creator and father of all people, is the basis for the belief in one humanity. For the Bible, Adam is not simply the first human being; Adam is 'the' human being – Adam that is all of us.

Humanity forms one large community of fate (Acts 17.26; Rom. 5.12.15–19). As all have alienated themselves from God and entangled themselves in sin, we have also become alienated and estranged from each other. Through the one saviour and mediator, Jesus Christ, God intends to gather humanity which is, through sin, estranged from God and from each other into a new humanity. (Eph. 1.10). Jesus wanted to make a new start with the gathering of the scattered sheep of Israel, such that there would be one shepherd and one flock (Jn 10.16).[29]

The Church Fathers frequently emphasized the connection between monotheism and the unity of the Church.[30] The Second Vatican Council built upon this[31] and spoke of the one family of humanity.[32] In this it unmistakably rejected all ethnic, cultural, national and also religious hostilities and discriminations, and laid the foundation for solidarity of the whole human race.[33] This brings us again to a question which has become newly acute in the context of globalization and global migration and networking. Vatican II called this globalizing unity a sign of the times.[34] Particularly in this new situation, the Church is to be a sign and instrument of one humanity.[35] As the messianic people of God,[36] the Church is to be the seed – we could also say the heart – of the one new humanity.[37] From this, one cannot deduce a political theology or a horizontal, secular ecumenism.[38] The service of unity which the Church can render to mankind has its theological basis in its unity with God. The Church has to demonstrate to humanity this theological foundation of unity and, consequently, to live with it. Only as the sacrament of the unity with God is the Church also the sacrament of the unity of mankind.[39]

The scandal of divisions

From the very beginning there have been controversies and also divisions in the Church. This can already be seen in the controversies between Peter and Paul (Gal. 2.11–15), then in the factions and divisions criticized by Paul in the church of Corinth (1 Cor. 1.10–14; 11.19), as well as in the strict warnings and demarcations in the Johannine epistles (1 Jn 2.18–27; 2 Jn 7–11; 3 Jn 9f.). For Paul, such divisions are not the work of the Spirit but of the flesh (Gal. 5.20). They touch the fundament of the Church and are in opposition to its nature.[40] They are not the expression of a legitimate diversity in unity, but separations from the unity into a mutually contradicting plurality. It is therefore essential to distinguish between a legitimate, complementary diversity and a plurality which destroys unity through contradictory differences, which is in opposition to the will of Jesus Christ and a scandal. Expressed in the symbolic language of the Church Fathers, the seamless tunic of Jesus has been cut through by divisions (Jn 19.23f.).

If, according to Paul, divisions serve to test the faithfulness and trustworthiness of Christians, and the apostle says that factions do and must exist (1

Cor. 11.19), then this is obviously not to be understood as encouragement for divisions or a justification of factions. On the contrary, the 'must' (δεῖ) of which Paul speaks has in the context of the Bible a deeper meaning of a salvation-historical-eschatological necessity.[41] It is an eschatological-dogmatic statement.[42] The divisions are the work of man, yet they are also in existence according to divine decree. In them the discernment of the spirits occurs through which the faithfulness of the Christians is to be revealed. They are eschatological examinations.

In the later writings of the New Testament the concept of heresy (in contrast to schism and apostasy) developed, which became efficacious in history – that is, heresy in the sense of erroneous teaching and a different doctrinal opinion (2 Pet. 2.1; cf. Tit. 3.10).[43] Yet, one can only speak of heresy if it is a case of intentional and obstinate contradiction to the authoritative doctrine of the Church. Consequently, since Vatican II the term heresy cannot be applied to those who are born into another church and who are baptized and at home in it. It can only be applied to those that once stood in full communion with the Catholic Church and who gave this up out of a free and conscious decision. Obviously, as we are more aware today of the historical conditioning of doctrinal statements, the term heresy has also become less clear-cut and difficult to apply in this context. Nevertheless, the Church as pillar and fundament of truth (1 Tim. 3.15) cannot give up denouncing grave deviations from the truth as such and excluding stubborn dissenters from its community.

The primal division between Jews and Christians occurred due to the separation of Church and synagogue.[44] This was followed by a large number of divisions within Christianity. In all of these separations, besides questions of faith there were also non-theological (cultural, political, etc.) factors, and, additionally, often regrettable lapses of mutual understanding and love. Although some of them lasted relatively long and affected large parts of the Church, many of the splits within Christianity have not endured, for example the separations of the Arians and the Donatists. Mainly three major schisms have remained until today.

First, there was the separation of the Assyrian Church of the East after the Council of Ephesus (431) and the Oriental Orthodox Churches (Coptic, Syrian, Armenian, Ethiopian, Malankara) after the Council of Chalcedon (451). Then came the separation of the Orthodox churches, often identified more symbolically than historically with the excommunication of 1054; in reality it was a process of mutual estrangement which became visible in a horrible way in 1204 during the fourth crusade at the capture and destruction of Constantinople. Finally we must mention the schism of Western Christianity in the wake of the Reformation of the sixteenth century which in itself led again and again to further separations. As a result Christianity today presents itself as a very colourful, indeed confusing and contradictory kaleidoscope that does great damage to its credibility and missionary appeal.[45]

The Eastern and Western schisms are two different types of schism which cannot be considered on the same level. In the Eastern schism the basic sacramental and episcopal church structure was retained. This entails injuries on both sides. Still, although in an wounded way, we are basically one Church. The situation is different in the case of the Western schism. It touches the fundamental structure of the Church itself and has therefore gone deeper. Yet, ultimately it has also not gone to the final root. Through one baptism a deep unity with its base in Jesus Christ remains.

Divisions that contradict the nature of the Church are a serious issue and must not be taken lightly or excused. They are an expression of God's eschatological judgement upon the Church. For this reason, divisions cannot, so to speak, be patched up by human diplomacy and compromises or through minimal consensus. The ecumenical movement of the twentieth century, which initiated a countermovement to the history of divisions, was thus not simply human work but an impulse of the Holy Spirit.[46] There is no other way for it but the way of prayer and penance,[47] thereby taking the poison out of the divisions so that inflexible, life-destroying contradictions can become fruitful tensions. The movement is to overcome the contradictions but maintain the diversity of legitimate, mutually complementing and enriching traditions.[48] This way from multiplicity to diversity is not easy, but rather painful and difficult. Following the image of the Trinitarian unity, the unity to which it should lead can be no uniform church but only a unity in diversity and a diversity in unity.

Catholic and Reformation understandings of the unity of the Church

The basic difficulty of the trajectory of modern ecumenism way lies in the fact that Catholics and Protestants proceed from different concepts of unity. From a Catholic perspective, unity has its foundation ultimately in the incarnational, i.e. the divine-human sacramental nature of the Church. It thus includes both the invisible divine dimension of the Church, which can be grasped only in faith and in the unity in Christ's spirit, as well as its visible human dimension which, according to Catholic understanding, is constituted in the world as society. Besides the unity in preaching and in the sacraments, the communion with the successor of Peter and the bishops in communion with him pertain to the visibility of the Church.[49]

This gives unity a concreteness which is sometimes admired but also provokes opposition in other churches and church communities. From a Catholic point of view this concreteness corresponds to the concreteness of salvation history. God did not just become man, he became in fact 'this' man, Jesus of Nazareth, who lived at a specific time in a specific country within a specific people. That was already then a stumbling block and cause for contention for many (Mk 6.3 par.; Jn 4.4). In some respects this Christological concreteness continues in the scandal of the ecclesiological concreteness in 'this' church.

It is at this point that we probably touch the toughest issue in the Catholic-Protestant controversy. Also in Lutheran perspective the Church is no *civitas platonica*.[50] Luther spoke not so much of an invisible but of a hidden church.[51] In contrast, the distinction between invisible and visible church goes back to Zwingli and has gained particular importance in Neo-Protestantism.[52] Against the latent ecclesiological Docetism of this position, Karl Barth emphasized that the Church or the community was Jesus Christ's own earthly-historical form of existence.[53] Similarly, Dietrich Bonhoeffer spoke of Christ as existing in the community.[54] The difference – which still remains – becomes apparent when Reformation confessions say that for unity it suffices (*satis est*) to agree in the Gospel and the administration of the sacraments according to the Gospel.[55] Catholics will willingly accept that both pertain to unity. The difference concerns the institutional unity in the episcopal office which is in communion with the bishop of Rome.[56]

The question thus comes to a head if one asks not only about the nature (what) of unity but also about the concrete place (where) of the visible unity. Is the Church a somewhat free-floating entity which here and there in word and sacrament becomes event in the local churches or does unity beyond the community have a concrete place in history where it can be indentified?[57]

'*Subsistit in*'

The question about the 'where' of the Church confronts us with the much-discussed and controversial issue of the *subsistit in* in the Constitution on the Church of the Second Vatican Council. The Council declared that the one and only Church of Jesus Christ subsists in (*subsistit in*) the Catholic Church. In other words, the one Church is concretely present and remained to be concretely found in the church which is in communion with the bishop of Rome and in the communion of bishops among themselves.[58] Already immediately after the conclusion of the Council the main editor of the Constitution on the Church, the Belgian theologian Gérard Philips, predicted that a lot of ink would flow over this *subsistit in*.[59] This happened indeed. Several times the ecclesial magisterium has seen reason to interpret, in an authoritative way, the statement of the Council.[60] The amount of literature on this issue is enormous.[61] It contains in essence the whole doctrine of ecumenism. We can only summarize briefly here the most important aspects:

(1) The traditional position of the Catholic Church is that the Church of Jesus Christ is (*est*) the Catholic Church. This was the position advocated in the encyclical *Mystici corporis* (1943) and it was explicitly reiterated in the encyclical *Humani generis* (1950). This stated the total identity

of the Church of Jesus Christ and the Catholic Church. It left no space for the recognition of ecclesiality outside the boundaries of the Catholic Church. As unity was already given within the Catholic Church, a greater ecumenical unity was conceivable only by the other Christians returning into the fold of the Catholic Church.

The Second Vatican Council replaced the word '*est*' with '*subsistit in*'.[62] This wording was to achieve two goals. On the one hand, it should retain the claim that the Catholic Church is undetachable from the one true Church. On the other, at the same time it should create space for the recognition of elements of the true Church beyond the boundaries of the Catholic Church.[63] For this reason the *subsistit in* can be called an opening clause. With this, the claim of the Catholic Church was neither relativized nor taken back, but it is now no longer advocated in the sense of all or nothing. It was to say that outside the Catholic Church there was not simply an ecclesiological vacuum.[64]

(2) The following were named as ecclesial elements beyond the boundaries of the Catholic Church:[65] the written Word of God, the life of grace, faith, hope and love and other gifts of the Holy Spirit and visible elements of sanctification and truth.[66] In addition, *Lumen Gentium* 15 names baptism as an institutional element. One may assume that this is not intended as a comprehensive list. The Holy Spirit is at work in these elements in such a way that they have salvific significance.[67] The encyclical *Ut unum sint* even says that, to the extent that these elements are present, the Church of Jesus Christ is efficaciously present in these churches.[68] Although it is sometimes insinuated, this does not say that there is no salvation possible outside the Catholic Church. As these elements pertain to the Catholic Church and strive towards catholic unity, the non-Catholic Christians participate in an imperfect sense in the Catholic *communio*. The Council thus advocates a graded concept of Church according to which the non-Catholic churches and ecclesial communities participate in a graded way in the unity and catholicity of the Catholic Church.

(3) The Catholic Church is convinced that in it alone fullness of all means of salvation are present. Only in it the Church of Jesus Christ subsists in an undetachable and lasting way.[69] Therefore, the essential unity of the Church is already reality in it. Yet, its unity is flawed because of the divisions. The ecumenical dialogue is to heal these wounds. Through it the imperfect unity is to be brought to full unity. This dialogue is not only an exchange of ideas but also of gifts.[70] The goal of ecumenism is therefore not the return of the others, but a joint growth in catholic unity.

(4) This position of the Council is incompatible with the view that unity has been lost and still exists only in fragments and that first it has to be rediscovered and restored through ecumenical dialogue. In addition,

any form of ecclesiological relativism or pluralism is also incompatible, according to which the Church of Jesus Christ also subsists in other churches and ecclesial communities. Likewise the position advocated today by most of the Protestant churches and ecclesial communities, that all churches are part of the one Church of Jesus Christ and thus the one Church was more less the sum of all churches, is incompatible.[71] As these churches and ecclesial communities contradict each other in many respects, such a unity would be a sum of contradictions that could not last.

(5) As the Orthodox churches have retained the essentials for being the Church, the Catholic Church calls them true churches and recognizes them as such in the sense of local churches that are called sister churches of the Catholic local churches. The Council even declares that through the celebration of the Eucharist they build up the unity of the Church.[72] Even though they are not in full ecclesial communion, the Catholic Church and the Orthodox churches are practically already now the one Church. The Orthodox churches claim no less decisively than the Catholic Church to be the true Church of Jesus Christ; so far they have not officially adopted these clarifications of the Second Vatican Council. Anti-ecumenical Orthodox groups conclude that the Catholic Church was no true church but a heretical one. Hopefully a future pan-orthodox council will clarify this question.

(6) The situation is different with the churches and communities of the Reformation. They lack the apostolic succession understood in the historical sense and thus the full substance of the ordained ministry.[73] When they call themselves churches, they do not understand their church being in the same sense as the Catholic Church claims for itself. Hence, the declaration *Dominus Jesus* has stated that they were not churches in the actual sense (*non proprio sensu*) but ecclesial communities. '*Non proprio sensu*' does not mean that they were not churches at all, yet they are not churches in the actual sense, as the Catholic Church claims for itself.

Even though one can point to the fact that Luther himself did not like the word 'church' and instead spoke of community, in Latin *communitas*,[74] one must admit that this factually correct statement was quite brusque in form. It has hurt many Protestant Christians. One cannot deny the communities of the Reformation the right to call themselves churches according to their understanding and to use the title 'church' in their names (World Council of Churches, Church of England, Evangelical Church in Germany and so forth). Not to call them by their name was perceived by many as rudeness. Obviously, they then did not intend to refrain from answering with perhaps similar rudeness.[75] To avoid such irritations, in everyday usage one will speak of the evangelical churches while being aware that the word 'church' is used in a different sense.

(7) One must be aware that the difference becoming apparent here between the Catholic and Protestant positions is of essential nature and cannot be levelled because of some false irenic. As this difference concerns the respective understanding of the Church, it will not be easy to overcome. Fortunately, there are also converging tendencies on both sides. On the one hand, one speaks of elements of the true Church and, on the other, one says that non-Reformation churches can be part of the one Church. On this basis a respectful ecumenical conversation on this essential ecclesiological point of controversy should be possible for the sake of restoring full unity. This holds true even though today's mostly peaceful coexistence of different communities all claiming the title church for themselves is, in the eyes of the New Testament, an unbearable state we must not get used to.

We cannot be grateful enough that because of the one baptism and the many other elements of being the Church, by now the awareness of a great commonality has grown and, although not the one Church, what could be called the one Christianity has taken shape.

4.2 The holiness of the Church and sin in the Church

Holiness is considered the oldest attribute of the Church.[76] Already Ignatius of Antioch speaks of the holy Church.[77] This title was already among the earliest symbols.[78] In the Apostles' creed, holy is the only attribute of the Church[79] which finally entered the Nicene and Constantinopolitan creed.[80] With Hippolytus the original wording of the formula was probably: 'do you believe in the Holy Spirit in the holy Church?'.[81]

Holiness as the *mysterium tremendum* of God

In the liturgy we often confess to the holy Church quite thoughtlessly without reflecting much upon how little self-evident, indeed even irritating, this statement is today. The irritating aspect does not only concern the holiness of the Church, which is at times difficult to perceive behind the secular entanglements and different scandals, but the holy and the holy one as such. The holy as *mysterium tremendum fascinosum*,[82] a primordial experience of mankind, has largely been lost. In our world everything has become profane. In consequence, we have lost the fundamental (for all religions) distinction between holy and profane; there is no more space for the holy and the holy one. Holy signs have often degenerated into consumer items or folklore or they only serve to decorate and make solemn special moments of our personal and communal life.

The biblical word 'holy' (Hebrew *kados*, Greek ἅγιος, Latin *sanctus*) is derived from the root 'set apart, select, mark out and exclude'.[83] Holy in the sense of the Bible thus means what is set apart and excluded. Therefore the word 'holy' is related to the word 'pure' and 'clean' (ἁγνός).[84] God as the Holy One is the one different and separate from all that is worldly; he is the one totally other, or – in more abstract terms – the transcendent one. Holiness is his nature. He is the 'holy One of Israel' (Isa. 12.6), he alone and nobody and nothing else. When celebrating the Eucharist we sing in the glory '*tu solus sanctus*!'

For this reason, to meet the holy God is something terrible for Old Testament people. Like Moses at the burning bush, we can encounter God only with our faces veiled (Exod. 3.6), for no one can see God or he must die (Exod. 20.19; 33.20). One must not create an image of him, and his name must be kept holy (Exod. 20.4.7; Deut. 5.8.11). In Isaiah's temple vision, God appears in the full power of his divinity (*kabod*) as the three-times Holy One which fills the prophet with terror and fear and shakes him to the depths of his existence (Isa. 6.1–5). The grandeur of this experience shines through again in the last book of Scripture where the prophet of Patmos sees the many living things at the throne of God who all sing to him three-times holy (Rev. 4.8).

For Hosea, the experience of God's holiness is the experience of his mercy and love which upsets all worldly-human categories and literally turns them upside down (Hos. 11.8f.). Yet, even under this aspect of love and mercy God does not become the good-natured friend. Rather, his love and mercy illustrate his total otherness. On the other hand, as will be shown, through his holiness in unfathomable mercy and self-communicating love, the religious understanding of holiness as the total otherness of God is inwardly reshaped and changed. In his love, he, the Holy One, is close to man and lets him participate in his life (2 Pet. 1.4) and his holiness (Heb. 12.10).

The Church as the holy people of God

Only against the background of this understanding of God's holiness is it possible to comprehend what is meant when we speak of the holiness of God's people and the Church. When the Old Testament says that God chose a holy people out of pure grace (Exod. 19.6; Deut. 7.6; 14.2 et seq.), such an choice means the setting apart from all other nations and, at the same time, the obligation to be different from all the other peoples and to worship exclusively the one and only God. In addition to the first tablet of the Ten Commandments which decrees the worship of the one and only God, the second tablet demonstrates that worshipping the one and only God has fundamental consequences for respect for the sanctity of life, marriage and family and for the whole social life of the nation. That is why holiness is not possible without justice.

Finally, everything is holy that is linked with the cult of the one God: special holy places (such as the tent of the covenant, the temple, Jerusalem), holy times (in particular the Sabbath) and holy rites. It is not without reason that the cultic laws of holiness are given so much space at the covenant at Sinai. Holiness is therefore a relational term that can be understood only from the relation of the holy God with his people and the relation of the people to God as the Holy One.

The New Testament adopted the Old Testament perception of holiness and expanded it Christologically. Now Jesus the Christ is God's Holy One (Mk 1.24; Lk. 1.35 et seq.). According to the messianic prophecy (Isa. 11.2; 42.1), he is anointed with the Holy Spirit at his baptism in the Jordan (Mk 1.11 par.). At Pentecost the Holy Spirit is poured out over the Church (Acts 1.8; 2.2–4). Built upon the cornerstone Jesus Christ, all those who are baptized can now be built as living stones to a spiritual house. The Old Testament theology of the people of God can thus be transferred, on a Christological basis, to the Church: 'but you are a chosen race, a kingdom of priests, a holy nation, a people to be his personal possession' (1 Pet. 2.9). The Church is to become a holy priesthood to bring through Jesus Christ spiritual sacrifices which please God (1 Pet. 2.5) and to proclaim the great deeds of God (1 Pet. 2.9). In this sense the Christians perceived and called themselves 'the saints' (1 Cor. 16.1; 2 Cor. 8.4f.; 9.1f.; Rom. 15.25f. et seq.).

They are holy because they are sanctified through God's Spirit and the Holy Spirit lives in them. Hence, the Church is the temple of God and the temple of the Holy Spirit (1 Cor. 3.16f.).[85] As a result, the temple is no longer a house of stone but the Church as the community of believers. In fulfilling the prophetic criticism of the superficial cult and the promise of the new covenant which God has written in the heart through the Spirit (Jer. 31.33; Ezek. 1.19f.; 36.26f.), the letter to the Hebrews considers the external cult as abolished through the once-and-for-all performed sacrifice of Christ (Heb. 7.25–8.13; 9.11–28; 10.1–18). It is about spiritual sacrifices (1 Pet. 2.5), about the liturgy of faith (Phil. 2.17), about a living and holy sacrifice in which we offer ourselves to God (Rom. 12.1). Sanctified in the Holy Spirit, the Church is to administer, in a priestly manner, the Gospel and become a sacrifice that pleases God (Rom. 15.16).

These statements must not be misunderstood in a spiritualistic sense. Concretely, sanctification happens through the purification in the waters of baptism through the word (Eph. 4.26f.). As a holy temple which is to be built up in the Spirit into a dwelling place (Eph. 2.21f.) the Church has a structure like any other building, even though this is eschatologically preliminary. There will no longer be a temple in the new Jerusalem, for the temple is the Lord God and the Lamb (Rev. 21.22). Already now the earthly liturgy of the Church points to the heavenly liturgy of the lamb and makes it anticipatingly present (Rev. 4.1–11; 5.1–14 et seq.), so we can also call holy the liturgy of the Church and that which takes place in the liturgy. The Eastern church speaks of the divine liturgy, the Western church of holy mass.

To comprehend the whole deep dimension of the confession to the holy Church, we must return again to the idea of the Church as the temple of the Holy Spirit (1 Cor. 3.16; cf. 6.19). This statement takes up the Old Testament promise that God is with his people and dwells among them (Lev. 26.11f.; 2 Cor. 6.16–18). In John's gospel it is taken up again in the farewell discourses: 'Anyone who loves me will keep my word, and my Father will love him, and we shall come to him and make a home in him' (Jn 14.23).[86] The first letter of John speaks of the community (κοινωνία) we have with the Father and his son Jesus Christ (1 Jn 1.3).

From this there developed the doctrine of the indwelling of God and particularly of the Holy Spirit in the baptized and in the Church. Already early Eastern symbols speak in the third article of the Holy Spirit who lives in us.[87] Johann Adam Möhler in particular developed, in his early volume, *Unity in the Church* (1825), an explicitly pneumatocentric ecclesiology. He expressly distanced himself from Friedrich Schleiermacher and stressed that the Holy Spirit could not be identified with the community spirit of the Church.[88] He refers to Dionysius Petavius († 1652), who, like later theologians of the nineteenth century (Carlo Passaglia, Clemens Schrader, Matthias Joseph Scheeben), spoke of a non-appropriated indwelling of the Holy Spirit, that is, of an indwelling pertaining to him as Trinitarian person.[89] For Möhler, the nature of Catholicism is based upon this mysticism. The actual mystery of the Church is participation in the life of God and the vitality of God's Spirit in us.

One must let these statements sink in to comprehend in depth what the holiness of the Church means. If God's Spirit indeed dwells in the Church, then we must say of it (sentences said or sung at each church consecration or church blessing festival): 'How awe-inspiring this place is! This is nothing less than the abode of God, and this is the gate of heaven!' (Gen 28.17). Then Paul's warning will also be understood: 'If anybody should destroy the temple of God, God will destroy that person' (1 Cor. 3.17). At the very least, the result of this should be a more reverent way of speaking about the Church and a more respectful behaviour in the Church than is often the case.

Structural holiness

No matter how strong the powers of evil, lies and death may be, because of the eschatological finality of Christ's coming they will not be able to destroy the salvific work of Christ and remove it from the earth. They might cause severe damage in the Church but they cannot destroy it. It is true for the Church that the gates of the underworld – that is, of death – cannot overpower it (Mt. 16.18). The irreversibility of God's coming into the world entails the indefectibility (indestructibility) of the Church. No matter how many storms blow over and through it, it will always exist until the end of time. 'I am with you to the end of the world' (Mt. 28.20).

This indefectibility of the Church means its indefectibility as the Church of Jesus Christ. It is therefore more than an institutional guarantee for continuity. If it continued to exist only as an external structure and institution, it would be only a ruin or, at best, a museum. Yet, as Christ continues to live in the Holy Spirit in the Church, the Church can never stop being the Church of Jesus Christ. It may be wounded in many aspects of its being, but its fundamental nature as Church can never be lost. This means that the principles of the Church, its testimony and its doctrine of the Gospel and its sacraments are 'infallible' and cannot miss their purpose. The Church as a whole cannot fall into error, that is, it cannot lapse from the Gospel and proclaim a different gospel (Gal. 1.6.9).[90] Its sacraments cannot become empty rites which no longer mediate salvation. They are valid sacraments even if those administering them are totally unworthy.[91]

This structural holiness must not be misunderstood in the sense that the Church owns the holy and the means of salvation. Rather God has decreed about them that his mercy always proves stronger than any human weakness, however big. Indeed, the structural holiness presupposes that the sacraments are actually administered by the exalted Jesus Christ in the Holy Spirit.[92] Ultimately, the structural holiness of the Church means the indissoluble connection of Christ and the Church.

Of course, one may ask if the adjective 'objective' is a an appropriate choice for this. It has its legitimate place for the distinction between the subjective holiness of a holy and saintly life. Yet, in our linguistic environment, 'objective' has the aftertaste of factual, sober, prosaic, dry, unpoetical inelegance and independence of personal affectedness. In consequence, the term 'objective' creates the idea that holiness is simply an 'object' which is indeed given to us, but which we then 'have and own'. This term does not let one feel the affectedness which reaches down to the ultimate depths of existence, the affectedness by God's holiness, by his presence, by the participation in him, by the joy of eschatological hope. Yet it also does not let one feel its character of judgement about all uncleanliness and sin. We must overcome this objectification and discover the deeper personal sense, to regain the joy of faith and of the Church.

All are called to holiness

The holiness given by the Spirit is above all a gift; yet it is then also a vocation, and so becomes the challenge to live a holy life in accordance with the given holiness. Already in the Old Testament we repeatedly find the warning: 'you must be therefore holy, because I, your God, am holy' (Lev. 11.44f.; 19.2; 20.7.26). The New Testament adopts this admonition (1 Pet. 1.16; 1 Jn 3.3). Jesus says in the same vein: 'you therefore must be perfect, as your heavenly Father is perfect' (Mt. 5.48). Luke writes: 'be compassionate just as your Father is compassionate' (Lk. 6.36). With the commandment to love God, holiness includes also love for the neighbour and so also justice. It is even more than all burnt offerings and other sacrifices (Mk 12.31f. par.). All are called to this holiness (1 Thess. 4.3; Eph. 1.4). For Paul, the holiness of the Church as temple of God entails that we cleanse ourselves from all impurities and strive God-fearingly for perfect sanctification (2 Cor. 7.1).

Unfortunately, this primordial biblical statement has often been forgotten. The call to holiness was often not perceived as vocation for the 'normal' Christian in the daily life of the world but only as a call for a few chosen ones. As a result, the saints were often and still are seen as exceptional Christians. Colloquially we even speak of 'funny saints', by which we mean eccentric Christians. In contrast, Vatican II emphasized again the general call to holiness.[93] The beatitudes of the Sermon on the Mount apply to all and the evangelical counsels apply[94] in a specific way to those in religious orders, but they are addressed to all who follow Jesus Christ. Charles Journet pointed out impressively and profoundly that sanctification and holiness are the purpose and objective of the Church and the why of its existence.[95]

So we must ask even more: what do holiness and sanctification of life mean? In the light of what has been said previously, it should be obvious that, because of Jesus' criticism, this excludes a purely external, cultic-ritualistic holiness. It is about a liturgy of faith (Phil. 2.17), a living and holy sacrifice in which we offer ourselves to God (Rom. 12.1). It is thus not about an occasional excursion into spirituality but about the sanctification of the whole life. In the Lord's Prayer, Jesus speaks of the sanctification of God's name (Mt. 6.9; Lk. 11.2). What this implies emerges out of the Jewish context,[96] namely, that God himself is subject and reveals his name (Lev. 10.3; Ezek 36.2f.; 38.23; 39.7), as well as that we become subjects who keep his name holy and live according to his will and commandment (Exod. 20.7; Lev. 22.32; Isa. 29.23).

Very early on the Lord's Prayer had its place in the liturgy and the baptismal catechesis. This highlights that its fulfilment was not perceived in the sense of a justification by works, but as a work of the Holy Spirit in us and through us. It is only the Spirit that can make us a new creation (2 Cor. 5.17; Gal. 6.15) which has fundamentally happened through the new birth in baptism (Jn 3.5). Understood in this way, sanctification would mean to let the truth of baptism become reality in life and to live as new human beings. Paul describes it in this way in Romans 6.3–11 and 1 Peter 1.13–25 in his baptismal paraenesis: 'all who are guided by the Spirit of God, (i.e. not by their own will, but let themselves led and driven by him in their lives), are sons of God' (Rom. 8.14). In contrast to those of the flesh, holiness shows itself in the fruits of the Spirit: love, joy, peace, peace, patience, friendliness, mercy, faithfulness, gentleness and self-restraint (Gal. 5.22; cf. 2 Cor. 6.6; 2 Pet. 1.6f.).[97]

In the course of church history there have been many charismatic awakenings and movements which have shaken the Church out of the danger and temptation of becoming bourgeois. It is thus impossible to write the history of the Church only as an institutional history, and certainly not as criminal history. It is above all a history of saints and of sanctification and renewal movements. They are a sign that the power of the Holy Spirit has remained efficacious in the Church. For this reason Vatican II stressed its appreciation of monasticism and religious orders and spiritual communities that commit themselves in a special but not exclusive way to a life according to the beatitudes. The Council also recognized their significance for the present time.[98]

It is also part of the good fruits of the Council that, since then, awareness has grown of holiness in the world and the piety of the laity on the basis of baptism and confirmation, also of the sacrament of marriage.[99] Part of such a lay spirituality is the tension between 'in the world' but not 'of the world' of action and contemplation, profession and vocation, work and prayer, mysticism and politics (Johann Baptist Metz). Depending on each situation of life, it has manifold places: marriage and family, friendship and job, voluntary commitment in Church and society. Although the Christians and the Church live in the world, they are not of this world (Jn 17.14f.). They are set apart and are therefore in many respects different and they must not deny their difference. They live in the world under the normal conditions of the world and still they strive to be different in that they try to be everything for all.

The *Epistle to Diognetus*, an apologetic text from the second century, describes this tension beautifully: 'For the Christians are distinguished from other men neither by country, nor language, nor the customs which they observe. For they neither inhabit cities of their own, nor employ a peculiar form of speech, nor lead a life which is marked out by any singularity. [...] They dwell in their own countries, but simply as sojourners. As citizens, they share in all things with others, and yet endure all things as if foreigners. Every foreign land is to them as their native country, and every land of their birth as a land of strangers. They marry, as do all [others]; they beget children; but they do not destroy their offspring. [...] They pass their days on earth, but they are citizens of heaven. They obey the prescribed laws, and at the same time surpass the laws by their lives. They love all, and are persecuted by all. [...] They are poor, yet make many rich; they are in lack of all things, and yet abound in all'.[100]

In recent times, the Church has beatified and canonized a whole group of laypeople and elevated them to the honour of the altar. They lived in the middle of the world and yet they were not of the world, but lived the ideal of a Christian life in a most impressive way. In the year for priests 2009–10 Pope Benedict XVI called to mind the Curé of Ars, Jean Marie Vianney († 1859) and he called thereby again to mind also the vocation to holiness of 'world priests'.

Sin and sinners in the Church

If one considers the confession to the 'holy Church' and the general call to holiness, one can only notice with horror that there are sin and sinners in the Church. Sinners are not just some really 'bad Christians'. We are all sinners. This is not only the case today; it has been so from the beginning. Jesus already spoke of the weed among the wheat (Mt. 13.24.40) and of the good and bad fish caught in the net of discipleship (Mt. 13.47–50). The Acts of the Apostles and the Pauline Letters do not hide the fact that there was sin in the early communities of the Church.

We hear of the fraud of Ananias and Sapphira (Acts 5.1–11), of disputes between Paul and his collaborators (Acts 13.13; 15.36–41), controversies concerning the circumcision of the gentiles (Acts 15) between Paul and Peter (Gal. 2.11–15), factions (1 Cor. 1.10–17) and legal disputes (1 Cor. 6.1–11), grave moral failures in the communities (1 Cor. 5.1–12; 6.12–20), of misuse and disorder during worship (1 Cor. 10.14–11.34; 14.26–40) and of lapsing in faith (Gal. 1.5f.; 3.1; 5.4). The Johannine epistles even speak of anti-Christian movements (1 Jn 2.18–27; 2 Jn 7–11; 3 Jn 9f.). Above all, the Letter to the Hebrews shows that there was already at that time lukewarmness and weariness and the danger of lapsing from faith in the tribulations of the beginning of persecution. The many warnings we find in the New Testament letters demonstrate that even in the primordial apostolic period not everything was ideal and in order. The Church has never been only a church of the pure and saints. It has always included sinners also in its fold. If this was not the case, we all would not belong to it.

So it was clear from the beginning that there are sin and sinners in the Church. Yet, very soon it obviously also became a problem for the Church. How can one be a part of the Church, part of the body of Christ, if one does not have the Holy Spirit and love, if one loses or denies faith, if one returns in his life to pagan and also for heathens scandalous behaviour? In the latter case Paul reacts decisively: 'you were not to have anything to do with anyone going by the name of brother who is sexually immoral, or is greedy, or worships false gods, or is a slanderer, or a drunkard or dishonest; never even have a meal with anybody of that kind. [...] you must banish this evil-doer from amongst you' (1 Cor. 5.11–13). In a different passage he lets leniency prevail instead of punishment (2 Cor. 2.5–11). In other words, punishment is temporally limited and is the last resort, the drastic last means of mercy to achieve the conversion of the sinner. One can speak here rather of an educational and medical significance. In this sense Paul acknowledges what came later to be known as church discipline and church order.

Binding and loosing, i.e. banning and lifting the ban, pertains to the Church (Mt. 16.18; 18.18).[101] Yet, it is not a sign of a strong church but of one that has become weak and feeble if church discipline is not exercised. In that case, together with the holiness of the Church, God's holiness is not taken seriously either. Who plays God's mercy against his holiness has also misunderstood mercy. With the warning against cheap grace, Dietrich Bonhoeffer also warned of the loss of church order and church discipline. 'Cheap grace means the justification of sin without the justification of the sinner.' 'Cheap grace is the preaching of forgiveness without requiring repentance, baptism without church discipline, Communion without confession, absolution without personal confession.'[102]

This has nothing to do with rigorism which, beside the danger of laxism, appeared repeatedly throughout church history. The rigorist trends such as Montanism wanted a church of the pure and the saints. After the persecutions the problem became pressing in the controversy over the rebaptism of heretics, in the disputes with the Donatists, the Cathars, with Wycliffe and Hus and with the Jansenists. The Church called to mind Jesus' admonitions to forgiveness (Mt. 6.14f.; 18.21f.23–35 et seq.) and also the line in the Lord's prayer, 'forgive us our trespasses as we forgive those who trespass against us' (Mt. 6.12; Lk. 11.4). This rules out a hard-hearted rigorism. Therefore, against initial opposition the Church allowed for the possibility of a second conversion and developed for this a special order of penance which took shape particularly in the sacrament of penance. The neglect of penance and the sacrament of penance are therefore an alarming indication of crisis which touches the Church to the core of its nature as holy Church.[103]

In order to solve the problem of sinners in the Church theologically, it is necessary to make important distinctions. Only those who have the Holy Spirit and live in faith and in love and with the Church can belong fully to the Church. Whoever dissociates himself from it through grave sin, because of God's faithfulness, does not fall out the efficaciousness of the Spirit which calls him in his conscience to repentance. Yet, as long as he suppresses the voice of the Spirit in his conscience and does not follow it, he is, so to speak, a dead member of the Church and, as such, a wound in the body of the Church.[104] Also the everyday sins of Christians wound the membership in the Church and weaken the radiance of the Church in the world.[105] If sin in the Church becomes rife, it can cause schisms,[106] as it has caused modern atheism.[107] These distinctions were theologically reflected with the statement that the baptized can lose baptismal grace, yet there remains the character *sacramentalis*, i.e. the baptized retains lastingly the character of the vocation given to him once and for all in baptism by God who is faithful even if we are unfaithful.

A sinful Church?

As Augustine realistically demonstrated, the Church is a *corpus permixtum*.[108] The Church Fathers did not hesitate to say that the pure bride of Christ can also take on the features of an unfaithful prostitute and that the spirit of Babylon can enter it.[109] Clearly, there is no reason for ecclesial triumphalism and under no circumstances can it be about remaining silent or glossing over scandalous behaviour of official representatives of the Church.

Against much opposition within and outside the Curia, during the liturgy for the first Sunday of Lent in the Jubilee Year 2000 Pope John Paul II did not hesitate to speak in an impressive service of repentance the *Mea culpa* of the Church.[110] He did not only speak of individual sinful errors within the Church but also of structures of sin (not sinful structures!) in the Church. He meant structures, mentalities and ways of behaviour in which sinful deeds of individuals have become structural and in terms of attitude habitual and have been strongly established.[111] They then concern not only individual acts but a habit of social life, exercise of ministry and teaching office, and the administration of sacraments.

The terrifying dimensions such habitual structures and mentalities can take on shows, for example, in the talk of the 'Babylonian captivity of the Church', which was common even before Luther and lasted 68 years. The poet Petrarch called the fortress-like papal palace at Avignon a 'hell of ghosts and devils' and 'the sink of all vices'. Another example is the hysteria of the witch-hunting era (which occurred also in non-Catholic regions) in early modern times. These are terrifying phenomena that one cannot gloss over and which one should not explain away all too easily with reference to the historical situations. Not only individual 'sons and daughters of the Church' but holders of highest office and the earthly church consisting of sinful humans can err and get stuck in behaviours, structures and mentalities which are expressions of being entangled and caught in sin.

Such horrifying experiences have led to the question: does it suffice to speak of sin and sinners in the Church, or does this not rather necessitate to speak of a sinful Church? The counter question is: can we indeed call the Church, which we confess as the body of Christ and temple of the Holy Spirit, the subject of sinful behaviour and thus sinful Church?

The Reformers could speak from their ecclesiological basis of the sinfulness of the Church. Luther even called the Church the greatest sinner, saying in a sermon: 'there is no greater sinner than the Christian Church'. It is simultaneously just and sinner for, because it is holy, it can pray for the forgiveness of its sins. The saint prays appropriately for the forgiveness of his sins. It is therein that he shows his holiness.[112] Luther here applies hereby to the Church the *simul iustus et peccator* from the doctrine of justification. From a Catholic point of view, both are not possible. Despite the basic agreement concerning the doctrine of justification, it has not been possible to completely solve the problems regarding the *simul iustus et peccator*.[113] Likewise similar problems arise in the application of the axiom to ecclesiology.

When we speak theologically of the Church, for Catholic understanding, the Church is not in sociological terms the total and sum of its members – including priests, bishops, Christians in religious orders, together with the pope. If one spoke of the Church in this sociological way, then one could speak of the sinfulness of the Church in an analogous way, in the actual sense that only a human being can be sinful. For this reason it is better, in the sociological sense too, to speak of structures and mentalities of sin in the Church rather than sinfulness. Yet, the Church is more than a sociological entity. It is the body of Christ, its head is Jesus Christ and its soul is the Holy Spirit. Not only the earthly church belongs to it but also the heavenly Church, the angels and saints, especially Mary whom we call Immaculata and who as such is the type of the Church. Proceeding from this theological understanding of Church, it is not then possible to call the Church sinful, for neither Christ nor the Spirit can be the subject of sin. So if we say that the Church is free from sin but sinful in its members, then the holiness and sinlessness of the Church are based on the sinlessness of Jesus Christ. We can likewise say that the Church as *ecclesia congregans* is free from sin, but as *ecclesia congregata*, as sociologically measurable earthly people of God, it is sinful.[114]

Karl Rahner advocates a different theory. Together with the Second Vatican Council he starts from the sacramental divine-human nature of the Church and claims that the visible human dimension of the Church is a constitutive part of its sacramental nature. The human dimension of the Church is the quasi-sacramental, real-symbolic form of expression of what it is. It is in this sense that Karl Rahner wants to speak of the sinful Church.[115] To do justice to this thesis, which he unfolds very differentiatedly, one must take into account that, strictly speaking, it intends to speak of the sinful Church for only one – albeit essential – aspect for being Church, the earthly human aspect. There is nothing to be said against this. However, the weakness of his thesis is that it does not take into account the fact that, as head, Jesus Christ is the subject of the Church and the Holy Spirit is its soul, which is an even more essential dimension for the sacramental understanding of Church. It also does not consider the heavenly Church which is essentially connected with the earthly church. If these aspects, all constitutive for the theological nature of the Church, are included in the consideration, it is totally impossible to speak of the sinful Church. This does not rule out the possibility of speaking not only of sinners in the Church but openly and honestly of sinful structures and mentalities in the earthly church.

Ambrose expresses this idea in a less abstract and far more concrete manner. As Christ, who is himself without sin, nevertheless took our sins upon him, in fact he made himself to be sin on our behalf (2 Cor. 5.21), so does the Church in an analogous way carry the sins of many.[116] Together with some mystics we can say that Jesus suffers in and with his Church the sins in the Church; they are painful wounds of his own body which is the Church. Many saints consider it their vocation to suffer vicariously with Christ the sins in the Church. Indeed, because the Church is holy, there is no other way for it than to carry and suffer vicariously the burden of the sin of its members and of the world in order to heal and sanctify them. In its service for the sanctification of the world and its own members, the Church has no other option than to enter the field of sin and to act in it.[117] This exposes it to temptation to which many often fall victim. Still, it pertains to the paradoxical nature of the Church that precisely its holiness makes it appear as a sinner, which makes it thus open to attacks and injuries. To put it pointedly: it is holy not although, but because, sinners belong to it and it bears their sin to heal and sanctify them.

Ecclesia semper purificanda

The Church, which has sinners in its fold and displays sinful structures, exists between the already and the not-yet. Now we carry our treasure in earthen and fragile vessels (2 Cor. 4.7). Only eschatologically will the Church be 'without stains and wrinkles' (Eph. 5.27) in its full splendour and full beauty.[118] Therefore, the Church can only be credible in calling itself the holy Church if it continuously goes the way of repentance, renewal and reform.[119]

Vatican II speaks of the *ecclesia semper purificanda*.[120] In fact, throughout history there have constantly been renewal movements. There was the emergence of monasticism in the Old Church, medieval renewal movements triggered by Bernard of Clairvaux and Francis of Assisi, the *Devotio moderna* in the late Middle Ages, the Catholic renewal movement even before and after the Reformation, the biblical, liturgical and ecumenical renewal in preparation for Vatican II, as well as the post-conciliar beginnings and spiritual movements. In each congregation every celebration of the Eucharist begins with the general confession of sins and the prayer for forgiveness. It is absolutely impossible even to imagine something similar for a secular gathering like a party conference or a parliamentary debate.

Of course, it must not stop at ritually repeated or publicly proclaimed confessions of sin and prayers for forgiveness. It necessitates an inner conversion and a 'renewal of the inner life of our minds'.[121] It must become concrete. This entails the purification of awareness and the admission of historical faults. The Church must change if it does not want to be changed by others. There is no way for it to keep its Tradition other than by renewing it and itself. This is not possible without painful processes of repentance and purification, nor without personal sanctification.

Regarding renewal, it is necessary to distinguish true renewal from innovations and false renewal. True renewal means something totally different from building a new church. It is not about a new church, but a Church renewed out of the spirit of Scripture and Tradition. This renewal cannot be accomplished by secular means, above all not by violence; in this one would only pull out the good wheat together with the weed (Mt. 13.29) and destroy more than build up. True renewal cannot happen according to worldly motives and aspects such as appearing good and advantageous before the world and being applauded by the world. These can only be a short-lived flash in the pan. It is about becoming evangelical in the original sense of the word; that is, not only to preach the Gospel with the call to follow and the Sermon on the Mount, but also to live it.

Whoever wants to renew does not only make himself friends in the Church; he will also have to survive opposition from within its ranks, misunderstandings and false accusations. He will have to bear this with forbearance and generosity, with impatient patience and patient impatience without becoming embittered inside. Love is patient and kind, love is never jealous. It is not irritable or resentful (1 Cor. 13.4f.). The renewal of the Church thus presupposes one's own renewal, conversion and sanctification. At all times it has been the saints who renewed the Church. Time after time they have succeeded in making shine anew the undetachable holiness pertaining to the Church.

4.3 The greatness and scandalousness of the catholicity of the church

What is the meaning of 'catholic'?

After unity and holiness, the creed names 'catholic' as the third property of the Church.[122] However, the term 'catholic' is not found in the New Testament. Still, the term 'catholic Church' is already found in some early symbols[123] and in the *canones* of the first ecumenical council of Nicaea (325).[124] It then found its place in the Nicaean-Constantinopolitan creed (381).[125]

Today, when we speak of the Catholic Church, it occurs usually as a name for a denomination. We then understand 'Catholic' as distinct from the Orthodox and Protestant churches and church communities. Naturally, as the early symbols are in fact jointly ecumenical until today, such a denominational understanding aiming for distinction is alien to them. In the original literal meaning 'catholic' did not have a distinguishing connotation, rather it meant the whole and total which is more than the sum of its parts. 'Catholic' meant wholeness in the sense of fullness.[126]

Even though the word 'catholic' is not found in the New Testament, there are factual equivalents such as the comprehensive fullness of salvation (πλήρωμα) in Jesus Christ (Col. 1.19; 2.9). The term itself is used for the first time by Ignatius of Antioch. 'Where the bishop appears, there let the people (πλῆθος) be, just as where Jesus Christ is, there is the catholic Church (ἡ καθλικὴ ἐκκλησία).'[127] In contrast to the individual community, whose legitimate head is the bishop, catholic Church means here the whole Church which is everywhere where Jesus Christ is and where he is heard.[128] Jesus Christ is the fullness and the Church is catholic insofar as it participates in this fullness.

We find the same Christological rationality for catholicity in the *Martyrdom of Polycarp* (circa 160). Yet, while for Ignatius 'catholic' does not yet have a specific ecclesiological meaning, now, as it were, the conclusion is drawn from the general participation of all individual communities in Jesus Christ. The epistle is addressed to all communities of the holy catholic Church in all places.[129] The catholic Church is the one Church scattered on the whole world.[130] Jesus Christ is the shepherd of the catholic Church throughout the whole wide world.[131] As the scattered individual churches participate in the fullness, they are called catholic beyond the epistles of Ignatius. Polycarp is thus called the bishop of the catholic church in Smyrna.[132] This shows that from the beginning the name 'catholic' was connected with the episcopal structure of the Church and the unity of the episcopate.

Augustine was completely inspired by the idea of unity. As bishop, the controversy with the Donatist schism became for him the mission of his life. He denies the Donatists that they were the true Church because they were not in universal *communio*. Catholic meant for Augustine the worldwide universal Church in contrast to the schismatic, solely local divisions.[133] *Catholica* comes from καθ' ὅλον and means *secundum totum*, spread over the whole world.[134] In the case of Augustine, this geographic understanding must be seen in a wider context. For him unity is the basic principle of every community and the unity of the Church consists of love: love is at the heart of the Augustinian understanding of Church. Divisions that fall from love therefore destroy the Church and one's own church being.

Cyril of Jerusalem brings both meanings together, though the emphasis is clearly on the qualitative understanding. 'It is called Catholic then because it extends over all the world, from one end of the earth to the other; and because it teaches universally and completely one and all the doctrines which ought to come to men's knowledge, concerning things both visible and invisible, heavenly and earthly; and because it brings into subjection to godliness the whole race of mankind, governors and governed, learned and unlearned; and because it universally treats and heals the whole class of sins, which are committed by soul or body, and possesses in itself every form of virtue which is named, both in deeds and words, and in every kind of spiritual gifts.'[135] According to the axiom of Vincent of Lérins († around 435), catholic is that which has been and is believed everywhere, always and by all.[136] According to this, catholicity has a diachronic and synchronic meaning.

The adjective 'catholic' has thus a qualitative meaning in the sense of the fullness of salvation as well as a geographical meaning in the sense of universality. It means truth as well as authenticity, believing the whole and the orthodox [in the sense of correct, T.H.] faith and also geographical universality. Thomas Aquinas still understood catholicity not primarily quantitatively and numerically but in the sense of fullness.[137]

Denominational narrowness

The tragedy that marks the story of the development of church history is that the property of the Church which should express its universality and participation in the Christological fullness has become the symbol of denominational exclusion and division.

The origins of denominational narrowness reach far back. Already in the *Codex Theodosianus* (438), through which the Church formally became the imperial church, only the proper church is recognized by imperial law; it alone was allowed to bear the '*nomen christianorum catholicorum*'. This rule was incorporated in the *Codex* of Justinian (529–34) and also had legal validity within the imperial law of the Holy Roman Empire of the German Nation. It made it possible to punish heresies and schisms according to imperial law. In addition, the popes after the Gregorian reform in the eleventh century laid exclusive claim for the Roman Church as *mater omnium catholicorum*. The *ecclesia catholica* was thus identified with the *ecclesia romana* until its exaggeration by Boniface VIII, who declared in the bull *Unam sanctam* (1302) that there was no salvation outside the Roman church and in obedience to the successor of Peter.[138]

Yet, this ideal and reality drifted increasingly apart. The Orthodox churches separated from Rome have naturally always regarded themselves, and still do, as explicitly catholic. Above all, they do this in the qualitative sense of the word as participation in the fullness of God's Trinitarian life. Catholicity is for them, because of the *Urbild-Abbild* scheme, a spiritual as well as an empirical reality. In particular the more recent Orthodox theology often connects the term 'catholic' with the Eucharistic *communio* ecclesiology whereby the local ecclesial Eucharist communities are connected through councils and synods and are thereby one church. It is also often combined with the sobornost-doctrine of the trans-individual unity and wholeness of a people and the Church (Vladimir Soloyev, Sergei Bulgakov, Nikolai Lossky et seq.).[139]

The reformers of the sixteenth century also kept, together with the common symbol of the old Christianity, the confession to the catholic Church. Although they interpreted the attribute 'catholic' according to their own ecclesiological conviction, they did not want to dissociate themselves from the old catholic Church, but from the Roman church of their time.[140] Already for imperial legal reasons they had to struggle to be called and recognized as the catholic Church. Only when integration in imperial law became obsolete with the secularisation of 1803 did catholic become a distinguishing and separating denominational name that on the Protestant side has had negative connotations from then on.

On the other hand, Catholic apologetics tried to demonstrate that all four *Notae ecclesiae* are realized in the Catholic Church, which led to a denominationally separating catholicity that was often practically identified with being Roman. In the situation of denominational pluralism the name

Catholic no longer sufficed without the complement Roman-Catholic. So the *Confessio fidei Tridentina* (1564) confessed explicitly the *sancta catholica et apostolica Romana ecclesia.*[141] In contrast to the Protestant focus on the *particula exclusiva* (*sola fides, sola gratia, sola scriptura*), the Catholic 'and' (faith and love, grace and works, Scripture and Tradition) was emphasized as sign of true catholicity. The inconsistency of this attempt becomes apparent in the fact that, precisely by intending to demonstrate one's own catholicity, one set oneself apart again and became particularistic.

Overcoming denominationalism

Out of the spirit of Romanticism and its holistic thinking, Johann Sebastian Drey and Johann Adam Möhler tried to lead the Church out of denominational narrowness and renewed again the original patristic understanding of catholic.[142] Representatives of a high-church neo-Lutheranism followed them in this (August Friedrich Christian Vilmar, Wilhelm Löhe, etc.). Within the Anglican Communion, a similar return occurred in the Oxford Movement. In the Catholic Church in the wake of the ecclesial renewal, inspired by Möhler among others, it was Henri de Lubac and Yves Congar and, in Germany, Karl Adam in particular who rediscovered the original holistic meaning of catholic.[143] Indeed, catholic frequently became an overall attitude, a holistic world view.[144]

The Second Vatican Council adopted the renewed holistic view. The Council emphasized anew the all-inclusive extent of the catholic as well as its unity within the inner diversity of nations, cultures, local churches and charismas,[145] without, however, giving up the particular connection to the Catholic Church in the institutional sense which alone has the fullness of the means of salvation.[146] Although the Orthodox do not recognize the primacy of the bishop of Rome as taught by Vatican I and II, this led to a new relationship with the Orthodox churches. Already the council of Florence (1439–45) spoke almost naturally of the unity between the Western and Eastern churches.[147] Vatican II finally acknowledged that the whole spiritual, liturgical, disciplinary and theological heritage of the Eastern churches with their different traditions belongs to the full catholicity and apostolicity of the Church.[148]

A similar change occurred in the Protestant ecumenical context. The first plenary assembly of the World Council of Churches in Amsterdam (1948) still understood catholic in the sense of a sacramentally, episcopally and centrally constituted type of church which was in contrast to the Protestant one, seeing the Church more as an event. Yet, even before that, renowned Protestant theologians (Nathan Söderblom, Friedrich Heiler, Paul Tillich, etc.) had already spoken of a Protestant catholicity. This was taken into account by the plenary assembly of the World Council of Churches in Uppsala (1968), which saw catholicity as a quality pertaining to the nature of the Church. Of course, this brought the World Council of Churches in danger of drifting towards a secular catholicity.[149]

Meanwhile, important representatives of Protestant theology claim the name 'catholic' naturally for the Protestant churches (Karl Barth, Werner Elert, Ernst Kinder, Edmund Schlink, Ulrich Kühn, Gunther Wenz, etc.).[150] It is therefore a specific German development that German-speaking Protestant Christians replace the phrase 'catholic Church' in the joint creed with the confession of the 'common' or 'Christian Church'.[151] On a global scale, today the term 'catholic' has lost its function for denominational demarcation and also its function as a deterrent. Today we can assume on all sides a holistic understanding of catholicity. With this, the continued existence of separated churches has become an even more pressing problem.

Catholic fullness

Let us first ask: what does the catholic fullness of the Church mean? Ultimately, it has a Trinitarian and Christological basis. After all, in Jesus Christ, the Godhead dwells bodily in its entire fullness (πλήρωμα, Col. 2.9; cf. 1.19). God desires to permeate everything (τὰ πάντα) in and through Jesus Christ (Eph. 1.10). The Church is his body; it is the fullness (πλήρωμα) of the one who in and through it fills the cosmos (Eph. 1.23). The universalization and concretizing of this essential catholicity is the work of the Holy Spirit, who leads the Church into all truth (Jn 16.13) and urges it to mission and thus to the involvement of all peoples and cultures.

On the one hand, the catholicity of the Church is thus in Jesus Christ and in the Holy Spirit a gift from God. On the other, it is a vocation through which the Church must fulfil, by way of mission, its own catholicity and realize it concretely. The Church's essential catholicity has therefore an eschatological dimension. Catholicity is the pre-occurrence of eschatological fullness in the particularity of the still-imperfect course of history.[152] Catholicity is not a static but a dynamic reality. Throughout history, the Church remains behind its own perfection. It is on the way to growing in the knowledge of the fullness and riches of Christ and to realizing them in all dimensions of its life and of human existence, to make them present in mission among all peoples and in all cultures, to become everything for everyone and to therefore be particularly with the poor and oppressed to make space again and again in its own ranks for the diverse charismas and to overcome divisions, narrowness and encrustations.

We can thus say that the Church is catholic wherever there is no selective gospel and no party ideology but where the whole faith of all times and places is held without reductions in its fullness, where it is confessed to all peoples and in all cultures for all people regardless of their nationality, sex, ethnic group or culture, where the faith refers to and is lived for all dimensions of humanity, where within the unity space is given to a broadest possible diversity, and where one is prepared in the Holy Spirit to listen to and learn of the ever greater and new of the fullness of Jesus Christ. Catholicity means therefore the opposite of narrowness and short-sighted stubbornness, of a polemic and apologetic mentality of separation; it means broadness, wholeness, fullness and universality. 'Catholic' is a fascinating 'object' to which one can confess without arrogance but with legitimate pride.

The Church as *concretum universale*

This understanding of the Church as universally open and holistic must not be understood in the sense of an undefined generality and an openness that is drifting towards being diffuse and unspecified. It does not mean a syncretism of all possible religions and world views in which positions alien to each other and that contradict each other are mixed to form a nondescript amalgam so that the uniqueness and distinctiveness of the Christian is distorted and lost. On the contrary, catholicity has its identity in Jesus Christ and cannot be detached from the unity, holiness and apostolicity of the Church.

Analogous to the perception of Jesus Christ as *concretum universale*, catholicity does not mean some undefined generality but concrete, visible and embodied universality; it is about catholicity in a concrete form.[153] Just as in Jesus Christ God has taken form not in any general humanity, but by becoming concretely 'this' man Jesus of Nazareth, it is analogously true that the fullness of salvation revealed in Jesus Christ is also present in the Church in a concrete, visible form. Thus, the Catholic Church is convinced that in it – which means in the church in communion with the successor of Peter and the bishops who are in communion with him – the Church of Jesus Christ is historically realized in a concrete, visible form, so that the Church of Jesus Christ subsists in it – in other words, it has its concrete form of existence.[154]

With this thesis the Catholic Church causes objection in the Orthodox churches as well as in the churches coming from the tradition of the Reformation. At first sight, it could seem that the communion with the successor to Peter, which is recognized by no other church, signifies a denominational narrowness.

Indeed, there is a pathological form of catholicity, a restricting and narrow-minded bureaucracy the thinking of which is ultimately un-Catholic and totally alien to reality, in that it has to regulate everything with one single pattern and which leaves little space for local ecclesial and cultural diversity and charismatic freedom. Understood properly, the connection to the historical succession in the episcopal office means that the Church is all-embracingly catholic not only in its presence (synchronic) but also with the Church of all times back until the apostolic origins (diachronic).

The communion with the successor of Peter creates a catholic universality, embracing all peoples and cultures, and, at the same time, an inner unity that no other church can present. The communion with the successor of Peter and with the bishops in communion with him does not mean therefore a narrowing of catholicity; it can and should rather be a sign and instrument of true catholicity.

Ecumenical catholicity

The ecumenical situation confronts us with the fact that not only the Catholic Church but all churches confess to belief in the one catholic Church. The Protestant churches speak of an evangelical catholicity, orientated to the norm of the Gospel, and they accuse the Catholic Church of a syncretistic understanding of 'catholic' which they contrast with evangelical definiteness and uniqueness. On the other hand, the Catholic side has spoken of a catholic 'evangelicity' [Evangelizität, T.H.], an understanding of the Gospel in the universal catholic consensus.[155]

The aforementioned principle of Vincent of Lérin appeared as a mediator. The principle was now understood in such a way that everything which is common to all churches in the creed or in the first centuries was authoritative. On this basis, early humanistic and irenic-orientated ecumenists aimed for an understanding that was often described by the term '*consensus quinquesaecularis*'. Their aim was to reach unity by way of a universal Christian council on the basis of the common fundamental articles of faith of the first five centuries and to regard the later additional articles as adiaphora.[156] Already in the sixteenth and seventeenth centuries this irenic concept met with opposition within its own ranks and was opposed as crypto-Catholic and syncretistic.

The concept of the *consensus quinquesaecularis* is found in a similar way in the concept of a *via media* as it was especially advocated in the context of the Oxford Movement in the Anglican Communion and which finds expression in the Anglican idea of comprehensiveness, which is a catholicity accepting every doctrine that does not contradict the basic principles of the Christian community.[157] This concept entered in substance the concept of ecumenical unity of the *Porvoo Common Statement* (1992).[158] It is also found in a substantially modified form in the concept of Protestant unity of the *Leuenberg Agreement* (1973) as a unity in reconciled differentness.[159] Also, in the Catholic enlightenment theology of the eighteenth century, in early Johann Adam Möhler and Ignaz von Döllinger († 1890), we encounter the classicistic idea of a normative initial period of the first centuries.[160] This idea also plays an important role in the ecumenical dialogue with Orthodox theology and their reference to the first millennium.[161] Still, it is also more or less explicitly spread far beyond ecumenical theology.

With the aid of the development idea according to which historical development cannot be fixed on one classical period, the classicistic idea was overcome by the later Möhler and John Henry Newman. On the other hand, a unity which tolerates contradictions as 'indifferent and equally valid' cannot last. Sooner or later, this causes new divisions or leads to indifference and relativism in the question of truth. For this latter reason, Pius XI, in the encyclical *Mortalium animos* (1928), rejected the ecumenism of the beginning of the twentieth century as 'pan-Christianism'. The Catholic Church's participation in the ecumenical movement became possible only after this relativizing momentum tending towards indifferentism could be overcome and 'Catholic principles of ecumenism'[162] could be formulated.

These Catholic principles proceed from an understanding of catholicity in a concrete embodiment which is given in the Catholic Church. And yet, they do not regard this as exclusive. They acknowledge in other churches and ecclesial communities manifold elements of sanctification and truth, elements that are not absent in the Catholic Church but which at times can be better developed in other churches. In this sense the other churches and ecclesial communities have, in different degrees and in different density, a share in the Church reality of the Catholic Church.[163] The ecumenical dialogue as an exchange of gifts can also help the Catholic Church to a more perfect realization of its own catholicity.[164]

In contrast to the model of mutual recognition of equal churches, this results in an ecumenical understanding of catholicity in concentric circles and a graded participation in catholicity. Whereas according to the previous model all churches are a part of the one catholic Church, the Catholic Church (similarly the Orthodox churches) teaches that, in it, the catholicity is given in a way of concrete shape (subsists), that other churches already participate in this to different degrees and should on the way of the ecumenical exchange participate in it ever more. Of course, the still-unsolved problem of ecumenism is that, because of the essential difference of both positions, a mediation of both concepts has not been possible so far.

On his way from Anglicanism and the Oxford Movement to the Catholic Church, John Henry Newman strove all his life for an adequate understanding of catholicity. He saw more and more that a via media was not possible and that catholic and Roman meant the same.[165] He concentrated this idea further and came to the conclusion that 'there was no medium [...] between Atheism and Catholicity, and that a perfectly consistent mind, under those circumstances in which it finds itself here below, must embrace either the one or the other'.[166] For him this conviction had its foundation in the faith in the one and only God and the one and only saviour Jesus Christ. This view might easily provoke opposition. Yet, whoever sees the powers of self-dissolution and self-destruction that repeatedly afflict Protestantism will not put this idea aside easily. Of course, one must add that Newman, after his conversion to the Catholic Church, complained about the narrow-mindedness, bureaucracy and senselessness of Rome and that it was against such faults that he articulated his hope for change.[167]

In the concreteness of its form, the Catholic Church will remain a scandalon, that is, a stumbling block, be it that one objects principally to its irritating concreteness, or takes offence in its sinfulness, weakness and narrow-mindedness, also of some of its representatives, which is factually not in line with its claim to catholicity. For this reason it pertains to catholicity and ecumenicity the willingness to repentance, renewal and reform. Without them, ecumenism is not possible[168] and catholicity is a claim which is hardly believable.

4.4 Apostolicity as a unique foundation and a perpetually new task

The fundamental significance of apostolicity

The attribute 'apostolic' as a description of the nature of the Church[169] is not yet found in the New Testament. We encounter it for the first time with Ignatius of Antioch who, in his epistle to the church in Tralles, characterizes this as apostolic.[170] The *Martyrdom of Polycarp* gives Polycarp not only the title 'catholic bishop of the catholic Church' but also 'apostolic teacher and prophet'.[171] Already the early symbols[172] and then the Nicaean and Constantinopolitan creed[173] confess the apostolicity of the Church.

The lasting authority of the apostles and the apostolic origin has its foundation in the nature of the revelation itself and in particular in the Christological fundament of the Church. Jesus Christ is the one sent by the Father; he is the *Apostolos katexochen* (Heb. 3.1). As he was sent, so he now sends the apostles: 'As the Father sent me, so I am sending you' (Jn 20.21). That they can fulfil their mission he sends them the Holy Spirit; he will remind them of everything he told them (Jn 14.26; cf. 17.18). So the Church is built upon the fundament of the apostles and prophets (Eph. 2.20). The lasting authority of the apostles can be understood against the background of the rabbinic schaliah-institute. This is based on the following principle: the sent one is identical to the sending one. That means the emissary is not just a simple delegate; he is rather representative of the sending one.[174] This view is also found in the New Testament: 'Anyone who listens to you listens to me; anyone who rejects you rejects me, and those who reject me reject the one who sent me' (Lk. 10.16; cf. Mt. 10.40; Jn 13.20).

The apostles are the original and first witnesses of Jesus' message and his resurrection. It is only through their testimony that we know at all of the resurrection. Without them, the message of Jesus' life and resurrection might have faded away totally unheeded and might be largely forgotten. For this reason the apostles and the apostolic testimony pertain constitutively to the revelation event. They and their testimony are therefore the fundament upon which the Church stands, indeed with which it can stand or fall. The Church is built upon the fundament of the apostles and prophets (Eph. 2.20).

The Apostolicity of the Church means that there can be no other and no new Gospel (Gal. 1.7). We are tied to the once-and-for-all, handed-down faith (Jude 3), the apostolic teaching and heritage (παραθήκη; *depositum*) (1 Tim. 6.20; 2 Tim. 1.12.14), and we must pass it on faithfully. It is for this reason that 'keeping' (Lk. 11.28; Jn 12.47; Acts 16.4; 1 Tim. 5.21) and 'remaining' (Jn 8.31; 1 Jn 2.6.27 et seq.) are basic words of the New Testament. The last book of the New Testament formulates the principle already documented in the Old Testament: add nothing and take nothing away (Deut. 4.2; 13.1; Rev. 22.18f.; *Didache* 4.13).

The confession to apostolicity is thus based on the idea that the Church is founded on the revelation which happened once and for all and that the Church is one and the same in all centuries. Apostolicity expresses the – for the Church essential – self-consciousness to be the Church of Jesus Christ in which Jesus Christ himself is heard through the mouth of the apostles. Whereas the properties of unity and catholicity refer to the synchronic *communio* of the Church existing in the present and whereas holiness emphasizes the transcendent connection, i.e. the community with God through Jesus Christ in the Holy Spirit, apostolicity is about the diachronic identity and continuity of the Church with the Church of the apostles and the Church of all times. While it might be tempting to swiftly write this off as dogmatic conservatism, a lack of flexibility, or the rejection of progress, it is, in fact, this faithfulness that prevents one from being exposed to all kinds of fast-changing trends and opinions (Eph. 4.14). With the apostolic foundation the Church has a good and reliable basis.

Different theologies of apostolicity

According to the synoptic gospels, Jesus chose the Twelve that they would be with him and he would send them (ἀποστέλλειν, Mk 3.14 par.).[175] Already during his earthly ministry, Jesus sent out his disciples to support his own mission (Mk 6.6–13 par.). Jesus probably only used the verb 'to send out', but he probably did not summon the Twelve apostles. The word 'apostle' (ἀπόστολος) is not contained in Mark's observation of sending out the Twelve. For the time of Jesus' earthly ministry, it is otherwise found only occasionally and then only secondarily in the first two synoptic gospels (Mk 6.30; Mt. 10.2).

It is not until Luke that the title apostle appears more frequently during the time of Jesus' earthly ministry (Lk. 6.13; 17.5 et seq.). With this, Luke wants to demonstrate the continuity between the ministry of the earthly Jesus and that of the risen and exalted Lord. This also becomes apparent in the criteria which the Lucan Acts of the Apostles present for the choice of Matthias: he should be 'out of the men who have been with us the time that the Lord Jesus was living with us, from the time when John was baptising until the day when he was taken up from us' (Acts 1.22f.; cf. 4.20; 10.38f.; 13.31). The later common tradition to speak of the twelve apostles goes back to this Lucan concept.

It is different for Paul. He was not an eyewitness to the proclamation of the earthly Jesus. He is not one of the Twelve. He calls himself the 'child untimely born' (1 Cor. 15.8). Paul therefore does not fit into the Lucan concept of the twelve apostles. Nevertheless he claims in his letters to be 'called to be an apostle, set apart for the service of the gospel' (Rom. 1.1; 1 Cor. 1.1; 2 Cor. 1.1 et seq.). The letter to the Galatians is the most explicit one: 'Paul, an apostle appointed not by human beings nor through any human being but by Jesus Christ and God the Father who raised him from the dead' (Gal. 1.1). Paul explains his claim to be an apostle with the fact that he saw the Lord (1 Cor. 9.1f.; Gal. 1.15f.). The direct encounter with the risen Lord is thus, for Paul, the decisive criterion for being an apostle. Yet, Paul is aware that he can fulfil his service only in continuity and communion with the other apostles. So, in order not to have run in vain, he seeks the approval of the apostles before him, in particular Kephas and James (Gal. 1.17–19; 2.1–15; Acts 15). So with him the criterion of historical continuity is complemented with that of community and collegiality. One is never an apostle as a private individual. The office of apostle can only be exercised in diachronic and synchronic community.

The eschatological-missionary dimension

The criterion of origination is not the only one for, in addition to the origin motif, there is the eschatological one.[176] The Twelve are chosen to represent the eschatological people of twelve tribes and they are later to judge the twelve tribes of Israel (Mt. 19.28; Lk. 22.30). Peter is already now given the keys to the heavenly kingdom (Mt. 16.17). The heavenly Jerusalem is built upon twelve stones bearing the names of the twelve apostles (Rev. 21.14). This is an aspect that takes us back to the essential idea of the heavenly Church. Beyond the solely linear authority derived by historical-linear succession from Jesus Christ and his mission, it gives the apostolic authority a certain vertical legitimation or representation. The apostles anticipate the eschatological judgement and participate in the power of the Kyrios, exalted to the right hand of the Father, as the head of the Church and ruler of the world. It is he who gives from heaven the ministries, including the office of apostle, and so builds up the Church (Eph. 4.11) and in whose name the apostles speak and act (Lk. 10.16; Jn 13.20) here and now.

In addition to the origin relation of the apostolic office, there is, so to speak, a vertical-eschatological relation. This is no longer just about the linear continuity with the origin but about its presence, in fact the identity of the exalted Lord speaking and acting here and now in the Holy Spirit.

Apostolicity does not only mean continuity but identity; it is the history in historicity.[177] One could speak of present-making memory (ἀνάμνησις) that is at the same time *memoria futuri*, anticipating present-making of the coming kingdom of God. Therefore, the apostolic dimension of the Church stands in the great context of the sacramental dimension of the Church, in particular the Eucharist, in which we celebrate the *memoria passionis et resurrectionis* and, at the same time and in anticipation, make present the heavenly Jerusalem.[178] In the West, this (dare one say) vertical eschatological dimension was largely lost in the second millennium in favour of a one-sidedly linear perspective.[179] Recovering it from the spirit of Scripture and the Church Fathers and above all from liturgy is of great ecumenical importance for the dialogue with the Orthodox churches.

Between the apostolic origin and the eschatological goal there is the time of the Church and its mission until the end of time (Mt. 28.18–20 et seq.). In addition, mission is not just an activity of the Church for spreading the Church; according to the testimony of the Acts of the Apostles, mission is carried, continued and initiated again and again by the Holy Spirit. He is the champion of mission. Mission thus does not simply mean passing on and spreading the apostolic message; it means making it present in each respective context. Such apostolic activity is not about external activities but about radiance from within; it is about a mission of dynamic attraction and presence. We are to make present and make shine the message of the Gospel in continually new encounters with old and new cultures.[180]

This eschatological foundation means that the transmission of the once-and-for-all transmitted Gospel does not happen in the manner of a coin passed on from one hand to the next whereby it gets more and more worn. In fact, the transmission is the work of the Holy Spirit who calls to mind and keeps present the word and work of Jesus Christ. He is to remind us of all that Jesus said and did; and on the other hand he is to lead us constantly into the truth (Jn 14.26; 15.26; 16.13). He is to keep the once-and-for-all transmitted teaching continually renewed so that it never becomes the old truth but remains young and fresh in indestructible and unspent newness.[181]

So the eschatological motive becomes foundational for the proper understanding of the apostolic Tradition. The once-and-for-all received apostolic message is not dead property. We cannot pass it on like a dead coin, we must not bury it timidly (Mt. 25.18.25); on the contrary we must make it fruitful and pass it on alive towards the future. On the one hand, the apostolic heritage is predetermined for us and, on the other, it is continually newly given to us in the Holy Spirit. It is *traditum* which is only present in the *actus tradendi*, in the act of faithfully receiving and actively passing on in the Church. This continuity with the apostolic origin is creative and innovative; it includes the history and development of dogma.[182]

This illustrates that the usage of the term apostle could expand already in the New Testament period. Missionary men who planted and built up churches such as Barnabas, James and others are also called apostles.

Similarly, the title apostle could likewise be applied to emissaries of the communities (2 Cor. 8.23; Phil. 2.25).[183] In the *Teaching of the Twelve Apostles* (*Didache*) we find rules for the reception of wandering apostles who were not tied to specific places but moved from one to another (*Didache* 11.3–6). In a further sense we speak also today of apostolic mission, apostolic zeal, apostolic commitment, etc., and, in addition, call certain Christians apostles of the poor, of the lepers, of the workers, of the youth and so forth. In this context, apostolic could also become the name for orders and institutions with such apostolic orientation (Apostolic See, apostolic vicar etc.) or documents (apostolic canons, apostolic constitution etc.). Accordingly, the terms apostle and apostolic can each be used in an analogous way quite diversely, whereby, however, the normativity of the unique apostolic office must not be obscured.[184]

In order that the living transmission of the apostolic Tradition does not become arbitrary, wildly sprawling and out of hand or curtailing the original message, it is necessary to point again to the motive of the *koinonia* which was crucial for Paul's understanding of apostle. Already the second letter of Peter rejects the unauthorized interpretation of Scripture (2 Pet. 1.20). Authoritative is the joint testimony of all. The apostolic testimony must be transmitted in consensus of all. Apostolicity is therefore inseparably connected with the criteria of unity and catholicity.

Apostolic succession

It was not before the transition from the apostolic period to the post-apostolic time that the question of faithfully keeping the apostolic heritage became urgent for the Early Church,[185] yet a development had already begun to emerge in the New Testament. This becomes clear at the farewell of Paul from Miletus. He knows what awaits him in Jerusalem and that he will not see the community again. In this situation he admonishes the presbyters of the church: 'be on your guard for yourselves and for all the flock of which the Holy Spirit has made you bishops, to feed the Church of God' (Acts 20.28). Paul does not leave the community behind as orphans; he admonishes the bishops/presbyters to care for the community after his departure.[186]

It is even more obvious that Paul – or, as is usually assumed today, one of his pupils – exhorts his (or their) pupils Timothy and Titus to be faithful to the apostolic heritage and to keep and defend the pure doctrine (1 Tim. 1.10; 4.6.16; 2 Tim. 4.3ff.; Tit. 2.1.7). He exhorts Timothy not to neglect the grace which is in him through the laying-on of hands by the elders (1 Tim. 4.14; 2 Tim. 1.6; cf. Acts 6.6; 14.23). He exhorts Titus, as he had done before him, to appoint elders himself (Tit. 1.5). Succession is not explicitly mentioned, yet factually the texts speak about it.

It is in the epistle of Clement to the church in Corinth that the term succession is explicitly mentioned for the first time. With reference to the divine order (τάξις) he calls the community to order. In such order God sent Jesus Christ and he sent the apostles. These appointed, after examining them in the Spirit, bishops and deacons for the future faithful.[187] With this, the first letter of Clement established a chain of succession for the first time. Ignatius of Antioch has a different point of view. He does not emphasize the historical succession but the presence of Christ in the bishop who presides in the council of the presbyters in the place of God, whereby the presbyters are to function as the council of the Apostles.[188]

We find the actual foundation of the doctrine of succession in the writings of Irenaeus of Lyons, who combined both perspectives. For him, apostolic succession is crucial in the controversy with the Gnostics who appeal to their own sources of revelation. Against them, Irenaeus emphasizes as criterion of truth that the Church has received the only true and life-giving faith from the apostles.[189] The apostles are the ground and the pillar of our faith; they were invested with the power of the Holy Spirit and so received from all and had perfect knowledge.[190] The apostolic Tradition is preserved by means of the succession of presbyters in the Church.[191] 'It is within the power of all, therefore, in every church, who may wish to see the truth, to contemplate clearly the Tradition of the apostles manifested throughout the whole world; and we are in a position to reckon up those who were by the apostles instituted bishops in the churches, and the succession of these men to our own times.'[192] 'Through this they received from all and had perfect knowledge.' 'It [the truth] is easy to obtain from the church; since the apostles, like a rich man [depositing his money] in a bank, lodged in her hands most copiously all things pertaining to the truth.'[193]

Irenaeus then mentions in particular the Roman church and the line of its bishops, saying that 'it is a matter of necessity that every church should agree with this church, on account of its pre-eminent authority'.[194] 'In this order, and by this succession, the ecclesiastical Tradition from the apostles, and the preaching of the truth, have come down to us. And this is most abundant proof that there is one and the same vivifying faith, which has been preserved in the church from the apostles until now, and handed down in truth.'[195] 'True knowledge is [that which consists in] the doctrine of the apostles, and the ancient constitution of the church throughout the world, and the distinctive manifestation of the body of Christ according to the succession of bishops, by which the apostles have handed down that church which exists in every place.'[196]

Of course, Irenaeus immediately adds that the apostles went into the world after they had received the power of the Holy Spirit.[197] Yet, the bishops have received, together with the succession of the episcopate, the certain charisma of truth.[198] Irenaeus is thus not concerned with a line of succession as a formal criterion which, as it were, would automatically guarantee the right doctrine. For him there is in addition a pneumatological aspect which enables him to see the apostolic succession in the episcopate in the context of the witnessing of many and to see the apostolic succession of the Church as a whole. He believes that 'for where the Church is, there is the Spirit of God; and where the Spirit of God is, there is the Church, and every kind of grace; but the Spirit is the truth.'[199] 'Without paper and ink, they [the leaders of the churches] have written salvation in their hearts by the Spirit and carefully preserve the ancient tradition.'[200] It is the Spirit that, by means of the apostolic succession, effects the remaining in truth, guarantees it and thereby constantly renews it.

What Irenaeus explicated so impressively, did not remain isolated in the Church of his time. Similar statements are found in Tertullian.[201] Eusebius collects in his *Ecclesiastical History* the lists of the bishops of Rome, Alexandria and Jerusalem,[202] similarly Hegesippus.[203]

The *Traditio apostolica* (circa 215) ascribed to Hippolytus is particularly important. According to it, the threefold ministry of bishops, presbyters and deacons is conferred by the laying-on of hands and a consecration prayer which represents a solemn *epiclesis* of the Spirit.[204] This emphasizes that the apostolic succession has an epicletic structure. It is not that in the ordination power is simply passed on in quasi-linear fashion from bishop to bishop. The fact that the consecrating bishop (or consecrating bishops) prays together with the assembled congregation to the Holy Spirit that he may fill the ordinant with the charisma of truth[205] adds (if one likes to say so) a vertical element.[206] Because of this, the apostolic succession as institution is, at the same time, a spiritual event and far from any kind of automatism. As the ordination takes place within the celebration of the Eucharist through the gathered congregation, it is also integrated into the whole of the Church's sacramental structure.[207]

Joseph Ratzinger worked out in detail the inner connection between apostolic Tradition and apostolic succession, especially for Irenaeus of Lyons, and presented the thesis: the succession is the concrete form of the Tradition; the Tradition is the authoritative content of the succession.[208] From this reciprocal relationship it follows that Tradition and succession interpret each other. The apostolic succession is the authoritative order of the Church, but it is no automatism functioning out of itself. Also in today's view, ordination has an epicleptic and thus pneumatological dimension.[209]

The apostolic succession, therefore, must be understood in the sense of the Early Church within the whole of the Church's pneumatological and sacramental structure and its apostolic faith. One must not remove it from this overall context. One must not reduce it to a – at any rate, historically unprovable – chain of uninterrupted laying-on of hands and thus turn it into an almost automatic guarantee, functioning out of itself, of the identity with and continuity in the apostolic faith. The apostolic succession of a bishop does not go back to a certain individual apostle but to the college of apostles and its apostolic heritage in faith. This is why it can only be exercised properly in the *communio* with all other bishops. The apostolicity of the Church is thus not a purely historical category but a structural whole within a sacramental overall understanding of the Church.[210]

Ultimately, continuity and identity in apostolic faith is the work of the Holy Spirit. The apostolic succession of the bishops is sign and instrument for this conferred and carried by the Holy Spirit, but it is not the 'object' (*res*) of continuity and identity in apostolic faith itself. The individual bishop can become unfaithful to his mission and the Holy Spirit conferred to him in ordination and can drop out of the apostolicity in faith. Already the history of the Early Church knows numerous examples for this. Such a bishop leaves the basis on which he stands and, if he proves stubborn and inaccessible to fraternal exhortation, must be removed from his office by the community of bishops or by the bishop of Rome as the head of the episcopal college. So that it does not come to this and so that the bishop can exercise his mission in the right and fruitful way for the Church, he needs the prayer and support of all faithful.

The debate concerning early Catholicism; or, once again: institution and/or charisma?

At the beginning of the twentieth century, the question concerning the Early Church's conception of the apostolic succession caused the famous controversy between Sohm and Harnack. Rudolf Sohm († 1917) believed he could demonstrate that, at the turn of the second century, the original purely charismatic order was replaced, especially through Clemens of Rome, by the sacrament law of the Old Church and its tie to the authority of the bishop.[211] For him, there is an essential contradiction between Church and law. Against Sohm, Adolf von Harnack († 1930) defended canon law. Yet, he understood it as a purely sociological necessity and the fact that, in Catholicism, it became divine law.[212] By contrast, Erik Peterson, for his part, showed that the first congregations, according to the pattern of the ancient ekklesia, were not structured according to the law of associations, but that they saw their order founded upon the holy law of the eschatological city in heaven. For Peterson there was divine law from the beginning.[213]

In terms of content, this discussion became acute again in a new form in the 1960s through Ernst Käsemann. Käsemann discovered not just with Clemens of Rome but already within the New Testament (in the Lucan writings, the letters from prison and the pastoral letters, especially the second epistle of Peter) a churching of the originally eschatological-charismatic message.[214] The result was a heated debate as this thesis raised again for Protestant theology the sensitive question of the canon and, at the same time, the problem of denominations. To claim an early Catholicism in the New Testament would in fact mean to deprive Protestantism in parts of its legal basis and conversely to concede a biblical foundation, at least partly, to Catholicism.

Naturally, this debate led to a dead end. The term 'early catholicism' proved to be indeterminate. The theses building upon it proved to be unreliable and thus controversial. This led to increasingly subtle but also increasingly absurd constructions of hypotheses. Meanwhile, modern biblical studies has left this largely behind and has turned to canonical exegesis which perceives the biblical testimony as a whole and interprets individual biblical passages in the context of the Old and New Testament.[215]

Reading and perceiving the Bible as a whole, there can be no doubt that from the beginning, the New Testament communities had communal ministries and that all essential elements of a so-called holy law developed very early during the New Testament period.[216] One must therefore not get lost in false alternatives. Holy law and sacramentally-epicletically mediated law are not in opposition to a charismatic order; rather the sacramentally understood Church and the ministry sacramentally mediated to the apostolic succession are the unity of institution and charisma.

'Apostolicity' used critically against the church – the controversy with the reformers

In the course of church history, the apostolicity founding and legitimizing the Church soon became a critical yardstick for the life and praxis of the Church. At first the criticism was not levelled against the apostolic doctrine but against the apostolic way of life. With reference to Jesus' message for the poor (Mt. 11.2–6; Lk. 7.18–22), his counsel to the rich young man to give up everything (Mt. 19.21) and to the simplicity and poverty of the first community and the poor in Jerusalem (Rom. 15.26), in fact, with reference to Jesus' own poverty, the monasticism of the Early Church saw itself as a kind of protest against the beginning of the Church becoming bourgeois. Origen was probably the first to speak explicitly of the *vita apostolica*.[217]

Changes criticizing the Church occurred already during the third century when sect-like movements appeared calling for a return to the simple apostolic way of life (*vita apostolica*) and thereby rejecting marriage and property in principle.[218] In the Middle Ages, we frequently find socio-critical poverty movements with criticism of the rich and powerful church and the demand for a poor church according to the apostolic ideal. We encounter such in the pataria of Milan, Arnold of Brescia, Apostolic Brethren (Gerardo Segarelli), the Cathars and Waldensians, with Wycliffe and Hus. In a sense they placed against the ecclesial hierarchy their own 'parallel hierarchy'. What was legitimate in these 'popular heresies' was taken up and integrated into the Church by Norbert of Xanten († 1134) and Rupert of Deutz († 1130) and in the thirteenth century by the mendicant order movement of Francis of Assisi and Dominic. The call for the simplicity of the *vita apostolica* thus received in a way the right of domicile in the Church itself.

The view is often advocated that the church criticism of the *vita apostolica* movement was a kind of forerunner to the Reformation of the sixteenth century. This ignores however the essential nature that the debate about apostolicity received through the Reformation. Luther himself argued along this line, claiming that the Reformation criticism applied not to life but the doctrine of the Church.[219] For this reason the Reformation criticism must not be reduced to criticism of then-existing ills and the Reformation to a church reform. It was and still is about the proper understanding of the apostolic church order itself.

This essential point of contention already became apparent in October 1518 in the Augsburg disputation between Luther and Cardinal Cajetan, which was, from Cajetan's perspective, more of a questioning than a disputation.[220] The controversy specifically concerned the pope's power of the keys when granting indulgencies, and, more fundamentally, the contribution of the Church in the mediation of salvation and the question of whether the efficacious reception of grace necessitates the subjective certainty of the faith of the recipient. As a perceptive Thomist theologian, Cajetan understood the consequences of this question and replied to Luther: 'this means establishing a new church.' For him, the question of the subjective certainty of faith pointed to a fundamental difference in the understanding of the Church.[221] As the pope, in Luther's view, suppressed the Gospel with his authority, after the Leipzig disputation (1520), Luther raised the question of whether the pope was the antichrist or at least his envoy. Later this question became a certainty for him.[222] Thus, in the same year, he arrived at the distinction between two churches: the essentially true, spiritual, internal Christianity and external Christianity.[223]

Luther did not want to call into question the apostolic Tradition as such. He understood apostolicity as faithfulness to Holy Scripture or the apostolically transmitted Gospel. For him this also included the proper administration of Baptism, the Lord's Supper, the office of keys and others.[224] He was committed to stand in communion with the Old Church while, in his opinion, the Roman church had detached itself from its origins. In other words, the controversy did not concern apostolicity as such, but its authoritative form in the ecclesial ministry.

It was fatal for the Catholic side that, because of the medieval development,[225] the Catholic Church of that time was also unclear about the significance of the episcopal office and the principle of apostolic succession. The writings of Irenaeus and his idea of succession were lost. They were rediscovered only relatively late and then were interpreted on the Catholic side with anti-Reformation emphasis.[226] By consequence, out of the antithesis on the Catholic side the ecclesial ministry often developed in modern times one-sidedly to a self-sufficient, purely formal criterion of ecclesial doctrine. The reciprocal tie between *traditio* and *successio* was largely ignored. Often one even restricted oneself only on the Petrine criterion. The ecclesial magisterium was in danger of becoming self-referential, of quoting only itself and of developing a purely magisterial theology.[227]

The question of the apostolic succession therefore became the decisive issue of the controversy. It was thus a consequence that the debate on this topic in the last decades has increasingly moved into the centre of ecumenical dialogues. The apostolicity of the Church in the broader sense of accordance with the teaching of the apostles is thereby not disputed; all churches claim to be apostolic in that sense. The problem is apostolicity in the narrower sense of apostolic succession in the episcopal office. The Second Vatican Council produced a number of aspects which carry this trajectory further.

The Second Vatican Council

The most important progress had occurred already in the Constitution on the Church *Lumen Gentium* which placed apostolic succession in the episcopal office within the apostolicity of the Church as a whole. Inspired by Möhler and Newman, Vatican II made clear that, according to the creed, the Church as a whole is apostolic and that all baptized participate in the truth in Jesus Christ and with this in the apostolic message. The first Letter of John even states that all participate in the anointing with the Spirit and that they do not need anyone to teach them (1 Jn 2.27). All have the *sensus fidei*. That is not to say that everybody can opinionatedly invoke one's own sense of faith; rather the *sensus fidei* is always also a φρόνημα ἐκκλησιαστικόν, a *sensus ecclesiaticus*.[228]

Vatican II can even say: 'The entire body of the faithful, anointed as they are by the Holy One (cf. 1 Jn 2.20.27) cannot err in matters of belief. They manifest this special property by means of the whole peoples' supernatural discernment in matters of faith when "from the Bishops down to the last of the lay faithful" they show universal agreement in matters of faith and morals. That discernment in matters of faith is aroused and sustained by the Spirit of truth. It is exercised under the guidance of the sacred teaching authority [...] Through it, the people of God adheres unwaveringly to the faith given once and for all to the saints (cf. Jude 3) penetrates it more deeply with right thinking, and applies it more fully in its life.'[229]

In addition to the Constitution on the Church, the Constitution on Divine Revelation *Dei Verbum* is particularly important. This constitution was severely contested at the Council, which is why the Council had to leave several things open.[230] Yet, all in all, this constitution is perhaps the most mature and best text of the Council, which, not least, meant a significant step forward in the ecumenical dialogue.[231]

The Constitution on Divine Revelation *Dei Verbum* already begins in the first sentences with a fanfare: 'Hearing the word of God with reverence and proclaiming it with faith'.[232] This describes the Church as a church listening to the word of God and from the listening it is a church testifying to the Word of God. It exists in the double gesture of listening and testifying. Even though it remained behind its own genial approach,[233] the Constitution on Divine Revelation unfolded this view in detail. It clearly demonstrates that with the Gospel as 'the source of all saving truth and moral teaching' the apostles left the Church not only teaching but, besides their oral word, they also left their example, as well as institutions established by them. They left the bishops as their successors and passed on to them their own teaching office.[234] 'So the Church, in her teaching, life and worship, perpetuates and hands on to all generations all that she herself is, all that she believes.'[235]

With the addition 'what she believes' the Council wanted to avoid the misunderstanding that the formula 'what she is' could cause. For authoritative Tradition of faith is not everything the Church is in its concrete existence but only what it testifies in faith. Not all traditions represent the authoritative apostolic Tradition.[236] The constitution excludes a mechanical identification with the introduction of pneumatological and eschatological aspects. 'For as the centuries succeed one another, the Church constantly moves forward toward the fullness of divine truth until the words of God reach their complete fulfilment in her.' 'Thus God, who spoke of old, uninterruptedly converses with the bride of His beloved Son; and the Holy Spirit, through whom the living voice of the Gospel resounds in the Church, and through her, in the world, leads unto all truth those who believe and makes the word of Christ dwell abundantly in them.'[237] The Tradition is a living process in which there are clarifications and progress; it is above all a living, historical process of conversation.

Finally, the Council states: 'Hence there exists a close connection and communication between sacred tradition and Sacred Scripture. For both of them, flowing from the same divine wellspring, in a certain way merge into a unity and tend toward the same end. For Sacred Scripture is the word of God inasmuch as it is consigned to writing under the inspiration of the divine Spirit, while sacred tradition takes the word of God entrusted by Christ the Lord and the Holy Spirit to the Apostles, and hands it on to their successors in its full purity [...] Consequently it is not from Sacred Scripture alone that the Church draws her certainty about everything which has been revealed.'[238]

The following section again emphasizes the belonging together, the harmony and, led by the Spirit, the interaction of Scripture, Tradition and teaching office. Then follows a further essential statement: 'This teaching office is not above the word of God, but serves it, teaching only what has been handed on, listening to it devoutly, guarding it scrupulously and explaining it faithfully in accord with a divine commission and with the help of the Holy Spirit, it draws from this one deposit of faith everything which it presents for belief as divinely revealed.'[239]

This text has repeatedly been criticized. It has certainly not solved all the problems, but it has undoubtedly done some groundwork. The old juxtaposition of Scripture and Tradition has been given up in favour of regarding them as intertwined and there can be no self-sufficiency of the teaching authority above Scripture and Tradition. Testifying must be preceded by listening – to the word of God as well as to the testimony of the universal

Church. Though testifying is the particular task of the magisterium, it is not its exclusive task. It requires the interaction of different instances of testifying.[240] All this leads further in a positive way. However, what the text of the Council lacks are concrete rules with criteria for this interaction.

Yet, another aspect is essential and leads further. Jesus Christ left the Church not only his teaching and founded not only its structure and then left it to itself. Rather, he gave it the Holy Spirit and poured it out over the Church at Pentecost that the Spirit calls to mind all what he had said and done (Jn 14.26; 15.26; 16.13). In this way, Jesus Christ remains present in the Church through the Holy Spirit. He makes himself and his teaching present through the service of the apostles and their successors. The apostolic succession in the narrow sense is neither isolated from the life of the Church nor is it a kind of automatic guarantee of remaining in the apostolic truth. In the context of a sacramental understanding of Church it can only be sign and instrument of the apostolic Tradition; it is always simultaneously institution and event.

Against this background, Vatican II was able to positively adopt the intention of the *vita apostolica* movement and state in an important passage, which is unfortunately too seldom cited: 'Just as Christ carried out the work of redemption in poverty and persecution, so the Church is called to follow the same route [...] Thus, the Church, although it needs human resources to carry out its mission, is not set up to seek earthly glory, but to proclaim, even by its own example, humility and self-sacrifice.'[241] It is on this basis that, since the general assemblies of the Latin American episcopate in Medellín (1968) and in Puebla (1979), the formula of the preferential option for the poor has been the critical and inspiring standard for a truly apostolic praxis of the Church.

The current ecumenical debate

Encouraged by the Second Vatican Council, more recent ecumenical dialogues with the churches of the Reformation have tried to liberate the question of apostolic succession from the denominational narrowness brought about through thesis and antithesis. Through this discussion, the controversial question has shifted towards integrating apostolic succession in the narrow sense of succession in office into the context of the apostolicity of the whole Church. In this question of integrating apostolic succession, the diversity of its ministries and charismata and the diverse instances of testimonies (testimony of the liturgy, the Church Fathers, the theologians, the sense of faith of the faithful, etc.), remarkable convergences have become possible.[242]

After several previous attempts, the Lima documents (1982) have become foundational in the multilateral dialogue. They acknowledge apostolic succession in the episcopal office not as a guarantee but as an efficacious expression of the Church's continuity through its history and identify it as the ministry, symbol and protection of the continuity of the apostolic faith. Yet they add that, as a sign, it is no guarantee for the continuity and unity of the Church. Churches that have not kept the succession should declare an awareness that it functions as a sign of the apostolicity of the life of the whole Church. This suggestion, however, is combined with the reservation that those churches which have not kept the succession in ministry cannot agree to a proposition that ultimately implies that the ministry which is exercised in their own tradition should not be valid until the time when it enters an existing line of the episcopal succession.

Not all Protestant churches have accepted this Lima text. At the very least, the bilateral dialogues have been able to highlight many converging elements in the different denominational positions which make it seem possible to acknowledge that, in the ministry of the respective other churches, a service for the apostolically transmitted Gospel is exercised.[243] Yet, because of that, to speak already of a differentiated consensus is difficult for that reason alone, as there is no consensus about the term 'differentiated consensus' and its suitability. The crucial question is whether an additive method suffices which brings together the individual elements on which there is agreement. The question regarding the apostolic succession in the ministry is, after all, like the tip of the iceberg of a fundamental difference in church understanding. This fundamental difference, until now unresolved, becomes obvious when, on the Protestant side, apostolicity is considered as a property of the invisible Church,[244] whereas, according to Catholic and Orthodox conviction, the content of the apostolic Tradition includes an authoritative apostolic embodiment.[245]

We find an intermediate position in the Anglican Communion and some Lutheran Nordic and Baltic churches for which apostolic succession in the episcopal office or of certain episcopal sees is essential.[246] They declared their ecumenical position in the *Porvoo Statement* (1992).[247] The Second Vatican Council acknowledged the special position of the Anglican Communion.[248] However, the Catholic Church maintains the decision of Leo XIII in the bull *Apostolicae curae* (1896)[249] which declared Anglican ordinations invalid. The question of whether this decision can be revised has not been discussed further after the decision of most provinces of the Anglican Communion, like most of the Lutheran churches, in favour of women's ordination.[250] An additional aspect is the fact that, in the Anglican Communion today, the episcopal office is integrated into synodal structures which accord largely with the Reformer's understanding of the relation between the common priesthood and the ministry.[251]

The future discussion of the apostolicity of the Church and apostolic succession in the episcopal office can only reach its goal beyond the things achieved so far if it succeeds in overcoming a latent ecclesio-docetism and a widespread phobia (also present in the Roman Catholic Church) against law in the Church and in perceiving the visible embodiment of the apostolic ministry as quasi-sacramental sign and instrument of the work of the exalted Christ in the Holy Spirit in the Church. According to Catholic conviction, apostolicity in faith can be distinguished from apostolic succession in the sense of succession in ministry but they cannot be completely separated from each other. Apostolic succession in the narrow sense belongs to the nature of the Church.

Hence, the question we must face is: how does the Gospel, transmitted once and for all by the apostles, speak in the Holy Spirit concretely to us today and how does it make itself heard in the Church and through the Church today? What does the Spirit today have to say to the communities (cf. Rev. 2.7.11.17.29 et seq.)? This brings us to the question which will concern us in the following chapter.

5

The concrete [illegible] e Church as [illegible]

5.1 The Church *of* the people of God

Preliminary considerations

The present chapter on the concrete form of the *communio* of the Church deals with the most difficult and most controversial part of ecclesiology. After the exploration of the properties of the Church has demonstrated that a nature pertains to the Church which is given to it by Jesus Christ and unfolded in the Holy Spirit, we must now look at the concretion of the *communio*-form of the Church – to be specific, at the offices, ministries and charismata. It is about the common priesthood of all of the baptized and the special priesthood of service, the offices of priests and bishops and the Petrine office. One only has to name these topics to realize immediately that in these questions there are not only difficult biblical and historical problems to be dealt with but that there are also differences between the denominations which unfortunately have not yet been fully resolved. It is still today a contested field of ecclesiology.

In dogmatic handbooks, Catholic presentations of the structure of the Church's nature normally begin with ecclesiastical ministry, concretely with the Petrine and episcopal office, only to deal with the vocation of laypeople in the Church afterwards in the context of the common priesthood of all baptized. This order turns things on their heads. The common priesthood of the baptized is foundational, not only for the service of laypeople, but also for the service of the ordained ministry. Therefore, we must begin with that which unites both, the ministry of the laity and of the ecclesiastical offices, and then, on this basis, we must clarify their differences and their reciprocal correlation.

When we place the exploration of the vocation of the laity immediately after the exposition of the common and uniting basis, this is not because the ecclesiastical office is to be derived from the service of laypeople. The reason is rather that neither the ordained ministry nor the Church as whole exists for themselves. The Church, rather, is sign and instrument for God's working in the world and for the coming of his kingdom – the Church serves the sanctification of the world and of life. Yet, the sanctification of the world and of life is, in a special way the vocation of the laity. The vocation of the laity concerns the goal and purpose of the Church, whereas the Church's offices do not pertain to the category of the purpose but to the category of media, as they are to serve the realization of the Church's goal and purpose. As, according to Aristotelian-Thomistic teaching, the means must be determined by the, that is,[1] we must begin with the vocation of the laity in the Church and relate to it the service of the ecclesiastical ministry. This teleological way of thinking stands in contradiction to the mechanical-causal world view that has largely established itself since Descartes.

The order would be misunderstood if it were called an ecclesiology from below that intends to deduce the vocation of the ecclesiastical office from that of the laity. It is neither about an ecclesiology from above (in the sense of a hierarchical above), in which the service of laypeople would be an extended office of the clergy, nor from below, in which the ministry of the office would be formed out of or commissioned by the community. It is about an ecclesiology *from the goal of* the Church that is determined by the coming of God's kingdom and by the permeation and sanctification of the world through Christ's Spirit. It is in this big context that we look at the proper correlation of office and community.

This was also the way of the Second Vatican Council. In opposition to the prepared draft it did not begin its exposition of the Church's nature with the hierarchical structure of the Church. However, it also does not begin with a so-called ecclesiology from below. It rather begins with the joint participation of all in the prophetic, priestly and royal ministry of Jesus Christ. In doing so, the Council begins with that which is common to laypeople, priests and bishops and which precedes all later distinctions, encompasses them and continues in all of them: with the common priesthood of all baptized.

The common priesthood of the baptized – biblical foundations

Today, for the foundation of the common priesthood of the baptized, one usually refers to the statements in the first letter of Peter (1 Pet. 2.4–10).[2] This text is a baptismal paraenesis, that is, an exhortation directed toward the newly baptized. In it, the Church is described with the image of the house of God. It speaks of Jesus Christ as the living stone rejected by the builders but upon whom the house of God is built out of living stones to a spiritual house. The living stones are the baptized. They are typologically rewarded with the titles of honour from the Old Testament covenant people

(Exod. 19.5f.). They are called a 'chosen race (γένος), a royal priesthood (βασίλειον ἱεράτευμα), a holy nation (ἔθνος) and a people (λαός) to be a personal possession to God'. It is to be a holy people set apart from the other nations, which belongs totally to God and lives according to his commandments. In other words, for the New Testament community all basic statements apply which we have made about the Old Testament people of the covenant.

Yet, the first letter of Peter also highlights the difference from the Old Testament covenant people. The whole argument of this text is Christologically constructed. The New Testament priesthood is determined by the once-and-for-all offered sacrifice of Christ through which we are taken into this priesthood in baptism and which we are to realize through a life that makes this baptismal reality efficacious (Rom. 6.3–14). So the people of the new covenant are not to offer with external cultic sacrifices such as food, incense, lambs and bulls but through Christ with spiritual sacrifices pleasing to God (1 Pet. 2.5). Already the Old Testament knew that the true sacrifices are prayer, thanksgiving, praise and repentance (Ps. 49.14; 50.19; 140.2; 106.22). Still, one can speak only to a certain extent of a spiritualization of the cult, for they are sacrifices in the Spirit (πνεῦμα) who is the most powerful reality.

Calling the priesthood a royal priesthood is to say that the privileges of kings apply to all baptized; to all pertain sovereignty and self-determination of life and all have direct access to God. In other words, this states the freedom of the Christian. The baptized are called to the freedom of God's children (Gal. 5.1.13), yet they are not to abuse this freedom and not to fall into new dependencies. The Christian freedom becomes efficacious in love (Gal. 5.5): 'Carry each other's burdens; that is how to keep the law of Christ' (Gal. 6.2). Hence, Christian freedom must not be individualistically misunderstood. On the contrary, the baptized participate in the one priesthood because of the common baptism not as individuals but corporately. It does not speak of priests in the plural but of priesthood (ἱεράτευμα) in the singular. It is only the last book of the Bible that speaks of priests in the plural (ἱερεῖς), yet this happens there only in a way that all individuals are viewed together in the one royal reign (βασιλεία; Rev. 1.6; 5.10; 20.6). The language of the royal priesthood has, from its foundation, a corporate-ecclesial structure.

The testimony of the Church Fathers and of high scholastic theology

The passages of 1 Peter find a broad echo in patristic literature. Origen speaks extensively of the service the Christians perform as priests, especially through their prayers for the benefit of all.[3] Each Christian carries his offering within himself.[4] This motif of the altar of the heart is taken up again by Augustine. Our altar is our heart where we offer the sacrifice of humility and praise through the fire of burning love.[5] We encounter the same motif again with reference to 1 Peter with Leo the Great[6] and much later with Bonaventura.[7] With reference to 1 Peter, Augustine says in addition that not only the bishops and presbyters are priests, 'but as we call all believers Christians on account of the mystical anointing, so we call all priests because they are members of the one Priest'.[8] The same is repeated by Leo the Great.[9] Unlike in Gnosticism, according to the testimony of the Church Fathers there cannot be two classes of Christians, spiritual and bodily ones, common believers and perfect ones.

In accord with the language of the biblical text, the Church Fathers interpret the first letter of Peter in its typological and spiritual sense. They do not deduce concrete rights for participation or sacramental authorities for the laity. The Church Fathers are concerned with the Old Church's ideal of holiness, with a priesthood at the altar of the constantly burning heart that is dedicated to God.[10]

In this sense, the idea of the common priesthood was not forgotten in the post-patristic period. Thomas Aquinas, too, knew about the participation of all baptized in the priesthood of Christ. He deals with this question when he speaks of the sacramental character that is impressed upon the Christian in baptism. This sacramental character distinguishes the baptized from the non-baptized. It signifies that one is numbered among God's people,[11] a conforming likeness with Christ and a commissioning to serve God in worship in the sense of the Christian religion (*deputatio ad cultum*).[12] Thomas distinguishes the baptismal ordination of each Christian from the ordination to the priesthood, the latter of which grants the authority to say the words of consecration *in persona Christi*.[13] Still, Thomas can also say that, even though the priest says the words of consecration *in persona Christi*, he also prays in the person of the whole Church, so to speak, *in persona publica*.[14] Hence, the priest stands praying in the congregation and, in some respects, also stands with authority in opposition to it *in persona Christi*.

What Thomas describes in seemingly dry words as commissioning of all baptized to the Christian cult appears in the so-called Roman Canon which, in contrast to Vatican II, many today consider as being antiquated or misunderstand as being obsolete. The first Eucharistic prayer says, in the commemoration for the living, not only that the Eucharist is offered for the 'servants', but also that they themselves offer this sacrifice of praise. It speaks of an offering of the whole family (*cunctae familiae*) of God and of a *memoria* of the whole holy people (*plebs tua sancta*). The liturgy has retained the idea of the common priesthood of all baptized up the present. It is therefore no coincidence that the renewal of the idea before the Second Vatican Council originated not from a democratic awakening in the Church but from the liturgical movement.

Luther's doctrine of the universal priesthood

A far-reaching change in the understanding of 1 Peter was initiated by Luther's over-interpretation. Luther did not understand this text in the sense of the common priesthood but as the universal priesthood of all the baptized that is as competence of all Christians in the interpretation of God's word. This interpretation is found above all in the reform tract of 1520 *To the Christian Nobility of the German Nation Concerning the Reform of the Christian Estate*. There Luther deduces from 1 Peter and the Revelation of John that all Christians are ordained priests through baptism. 'For whatever issues from baptism, may boast that it has been consecrated priest, bishop, and Pope.'[15] We find the same line of argument again in the two other main Reformation texts of that year, *The Babylonian Captivity of the Church*[16] and *Concerning Christian Liberty*.[17] A little later Luther wrote *That a Christian Assembly or Congregation Has the Right and Power to Judge all Teaching and to Call, Appoint, and Dismiss Teachers, Established and proven by Scripture* (1523).[18] However, according to Luther, the authority given to the whole community cannot be seized by an individual; rather it must be orderly conferred upon an individual in accord with the order given by Christ and then it must be exercised by this person.

Whereas the above-mentioned early texts by Luther convey the impression that the ministry emerged from the common priesthood, the later Luther speaks of the institution of the preaching office by Christ. In *On Councils and the Church* (1539) Luther counts the ordination and vocation of bishops, priests and preachers to be the signs by which the Church is recognized. Thereby he does not derive the ministry from the people but from the institution by Christ.[19] This view was also adopted by the *Confessio Augustana* (1530)[20] and was authoritative for Lutheranism until the nineteenth century. The *Augsburg Confession* and other confessional texts do not even mention the common priesthood. It was only in pietism that we see the development of the doctrine of the common priesthood in the sense common today and of an independent piety of the laity.

As a result of the different lines of thinking, Luther's teaching of the common priesthood has found different interpretations within Lutheranism and is still controversial today.[21] On the one hand, there is a theory of institution that could be called high-Lutheran which is very close to the Catholic understanding and today is also usually found in ecumenical documents.[22] On the other hand, there is a theory of conference which is probably the dominant teaching within Lutheranism today. It remains behind the ecumenical convergences which have already been reached and causes difficulties in the ecumenical conversation.[23]

The interpretation of cultural Protestantism, current again today, which tries to read the early Luther and his teaching of the common priesthood from the perspective of the modern idea of liberty, is hardly sustainable. After all, in his text *To the Nobility* Luther is in fact not concerned with a kind of democratic view; instead, with the aid of his teaching of the common priesthood, Luther placed church reform into the hands of the counts. In this, he was still firmly rooted in the unity idea of medieval Christianity where the spiritual and temporal authorities formed one unity.[24] Luther's appeal to the nobility led soon to the regional rulers' church rule. What is presented as liberation from clerical dominance led thus to a different, even stronger dependence which lasted in Germany until the end of the monarchy in 1918 and which then led with the 'Deutsche Christen' into an even worse ideological dependency.[25] If one wants to call Protestantism a church of liberty understood in the modern sense, then one can refer to the Baptists, Pietism, the free churches and, in other ways, to enlightened liberal Protestant tendencies in the nineteenth century, but hardly to Luther himself.[26]

After 1918 and again after 1945 the Protestant churches in Germany made a new start. Prepared through Pietism and through Friedrich Schleiermacher's reform plans, they emphasized the common priesthood in a new form within a synodal church order in combination with a synodally integrated episcopal office.[27] With the Leuenberg Agreement of 1973, the Lutheran churches recognized the synodal-presbyterial order of the Reformed churches, which had the synodal order from the beginning.[28] Today the synodal constitution is more or less common to all Reformation churches. However, these synods, whose majority are non-ordained people, are not synods in the sense of the Old Church. Basically they are church parliaments which are largely in charge of church leadership. So these more recent church orders express Luther's original teaching of the common priesthood in a new form.

The Second Vatican Council

On the Catholic side, it was the Second Vatican Council that newly emphasized the biblical, patristic and high-scholastic doctrine of the common priesthood. The text from 1 Peter plays a prominent role in the documents of Vatican II. Since then this text has been considered in Catholic theology as the Magna Carta of the common priesthood of all baptized. Already the language highlights the difference from the Lutheran interpretation insofar as the Council does not speak of the general priesthood but of the common priesthood of all baptized – meaning not only the laity, let alone the laity in opposition to the clergy, but all members of the Church, including the priests and bishops as well as those in religious orders.

According to the Council, all baptized participate as parts of the one people of God and of the one body of Christ in the priestly, prophetic and royal office of Jesus Christ.[29] All are to give witness of the Gospel, all are called to full, conscious and active participation in the celebration of the Eucharist,[30] and all shall consider themselves as jointly responsible in the Church.[31] Yet, in all texts where the Council refers to the passage in 1 Peter, though it deduces 'co-responsibility', it does not deduce rights or authorities; it rather follows the line of the Church Fathers' interpretation that spoke of spiritual sacrifices of a holy life.

Still, one must not underestimate the significance and range of the Council's statements. For with its doctrine of the common priesthood of all baptized, the traditional language has become obsolete which spoke of two states, distinctly separated from each other, the clergy and the so-called 'common', 'simple' people (plebs) that in matters of the Church had nothing to say and were not competent. The mission of the Church is entrusted to the whole of the Church and thus to all Christians together. Nobody is only object; all are also subject in the Church. All are in their respective way responsible for the Church and the exercise of its mission. The common priesthood is the basis of the brotherhood or sisterhood of all in the Church as the one family of God.

In the view of the Council, the joint participation in the ministry of Jesus Christ as prophet, priest and king must not be misunderstood, however, as some abstract equality of all. As will be shown later, it does not abolish the distinction between offices and charismas that is often testified in the New Testament (1 Cor. 12.4–31; Rom. 12.3–8; Eph. 4.7–12); the joint participation rather precedes these distinctions and continues in them. There exists a unity of mission, but distinctness in participation in the common mission.

The fundamental common ground is therefore misunderstood if it is perceived in a temporal-democratic sense. This is already linguistically excluded. After all, it is telling that for 'people' in the biblical-theological sense the Greek language does not use the political term δῆμος which is found in the term democracy, but the salvation-historical term λαός taken from the LXX. In particular according to 1 Peter, the people of God is not a people like all the other peoples but God's people (λαός τοῦ Θεοῦ), the people chosen and set apart by God. It does not assemble like the political nation to decide what is to be done; rather it gathers to hear and to celebrate what God has decided and done. It is to proclaim God's great deeds (Acts 2.11) and to offer sacrifices of praise (Heb. 13.15).

It belongs to the good fruit of the Council that after the Council the people of God ecclesiology has enriched the concrete life in the Church, in particular in the parishes and dioceses. It has led to a new style and a new brotherly and sisterly togetherness of bishops, priests, laity and Christians in orders. Together all bear responsibility for the realization of Jesus' mission and the sanctification of the world. This does not mean that any one person is able to do everything. Rather, the Church in the New Testament can be compared to an organism in which different organs have to perform different tasks for the welfare of the whole. It can also be compared to a house that has a structure as such and only lasts if the individual parts are well put together.

Some might be afraid of such a colourful Church of the people of God and may long to return to the times when the reverend determined, did and ordered nearly everything. Yet, for theological reasons as well as changes in society's mentality, there can be no way back. Anyone who has experienced a living community with its multifaceted activities and the co-responsibility of many will also not want to go back. He or she will welcome the development towards the Church of the people of God as enrichment. Initial teething problems and some adolescent excesses of arrogant appearance of individual laypeople that have happened and, in parts, still happen will also occur again in future, just as there is and will occur again arrogant clerical behaviour. Those can and should be overcome in a patient, even though not easy, maturation process and lead to responsible true maturity and to collaboration in solidarity and in partnership of all in the one people of God. I will return to this when exploring the offices in the Church.[32]

5.2 The vocation of the laity

Historical overview

During and after the Council, the ecclesiology of the people of God and common priesthood of all baptized have become the foundation for determining the place and vocation of the laity in the Church.[33] The growing awareness of the laity belongs to the positive results of the Council. Yet it has also become the source of many subsequent misunderstandings and new controversies. Criticism of the traditional, divisive understanding of the laity as non-clergy not in religious orders and the attempt of a positive assessment and appreciation of the state of the laity, as well as new controversies concerning a healthy determination of the relation between clergy and laypeople, can only be comprehended against the background of the change-prone history of the laity in the Church.

The word 'layperson' is often derived from the biblical word 'λαός', meaning the people of God. This is to award the layperson the title of honour 'member of God's people' in contrast to the heathen nations. This establishes the context in which we can speak theologically of laity – the theology of the people of God. Yet, etymologically this derivation is not correct. The word 'layperson' (λαικός) is contained neither in the LXX nor in the New Testament.[34] The term appears for the first time in the first epistle of Clement[35] as a description of those in the people of Israel who were neither priests nor Levites. With Tertullian, Clement of Alexandria and others, this soon developed into an understanding analogous to the profane usage distinguishing between office-bearers and the plebs, the normal people. Laypeople were seen as those dealing with their private business (ἰδιώτης), and had nothing to do with and had no knowledge of public affairs.

With the appearance of monasticism, a third category of Christians emerged: the monks and the Christians in religious orders. Unlike the laity, they did not concern themselves with temporal affairs but with spiritual ones. Additionally, the members of the clergy were already seen very early on as 'spiritual people', who do not live after the fashion of the world but are set apart for a spiritual life and state. It thus becomes comprehensible that the great idea of the brotherhood of all Christians stepped more and more into the background and the name remained reserved for describing the relation among clergy as confreres.[36] The actual relations were, of course, much more differentiated. Factually, the laity participated in the election of bishops, at synods and councils; the ruling nobility as well as the congregations themselves played a role in shaping the life of the Church; and finally, the laity participated in the executive power of the Church. These are all facts that also have theological weight as such.[37]

Since the debates during the Investiture Controversy about the freedom of the Church from the intervention of the ruling nobility, there have been attempts to exclude the laity from any active role in the Church. So Gratian († 1160), who is considered with his *Decretum Gratiani* as the father of canon law, distinguished two types of Christians, the clergy and the laity, that is, servants of the cult and people of the world.[38] Consequently, a layperson was somebody who was neither clergy, nor monk, nor in religious orders. The life of the laity in the world was often seen as compromise and concession to human weakness. There was also a development in the self-conception of the clergy, which increasingly was no longer seen as spiritual from the perspective of monasticism but as 'clergy in the world' from the office as a member of a social and cultural state.[39]

If one wants to do justice to the medieval ecclesial life, one cannot rely alone on the history of words and theological definitions and disregard the real life of the Church. This leads to an inappropriate black and white perspective. The Gelasian perspective must be perceived within the perspective of unity between spiritual and secular matters in the Christianity of that time and within the framework of the medieval system of estate. In particular, one must not understand the notorious bull of Boniface VIII, *Clericis laicos semper esse infestos* (1296) *The laity and clergy have always been bitter enemies*, as a fundamental statement about the relation between clergy and laity in the modern sense. The laypeople referred to here were lay jurists of the French King Philip the Fair who challenged the pope's rights.

Within the system of estates and also within the guilds, there was an active religious life of the laity. In the context of the mendicant order movement in the thirteenth century the third orders emerged in which lay Christians participated in the charisma of the orders. The late medieval period knew pious lay movements (Beguines and Beghards). In addition, the awareness of the Church as *congregatio fidelium*, as *communio sanctorum* and as holy people of God remained alive with the best medieval theologians and in the liturgy. It is true, of course, that in the Middle Ages the role of the laity in ecclesiastical affairs was seen as edifying and spiritual.

A decisive moment was the Reformation of the sixteenth century. With the idea of the immediacy of each Christian to God, the Reformation broke through the concept of states within the religious order, yet retained it sociologically.[40] Against the Reformers, the council of Trent defended the hierarchical constitution of the Church.[41] By consequence, the common priesthood was hardly mentioned in post-Tridentine theology.

Still, also at that time, theology did not reflect the whole life of the Church. Already Saint Francis de Sales († 1622) aimed for a lay spirituality; others, such as Saint Vincent Pallotti († 1850), followed. In the nineteenth century one can point to the Münster circle of Princess von Gallitzin († 1806), the Salesian Society founded by Don Bosco († 1888), the Association of Journeymen founded by Adolf Kolping († 1865), reform Catholics like Friedrich von Hüngel († 1925) and others. In the twentieth century even before Vatican II, it was the German youth movement (Bündische Jugend) and, connected with it, the liturgical movement (particularly the group around Romano Guardini), the Schoenstatt Movement, the Opus Dei, then the pre-conciliar spiritual movements that aimed in different ways for a Christian way of life of the laity and the holiness of the people in the world.[42]

As with the medieval understanding of the laity, modern approaches to this problem must be seen against the background of developments in modern society, particularly the evolution of modern secularization. The wars of religion which followed the Reformation could be ended only by considering religion as a private affair. This resulted in what is known as laicism, i.e. the attempt of the Enlightenment and liberalism to push the Church or the clergy out of the temporal sphere. This led to a laicistic culture. The laity were accordingly considered as those who, in secular affairs, have their own judgement independent from the doctrine of the Church.

To counter the resulting privatization of faith, Pius XI supported in his inaugural encyclical *Ubi arcano Dei* (1922) the Catholic Action which he defined as participation of the laity in the hierarchical mission of Church. Laypeople were seen therein as the extended secular arm of the hierarchy. This resulted in a double logic and culture, an ecclesial-lay and a secular-laicistic culture, especially in Romance countries, where these patterns of thinking can still be found in parts today. In contrast, there was a different development in German-speaking countries. In the nineteenth century lay associations developed 'from below' out of the commitment of the laity who, after the collapse of the imperial church, worked for the liberty of the Church against liberalistic trends and thereby kept free the back of the official church. This was a relatively independent commitment of the laity in the political-cultural and social field. Therefore, the Catholic Action could never really take hold in German-speaking countries; conversely, the German development has not always met with understanding in Rome.

An independent theology of the laity developed only after the First World War in connection with the then-contemporary renewal movements. Indeed, in terms of the liturgy the awareness of the people of God as the subject of liturgy had been kept. Pope Pius X had originally coined the term *actuosa participatio*. The Council then made it a key term of the liturgical reform. This term expressing the full, conscious and active participation of the faithful[43] in that which is the centre and climax of ecclesial life could thus become not only a key term for liturgical reform but for renewal of the whole of ecclesial life. In France the secularization had progressed furthest. Here came an additional aspect. Under the keyword 'France, pays de mission' there occurred a new pastoral orientation which was soon taken up in Germany.[44] With this it also became obvious that now was the hour of the laity to give witness for Jesus Christ in the world of today.

What was, in particular, theologically decisive was Yves Congar's *Jalons pour une théologie du laïcat* (1953; English: *Lay People in the Church. A study for a theology of the laity*, London: Bloomsbury, 1957), a book which is rich in biblical material and in material from the history of theology and has remained inspiring until today. Congar proceeded from the common active participation of all baptized in the threefold ministry of Jesus Christ as teacher, priest and shepherd or king, and thus stressed the subject status of the laity in the Church. He saw the service of the laypeople in the ministry in the world and the vocation of the clergy as service for the kingdom of God. This distinction led to an unsatisfactory dualism of secular and salvation service that could only be overcome in the period immediately before the Council. The basis for the idea that the permeation of the world was the vocation of the whole Church had actually already been laid by Pius X with the programme applicable to the whole Church, '*Omnia instaurare in Christo*'.

The Second Vatican Council

The Second Vatican Council took up the renewal efforts of the first half of the twentieth century. Still, it is historically absurd to pretend that the dignity and significance of the laity had only been newly discovered by the Council. With its statements the Council moved on the ground of the Tradition which was more practical than theoretical. Here and in many other passages it expressed what had already been lived and taught in the centuries before. It formulated more explicitly and coherently what is also found scattered throughout the doctrinal Tradition, and, precisely so, the Council borrowed impulses from the preceding renewal movements.

The Council placed its statements about the nature and vocation of lay Christians in the context of the doctrine of the common priesthood of the baptized.[45] The intention thereby was to overcome the negative description of the laity as non-clergy and not in religious orders and to present a positive description. It called laypeople '*christifideles*', Christ's faithful people. As such they belong fully to the Church through baptism and its completion in confirmation. Indeed, they *are* the Church and participate in the Holy Spirit in the threefold office of Jesus Christ as prophet, teacher, priest and king or shepherd.[46] This sacramental foundation of the place and mission of the laity means that the Council could no longer regard laypeople as commissaries and the extended arm of the clergy. They have received their vocation and mission not through commissioning by the ordained ministry and participation in its mission, but because of baptism in the Holy Spirit from Jesus Christ himself. Therefore, they should exercise their mission in the freedom of the Holy Spirit, but within the community alongside their brothers in Christ.[47] Their dignity and vocation are ontologically based in baptismal reality and result from the inner dynamism of baptism. For this sacramental-theological and ontological reason, it does not suffice to ground the mission of the laity as purely functional on today's missionary situation or to determine it from individual functions or rights.

After this basic approach with baptism (and confirmation as completion of baptism), the Council wanted to determine the particular vocation of the laity within the common participation of all Christians. In the eyes of the Council, 'the laity, by their very vocation, seek the kingdom of God by engaging in temporal affairs and by ordering them according to the plan of God', so 'what specifically characterizes the laity is their secular nature'.[48] However, this statement is often used to one-sidedly assign the laypeople the function to engagement in secular affairs. With this statement the Council did not intend to present an actual definition of the laity but rather a description of their vocation.[49] After all, engagement in secular affairs is not exclusively the task of the laity. The Council very precisely states that the secular nature 'specifically characterizes the laity', in other words not exclusively. The permeation of the world pertains as a task to the whole Church. The ordained person does not lose through ordination what he has received through baptism and confirmation. Thus, one cannot construct a dualism between the salvific service of the clergy and the secular service that is reserved for laypeople. On the contrary, it is important to maintain in the 'diversity of ministry the oneness of mission'.[50]

At this point, the difficulty, indeed the impossibility, of clearly demarcating and defining the mission of the laity within the Church becomes obvious. Additionally, the term *christifideles*, Christ's faithful, applies in fact to all belonging to the people of God. If one specifies more precisely that laypeople were those *christifideles* living in the world under normal circumstances such as marriage, family, world of work, culture, politics and so forth, then it does indeed apply to the majority of cases. However, this statement would also apply to permanent deacons and priests who were not directly active in pastoral care, but instead in areas such as politics in past times or, for example, in culture and research today. In a basic sense, priests and bishops also fulfil their responsibility in the world. Although they should keep out of concrete political and other temporal issues, they are still responsible if it concerns the basic theological orientation of the secular areas and their moral order. What the Council highlighted as the legitimate independence of secular realities,[51] for which the laity are particularly responsible, is often misunderstood as if these temporal realities were neutral and were not in need of purification, sanctification and orientation towards the universal saving design of God through the ministry of the Church through Christ and in the Holy Spirit.

Conversely, the ordained ministry depends upon the participation of the laity. The Council explicitly stated that the laity can participate in certain official services. This applies to liturgy, catechesis, theology, welfare and social work and building up communities.[52] Thus, there are laypeople who are not ordained but participate in certain tasks of the ordained clergy and who do so as their main profession. Without such services and without the generous voluntary commitment of many men and women in the pastoral areas mentioned above, in many cases the ecclesial life could no longer be sustained. To the same extent that clergy are not fundamentally excluded from temporal affairs, the faithful are not basically excluded from any kind of participation in the official priesthood.

Just as, in the secular order, there is no collective term for citizens exercising no official or sovereign function – they are simply citizens of the state – so in analogy there is no strict and exclusive collective term for lay Christians without official ecclesial function. They are simply members of the Church with all rights and duties connected with it. One can give only a kind of typological or working definition and say that within the common mission of all baptized it is the particular and normal task of the lay Christian to sanctify the temporal reality from within, while within the common mission it is the *proprium* of the special priesthood to support the laity in their mission (Eph. 4.12) – that is, to inspire them spiritually and to motivate them, to accompany them and, above all, to strengthen them through the administration of the sacraments.

In this the special priesthood is literally a *sacerdotium ministeriale*, a priesthood of service for the task of Christians living in the world.[53] Therefore, those bearing offices in the Church should respect the personal dignity of the faithful and listen to their counsel.[54] This applies, in particular, to secular issues in which Christians living in the world are at home and have their own professionalism. In a different way this pertains also to questions of faith. For each baptized one was given the Holy Spirit and each is taught by him (1 Jn 2.27); therefore the sense for faith (*sensus fidei*) pertains to all of those who are baptized.[55]

Finally and above all, the distinction between spiritual person and secular Christian is obsolete. For according to Scripture, all of the baptized are 'spiritual people' and the vocation to holiness is common to the baptized.[56] Also, the 'normal' Christians living in the world should not be of the world (cf. Jn 17.14f.), but, rather, they should sanctify themselves and the world in their temporal existence and service. In addition, the 'world Christians' should not be worldly or secularized Christians, but they should sanctify the temporal reality from within. They are to be leaven in the world and permeate the world with the spirit of the Gospel.

Post-conciliar developments

The Council's statements about the life and mission of lay Christians in the Church and the world had been prepared in the pre-conciliar renewal movements and in theology. They did not, so to speak, appear out of the blue. Still, for general awareness they seemed nevertheless revolutionary, just as if all distinctions had been abolished. Also, as will be discussed later, many priests were unsettled in their self-understanding. In particular, in connection with the debate on fundamental democratization after 1968 there was a lot of discussion on democratization in the Church and on the question of the rights of the laity.

The episcopal synod of 1987 on the *Vocation and Mission of the Laity in the Church and in the World* was to clarify and explore the questions that had arisen. The post-synodal exhortation *Christifideles laici* (1988) further explored some aspects of Vatican II. Though demanded in parts, it did not give up the term laity, but tried to give it a deeper, positive dimension. It says: 'the entire existence of the lay faithful has as its purpose to lead a person to a knowledge of the radical newness of the Christian life that comes from Baptism, the sacrament of faith, so that this knowledge can help that person live the responsibilities which arise from that vocation received from God.' To describe the essence of the layperson, the exhortation refers therefore to baptism: 'Baptism regenerates us in the life of the Son of God; unites us to Christ and to his Body, the Church; and anoints us in the Holy Spirit, making us spiritual temples.'[57]

Consequently, the laity do not only belong to the Church, they *are* the Church. They are so because of the common participation based on baptism in the mystery and vocation of the Church, and yet, at the same time, they are Church only in community with the ordained clergy and those in religious orders. 'Among the lay faithful this one baptismal dignity takes on a manner of life which sets a person apart, without, however, bringing about a separation from the ministerial priesthood or from men and women religious.'[58]

The call for a democratization of the Church departs not from the *communio*-concept but instead from a non-theological and thus inappropriate criterion.[59] Of course there can be no doubt that human and personal rights based on natural law are also valid in the Church.[60] Still, the question of the laity's rights in the Church cannot be discussed with the criteria of today's democratization processes. Rather, they result, on the one hand, from the *communio* because of baptism and confirmation and, on the other, by way of inference from the serving nature of the ecclesial ministry.[61] Without any claim to comprehensiveness, laypeople have the right to Christian education and to a proclamation in which they hear the doctrine of the Church and not the private views of the preacher; insofar as they are properly disposed, they have the right to receive the sacraments, particularly the Eucharist, in accordance with the order of the Church;[62] they have the right to speak and to be heard in questions of faith; they have the right to participate in building up the people of God and in shaping temporal affairs in the spirit of the Gospel; as parents they have the right and with it also the duty to educate their children in a Christian manner; they have the right to assemble into Christian associations.

To do justice to the *communio*-character of the Church and the vocation and responsibility which is in common but to be realized in different ministries, it is necessary – and this is a far-reaching consequence – to develop a communicative and participatory style of life and of leading the Church which takes seriously the personal responsibility of the ministry as well as the dignity of the laity who are never just object but also responsible subject of the salvation mission of the Church. It is important to give space and to listen to God's spirit through an ordered cooperation of all charismas and by listening to each other.

The unity of vocation, while distinguishing and not confusing the different ministries, necessitates bodies of joint consultation and consensus-building.[63] Bishop Cyprian of Carthage gave this participatory and collegial style a classic expression. He writes that he wants to do nothing on his own judgement without the counsel of the presbyters and the consent of the people, indeed he only wants to decide on the basis of joint consultation and examination.[64] The same wisdom is also found in the Rule of St Benedict. Although he emphasizes very much the role of the abbot, the abbot is to decide nothing in matters of importance without having heard before the counsel of the brothers.[65] John Henry Newman explored this aspect beautifully in his treatise *On Consulting the Faithful in Matters of Doctrine*, showing that, during the Arian crisis of the fourth century, it was not the hierarchy but the laity who maintained and saved the true faith.[66] Also, in the present crisis, it is absolutely vital for the Church that the official ministry listens to the testimony of the laity and takes it seriously. This applies not only to public and published opinion, in the Church as well, but also and in particular to the testimony of the ordinary people, the quiet people, the praying women and men, the young and the old.

Unfortunately, the post-conciliar debate has not always distinguished between a legitimate and illegitimate de-clericalization. It is legitimate that worldly tasks in the Church such as economy, administration, public relations, education, formation and others which were traditionally done by the clergy are given today to trained laypeople. This division of tasks accords with the specific responsibility of the laity as well as with increased complexity and differentiation in the sectors mentioned. However, the case is different when the interest focuses on the most extensive participation possible of the laity in specific tasks of the ministry. This leads to the danger of clericalizing the laity and laicization of the clergy.[67] The consequence of such an – unfortunately widespread – ecclesial inward focus is that responsibility for the sanctification and permeation of the world, as emphasized by the Council, and the orientation to God's saving plan is no longer the centre of attention. Yet this is a task that is today more than urgent.

Laypeople in pastoral service

The number of laypeople who work as full-time staff in the pastoral service of the Church has increased significantly since the Council. For quite some time now, especially in missionary areas, there have been catechists and, because of the particular development in Germany, pastoral and parish assistants.[68] In the USA one speaks instead of lay ecclesial ministers.[69] This question is not about the dignity and vocation of the laity as such but about laypeople who, after a special training because of an explicit mandate (usually conferred ecclesially in a liturgical form), participate, for a specific time, in tasks which are not only traditionally but specifically tasks of the ecclesial ministry.

The Council basically envisages such commissioning and respective forms of collaboration.[70] One has to attest that many people who perform these tasks do so with dedication and their work has been fruitful with a lot of success. As Christians who live and work in the world they can bring aspects of today's life into the ecclesial service and conversely they can live out the Gospel in the contexts of life and the world. And, moreover, one will be grateful for such 'fresh air'.

Yet, by now these services have taken on a dimension that goes far beyond the originally envisaged special situation and emergency and has become in many parishes the normal state of affairs. This poses some basic problems. The laypeople who work commissioned by the Church full-time in the pastoral field are considered factually as clergy by some (K. Rahner); others argue for the creation of a new level within the ordo, in other words a new form of the lower clergy (Peter Hünermann).

Both suggestions are theologically problematic. Leaving aside the fact that both concepts can only lead to a subordinated rank of a substitute office and can thus be regarded as discrimination, they both lead to a new separation of ordination, leading and teaching authority which the Council rightly intended to overcome.[71] What is seemingly progressive reveals itself literally as a step back into the Middle Ages. Above all, such mixed forms obscure the sacramental basic structure of the Church. This causes uncertainty among priests and ordinands as well as laypeople themselves in their respective self-understanding. This in turn does not lead to the desired fruitful cooperation. Instead, it leads to bad fighting for prestige and competences, to tensions and, in the end, to frustration on all sides.

If the commissioning of laity for full-time participation in certain tasks of the ordained ministry is to have a future in a responsible way, of which there can be no doubt in the case of the catechists, and if theological ambiguities and bad practical tensions are thereby to be avoided, then it would be recommendable to entrust to the professional pastoral services of the laity such areas of pastoral care in which, because of baptism and confirmation, the layperson is able to assume relatively independent responsibility. This includes, among others, catechesis, education, caritas, group work, missionary witnessing in milieus far from the Church, and so forth.[72] All this is sensible and useful. In contrast, the proclamation within the liturgy (homily) and the leading of public, liturgically formed worship services of the Word cannot be the normal task of the laity and laypeople can be commissioned only in individual cases. Finally, it is absurd to base the fundamental question of the place and appreciation of the laity on questions concerning the profession of one group. As will be shown directly below, the real and pressing challenges lie somewhere else.

Marriage and family as the particular place of the vocation of the laity

Because of its nature, the laity's responsibility lies particularly and distinctively, though by no means exclusively, in the area of marriage and family. Marriage and family have their foundation already in the order of creation (Gen. 1.27f.); they are God's good gift and order and they were sanctified by Jesus Christ (Mt. 19.3–9). The Church considers the marriage bond as the sacramental sign of the covenant between God and his people and of the covenant between Christ and his Church (Eph. 5.21–33; cf. Col. 3.18–21; 1 Pet. 3.1–7). The Council calls the family a kind of domestic church.[73] Marriage and family are the fundamental centre of ecclesial and social life; they build up the Church and enrich it.

In matrimony and family, life is transmitted not only physically. Rather, normally there occurs also the second, social birth, the intellectual and spiritual formation of the young human which is of fundamental importance for the building of human society and for the Church. In matrimony and family, faith is to be passed on, lived and practised. Matrimony and family are therefore the distinct location for the social and ecclesial commitment of the laity.

Matrimony and family are about the creational determination of humanity who, as man and woman, is called to a lifelong partnership which normally finds its fulfilment in children. Accordingly, family happiness is, for most people today, dream of their lives. God's blessing rests upon it (Gen. 1.28; cf. 2.22–4). Alternative concepts of partnership may realize some values of matrimony and family in a similar way. Yet, as they do not accord with God's order in creation, they also do not accord with God's vocation for humanity. God's blessing does not rest upon them, and therefore they cannot become a blessing for man or society. One may not socially discriminate against them. Still, the Church cannot approve of them and bless them.[74] If the Church did that, it would become untrustworthy in its task to testify God's order for the benefit of mankind.

The present crisis of matrimony and family must be seen in the shift in global demographics, in the problems concerning education and Christian initiation of children and youth and in the high number of divorces. This is a crisis which threatens the future of society and the Church from within. If anywhere, then it is here in this area that laypeople, men and women, are particularly called.

The place of women in the Church

Together with the question of the place of the laity in the Church, today there is often discussion of the place of women in the Church.[75] Usually this does not happen without a tone of criticism of the Catholic Church. In all honesty, one cannot deny that in the Catholic Church, though unfortunately not only here, there have been – and still partly are – misogynist tendencies and discrimination against women. Yet one should also not deny that the Catholic Church has moved on this question and that some common stereotypes no longer accord with reality.

It was the first official breakthrough when Pope John XXIII counted in the encyclical *Pacem in terris* (1963) among the 'signs of the time' the growing awareness of the woman, of her human dignity and her participation in public life, and he demanded general recognition of her human rights.[76] The Second Vatican Council took up this impulse and spoke clearly against any kind of discrimination and for the responsible collaboration of women in the Church and in society.[77] It admonished to take care that women in the Church are given space and attention and that they have possibilities of participation.[78] In the final declaration of the Council it says: 'The hour is coming, in fact has come, when the vocation of women is being achieved in its fullness, the hour in which woman acquires in the world an influence, an effect and a power never hitherto achieved. That is why, at this moment when the human race is undergoing so deep a transformation, women impregnated with the spirit of the Gospel can do so much to aid mankind in not falling.'

Several post-conciliar documents have taken up this issue and adopted the new tone, which is announced here, and have extensively addressed the topic. This applies in particular to the apostolic letter by Pope John Paul II *Mulieris dignitatem. On the Dignity and Vocation of Women* (1988)[79] and the document resulting from the Synod on the Laity, *Christifdeles laici*

(1988).[80] All of these documents speak a new language and breathe a new spirit.

If one looks back from these recent magisterial statements to their theological origins, especially to the testimony of the Bible, then one will find in the Old Testament and still in the New Testament sentences that mirror the patriarchal culture of their time. Yet, one can also notice that the Old Testament and especially the New Testament transcend these culturally conditioned schemes. Already on the first pages of the Old Testament, the story of creation states that God created man and woman in his image and likeness (Gen. 1.27). Both, therefore, have the same dignity, and the woman has the same immediacy to God as the man.

Thus the Old Testament knows great and outstanding women who in decisive moments of Israel's history courageously intervened and who were independent subjects in the salvation history: Sara, Hagar, Rebecca, Rachel, Debora, Miriam, Hannah, Esther, Judith and others. In the New Testament we have to mention in first place Mary, the mother of the Lord and mother of the Church. With her yes she acted for the whole of humanity; in her the Church already existed, even before the first men were called; she is the lasting archetype of the Church and of being Christian.[81]

The way Jesus himself encountered women and dealt with them was perceived as new among his contemporaries. It is reported that the disciples were surprised that Jesus spoke to a woman (Jn 4.27). No contemporary rabbi did this. It was especially impressive and indeed shocking for his opponents how he dealt with sinners and adulteresses (Lk. 7.36–50 par; Jn 8.1–11; 12.3–8). During his wanderings he is also accompanied by women supporting him; among these Mary Magdalene stands out in particular (Lk. 8.2f.). There seems to have existed a personal friendship between Jesus and both sisters of Lazarus, Mary and Martha (Lk. 10.38–42; Jn 11.1f.). Yet, it is this relationship that highlights that Jesus sees women not just as handmaids, but as listeners of his word equal to the disciples. Courageous women followed him until under the cross (Lk. 23.49.55); they were the first witnesses of the resurrection (Mk 16.1–8 par; Jn 20.1f.11–18). For this reason Mary Magdalene is often called apostle of the apostles.

Jesus' most important statement in this context is his word about the indissolubility of marriage and the life of celibacy for the kingdom of heaven (Mt. 19.3–12). With this word, Jesus puts an end to the double moral standard whereby the husband can divorce his wife but not the wife her husband. For Jesus, this inequality of man and woman is expression of hard-heartedness. It does not correspond to God's original will of creation. For Jesus the wife is not at the disposal of the husband. The word celibacy for the sake of the kingdom of heaven goes one step further. It frees the celibate one from the obligation of marriage and from the destined role of the woman as wife. With this word the woman is 'somebody', even without a husband. She has here own 'status', that is, is respectable and respected apart from a relationship to a husband. This does not mean a devaluation but an increased appreciation of marriage, for marriage is thereby neither for the man nor for the woman a socially almost compulsory necessity. It is now a freely chosen option to celibacy (cf. also 1 Cor. 7.32–4).

On the basis of such Jesuanic statements and his own praxis, it is not surprising that in the Early Church women played an important role in spreading Christianity and building up communities. In his letters Paul mentions many names of women who supported him on his journeys and played an important role in the early communities, such as Lydia who after her conversion became the centre of a house community (Acts 16.14f.). For Paul, these women are not anonymous beings; he calls them by name and thanks them personally: the couple Priscilla and Aquila; Phoebe and many others (Acts 18.26; Rom. 16.1–16; 1 Cor. 16.19; Phil. 4.2f.; Col. 4.15; 1 Tim. 5.3–18).[82]

Paul was not the misogynist as he is sometimes portrayed.[83] For him, in Christ there is no longer male or female. Even though the natural, creational differences continue to exist, they have lost their separating and discriminating significance (Gal. 3.28). In 1 Cor. 11.11 he says the woman should not be without man nor the man without woman; even though according to Genesis the woman stems from the man, still man comes through the woman into the world. In Eph. 5.23 Paul adopts the patriarchal house rule according to which wives should be ruled by their husbands, yet he immediately corrects it by saying that men should love their wives as Christ loved the Church, indeed husbands should love their wives like their own body (Eph. 5.25.28). Paul goes even further. He describes the Church with female images. For him the Church is Christ's bride (2 Cor. 11.2). So, the woman and the female nature characterize the ecclesial community as a whole. The woman thus becomes a symbol for the Church and expresses the soul of the Church, the bridal love for Christ. The dedicated piety of many women indeed applies today to many men, including many priests.

Later on in church history there are many great and outstanding women to be named who made an independent contribution to mission and the history of piety: Monica, the mother of Augustine, Macrina, sister of Basil, Scholastica, the sister of Saint Benedict, Olga of Kiev, Walpurga and Leoba, Hildegard of Bingen, Hedwig of Silesia and Hedwig of Cracow, Elizabeth of Hungary, Birgitta of Sweden, Catherine of Siena, Joan of Arc, Rosa of Lima, Teresa of Ávila, Mary Ward, Margaret Mary Alacoque, Elizabeth Seton, Jeanne Françoise de Chantal, Thérèse de Lisieux, Edith Stein, Mother Teresa of Calcutta and many others. One cannot write the history of the Church without mentioning and appreciating these and many other women. Just as Mary Magdalene carried at Easter the message of the resurrection to the disappointed and depressed apostles, among them there have been, time and again, courageous women who roused and encouraged priests, bishops and even popes.

On the other hand, these great women cannot hide the fact that there are, in the history of theology and in canon law, numerous statements and regulations which degrade, disadvantage and discriminate against women in their relation to men with historically and culturally conditioned views that are, from today's perspective, obsolete. Although they are usually no longer publicly articulated, in parts such discrimination has an effect on mentality and praxis, even today. This does not devalue the examples already mentioned and the more recent doctrinal statements quoted above, but they provoke impulse to achieve a change of attitude and praxis.

If we look at today's teaching of the Church, then it proceeds from the statements of both of the creation narratives in Genesis about the dignity and place of the woman. They clearly state the same dignity for men and women. Both are created in God's image and likeness and therefore both are equal to each other (Gen. 1.27). The woman has the same human rights as the man. Because of their immediateness to God one cannot define the woman from the man nor to the man. Both can only be defined from God and towards God. The dignity of the woman is even less limited to her role as wife, mother, partner and colleague or only as worker. To this first statement, the creation narratives add a second one: man and woman were created for each other; they are to complement each other and to become one and fruitful in their children (Gen. 2.24). So equal dignity does not mean some abstract equality but one which is reciprocal and complementary. In this context, woman becomes the companion of the man and the man the companion of the woman. For us today, this means a relation of partnership between men and women.

This partnership and complementarity must not be reduced to bodily-sexual partnership, nor must it be defined, as has been common since Romanticism, by supposedly typically female or male characteristics. It has to be seen from the whole human, that is, both bodily and mentally. Body and soul form a unity: the soul is the essential form of the body and the body is the real symbol of the spirit. From this it follows that being woman or man is determined by creation and nature and is also given for responsibility and cultural shaping. The given biological-sexual determination (sex) can be shaped in the history of culture and society to different cultural and social roles (gender). That is why no woman can be imposed upon one historical image of woman. This does not mean arbitrariness or even freedom for manipulations of any kind. From a bodily-spiritually holistic perspective, the different bodily determination of man and woman is not irrelevant for unfolding the being of a person. Making the bodily dimension indifferent or manipulating it leads to a Gnostic or Cartesian duality of body and spirit which contradicts the holistic and personal approach of Christian anthropology.[84]

It is only against this background of the integral human, bodily-spiritual and personal determination of the relation between the sexes that we can understand the biblical symbolism for gender that has become largely alien for us today. The Bible sees the relation of husband and wife as a parable for the bridal relation between Christ and the Church (Eph. 5.32).[85] In this respect, the woman in the Bible virtually becomes the symbol and representative of the Church as Christ's bride. This highlights the fact that the woman as woman is 'somebody', an independent and autonomously responsible subject in the Church. Through her womanly nature she has something to give to the Church and to say what the Church would lack without her. For this reason, John Paul II speaks of the prophetic significance of the woman as woman.

It is thus essential that life in the parishes and on all levels of ecclesial life lost its largely male-shaped form and the female dimension was given more space. Prayers, hymns and forms of worship and the whole style of ecclesial life must become receptive for the experiences of happiness and sorrow, joy and pain of women; theological tenets must be complemented by images and symbols that reflect the concrete life and the experiences of women.

Yet, depending on their respective vocation, women can live their human, Christian and ecclesial existence in different ways. Departing from the order of creation and salvation, the Church appreciates the woman as wife and mother. As Eve, woman is the mother of all living (Gen. 3.20). Of course, the care, the affective home and the human and Christian education are entrusted jointly to fathers and mothers. Still, they are a particular essential, social and ecclesial service of the woman, which deserves ecclesial and social recognition. The Church also appreciates the dignity and contribution of those women who voluntarily or because of their destiny remain unmarried, especially of those women who, within or outside religious orders, live according to the evangelical counsels and thereby offer an irreplaceable and valuable service in the Church and society in education and caritas, often in the care for the poorest of the poor. Beyond the field of the family, women can and should be publicly active in the Church and in society in a responsible way.

Parish life today is no longer conceivable without the responsible voluntary and full-time commitment of women in community work, in catechesis, in pastoral care for families, sick and elderly and in many other fields. This engagement deserves to be appreciated much more than usually happens. During the last decades many things have come to be taken for granted, also on 'higher levels', and deserve to be supported further. Women today are no longer only active in the charitable field typically considered as womanly, but also in theology, in responsible positions in church leadership as councillors of the diocesan curia, chancellors, judges, heads of the diocesan caritas, responsible for the sector of education and formation and so forth. Also, in the Roman Curia qualified women could contribute in responsible positions a new style and new perspectives and help to overcome the clericalistic sphere and the atmosphere dominant there. It is therefore absurd and in itself again a clericalistically narrowed perspective if one intends to focus the issue of women in the Church exclusively on the question of women's ordination.[86]

If I am not completely mistaken, regarding the issue of the place and vocation of women in the Church, we are just at the beginning of a development. It will probably need charismatic and prophetic women who show with imagination and courage, but also with determination and patience, new forms and ways for the service of women in the Church, women who live exemplary lives and thereby enrich the ecclesial life. The eventful life and work of Mary Ward († 1645) was exemplary.[87] When she founded the Institute of the Blessed Virgin Mary (today: Congregatio Jesu), in which her sisters did not live in monastic seclusion as nuns, but instead lived according to the adapted rule of St Ignatius of Loyola, Mary Ward met with much opposition and hostility, not least from the Jesuits themselves. She did not give up and persisted. Still, it was only more than fifty years after her death that her order received ecclesiastical recognition. By now, the beatification of Mary Ward is within reach, although we still have to wait for it.

This shows again that the topic of women in the Church is far from finished and there remains much that can and must be done – in the interest of women, but also in the interest of the Church that cannot dispense with the charisma of women. Only if the Church gives space to the charisma of women can it reach the full realization of its catholicity and of its own nature as bride of Jesus Christ. The Church can shine into today's world only as a community based on partnership of men and women.

5.3 The offices of the Church as nexuses of service for the *communio*

Ministry as service

Emphasizing the dignity and mission of the laity in the Church raises the question about the ministries in the Church, their foundation and the concrete way of exercising their mission in relation to the mission of the laity. Obviously, if one looks in the New Testament for the foundation and understanding of ministry and ministries in the Church, one encounters immediately the difficulty that the New Testament does not know our term 'ministry' in the sense of a social position invested with certain competences. The New Testament does not use any contemporary Greek language term for community functions (ἀρχή, τιμή, τέλος, λειτουργία).[88]

Instead of the terms available in the language of that time, the New Testament speaks of service (διακονία). In other words, it uses a term that points in a completely different direction from the word 'ministry'. *Diakonia* does not mean the exercise of rights and competences, nor ruling, but helping action and behaviour that accords with what is indeed, in this respect, the revolutionary example of Jesus (Lk. 22.27) as he explicitly commissioned his disciples in contrast to ruling and dominating: 'Among you this is not to happen!' (Mk 10.43).[89] The New Testament idea of service, however, must be understood in a comprehensive sense. It reaches far beyond the charitable-social area; it does not only mean service at the tables but also the service of the word (Acts 6.2.4) as well as the commissioning to make present the ministry of Jesus who gave himself in service up to his own death: 'Do this in memory of me!' (Lk. 22.19; 1 Cor. 11.24).

Still, even with the help of the term *diakonia* we find in the New Testament no uniform order of ministries or services and no fixed structure of service. These developed only in the wake of the later New Testament writings in the third generation. In the New Testament we encounter an emerging Church. As far as this is possible, the reconstruction of this development process reveals some features that were not only authoritative from the beginning but also fundamental for the later Church. Ultimately the Church is always moving and it is so today in a totally new and in some respects quite dramatic way. Its historical way is not just a day out. The New Testament presents no detailed map for this way, but it offers the Church a kind of compass.

The foundation of Church offices in Jesus' calling of the disciples

With his message of the coming kingdom of God and his call to faith and repentance, Jesus addressed all who came to hear him (Mk 1.15). However, he called only certain chosen ones to follow him more closely. The vocation was radical; it entailed separation from occupations (Mk 1.18; 2.14), from the family (Mt. 8.21f.; 10.37) and from possessions (Mk 10.17–22). Again from the great number of his disciples Jesus chose in a special way twelve disciples (μαθηταί) mentioned by name. He called them to follow him more closely in order to send them out. All four gospels testify to this closer call to discipleship (Mk 1.16–20 par; 3.13–19 par; Jn 1.35–51).[90]

Mk 3.13–19 reports how Jesus, seeing the crowds of people, climbs up a mountain to pray. That is what he always did when important decisions had to be taken. Then he called those to him 'whom he wanted'. The appointment of the 'Twelve'[91] to special discipleship is thus a sovereign act of free and sovereign election. The disciples do not put themselves forward or apply to become disciples. The call addressed to them is an effective word that ultimately makes the disciples into disciples. It says in the text 'he made' (ἐποίησεν), in other words he created them his disciples. This does not annihilate the freedom of those called in this way; they must follow the call out of their own decision. Of them it says: 'they came to him'. This decision is radical. They leave everything behind: home, family, income, and share Jesus' itinerant life. This radical nature goes far beyond what the rabbis of that time demanded from their disciples.

The vocation is followed by the double determination of the goal of special discipleship: the disciples are to be with Jesus and his community to be then sent out. In other words, gathering and sending belong together. The mission can be lived and realized only out of the community with Jesus. Finally, the disciples are individually mentioned by name. They are not anonymous, exchangeable, impersonal functionaries. They have a name; they are accountable with their person for their 'object'. They are witnesses who stand with their whole person for that to which they testify. They can be convincing only as witnesses; only as such they can win other people, i.e. be fishers of men (Mk 1.17).

Quite likely, Jesus himself did not yet call his disciples apostles.[92] The call to follow more closely in special discipleship does not yet signify the institution of certain offices. Yet, after Easter this call became the basis for the office of apostle. After Easter the exalted Lord sent out the Twelve into all the world to proclaim the Gospel and to make all people his disciples (Mt. 28.16–20; cf. Mk 16.15–18; Jn 20.21–3; Acts 1.8). The mission is to last until the end of the world (Mt. 28.20). Yet, the apostles were also mortal. Therefore, after their deaths others have to take up their mission and continue their vocation. These 'others' are no apostles, for the office of apostle is unique, going back to the immediate commissioning by the resurrected one. So these 'others' are not new apostles, but only they exercise certain apostolic functions. They do not have the office of apostle, but rather the office. It is only in this analogous sense that they can be called successors of the apostles.

The development of the apostolic Church

If one asks who these others are who, according to the testimony of the New Testament, exercise the apostolic functions of the apostles, one does not receive a uniform answer in the New Testament.[93] At first the authority of the apostles was still so much immediately present that the question of a clear structure of ministries arose only towards the end of the apostolic time and in the immediate post-apostolic period. Initially this development was obviously quite diverse and led only in the second and third generation to fixed institutional forms.

Even though there were no uniform structures of ministry and community in the initial period, it cannot be denied that from the beginning there have been special ministries in the communities that can be called community offices. There can be no talk of a purely charismatic beginning out of which more institutional forms developed only later. Also the situation of the church in Corinth which is often referenced cannot be used to support the thesis of an initially purely charismatic order. The list of charismata in 1 Cor. 12.28 displays a clear structure: it explicitly mentions in first place the apostles, in second the prophets and in third the teachers. These are apparently ministries constitutive for the community. They are followed by other charismata which are introduced with 'in addition' and which are obviously not granted the same importance. In addition to the apostles, prophets and teachers the list mentions shepherds; in the early period they played an important role in other communities (Acts 13.1; Eph. 4.11). We are obviously looking at a relatively widespread early constellation.

At first the early community in Jerusalem was led by the apostles (Acts 1.42; 4.33.36f.; 5.2; 6.6; 8.14 et seq.), among whom Simon/Peter particularly stood out as the decisive authority.[94] Together with him John steps forward repeatedly (Acts 3.1–11; 4.13.19). Later we encounter the three 'pillars', James, Kephas and John, as those with special esteem in the community (Gal. 2.9). After Peter's departure from Jerusalem, James was responsible for the church in Jerusalem (Acts 12.7; 15.13; 21.7 et seq.). He also could claim an immediate appointment by the resurrected (1 Cor. 15.7).

Quite early on we hear that, as the burdens increased and there was the danger of divisions in the community, the apostles appointed by laying-on of hands the 'Seven' as assistants. In this context, service (διακονία) is mentioned. However, the Seven cannot be regarded as deacons in the later sense. They are, rather, to be seen as the leaders of the Hellenistic gentile Christian communities (Acts 6.1–7). In any case, their ministry cannot be restricted to service at the tables. In particular, Stephen worked as a charismatically gifted evangelist (Acts 6.8–60). Philip worked as a missionary and catechist and he baptized (Acts 8). The early Christian literature mentions the deacons at the side of the bishops (Phil. 1.1; Didache 15.1f.). Later the same demands are required of them as of bishops (1 Tim. 3.1–7; 3.8–12).

According to Acts of the Apostles, wherever Paul came he appointed elders (πρεσβύτεροι) by laying hands on them and with fasting and prayer (Acts 14.23). In addition, in the prescript to Philippians we read of overseers and deacons in that community (Phil. 1.1). Still, for that time, both titles should not be understood in their later meaning. Initially, the difference between *presbyteroi* and *episkopoi* seems not to have been really clear-cut. When at his departure from Miletus, in anticipation of his death, Paul appointed shepherds nominated by the Holy Spirit who were called *episkopoi* as well as *presbyteroi* (cf. Acts 20, verse 17 with verse 28).

It is generally assumed that, following the respective synagogue tradition, those presiding over the community in the Hellenistic-Judaeo Christian milieu were called *presbyteroi* (Acts 14.23; 15.2; 20.17.28; 21.18; Jam. 5.14; 1 Tim. 5.17.19; Tit. 1.5; 1 Pet. 5.1). By contrast, the gentile Christians spoke Greek. Here, one speaks of *episkopoi*, literally overseers, i.e. people having control and oversight (Acts 20.28; Phil. 1.1; 1 Tim. 3.1f.). It is remarkable that in the pastoral letters the title *episkopos* is always used in the singular, whereas for *presbyteroi* they use the plural. The presbyters seem to have formed a kind of senate, a council of elders. It is contested whether we can perceive therein already an indication of a development towards the monepiscopate.

Both *presbyteroi* and *episkopoi* are defined more precisely in the New Testament with the help of the term shepherd (Acts 20.28; Eph. 4.11; 1 Pet.

2.25; 5.2). As pastors and shepherds, a pastoral service pertains to them. In this sense 1 Peter emphatically admonishes the elders: 'give a shepherd's care to the flock of God that is entrusted to you: watch over it, not simply as a duty but gladly, as God wants; not for sordid money, but because you are eager to do it. Do not lord over the group which is in your charge, but be an example for the flock' (1 Pet. 5.2f.).

If we consider the context of all these different statements, then it is hardly possible to regard these services as purely functional ministries. The fact that their commissioning happens with the laying-on of hands and prayer speaks against such a functional view. In the Old Testament-Jewish tradition (cf. Num. 27.18–23), the laying-on of hands (ἐπίθεσις τῶν χειρῶν) is not just a formal, purely legal gesture. It means conferring blessing and authority. It grants a gift of the Spirit, the spirit of power, love and consideration (2 Tim. 1.6f.; cf. 1 Tim. 4.14; 5.22). So the laying-on of hands is the technical term for the ordination as transferring a charisma of ministry.[95] With this, the institution and the sacramental understanding of ordination already have their foundation in the New Testament.

Generally, exegetes today consider the pastoral letters and 1 Peter not to have been written by the apostles themselves but by their pupils. In the world of that time such pseudepigraphy was fairly common. From a theological perspective, it indicates that from the beginning – and in fact without problems – there was what later came to be called apostolic succession. The New Testament itself reflects in some passages upon this transition. In Paul's farewell speech from Miletus, the apostle envisages the post-apostolic time. He determines that the overseers or presbyters should care for the flock after his departure (Acts 20.28f.). This farewell speech of Paul could also be called his testament for the post-apostolic time. According to the pastoral letters, Paul commissioned Timothy and Titus to pass on their ministry with the laying-on of hands (1 Tim. 4.14; 2 Tim. 1.6; Tit. 1.5).

The appointing of shepherds of the communities not only has a 'horizontal' dimension. Ultimately, it is the exalted Lord himself who guarantees the continuity. It is he who appoints shepherds in the Church (Eph. 4.11). So the community ministries are more than just an ecclesiastical or communal institution; ultimately they have a Christological and pneumatological foundation. Already in the Old Testament, God himself is called shepherd of his people. The New Testament calls Jesus shepherd (1 Pet. 5.4) and shepherd and bishop of the souls (2 Pet. 2.25). It is he who, as the exalted one, gathers the flock. In this way Paul can speak of God's fellow workers (συνεργοί; 1 Cor. 3.9; 1 Thess. 3.2; cf. 2 Cor. 1.24). All of this highlights that the shepherds fulfil their ministry in the name and service of God who gathers the flock through Jesus Christ, who feeds it and keeps caring for it.

The community participated in the commissioning of the shepherds in the New Testament time and the time of the Early Church, but they were not appointed and commissioned by the community. In this way the shepherds can claim authority in their ministry. There are good reasons why they are called overseers (προϊστάμενοι, 1 Thess. 5.12) and leaders (ἡγούμενοι, Heb. 13.7.17.24). Paul repeatedly admonishes to show respect to them and to subordinate oneself to them (1 Thess. 5.12f.; 1 Cor. 16.15f.; Heb. 13.7). It applies to them what Paul claims for himself: 'we are ambassadors for Christ; it is as though God were urging you through us, and in the name of Christ we appeal to you to be reconciled to God' (2 Cor. 5.20). Jesus Christ invests them with authority (ἐξουσία) to prepare the people for his service, to lead it and strengthen it (Eph. 4.12). Hence, 'anyone who listens to you listens to me; anyone who rejects you rejects me, and those who reject me reject the one who sent me' (Lk. 10.16; cf. Mt. 10.40; Jn 13.20).

So we find already in the New Testament clear outlines of the later understanding and ordering of the official ministries. Still, despite the fact that ministerial structures already began to become fixed, the development remained in flow for some time. This can be seen in the fourth gospel that does not know of presbyters and overseers. Here, the charismatic figure of Jesus' favourite disciple dominates, who is placed concurrently against Peter (Jn 12.23; 20.8f.; 21.7ff.20ff.). While we find in the *Didache* apostles, prophets and teachers, we also hear of charismatic wandering apostles (*Didache* 11–15). Also, in some post-New Testament writings of the Early Church[96] the development seems not to have been completed. According to the first epistle of Clement, the church of Corinth appears to have been led by a group of presbyters and, remarkably, Ignatius of Antioch speaks nowhere in his letter to the church of Rome of a bishop of this church, as he normally does elsewhere.

Therefore, we must assume a variegated development which happens by no means synchronously but quite differentiatedly. However, nowhere were the different orders perceived as essentially conflictive, but rather as legitimate diversity within a greater common ground. Viewed as a whole, we may well speak of a shift from more charismatic to more institutional forms. Still, nowhere is there a conflict between charisma and institution, for the ministries are also not perceived as institution but as gifts of the Spirit. So the Church is always both charismatic event and institution.[97] For this reason it would be anachronistic and would display a static and unhistorical understanding of the Church if one wanted to find all later developments already in the New Testament, as it would be equally anachronistic if one intended to find the later different episcopal and presbyterian denominational church orders already in the Early Church and, with this, legitimize denominational differences.[98] The New Testament presents us with the image of a dynamic church in progress with charismatic as well as already clearly developed institutional elements and, as a church in progress as such, it is the standard for later developments.

The development of the episcopal office in the Old Church

On the basis of the New Testament and, in particular, the development observable in the pastoral letters, it seems clear that the threefold ministry of bishop – priest – deacon and the so-called monarchic episcopate emerged in the post-apostolic period.[99] We find the earliest evidence for this development in the letters of Ignatius of Antioch, who probably died a martyr's death in Rome during the final years of Emperor Trajan (110–7). It is noteworthy that the letters of Ignatius of Antioch were written almost at the same time as the last books of the New Testament.

For Ignatius, the monepiscopate belongs definitely to the ecclesiastical structure. However, unlike today, for him the bishop is not the overseer of an ecclesial region but the overseer of a local city community. In this sense he writes: 'I exhort you to strive to do all things in harmony with God: the bishop is to preside in the place of God, while the presbyters are to function as the council of the Apostles, and the deacons, who are most dear to me, are entrusted with the ministry of Jesus Christ, who before time began was with the Father and has at last appeared.'[100] He writes to the Ephesians: 'it is therefore proper in every way to glorify Jesus Christ who has glorified you, so that you, fully trained in unanimous submission, may be submissive to the bishop and the presbytery, and thus be sanctified in every respect.'[101] The presbytery is to be united with the bishop like the strings on a harp, and they are to harmonize as in a single chord.[102]

With these statements Ignatius presents an idealized image which, already in his time, hardly matched with reality everywhere, including Rome. It seems that there was not yet a bishop in Rome, while in Corinth we hear of presbyters. And we have no information on this issue from such an important church as that of Alexandria. It is thus even more remarkable that this idealized image prevailed in the East and West very quickly and without any significant opposition.

Towards the end of the second century, there was Irenaeus of Lyons († about 202), a pupil of the Apostolic Father Polycarp of Smyrna who in turn, as Irenaeus tells us, was a pupil of the apostle John. Already for Irenaeus it is incontestable that the bishop is the head of a local church.[103] With his text *Adversus haereses*, Irenaeus – his name means the peace-loving one – is, so to speak, the first systematic theologian whose authority corresponded to his employment of a rule of faith (κανὼν τῆς πίστεως, *regula fidei*) a term coined by him that is significant for the subsequent theological Tradition. What is meant is the normativity of the apostolic kerygma in the ecclesiastical form of proclamation. With this rule, Irenaeus opposed the gnosis which pressed and threatened the Early Church and which appealed to private apostolic revelations. By contrast, Irenaeus refers to the apostolic succession of bishops which the Gnostics do not have. For him, the apostolic succession is the concrete embodiment, the content of which is the apostolic Tradition. Obviously Irenaeus is thereby aware that keeping the Church in the one apostolic faith is not guaranteed by a chain of laying-on of hands, but that it is, ultimately, the work and gift of the Holy Spirit.

Already the *Traditio apostolica*, ascribed to the Roman presbyter (and counter bishop) Hyppolytus († 235), offers in the third chapter a description of an episcopal ordination. It takes place with the laying-on of hands and the prayer for the spirit of leadership and is intended to fulfil, in a dignified manner, the mystery of the high priest.[104] On the basis of this description, Hyppolytus goes on to refer to the bishop with sacerdotal terminology 'high priest'. This terminology was taken up by Cyprian of Carthage († 258) and became common usage from then on.[105] With this, the celebration of the Eucharist is moved into the centre of the episcopal ministry.[106] Cyprian also considers it essential that the episcopate is one and undivided and is exercised by the bishops together (*in solidum*).[107] So the *communio* structure of the Church becomes apparent in the episcopal office. The bishop is in the Church and the Church is in the bishop.[108]

We see, then, that the development of a doctrine of episcopacy was more or less complete by the first half of the third century. The Council of Nicaea (325) already unmistakably presupposed this development and adopted the rule already found in the writings of Hyppolytus,[109] namely, that all bishops of a province should participate in the ordination of a bishop.[110] This rule is more than a rule of protocol, but rather symbolizes that the bishop is ordained for a particular local church and that through ordination he is placed at the same time into the college of bishops. This also expresses sacramentally and symbolically in the ordination the *communio* shape of the Church and the episcopal office.

This super- and subordination is described by Clement of Alexandria († about 215), Origen († 253/254) and then especially by Pseudo-Dionysius the Areopagite (about 500) as an image of the hierarchy of angels; a move that exemplifies also, but certainly not only, a platonic form of speculation and an allegorical exuberance.[111] Such statements illustrate that, in this early time, the Church understood itself not only as an earthly institution and organization, but also as a community connecting the earth with heaven. It saw itself as *communio* sanctorum where, particularly in the liturgy, the heavenly world reaches into the earthly one and, vice versa, the earthly world reaches into the heavenly one.

The matter-of-course naturalness and speed with which the conception of the threefold ministry could prevail in such a short time has often astonished scholars and has led to the question of the origins of this impetus.[112] A number of historical reasons can be identified. Yet, the sociological explanations suffice only at first sight, for despite all links with existing sociological and religio-historical concepts in terms of content, the episcopal office of the Old Church was something new that accorded with the eschatological novelty of the New Testament people of God. Hence, one is compelled to conclude that the development was generally received without problems and quickly and without noticeable opposition, mainly because it accorded with the intrinsic law of the Church's nature and of the ministry.

Despite this quick and remarkable concord, regarding the threefold ministry the Council of Trent did well not to speak of divine institution (*institutio*) but of *divina ordinatio*, i.e. of divine order or providence.[113] Also Vatican II expresses itself carefully, saying that the one ministry instituted by Jesus Christ is exercised of old (*ab antiquo*) in this threefold order.[114]

Medieval developments

This rapid consolidation in the understanding of the threefold ministry by no means excluded further developments. On the contrary, in the second millennium during the early Middle Ages, a form and understanding of ministry prevailed that had been prepared in some respects in the first millennium, but was substantially different from the ideal image we have with Ignatius of Antioch, Irenaeus of Lyons and Cyprian of Carthage. One has to speak of a deep-reaching change of form.[115]

As Christianity expanded from the cities to the surrounding country and as presbyters were entrusted with rural communities, the presbyters who had previously been a council of the bishop became under the authority of the bishop overseers of communities and the Eucharist. This led to an increasingly sacerdotal understanding of the office of the presbyter. The episcopal office developed from the office of an overseer of a community of churches in a city to one of regional oversight which, in the Middle Ages, was additionally tied into the feudal system.

This development was one reason why, in the Middle Ages, the bishop was ascribed not only sacramental priority but also a priority of dignity, i.e. jurisdiction. To this Hieronymus contributed particularly with a passage in his commentary on the letter to Titus, according to which the presbyters had originally been on equal standing with the bishops, and placing them higher was therefore to be regarded more as custom than an order of the Lord.[116] This statement had an enormous effective history. Through Isidor of Seville and the Pseudo-Isidorean Decretals it quickly gained great influence in medieval theology. The consequence was the separation of judicial authority from the sacramental power of ordination which led to the unfortunate distinction between power of ordination (*potestas ordinis*) and power of jurisdiction (*potestas jurisdictionis*).[117] This doctrine was adopted by the *Decretum* (around 1140) of Gratian and then by the influential *Sentences* of Peter Lombard († 1160).[118] In this way it became authoritative for the whole medieval period.

The great systematic theologian of the Middle Ages, Thomas Aquinas, attempted a synthesis again in his later work.[119] Basically he remained confined within the medieval perspective that bishops were on the same level as presbyters concerning the power of Eucharistic consecration (*corpus Christi verum*) and that the episcopal ordination was no sacrament in and of itself. However, Thomas would not have been the genial systematic that he was if he had not felt the inadequacy of this theory and had at least indicated a way out of this inextricable situation. For him, concerning the *corpus Christi verum* in the Eucharist, the power of consecration, priests are placed on the same level as bishops; still with regard to the *corpus Christi mysticum* of the Church a greater authority pertains to the bishops, which includes also the administration of ordination – in other words, a sacramental authority. Yet, for Thomas, in the tradition of Augustine, the *corpus Christi verum* is only an intermediate reality of the Eucharist (*res et sacramentum*) whereas the *corpus Christi mysticum*, the unity of the Church is the actual object and goal of the Eucharist (*res sacramenti*).[120] The higher authority of the bishop regarding the *corpus Christi mysticum* is thereby moved out of the purely judicial sphere and stands in an intrinsic sacramental relation to the Eucharist and embraces and reaches above the power of ordination of the priest.

Unfortunately, this perspective and the possibilities it contained could not prevail in the late Middle Ages. On the contrary, the judicial dimension became even more independent. As in the medieval view the priest, even though in a similar way, had the same authority as the bishop, the opinion spread among theologians and canonists that with a dispensation from the pope priests could also, in exceptional cases, administer the ordination. This indeed happened in some cases.[121]

This theological view and the cases based on it have to be regarded as, at best, marginal. One may not deduce from such theological opinions and from such borderline cases a further theory of a possible presbyterial succession beyond the episcopal succession. The fact that these presbyterial ordinations required papal dispensations shows that, even though in a problematic way, incorporation into the *communio* net of the episcopate, as we would say today, was also basically maintained in these cases. Together with the many grave ills in the late Middle Ages, these borderline cases highlight the large extent of theological uncertainties and ultimately the dead end which had been reached. Both were to have a fatal effect in the Reformation.

The critiques of the Reformers and the reply of the Council of Trent

The Reformers' criticism of the understanding of ministry concerned the unmistakable abuses of which there was no shortage at the end of the medieval period. And yet the Reformers went beyond the problem of abuses to call into question the sacramental understanding of the ecclesial ministry itself. This criticism was even more fundamental as it was linked to a related criticism concerning the understanding of the Eucharist as sacrifice of the mass which Luther considered 'the greatest and most horrible abomination' and a 'papal idolatry'.[122] In other words, the criticism of the ordination was ultimately a criticism of the ordination to the 'sacrificial priesthood'.

In his writing *Of the Babylonian Captivity of the Church* (1520) Luther called the sacrament of ordination a human invention containing no promise of grace.[123] For him, all believers are priests by virtue of baptism. That a priest wants to be more than everybody else because of his ordination is, for Luther, a contradiction of the liberty of the Christian and of the Christian brotherhood and is therefore an expression of shameful tyranny. With this, Luther did not abolish ordination, but understands it as a commissioning for the ministry of the word. It is only this ministry of the word that constitutes a priest or a bishop; one who does not preach is no priest. For Luther as well as for the other Reformers, ordination was thus the commissioning to the ministry of the word and the sacraments which were regarded as intensification or, in the case of Calvin, as confirmation of the word.[124]

Although all have the same authority in God's word and sacrament, they should exercise it only with the consent of the community or because of commissioning by superiors. So the sacrament of ordination is nothing but the custom of calling somebody into the service of the Church.[125] With the thesis that whoever does not preach is not a priest, Luther also turned against the doctrine of the indelible sacramental character of ordination. Melanchthon was at least prepared to recognize ordination as a sacrament in the wider sense as long it was not seen as the authorization to sacrificial service but to the ministry of word and sacrament.[126] Similarly Calvin also knows that the apostolic custom of the laying-on of hands at ordination is not ineffective.[127] However, the Reformers rejected all rites of ordination that could have been understood as conferring the power to offer the sacrifice of the mass.

Regarding the administrator of the ordination, the Reformers basically maintained that the bishop was, in normal circumstances, the person to administer it. Yet, as no bishop of the 'old faith' confessed to the Reformation and was prepared to ordain pastors for the Reformation communities, Luther saw himself forced to perform ordinations himself.[128] In a letter to the Bohemian communities that were without pastors, he recommended that they should elect one or several from their midst and appoint them with prayer and laying-on of hands.[129] For Melanchthon also, the ordination pertains primarily to the bishops. Because of the refusal of the Catholic bishops to ordain pastors for the Reformation communities, he called the ordination by non-bishops as a right of emergency and to support this referred to respective late medieval canonistic theories and their biblical and patristic lines of argument.[130]

The Reformation criticism, in particular the criticism of the sacrificial character of the mass and of the priestly ministry resulting from it, was perceived by the Catholic side as a fundamental challenge to the sacramental order and the perception of how this had historically developed. Thus the Council of Trent took recourse to the medieval understanding and defined the priestly ministry from the Eucharistic power.[131] It rejected the Reformation position that ordination was only a human invention and a rite created by humans for instituting into the ministry and the council defended ordination as a sacrament instituted by Jesus Christ that confers grace through word and signs.[132] It impresses an indelible character and confers a priestly authority unlimited in time such that once somebody has been ordained he cannot return to the state of a layperson.[133]

Still, in Canon VI and the doctrinal text belonging to it, there is also a different tone. It says that not all Christians are in the same way priests, rather there is according to divine will (*divina ordinatione*) a hierarchical order.[134] The bishops as successors of the apostles are thereby superordinated to the priests.[135] Although it is not said what this superordination is – in other words, it does not say if it is of sacramental or juridical nature – one can still detect in this wording a reorientation in the theology of the episcopal office.[136] Such a reorientation was already taking place in the late medieval period.[137] Yet, at that time a clarification of the bishop's position was not possible because of the embittered dispute with the curia.[138] In addition, the council stated that for the legitimacy of the ordination the consent of the people or the secular authorities was not necessary.[139] Finally, it declared the ordination of the reformers as illegitimate but not explicitly invalid.[140]

In the reform decrees, then, the council succeeded in clearly overcoming the sacerdotal narrowness and in outlining a more comprehensive pastoral model of the bishop and priest, orientated at the *cura animarum*, which included, besides the offering of the sacrifice of the mass and the sermon, the administration of the sacraments and care for the poor.[141] In the following period, the pastoral model had great influence on the pastoral praxis and the spirituality of many bishops and priests. The post-Tridentine reform bishops such as Charles Borromeo († 1584) and Francis de Sales († 1622) realized this model in exemplary fashion. However, in post-Tridentine theology the anti-Reformation sacerdotal view dominated almost exclusively. In consequence, two different models stood unreconciled next to each other.

In addition, in the post-Tridentine era the bishops, especially the German prince bishops, were tied into the feudal order. The feudal shape of the episcopal office ended only with the French Revolution and the end of the imperial church at the beginning of the nineteenth century. It was in this new situation that the First Vatican Council intended to clarify the question of ecclesiology as a whole. However, due to the untimely end of the council, it could deal only with the primacy of the bishop of Rome but not with the episcopal office. The abolition of this imbalance and the clarification of the theology of the episcopal office were therefore some of the expectations expressed most often for the Second Vatican Council.

The episcopal office at the Second Vatican Council

The Second Vatican Council signified a Copernican Revolution against the medieval tradition.[142] It went back to the Tradition of the Old Church and no longer defined the episcopal office as extended priestly ministry but, conversely, as the fullness of ministry and the priesthood as graded participation in the one *ordo*. With this, it renewed the understanding of the Old Church, the sacramental understanding of the episcopal ministry. It saw the bishop as the successor of the apostles[143] upon whom the fullness of the sacrament of ordination is conferred through episcopal ordination.[144]

Episcopal ordination confers upon the bishop the threefold ministry of priest, teacher and pastor, meaning that it basically also confers the jurisdiction which is meant by authority of the shepherd, even though this still requires the assignment (*determinatio*) to a diocese or, in exceptional cases, to an important task.[145] Bringing again together *ordo* and *iurisdictio* which had been separated in the early Middle Ages must be regarded as one of the most crucial decisions of the last council.

A further important step was that the Council perceived the episcopal ministry again in the sense of the Old Church, especially of Cyprian of Carthage, as participation in the one episcopate, which means in its integration into the whole episcopate and its head, the bishop of Rome.[146] According to the Council, because of their nature the three ministries can only be exercised in the hierarchical community with the head and the members of the episcopal college.[147] Thereby the problem, which Trent had not been able to solve, of the relation of the episcopal office to the Petrine office was not yet solved but was put on a new basis and brought closer to a solution.[148] Having stressed the sacramental and collegiate character of the episcopal ministry, the Council then drew the practical consequences for the renewal of synodal elements in the Church and for a new emphasis on the significance of the local or individual church within the universal Church.[149]

On the basis of *Lumen Gentium*, the decree *Christus Dominus, On the Pastoral Office of Bishops in the Church* elaborated the practical pastoral consequences of the renewed view of the episcopal office. It thereby placed in the foreground the bishop's duty as pastor and of proclamation and his apostolic missionary duty in the present world. The bishop is to present the Christian doctrine adequately adapted to the needs of the time and is to be in conversation with the people, especially those in difficult situations, with the separated Christians.[150] Following a line already sketched out in the Tridentine reform decrees, this draws an apostolic and missionary image of the bishop which went hand in hand with an explicit rejection of secular rights and privileges.[151]

Returning to the Old Church's conception of the episcopal office and simultaneously turning to today's missionary situation triggered an exploration of several issues: the foundation of a clarification concerning the problem, unresolved in Trent, of the relation between the episcopal office and the Petrine office and, together with this, the adoption of the pastoral intention of the Council of Trent. The emphasis of the Old Church unity of *ordo* and *iurisdictio* met the Orthodox perspective. Stressing the bishop's task of proclamation corresponded with present pastoral challenges and at the same time with a legitimate issue of Protestant theology. All in all, pastorally and ecumenically this opened a new post-Constantine chapter of Church history.

The ministry of the priest

On the one hand, the reorientation of the episcopal ministry and, on the other, the emphasis placed upon the participation of all baptized in the mission of the Church had to have consequences for the understanding of the priestly ministry. Important as the episcopal office may be, what would a bishop be without priests? He would be a head without arms and legs. The bishop is usually far away from the congregations; in contrast, how the Church is locally concretely represented and how it becomes pastorally efficient depends to a large extent on the priest. Yet, what is a priest? He is certainly not just a deficient edition of the sacrament of ordination. So what is his actual proprium? In addition, there are problems for the priest resulting from the changed situation within the Church and from a rapidly changing situation in society. These problems began to emerge already during Council. Thus it was appropriate, indeed necessary that the Council speak explicitly about the ministry of the priests.[152]

The Council began in the doctrine of the priestly ministry from the point that the priest becomes, through ordination, conformed to the likeness of Jesus Christ and shares in the ministry of sanctification, proclamation and leading. However, the priests do not have the fullness and highest level of priestly ordination, but rather depend upon the bishops for the exercise of their power. As it were, they represent the bishop in their local congregation and so make the universal Church visible. They are an aid and organ of the bishops and together with the bishop they form one presbyterium. Conversely, the bishops are to regard their priestly collaborators as sons and friends, just as those recognize the bishop as their father and are respectfully obedient to him. Among themselves, the priests are to be united in brotherliness.

On the other hand, the Council does not simply regard the priestly ministry as outflow from the episcopal ministry. Like any other sacrament, priestly ordination is also primarily administered by Jesus Christ himself.[153] Thus, because of ordination the priest is shaped according to the image of Christ the High Priest and called to the participation in his threefold ministry. He acts *in persona Christi*, especially in the celebration of the Eucharist, the central and focal point of the service and life of a priest.[154]

With this, the sacrament of priestly ordination gives the priest a relative independence and personal responsibility, even though he has to exercise this within the communion with the bishop and the presbytery. Similarly to the episcopal office, the Council emphasized extensively in the constitution on the Church, *Lumen Gentium*, and in the decree *Presbyterorum ordinis, On the Ministry and Life of Priests*, the apostolic-missionary duty of the priest in today's world.[155]

At this point it becomes clear that, in its recourse to the Old Church Tradition, the Council could not simply ignore the medieval tradition. Already in the Old Church the development began which led to the situation that relatively independent duties pertained to the priest as parish priest and in various other pastoral areas. This development is irreversible. Yet, the Council did not reach a satisfactory new synthesis, even though the approaches of Thomas Aquinas could have built a bridge. Continuing these concepts further, one could say that the Eucharistic power which the priest has together with the bishop is conferred upon the priest in view of the concrete local congregation (or in the case of a priest entrusted with a special task for a specific group of Christians). By contrast, it is conferred upon the bishop in view of the greater and ultimately universal *communio* of the Church and its unity which is the actual intentional purpose of the Eucharist. It is thus not about more or less participation in the one ministry, but about two dimensions orientated towards each other of the one Eucharist and of the one ministry in the one Church which is present in different ways but essentially interrelated with each other in local communities, in local or individual churches as well as in the universal Church. The Council did not think these questions through to the end; it has left questions unanswered which broke open after the Council in a dramatic way.

The post-conciliar identity crisis and a new orientation of the priestly ministry

Not only the new orientation in the perception of the episcopal office but also the emphasis on the participation of the laity in the mission, of the Church created a new situation for priests. It meant saying farewell to 'reverend', and entailed a new understanding of the priest as a brother among brothers. Both developments led to uncertainty, in fact, to an identity crisis for many priests. They asked themselves: who are we? Not bishops, not laypeople, what then?

In particular, the sacerdotal dimension of the priest, which had stood so much in the centre during the Middle Ages and in the post-Tridentine epoch, was now met with incomprehension by many, if not rejection. This often led to a more or less purely functional self-understanding of the priests as leaders of the congregation, and caused for many priests a crisis regarding their self-understanding and way of life, leading to an exodus during which many left their ministries. This dramatic identity crisis among priests ultimately highlighted the post-conciliar crisis of the Church itself. This was and is about nothing less than a new, local, concrete reshaping of the Church in an essentially changing, and largely secularized, world in which there no longer seems to be any space for priestly existence.

Post-conciliar theology has gone different ways to make the proprium of the priestly ministry newly comprehensible from the centre of faith.[156] There have been attempts to comprehend being a priest either from the vocation to proclamation, from the celebration of the Eucharist or from the pastoral ministry and to integrate respectively into each of the other aspects. The different attempts thus do not exclude each other. Still, they only become really convincing if the priest is perceived from the centre of his vocation and mission, from Jesus Christ and the sacramental likening to him.

Like the first disciples, every priest is called personally, insofar as he is with Jesus Christ and is sent by Jesus Christ (Mk 3.13 par). Gathering and sending therefore constitute the two poles of priestly existence. To put it in other words: growing in personal friendship with Jesus, and becoming, like Jesus, the friend of all people and to mediate to them through word and sacrament the friendship and communion with God. No one can have greater love than to lay down his life for his friends (Jn 15.13). For a deeper understanding of the priestly ministry we can depart from Jesus' farewell discourses in John's gospel: 'I shall no longer call you servants ... I call you friends' (Jn 15.15).[157] The basis and centre of the priestly existence is the personal friendship and likening to Jesus. This means that the priest, especially in the celebration of the Eucharist in which the death and resurrection of Jesus Christ become present, is taken in an existential way into the mystery of the death and resurrection of Christ so that by following Jesus he gives his life completely to God and his kingdom and as good shepherd for the people entrusted to him. In this Jesuanic and New Testament sense, the sacerdotal dimension pertains existentially to being a priest and constitutes its innermost centre.

The priestly ministry which takes shape in the manifold ministries of proclamation, in the sacramental-liturgical ministry as well as the pastoral ministry and the ministry of reconciliation is not just mere function. Vocation and mission by Jesus Christ shape the whole existence of the priest. He is to witness for Christ with his whole life. Through ordination he is taken lastingly by Christ and for Christ into service. This taking into service lastingly shapes his whole being. This is the deeper meaning of the indelible character of ordination. It is not a scholastic speculation but an expression of eschatologically final taking into service. Simultaneously it means the effective promise that Jesus Christ, who has chosen the priest for this service, remains lastingly with him and that his friendship will last throughout the whole life of the priest, also in difficult situations.

Such self-understanding is in contrast to that which is today commonly seen as self-realization and self-fulfilment. However, is that not also true for the beatitudes of the Sermon on the Mount and thereby for the whole Christian existence in general? The beatitudes are not a message of mourning but of joy. The friendship through Christ with God and with mankind brings joy into the life of the priest and is to radiate joy. In this sense the priest is to live representatively and exemplarily the Christian alternative to what 'one' today generally expects from life as happiness. It is only in this large context that the issue of celibacy can be comprehended and meaningfully discussed.

Celibacy – a permanent topic of controversy

In the context of public perception and debate, the issue of celibacy continues to dominate all other questions.[158] The voluntary choice of living unmarried can only be understood if it is not seen exclusively from its negative aspect, the voluntary renunciation of something that is among the greatest joys of human life, the renunciation of marriage and having your own family. This renunciation has to be seen from its positive aspect, from the friendship with Jesus and following him, from serving the kingdom of God and the people. Only the one for whom God is everything can renounce everything else as far as is humanly possible. It is only from this theological, Christological and ultimately eschatological perspective that one can comprehend the intrinsic affinity of priestly ministry and voluntary celibacy. A purely inner-worldly perspective must declare this as madness.

The celibacy of a priest belongs in the context of the special following of Jesus who, unlike his contemporary rabbis, himself lived celibate. It belongs in the context of the vocation to leave everything behind for the sake of Jesus and the Gospel, including one's own family, and for the sake of the kingdom of heaven to be present totally and undivided but also unhampered by family concerns (1 Cor. 7.33f.) in the service 'for the many' (Mk 10.45). Ultimately, the priest is to represent Jesus Christ in his bridal love to his bride, the Church,[159] and to express the eschatological novelty of the Gospel. Thus voluntary celibacy has a witnessing nature that is highly appropriate to the priesthood.

Against widespread opinion, according to more recent research, the demand of abstinence for the clergy goes back to the time immediately after the apostolic period. Already the statement in 1 Tim. 3.2, that the bishop is to be married only once (cf. Tit. 1.6), is, according to several scholars, not to be interpreted against the commandment of celibacy, but, on the contrary, points in its direction. It says, in fact, that, after the death of his wife, a bishop should not marry again but live in abstinence.[160] We know for certain that the Synod of Elvira (circa 306) confirmed with the rule of abstinence for the clergy[161] an already existing discipline and newly inculcated it. This was confirmed at the first ecumenical council of Nicea (325).[162] So this discipline was in force in the churches of the West and the East. The different way of the Eastern churches began only with the decision of the Council in Trullo [Quinisext Council, T.H.] of 691. Thus, the discipline of the clergy's celibacy does not only go back to the Gregorian reform and the second Lateran Council (1139). What was new then was only the canonical regulation that ordination constitutes a impediment to marriage and clergy having taken wives or concubines are to be deprived of their office.[163] This was later reaffirmed by the council of Trent against the Reformers.[164] Even though ideas of cultic purity and also, in the early Middle Ages, political dynastic considerations played a role in this development, it can only really be understood in the light of the novum of Jesus' eschatological message.

As much as the rule of abstinence or celibacy is, in fact, not a rather late 'reinvention', the present debates about celibacy are nothing new. There were serious arguments already in the twelfth century, then in the late Middle Ages, at the time of the Reformation, and then again in the eighteenth and nineteenth centuries. In the period following secularization, the lack of priests was by no means less but even far greater than is presently the case in some European countries. Still, each time the crisis was followed by a renewal and a new revival. In view of the recent celibacy debates Vatican II spoke clearly in favour of keeping celibacy in the Latin Church.[165] Together with three post-conciliar episcopal synods, the post-conciliar popes have emphatically reaffirmed this view several times.[166]

Still, the Church can more precisely determine traditions which, although they have a biblical foundation, are not of divine law (*ius divinum*). Hence, the Church knows married presbyters in the Eastern churches that are in full communion with Rome. In individual cases it has admitted into the ordained priesthood Anglican and Lutheran married pastors who had converted to the Catholic Church. Initiated by the Council, it has introduced married permanent deacons.[167] So, people often ask, in a situation of a continuing shortage of priests where many parishes are without priests, why not admit men proven in profession and marriage (*viri probati*) to the ordination to the priesthood?

When all aspects are taken into account, an affirmative positive answer to this question is not as straightforward as it might at first appear. Globally, the number of priests is increasing. In addition, the decrease in vocations to the priesthood in some European countries is not solely a problem of celibacy. The decrease has manifold and complex reasons that have, above all, to do with the situation of faith and the decrease in religious practice. So one has to ask if *viri probati* would not rather be a pseudo-solution which would obscure the underlying problems and their solution and would weaken the testimony of voluntary celibacy, which is pastorally necessary today. In this respect a comparison with the Protestant churches having no celibacy can have a sobering effect. At present they still have the higher number of candidates. Yet, despite the higher number of pastors, are they indeed in a better position if we look at the all-decisive question of efficacious witness to the Gospel?

The issue of celibacy is obviously not suitable as a focal point for church reform and renewal of the Church. Rather, the present social and ecclesial situation necessitates considerations and efforts in the vocations, in the selection and the overall human and spiritual formation of candidates for the priesthood and in accompanying priests. After the end of the old-style presbytery, we should reflect about the general conditions of life of their ministry. Above all, continued prayer for vocations in the parishes (Mt. 9.38; Lk. 10.2) and a supportive atmosphere for the growing and maturing of vocations is necessary. The permanent discussion of celibacy is thereby only harmful and counterproductive.

Ordination to the priesthood for women?

Against the background of the anthropological, sociological and ecclesial change in the perception of the role of women today, the question is often raised whether women can and should be admitted to the ecclesiastical ministry.[168] This question too has not been posed in the Church for the first time. Yet, previously it originated mostly from Gnostic movements on the edge of the Church or outside of it, while today, in the Western world, it is also asked from the centre of the Church. The Church's position not to admit women to the priesthood is, for many Catholics, incomprehensible, and not only to women, but also to men. In other cultures, of course, there is often the contrasting difficulty of understanding us 'Westerners' with this question.

Despite initial opposition and controversies lasting in parts of the Church until today, for most of the Reformation churches, because of their different understanding of ecclesial ministry, it was no basic problem to follow the social developments.[169] The Catholic Church and the Orthodox churches are in a different position because of their sacramental understanding of ministry. With regard to the ecclesial ministry, they see themselves tied to the will of Jesus Christ as they perceive it from Holy Scripture and the Tradition of the Church. Admittedly, in the Tradition we undoubtedly find patriarchal and misogynist ideas that must be regarded today as obsolete. However, if one takes a closer look, one discovers that these obsolete ideas were not the only and decisive reasons that led, in both Holy Scripture and in the theological Tradition, to the conviction that women cannot be ordained to the priesthood. Ultimately, Christological reasons were decisive for Holy Scripture and Tradition.

The Catholic Church is not at liberty to decide arbitrarily about its order, and, as there is no indication of women's ordination in Jesus' own teachings or in Holy Scripture or in Tradition, the Church does not consider itself authorized to ordain women priests or bishops. By now, this has been clearly stated by high-ranking ecclesiastical decisions.[170] Concerning their level of authority, these decisions are so decisively authoritative that I can hardly envisage a change in the Church's teaching. They are of a binding and final character.

The Christological reasoning is not to be perceived only positivistically. Theologically, it assumes that the priest represents Jesus Christ to the congregation. Thereby, Jesus Christ being a man is not decisive as such, but the biblical statement evidenced also amply in Tradition that Jesus Christ stands opposite the Church like a bridegroom to his bride and turns lovingly towards her. This biblical gender symbolism is more than just an image and a metaphor; it expresses a deep reality that was elaborated particularly in women's mysticism of the Middle Ages.[171] The bishop and the priest are to represent Jesus Christ in a holistic, bodily and symbolic way. At the episcopal ordination the bishop has the ring placed on his finger with the words: 'Take this ring, the seal of your fidelity. With faith and love protect the bride of God, his holy Church'.

Today, thinking in symbols and the employment of gender symbolism have become largely alien to us. Such thoughts are hardly or not at all accessible for many today. Thus the discussion of women's ordination will continue for some time. Thereby it will not be enough merely to defend the Church's doctrine. It is essential to make comprehensible the deeper biblical and spiritual aspects contained therein. It is, however, also necessary to understand and take up positively the concerns of those who advocate women's ordination. This is only possible if we realize that which is theologically clearly possible and indeed which is urgently necessary and if we give more space in the different areas of ecclesial life to the charisma of women in the Church than is presently the case.[172] Only in this way will it be possible to bring peace to the situation in the Church regarding this question.

The permanent diaconate

Besides the renewal of the theology of the episcopal office and the priestly ministry, with the renewal of the permanent diaconate the Council took another step towards renewing the understanding of ministry in the spirit of the Old Church's Tradition.[173] In the Old Church the deacons fulfilled manifold liturgical, catechetical, charitable and administrative tasks at the side of the bishop and as his helpers. They were considered to be the eye and arms of the bishop. They were distinguished from the presbyters and, above all, could not preside at the Eucharist. Nevertheless, in Rome as leaders of various regions they were at times more powerful than the presbyters. The diaconal tasks were later taken over by the presbyters. Thus, in the Latin Church, since the end of the first millennium the diaconate was only a transitional stage on the way to the presbyterate.

Already the Council of Trent tried to renew the permanent diaconate, yet without success.[174] If Vatican II re-established the diaconate as 'a proper and permanent rank of the hierarchy', then there were also pastoral and missionary concerns decisive for this.[175] It was not simply about the mere restoration of the Old Church's practice but about a true renewal in view of the challenges of the new pastoral situation.

The Council's text makes it unmistakably clear that the diaconate is a sacramental rank of ordination of its own and thus shares in the threefold service of ministry. About the personal profile of the deacon within the ministry, the Council only says that the deacon is commissioned 'not unto the priesthood (*sacerdotium*), but unto a ministry of service (*ministerium*)'.[176] This clarifies that the deacon cannot perform particular priestly services, especially the Eucharist and the sacrament of penance. However, it remains undetermined what is precisely meant by *ministerium*. After all, service applies to all Christians and to all ranks of the ministry. By way of explanation, the Council only offers an enumeration of individual tasks. This list is probably meant to be exemplary rather than exhaustive. A theology of the diaconate and a specific profile of the deacon do not result from this. Again, the Council has left open questions that still await full clarification.[177]

If one wishes to get closer to the proper profile of the deacon, it is necessary to distinguish him, on the one hand, from the priest. The deacon is neither a substitute priest nor an emergency priest, and by no means a defective priest. On the other, as sacramentally grounded service, the diaconate is to be distinguished from the lay services. The deacon is thus no 'lay deacon' and certainly not an ordained social worker. It is best to think of the deacon as a kind of bridge between the bishop or the presbyter and God's people.[178] Yet this description also contains some ambiguities. After all, in cases of emergency the deacon can take over certain functions of the priest (such as leading a congregation), just as, in cases of emergency, laypeople can take over certain functions of the deacon (emergency baptism, exceptional administering of holy communion). However, it would be wrong to try to define the specific profile of the deacon from these exceptional cases.

The most plausible solution for me still seems to be to understand the deacon from the *diakonia*. It is thereby essential to understand *diakonia* in the comprehensive biblical sense. It must not be regarded only as charity and social work, but includes the ministry of the Word and of the sacraments (baptism and administering the Eucharist), as well as the lived testimony of the personal attitude of serving and dedication. In this perspective the deacon can be understood as the official representative of Christ's *diakonia*.

Concerning the controversial issue of deaconesses, I can make only a few remarks in this context.[179] Deaconesses have been known in the East (except for Egypt and Ethiopia) since the third century, in the West from the sixth until the thirteenth century.[180] Yet, in the East and the West their status was different from that of the male deacon. In Syria, where deaconesses are especially attested, this was the case against the background of a society with a strict separation of women and men, so deaconesses were commissioned especially for the pastoral care of women. For reasons of decency they were called to assist at the baptism of adults, but they were not to serve at the altar. Accordingly the rite of ordination was different from that for male deacons. In the West, the Eastern diaconate of women was rejected by several synods.[181] When there is talk of the ordination of deaconesses in the West, it is either the appointment of abbesses or the solemn reception into the state of widowhood.

In other words, there is no continuous uniform tradition that could be taken up. Given the present conditions, the introduction of the ordination of deaconesses would be a new creation which would found a new practice. At best it would be possible as a sacramental but not as a sacrament. However, this would not signify an elevation of the status of women as wished by those who plead for the introduction of deaconesses. On the contrary, it would lead to regarding women as inferior to male deacons. Demanding the ordination of deaconesses is therefore not a suitable approach to realize the legitimate issue of giving women more space and public status in the Church. This can be done better, more effectively and more independently in a non-clerical context. As has already been demonstrated, there are numerous possibilities for such a context.[182]

In the end: ministry and community

The Council emphasized the common priesthood of all baptized and stressed anew the position of the laity in the Church. It likewise set new tones and aspects for the question of offices. This raises once more the question concerning the relation of the two. This question has been extensively and at times fiercely discussed at the Second Vatican Council and after the Council.[183]

The Council Fathers took great pains to arrive at an exact determination of the relation between the common priesthood and the special priesthood of service. They wanted to distinguish within the common priesthood so that neither the common priesthood would be degraded nor the special dignity and position of the ministerial priesthood would be called into question. Many suggestions were made and rejected. Nevertheless we cannot say that the formulation the Council ultimately arrived at was already fully mature. In order to determine within comprehensive common ground the difference between the common and the special ministerial priesthood, the Council took recourse to the scholastic terminology well known to theologians. It said: both differ not only in degree (*gradus*) but also in essence (*essentia*).[184]

For those used to scholastic terminology this wording is clear; for everybody else it is, however, misleading. It can only be understood properly if the scholastic terminology is exactly interpreted and the context is taken into account, which is much clearer in the Latin text than in the German translation. If the context is taken into account, it becomes clear that the identified distinction is made on the basis of what is common to both and in the context of mutually ordering both to each other. In this context it is intended to say that the laity and ordained office-bearers participate in the one priesthood of Jesus Christ not in a different degree but in a different way.[185] The difference between them is not that the special priesthood was shaped out of the common priesthood, nor is it an increase or intensification of the common priesthood. Who holds the ministerial office in the Church, so to speak, is not automatically a better Christian. Rather, both belong to a different level and a different order. The common priesthood belongs to the order of goal, i.e. the realization of Christ's priesthood for the sanctification and transformation of the world. The ministerial priesthood belongs to the order of media, that is, to serve and further the common priesthood.[186]

The letter to the Ephesians states this special task of the ministry very precisely: the offices are to equip the saints (i.e. the faithful) for the fulfilment of their vocation (Eph. 4.12). They are to inspire and motivate the faithful, also to correct them if need be; they are to accompany them spiritually, fortify and encourage them and through the administration of the sacraments they are to strengthen the faithful gracefully.

Proceeding from the Pauline doctrine of charismata, the teaching of Vatican II can be intensified and made more comprehensible.[187] Paul speaks of a great number of different charismata, offices and ministries in the Church and he likens the Church or the community to an organism in which each part has its own function which it can only realize through interaction with all the others (1 Cor. 12.4–27; cf. Rom. 12.4–8; Eph. 4.15f.; Col. 2.19; 1 Pet. 4.10f.). Like in an organism, there should be in the Church an ordered interaction and cooperation between the different charismata, offices and ministries. Paul also calls the Church a house of the Holy Spirit (Eph. 2.21f.; 1 Pet. 2.5; cf. 1 Cor. 3.9). In other words, the Church is a structured fabric in which the individual parts mutually carry and hold each other. As there are sinful humans involved, such an interaction can be disturbed by the breaking of rules and can indeed become pathological. The house can at times also fall out of kilter and the wood can creak, and it is then necessary to restore and renew it. However, on the whole it has its own order, structure and logic and therein an internal and external beauty.

Within the Christologically and pneumatologically based structure of the Church, the ministries have their own charisma. The office-bearer stands in the middle of the community and depends on the prayer, cooperation, encouragement and, under some circumstances, the criticism of the other charismata. Together with all other Christians, he must listen to the word of God and, like all the others, he depends on grace and forgiveness. Therefore, the offices are to respect the dignity of the other charismata and to give them liberty and space to act; they are to encourage and support the charismata; they are to hear their concerns and to accede to their wishes.[188] On the other hand, within the context of the whole, the offices have their own task and place that cannot be derived from the community to which they have been appointed and authorized by Jesus Christ (Eph. 4.7–12). They speak and act neither in their own name nor in the name of the congregation nor as commissioned by it but in the name of Jesus Christ himself. 'Anyone who hears you hears me' (Lk. 10.16; cf. Mt. 10.40; Jn 13.20; 2 Cor. 5.20). In exercising their mission they stand authorized opposite their congregation and may therefore expect respect and obedience (1 Thess. 5.12f.; 1 Cor. 16.15; Heb. 13.7).

This tension of the relation and fabric of common priesthood and ministerial priesthood mirrors, in an analogous way, the in/above of Christ and Church. The ministry stands in the Church and the congregation but in the exercise of its ministry it stands, *in persona Christi*, opposite the congregation.[189] Therefore, there is a double representation of the office: it represents the congregation and it also represents Jesus Christ against the congregation.[190]

Speaking and acting in the name of Jesus is a considerable challenge that must not be misunderstood and abused. One can only speak and act properly in the name of Jesus if one also speaks and acts in the way of Jesus. Jesus did not come to be served but to serve (Mk 10.42–5). The Christological and pneumatological foundation of the ministerial office is thus not only decisive for the foundation of its specific authority but also for its proper exercise. It should accord with the basic attitude of Jesus. The offices are not the exercise of sovereignty and power but, by following Jesus, they are service for the people of God and its mission. They are not to exercise their charisma of office high-handedly or domineeringly, but they should understand it as service for building up the community (1 Cor. 12.7; Eph. 4.12). They are not to be lords over faith but servants of joy (2 Cor. 1.24). With the washing of the feet on the evening before his suffering and death, Jesus gave a vivid example of this servant's service (Jn 13.1–17).

The first letter of Peter expresses this idea concisely: 'give a shepherd's care to the flock that is entrusted to you: watch over it, not simply as a duty but gladly as God wants; not for sordid money but because you are eager to do it. Do not lord over the group which is in your charge, but be an example for the flock' (1 Pet. 5.2f.). This highlights a new and yet old image of the Church which alone allows for a future of the Church.

Excursus on the ecumenical discussion of ministry and the mutual recognition of ministries

The Second Vatican Council and the theological developments that have taken place in its wake have made it possible that today, compared with the sixteenth century, the question of ministry can be discussed in a new situation. Many multilateral and bilateral conversations have begun which have led to a number of positive results.[191] The dialogue documents do not have a doctrinal or official church character but to a very high degree an exemplary character. Due to the diversity of the conversation partners and their different positions, it is quite difficult to summarize the conversations. A summary is also difficult as it has become apparent in these conversations that there are unresolved questions and different positions not only between the churches but also within the respective churches and their theologies.

Nevertheless, some important and positive results can be named. For instance, in the conversations there is agreement that the ministry is not to be understood as a delegation of the congregation but as a foundation of Jesus Christ and, as such, as constitutive for the Church. The ministry is within the community, but, in exercising its mission, is *in persona Christi*, in opposition to the community. Though it is not regarded as a sacrament everywhere, ordination with prayer and laying-on of hands is, however, recognized as a liturgical act which efficaciously grants the ordinand a charisma of office. In all churches proclamation is seen as an essential task of the ministry, and thus a one-sided sacerdotal understanding of the ministry is overcome. The question of the 'ordained priesthood', which was highly controversial in the Reformation, has become substantially defused through theological consensuses regarding the question of the sacrificial character of the mass. Today there is broad agreement that the Eucharist is not a new sacrifice, nor a repetition of the unique sacrifice of Christ, but that this sacrifice is sacramentally made present in the Eucharist.[192]

What is also positive is the reconsideration of episcopacy and the episcopal office that is emerging in ecumenism and especially in the Lutheran churches.[193] In this context we must mention the emerging consensus that the succession in office can only be correctly understood within the apostolic succession of the Church as a whole, and the corresponding consensus that the succession in office must not be restricted to a chain of laying-on of hands, but that it includes succession in the apostolic faith. The apostolic succession is thereby understood as an overall structure in which all of these elements belong together.[194] Within this overall structure, the succession in ministry is not a guarantee but sign and instrument. The continuity and identity of the Church in faith has its basis ultimately in the promise of the Spirit who leads into all truth (Jn 14.26; 15.26; 16.13).

In a number of cases, such as the first phase of dialogue with the Anglicans, these are consensuses, yet, in general, they are, rather, only convergences. There still remain questions to be clarified, especially concerning the sacramental character of ordination and the concrete form of the apostolic succession. The different positions, however, have highlighted deeper differences. These concern the ordination of women, the commissioning of non-ordained people for public proclamation, the administration of sacraments and the presidency at the Eucharist or the Lord's Supper, as it is the case in some ecclesial communities. They have also forced to the surface new, previously non-existent problems that have, in the meantime, complicated the dialogues.

Despite the differences which undoubtedly still exist and the open questions, the positive results of the dialogues must not be underestimated, whether theologically or practically. Pope Leo XIII had spoken of the invalidity of the Anglican ordinations,[195] and Vatican II still spoke of a '*defectus ordinis*' in the ecclesial communities of the Reformation.[196] This was originally meant in the sense of a total absence. As a result of the dialogues that have taken place since then, however, the term *defectus* must be understood as deficiency. Just as we speak of elements of the Church, so we can also speak analogously of the recognition of essential elements of the ministry in the ecclesial communities of the Reformation. On this basis, by now a fraternal relation has developed between priests and bishops of the different churches and ecclesial communities, and this is not merely a matter of protocol or inter-personal politeness, but rather shows that, despite all differences that still remain, the ministry in the respective other church is not 'nothing', but rather that, in a non-quantifiable way, 'something' is recognized as being there – namely, something of the ministry that Christ established for his Church. This is a result leading far beyond the polemic of the sixteenth century and is of crucial importance for practical cooperation.

Because of the positive results, especially in relation to the Anglicans and the Lutherans, there are some who already want to speak of a differentiated consensus or who even consider possible a mutual recognition of the ministries.[197] Yet, as there is no consensus about the term 'differentiated consensus', this demand only leads to new misunderstandings. It also runs the risk of inappropriately minimizing the remaining differences.

It does not suffice to refer to the (historically undeniable) change of form that occurred from the New Testament to the episcopal office in the Old Church, and from there to the medieval and modern form up to Vatican II.[198] This change of form accords with the historicity of the Church and is a historical necessity. For precisely this reason, it is an anachronism to try to re-establish the local episcopal office, as we have with Ignatius of Antioch, in the form of the pastor's office of the sixteenth century, or to try to rediscover it in the Protestant pastor's office of today. After all, the decisive question is whether, in the change of form, the continuity and identity of the basic principles have been maintained or not. If the question is put like that, then today's Catholic episcopal office is undoubtedly more in line with the local episcopal office described by Ignatius than the present Protestant pastor's office. Similarly, this holds true for the 'emergency situations' claimed by the Reformers. Because a denomination has formed that assumes this claim, what was then an emergency situation is now the *standard* situation, according to the confession of the Reformation churches and has thus become a question of faith.[199]

The issue of identity arises in particular with the question of determining the relation of common priesthood and the ordained ministry as it has prevailed in the praxis of many Lutheran and Reformed churches.[200] It has consequences for the present form as well as for the understanding of the synodal episcopal office in the Lutheran churches that is, in fact, also found in the Anglican Communion since the second half of the twentieth century.[201] This is because, in the form of the synodal episcopal office, the episcopate is exercised not only in the interaction with synodal bodies but largely by synodal bodies that consist mainly of non-ordained people. So it was significant that, for determining the Magnus consensus on the doctrine of justification, it was not the Lutheran bishops who were asked, but the Lutheran synods, and they also decided. In other words, not the bishops but the synods had a magisterial function.[202] This is an understanding of the episcopal office that corresponds neither to that of the Old Church nor to today's Catholic or Orthodox episcopal office. It is rather a new creation of the twentieth century based on the determination of the relation between the common priesthood and the ministry, especially in the early Luther. As long as this question is not clarified, a full recognition of the Protestant episcopal office, as it presents itself today, is fundamentally impossible.

After all, ordination is not a quasi-magically efficacious act, but a sacrament of faith. Its recognition therefore depends decisively on the intention. What is meant is not the personal faith of the ordaining person – what he subjectively thinks or believes – but what the creed of his church objectively says, the creed on whose basis he acts, to which he is obliged and upon which he obliges the one to be ordained. The Catholic Tradition speaks of the *intentio faciendi quod facit ecclesia*, the intention to do what the Church does.[203] From this perspective a Protestant administrator of the rite of ordination cannot at all intend to confer the office that exists in the Catholic Church and as it is understood in the Catholic Church. Strictly speaking, he must even exclude this on the basis of the confession of his church. It is therefore telling that, for declaring the invalidity of Anglican ordinations, the reasons given were not the interrupted chain of the laying-on of hands, but the lack of intention and thus of the right faith.[204]

This brings us to the heart of the problem. The mutual recognition of ministries is not a problem that can be solved on its own. In particular, it cannot be solved alone by the nevertheless useful and instructive historical exploration of historically given freedom. The ecclesial ministry, especially the episcopal office, represents the Church and its authoritative confession. Each mutual recognition presupposes, therefore, the full recognition of being Church and of the faith of the other church. To make progress in the question of ministry, the ecumenical dialogue must therefore, as a next step, positively address the question of the Church in order to then discuss the question of ministry again in this context of the question of the Church. Not only from a theological perspective, but also from the perspective, of general public perception, this problem culminates, in particular, in the question of the Petrine office.

5.4 The Petrine office – the ministry of unity

Ecumenically, the Petrine office is probably the most delicate and difficult aspect of ecclesiology. For the Catholic Church, the Petrine office is, as the ministry of unity, a gift of the Lord to his Church. And yet, all other churches reject the claims connected with this office and consider it an obstacle to unity. So the Petrine office, intended as an service to unity, has become, for most other Christians, a cause for separation. To overcome this paradox, Pope John Paul II called for a fraternal dialogue concerning how this ministry, while keeping its essence, can be exercised so that it is acceptable for all. Pope Benedict XVI also embraced this issue.[205] To make progress in this question we must first ask: what is the essential, in other words foundational, substance of this office?[206]

Biblical foundations

The biblical foundation of the Petrine office poses a whole range of exegetical and historical questions which cannot all be dealt with in detail in this context.[207] What might serve as a point of departure is the historically indisputable fact that Jesus gave the fisherman Simon Barjona the surname Kephas, which means the rock (πέτρα), which became in Greek Peter (Πέτρος). This conferring of the name is unanimously reported by all four evangelists (Mk 3.16; Mt. 10.2; Lk. 6.14; Jn 1.42), such that it is difficult to doubt its historical reliability. Yet, at that time names were not just hollow words. Rather, names signified a vocation and a position. The rock is regarded as, symbol of firmness and stability, as it gives footing and refuge. This is Peter's essential task and that of the ministry named after him.

Because of this vocation, Simon/Peter is mentioned in the first position in all lists of the apostles (Mk 3.16 par). In the circle of the disciples, he is the leader and spokesman of all the others (Mk 8.29.32; 10.28). In all gospels he is the first one who speaks the confession of Jesus as the Messiah, i.e. as the Christ (Mk 8.29; Mt. 16.16; Lk. 9.20; Jn 6.68f.). He is thus the decisive witness for Jesus Christ and the archetype of the Christian teacher. For all this it is foundational that, according to oldest Tradition, Peter is the first and primal witness of the resurrection (1 Cor. 15.5; cf. Lk. 24.12.34). With his testimony, he is the rock upon which one can build in faith and to which one can hold on in faith. He is to strengthen his brothers (Lk. 22.31f.). Indeed, in the first church of Jerusalem Peter was the decisive person and its leader (Acts 1–12). He was the first to dare to speak of the transition from Jewish Christianity to Gentile Christianity (Acts 9f.), and at the council of the apostles in Jerusalem he spoke the decisive word hereto (Acts 15). In other words, Peter was not only keeper; he also courageously showed the Church the way toward its future.

Paul recognized the authority of Peter. He counts him together with James and John as the pillars (Gal. 2.9), and attaches great importance to meet him, to stay fifteen days with him and finally to be acknowledged by him (Gal. 2.8f.). Despite the severe conflict he had with him in Antioch (Gal. 2.11–14), Paul recognizes the authority of Peter. For Paul he is the decisive bearer and guarantor of Tradition.

Thus, Jesus' words at Caesarea Philippi, written in large letters in the dome of St Peter in Rome, do not stand in isolation, but point beyond themselves to a much larger context: 'You are Peter and on this rock I will build my Church' (Mt. 16.18). Among exegetes, there is widespread agreement that this text, in its present form, does not go back to the historical Jesus, but that it is a composition of the evangelist. Of course, there is also widespread agreement that this composition was not a pure invention of Matthew; that it rather goes back to older traditions which ultimately hearken back to the conferring of the name through Jesus and the appearance of the Resurrected before Peter.

This text contains the essence of the special mission of Peter. He is the one who, as the first and representing the others, formulates the confession to Jesus Christ: 'You are the Messiah, the Son of the living God.' Jesus then says that no human agency revealed this confession, but that it stemmed from a special revelation of God the Father. In other words, Jesus recognizes Peter's special charisma as a teacher given to him by God. This is followed by the promise to Peter: 'You are Peter and on this rock I will build my Church' (Mt. 16.16.18). One can ask if, with this word, Peter as a person or the confession of Peter has to be regarded as a rock. Already the Church Fathers give different answers to this question. They also provide a third answer that is probably the majority opinion of today's exegetes. It says that we can distinguish between the confession of Peter and the person of Peter, but that the two cannot be separated. The confession is tied to the person and the person to the confession. Thus, with his confession and because of it, Peter becomes the solid foundation of the Church.[208]

What this function as rock concretely means is explained by Jesus with the image of the 'keys of the kingdom of heaven'. With his confession to Jesus as the Messiah and Son of the living God, Peter unlocks for those who accept this confession in faith the gates to the kingdom of God. So the authority of the key means teaching authority; Peter is the rock as authoritative witness and teacher of Jesus' message. The idea of 'binding and loosening' points in the same direction.[209] 'Binding and loosening' are rabbinic *termini technici* that signify the teaching authority and the power to decide, to forbid and to permit. The mission of Peter is, therefore, not only a pastoral ministry and pastoral primacy (in the sense that pastoral is normally understood today). Rather, a special authority given only to him is conferred upon Peter, because of which he is, as witness and guarantor of Jesus' teaching, the solid foundation upon which the Church is built. With this power Peter is also called to strengthen the brothers (Lk. 22.31f.).

One cannot object to this special authority of Peter simply by pointing out that, in a different passage in Matthew, the power to bind and loosen is also given to all disciples (18.18). This second passage is clearly a community rule and consequently it is power on a local level, whereas the word of the rock is about a special authority which is to be exercised on the level of the universal Church.

The special commission to Peter found in Matthew is also found in a different form in the gospel of John. On Easter morning, although the favourite disciple arrived first at the tomb, he lets Peter enter first, thus giving him precedence (Jn 20.1–10). After the resurrection, Simon/Peter is called as shepherd to look after the sheep, that is, to lead and guide the community of the disciples (Jn 21.15–17). The thrice times conferring of the shepherd's office shows that this is a legally binding act of lasting validity.

The New Testament speaks nowhere of passing on the special authority given to Peter. However, the continuation of the power given to Peter can be based implicitly on biblical grounds, for the fact that Mt. 16.18 as well as Jn 21.15–17 were written in their present form only after his death shows that Peter was of special significance beyond his death in the post-apostolic Church. The same results from the rest of the New Testament, especially from the fact that the first and second letters of Peter were obviously written by a pupil (or pupils) of Peter from Rome. There Peter is called eldest among the elders, witness and shepherd (1 Pet. 1.1f.; 2 Pet. 1.16–19). Also the fact that no other name is mentioned as often in the New Testament as that of Peter shows that already in the New Testament the mission of Peter was regarded as lasting Petrine ministry and as a Petrine office. Otherwise, the veneration of Peter which soon began would also be inexplicable.

The Petrine office in the first millennium

The historical development of the Petrine office poses as many questions as its exegetical basis.[210] Undoubtedly there were historical developments already in the first millennium and then in the second millennium. It would thus be anachronistic to apologetically project the doctrine of primacy of the First and Second Vatican Council back to the beginnings of church history. However, the Church has been the same in all centuries. It realizes its constant nature depending on changing historical necessities in a historically different way. It is thus a creative and innovative continuity for which, according to John Henry Newman's doctrine of development, it suffices that the basic type – that is the proportions, the basic form and the principles – are maintained.[211]

Already in the first millennium the development occurred in different steps:

(1) The point of departure and the lasting basis of the Petrine tradition is not a motive of power, nor of the political position of Rome as capital of

the Roman empire, but a decidedly spiritual motive. A special veneration of Peter and his grave developed very early on. This veneration of Peter and the pilgrimage to his tomb is the spiritual breeding ground for all later theories about the continuing efficacy of Peter in his successors, the respective bishop of Rome.[212]

Also very early on, in the letter to the Corinthians ascribed to Clement of Rome (about 96 AD), we see a special responsibility of Rome for non-Roman communities as well. This letter intercedes with authority in conflicts of the church in Corinth and urgently admonishes peace. The special importance of the church of Rome appears again in the letter bishop Ignatius of Antioch writes to the church in Rome (about 110 AD). In this, he says that it has the presidency in love (προκαθημένη τῆς ἀγάπης).[213] What is then particularly important is the testimony of Irenaeus of Lyons in the second century. In the controversy with Gnostic tendencies he establishes an important criterion: 'it is a matter of necessity that every Church should agree (*convenire*) with this Church [of Rome, T.H.], on account of its preeminent authority, that is, the faithful everywhere (*undique*), inasmuch as the apostolic Tradition has been preserved continuously by those who exist everywhere (*undique*).'[214] Tertullian speaks similarly.[215]

These testimonies are interpreted in different ways. In any case they must not be over-interpreted in view of the later claim to Petrine primacy. Still, they clearly highlight that, from very early on, Rome was regarded as home and guarantor of the apostolic faith, and that it was an important centre of the *communio* and of the communication in the Church. Soon Rome became the refuge of those who got into trouble because of their faith. Rome became thus an important instance that could be appealed to in questions of controversies. The synod of Sardica (343/344) expressly affirmed this practice.[216]

The first ecumenical council of Nicaea (325) summarizes the early development. It speaks of the ancient custom whereby Rome has priority (πρεσβεία) in Italy, Alexandria and Antioch in their respective provinces.[217] At the council of Constantinople (381), it was not so much the ecclesiastical but the political aspect that was decisive. The council placed the larger areas of the Church parallel to the administrative units of the state and said that the bishop of Constantinople is to enjoy the privilege of honour after the bishop of Rome.[218] Against this political interpretation, a Roman synod under Pope Damasus (382) placed the theory of the three Petrine sees, Rome, Alexandria and Antioch, which from then on would be decisive for Rome. He was thereby especially supported by Jerome, the most biblically learned Church Father. He wrote to Damasus: 'As I follow no leader save Christ, so I communicate with none but your blessedness, that is with the chair of Peter. For this, I know, is the rock on which the church is built!'[219]

(2) The position of the Roman bishops became foundational for subsequent developments. The statement of Pope Damasus shows that, early on, Rome

was recognized not only from outside as centre of the *communio* but actively claimed leadership. This becomes apparent for the first time with Pope Victor (189–98) in the controversy over the Easter date. Pope Stephen (254–7) invoked for the first time Jesus' word to Peter in Mt. 16.18ff. We find a claim to primacy with the popes Damasus (366–84), Siricius (384–99)[220] and Innocent I (401–17),[221] Rome is now called the caput of the whole Church and the bishop of Rome is perceived as *vicarius* [vicar, T.H.] of the Prince of the Apostles, Peter.[222]

Pope Leo the Great (440–61) summarized the early Roman Petrine and papal theology. Basically, with him we have all the essential elements of the later primacy doctrine. According to Leo, Peter is efficaciously present in his successors and continues to preside on his cathedra. In this sense the bishop of Rome is *vicarius Petri*.[223] He describes his position with the terms *caput, princeps* and *principatus* and speaks for the first time, though not yet in the later sense, of the *plenitudo potestatis*.[224] Leo therefore decidedly rejected canon 28 of the council of Chalcedon (451), which granted Constantinople, as the new Rome, the second place (the Greek text even speaks of the same rank) after Rome.[225] Like Damasus before him, he insisted on the theory of the three Petrine sees. We find a similar position again later with Pope Gelasius (492–6).[226] In this we can see, already very early on, different developments and rifts in the relationship of East and West.

(3) Besides the line of primacy emerging in the third and fourth centuries, there is also the line of episcopal and collegiate tradition. This was advocated in particular by Cyprian of Carthage.[227] Thus the bishops should act in harmony and mutual love. Nevertheless, Cyprian can also say that the Church was built upon One (*unum*) and that, based on the commandment by Christ, it has its unity from the origin.[228] Hence, Cyprian sees the Church of Rome as the '*matrix et radix ecclesiae catholicae*',[229] and the see of Peter as the primordial church (*ecclesia principalis*) and as the source of episcopal unity.[230]

The position of Augustine, the most influential Church Father in the Latin tradition, must not be reduced to the later statement '*Roma locuta, causa finita*'.[231] For him, the rock (*petra*) upon which the Church is built is Christ (1 Cor. 10.4; cf. 3.11). Thus he stresses again and again: '*non enim a Petrus petra, sed a petra Petrus*'.[232] According to Augustine, Peter does not receive the power of keys for himself alone, but as representative of the Church. Augustine sees Peter as *figura ecclesiae, sacramentum ecclesiae, typus ecclesiae* and *typus unitatis ecclesiae*.[233] This view remained influential until the Middle Ages and, with reference to Augustine, is still found with Thomas Aquinas.[234]

The balance between the two principles of primatiality and collegiality appeared particularly at the council of Chalcedon (451). The council fathers acclaimed when the dogmatic epistle (Tomos) by Leo was read: 'this is the faith of the fathers, this is the faith of the apostles! We all believe this ... Peter has spoken through Leo!'[235] Yet, then they formulated the Christological confession independently. Though they took up Leo's contribution, they integrated it, however, into a confession strongly influenced by the Alexandrian theology, especially that of Cyril's second letter to Nestorius. This balance was in line with the views of Leo the Great himself.[236]

Gregory the Great (590–604) summarized the development in the late period. He sees himself as heir of the apostle Peter, the *princeps apostolorum*, who is entrusted with the care of the whole Church.[237] Still, he also knows that his honour is the honour of the whole Church and the strength of his brothers. That is, he acknowledges himself as honoured, if the honour which is due to them is not refused.[238] Thus, he objects to the title 'ecumenical patriarch' which had become common usage in Constantinople, and also decidedly refuses for himself the title *papa* or *epsicopus universalis*.[239]

(4) In the late period, the differences between East and West became increasingly obvious. They were intensified as the Western Roman empire collapsed in the turmoil of the great migrations while the East remained tied into the imperial church system for almost one millennium longer than Rome. In Byzantium, there was the Christianized Hellenistic ideology founded by Eusebius of Caesarea († 339) (Francis Dvornik) which saw the unity of empire and Church represented and guaranteed in the sacral understood emperorship. In the wake of an imperial reform, Emperor Justinian (527–67) introduced the system of pentarchy as an instrument of imperial church rule. This gave the five patriarchates of Rome, Constantinople, Alexandria, Antioch and Jerusalem constitutional importance. Still, also after Justinian, the bishop of Rome had a special position within the pentarchy. He called the pope 'head of all priests of God' and 'keeper of the faith'.[240]

The importance of the Roman bishops demonstrated itself always when there were questions of faith. Pope Julius I (337–52) proved himself champion of the Nicaean orthodoxy and defender of Athanasius when Athanasius was condemned and deposed by an Arian synod in the East (Tyre 335; Alexandria 341). Similarly, Leo the Great (440–61) positioned himself against Nestorius and stood up for bishop Flavian of Constantinople, who had been deposed in 449 at the 'Robber Synod', and defended the true faith at Chalcedon (451).

In this late period the popes proved to be champions of Chalcedonian orthodoxy, so in the controversy about Monophysitism and in ending the Acacian schism (484–519) through the formula of unity (formula Hormisdae) of Pope Hormisdas (514–23). It says that the promise given in Mt. 16.18 to Peter had been confirmed by historical experience, 'in the Apostolic See the Catholic religion has always been kept unsullied'; in communion with it 'the whole, true, and perfect security of the

Christian religion resides'.[241] The same firmness was shown in the conflict about Monenergism and Monothelitism where at the third council of Constantinople (680/681) the letters of Pope Agatho (678–81)[242] were confirmed by acclamation just as at Chalcedon the dogmatic letter of Leo the Great had been acclaimed. In this controversy, Maximus the Confessor (580–662), one of the most important church fathers of the East, turned out to be a bridge-builder between East and West.[243] Also the iconoclastic controversy could be solved at the second council of Nicaea alone with aid from Rome through a letter by Pope Hadrian I (772–95).

In the ninth century there was a severe conflict concerning Patriarch Photios, who was wrongfully seen for centuries as the instigator of the schism between East and West. In the tug of war about the belonging of Bulgaria, he was condemned by Pope Nicholas I (858–67),[244] by Pope Hadrian II (867–72) and by the fourth council of Constantinople (869/870), recognized only by the West.[245] When he tried during his second time as patriarch to find a modus vivendi with Rome and thereby recognized the bishop of Rome as the first among the five patriarchs while maintaining that each patriarch was in his sphere the final instance concerning administration and liturgy, he was rehabilitated by the synod of 879/880 with the consent of Pope John VIII (872–82). This was the last joint synod of East and West. It was indeed a true synod of unity that deserved to be recognized as ecumenical.[246]

Despite this agreement, the mutual alienation between East and West widened for political and cultural reasons. There were schisms time and again that could then be resolved once more. It was only the mutual excommunication of Cardinal Humbert of Silva Candida and Patriarch Michael Cerularius of Constantinople in the year 1054 which led to a non-communion (ἀκοινωνία) lasting until today. Only those two were directly affected by this conflict. No one at that time considered the excommunications to force a final separation. There was also no controversy about dogmatic questions such as the question of primacy or the issue of the addition of the *filioque* to the creed. At stake were only matters of discipline that would today no longer justify any separation of churches. Nevertheless, in fact the excommunication led to a schism lasting until today, and over time the alienation between East and West has widened considerably.[247] It was not until the Second Vatican Council that one succeeded in eradicating this excommunication from the memory of both churches and initiating, in the opposite direction, a process of reconciliation.

The Latin West in the second millennium

(1) After the fall of the Western Roman, empire, there was an independent development in the West during the Migration Period. Rome's turn towards the Franks was sealed with the imperial coronation of Charlemagne (800). The Church became dependent on the respective princes in the new feudal

imperial church system. The reform movement after the end of the *saeculum obscurum* in the tenth century became decisive for the further development and in the controversies about the freedom and independence of the Church (*libertas ecclesiae*). This happened in the Investiture Controversy of the eleventh century during the pontificate of Pope Gregory VII (1073–85). He articulated his understanding of primacy concisely and provocatively in the 27 theses of the *Dictatus Papae* (1075). For him the Roman Church is '*mater omnium Ecclesiarum*' (mother of all churches). It is pivotal point, source and origin, pinnacle and fundament. The synods now became advisory bodies of the pope. According to Yves Congar, this was perhaps the biggest radical change in the whole history of the Church and the papacy.[248]

The claim to primacy of Gregory VII was intensified again by Innocent III (1198–1216). He no longer called himself only successor and *vicarius Petri*, but *vicarius Christi*.[249] The fourth Lateran council (1215) confirmed the privileges of the patriarchates. However, it stresses the primacy of the Roman Church based on divine commandment and it calls Rome the *mater* and *magistra* of all Christ's faithful.[250] The second council of Lyons (1274)[251] then undertook one more attempt to achieve unity with the East. Politically under pressure, the Eastern Roman Emperor Michael VIII Palaeologos declared that Rome had the highest and fullest primacy and the rule over the whole Catholic Church, and that the bishop of Rome had the *plenitudo potestatis*.[252] However, the confession was not a document of dialogue but a dictate in the sense and language of the Latin doctrine of primacy and was immediately rejected by the East. Finally, Boniface VIII (1295–1303) increased the papal claim once again. In the (not infallible) bull *Unam Sanctam* (1302) he declared 'it is absolutely necessary for the salvation of every human creature to be subject to the Roman Pontiff.'[253]

(2) The Middle Ages were by no means as uniform as they are often presented. During the medieval period there was no shortage of counter-movements. In particular, Bernard of Clairvaux, who was basically on the side of the reformers of the eleventh century, warned his pupil Pope Eugene III (1145–53) of exaggerated claims and criticized Roman centralism.[254] Traditions of salvation history continued in monastic theology and synodal traditions continued in canon law. In addition there emerged spiritualistic movements.[255]

Among others, the exaggerations of the Roman claim to primacy were a reason for the Western schism. At the beginning two and at the end three popes opposed each other. They mutually excommunicated each other and their respective obedience so that the whole of Western Christianity was excommunicated. In this hopeless situation attempts were made through conciliar theory to revive older synodal elements and to take up more recent cooperative ideas to demonstrate the superiority of a general council above the pope.[256]

On this basis the Council of Constance (1414–8) formulated in the decree *Haec sancta* (1415) the superiority of the council above the pope.[257]

This decree was not a dogmatic decision of faith but an emergency measure to restore the unity of the Church and to ensure the survival of the papacy with the election of Martin V. Pope Eugene IV declared the decree invalid in 1441. Yet, even though *Haec sancta* did not formulate a conciliaristic dogma, ecclesiologically it is not insignificant. As emergency law, it belongs permanently to the possibilities of the Church and in extreme situations (which hopefully will never happen) it can serve as a model.[258]

The union council of Florence (1439–45) was to overcome the conciliaristic ideas and to reach a union with the Greeks. This resulted in the first formal definition of the primacy. The Greeks were prepared to recognize the pope as the first among the patriarchs with respective powers if such a definition contained also limitation of the papacy through the rights of the patriarchs. So a compromise was reached in the decree *Laetentur caeli* (1439): first the Western doctrine of primacy was presented and it expressed the universal primacy of the pope as successor of Peter and representative of Christ, head of the Church, father and teacher of all Christians who is invested by Jesus Christ with the *plenitudo potestatis*; the second part confirmed the privileges and rights of the patriarchs.[259] Placing these positions side by side left room for different interpretations. The Western representatives considered only the first part to be a dogmatic statement and the second they regarded as an honourable custom. For the Greeks the second part signified a restriction of the papacy. Also in the West, conciliaristic ideas could live on in Gallicanism and later in Febronianism.

(3) From the beginning, the Reformation of the sixteenth century was influenced by a severe polemical controversy about the primacy which culminated in the accusation that the pope was the Antichrist prophesied in 2 Thess. 2.1–12. In the Middle Ages, this was a common topice of controversy.[260] Yet, for the Reformers, it had a precise theological sense and meant that the pope suppressed the Gospel of Jesus Christ, which the Reformers saw concentrated in the doctrine of justification alone through grace. Luther thought that therein the final eschatological battle had begun. Ultimately, the polemic is understandable only on the basis of this perspective.[261]

Despite this poignant polemic of the Reformers, the Council of Trent saw itself in no position to arrive at a clear statement about the primacy. This was due to inner-Catholic differences of opinion. The question could be discussed only indirectly in the context of one of the then most urgent reform issues – the residential obligations of bishops. This was about the reform of the practice by which popes granted positions, the restriction of appeals to Rome and others. Ultimately, behind all this was the question of whether the power of a bishop was derived directly from Christ or from the primacy. The time was not yet ripe for a solution. So, after long debates only a compromise could be reached. It was declared that the residential obligation was no *ius divinum*, but a divine commandment and severe punishments were placed on its infringement. However, the basic ecclesiological question was left open.[262]

The vehement polemic of the Reformers against the papacy caused, as it were, an antithesis in the post-Tridentine theology, such that now the primacy was more strongly emphasized than ever before. In its anti-Reformation attitude it became not only theologically but also psychologically, and indeed sociologically, a sign of identity of the Catholic Church, just as it pertained and still pertains to the identity of the other churches and communities to have no pope. Still, it was not for three-and-a-half centuries after the beginning of the Reformation, in a completely different situation, that there was a binding definition of the papal primacy.

The First Vatican Council

The First Vatican Council (1869/1870)[263] took place under conditions unprecedented in the history of the church councils. All preceding councils had been imperial councils; the Congress of Vienna (1814/1815) had sealed the end of the imperial church. In these upheavals many, especially those swayed by the restoration philosophy of Joseph de Maistre († 1821), considered the papacy the last bastion and the only remaining ground. This ultramontane atmosphere, which proceeded not so much from Rome as from the 'base', was the context for the council's definition of the primacy of the bishop of Rome.

It is thus even more remarkable that in the preface, which is crucial for the interpretation, the dogmatic constitution *Pastor aeternus* does not begin ideologically but Christologically. It calls Jesus Christ the eternal shepherd and bishop of our souls (1 Pet. 2.25). He is the actual invisible head of the Church. For this reason the primacy is consciously called the 'visible fundament' of the Church. After this Christological foundation, the primacy is ecclesiologically integrated as the ministry for the unity of the Church through the bonds of faith and love. This ministry of unity occurs concretely – and therein the finality of the primacy is concretely expressed – as ministry of the unity of the episcopate. Therefore the constitution speaks in the sense of the old Tradition of the priority of the Church of Rome,[264] of the pope as bishop of the *sedes* or *cathedra Romana*[265] and calls him throughout *Romanus Pontifex*. The constitution sees the foundation for the primacy of the pope in his capacity as bishop of Rome, and thereby rules out a one sidedly universalistic view of the primacy.

Finally, the preface serves as an essential principle for the interpretation of papal dogmas. It says that it intends to define the primacy in the sense of the old and continuous faith of the universal Church.[266] This means that the definitions of the council must be interpreted in the context and in the sense of the previous Tradition, especially the Tradition of the Old Church.

After this preface, the dogmatic constitution elaborates the primacy doctrine in four steps: it first defines the institution of the primacy in the apostle Peter not only as honorary primacy but as primacy of jurisdiction,[267] then its continuation in the Roman bishops as the successors of Peter,[268] after that its nature,[269] and finally the infallible teaching primacy of the pope.[270] Thus, the council teaches that the Roman Pontifex is the successor of Peter, representative of Christ, head of the whole Church, father and teacher of all faithful. To him pertains an ordinary, episcopal and immediate authority and power over the whole Church to care for it, to lead and to guide it.[271]

The three adjectives which more precisely determine the universal jurisdiction of the Roman bishop are essential. It is called ordinary not because it was the normal case but because it is not delegated, because it is given with the office itself. It is determined as episcopal which says that it is to be understood, not in a purely functional sense, but pastorally, and that it is sacramentally grounded in the office of the bishop of Rome. Finally, it is immediate as it can refer to all shepherds and faithful of all rites and rank without any need for intermediate instances. It applies not only to matters of faith and morals, but also to such spheres as discipline and leading. It can be exercised freely and independently from any secular power. Beyond the decision of the pope there is no higher authority, such as a general council, to which one could appeal.[272]

It might seem that, with this, the universal jurisdiction was to be understood in the sense of an absolute monarchy. Yet, the council rejects the view that the bishops were merely officials of the pope. It calls the bishops appointed by the Holy Spirit (Acts 20.28) and quotes Pope Gregory the Great that his honour was the honour of the whole Church and the unbroken vigour of his brothers: 'I am truly honoured when due honour is paid to each and every one'.[273] In this sense the German bishops rejected, after the council, the recommendations of the German chancellor Otto von Bismarck. He argued that through the definition of the council the rights of the bishops had been absorbed by those of the pope and that the bishops were only instruments and officials of the pope. The German bishops stressed in their reply that the pope did not take the place of the jurisdiction of a diocesan bishop but that he affirmed this. This declaration was expressly confirmed by Pope Pius IX.[274] It can therefore be regarded as authentic interpretation of the council. It says that the primacy does not replace the ordinary and normal church government of the bishop and is not in competition with it. It says that the primacy respects and supports it and a direct intervention happens only in extraordinary situations such as when another instance fails, is impaired or overextended, does not seriously fulfil its obligation, or if there is a question concerning the whole Church.

Regarding the definition of infallibility, one must note that the council consciously does not speak of the infallibility of the pope. Instead it speaks of the infallible teaching office of the pope.[275] It thereby referred to the Tradition common to East and West. It demonstrates that the Roman see had always maintained that the apostolic primacy also contained the highest teaching authority of the magisterium.[276] Yet, to avoid misunderstandings the council states that the infallible magisterium does not mean that the pope could proclaim a new revelation. Infallible magisterium rather means that Peter and his successors were given a special charisma of keeping and interpreting the revelation and heritage of faith passed on by the apostles.[277]

The exercise of infallibility is tied to concrete conditions. It does not apply to normal doctrinal statements and certainly not to personal theological and other opinions of the pope. It applies only under clearly defined conditions: 1) when the pope speaks ex cathedra, when he exercises his office as shepherd and teacher of all faithful; 2) when he proclaims a truth of faith and morals; and 3) when this doctrine is proclaimed to be kept (*tenedum*) by the whole Church.[278] If these conditions are fulfilled, then the infallibility given to the Church pertains to the judgement of the pope because of the divine advocacy promised to him in defining doctrine of faith and morals. In other words, the pope does not have an infallibility detached from the Church, but he exercises the infallibility given to the Church. He is then an authentic witness of the faith of the Church.

At the last moment it was added to this definition that such ex-cathedra decisions are unchangeable 'ex sese' and not because of a subsequent affirmation through the Church.[279] This is a highly ambiguous wording. It does not say that the pope could take magisterial decisions independent from the previous faith of the Church. It should only say that the validity of such decisions cannot be made to depend on the subsequent affirmation through a council or any other instance. This was to condemn Gallicanism and its offshoots (whereby Gallicanism is itself an offshoot of conciliaristic theories). In other word, the 'ex sese' excludes the possibility of an appeal from the decision of the pope to another instance (such as a general council). Still, the council maintains that the pope is tied in content to the faith of the Church. The council did not intend to tie the pope to certain procedures of how he is to explore the faith of the Church. He should be free to do this appropriate to the circumstances of each time and situation. To meet respective wishes, the council recounts the ways popes proceeded in the past. It mentions ecumenical councils, explores the view of the Church scattered throughout the world, partial synods or other sources.[280]

In other words, the definition of infallibility has nothing to do with the spectre of a personal infallibility of the pope detached from the Church. Concerning infallible magisterial decisions the pope is no oracle, but the official witness of the Church's faith. Thus the intention of the first Vatican Council was to be understood in the tradition of the fourth council of Constantinople, the second council of Lyons and the Council of Florence as an authoritative expression of the Tradition.

Taking everything into account, the two papal dogmas, the primacy of jurisdiction and the infallibility of ex-cathedra decisions, can be seen as valid expressions of the Tradition. They want to state authoritatively what Jesus Christ wanted for his Church as the ministry of unity and of faith, what has been historically transmitted and has proven itself historically and what has emerged increasingly clearly as the sign of identity of the Catholic Church.

The dogmas of the first Vatican Council as the sign of identity of the Catholic Church met with resistance within the Catholic Church and led to the schism with the Old Catholic Church. They were met with opposition from all other churches until the present day. Also within Catholic theology, despite all basic recognition of their binding nature, the limits of both dogmatic formulas have been highlighted then and now. They express and promote the Tradition of the Church only under a certain aspect. They could only indicate but not unfold the doctrine of the episcopate. In the doctrine of primacy, both use with the term 'jurisdiction' a one-sidedly judicial language as was common for the contemporaneous academic theology. The term 'infallible' is ambiguous, emerging in this sense only in the Middle Ages. It can be misunderstood in the sense of freedom from sin or that a dogmatic formula was of a complete perfection detached from any historical conditioning and limitation and thus totally incorrigible. Finally, the formula '*ex sese non autem ex consensu ecclesiae*' is rather ambiguous, as this might be misunderstood in the sense of an infallibility detached from the Church.

Above all, it is unfortunate that because of the outbreak of the Franco-Prussian war the council was not able to integrate the doctrine of primacy into the whole of ecclesiology. The council remained in limbo. This resulted in a sensitive imbalance regarding the reception and interpretation of the council. The council was interpreted theologically and canonistically in a maximalist and one-sided papalistic sense and fell thus behind the differentiation that the council itself had established. What the council defined for exceptional situations, in which the normal instances break down or fail and the normal ways of communication are not possible, became the standard for Church government.

Thus, Vatican I poses a difficult interpretation problem for us. The basic question is how to succeed in interpreting, according to the interpretative rule set by the council, in the sense of the whole Tradition, the great gift which the ministry of unity of the Petrine office means for the Church and in retranslating the judicial language into the sacramental language of the *communio* ecclesiology of the Old Church. The Petrine ministry must be led out of a historically conditioned narrowness and must be integrated again into catholic wideness of the *communio ecclesiarum*. In this respect, Vatican II made an essential step forward.

The Second Vatican Council

Among the expectations for the Second Vatican Council (1962–5), there was from the beginning the suggestion and wish that the Council should continue Vatican I, complement it and especially place the two papal dogmas into the whole of Catholic ecclesiology. For the sake of such expectations, the liturgical, biblical, patristic and ecumenical renewal movement between the two world wars had laid substantial groundwork and provided a more intense knowledge of the biblical and patristic Tradition that had not yet been available at Vatican I. This had opened the possibility of placing the doctrine of primacy and of infallibility of the popes into the full horizon of the *communio*-ecclesiology.[281]

In this sense the Second Vatican Council perceived itself not as a break with the first Vatican Council, but as its continuation. It placed itself decidedly in the tradition of Vatican I and explicitly received its decisions in the third chapter.[282] Any attempt to construct, in this issue, a contradiction between both councils is therefore absurd. However, Vatican II placed the doctrine of Vatican I into a more comprehensive perspective. Unlike Vatican I, Vatican II does not begin with the hierarchical structure of the Church but with the Church as the people of God and as *communio*, thereby placing the doctrine of primacy into the whole of ecclesiology. In this large context statements about the primacy are complemented with statements about the bishops as successors of the apostles[283] and the collegiality of the episcopal office.[284] Also according to Vatican II, the pope is the visible fundament of the unity of the Church, but the Church no longer appears simply as a papal church, as which it had been previously polemically apostrophized.

However, although often considered as such, the actual change of perspective of Vatican II was not the doctrine of the collegiality of the episcopal office.[285] The change was the fact that the Council no longer expressed the primacy with the terminology – and therefore no longer with the perspective – of jurisdiction, but within the framework of the sacramental structure of the Church. One of the most important decisions of the Council was to correct the distinction, common since the Middle Ages, between *ordo* and *iurisdictio* and to embed the *iurisdictio* in the *ordo* in the sense of the Old Church sacramental view of the Church. This goes so far that the constitution on the Church of Vatican II no longer speaks at all of the primacy of jurisdiction. Diverging from Vatican I, Vatican II and following it the post-conciliar canon law no longer speaks of a universal primacy of jurisdiction but of the *sacra potestas* of the bishop of Rome, a term the Council also uses for the authority of the bishops.

This general course means that the jurisdiction is not conferred upon a bishop by the pope after his ordination, but with the episcopal ordination itself. It is not derived from the papal jurisdiction; it is only determined by the pope, that is, it is assigned to a specific diocese or, in special cases, to an important super-diocesan task.[286] This definitely excludes the authority of the bishop from being perceived as emerging from the authority of the pope. The Council also orders the pope as bishop of Rome into the sacramental and episcopal structure of the Church and also calls him, like Vatican I previously, bishop of Rome.[287] He is not pope and then in addition bishop of Rome (*Papa qui episcopus Romanus*); he is rather pope as bishop of Rome that is universal shepherd of the Church with all the authority and powers already ascribed to him by the first Vatican council (*Papa qua episcopus Romanus*).[288]

The language of the collegiality of the episcopal office is relatively new. Still, it accords with the Old Church Tradition that the ordination of a bishop is to be performed by at least three bishops;[289] in other words, through his ordination the bishop is received into the college of episcopate. According to Cyprian, the mission is given to the episcopate *in solidum*.[290] Finally, the doctrine of the collegiality in the episcopal office must be understood in the context of the sacramental *communio* ecclesiology. This is not a new doctrine but the clarification of an ecclesial practice rooted in the Tradition. Already Vatican I intended to teach the collegiality of the episcopate.[291] The fact that this now happened through Vatican II is of great importance within the Church as well as ecumenically.

According to Vatican II, the highest and full power in the Church pertains to the episcopate as whole. This does not mean that there was a second highest and full power besides the highest and full power of the pope. The Council rather states that the college of bishops together with its head, the bishop of Rome, but never without this head, is the bearer of the highest and full power in the Church. Conversely, the pope can always exercise the highest and universal power freely and by virtue of the office given to him by Christ; if he does this, he always does this as head of the episcopal college.[292] The assumption of the two independent – and even competing with each other – highest authorities is thereby ruled out. The pope and the entire episcopate do not oppose each other like two independent powers; rather the one highest power can be exercised in two different forms. It is for the pope according to his best judgement to decide which form of exercise is appropriate for the different and changing situations of the Church.[293]

It is obvious that, at this point, the Second Vatican Council has left open inner-church and ecumenical questions. Without questioning the basic liberty of the pope, a more explicit collegial or synodal integration of such decisions would be conceivable and also desirable.[294] Thus, despite all positive progress, the Council also has its limits.

Nevertheless, it remains true that the Second Vatican Council opened many doors into the future and by far not all open doors have been walked through yet. The practical reception remains a wide field beyond the post-conciliar canon law of 1983.[295] This concerns in particular the collegial and synodal praxis on the level of the local church and the universal Church. At least temporarily, here some of the doors have also been closed again after the Council. The post-conciliar confusions together with the new communication possibilities have led to a new curial centralism which the majority of the Council did not, in fact, want. Thus, not only Vatican I but also Vatican II is in need of a re-reception and further development that is presently only at its very beginning.

Open and ongoing questions

An important step for the further development concerning the practical reception of Vatican II was taken by the Congregation for the Doctrine of Faith with *Considerations*, produced and published in 2002. The Congregation notes that primacy must be exercised depending on changing historical necessities and always for the good and in the best interest of the ecclesial unity.[296]

In just this respect, in a globally networked world, the Petrine office as ministry of unity will increase in importance today and undoubtedly in the future and will prove to be a gift of the Lord to his Church. It provides the Church and the work of Jesus Christ in today's pluralism of opinions and interests with a publicly, globally audible common voice; it serves the unity of the Church as well as its freedom and independence; it proves to be helpful for furthering ecumenical dialogue and dialogue with other religions and modern culture; it stands up for the protection of human life, for furthering the dignity and rights of the human person, for social justice and for peace in the world. Nothing would be more foolish than to think that the significance of the Petrine office was decreasing in the new millennium. Since the Second Vatican Council, it has stood at the beginning of a new epoch and it will gain in significance.

The same aspect could also open the way for a future possible – and probably also necessary – exercise of the Petrine office. In view of the constantly increasing complexity in the world and the global Church, it is becoming more and more difficult to have all – particularly crucial – decisions taken adequately by a central authority. In the future, the pope will thus, in a self-restriction of his power, leave many decisions to regional authorities such as national or continental episcopal synods, and will only intervene in exceptional situations affecting the whole Church. This is also necessary from an ecumenical point of view because, in the sense of the Council of Florence, in this way the traditional rights of the patriarchs and their synods can be respected while recognizing the primacy.[297]

An important point both within the Church and ecumenically is the appointment of bishops. Clearly, the election of a bishop through the people, as it existed in the Old Church, cannot be re-established under today's circumstances. Even less can one reach back to the influence of princes or secular authorities. Still, the independent appointment of bishops by the pope (with few exceptions) has existed in the whole Church only since the end of the imperial church in the late eighteenth century.[298] Therefore the stronger participation of local churches would be quite in line with the Tradition and would be anything but a new practice – rather the re-establishment of the traditional way in a manner appropriate to the changed situation. The concordats between the Holy See and several countries which contain forms of participation or approval by the local church and the State for the appointments of bishops already point in this direction. In contrast, attempts to force a bishop upon a diocese against its pronounced will have proven to be pastorally damaging and counterproductive for the authority of Rome.

Apart from such important issues of practical reception, there remain also theological questions. The Council did not succeed in articulating and interpreting the universal pastoral responsibility of the bishop of Rome in categories of a Eucharistic *communio* ecclesiology. There are two approaches here. On the one hand, one can proceed from Peter's confession of Christ and consider the essential Petrine function of the bishop of Rome to be, for the whole Church, witness, teacher and guardian of the faith in Jesus Christ, his death and resurrection, and to watch over the keeping of and unity in the faith. On the other, one can depart from the famous formula of Ignatius of Antioch, according to which it pertains to Rome to preside in love (ἀγάπη).[299] In this context, *agape* means not some kind of non-committal feeling or organizational association. As an expression of the essential nature of the Christian, *agape* is, rather, a Eucharistic term which means solidarity in the love of God revealed in Jesus Christ given through joint participation in the Eucharist. Coming from the word of Ignatius, one could understand the universal pastoral office of the pope as having special responsibility for the Eucharistic community in the Church and between the individual churches.[300] From both perspectives, further developments within the Church and ecumenically are necessary but also possible.

On understanding infallible ex-cathedra decisions

Departing from the Petrine function to be witness, teacher and guardian of the faith in Christ and of the unity in faith, the dogma of infallible ex-cathedra decisions necessitates some consideration of its own. After all, the term 'infallible' is ambiguous and totally incomprehensible for many people today. Indeed it has almost become a dogma of sceptic and pluralistic modern and postmodern thinking that we can discern truth, above all God's truth, only approximately and perspectively, if at all. In this respect, the claim to infallibility appears arrogant and intolerant.[301]

A closer look shows that this criticism is directed not only against the infallibility dogma, both fundamentally and generally, against the biblical faith in revelation. After all, it is, so to speak, the basic dogma of the New Testament that God revealed himself definitively in Jesus Christ once and for all, historically unsurpassable and for humans of all cultures. There can be no doubt for the New Testament that the Truth which Jesus is in person remains present through the Holy Spirit in the Church. For the New Testament this is not an arrogant claim but a great gift through which, together with the Truth, the light of life definitely has risen above us so that we no longer live in darkness, but are freed from the powers of darkness and untruths, of changing fashions and, not least, from our own life, falsehoods and self-deceptions.

The Truth is concrete and must be concretely interpreted in the specific situations of the Church and the Christian life. For this, Jesus entrusted Peter with the words 'binding and loosening' (Mt. 16.19) the authority for doctrinal decisions.[302] Jesus promised to Peter that these decisions made on earth would also be valid in heaven. He gave him an authority to teach and decide with eschatological validity and finality.

Thus, according to the will of Jesus, there are decisions in the Church which are eschatologically final. Of course, the term 'infallible' for such decisions emerged only in the mendicant controversy in the thirteenth and fourteenth centuries.[303] However, what is factually meant is older and based on the biblical understanding of the faithfulness-truth (*emeth*) of God.[304] It is a fundamental conviction of the Bible that God is faithful and we can rely on him unconditionally. God can neither err nor lead into error (*nec falli nec fallere potest*).[305] Infallible in the sense of the original word *infallibilis* is therefore God. With this infallible fidelity, God stands by his Church and makes it the pillar and fundament of the Truth (1 Tim. 3.15). Because of Christ's promise and through the assistance of his Spirit, the Church will endure in the fight with the powers of lies and death until the end of time (Mt. 16.18; 28.20). Despite all persecutions and inner weaknesses, the Church will endure until the end of time because of God's faithfulness. This promise means more than an institutional guarantee of existence. After all, the Church is only the Church of Jesus Christ if it keeps the confession to Jesus Christ, if it does not abandon the revealed truth but remains faithful to it. Thus, there can be error and sin in the Church but as a whole it is not only *indefectibilis* but in an analogous, i.e. in a derived way, because of God's promise it is also *infallibilis*.[306]

This infallibility applies to the Church as a whole.[307] It applies to the Petrine office insofar as this, in the sense of Augustine, is *typus ecclesiae*, that is, insofar as the bishop of Rome speaks as official witness to the faith of the Church.[308] So the pope is infallible neither in his personal and private opinions nor in his personal actions and behaviour; in all these, he is fallible like any other human being and Christian. He is only infallible when he speaks ex cathedra – in other words, when he exercises his magisterium and teaches the faith of the Church definitively and generally authoritatively for the Church.

This reasoning and interpretation also already highlights the inherent limitation of papal infallibility. Not only personal and private opinions of the pope are excluded; also not all his magisterial statements are infallible. They are only infallible if the pope speaks expressly as *typus ecclesiae*, as the holder of the Cathedra Petri in questions of faith and morals in a way that is authoritative for the whole Church. This does not apply to sermons and catecheses, speeches, letters, nor to encyclicals (unless the pope used expressly an encyclical for an ex-cathedra decision). All of these magisterial statements have their own specific authority, but they are not infallible. There is also a restriction to infallibility with respect to content. It does not apply to scientific, historical, political and other questions. Instead, 'this infallibility with which the Divine Redeemer willed His Church to be endowed in defining doctrine of faith and morals, extends as far as the deposit of Revelation extends, which must be religiously guarded and faithfully expounded.'[309]

This explanation highlights that the infallibility of the pope while exercising his magisterium is not detached from the Church. The infallible magisterium of the pope exists, rather, to testify the faith of the Church and nothing but the faith of the Church. It is tied back to the preceding consensus of the Church in faith. It expresses the faith of the Church with eschatological validity and through the assistance of the Holy Spirit it cannot err nor lead into error. As Johann Adam Möhler puts it, it is unerring.[310]

As such decisions are true, they are also irreformable,[311] for what is true today will also be true tomorrow and cannot be wrong tomorrow. Thus, the dogma testifies within history the truth, which transcends all historical conditioning, of the truth that appeared eschatologically definitely in Jesus Christ and of God's unconditional love. Such a decision puts an end to all dialectics. Therefore, it is not legitimized through subsequent reception in the Church. Still, such decisions are interpreted in a subsequent process of reception and are integrated into the whole of the faith and life of the Church.[312]

The infallibility and irreformability of such decisions accord with the historicity of the Old and New Testament order of salvation. The eschatological definite occurs in historical conditions. Thus, dogmatic decisions always take place in a specific historical situation, they use historical human language and ways of expression and are insofar historically conditioned.[313] It pertains also to the historicity that dogmas can subsequently be deepened and complemented, obviously always in the same sense and the same meaning.[314] In other words, there is growth and progress in understanding the faith.[315] However, within all this historical conditionality they express something that is valid and binding for all times. Hence, dogmas must be historically interpreted in the sense that the historical situation, the context and the historical way of speaking must be considered in the interpretation and thereby what was said at the time must be interpreted in today's context and language with a mind attentive to the Spirit. Heinrich Schlier expressed this beautifully with the idea that dogmatic statements remain worth reflecting.[316]

For this historical hermeneutic of dogmatic statements, there are rules recognized by the Church which we can outline only briefly in this context. The basic rule says that dogmatic statements must not be considered in isolation, but they must be regarded in the context and connection with the whole of faith (*ex mysteriorum ipsorum nexu inter se*).[317] Thereby the hierarchy of truths must be respected,[318] which means that the individual truths of faith are to be understood in connection with and in the light of those Christological and Trinitarian statements of faith that are fundamental for them.

A second rule says that the faith of the Church as a whole is not an abstract construction of doctrine but the faith lived and witnessed in the Church. It manifests itself in the *sensus fidelium* guided by the Holy Spirit and in the different forms of his ways of expression.[319] This includes in particular the liturgy. The liturgy celebrated together is the most important interpretation instance of the Church's faith. Thus, *lex orandi statuit legem credendi*.[320]

The liturgy teaches us to understand and interpret the creed as doxology, as praise of God.[321] It is rather telling that, in the solemn liturgy, the creed is not simply read or said; instead it is sung and regarded as praise of God. This leads to the third rule, which comes mainly from Thomas Aquinas. According to him the actual goal faith seeks to express is not a sententious formula as such but the 'object' expressed in the sentence – in other words, God himself.[322] Statements of faith must be interpreted in view of this theologically intended purpose.

This leads to a further interpretative rule. The dogma is about interpreting the message of God as the eschatological salvation of man. Dogmas are thus not simply theoretical matters but saving truth. Therefore they must be interpreted from the final goal of man to the existential question of man's salvation.[323] As theological statements, they are to be explained soteriologically and their spiritual significance must be shown.[324]

Finally, as statements of salvation, statements of faith are not dictates imposed upon man. The Christian faith does not consist of total and blind obedience but reasonable worship (Rom. 12.1). Statements of faith, though, contain mysteries of faith that transcend human reason and cannot be kept as rational truths.[325] Still, they can be understood in analogy to human rational truths.[326] The basic theological principle '*fides quaerens intellectum*' applies also to papal ex-cathedra decisions. This principle demands an interpretation of faith as opening understanding and liberating man and accordingly it demands a comprehending and responsible answer from faith.[327]

To sum up: if the doctrine of the infallibility of the pope is perceived in the broad context demonstrated here, then it is not the despotic spectre which it often appears for many. It is expression of the central truth of our salvation that God revealed to us in Jesus Christ once and for all the truth of our life and that this light of truth remains victoriously present in the Church and cannot be darkened again. It is a salutary and liberating truth. As such we can and should bring it as our contribution into the ecumenical dialogue.

The Petrine office in the ecumenical dialogues

The more the world comes together as one, the more pressure there is on nationally constituted churches, and the ecumenical dialogue about the ministry of unity of the Petrine office becomes more urgent and peremptory. This dialogue has long since begun in the new climate made possible by the Second Vatican Council.[328] Pope John Paul II took the initiative himself and, in the encyclical *Ut unum sint* (1995), invited a new ecumenical dialogue concerning the future form of the Petrine office. He inspired a conversation about how a new form of exercising the primacy could be found that can be recognized by all sides without renouncing what is essential to its foundational nature.[329] Pope Benedict XVI repeated this invitation verbatim during his visit to Phanar (2006).

This dialogue is a sensitive issue for all sides. After all, for Catholics the Petrine office is a sign of identity of their church, as, conversely, non-recognition is a sign of identity for all other churches. Thus, the problem is not only theologically difficult, but also carries an emotional and historical burden. It requires from all sides sensitivity and a willingness to listen and to rethink.

The conversation about the Petrine office takes place in particular with the Orthodox churches.[330] With them we have in common the apostolic and sacramental form of the Church of the first millennium, and therein have a joint basis upon which we can build and look for a form of the Petrine office recognized by both sides.[331] The point of departure for the conversation is the common episcopal structure of the Church.[332] Primacy (πρῶτος, *Primas*) and synodality or collegiality are thereby constitutive on each level of the Church, local as well as universal. The Orthodox churches basically recognize, in this sense in the Tradition of the first millennium, the primacy of the bishop of Rome. Yet, the question is: of what kind was this primacy and of which kind should it be?

The formula frequently used by the Orthodox side of '*primus inter pares*' remains ambiguous as long as it is not clarified what *primus* in fact means.[333] Does *primus* mean only an honorary primacy to which only outward signs of honour pertain and is thus only a primacy of protocol? A primacy of honour understood in this way would not do justice to the Catholic understanding of primacy. It would also be of little use and biblically it would be more than problematic. Thus one will have to take seriously that 'honour' in the sense of τιμή or *honour* also included in the old world the meaning of authority. Hence it must be clarified which kind of authority this is.

In order to clarify this question, one can depart from the practice of the first millennium. Still, one must thereby take into account that history did not stop in the second millennium, but has moved on for both sides. The Christendom concept of the Church, with the emperor as a decisive symbol of unity is, at least in the East, irretrievably lost. Even if we so desired, we cannot go back to the first millennium. The Tradition is a living process that did not simply freeze with the end of the first millennium. Therefore, the normative Tradition of the Church cannot be restricted to the first millennium.

Surprisingly, the medieval councils of Lyons II (1274) and Florence (1439–45) give us an indication of a direction in which an answer might be found. Florence defined, for the first time, the Roman claim to papacy, but, at the same time, recognized the traditional rights of the patriarchs.[334] In other words, the primacy is basically reconcilable with the recognition of the patriarchs and their synods. The Roman primacy thus lies on a different level from the authority of the patriarchs. The recognition of the authority of the pope and that of the patriarchs in their respective churches are thus, as was the case in the first millennium, basically compatible with each other.[335] This is also in line with the First Vatican Council which says, following Pope Gregory the Great, that the pope's authority was not in opposition to that of the bishops over their flocks. On the contrary, the former strengthens and defends the latter.[336] From this it follows that, by way of self-restriction of his authority, the pope could limit himself when exercising his primacy in the Eastern churches in disciplinary matters concerning extraordinary cases. The normal church government in the Eastern churches could then happen as before within the framework of the traditional patriarchal-synodal church order. This would not be a novelty but a renewal of the Old Church practice.

Though this is just a rough sketch, taking all this into account I could envisage, in the long run, the following consensus: (1) The Petrine office is primarily, in the sense of Peter's confession, a witnessing office for Jesus Christ. It watches over the true faith. Questions of faith cannot be decided without the bishop of Rome. (2) In cases of discipline, the pope normally does not exercise direct jurisdiction in the East. He watches over proper practice in all churches, yet he intervenes only in extraordinary cases such as the case of recourse or if a local church can no longer solve its own problems or gravely fails to solve them. In such situations, the pope could commission other instances of the Eastern churches with the solution or, if appropriate and necessary, could decide himself. (3) Only the pope can call a general council, as the presidency pertains to him and without his assent the council's decisions have no authority.[337]

On the basis of many experiences, I know very well that it will be a difficult and, as far as we can judge, also long way until such a solution is reached. Too many misunderstandings and negative experiences have accumulated in a thousand years of separation, and these have had, for many, lasting and traumatic effects. In addition, the understanding of interpreting Scripture and of the first millennium which developed in the second millennium are also too different. The alienation which led to the separation did not only consolidate in the second millennium, it also grew. To overcome all these difficulties and achieve a healing of the historical memories, it necessitates conversion and reconciliation of the hearts on both sides. It is only then that a solution will be possible with God's help and good will on both sides.

What is theologically and spiritually true for the dialogue with the Orthodox churches applies also to the dialogue with the churches and communities of the Reformation. Yet, the dialogue about the question of primacy is obviously more difficult. In contrast to the Orthodox, despite all convergences, we have with these churches and communities no common sacramental-episcopal understanding of Church and ministry which would be the basis and framework within which alone the question of primacy could be brought to a solution. Nonetheless, in past centuries there were already occasional conversations about a possible agreement.[338] In the changed situation after the Second Vatican Council a new atmosphere emerged in which theologians from both sides could deal repeatedly and intensively with the question of primacy in official as well as informal ecumenical dialogues in an open-minded and emotionally relaxed way.[339] Fraternal encounters between bishops as well as between the pope and bishops and leaders of other churches have become almost commonplace. In addition, in many areas there is, by now almost natural, cooperation on the local and universal level.

On the Protestant side, there are important voices who highlight that despite all severe and – towards the end of his life – hateful polemics, Luther himself never questioned the papacy of his time as such. His polemical utterances are rather conditional; that is, he could recognize a papacy if this permitted and did not suppress the preaching of the Gospel. Luther's statements in his commentary on Galatians (1531/1535), that he would not only carry the pope on his hands but even kiss his feet if he only set conscience free and permitted the preaching of the gospel of justification, are famous.[340] Also Melanchthon's supplement to the Schmalcald Articles, that if the pope allowed the Gospel, he would recognize the pope, in his position by human right, for the sake of peace, is well known.[341] Thus, today the Protestant churches can recognize and accept in today's papacy a ministry of the Gospel, as conversely it is recognized by the Catholic side that important elements of the apostolic ministry are realized by the bishops and leaders of the other churches.

The furthest progress has been achieved in the conversations with the Anglican Communion. Even though it has been impossible to achieve a consensus going beyond many convergences, it is possible to build upon the results reached.[342] Unfortunately, because of recent developments and internal difficulties within the Anglican Communion, a consensus is unlikely for the foreseeable future. In the Catholic/Lutheran dialogue, the formula has become standard 'that also the Petrine office of the bishop of Rome does not have to be excluded by Lutherans given that it is subordinated to the primacy of the Gospel by theological reinterpretation and practical restructuring'.[343] The document of the Groupe de Dombes between representatives of the Catholic and Reformed churches came to similar conclusions.[344] The document *Communio Sanctorum*[345] that has emerged from the Catholic/Lutheran dialogue in Germany goes a positive step further, likewise the document recently emerging from the informal international theological Catholic/Lutheran dialogue *Gemeinschaft der Kirchen und Petrusamt.*[346]

In all these documents we have positive steps of approximation, a better understanding free from prejudices on all sides and mutual respect and cooperation, but we are still a long way from a consensus. After all, what exactly is the meaning of theological reinterpretation and practical restructuring? Of course, similar to the Orthodox side it means, among other things, the binding integration into a collegial-synodal structure. Yet, how far could this go without touching the identity of the Petrine office? These are questions which raise again the open ecclesiological basic questions concerning the sacramental episcopal nature of the Church that require a theological and above all practical rethinking on all sides. With this we are only at the beginning of a beginning.

If the ecumenical dialogue is to be not only an exchange of ideas but of gifts, then the Catholic dialogue partners can contribute the Petrine office as a gift for the whole Church and its unity in diversity and their service for the one mankind. This requires of course that we address anew the question of collegiality and synodality in the life of the Church.

5.5 Collegiality, conciliarity and synodality in the life of the Church

Historical significance

The Acts of the Apostles tells us of the fundamental controversy important for the young incipient Church and for the whole of church history, namely, the questions of whether circumcision is necessary for Gentile Christians. We read that the apostles, the elders and the brothers came together to discuss the issue (Acts 15) and, after consultation, unanimously decided: 'it has been decided by the Holy Spirit and by ourselves' (Acts 15.28). From the second century onwards this so-called Apostle Council become the prototype in cases when it was necessary to act together in disputes with heretics, to define church order or in disputes among bishops.[347] We hear for the first time of a synodal life in Asia Minor (against Montanism and in the Paschal controversy), then in the letters of Cyprian of Carthage in Northern Africa (in the rebaptism controversy).

For Cyprian, the '*in unum convenire*' does not only mean the actual gathering but the *unanimitas* the consensus horizontally and vertically, in other words in the present Church as well as with the past Church.[348] With Augustine, we hear the controversy with Donatism of synods or councils.

He sees their function as the strengthening of limited human knowledge, the affirmation of Truth and the confirmation of customs.[349]

The Roman bishops, too, regularly held synods. Other important particular synods took place among others in Arles (314, 473), Carthage (418), Orange (Arausicanum) (529), and several times (the first in 400) in Toledo. The synodal tradition also played an important role in the Middle Ages. After the crisis of conciliarism and the Reformation the synodal tradition was revived by the Council of Trent. It played an important part for the Catholic renewal after the Reformation. One has only to think of the important reform synods of Charles Borromeo († 1584) in Milan.

Whereas synods or particular councils pertain – or at least should pertain – to the normal life of the Church, ecumenical councils are extraordinary events. It came to them for the first time after the emergence of the imperial church under Emperor Constantine the Great in Nicaea (325). The recognition of a council as ecumenical depended largely on its reception. Criteria for the recognition were established by the second council of Nicaea (787) and thereby it recognized the special significance of the bishop of Rome.[350] The Eastern and Western churches both recognize together seven ecumenical councils. The list valid in today's Latin Church prevailed only through Robert Bellarmine so that, including the Second Vatican Council, there have been twenty-one ecumenical councils to date. They are practically all key events, foci and points of orientation in the life of the Church.

Theological understanding

While Catholic theology speaks of collegiality, Orthodox theology uses the term synodality. Both have in common the notion that synods or councils are assemblies of bishops even though laypeople can participate and contribute without voting and have already done so in history so far in a manifold and effective way. On each level, a synod is to have a primate (πρῶτος) who convenes it and confirms it. Synods of the third and fourth centuries began to inform the bishop of Rome about their decisions, just as he claimed to reject decisions that contradicted a general council.[351] In this question we notice already very early on a difference between East and West which, among other reasons, led to the separation in the second millennium.[352]

Totally different from the understanding of synods of the Old Church is the synodal-presbyterial understanding of synods and of the synodal episcopal office that, by developing further concepts of the Reformation prepared by Friedrich Schleiermacher († 1834), generally prevailed in the twentieth century in Reformation churches. It highlights the specific Reformation understanding of the common priesthood and the ministry.[353] Accordingly, the synods which have a lay majority perceive themselves as church governing bodies which do not only participate under the supervision of the bishop, but which exercise power themselves. The bishop or president is integrated into the synod and is largely tied to its decisions. In the twentieth century, synodal government was also introduced in the episcopally structured Anglican Communion.[354] These are neither synods in the sense of the Old Church nor in the understanding of the Catholic Church or the Orthodox churches, but church parliaments.

The Catholic theology of councils or synods springs from the *communio* structure of the Church and from the collegiality of the episcopate contained therein, i.e. in communion with the Petrine office the joint participation in the one episcopate.[355] The conviction that the Church is a creation of the Spirit and that it cannot totally fall away from Truth was expressed in Patristic times in the conviction that the doctrine of faith definitely proclaimed by an ecumenical council was given by the Spirit and that the highest authority pertains to it after Holy Scripture. The erroneous term 'infallible' did not appear until the fourteenth century and became, in reaction to the Reformation criticism, an important axiom of Catholic theology.[356]

Collegiality/synodality is not only about conciliar assemblies and finding decisions (*collegialitas effectiva*) but also about the collegiate and synodal spirit and the corresponding fraternal practice in the whole life of the Church (*collegialitas affectiva*). The word synod (σύνοδος) originally means gathering as well as companionship along the way. Therefore, collegial or synodal structures in the Church are not only a problem of purely external structures or simply organizational questions, neither are they a question of distributing powers in the Church. They are rather rooted in the nature of the Church as *communio* and must shape its life and style on the whole.

The Second Vatican Council and the post-conciliar development

The Second Vatican Council laid the foundations for the renewal of synodal life with the help of the doctrine of the collegiality of the bishops.[357] The post-conciliar canon law provides for diocesan and regional synods.[358] In addition, the Council suggested presbyterial and pastoral councils at diocesan and local levels[359] and demanded episcopal conferences.[360] These cannot replace or restrict the responsibility of the individual bishop, but they should support it. Unfortunately, the development of collegial/synodal structures was only hesitatingly followed up after the Council, so the respective possibilities of the post-conciliar canon law have so far only been realized to a small extent. It would have been desirable to see on the level of particular churches a revival of the practice, steeped in tradition, of particular synods. Useful and important as they might be on a working level, episcopal conferences and the post-conciliar presbyterial and pastoral councils cannot replace synods in the theological sense and in the sense of canon law.

On the level of the universal Church, the Council recommended the institution of an episcopal synod.[361] It was established by Paul VI with the Motu proprio *Apostolica sollicitudo* (1965). Since then, the universal and regional episcopal synods have become important instruments to strengthen affectively and effectively the collegiality of bishops. A further development of their way of working and functioning would be desirable. The call for the strengthening of synodal life on the universal level must not be misunderstood as an attempt to restrict the Petrine office. As the visible centre and basis of the unity and the freedom and independence for the Catholic Church, the Petrine office is a gift of the Lord to his Church. Therefore, it cannot be about synodally weakening the Petrine office but supporting it collegially. The pope alone can convene a synod and he must also confirm it. The synodal consultation is of great importance for him, but it cannot commit him or even overrule him. Leading the universal Church is only possible in trusting cooperation of pope and synod.

Another form of expressing collegiality on a universal level is the College of Cardinals as senate of the pope.[362] Cardinals (from *cardo*, pivotal point) were originally the suburbicarian bishops, the representatives of the Roman clergy and the deacons of the ecclesial districts of Rome. Pope Alexander III finally granted them the exclusive right to elect the pope in 1179. In the Middle Ages, they had considerable influence through regular consistories and often through electoral capitulations. The institution of cardinal congregations with assigned subjects by Sixtus V (1588) was in line with the demands of a more modern, functional church government. Obviously, this diminished the influence of the College of Cardinals as such and it transformed the Curial Cardinals residing in Rome into leading curial officials. The now-internationalized College of Cardinals should perform today again more clearly its original role as senate of the pope. The College of Cardinals and the episcopal synod can thereby complement each other as two synodal bodies.

The strengthening of the synodal principle on a universal level would be an important contribution to the dialogue about the new way of exercising the Petrine office to which Pope John Paul II emphatically encouraged.[363] Pope Benedict XVI repeated this encouragement during his visit to Phanar (2006). Instead of being an obstacle for the other churches and church communities, the Petrine office, synodally and collegially strengthened, could become an important ministry for the greater ecumenical unity of the Church as well as a gift for the other churches and ecclesial communities that often suffer from internal fragmentation.

Through the renewal of the synodal principle on all levels and by strengthening it on a universal level, the Catholic Church could profit greatly without giving up the least of the essential nature of the Petrine office. In particular, the strengthening of the synodal principle would enable a fruitful, regular exchange of information and experiences between local churches as well as between local churches and the centre. This appears indispensible in a world and Church that is constantly becoming more global and at the same time more pluralistic and confusing. It would help to avoid present communication weaknesses and blunders. It does not pay if there are internal consultations by a handpicked staff of obedient advisors and critically-constructive loyal voices are carefully filtered out from the start. A more participatory and dialogical style would make the *communio* nature and universality of the Church appear more visible, tangible and trustworthy. Finally, it would also be necessary and beneficial to have more mutual information within the Roman Curia.[364]

5.6 The one Church and the many individual churches

The question of primacy as well as that of collegiality/synodality raises the issue of the relation of the one universal Church to the many local or individual churches. The New Testament uses the term church (ἐκκλησία) in the singular[365] as well as in the plural in the sense of the many local churches.[366] For the New Testament, the one Church is present in each local church. Paul speaks of the 'church of God in Corinth' (1 Cor. 1.2; 2 Cor. 1.1). Similar statements can be found in the early Church Fathers.[367] Thus, one cannot help but say that in each local church celebrating the Eucharist there is not only a part but there is present the one Church of Jesus Christ.[368]

Yet, as it is in each case the one Church that is present in the many local or individual churches, no individual church can isolate itself from the one Church. Each local church, rather, is a concrete manifestation of the one Church and depends on the communion with all other local churches. There are many churches, yet they are not the one Church because of a subsequent association but because of their nature. As such they grant each other peace (*pax*), call themselves a brotherhood and offer each other hospitality. Above all, they agree in the transmitted doctrine of faith.[369] Cyprian of Carthage, in particular, highlighted the unity and undividedness of the episcopate.[370] In the Eastern church, Basil often stressed in his letters the necessity of unity and cooperation among the churches of East and West.[371]

The question about the relation between unity and diversity in the Church has been asked time and again in the course of church history. It was in the background during the gradual separation of the Eastern and Western churches, and emerged again in medieval conciliarism, in debates during the Council of Trent about the residence obligation of bishops and in modern times in controversies with Gallicanism and episcopalism. Among others, the definition of primacy by the First Vatican Council was addressed against offshoots of the latter-mentioned trends. Yet, already the letter of the German bishops in response to the circular telegram by the German Chancellor Bismarck, which was expressly confirmed by Pope Pius

IX, made it clear that the primacy definition of Vatican I did not intend to abolish personal rights of the bishops and did not want to deprive local churches of their rights in this way.[372] However, an extensive treatment of this question was not possible because of the premature termination of the council due to the outbreak of the Franco-Prussian War.

Referring to the ecclesiology of the Old Church, the Second Vatican Council took up the question again in many places. It referred thereby explicitly to the tradition of the Eastern Church and emphasized anew the significance of local or particular churches. The Council expressly declares: 'within the Church particular Churches hold a rightful place; these Churches retain their own traditions, without in any way opposing the primacy of the Chair of Peter, which presides over the whole assembly of charity and protects legitimate differences, while at the same time assuring that such differences do not hinder unity but rather contribute toward it.'[373] The one and only Catholic Church consists in and of particular churches fashioned after the model of the universal Church.[374] 'This Church of Christ is truly present in all legitimate local congregations of the faithful which, united with their pastors, are themselves called churches in the New Testament.'[375]

After the Council, the discussion partly turned into a local ecclesial particularism. The Congregation for the Doctrine of Faith considered it necessary to explain in the letter *On some Aspects of the Church understood as Communion – Communionis notio* (1992) the meaning of *communio*-reality. The letter explains that, just as the Church exists 'in and from' the many local churches,[376] so the many churches exist 'in and from' the one Church. It says that the universal Church is 'a reality *ontologically and temporally* prior to every *individual* particular Church'.[377] This last sentence caused a fierce discussion which also led to a debate about the relation of local church and universal Church between the then Cardinal Joseph Ratzinger and myself.[378]

In this debate, I was not concerned about church politics. My concern was a pastoral one, namely, the question of balancing the imbalance of the, at times excessive, Roman centralism. This is, theologically, thus referred to the position of Henri de Lubac. In his view, we can speak neither of a priority of the local church against the universal Church nor vice versa, but only of the simultaneity and mutual permeation of both. Thus, I spoke nowhere of a priority of the local church and a subsequent federation of the particular churches to the universal Church. My position was that of the simultaneity of universal Church and local church. So also Henri de Lubac: 'A universal church which would have a separate existence, or which someone imagined as existing outside the particular churches, is a mere abstraction.'[379]

Similarly, Pope Paul VI compared the universal Church to a large tree in whose branches the birds of heaven lived (Mt. 13.32), and to a net that caught all kinds of fish (Mt. 14.41). Every particular church would become poor if it cut itself off voluntarily from the universal Church, but 'at the same time, a Church *toto orbe diffusa* would become an abstraction if she did not take body and life precisely through the individual Churches. Only continual attention to these two poles of the Church will enable us to perceive the richness of this relationship between the universal Church and the individual Churches.'[380]

I was therefore surprised by the fierce reaction. It built up to the accusation that I no longer could or wanted to see God's great idea of Church. All would therefore end in theological enthusiasm that left only the empirical reality of the churches with and against each other, yet Church as theological issue would be crossed out. 'If one can see the Church anymore only in human organisations, this leaves indeed only desolation.' I could only agree to this. Still, anyone who knew me and knew what I had written in many places following the spirit of Möhler about the Church could regard these accusations only as severe misunderstanding that, thank God, could soon be largely clarified.

In the course of the debate it became evident that the term 'local church' as well as 'universal Church' required clarification. Vatican II uses the first term to mean the particular church (*ecclesia particularis*) that is the diocese, and also in the sense of the church of one country or continent. In our context it means the local church in the sense of the local church gathered around and led by its bishop. The Council normally uses for this the term *ecclesia particularis* which should not be translated by 'particular church' but 'individual church'. It is not only an empirical but also a theological entity. The term 'universal Church' appears in the Constitution on the Church, *Lumen Gentium*, only in three places and each time with a different meaning.[381] It can refer to the pre-existing and eschatological Church of all times and to the whole empirical church. These are different levels that are interrelated but which were unhealthily mixed in the debate.[382] According to the pastoral perspective, my concern was the earthly church and the relation within history of the one Church to the many individual churches. The teleological priority of the one pre-existing and eschatological Church was never up for discussion and thus has never been denied by me.

To reach a solution, we can start by stating that *the one* is not simply the first number in a row of numbers. Rather, *the one* is the measure of numbers and of multitude[383] and, in the sense of Thomas Aquinas, a transcendental determination of being.[384] In the finite sphere, however, unity can only be conceived as unity of a plurality, for without plurality a finite measure would be unrelated and in the original sense absolute. Conversely, plurality presupposes unity as its measure. Theologically this is analogous to the relation of the one Church within history to the many individual churches. From eternity God wants and founds in Jesus Christ the one Church but he wants it as unity in many individual churches. This unity does not emerge from an association of individual churches, it is rather historically present in the many local or individual churches. On the other hand, local or individual churches are no spin-offs or emanations from one Church within history. Instead, both are present in each other and with each other; they permeate each other and exist perichoretically.

Concerning a historic precedence of the one Church before the many local churches, it cannot be verified biblically or historically in the Early Church. From a historical perspective, the account of Pentecost in the Acts of the Apostles (Acts 2) is a construction of Luke which does not seek to rule out that there were probably from the beginning, maybe in Galilee, also communities outside Jerusalem. Thus, the Church within history must be regarded historically and philosophically as unity in the diversity of individual churches as well as diversity in the unity of the one Church. Unity and diversity are always present in the earthly Church simultaneously, together and in each other in mutual perichoretic permeation.

The perichoretic unity of universal Church and individual church beyond centralism and federalism is something unique that does not exist in any other secular constitutional structure. Yet, as the Church is a divine-human reality, it cannot be forbidden also to ask about the practical consequences.[385] The earthly Church must strive in its praxis, such as canon law or the appointment of bishops, to do justice to both ecclesial aspects, universal and local, and it must strive for the proper balance between unity and legitimate diversity. In everything that is essential, the Church must make efforts for unity while allowing independence and diversity in everything else. No burdens are to be imposed beyond the essentials (Acts 15.28). It is self-evident that this principle is also of ecumenical importance, in particular in relation to the Eastern churches.[386]

In any form of centralism, it is to be feared that, sooner or later, it turns into its opposite. Despite all globalization, the situations and challenges in the world are so different that it is becoming increasingly impossible to regulate almost everything as centrally as possible. If it is nevertheless attempted, then centralism becomes only hardly bearable with the time. It will cause increasing annoyance and in practice it will sooner or later lead to a silent termination of the unity. In contrast, wise balancing of unity and diversity could overcome some built-up annoyance and mistrust.[387]

Möhler's famous words hold true: 'Two extremes are possible in ecclesiastical life, and both are called egoism. They arise if *each as an individual* or *one individual* wishes to be all. In the latter case the bond of unity is so narrow and love so warm that one cannot free oneself of its strangling grasp. In the first case, everything falls apart, and so love grows so cold that one freezes. One egoism begets the other. Neither one not another must wish to be all. Only all can be all and the unity of all can only be a whole. This is the idea of the Catholic Church.'[388]

5.7 The future of the parish structure

The parish and the community/congregation

There are not only problems and developments on the level of the universal Church and the local church but also on the level of the local community. It is there that they are felt most directly, for the majority of faithful is at home in the Church through their parish or local community. Yet, this home is increasingly dissolving in the context of the present social and ecclesial change because parish, political community and social environment no longer form a unity. There are regional differences in this situation, but, generally, it is almost the same tendency in the countries of Western Europe.

The concentration of ecclesial life in the local community was not there from the beginning. Originally, the Church was an urban institution and the church of the bishop was the centre of ecclesial life.[389] When the Church spread from the cities to the surrounding country, the bishops saw themselves increasingly forced to send presbyters into the country to take over there certain pastoral tasks under their authority. In Rome it came to the establishment of the so-called titular churches. From about the sixth century onwards there were country parishes throughout the whole Western church. The term parish (παροικία, *parochia*) that came to be used originally meant to live in a foreign land, in a place without civil rights. The term parish thus originally expressed the eschatological orientation of the Church and of Christian existence and the Christian pilgrim existence (1 Pet. 1.17; 2.11). Within the western world, the parish then became the normal unit for Christians. The Council of Trent in particular regarded them as important centres of pastoral care.[390]

In the wake of the pastoral renewal between the two world wars, the change from the parish to the community occurred. The latter term was typical of Protestant theology and expressed the specific Protestant understanding of Church. In Catholic usage, it meant a turn from a territorial understanding to a more personal and interpersonal understanding. Out of this view, a specific community theology and pastoral care emerged with the greatest possible participation and co-responsibility of the laity.[391]

The Council speaks of the local community and pays great attention to it in a separate section in the Constitution on the Church, *Lumen Gentium*. It strives to determine the local communities (*congregationes fidelium locales*) theologically within the framework of the people of God ecclesiology and the *communio* ecclesiology.[392] Pope John Paul II's post-synodal exhortation *Christifideles laici* (1988) says of the local community that in it the *communio* of the Church finds its immediate and visible expression. The parish is for most Christians the concrete form of the local realization of the Church. 'In a certain sense it is the Church living in the midst of the homes of her sons and daughters.'[393] Post-conciliar canon law has followed this development. It defines the parish no longer as an administrative unit but as a pastoral community of faithful.[394]

Since the Council, the local community has found itself confronted with the change in society as a whole and also within the Church. Social change leads to urbanization and largely to the dissolution of the traditional village structure, to an unprecedented mobility of the population and in society to cultural-religious pluralism that results in the dissolution of the traditional *Volkskirche* form with its relatively homogeneous ecclesial-denominational milieu.[395] Today we live again, like the first Christians, increasingly as aliens and in a diaspora situation. A consequence of this social and ecclesial situation is that, to a large extent, the traditional parish structure and parish pastoral care in Western Europe (under different conditions partly also on other continents) can no longer be maintained.

The end or the ending of the *Volkskirche* supported by the milieu is one reason among others that the number of practising Catholics has decreased. This in turn is one reason among others for the decrease in vocations to the priesthood. What is referred to as a shortage of priests is therefore not calculated in relation to practising Catholics but in relation to the traditional parish structure as it developed under the conditions of the *Volkskirche*. Most dioceses try to solve the resulting problems by amalgamating parishes or so-called pastoral care units or parish units whereby the old parishes continue to exist. There are some successful examples. Yet, in the long run this is an unsatisfactory situation for the communities, and it creates an excessive demand for priests. In the long run, the *Volkskirche* cannot be simulated if, for various reasons, it continues to dissolve further.[396] Obviously, the answer to the question about the right way to a new social form and form of life of the Church cannot simply come from behind a desk. The answer cannot be only administrative and organizational measures ordered by a decree. A new social form must grow on the basis of the ecclesiology of the people of God and this is only possible through a long process.

Volkskirche – the church of the people

The idea of *Volkskirche* developed through a long process into the popular church. The traditional *Volkskirche* is characterized by a more or less given identity between the church and the respective society or by the fact that the established society is, as it were, duplicated through its own institutions from kindergartens and schools to hospitals. This social form is dissolving today and in many cases it already belongs to the past. In traditionally Catholic countries and regions, social and cultural development leads also to the fact that practising and confessing Christians become a minority.

Still, this is no reason to panic. Minority situations do not necessarily have to lead to sectarian milieus. If they are alert and alive, small communities can, by all means, radiate. A good example of this is modern European and North American Judaism. Similarly, Christian minorities too can be creative and communicative minorities that practise a new, Christian-inspired model of life and thereby can bring about change in society.[397] With the ending of the old *Volkskirche* structure, the Church must regain a missionary radiance to become home for as many people as possible. To be the church of the people, the Church must not be satisfied with the remaining faithful and with those 'still' practising as a wrongly understood 'holy rest'. A church that no longer wants to grow will die and ultimately become extinct.

Therefore, the thesis of the end of the *Volkskirche* must not be misunderstood. The Church will always have to remain a *Volkskirche* in the sense that it is rooted in the people and exists for all. All must feel at home in the Church: the educated and the uneducated, rich and poor, young and old, healthy, sick and handicapped, locals and strangers, dumb and intelligent people, zealous, pious Christians and sceptics and seekers, etc. Thus, the Church must never become an elite church of the religiously assured, those totally committed to the Church and marked by, as it were, religious 'talent'. Yet, as church of the people it, must not lack profile and become simply a service church which submits to the laws of the market with as broad as possible a range of charitable-social offers for a potential clientele. The Church must remain a communion of faith and a community of worship. It is only from this centre that it can radiate into its environment.

Hence, after the end of the traditional *Volkskirche*, the model for a new ecclesial social form is neither the homogenous community church defined by territory nor the elitist church of decision, but the 'church of the people' which is already emerging along rough outlines. It will be a community of faith of those identified to different degrees, which has the joint celebration of the Eucharist at its centre, and which sees itself in solidarity with existential problems, the joys and hopes, the fears and sorrows of the people.[398] In the sense of the ecclesiology of the people of God of Vatican II, priests and laity will work trustingly together in it. Such a church of God's people cannot be planned. Yet, one can notice its emergence and should further it carefully. Still, what can it concretely look like?

The future parish – the centrally located church and many surrounding communities

It will not be possible to design the concrete shape of the future church of the people from the lack, specifically, of priests and community. Simply spreading out the lack evenly and thinning out ecclesial presence evenly across the territory is a method which is not orientated towards the future but towards the past and which can, for this reason alone, have no future.

We must approach the issue positively and ask: how can the Church exercise its mission in the sense of the people of God theology within the fast-changing social structure and correspond to it pastorally?

Nobody will want to dissolve or intentionally destroy the traditional village community, where it still exists. Yet, it is obvious that it will not be the social form of the Church leading into the future. However, we must not look back nostalgically but we must look ahead.[399] Still, in this new situation we must not wear out the remaining resources, we must rather concentrate them. The first evangelization of Europe originated from spiritual centres (churches of bishops, urban churches, monasteries, and others). In the missionary areas and in the young churches in the Third World, this structure has remained alive until today. I cannot see any other way for the new evangelization of the old Christian countries. Instead of thinning out across the regions there should be a concentration on the centre. To the extent as larger social living areas develop, the creation of central churches will be essential. A new description of parishes, as is already happening to a large extent in France, can evolve more or less organically from this.

These central churches should be oases where vigorous powerful ecclesial life radiating missionarily anew can be experienced on Sundays and feast days. One should find there on Sundays and feast days a well-designed liturgy and during the week catechetical, charitable and other events and, above all, always a person one can talk to at any time and who can give information.

This concept meets with the serious objection that in consequence it dries up the surrounding environment and turns it into a pastoral desert. Of course, this cannot be the intention. To avoid such pastoral desertification we should take recourse to a second model of the Early Church that has stood the test in the further course of church history, especially in times of emergencies and of persecutions (such as presently in China, or as I experienced in Prague during the Communist era). It is what the New Testament calls house churches.[400] It had already been revived by Methodism and pietism. Among others, house churches play an important role today in charismatic renewal, in the base communities (Latin America) and in the Little Communities in Africa.[401]

Transferred to our situation, it means that there should be and must be many kinds of communities gathered around a central church. They can have manifold forms. Where possible, the former parish can continue a vibrant community life. Manifold transitions are possible. In addition, there can be house circles, base communities, spiritual communities, and groups for Bible reading, prayer, catechumens, families or friends, women, youth and so forth. All these more or less fixed communities can be biotopes of faith, places where Christian life can be concretely experienced and learnt and where it is lived so that it radiates. The future parish will thus be a community of communities, a network of circles, groups, formal or informal associations that can be called house churches in the sense of the New Testament. In them, Christians can have an ecclesial home in a new way. A religious nomadic existence in the middle of the modern diaspora is not the ideal way of being Christian. This is only possible in the 'we' even though the attachment to this 'we' can be of different intensity. This necessitates comprehensible community forms in which the Church can be concretely experienced and lived.

Building up this web of communities, focusing them on the Gospel and bringing them together on the Sunday for the joint celebration of the Eucharist will in future require the ministry of unity of the bishop and the priest in a new way. The office of the bishop and priest as ministry of the unity will thus not be less important but it will be crucial in a totally new way. In a world that has become increasingly pluralistic, it is necessary to gather the people of God that live not only scattered across the world but also across a whole region, to bring them together in joint worship and so to build up diaspora communities.

Priests will only be able to see this through humanly and spiritually if they do not act in a solitary way and do not live as hermits in their presbyteries or homeless like vagrants. They must live communally in the central parish and they must be able to be at home there. Such communal living and eating do not necessarily have to take the form of an order or oratory.[402] You could well see how this might function in the 'rectories' in the United States. There several priests, despite different roles such as parish priest or chaplain, live together. Each has his own sphere but they eat together and there should be, if it is to work well, forms of joint prayer.

All this has to grow. It cannot be decreed from above overnight. Yet, priests as well as communities must let themselves be challenged by the new situation nowadays. We must hear what the Spirit tells the communities today (Rev. 2.7.11 et seq.). As the eschatological people of God they live continuously less in the environment of a cosy familiar congregation but in parishes which become new alien entities in a pluralistic world that is uncomprehending and indifferent towards Christianity, if not even hostile. There they are to be the agent that transforms the environment from within and the light that radiates and attracts. In this way, as diaspora churches they can be new missionary churches.

5.8 Monasticism, religious orders and spiritual communities

It would be a most incomplete presentation of the concrete form of the Church if it spoke only of the universal Church and individual churches as well as local communities and did not also speak about monasticism, religious orders and the new spiritual movements. They are not phenomena on the fringe of the life of the Church. On the contrary, they play an important part in the history and present life of the Church and they are an essential part of ecclesial life. The religious communities are joined 'to the Church and its mystery in a special way'; they belong 'undeniably to its life and holiness'.[403] They must, therefore, also be a subject of ecclesiology.[404]

Religious orders – charisma and institution

It is not possible to derive a theology of religious orders in a theologically abstract way. It can only be developed as reflection of the history and reality of the orders. In each case they came into being at the crossroads of church history, often as an answer to situations in which faith was put to the test, or – as in modern times – often as an answer to missionary, pastoral or social emergency situations. As incursions and awakening of God's Spirit in the Church they are God's answer to the respective cry of each time.

This situational and charismatic-prophetic origin makes it difficult to subsume the orders under one common generic term or to reach a satisfactory, generally accepted classification of the different religious orders. The independent monastic communities of the Old Church were not yet religious orders in the later sense. These have existed only since the Middle Ages. In modern times, orders emerged that are apostolically orientated pastoral associations, missionary societies or apostolic-charitable communities. Since Vatican II one has tried to subsume the different religious communities with the term 'institutes of the consecrated life' whereby the relation to societies of the apostolic life remains open and the orders are distinguished from secular institutes and new spiritual movements. Thus it becomes again apparent, as Vatican II said, that 'on a tree which has grown in the field of the Lord, various forms of solidarity and community life, as well as various religious families have branched out in a marvellous and multiple way from this divinely given seed'.[405]

The common field is the Church and the beatitudes entrusted to it in the Gospel, the call to follow Jesus and the evangelical counsels of chastity, poverty and obedience. They apply generally to all Christians but are observed by the religious in a special, particularly intensive and communal way according to the respective rule of each order. Thus, following the Council, the theology of the orders builds upon baptism as the foundation of each Christian existence. Through baptism all Christians have died with Christ for this world and are resurrected to a new life.[406] It is this new life and the common vocation to holiness in the spiritual struggle with the powers of sin in the old world that the religious want to live because of their personal vocation and special grace by accepting the vows or promises to live in a particularly intimate way following a communal rule and so to dedicate their whole life to God. The resulting separation from the world includes as participation in Christ's mission and of the Church a new, representing, interceding, and – especially in the active orders – a missionary, pastoral, educational or charitable turn to the world and a service in the Church and for the Church. Contemplation and action, or to be more precise, action resulting contemplation and contemplation that becomes action belong together.

In this sense, the religious orders perceive themselves as a 'splendid sign' in the Church.[407] They are a sign of the beginning kingdom of God and a sign of brotherhood which will be as a sign lived by sinful humans, always also a broken sign. For Pope John Paul II, the consecrated life, if lived consequently and convincingly, is a decisive element of the Church at its heart and centre, for it reveals and represents the innermost nature of the Christian vocation and expresses that striving of the whole Church as bride after the union with the one bridegroom. The orders are therefore a precious impulse for an increasingly consequent realization of the Gospel.[408]

The religious orders show that the life and the shape of the Church are not one monolithic institutional structure but a diverse and living reality in which institution and charisma permeate each other. They do not see themselves as dialectically and charismatically opposite to the church as institution. In fact, the orders are themselves, as permanent charisma, institutions that can represent their legitimate institutional interests, as, vice versa, the ecclesial office is institution and charisma that has the task to test the charismata and, where appropriate, to recognize them publicly. Just so, both belong to the orders: their own prophetic charisma as well as the canonical ecclesiastical recognition. This gives the orders their independence within the Church which is not absorbingly integrated into the institutional structure of the Church and which must be recognized and maintained by the ecclesiastical office. At the same time it expects from them a '*sentire in ecclesia*'. It is only in this way that they can be quasi fresh cells of the Holy Spirit in the organism of the Church that enrich and renew the life of the Church with the wealth and diversity of their spiritual gift again and again. Yet, they can also affect the life of the Church through internal crises, so that they become like festering ulcers. In this case they must be admonished and called to order by the Church.[409]

The orders do not belong only to the past. They are – particularly in the present, spiritually dry and barren time – urgently necessary. They correspond to a widespread search for an alternative spiritual life to which they try to do justice as spiritual centres and with spiritual hospitality. It is to their missionary commitment, which deserves to be called heroic especially in the initial period and in times of persecution, that whole continents owe the light of the Gospel until today. In addition there are the cultural and educational achievements of the old as well as the new orders. The charitable and apostolic service of the sisters for children, sick, disabled people, often among the poorest of the poor, requires special mentioning. From the beginning, orders played an important part in the ecumenical movement, today especially through their proximity to the growing spiritual communities in the Protestant churches. Outside Europe they are indispensible for the interreligious and intercultural dialogue which is impossible without spiritual encounter and spiritual exchange. Through their simple life they are close to the poor and represent them. Thus, they have indirectly in the sense of Christian freedom a special social-critical importance. For all these reasons we can say that today, in particular, is the era of the religious orders.[410]

Monasticism

The origin of and basis for the religious life is the monasticism that developed in the early period of the Church and has remained vibrant until today.[411] According to the original meaning of the word (μοναχός/*monachus*), being a monk means a life of outward and inward separation. In his *Vita Antoni*, Athanasius impressively describes the work of the father of monasticism, Anthony the Great († 356).[412] In a situation of an already-beginning bourgeoisification of Christianity, the first monks wanted to follow the call of the Gospel and leave everything behind for the sake of God's kingdom. They only looked for the 'one thing which is indeed necessary' (Lk. 10.42). They retreated alone (anchorites, hermits), in communities (coenobites) and later in monastically organized communities from the inhabited and then inhabitable regions into the solitude of the desert or barely accessible mountain regions. They searched for an ascetic life in solitude, guided by the motive of searching God (*quaerere Deum*) and the undivided love of God.

Monasticism unites the churches of the East and the West. We find the theology of Eastern monasticism in particular in Basil the Great († 379) and in the various manifestations of his rule. It shows that Basil did not intend a monkish special existence but, for him, it was about the full realization of the Christian existence. We have a similar position one hundred years later in the West with Augustine († 430) and his later influential rule, which is dominated totally by the love of God and the resulting brotherly love.[413] The rule of St Benedict draws from these older paragons (besides Basil and Augustine especially from the *Rule of the Master*). It is characterized by wise moderation and could thus become the decisive monastic rule in the occident.

The monasticism which had developed in the East came to the West with Athanasius († 373), having being banished to Trier. In particular Martin of Tours († 399) is considered the Anthony of the West. We know about his life mostly through Sulpicius Severus († circa 425).[414] Martin combined monastic life with missionary itinerant monasticism, becoming the model for early medieval wandering monks (Kilian, Emmeram, Corbinian, Eberhard, Rupert, Fridolin). The ideal for the Irish wandering monks (Columba, Gall) was the leaving of home (*peregrinatio*) for Christ. We owe to monasticism the mission of northern Europe. Important missionaries were Pirmin (Abbey at Reichenau), Willibrord, Boniface, and Walburga. In addition it was through the monasteries that the humanist inheritance was handed down from ancient times through the turbulence of the great migrations down to the Middle Ages. Benedict of Nursia († 547) then became the great father of monasticism in the West. Pope Gregory the Great († 604) created a monument to him. Benedict must be regarded in conjunction with his sister, St Scholastica († about 542), at his side. It is that Benedict is venerated as one of the spiritual founding fathers and a patron saint of the West or Europe.

Important monastic theologians are above all the Venerable Bede († 735) and Anselm of Canterbury († 1109). Important reformed orders of the Benedictines are the Carthusians (founded by Bruno of Cologne, † 1101) and the Cistercians with Bernard of Clairvaux († 1153) and, emerging from them in the seventeenth century, the Trappists. In addition there are great women, such as Leoba of Tauberbischofsheim († 782) and Hildegard of Bingen († 1179); other, more independent female personalities were Birgitta of Sweden († 1373) and Catherine of Siena († 1380). They all had a significant impact on church history and especially on the history of piety.

All of these different monastic communities perceive themselves as realizations of the first Christian community of Jerusalem (Basil), as realizations of the love of God (Augustine), as education for following Christ (Benedict) and as eschatological existence in anticipation of the heavenly Jerusalem. They do not want to be a higher class or privileged caste of Christians. Both symbolically and as witnesses in the Church and for the Church, they want to live the eschatological existence pertaining to being Christian in the sense of the beatitudes of the Sermon on the Mount and the evangelical counsels of poverty and chastity in brotherly community in obedience to the rule. At the same time, monasticism produced in the sense of '*ora et labora*' (pray and work) magnificent missionary, theological, pastoral, cultural, pedagogical and charitable-social achievements that have had a lasting effect on European culture. Still, basing monasticism only on cultural and social motives is insufficient. Ultimately, monasticism can only be comprehended from the radically lived eschatological existence which recognizes that our home is not here but in heaven (Phil. 3.20).

So to speak, the monastery wants to be a cell (*cellula*) or an oasis in the Church, which is, through prayer, the celebration of the liturgy and testimony of life also a ministry for the Church and for the world. By offering hospitality, the monasteries provide other Christians with space for spiritual retreat and reflection. Usually they gather a circle of laypeople (the so-called third order) around them who attempt to fulfil the monastic ideal under the conditions of life in the world. Still today, the rules of St Basil, St Augustine and St Benedict (to name just the most important ones) can serve as inspirations and encouragement for the spiritual life beyond the sphere of monasticism.

Religious communities

It was against the intention of their founders that the old monastic orders developed during the Middle Ages into powerful and rich institutions deeply tied into the feudal system of the time. Typically, such institutions were void of the original charasmatic impulse. In this crisis, the call for a *vita evangelica* or *apostolica* was often articulated in a dangerously church-critical way. Francis of Assisi († 1226) took up this call. Like his spiritual sister, St Clare († 1256), he wanted to live the Gospel *sine glossa*, without addition or cuts. Yet, in contrast to the desert fathers, he did not retreat into the desert of sand and stone, but into the 'desert' of the poor and poorest in order to live there with his 'Friars Minor' among the poor of the Gospel according to Mt. 10.5–14.[415] Coming from Castile, Dominic (Domingo de Guzmán) († 1221) was also concerned about the by then mighty heretical poverty movement (Cathars, Albigensians), and chose with his brothers the poor, preaching itinerant life.

The male and female mendicant orders which then emerged are, in contrast to monasticism, a new form of religious life. They have no structure tied to a place but they have a central structure likened to the universal Church. As such, they made a crucial contribution to the awareness of the universal Church and for the consolidation of the primacy. In the then-developing urban milieu they are pastorally more outward-orientated. Following the Gospel, they desire to live the spirit of poverty and simplicity and to keep it alive in a church that is time and again in danger of succumbing to the temptations of power, wealth and pomp.

The figure of the poverello St Francis of Assisi continues to fascinate Christians and non-Christians even today. Great theologians emerged out of the mendicant orders, such as Alexander of Hales, Bonaventure, Duns Scotus, Anthony of Padua from the Franciscans, Albert the Great, Thomas Aquinas, Meister Eckhart, Johannes Tauler, Heinrich Seuse of the Dominicans, from the related Carmelites Theresa of Avila, John of the Cross, and in the nineteenth century Thérèse of Lisieux. They all offer rich spiritual food for today's Christians as well.

As a reply to the crises of the Church in the late Middle Ages and the Reformation, a number of new orders emerged. From the Italian reform Catholicism we must mention the Congregation of the Oratory of Philip Neri († 1595) as well as the Franciscan reform order of the Capuchins. The Society of Jesus (Jesuits) became the most important and most influential of these orders. Following the spiritual exercises of Ignatius of Loyola († 1556), the Society of Jesus strives for the decision between the 'two banners', that is between the realm of this world and following Jesus, in order to live for the greater glory of God in radical availability for the ministry of the Gospel and for the Church.[416] The Jesuits contributed decisively to the Catholic renewal after the Reformation (Peter Canisius, † 1597) and to modern mission (Francis Xavier, † 1552). They have an enormous theological, spiritual, missionary and pedagogical radiation, and modern church history up to today is inconceivable without them. The Congregatio Jesu, the female branch of the Jesuit order founded by Mary Ward († 1645), has made important contributions, particularly to the education and training of girls.

The other, very different, male and female religious communities of modernity time are pastoral communities (Redemptorists, Passionists, Salesians, Pallotines, etc.), missionary societies (the Steyler Fathers, the Holy Ghost Fathers, the White Fathers, the Comboni Missionaries, Maryknoll, Marianhill, etc.) or educate young people such as the Brothers of the Christian Schools (founded by Jean Baptiste de la Salle, († 1719) and the Sisters of Charity (going back to Vincent de Paul and Louise de Marillac, † 1660) who dedicate their life to working for the poor and sick. The same is true for the manifold forms of the regulated Third Order of St Francis.

Today these communities ask themselves how they can realize their original charisma and their original vocation in the light of the new challenges of a changed situation in the Church and the world. Under this double aspect, Vatican II called the religious communities to a reflection on the sources of spiritual life and the spirit of their origin and to renewal by adaption to the changed circumstances of our time.[417] Clearly, the post-conciliar crises have left their mark on the orders. Yet, through the impulses of the Council, there are also many signs of a renewal in the spirit of Holy Scripture, the liturgy and in addressing, with willingness to listen, the new spiritual, pastoral and social challenges for the Church.

That the order movement is not dead today can be seen in the Little Brothers and Sisters of Jesus (going back to Charles de Foucauld, † 1916, founded by René Voillaume and Magdeleine Hutin) and the Missionaries of Charity founded by Mother Teresa of Calcutta († 1997), who combine an intensive contemplative life with a radical commitment to the poorest of the poor in the world. New orders of a monastic kind are the Ecumenical Monastic Community of Bose (founded by Enzo Bianchi in 1965) in northern Italy and, also inspired by Charles de Foucauld, the Monastic Fraternities of Jerusalem (1975).

Spiritual movements

After the Second Vatican Council, numerous spiritual movements and communities have unexpectedly developed like a new spiritual spring. Some of these have spread all over the world.[418] They are a precious fruit of Vatican II.[419] In contrast to the Catholic lay associations of the nineteenth and early twentieth centuries,[420] these are a new form of communal life for laypeople. They understand the Christian life as a communal way of faith (*itinerarium, camino*) and of Christian witness on the basis of their respective specific charisma and pedagogy founded upon it.

Founding figures such as Luigi Giussani († 2005) and Chiara Lubich († 2008) have not only influenced these movements; they have also opened a new dimension for the life of the Church. They desire to live and witness being Christian not in secluded monasteries but in the midst of the world. With this they have given, both *ad intra* and *ad extra*, a new missionary impulse where mission is not an external addition to Christian life, nor a programmatic strategy, but rather mediation (communication) of one's own experience of the encounter with Jesus Christ and of the joy and beauty of the Church's faith. In this way, through manifold forms of friendship and collaboration they have also become promoters of the ecumenical movement and the interreligious dialogue.

The novelty of these movements and communities has often led to tensions, and in parts it has also caused prejudices and incomprehension. In some respects the way of the new spiritual movements and communities is not yet completed and needs clarification and maturity. Maintaining a specific charisma must not become self-centredness and its connection to the Petrine office must not be placed in opposition to the willing integration into each respective local church and its needs. Conversely, local churches should perceive the new spiritual movements and communities not as a problem but as a gift. They can help them to transgress an often too narrow cultural, social and ethnic horizon towards a greater catholicity. They can also give them new impulses for a life according to the Gospel.

Thus we can say already today that the new spiritual movements and communities are a providential answer of God's Spirit to the difficult situation of the Church after the Council. In the ever-increasingly secular world in which many people live as if God did not exist, they want to live the Gospel and radiate the joy of faith. In this way they are important bearers of the new evangelization which has become necessary today. It is this topic of the Church's mission today that we must now address.

6

The missionary and dialogical Church

6.1 The missionary Church

We proceeded from the universal saving design of God for all nations and from the coming of God's kingdom that is already present and effective in the Church in the mystery.[1] Yet, the Church is not the end of God's ways. It is not an end in itself, but points beyond itself. It is sign and instrument of the coming kingdom of God. It is the messianic people of God.[2] This messianic nature of the Church becomes apparent in the call to mission, to go to all nations and to proclaim the Gospel and to baptize. When we speak here at the end of the Church's missionary mandate, we come back to our universal, eschatological point of departure. We come full circle in ecclesiology with a universal outlook.[3]

Biblical foundations

We find the call to mission at the end of all four gospels. The conclusion of Matthew is particularly impressive: 'Go, therefore, make disciples of all nations; baptise them in the name of the Father and of the Son and of the Holy Spirit, and teach them to observe all the commands I gave you' (Mt. 28.19f.). Similarly, we read in Luke: 'you are witnesses' (Lk. 24.47f.; cf. Acts 1.8). According to the supplementary chapter of Mark, the disciples are sent to the whole world (κόσμος) and to all creation (κτίσις) (Mk 16.15). John incorporates the mission mandate into his theology of sending: 'as the Father sent me, so I am sending you' (Jn 20.21). These few words, all placed in a prominent position, emphasize that the earthly church is missionary in nature.[4] The Church is missionary or it is no longer the Church of Jesus Christ.

If we look at the details, the testimony of the Bible is more differentiated.[5] The Old Testament does not yet know mission, though it does have a universal orientation. Abraham is called to be a blessing for all peoples

(Gen. 11.3 et seq.). For the messianic time the prophets expect a pilgrimage of the nations to Zion (Isa. 2.1–5; Mic 4.1–3) and the universal outpouring of the Spirit (Joel 3.1-5). The universal character of biblical monotheism is presented in a different way in the creation narratives and in wisdom literature. All of these impulses are taken up by Jesus. He considers himself to be sent only to the lost children of Israel and sends his disciples only to them (Mt. 10.5; 15.24). Yet, then he encounters several times among the non-Jews a faith he has not found in Israel. It becomes clear in the encounter with the centurion of Capernaum (Mt. 8.5–13) and with the Syro-Phoenician woman (Mk 7.24–30). Similarly, according to John (Jn 12.20), many among the Greeks turned to Jesus seeking help and found it. Jesus thus rejects a restrictive interpretation of the children of Abraham (Mt. 3.9; 8.11; Jn 8.30–47) and anticipates the coming pilgrimage of nations, and, thereby, the participation of non-Jews also in the promises to Israel (Mt. 8.11).

Thus, in the time after Easter, following difficult internal debates, a decision in favour of the gentile mission was reached (Acts 10f.; 15; Gal. 2). Peter himself led the way. However, it is Paul in particular who perceives himself as missionary to the gentiles (Rom. 11.13; cf. 1.5; Gal. 1.16; 2.7–9). He thereby takes up the motive of the filiation to Abraham, which is not based on descent but exists because of the faith (Rom. 4; Gal. 2.6–19). In this way the gentiles also share in the promises to Israel (Rom. 11.1–21). The ultimate reason is, for Paul, that the risen Jesus is, as the new Adam, not only head of the Church, but also of the new humanity (Rom. 5.14; 1 Cor. 15.45). In Christ God reconciled the world to himself and entrusted the apostles with the word and the ministry of reconciliation (2 Cor. 5.19). This universal nature finds its fullest expression in the later (deutero-)Pauline writings. Jesus Christ is the image of the invisible God. Through him, in him and towards him everything is created. It is in him that God dwelt in his complete fullness and reconciled everything to himself. He desired to bring everything in heaven and earth together in Christ (Col. 1.15–20). In him, he brought everything together in him in order to unite it (Eph. 1.10). He is the one mediator between God and mankind (1 Tim. 1.5).

The new situation and the new approach of the Second Vatican Council

Throughout history, the Church has realized its mission according to the particular changing historical conditions:[6] during the first centuries in the ancient world, but also early on as far away as India, then in the Anglo-Saxon and Germanic areas, in the Slavic and Nordic spheres, in the second millennium in Africa, Asia, Oceania and in both Americas. Many heroic achievements of holy and saintly missionaries, men and women, are admirable. The Christians in the former missionary countries are grateful to them up to today that they brought them the light of the faith through great personal commitment. This is not the place to recount this history and all its aspects in detail.

There was a fundamental change in the historical conditions of mission with the end of both European supremacy and the colonial era after the Second World War. In this context there was frequent criticism of modern mission and its methods.[7] It is often criticized as an expression of colonialism, the imperial urge to expand and blamed for suppressing autochthonous religions and cultures. Admittedly, the missionaries were, in many respects, also children of their time and their culture. In other words, there are also lost opportunities and dark sides to missionary history. Yet, appropriate as this criticism may be in individual cases, as a generalization it is unjust. After all, many missionaries defended the locals and their rights against the colonizers and furthered their local culture, often also being the first to research this culture. They also brought them, together with the light of the faith, schools, houses for the poor and infirmaries, so putting the locals in touch with the achievements of European civilization and thus contributing essentially to furthering the human and cultural development of these peoples.

Some theologians thought after the end of the colonial era that this new situation also meant the end of mission, or at least a moratorium on mission.[8] Others referred to the possibility of salvation for non-Christians[9] as an argument against mission and the duty to have dialogue with other religions.[10] This led them to the wrong assumption that it would suffice if a Buddhist became a better Buddhist, the Hindu a better Hindu, and the Muslim a better Muslim.[11] In addition, others criticized the ecclesial-centric character of previous mission theories and demanded emphasis on their political and social dimension.[12] Consequentially, for many Christians today the focus is no longer on the missionary proclamation of faith but on development aid, the promotion of liberation, justice, reconciliation and peace. All these are undoubtedly important challenges, aspects the missionary activity of the Church must not neglect. But they cannot replace mission itself.

The Second Vatican Council recognized the new situation but it drew different conclusions. It chose a new theological point of departure and thus initiated a turn in mission theology.[13] The Council no longer departs from the salvation of souls (Münster school) or the implanting of the Church (Leuven school), but integrates and reconciles these two traditional approaches into a larger theological context.[14] It perceives Christ as the sign and instrument and thus the mission in a Trinitarian, Christological and pneumatological context.

The Council proceeds from the sending of the Son by the Father who sent the apostles in the Holy Spirit (Jn 20.21) and thus from Jesus Christ, to whom all authority is given (Mt. 28.18) and who, in the power from above (Acts 1.8), sends out his disciples. The point of departure is thus the spring-like love of God who sent his Son as the new Adam, and who, in the Holy Spirit lets his saving work be effective from within.[15] He intends for the Church to be a sacrament of salvation,[16] that is, a sign and instrument of the most intimate union with God and for the unity of the whole of mankind.[17] 'Missionary activity is nothing more and nothing less than an epiphany, or a manifesting of God's decree, and its fulfilment in the world and in world history, in the course of which God, by means of mission, manifestly works out the history of salvation.'[18] The earthly church is thus missionary by its very nature.[19] John Paul II was therefore right to stress that mission had not yet reached its end today, but that it stood at a new beginning and had entered a new phase.[20]

A theology of mission

The theological foundation of the mission in the New Testament and in the Second Vatican Council clearly shows that the origin of the mission is God himself. Mission is first and foremost God's own work; it is *missio dei*.[21] It proceeds from the Father through the Son and is carried forward by the Holy Spirit. In second place, we must add that God's Spirit awakens and calls people and takes them into service for mission. In this respect, mission is a vocation and duty of the Church. The *missio dei* brought forth its first fruit in the Church and is now to be carried on through the ministry of the Church as the messianic people of God[22] in the Holy Spirit, leading to the building up of the new humanity after the primal image Jesus Christ. 'What we have learnt is not that the church "has" a mission, but the very reverse: that the mission of Christ creates its own church. Mission does not come from the church; it is from mission and in the light of mission that the church has to be understood.'[23]

The goal of mission is only indirectly the Church and the spreading of the Church. Its purpose is first and foremost to proclaim the kingdom of God that has come with Jesus Christ and that is now breaking through in the Church through the Holy Spirit. It is about the petition in the Lord's Prayer: 'hallowed be your name, your kingdom come!' Mission seeks conversion from the old and new idols to the one and true God (1 Thess. 1.9), it seeks that all have life and have it to the full. Thus it seeks to let all participate in the richness of God's life, in the light of the good news of Jesus Christ and in the gifts of the Holy Spirit. With this, mission seeks to gather the one people of God in the glorification of the one God, under the one Lord Jesus Christ and in the one Holy Spirit. As in the beginning, the Church emerges again and again out of the dynamics of the coming of God's kingdom.[24]

The kingdom of God is the kingdom of truth, justice, holiness, freedom and peace. Witnessing to the one true God is therefore also about witnessing to God as the God of humanity and of each individual human person, as the God of love, justice, freedom, reconciliation and peace. Without turning into a social gospel or even one of prosperity, mission thereby also serves peace, reconciliation and justice in the world. It frees from being tied and destined by birth to a certain culture and religion. Mission helps to overcome tribalism and nationalism, overturns the idea of development being limited to purely economic and technological progress, and helps to integrate independently legitimate causes into a larger, holistic and complete human development. Ultimately, mission is in the service of the transformation of the world out of the spirit of the dawning kingdom of God.

Mission may draw its strength primarily from the power of the Holy Spirit, but also from the testimony of many male and female missionaries, and in particular from the testimony of the many missionaries who have given their life as martyrs for Christ, the Gospel and for the brothers and sisters. The twentieth century was rich in martyrs in missionary churches. This is a promise for the missionary effort in the new twenty-first century, for the blood of the martyrs is the seed of new Christians.[25] We may trust that the many thousand-fold seed of the last century will grow one day and bear rich fruit.

Mission today

This renewed perception of mission must be put into practice in the changed situation of the world and of mission in our postcolonial globalized world. It is neither possible in this context nor within my competence to develop a method or strategy of mission. I can only sketch out some concise aspects without any claim to completion.

(1) The time of Western mission, when Europe sent missionaries into all the world, is now over. The European churches are no longer in a position to do this for lack of missionaries. Europe, where the traditional form of the Church is in crisis, requires a new mission itself.[26] It is necessary for the European churches to overcome this notion of status quo. They urgently need a renewal of missionary awareness and a new missionary beginning. Thus, Western mission has become world mission on all six continents.[27] The mission of the future will have to come from the respective local churches and it will have to be their responsibility.[28] Poorer local churches should be supported in solidarity by those local churches that are richer in financial resources and spiritual vocations. This applies in particular if a local church finds itself in difficulties as a result of persecutions and oppression or because of material suffering, war or natural catastrophes.

(2) Evangelization is the basic duty of the whole people of God. Therefore, the responsibility for mission will be borne today and in the future not

only by priests and religious orders but more than previously by laypeople. Because of their baptism and confirmation they want to bear witness to Jesus Christ in their respective environment and be 'salt of the earth' (Mt. 5.13f.).[29] They can let themselves be sent out temporarily or permanently to contribute their knowledge and expertise as craftsmen and professionals, as teachers, doctors and nurses, as engineers, as business advisors and many more and thereby profess their faith as Christians.

(3) At present, mission as proclamation of the Gospel is forbidden in many countries and even leads to persecution. This is not only confined to countries with a Muslim majority but also others prohibit freedom of religion and at times severely penalize missionary activities and changes of religion. In such situations mission is only possible through the testimony of Christian presence. Charles de Foucauld († 1916) gave a compelling and convincing example with his simple life among the Tuareg in the Sahara and on the Assekrem plateau in the Hoggar mountains. He never did missionary work. However, he made friends with the Tuareg, studied their language, worked among them for reconciliation and peace and witnessed to Christ through his spiritual life orientated on the Gospel. Until his violent death he did not find pupils or followers. Today the Little Brothers and Sisters live and work in his spirit in many parts of the world among the poorest of the poor and witness to them Christ's love.

(4) Finally, and above all, mission in the present and the future will be shaped by the spirit of dialogue with indigenous religions and cultures,[30] by the effort for inculturation,[31] and by the preferential option for the poor. In other words, it will be holistic and combined with the fight against injustice and oppression, persecution, poverty, hunger and illness as well as with furthering a whole human culture. In the light of common challenges for all Christians, mission cannot happen in competition with other churches and ecclesial communities but wherever and as far as possible in ecumenical cooperation.[32]

Mission and dialogue

It is not easy to determine the precise relation between mission and dialogue.[33] On the one hand, dialogue is an element of mission itself, for mission means inviting and courting communication of the truth received from God to others who should hear it and understand it and hopefully, with the aid of the inner graceful mediation of God, accept it in freedom. Yet, as much as mission is dialogical, it is more than dialogue. Mission is purpose-orientated. Following Jesus' commission, mission seeks to – and must – proclaim the Gospel to all creatures, to win and inspire people for God and his kingdom and receive people into the Church in baptism and, in turn, send them out as messengers of the Gospel. Mission desires to witness to God's love to all people and thus contribute to God's saving design becoming a reality for all people and making the Church present as eschatological sign of salvation among the nations.

In contrast, dialogue as such is purposeless and must also not be instrumentalized. Like love, it is unselfish and unintentional and therefore not in itself directed at the conversion of others. It cannot be 'made' or planned if the dialogue partner is touched by the testimony to the truth and becomes inwardly convinced; it lies within the freedom of God in the freedom of man. Both are a mystery which we cannot enter and should not even attempt to do so. Dialogue is a quasi-sacramental medium through which God can enter the conscience of the dialogue partner if he or she is open to and for it. It must be conducted with great discretion, respect and veneration for the other. In this respect, dialogue must be only an inner element of mission. It should precede mission, accompany, complement and deepen it. In this comprehensive sense, dialogue is an essential and indispensable task of a missionary church.

6.2 The Church in dialogue

Dialogue is a key term of modern thinking and became also a key term of the Second Vatican Council.[34] Dialogic thinking has biblical roots because the revelation[35] as well as the transmission of the revelation, i.e. mission, have a dialogic structure. Of course, dialogue must not be confused with a noncommittal conversation or even with mere chatting. Equally, dialogue is not about uncompromising negotiating, diplomatic concessions or some form of syncretism. A true dialogue can only be led by partners who each have their own identity, i.e. who have their conviction and position which they do not neglect or hide, on the contrary which they hold up in a dialogue and about which they want to enter into an exchange with the partner.

In contrast to a polemical and self-opinionated dispute in which everyone only presents his own position, dialogue tries to depart from a common human, religious or Christian basis without neglecting thereby one's own position, yet looking at one's own position with the eyes of the other. This can serve the purification, clarification and deepening of one's own position. In other words, dialogue is a serious way to draw closer together to each greater truth while also keeping differences and respecting the other in his otherness. If it was not about truth in this way it would not be a serious dialogue.

From this perspective the Church is, by its nature, dialogical. It is no self-contained entity. It is Church only from God and by listening to him, and it is Church in the re-enactment of God's loving turn to the other through the witnessing proclamation of his message. It is Church which is in following

Christ in solidarity with the joy and hope, fear and sorrow of the people, especially the poor and troubled ones of all kinds.[36]

Thus, the dialogues initiated by the Church after the Second Vatican Council are no betrayal of the truth; on the contrary, they are an expression of the innermost nature of the Church. They are not just an interesting academic exchange of ideas but an exchange of gifts. In them the Church communicates itself and through the Church God communicates himself. For that reason the dialogues have a global, holistic, existential, ultimately quasi-sacramental dimension.[37]

6.2.1 The dialogue with Judaism

The most fundamental dialogue takes place between the Church and the Jews.[38] This is because, for the Church, Judaism is not a religion outside of it but one which belongs to it intrinsically and pertains to its identity. Jesus himself was a Jew and lived out of the tradition of the Old Testament. Mary, his mother, was a Jewish woman and all the apostles were Jews. For this reason alone, Christians can never be anti-Semites. Jews and Christians believe the one God, maker of heaven and earth; both go back to the same father in faith, to Abraham; both have in common the patriarchs, Moses and the Decalogue, the psalms and the prophets.

Thus the Church is and remains related to Judaism in its origin and nature. On the other hand, Judaism and Christianity differ essentially when it comes to the centre of the Christian faith, the confession of Jesus as the Christ, his cross and his resurrection and as the Son of God. In other words, between Jews and Christians there is a relationship that is unique in the history of religion. On the one hand, there are the common root and substantial and fundamental common ground, on the other hand, there is the essential difference in the faith in Jesus Christ, the salvation for all people.

A complex history

Because of this unique relationship of fundamental commonality and fundamental difference, the history between Jews and Christians could only be difficult, complex and full of tension. The various writings of the New Testament do not present a homogenous picture. They rather show a multi-layered, historical development of the relationship.[39] Jesus clearly sees himself in the tradition of the Old Testament and refers to it in many cases. His messianic interpretation presented with authority (ἐξουσία) is soon recognized as new teaching (Mk 1.22.27; Mt. 7.29). This resulted in conflict with the representatives of Judaism of his time which increasingly worsened and led to condemnation through the Sanhedrin and to his violent death.

According the Acts of the Apostles there was an initial peaceful coexistence (Acts 2.46f.), but soon there were also conflicts and persecutions (Acts 4f.; 8 et seq.). On his missionary journeys, Paul repeatedly encounters resistance from the Jews, and their stubbornness is for him an unfathomable mystery (Rom. 11.7.25). He severely criticizes them (Rom. 2.17–29 et seq.), but he is also full of sorrow and suffers in his heart because of their disobedience (Rom. 9.2). Like no other New Testament author he knows about the Jewish roots of Christianity and the lasting significance of Judaism and its eschatological redemption (Rom. 11). Also, John's gospel says that salvation comes from the Jews (Jn 4.22), yet, in John 'the Jews' become wholesale 'the' opponents of Jesus and of the Gospel (Jn 7.13; 9.22; 10.24 et seq.); in fact, they are called sons of the devil (Jn 8.44). This might already indicate a later historical development apart from each other in the course of which the Christians were excluded from the synagogue (Jn 16.2–4; cf. Mt. 10.17) and increasingly went their own ways.

Some anti-Jewish statements (such as 1 Thess. 2.15f.) may reflect some non-biblical anti-Jewish prejudices of that time. Much more important, however, is the fact that they are along the line of the harsh prophetic criticism of Israel in the Old Testament itself. Thus, it is not possible to derive any basic anti-Judaism from the New Testament, but from the beginning there is a differing interpretation of the common sources, which led to conflict. The New Testament perceives itself thereby as the new, final interpretation and as the fulfilment of the Old Testament.

The difference in the interpretation of the Old Testament became fully apparent after the destruction of the second temple in the year 70 AD. It was only then that the rabbinic and Talmudic Judaism which we have today developed. It was only from then onwards that in a long process though on a common basis, yet in difference and distinction from each other, Judaism and Christianity each found their own respective doctrinal and institutional form, resulting in the so-called substitution theory according to which Christianity, as the new people of God, has taken the place of the old people of God.[40] This led to the theological anti-Judaism which is reflected in the tractates of the Church Fathers, *Contra Judaeos*. In this sense it was possible that the pre-conciliar intercession of Good Friday prayed for the *infideles Judaei* which, correctly translated, does not mean 'the unfaithful Jews' but 'the unbelieving Jews'.

Theological anti-Judaism must be distinguished from the popular anti-Judaism that already existed in non-biblical antiquity. It led, especially in connection with the crusades, to pogroms and outbreaks of violence against Jews as well as to the common derogatory, typecasting prejudices. Finally, one has to distinguish between anti-Judaism and anti-Semitism. Anti-Semitism is a primitive racial ideology that did not appear until the nineteenth century and which, at the time of National Socialism, caused the unspeakable cruelties of the Shoah, the murder of about six million Jews engineered and carried out by the state.

The basic distinction between anti-Judaism and anti-Semitism does not rule out that anti-Judaism partly prepared the ground for anti-Semitism to spread out in such a way and that the criminal National Socialist plan for the extermination of European Judaism did not meet with the consistent and decisive resistance which one could have expected from Christians. To be fair, one must also mention the numerous individual courageous Christians who supported the Jews to the best of their ability and at the risk of their lives.

After the Second World War, horrified by the Shoah, all churches began to become more conscious again of their historical Jewish roots. All major churches now strove to leave the 'language of disdain' (Jules Isaac) behind them and to begin a new positive relation with the Jewish people in mutual respect, esteem and cooperation.[41]

The new beginning of Nostra aetate

(1) The fourth chapter of the declaration *Nostra aetate* deals with Jewish-Christian relations. With this the Second Vatican Council opened a new chapter in relation to the covenant people Israel.[42] The declaration could take up the foundational statement the Council had already made in the constitution on the Church.[43] It demonstrated the common heritage of Jews and Christians and highlighted the spiritual connectedness with the tribe of Abraham. It called to mind again that the Church, according to Paul, is grafted on the root Israel and that it continues to be carried and nourished by this root (Rom. 11.17–24). Through the cross Christ reconciled Jews and gentiles and united both in him (Eph. 2.14–16). With this, theological anti-Judaism had been factually overcome and the substitution theory, that the New Covenant had taken the place of the Old, had been given up.[44]

(2) With reference to Paul, the declaration could demonstrate that, because of God's faithfulness, the covenant of God with Israel had never been recalled. The Jewish people are not condemned, but are still loved by God for the sake of the fathers, for God's gifts of grace and his calling are irrevocable (Rom. 11.2.29). Neither all the Jews of Jesus' time nor the Jews today can be indiscriminately blamed for the guilt of Christ's death on the cross upon which the Jewish leadership and their followers insisted. The theory of a collective guilt of the Jewish people, which has led to many regrettable consequences in the course of history, is also thus rejected. The declaration combines this rejection with the positive statement that Christ accepted his suffering and death in freedom and out of endless love for the sake of the sin of all people. The cross of Christ must therefore be proclaimed as the sign of God's universal love and as a source of grace.

(3) As the third important historical setting, of course, the declaration deplores all outbreaks of hate, persecution and manifestations of anti-Semitism that have been launched at different times by different people against the

Jews. On the first Sunday of Lent 2000, Pope John Paul II made a confession of guilt and said a prayer for forgiveness in St Peter's in Rome. During his visit to the Western Wall in Jerusalem on 26 March 2000, he expressed this regret with his prayer for forgiveness in an impressive symbolic act. Already before this, in 1998, the Commission of the Holy See for Religious Relations with the Jews had presented the document *We Remember: a Reflection on the Shoah*. It could be only a first but not a final word. Yet, which person would want to speak a final word about such a monstrous crime as the Shoah?

(4) Finally, the declaration *Nostra aetate* expressed the intention to further the mutual knowledge and respect of Jews and Christians. It suggested biblical and theological studies and pleaded for a fraternal conversation. This proposal met with an enthusiastic response at the Council and has led to an intensive and fruitful dialogue with religious Judaism on the level of different episcopal conferences as well as on a universal level.[45] In particular Pope John Paul II made the reconciliation with the Jewish people his mission. During his historic visit to the great synagogue of Rome on 13 April 1986, he called the Jews our older brothers in the faith of Abraham.

On this basis a fruitful cooperation between Jewish and Christian scholars was able to develop in the area of exegesis. It has influenced and changed the Catholic and Protestant researching of Jesus during the last few decades.[46] This new awareness of the Jewish roots of Christianity also went hand in hand with new research into the Jewish Christianity of the Early Church and the recognition of its significance.[47] Finally, there was historical research of the complex, often difficult, but also often positive relations between Jews and Christians and research into reciprocal influences in the course of liturgical history.

The rediscovery of Jewish roots is not only of historical but also of essentially ecclesiological significance. One realized that from its origin and nature the Church is the church of Jews and gentiles (Eph. 2.11–22). The break between the two was the prime schism which cut the Church off from its root that gave it life and strength, thus weakening it. For this reason, the historic turn to the dialogue with Judaism is of utmost world-historical and ecclesiological importance. Meanwhile, this dialogue has led to cooperation in practical, social and cultural questions. Jews and Christians have the ten commandments in common and represent the same or similar concepts of values. Just so, they can witness together to the one God who is the foundation of the dignity of each person. What is more, they can stand up together for justice and peace in the world.

The salvation of the Jews and the problem of missionizing the Jews

Fundamental differences and difficult theological problems remain. They concern, in particular, the question of the salvation of the Jews and the problem of missionizing the Jews.[48] Stating that the Jews are still God's chosen covenant people does not mean for Christians that there was, for Israel, a parallel way to salvation beside the salvation given to us in and through Jesus Christ.[49] From a Christian perspective, he is the one and universal mediator of salvation. The positive declarations in Rom. 9–11 about the lasting validity of the Abrahamic covenant must thus not be regarded in isolation from statements elsewhere in *Romans* which speak of Jesus Christ's importance for salvation through which the Mosaic law lost its importance for salvation (particularly Rom. 3.21–31).[50] Of course, this does not deny the Jews, just like the unbaptized among the heathens, the possibility of salvation.

It is only possible to understand correctly the continued validity of the covenant with Israel in the context of the whole history of the covenants: the covenant with Noah, then with Abraham and the fathers, with Moses and finally the eschatologically ultimate covenant through cross and resurrection of Jesus Christ. Each of these covenants does not suspend the one antecedent to it, but confirms it and at the same time interprets it anew.[51] This also applies to the relation between the Abraham and Moses covenant and the new covenant in Jesus Christ. From a Christian point of view, the continued validity of the old covenant has its foundation in Jesus Christ's affirmation of all the previously given promises (2 Cor. 1.20). The new and final covenant is thus not the abolition or replacement of the old covenant but its transcending confirmation and fulfilment. Through it the Abraham covenant has received its originally intended universality for all nations.

Conversely, the continuing schism between Jews and Christians reminds Christians that the full realization of the yes to the old covenant which has come in Jesus Christ is still pending. This yes will only become full reality when at the end of time all gentiles receive salvation and the whole of Israel is saved (Rom. 11.25f.). Until then the Church is still on the way and moves towards its eschatological perfection.

This unique complex relation of Christians and Jews raises the difficult question of whether, in the eschatological time, there should and can be missionizing of the Jews.[52] In faithfulness to the New Testament, one will maintain, as a Christian, that the call to mission has universal importance. Paul too always addressed the Jews first on his missionary journeys. Yet, the universal call to mission can and must be fulfilled differently among the Jews and the gentiles. Christians will also witness before Jews to Jesus Christ. Witness (μαρτυρία) is a theological and existential basic category of the Bible which comprises not only the witness of the word but also the witness of action and of life which, however, respects and watches the freedom of the other. Catechizing and baptizing Jews by force, which has, sadly, happened in the course of history, must therefore be categorically condemned as abuse. Testimony to the Jews must be distinguished from missionary witness to the gentiles. Apart from some evangelical movements, the Church maintains this distinction. The mission among the gentiles (*missio ad gentes*) calls to conversion from the idols to the living and true God (1 Thess. 1.9). There cannot be such mission among the Jews, who already believe in the one true God. Hence, unlike the specific mission of the gentiles in the past and present, the Church has never undertaken the systematic and specific missionization of the Jews. There will always be individual Jews converting to Christianity. The saving of the 'whole of Israel' (Rom. 11.26) is God's own work at the end of time.

Nevertheless, Christian mission among the gentiles is also of importance for the Jews. It makes the God of Israel known among the nations and gives biblical monotheism its own universality. It reminds the Jews of the promise of blessing to Abraham for all nations (Gen. 12.3; 18.18; 22.18 et seq.) and helps to prevent them from withdrawing into particularism. Vice versa, the Jews will remind Christians of their historical roots and so contribute that the Christian faith remains 'grounded' and does not become a speculation detached from history or become gnosis and, cut off from its root, become powerless and weak.

Jews and Christians have something to say to each other. 'Side by side' they wait for the coming of the messiah; in mutual respect they witness to their common ground and their difference in the messianic hope. Towards the world they give joint testimony of the hope that history, which cannot be fulfilled out of its own, does not run into the void but that it is moving towards a perfection in universal peace (*shalom*) which only God can give. On the basis of what they have in common, they can and should cooperate fruitfully together in many questions. Thus, there can be a manifold exchange of gifts and a mutual give and take between Jews and Christians. In many cases a friendly relationship has grown between the two. Still, because of historical burdens and even more so because of its essential complexity and differentiation, this relation will remain difficult also in future and may prove to be fragile at times. It requires a great amount of sensitivity and decisiveness on both sides to keep a friendly dialogue and a good and fruitful cooperation. On the side of the Catholic Church, the decision for it has been positively made with the declaration *Nostra aetate*.

6.2.2 Ecumenical dialogue

A short historical overview

According to the will of Jesus, the Church is one.[53] Yet, since the days of the apostles, there have been divisions in the Church. In the light of the Gospel and in view of the world, this is a scandal which the Church cannot accept. This fragmentation contradicts the will of Jesus and weakens the effectiveness of the Gospel in the world. Therefore, we must not get used to this state of affairs. Above all, as the Catholic Church claims for itself that unity is, in it, already, though not perfectly, realized and sees itself particularly committed to unity through the Petrine office, such fragmentation must be a challenge for the Catholic Church.

Thus, every century has seen efforts in one way or another for the unity of all Christians.[54] The Church Fathers of the East and West made efforts for unity. For Augustine, as bishop, overcoming the Donatist schism was in fact a mission in life. In the Middle Ages one can think of the second council of Lyons (1274) and the Council of Ferrara-Florence (1438/1439), in the Reformation period of the religious discourses of Augsburg (1530) and Regensburg (1541), at the end of the seventeenth century of the correspondence between Leibniz and Bossuet and, already prior to today's ecumenical conversations, of the Malines Conversations with the Anglicans (1921–5). In other words, what today is described in terms of ecumenism and ecumenical dialogue is as old as the Church itself.

Still, concerning the way it is exercised, ecumenism in the twentieth century has taken on new forms and an unprecedented dynamic. The modern ecumenical movement has developed out of many individual initiatives. Even though it was in a problematic state, the Enlightenment and liberalism prepared its ground with their relativizing of the dogmatic foundations of the denominations. In addition, there was Romanticism with its doctrine of opposites as mutually complementary polarities. After the time of polemics and apologetics a new irenic attitude grew out of it.[55] The most important impulses came from the awakening movements and the ecumenical prayer movements that developed independently from each other in the second half of the eighteenth century and in the nineteenth century in various churches on different continents and in different countries. From the beginning the Catholic Church was involved through prayer groups in the spiritual preparation of the ecumenical movement. Also, saints like Vincent Pallotti († 1850), Adolf Kolping († 1865) or Don Luigi Orione († 1940) called to the prayer for unity and participated in it. Spencer Jones († 1943) and Lewis Watson († 1944), who had converted from Anglicanism to Catholicism, launched the week of prayer for Christian unity. Since Leo XIII it has been repeatedly endorsed and recommended by the popes.[56]

This prayer movement was also in the background of the 1910 world missionary conference in Edinburgh. The missionaries assembled there came to the conclusion that the divisions of Christianity were the biggest obstacle for world mission. Because of this insight, the missionary conference of Edinburgh is considered as the starting point of the modern ecumenical movement, in which ecumenical concern was combined from the beginning with missionary concern. The two impulses of the modern ecumenical movement – *faith and order* and *life and work* – emerged from the impulses of Edinburgh. They represent two different but mutually complementary directions of the ecumenical effort. In 1948, after the Second World War, they resulted in the founding of the World Council of Churches in Amsterdam. This Council does not see itself as a kind of super-church but as a fellowship of churches that, according to its basic formula, believe in Jesus Christ as Lord and redeemer to the glory of the Father, Son and Holy Spirit. The basic formula of the World Council of Churches is thus determined Christologically and Trinitarian.

While very early on there were already important impulses from the Ecumenical Patriarchate[57] and the Anglican Church,[58] and while Swedish, German and Dutch Protestant theologians were leading the way in the early ecumenical movement,[59] the Catholic Church was initially cautiously critical of the ecumenical movement. Pius XI's encyclical *Mortalium animos* (1928) articulated fundamental concerns. As the Catholic Church has understood and understands itself as the one church of Jesus Christ, it saw in the ecumenical movement the danger of religious indifferentism and relativism. It took courageous theological pioneers to reach a theological clarification. The *Una-sancta movement* and various ecumenically minded monasteries contributed positive spiritual and practical experiences to this.[60] Theologically, one could take recourse to Johann Adam Möhler and John Henry Newman as well as to more recent historical research which led to a deeper understanding of the Eastern church traditions and a new objective assessment of Martin Luther.

In addition to the theological preparation there were the experiences of National Socialism and Communism, of the Second World War, of flight and expulsion, of emigration and immigration and of the new diaspora situation. This created a community of fate among the separated churches. Not least in the concentration camps, courageous Christians of all denominations met and saw themselves united against a godless, inhuman, totalitarian, Nazi or Communist system of injustice.

Thus, already under Pope Pius XII, a *Monitum* of the Holy Office in 1948 acknowledged an impulse of the Holy Spirit in the ecumenical movement. Pope John XXIII had lived and worked as a delegate for nineteen years in mainly orthodox countries. For him, unity with the Eastern churches was a matter particularly close to his heart. Advised by Archbishop (later Cardinal) Lorenz Jaeger (Paderborn), he launched already in 1960 – in other words, before the beginning of the Second Vatican Council – the Secretariat (today Pontifical Council) for Promoting Christian Unity.[61]

The ground had been well prepared for the Second Vatican Council and the decree on ecumenism, *Unitatis redintegratio* (1964). Pope Paul VI promulgated the decree on ecumenism together with the constitution on the church, *Lumen Gentium*, as its complement, so to speak. Already in the introduction to the decree on ecumenism the Council declared that the restoration of unity among all Christians was one of its principal concerns. Division contradicts the will of Christ and scandalizes the world and damages the holy cause of preaching the Gospel to every creature.[62] Therefore the Council saw in the ecumenical movement an inspiration of the Holy Spirit.[63] It established Catholic principles for ecumenism, thereby opening the door for the Catholic Church to enter officially into the ecumenical movement.[64]

Since the Council, the Catholic Church has led many bilateral dialogues at local, national and universal levels. At the beginning there were dialogues with the Protestant churches or their world federations, then came dialogues with the Oriental-Orthodox and Orthodox churches. By now, dialogues have been extended to the free churches. In addition, the Catholic Church is a member in the Faith and Order Commission of the World Council of Churches. As a result it is also involved in multilateral dialogues. The significant dialogue results of the Dombes Group are also important.[65]

The encyclical on ecumenism of Pope John Paul II, *Ut unum sint* (1995), was the official affirmation of this work. At the same time, it sought to deepen and continue the Catholic contribution to ecumenism. In order to clarify matters further, the pope issued the *Directory for the Application of Principles and Norms on Ecumenism* (1993). For him, the ecumenical concern had its foundation in the will the Lord prayed on the evening before his death that all may be one (Jn 17.21). For the pope it was an irreversible obligation,[66] not a supplement or a mere addition to the traditional activity of the Church. Rather, it pertained organically to its life and work and was an integrating part.[67] He wrote: 'To believe in Christ means to desire unity; to desire unity means to desire the Church; to desire the Church means to desire the communion of grace which corresponds to the Father's plan from all eternity.'[68] Pope Benedict XVI confirmed this obligation already on the first day of his pontificate[69] and added later that ecumenism was not an incidental undertaking for the Church but constitutive for the Church and every Christian.[70] The ecumenical concern is thus, by no means, a kind of novelty but stands upon a solid biblical, historical basis and, above all, on a solid theological as well as spiritual and magisterial basis and updates this according to the present historical necessities and possibilities.

Catholic principles of ecumenical dialogue

As theological foundation the Council established Catholic principles of the ecumenical dialogue.[71] It does not start with some abstract idea or even ideology of dialogue but from the self-understanding of the Catholic Church. It thereby takes recourse to the ecclesiology extensively unfolded in the constitution on the Church.

The Council begins with a universal eschatological perspective. It sees the Church founded in the love of God who sent his Son into the world to bring the whole of mankind into unity. This results in the Christological reason which refers to Jesus' prayer for the unity of his disciples and especially to Jesus giving himself on the cross for the salvation of all who believe in him. In a further step, the Council takes up the Eucharistic ecclesiology. For the Council it is through the Eucharist, the centre and culmination of the life of the Church, that the unity is symbolized and effected. Finally, the Christological and Eucharistic rationale is followed by the pneumatological perspective. The Holy Spirit is the principle of unity in the Church. It effects the unity and the diversity of the gifts and ministries. It is only after these foundational statements that the Council speaks of the office, founded by Christ, of teaching, leading and sanctifying. This office is entrusted in a special way to Peter upon whom Christ, after Peter's confession of faith, founded the Church. This perspective of the theology of office is established Christologically insofar as the Council insists that Jesus Christ himself is the ultimate cornerstone and remains the shepherd of the souls for eternity.

Within the framework of this comprehensive theological view, the Council names three elements of the nature of unity: unity in faith, in the sacraments and in the community in the unity through the ministry of the bishops and the successor of Peter. As such unity, the Church is, as it were, an elevated sign among the nations. Its highest model and primal image is the unity of the one God, the Father and the Son in the Holy Spirit in the trinity of the persons. With this eschatological, Christological, Eucharistic, pneumatological, ecclesiological and ultimately Trinitarian foundation the Council left a one-sided institutional, hierarchical view of the unity of the Church far behind and presented a very comprehensive theological foundation for the realization of the ecumenical cause.

This theological breadth led to a new – at least at that time perceived as new – tone in speaking of non-Catholic Christians and their churches and ecclesial communities. All belong to this Church who believe in Christ and who have received baptism in a valid way. Through this they are in some, though not full, communion with the Catholic Church. The guilt for the not-full communion lies on both sides. One cannot blame those who are born into other communities and have received their faith in Christ there. They are justified by faith and incorporated into Christ. They deserve the name of honour of Christian and they are recognized by the Catholic Church as sisters and brothers in the Lord.[72]

Thus many significant elements and endowments which together go to build up the Church can exist outside the visible boundaries of the Catholic Church. Christ's Spirit has seen fit to use them as means of salvation.[73] Still – and here the Council sticks to the teaching of Tradition – the fullness of these means of salvation is found only in the Catholic Church. It is the general means of salvation. The Church of Jesus Christ subsists in it, that is, it has in it its concrete historical form of existence and remains historically concretely present.[74] In it exists the unity which it can never lose. For the Council, this is not just a purely static but also at the same time a dynamic statement, for the Council adds that the unity continues to grow until the end of time.

In this non-static, but historical-dynamic, eschatological view of the Church, it is now possible to say – and this is the new aspect – that the statement about the Catholic Church as a general means of salvation must not be understood as exclusive in the sense that outside its institutional boundaries there was an ecclesiological vacuum. Instead, to the extent that outside the institutional boundaries of the Catholic Church the mentioned elements are found, the Church of Christ is efficaciously present.[75] Following the Council one can therefore speak of a graded membership and a graded realization of the one Church of Jesus Christ. In this grading, the Council sees an essential difference between the Oriental-Orthodox churches and the Orthodox churches which have kept the essential sacramental and apostolic basic structure, and those ecclesial communities having emerged out of the Reformation that belong through baptism to the body of Christ but that have not kept the apostolic succession in the episcopal office and the original and full substance of the Eucharist.[76]

It is the task of the ecumenical movement to overcome the obstacles to full communion and to lead from the imperfect to the full church communion that finds its expression in the Eucharistic community at the one table of the Lord.[77] In this respect, the Council presents a kind of definition or, better, a kind of working description of the ecumenical movement: 'The term "ecumenical movement" indicates the initiatives and activities planned and undertaken, according to the various needs of the Church and as opportunities offer, to promote Christian unity.'[78] This is, indeed, a theological rationale and task description for the ecumenical movement calling for a theology of the ecumenical dialogue.

Theology of the ecumenical dialogues

The task of ecumenical theology emerges out of the foundation and principles of the ecumenical movement.[79] From what has been said, it is clear that it is not a private affair of individual theologians, but theology on the basis of the ecclesial doctrine, in the spirit and vocation of the Church. It adheres to the same principles and methods that apply to Catholic theology as a whole and is under the same claim to truth as all Catholic theology. If, in contrast to dogmatics, it is, in its approach, less doctrinal, but proceeds more dialogically, it does not mean that it was not bound to the same ecclesial doctrine. It is not the theological truth that is different, but the methodological approach to truth.

In contrast to dogmatic theology and in particular to controversial theology, ecumenical theology does not depart from doctrinal differences but from the basis of common ground and tries from there to understand existing differences better, to place them correctly and to recognize possible convergences in order to then testify ecumenically to that which each church considers its treasure. As such, each individual question must be understood in the context of the whole and under consideration of the hierarchy of truths.[80] This should happen humbly, modestly, respectfully before the convictions of others (and, in this respect, ready to listen to the concerns and questions of others), but also clearly vis-a-vis one's own positions. Therefore, ecumenical theology is not to perceive non-Catholic witnesses and testimonies only as *adversarii*, as opponents and counter-arguments. Instead, it should learn from them and, as far as possible, integrate them into one's own theological argumentation, reception and forming of consensus.[81] This gives Catholic theology a truly catholic breadth.

Thus, ecumenical dialogue is dialogue, that is, exchange in truth and in love. As truth without love is repulsive, love without truth is equally not serious and dishonest. It is for this reason that the ecumenical paradigm shift attempted in the 1970s, marked by a move away from theological ecumenism and toward a secular ecumenism beneath the motto 'doctrine divides, service unites,' could not succeed.[82] After all, praxis is by no means as clear as is implied here. It only unites if it is borne by common convictions. If this is not the case, new 'ethical denominations' develop that cause new, unprecedented controversies, as was indeed the case and still is. Equally, the question of truth cannot be pragmatically avoided because of misunderstood ecumenical love.[83] The demand that the churches should find intelligent compromises departs from the error that truth could be quasi-newly developed through negotiations in a consensus which is to be reached diplomatically. Such an idea forgets that the truth of the Church is given and not a matter for negotiation.[84] One often hears the claim that the differences were only misunderstandings that have been overcome today with better knowledge or which could be easily overcome. Recent ecumenical developments question this view. Meanwhile, there is an increased awareness of basic differences that have remained unresolved until now. It becomes apparent that, especially concerning the understanding of Church, there are substantially more problems and difficulties than some would care to acknowledge. This will be addressed now.

The basic problem: different visions and objectives

Following the path outlined by the Council, many dialogues of recent decades to overcome misunderstandings have resulted partial consensuses and convergences, and also individual consensuses.[85] Ecumenical dialogues have, by now, however, also increasingly highlighted the basic problem of ecumenism: the Catholic Church, the Orthodox and the Protestant churches depart from a different understanding of the Church from which different understandings of unity result, as well as different views of the goal of ecumenism.[86] This is quite a dangerous situation. If the goals are unclear, then there emerges a danger that everyone will go in different directions and end up further apart than they were in the first place.

This problem has been discussed for some time under the heading 'ecumenical objectives and visions'.[87] Today, it is *communio* that is named as the goal of ecumenism by those involved in the ecumenical dialogue. The problem, of course, is that, because of the different ecclesiological bases, not everyone understands '*communio*' in the same way.

On the basis of an ecclesiology focused on the local church, the Protestant churches give unity in reconciled diversity as their goal. They thus follow article VII of the Augsburg Confession, according to which it suffices (*satis est*) to agree in the proclamation of the Gospel and the administration of the sacraments (baptism and Eucharist) in accordance with the Gospel.[88] On this basis the Lutheran, Reformed and United churches in Europe entered in 1973 into the *Leuenberg Agreement* communion, in the sense of church communion as communion of chancel and Eucharist. Since article VII of the Augsburg Confession does not go into much detail, these churches could reach a *communio* of consensus, even though clear differences remain concerning the understanding of Church and ministry.[89] For the Anglican Communion, the unity in the historical episcopate is essential (*Lambeth Quadrilateral*, 1888). It was on this basis that it reached an agreement with the Nordic and Baltic Lutheran churches, the result of which is the *Porvoo Common Statement* (1992).[90] However, it is such communions often appear content with a unity in the fundamental articles of faith even though the so-called adiaphora are not addressed, a position which is not possible for Catholics and Orthodox.[91]

For the Catholic and Orthodox churches, a separation between content and the official form of the Church in the episcopal office is not possible.[92] The Orthodox churches are similarly convinced, like the Catholic Church, if not even more decidedly so, that they are the true Church. For them, agreement on the doctrine and the sacramentally-episcopally constituted form of the Church in the first millennium is decisive. The difference results from the differing assessment of the development of the Catholic Church in the second millennium. In particular, the development of the doctrine of primacy is, for the Orthodox churches, an incomprehensible separate Western development. In contrast, the Catholic Church regards the Tradition of the second millennium as a living, developing Tradition and in this respect in continuity with the first millennium. It regards the dogmas of the second millennium on the basis of the joint first millennium and as their further development, and therefore considers them as authoritative.[93] Hence the question is whether we can reach agreement on a joint understanding of the primacy, whether we can agree on a new exercise of the primacy, accepted by both sides, and whether we can say together what communion with the Petrine office concretely means. This is the object of the present Catholic-Orthodox dialogues.

For the Catholic Church, the goal of the ecumenical movement is the full visible communion in the one faith, in the same sacraments and in the communion with the episcopal office in apostolic succession in communion with the successor of Peter. This objective must not be understood in the sense of a simple ecumenism of return. It does not mean a step back.

Likewise, it does not mean that the other churches must join the Catholic Church as it exists concretely today. The desired unity is neither fusion nor absorption.[94] As the Catholic Church knows the possibility of a development of doctrine, some individual aspects of being Church which are basically present in the Catholic Church, but which are only marginally developed or even withered, to the extent that they are more richly and fully developed in other churches, can be developed further through ecumenical dialogue. Ecumenical dialogue is not a one-way street, but rather an exchange of ideas and gifts and should so lead to a realized fullness of catholicity.[95] The dialogue is not about giving up one's own identity but about growing and enriching in one's own identity.

Therefore, the desired unity should not be a unity in the sense of uniformity, but a unity in diversity in which the separated churches retain their own legitimate traditions and can contribute them to the greater unity. Unity in diversity means, at the same time, diversity in unity. It is more than just a peaceful or controversial side-by-side, more than just living together, and it goes beyond an ecumenism of opposites. It is also not only constituted by the association or cooperation of the churches. Instead, the already given, but flawed and thus imperfect unity is to be healed by way of reconciliation so that full communion might be restored. Hence, Joseph Ratzinger has taken up the thought of Oscar Cullmann, who speaks of unity through diversity,[96] and writes that churches are 'to remain churches and yet they are to become one church'.[97] How this can be thought out was already demonstrated by Johann Adam Möhler in his early work *Unity in the Church* (1825). Möhler took up the dialectical thinking of German Idealism and developed it further, demonstrating thereby how opposites which egoistically lock themselves up, exclude each other and so become impoverished can, by way of reconciliation, give up their egoism and their obstinacy and become a fruitful unity in love. Neither outside nor beside, but within this unity, the opposites can move 'freely and easily'.[98]

With this there are many still-unresolved problems which show that there is still some tough work waiting for ecumenical theology. In the next phase of the dialogues, we will therefore make the understanding of Church our topic and we must ask what we mean by a *communio*-ecclesiology and what we mean precisely when we speak of the unity of the Church as a *communio*-unity.

Spiritual ecumenism and the ecumenism of life

Academic dialogue is important and indispensable for the progress of the ecumenical movement. However, ecumenical dialogue is not only an exchange of ideas but also of gifts. Therefore it is only possible in a spiritual atmosphere characterized by joint prayer. Ultimately, it must not remain an issue for experts alone. Rather it must be imbedded into an ecumenism of life, carried out by an ecumenism of prayer, and, finally, received by the whole people of God.[99]

This spiritual ecumenism was developed in particular by Abbé Paul Couturier of Lyons († 1953) and by Max Josef Metzger († 1944), who was executed by the Nazis as a resistance fighter. The Second Vatican Council took up the issue and stressed that spiritual ecumenism was the centre and heart of ecumenical efforts. This includes concretely conversion, repentance, examination of conscience, and, above all, prayer.[100] In 1983, Pope John Paul II beatified the Trappist nun Maria Gabriella (Sagheddu) of Unity († 1939) who was inspired by Paul Courturier. The pope called her an example and model of spiritual ecumenism.[101]

This ecumenism of life is ecumenism lived in the daily life of Christians and communities. Spiritual ecumenism takes seriously that the unity of the Church is not our work but the work of the Holy Spirit. As we have seen, already at the beginning of the ecumenical movement there was an impulse of the Holy Spirit, and this impulse can be continued and brought to its goal only in the Holy Spirit. As the first disciples prayed unanimously after Jesus' ascension into heaven together with the women and with Mary for the coming of the Spirit (Acts 1.12–14), so we should also pray for a renewal of the event of Pentecost. In this we should make Jesus' prayer our own that all should be one (Jn 17.21). It is promised to the prayer in the name of Jesus that it will be fulfilled (Jn 15.24). Yet, how could we pray more in the name of Jesus than if we make his prayer ours and, as is movingly expressed in the spiritual testament of Paul Courtier of 1944, if we pray for the unity of Christians and thereby pray for unity not as we want it but as he wants it, where, how and when he wants it?

Such spiritual ecumenism is a multifaceted reality. In the first instance, it means openness for the working of the Holy Spirit who alone can open the heart towards sympathy and empathy, which are basic prerequisites for any dialogue. The Spirit thus enables us to overcome prejudices, to admit and repent the errors of the past and our own faults. He gives us the grace of conversion and repentance which must take effect in reform and renewal. He helps to overcome the notion of competition and to recognize the gifts given to others and to accept them also as gifts for us. He leads us to carry the burden of others (Gal. 6.2) and to share in solidarity the joy, suffering, hopes and sorrows of others. Finally, the Spirit moves and inspires us in spiritual reading of Scripture (*lectio divina*) to exchange and communicate about the primal testimony and the primal message common to all Christians and about one's own praxis and experiences in faith. On these different ways we can grow more and more intensively in unity and prepare the way for full unity.

Spiritual ecumenism is the task of every Christian and every community. For this, one does not need to create special occasions or organize specific events. The good and bad moments of life, the course of the liturgical year (especially Advent, Lent and festive seasons) and ecclesial events and feasts offer many possibilities. Monasticism in particular, with its sources common in East and West, can make its own contribution.[102] In recent years, the spiritual communities, together with corresponding movements and communities of other churches, have taken up this task in local, regional and European encounters. This is, at present, the most fruitful and most promising form of ecumenical dialogue and a crucial construction site for the future of the Church.

How long is the journey?

Impatience, disappointment and scepticism concerning lack of progress mark the ecumenical journey. As far as we can judge, the way to the goal of unity of all Christians is indeed probably longer and more laborious than many had at first hoped during the first ecumenical new beginning. Still, there is no reason for resignation and scepticism. What has been achieved so far is no small matter, and we should thus be grateful and encourage us to press forward. Though the full unity of the Church has not yet been given to us, especially unity at the table of the Lord, yet there is already something like a new unity and a new awareness of unity of Christianity among Christians. In the last decades Christians and churches have moved closer to each other. No reasonable or responsible person can want to take back what has been achieved.

In view of these new challenges, Christians and churches cannot afford at all to stand against each other or to live detached and indifferent side by side. Considering the common challenges, they have no other option but to witness together in this world to the common Father and the common Lord Jesus Christ in the one common Holy Spirit and to cooperate in the service for mankind, peace, freedom and justice in the world.

If we are convinced that ecumenism is an impulse of the Holy Spirit, then we may be convinced, despite all difficulties, that the Spirit is faithful and brings to an end what it itself initiated. We may continue on the ecumenical way with hope. The little sister of hope is patience, which, however, is only then genuine if it is paired with courage and preparedness to take those steps which are already possible today. The specific how, when and where of the full Church communion is not in our hands, but in God's. If we make our contribution, it can be only given to us in a renewed Pentecost as a gift of the Holy Spirit.

6.2.3 Dialogue with the religions

The present situation of the world and mankind is characterized by globalization on an unprecedented scale, which goes far beyond the field of economic interrelations. Through the worldwide migration of millions of people, through unprecedented networking with the aid of electronic media, because of a previously impossible mobility and mass tourism, nations and cultures have come closer to each other. Religions that previously lived separately from each other are today present directly among us.

The position of the Church

The Second Vatican Council addressed, for the first time, the new situation which then was only beginning to appear with the declaration *Nostra aetate. On the Relation of the Church to Non-Christian Religions.* It says that 'day by day mankind is being drawn closer together, and the ties between different peoples are becoming stronger'. The Council saw the task in 'promoting unity and love among men, indeed among nations'. It wants to consider 'what men have in common and what draws them to fellowship'.[103]

The declaration speaks in particular of the dialogue with Jews and Muslims. Christianity is connected with Judaism in a special and, in the history of religions, unique way. The declaration *Nostra aetate* highlights the common roots of Judaism and Christianity and regrets and condemns any form of anti-Semitism.[104] The declaration speaks of the Muslims 'with esteem'. It speaks of 'quarrels and hostilities' of the past and advises mutual understanding and to cooperation for social justice, peace and freedom for all people.[105] The declaration mentions more briefly also the great Asian religions Hinduism and Buddhism.

To make this declaration effective practically, Pope Paul VI founded at Pentecost 1964 the Secretariat (today Pontifical Council) for Inter-religious Dialogue.[106] This dialogue found a mighty supporter in Pope John Paul II, especially with the two world prayer meetings in Assisi (1986, 2002). Various international movements (Sant'Egidio, Focolare and others) continue his ideas with great commitment. The same is undertaken by the national episcopal conferences. There are similar dialogues on the level of the World Council of Churches, the Conference of European Churches, the Protestant Church in Germany and other churches such as the Anglican Communion, the Ecumenical Patriarchate of Constantinople and the Russian-Orthodox Patriarchate of Moscow. The literature on this topic has by now become enormous.[107]

Ultimately, all churches involved consider dialogue as the only sensible possibility to avoid a clash of cultures, such as has been prophesied by some.[108] It does not seek to be a mission with different means. It aims for agreement on common ground and furthering what there is in common. Inter-religious dialogue is thus not just a purely academic concern like the discipline of comparative religious studies. Rather, it tries to respond practically to the new situation of mankind through the reduction of potential violence, misunderstandings and mistrust and through building mutual understanding and respect and joint furthering of social integration and of international peace.[109]

Of course, one must not have illusions about the difficulties of the inter-religious dialogue. Substantial cultural, in parts also political, differences must be considered. Above all, the religious and theological differences are bigger by far than in the ecumenical dialogue. There is a qualitative difference between the latter and the dialogue with the non-Christian religions. The ecumenical dialogue departs from common ground: the common confession to God and Christ, the common baptism and common Scripture, in the traditional churches and communities also the common symbols of the Old Church. There is no such common basis in the inter-religious dialogue – quite the contrary!

This raises immediately the first basic problem that must be addressed before all others: what is common to the religions? Does such common ground exist at all? In consequence, what can inter-religious dialogue mean and what can it achieve?

The general term 'religion'?

Today, many things are called religion: Judaism and Islam, the great Asian high religions, nature religions, religions that disappeared long ago such as that of the Maya, but also so-called new religions and new religious movements. Often the term is also extended to include mysticism, esotericism, New Age, so-called youth religions or other forms of free-straying religiosity. In parts, even explicitly a-religious or anti-religious attitudes are classified as religion or religious supplements, such as the idolization or setting absolute of earthly-finite aspects (race, nation, state, culture, sport and so forth).

So, what is religion? In reply to this question we must say that there is no religion in the singular; concretely there are only quite different religions in the plural. The question about a common core and a common substantial essence of religion in the religions is almost impossible to answer from an etymological perspective alone.[110] The Latin word *religio* is usually associatively derived from *relegere*, 'to observe carefully', and its meaning is similar to *pietas* or *cultus* the religious-cultic observance, in other words, the observing of religious-cultic rules (Cicero). Others see *religio* as derived from *religare*, 'tying back to', and understand thereby a personal connection to God or a deity (Lactantius, Augustine). However, this represents by no means an understanding of religion that can be generally presupposed and it does not apply to Buddhism, which does not know a personal or transcendent god. It becomes difficult, above all, when one searches for an equivalent of *religio* in other languages. The Greek language offers several different words. One can think of εὐσέβεια, the respectful behaviour towards religious orders, upon which life of the family, the State and between states rests.[111] Still, τιμή, λατρεία, θρησκεία are also possible, among others. It gets totally complicated when non-European languages are included in the discussion.

While the etymological derivation is already difficult, defining the content is even more difficult.[112] The general term 'religion' is a product of the Enlightenment and has only existed since the seventeenth or eighteenth century. It is an artificial construct that seeks to explore the common nature of religions but excludes their differences as historically, socially or culturally contingent accessories, or which wants to explain the differences with a lack of knowledge, misunderstanding or abuse. People who seriously practise their religion will consider such enlightened attitudes as misunderstandings or even insults, for they see themselves as not taken seriously in their religious practice.[113]

So it comes as no surprise that James H. Leuba could collect 48 definitions of religion.[114] Because of the extension of the term described above, more have been added to the collection. Agreement is not in sight. Because of this impossibility of a definition, quite early on there was the call to abandon the term 'religion'. Yet, without a general term 'religion' we could also no longer speak of religions. Thus, the general term 'religion' will have to be understood as a linguistic convention.

This conventional usage must be taken into account when one speaks, as has become common, of the three monotheistic religions: Judaism, Christianity and Islam. This is a collective term that appeared only through the French orientalist Louis Massignon († 1962).[115] It can point to the common aspects of the three religions mentioned, but it cannot obscure that the language of the one god is understood differently in Judaism, Christianity and especially in Islam. Islam does not know the god of history who turns towards us humans. It rejects therefore the incarnation, suffering at the cross and the resurrection of Jesus Christ, all truths of faith central to Christianity. The different understanding of God also results in a different idea of man that finds concrete expression the Islamic legal system, the sharia, which allows in some Muslim countries a certain freedom of cult but does not know of a true freedom of religion. The same applies to the oft-asserted parallelization of the Bible and the Koran. If one perceives the Bible as word inspired by God in and through human word or the Koran as the immediate word of God, this is a difference of fundamental significance for each respective hermeneutic and for the dialogue.

So, what is religion?

On the whole, religion today is no longer reduced religion-critically to anthropological, sociological, psychological and other factors (Ludwig Feuerbach, Karl Marx, Friedrich Nietzsche, Siegmund Freud et al.).[116] Today it is mostly perceived as a non-reducible, original and independent phenomenon (Friedrich Schleiermacher, Max Scheler, Rudolf Otto, Mircea Eliade et al.). It is thereby often described as experience of the holy as a *mysterium tremendum fascinosum*.[117] This is a term that has become alien to a secular thinking and understanding of reality. In consequence, proceeding from secular thinking, there is often an attempt to restrict religion to the purely private and personal sphere. This is not possible for any religion because each religion is inseparably connected with interpretations of the whole of reality. Thus, religions are always connected with a certain culture, in other words a certain way of personal and social life. For that reason, religions can be the object of religio-sociological research and theory development (Émile Durkheim, Max Weber, Thomas Luckmann, Niklas Luhmann et al.).

Religions make claims on society which can come into conflict with each other. As Europeans we have had painful experiences with this, from which we have learnt what we consider today as one of the most important achievements of our culture: freedom of religion as basis of our free constitutional and legal system and as foundation of a social order of peace. The basis for freedom of religion is not indifference towards other religions, but respect for other religions and attempting to live peacefully together.[118]

This positive freedom of religion is the basic prerequisite for inter-religious dialogue. It contains not only the right to personal religious conviction (freedom of conscience), which includes the right to change religions, but also the freedom to publicly exercise the religion, obviously in a way that the public peace (and so the freedom of others) is not endangered.

In this sense, we grant freedom of religion naturally to other religions existing among us. However, in many countries where these religions have originated, such freedom is not granted to the Christians living there. As a theologian, one may and must point out honestly such difficulties that Christians increasingly experience in other cultures, mainly (but not only) in countries with a Muslim majority. There is anti-Semitism which we decidedly condemn, and there is Islamophobia which we equally condemn expressly. Yet, there is also Christophobia that should likewise not be tolerated. The respect for the religion and culture of others and the freedom of others to live and exercise their religion are basic prerequisites for inter-religious dialogue and for peace in the world.

The openness and distinctiveness of Christianity – three theses

Once these conditions are clarified we must now address as a next step the following question: in view of this complexity of matters, what can inter-religious dialogue mean and what can it possibly achieve? Considering what has been said so far, there can be no answer in the sense of a neutral theory of inter-religious dialogue, but only on the basis of a specific personal option or position. Therefore in this context the question can only be answered from a Christian perspective, but not from a general religious perspective or from an Islamic or Buddhist view.

From a Christian perspective we can present three attempts at a solution as they are discussed at present.

(1) The first solution, abandoned in its absolute form today, can be called the exclusive approach to a solution. It stems from the fact that already the Old Testament, with its faith in the one and only God, turns against the veneration of other gods. The exclusive biblical monotheism is particularly expressed in the first commandment: 'You shall have no other gods to rival me' (Exod. 20.3; Deut. 5.7–10). The faith in one God is repeatedly emphasized quite clearly by the prophets. For Isaiah the idols are simply nothings (Isa. 41.29). Jesus confirmed the faith in the one and only God (Mk 12.29–32; cf. Jn 17.3; 1 Cor. 8.5f.).

Thus, from the beginning until today, the conversion to Christianity through baptism has meant renouncing idols and converting to the one true God (1 Thess. 1.9). The Church Fathers never hesitated to name and criticize the erroneous and superstitious belief in pagan religions. Paul reproaches the heathens that they had known God but that they had not honoured him; instead they had kept down the truth and had thus been slaves to nothings (Rom. 1.18–21).

These are statements that have lasting validity and exclude any kind of relativism, indifferentism and syncretism, especially the 'do-it-yourself' religion, widespread today, which chooses, like in a shop, the momentarily suitable things from the religious offer and gathers set-pieces from different religions.

(2) Of course we see today that these exclusive statements are only one half of the truth. Besides these exclusive statements there are already other positions in the Bible which are called inclusive today. Already the Bible knows of so-called holy heathens: Abel, Enoch, Melchisedek, Job. The Acts of the Apostles in the New Testament says that God is welcome in every nation that fears him and does what is right (Acts 10.34). Paul speaks of conscience and says that heathens have the law written into the heart and that their conscience testifies to it (Rom. 2.15). According to John's gospel, the light revealed in Jesus Christ shines for every person (Jn 1.9).

For this reason, in the Early Church the apologists of the second century could speak of the seeds of truth or the fragments of truth (λόγοι σπερματικοί) which are found in the cultures and religions of heathens. Yet, at the same time, they said that the truth appeared in the incarnated logos Jesus Christ in unsurpassable fullness.[119] Augustine spoke of the Church which '*ab Abel iusto*' – in other words, since the beginning of the world – runs through the whole of history. Thomas Aquinas adopted this theory in many passages of his work.[120] At the end of the Middle Ages and the transition to modern times one has to name the philosopher, theologian and polymath Nicholas of Cusa († 1464) with his tractate *De pace fidei*.

The Second Vatican Council spoke, following the Bible, of God's universal saving will (1 Tim. 2.4) and of a universal efficaciousness of God's Spirit. Accordingly, it interpreted the doctrine of *extra ecclesiam null salus* to mean that salvation is possible because of God's grace for everyone who seeks God and follows him as he can perceive him in his conscience.[121] The Council also maintains that the salvation of non-Christians is not mediated through Buddha or Mohammed or other saviours but alone through Jesus Christ. Yet, the Spirit of Jesus Christ is not tied to the boundaries of the visible church. God has ways which he alone knows.[122] We must leave the 'how' to God. John Paul II explored extensively the doctrine of the universal efficaciousness of the Spirit in his mission encyclical *Redemptoris missio* (1990) and also included other religions and cultures in this efficaciousness.[123]

(3) The theory recently presented that is based upon religious pluralism (Wilfred Cantwell Smith, John Hick, Paul F. Knitter, Perry Schmidt-Leukel, etc.) is distinct from the second thesis. It proceeds from the absolute transcendence of God and says, along the lines of Kant's critique of knowledge, that this transcendence cannot be grasped adequately by any religion. All religions grasp only a more or less important aspect of the divine. Thus, according to the theory, all religions must give up claims to absoluteness. In the sense of the thesis of religious pluralism it does not mean that all religions are equally valid. The criterion for their recognition, however, is not if they accord more or less to God's truth but if and to what extent they serve mankind and its liberation and support the fight against poverty, violence, discrimination and others. In other words, the criterion is not a theoretical one, but an ethical-practical one.

This pragmatic attempt at a solution seems plausible for many today and dominates public discussions. Of course, it is dependent on philosophical preconditions that can be questioned critically. It is above all worth noticing that there is simply no agreement over what serves mankind. The question of what helps mankind is answered differently by different religions and depends on each respective image of man, which in turn depends on the respective image of God. In other words, the question of truth cannot be excluded unless one wants to submit to an ideological dictatorship and simply accept what is today generally considered to serve mankind. In that, however, one then degrades god or the divine to a servant of one's own purposes.[124] In addition, none of the monotheistic religions can accept that it should grasp only one aspect of God and be one religion besides others. The pluralistic thesis therefore forces upon the monotheistic religions, not only orthodox Jews or Christians but also Muslims, a criterion which they could only accept at the price of their self-abandonment. Through this the dialogue with the thesis based on religious pluralism has been made impossible even before it has begun.

What does it mean to claim absoluteness for Christianity

How can we move forward here? To clarify this, we must first establish what is meant by the so-called claim to absoluteness of Christianity and what is not.[125] This is necessary particularly because the term 'Christianity's claim to absoluteness' does not originate from the traditional vocabulary of Christian theology, but from Hegel's speculative philosophy of religion. Already Ernst Troeltsch pointed out that, from a purely empirical perspective, one cannot speak of an absolute validity of Christianity but only of a supreme validity.[126] Still, it will be difficult to prove this empirically.

If we take a closer look, we can understand the absoluteness of Christianity in a double sense: on the one hand, as *genitivus subjectivus* – as self-evidence of Christianity or God who has revealed himself in an unsurpassable way in Jesus Christ; on the other, as *genitivus objectivus* – as the claim to absoluteness of the one whom Christianity represents and mediates, concretely in the claim of the Church to be in possession of the absolute truth. The first thesis cannot be given up by Christianity. In contrast, the second is problematic. In the actual sense, God alone is absolute and God is not possessed by anyone. Concerning the testimony of the Church, one must not overlook its historical dimension. In other words, one must distinguish between the claim of revelation itself and its historical mediation through the Church.

Instead of speaking mistakably of Christianity's claim to absoluteness, it would be better to proceed from the biblical use of language, which does not speak of the absoluteness of Christianity but of the fullness of time brought about by God in Jesus Christ (Mk 1.14 par.), and of the fullness (πλήρωμα) of God's revelation in Jesus Christ (Col. 1.19). This biblical terminology is not exclusive; rather it is inclusive, and means the final fulfilment of that which is planted and realized as hope in humans, cultures and religions. It is not a claim that the Church can make for itself in its empirical form, for in its empirical embodiment the Church often lags behind this claim. Thus it requires action of the Church itself as bearer of this message.[127]

The one God – the one humanity

The basic elements of the exclusive theory and especially the inclusive theory remain as points of departure for the Christian inter-religious dialogue, while acknowledging all essential differences, the inter-religious concerns, above all, the common ground between the religions. The religions have in common the recognition of the holy or the divine (in whichever way that is understood), and, among the monotheistic religions, the recognition of the one transcendent god as origin and orientation of human life. Despite all basic differences, this is common ground which is very important in view of a secular understanding of reality and life. The holiness of god or the divine also includes, for all religions, respect for the sanctity of life.

If we proceed like this from the question about God, then this might seem to many contemporaries like a problem far from the realities of life. That this is not the case can be read already on the first page of the Bible, which speaks of the one God who is the creator and father of all reality and all humans. The one God is the foundation for the god-like dignity of every human regardless of his ethnic, cultural or religious affiliation, independent also of gender (Gen. 1.27). He lets the sun rise and rain fall over good and bad (Mt. 5.43f.). The one God founds the unity of the human race. This unity of the human family based on the Creator is, for Christians, the foundation for common human values and universal human solidarity. It is also the foundation for cooperation, non-violence, tolerance, mutual respect, freedom of religion, justice, solidarity, freedom and peace, for the same dignity of men and women, for the reverence for life and for protecting the creation.

So, confessing to the one God of all humans has practical consequences. This applies not only to the order of creation but also to the order of salvation, beginning with Abraham. While Abraham is called out of the nations he is also called to be a blessing for all nations (Gen. 12.1; 18.18 et seq.). At the burning bush, God reveals himself to Moses as the God who is with his people on the way through history (Exod. 3.6.14.16). He is not a local or national god but a world god and a god of the way. He is present everywhere his people comes; he is a god of humans and present where there are humans who seek him. According to the prophetic promise, he will gather all nations (Isa. 2.2–5; Mic 4.1–3). Jesus took up this gathering movement and initiated it by sending out missions in all nations. Understood in this way, mission is the form of Christian globalization whereby humans and cultures are brought together not only economically, medially or in terms of traffic, but despite all remaining diversity to share the same basic convictions.

The Old Testament already drew two practical consequences from this universal perspective which can be relevant today in a new way. In the first place we can point to the Golden Rule which all religions, also the Bible (Tb 4.15; Sir. 31.15; Mt. 7.12; Lk. 6.31), know in one way or another. In its negative form it says: 'do not do unto others what you do not want them do to you'. The positive and more demanding form is: 'do unto others everything you want them to do to you'. This rule can become the foundation for the joint commitment for justice, freedom and peace in the world and for the joint fight against poverty, violence, discrimination and so forth. Despite all differences the religions can agree on this common ground and cooperate on this basis.[128]

A second point results from the fact that already the Old Testament knows and appreciates the common-oriental custom of hospitality (Deut. 10.18f.; Prov. 27.8; Sir. 29.21 et seq.).[129] Abraham, the father of faith, is presented as a shining example of such hospitality (Gen. 18). Hospitality means accepting and welcoming the alien and the stranger, giving room to the stranger in one's own house. Jesus set us an example for such an existence for others (Mk 10.45 par). It is not a peripheral issue but the centre of Christian existence and identity.[130] Thus, in the great judgement discourse, Jesus praised hospitality and, above all, hospitality towards persecuted ones, and he made it a criterion in the judgement (Mt. 25.35–43).

In this passage the Gospel poses a critical question: how is it with our hospitality for pressed and persecuted people? The question of hospitality is all the more pressing for Christians, as Christians in many parts of the world are strangers themselves. Being alien is, so to speak, a basic existential of being Christian and there is at present more than one situation where Christians live in and among other cultures in severe distress and urgently need our solidarity.

To be welcomed and accepted as a guest entails that I have to obey the house rules of the host. This is especially the case in a foreign country if I enjoy not only the rights of a guest but also citizen rights, for then it contains not only rights but entails also duties. To demand them has nothing to do with intolerance or xenophobia, but rather with self-respect and with our right to live according to our culture, to preserve it and to develop it further. Clearly, this cannot happen in separation from other cultures but only in historical encounter and exchange with them.

Back to the question of Christian identity

This brings us finally back to the centre of the inter-religious dialogue: the question of Christian identity. Dialogue presupposes partners who each have their respective identity but do not, however, perceive identity as a closed and locked up monad but as an open identity which realizes itself by way of dialogue and exchange. A properly understood Christian identity is not a timid, closed-up identity escaping into a circle of wagons or even some narrow-minded chauvinism. It is rather an identity open for others, transcending itself towards the other; it is indeed an identity which identifies with the other as the other. Yet, by identifying with the other it does not give up its own identity, but instead realizes, clarifies and deepens it and is at the same time enriched by the other.

Thus, asking the question of truth does not exclude dialogue, rather it opens it in its deep-reaching sense. After all, dialogue means more than a polite and non-committal conversation, more than some friendly interest. It does not mean a sentimental syncretism, nor an enthusiastic, utopian all-unity or universal religion in which one's own identity is dissolved and lost. Dialogue does not refrain from respectful argument aiming for agreement. Put positively, inter-religious dialogue strives to get to know the other and indeed to understand him, to eliminate prejudices and to build understanding and trust, to reach understanding about what is common and what separates, to respect what is different, and in this way to find ways of cooperation, at least in those parts that are essential and partly crucial to survival for all parties involved.

This dialogue is our task today as humans and as Christians for the sake of peace. It is not just an academic issue, but above all a cultural, social and ecclesial one which also involves concrete practical questions and decisions. Like any other dialogue, the inter-religious dialogue, too, will never come to an end. It remains on its way. This open way towards and with each other pertains to being human as well as to being Christian. In this sense the dialogue of religions truly realizes in its own way what also pertains to Christian identity.

6.2.4 Dialogue with the world of today

The objective of and problem with the pastoral constitution

The Second Vatican Council did not stop at dialogue with Jews, other Christians and other religions. It also initiated dialogue between the Church and the modern world. It did this particularly in the pastoral constitution *On the Church in the Modern World. Gaudium et spes.*[131] Many consider this to be the most distinctive and most significant document of the last council for, in the pastoral constitution, more than in any other documents of the Council, the extension of horizon which the Council accomplished becomes apparent. The dogmatic constitution on the Church, *Lumen Gentium*, was about the Church, its nature and its mission. The pastoral constitution now highlights the sense in which the Church, described therein *ad intra*, is also Church *ad extra*. It does not exist for itself, but is the Church in the world and Church for the humans in this world.

The Council consciously does not write 'Church *and* the modern world' for it intended to overcome the usual juxtaposition of Church and world as two parallel worlds. This touched upon a current problem which was then emerging newly emerging. Particularly in Catholic countries and regions, a Catholic lived from birth in family, parish, kindergarten and school, to party and trade union, hospital and old people's home in a more or less closed Catholic milieu. Yet, this milieu is increasingly collapsing. The Council intended to overcome the juxtaposition of the two worlds and said that the Church lives *in* the modern world and that, conversely, the modern world reaches into the Church. The Church thus confesses to contemporaneity. In fact, the members of the Church are, at the same time, also citizens of the modern world. This basic concern is articulated already in the first, oft-quoted sentence: 'The joys and the hopes, the grief and the anguish of the men of this age, especially those who are poor or in any way afflicted, these are the joys and hopes, the grief and anguish of the followers of Christ. Indeed, nothing genuinely human fails to raise an echo in their hearts.'[132]

This was a new orientation for which many Catholics were not prepared and which overwhelmed them. Thus, the consequences were at first a number of misinterpretations and short-circuits. Many jumped, so to speak, from the juxtaposition of Church and world abruptly to an, at first rather unclear, description of the Church and the Christian as being 'in the world' and after the ways of the world. There was obviously need for clarification. The question has been and still is: what does the purely empirically and phenomenological undeniable being 'in the world' mean from a normative perspective? In other words, how can Christian identity be maintained 'in the world'?

There was also no easy answer for the pastoral constitution because a pastoral constitution was also a conciliar novelty. No council had previously ever published a pastoral constitution. There were always doctrinal and/or disciplinary documents. It was clear to everyone what these were about. Hence the question is: what is the meaning of pastoral constitution and which kind of authority can it claim? The new orientation posed therefore a basic theological problem of method. For this reason the Council could agree on the title 'pastoral constitution' only after long debates. A special comment on the title made it clear that the pastoral character of the constitution rests on the principles of doctrine and that the constitution also has a doctrinal intention and is to be interpreted according to generally applicable theological interpretation rules.

Yet, this is only where the problem begins. The question is indeed: what is meant by 'the modern world'? The Council speaks of the 'signs of the times'. However, how are they to be determined and how is their relation to the theological principles to be determined?[133] How are the doctrinal principles and the modern world to be related to each other? How does the anthropocentricity of the pastoral constitution relate to the Christocentrism explicitly expressed elsewhere?[134]

Concerning this point, the Council did not think through to the end the question it raised itself – or, to be more precise, it could not think it through to the end. Opinions of interpreters and in theology in general differ until today about unresolved questions in the pastoral constitution.[135] In this way, the pastoral constitution highlights a problem which exists undeniably in the changed socio-cultural situation. However, it also confronts us with basic problems which it could raise but not fully resolve. What is missing in the pastoral constitution is a pneumatology. It is for the Holy Spirit to make the singular, for the relation to the world decisive, Christ-reality present in the Church and in the history of the world.[136] In this respect the rules for discerning the spirits are also significant for the question about dialogue with the world.[137] Ultimately, this is not about history as norm but as concrete place of theology, proclamation and Christian life.

What does 'modern world' mean?

When the Council speaks of the 'world', it does not, in line with its intention, think of the world as cosmos or universe, nor in the philosophical sense as the embodiment of all reality. It is about the world of humans, the human family which lives in the entirety of reality.[138] 'For the human person deserves to be preserved; human society deserves to be renewed. Hence the focal point of our total presentation will be man himself, whole and entire, body and soul, heart and conscience, mind and will.'[139] The focus of the pastoral council is an anthropocentric understanding of the world, the world as family, as cultural, social, economic and political world of modern humanity.

This anthropocentric understanding of the world is also in the background of the pastoral constitution's understanding of culture.[140] It was not the task of the Council to give a definition of the term 'culture'. Opinions on this problem differ substantially in the respective sciences.[141] In light of its objective the Council was not primarily concerned, as the German use of language might suggest, with 'sophisticated culture' (such as literature, art, law, science and so forth). Instead, it was focused on today's much more comprehensive family, cultural, social, economic and political world – in other words, today's culture of life, which is socially, aesthetically, spiritually and religiously differentiated, sophisticated and refined in the 'high culture'.

The same applies when the Council speaks of the 'modern world'. Again, one may not expect from the Council a comprehensive definition of the nature of modernity. Considering the complexity of modernity, such a definition is controversial in the history of philosophy and culture and is determined by each position.[142] The Council was concerned with the modern world in which we find ourselves and to which we as Christians must relate. Already the opening lines of the constitution show a distinct turn from the antimodernist mentality of the nineteenth century and the first decades of the twentieth century and the attempt to reach a constructive, though not uncritical, dialogical relation with the modern world and its culture.[143] Thus, the Council positively described various features of the modern world: its dynamic and evolutionary understanding, the growing socialization, personalization, communication and others. It acknowledged explicitly the positive humanitarian achievements of the modern world, in particular progress in the history of freedom, the freedom of religion,[144] human rights,[145] the recognition of the same dignity of men and women,[146] the legitimate autonomy of temporal cultural spheres,[147] the separation of Church and State and together with it the Church's renunciation of secular power and privileges.[148]

Nevertheless, in spite of any positive assessment of the modern world, the Council did not conceal critical aspects of today's world.[149] The Council knows the ambivalence of the modern world, crises of growth and disturbance of balance.[150] It counts atheism among the most serious facts of the present time[151] and complains about secular, indeed anti-religious humanism.[152] In the meantime the negative aspects of modern culture have become more apparent. John Paul II spoke in fact of a civilization of death and a conspiracy against life.[153] These are strong words. However, this critical view is found not only on the side of the Church, but also among many quite different modern thinkers.[154] Who wants to be modern and get into conversation with modernity, must also recognize criticism of modernity. Max Horkheimer and Theodor W. Adorno presented the *Dialectic of Enlightenment*[155] according to which each progress entails at the same time also a step back and a loss. Along similar lines, Jürgen Habermas and Joseph Ratzinger speak of the *Dialectics of Secularization*.[156] Habermas defends the unfinished project of Enlightenment, but speaks at the same time of a derailing modernity.[157] Modern subjectivity is in danger of turning into an objectivizing – in other words, a reification – of man and into a socially ruthless individualism, into immense injustice and a growing gap between poor and rich, into reckless exploitation of nature and destruction of the ecological balance, into practical materialism, into relativism down to nihilism.

In other words, since the eighteenth century, a new attitude towards life and new civilization have developed against the 'old' European culture. The positive sides of this must be acknowledged. Yet, they are also deeply ambivalent and can, as happened in the totalitarian systems of the twentieth century, turn into new barbarism. Even where this is not the case, the new civilization often tries to live as if God did not exist.[158] It is often indifferent and hostile towards Christianity. Therefore, the dialogue of the Church with modern culture must not be naïve. It does not help to replace anti-modernism with a modernistic cultural optimism. As little as the decadence model does justice to the modern world, so little does the progress model. What we call the 'modern world' is multifaceted and ambivalent.

The Church and the modern world

The dialogue with the multifaceted modern culture which the Council initiated was especially close to the heart of Paul VI. He considered the break between the Church and modern culture to be the drama of our epoch. Therefore, he called for a new evangelization of culture.[159] Following the preaching of the apostle Paul at Areopagus in Athens (Acts 17.22–31), Pope John Paul II spoke of a new missionizing of the modern areopaguses, the world of communication, of science and of the engagement for peace and development.[160] Pope Benedict XVI continued this question and deepened it. In his Regensburg lecture he took up the fundamental topic of faith and knowledge and he has stressed its importance since then.[161]

The dialogue of the Church and the Christians with the modern world and its culture has many aspects and contains many fields, for examples, with art and culture, science and economy, politics, media, and many more. The pastoral constitution and the many documents of the Church since then have addressed and dealt with this extensively. Each of these individual fields of dialogue raises its own specific problems which cannot be addressed in this context.[162] For the theologian, the prime consideration of the dialogue must be the question of God.[163] The God crisis is ultimately the root of the crisis of humanity, society and, as much as they are mutually dependent in some respects, the church crisis.

It was only by proceeding from the biblical understanding of God that the Council was able to recognize the legitimate concern of modern secularity. Because God is not a part of this world but is subliminally above all worldly things and distinct from it, and because he is present as the transcendent one in all reality and can be found in all things, he does not annihilate their own creaturely being but establishes it. In particular, to humanity he grants freedom. Yet, as soon as the reality becomes detached from its founding basc and secularity becomes secularism, a spiritual vacuum emerges in which everything becomes devoid of basis and sense. We are experiencing this vacuum at present. New religious trends or an intolerant and thereby absolutizing secularism – a contradiction in terms – try to enter this vacuum, implant themselves there and fill it. Whenever humanity itself becomes the ultimate point of reference, the result is egoism and disunity. If the final fulfilment of humanity, which can ultimately only be God, is lost, then the individual is left to pursue fortune wherever it might be found, or will renounce it in resignation. Godforsakenness leads inevitably to human self-forsakenness and to the decline of true human greatness. The death of God has not, as Nietzsche had hoped, led to the true life, but to the death of humanity.[164]

It is thus the first and most important task of the Church to remind humanity that God is the ground, goal and content of life and the guarantor of the dignity of every human person. The passion for the ever-greater God will then also become the passion for the dignity of every person and for justice among all people. To understand the world and life in light of God does not by any means entail falling back into the pre-modern period. Indeed a theological understanding leads, without turning into a one-dimensional secularism, to an affirmation of the world as secular world reality. So the Church can accept modernity as a positive development and, at the same time, prevent modernity from the threatening destruction of itself by itself.[165]

Inculturation as Passover event

The dialogue between the Church and culture cannot restrict itself to Europe and the European culture crisis. Since the Second Vatican Council, the Church has become, in a new and concrete sense, a worldwide church and is confronted with the whole diversity of cultures in today's world. The motto is: inculturation of Christianity into the different cultures. What does this mean?

The term inculturation is a neologism that expresses something very old.[166] We find it already in the Old and New Testaments, in Israel's encounter with the surrounding Canaanite and later Hellenistic culture, in the transition from Jewish to gentile Christianity, in the encounter of Christianity with the Hellenistic-Roman culture and later in the encounter with the Germanic peoples, with the Slavs, the China mission of Matteo Ricci and the mission of India by Roberto Nobili in the seventeenth century, which, unfortunately, had to be abandoned because of disputes over rites that threatened the missionization of Asia. Since Vatican II, inculturation has been a fixed component of doctrinal statements.[167]

In contrast to sheer acculturation, inculturation does not mean adaptation to an existing culture or taking over individual set pieces or individual rites, symbols, ways of living and especially the language of this culture, as much as this may evidently also be important. Inculturation means the permeation of a culture. This is not to say, however, that Christianity must be, as it were, culturally 'pitted', its centre then replaced by another culture. Christianity is never without culture. In each case it has a Judaeo-Christian, Hellenistic, Latin, Romanic, Germanic, Slavic or other cultural form. Inculturation occurs as transculturation, as a complicated and complex process of cultural encounter whereby Christianity does not only adopt language in individual cultural forms, but like leaven it permeates the other culture from inside, purifies it and forms it anew, as conversely Christianity thereby adopts legitimate values of another culture and so itself is enriched. In other words, inculturation is a complex historical event.

Theologically, one can speak concerning inculturation of a Passover event that occurs according to the law of death and resurrection in the Holy Spirit. It is about a kind of baptism where the old must die so the new can emerge, whereby the new does not simply destroy the old but it is lifted up in a threefold sense: it is purified, kept and brought to its innermost fulfilment. Dialogue proceeds in three steps: recognizing and keeping – purifying – fulfilling.[168]

It is obvious that the question of inculturation does not only apply to Africa, Asia and other non-European continents, but also in a special way to Europe itself. After the collapse of modern belief in progress, after the catastrophes of the twentieth century and the culture crisis of Europe at the end of the twentieth and the beginning of the twenty-first century, Europe is in need of a new evangelization and, in this context, a new inculturation of Christianity.[169] Our world needs again the breath and drive of hope, it needs orientation towards the true and great goals of humanity and it needs the magnanimousness overcoming of timidity, of the daring of great things and the making of sacrifices necessary for the accomplishment of great goals.

Small cells as biotopes of cultural renewal

In the modernism and anti-modernism crisis at the end of the nineteenth and the beginning of the twentieth century, open-minded laypeople and theologians aware of the problems stood up for an opening of the Catholic Church towards modern culture and for a renewal of Catholic culture.[170] After the end of the bourgeois age, the *Bündische Jugend* [German Catholic youth movement, T.H.] also wanted to contribute to a new, Christian way of living and thus also to a renewal of culture. This movement was brutally interrupted by National Socialism and the Second World War.[171]

After the crisis of European culture which has become manifest since then, this impulse cannot be simply repeated or continued. There can be even less a new retreat into a supposedly intact separate Catholic world. It is to be hoped that today we will also be given men and women who have something to say based on their Catholic faith in theological and secular sciences, in economy and politics, to say something that may sound alternative in many respects and that precisely through this makes people listen and convinces them. It will never be the masses but always individuals who begin with this.

Ultimately, only the lived message can convince. Therefore, small groups, which can also be called creative minorities, are of great significance today. They can become biotopes for a new culture and a new style of life.[172] They can be cells preparing the way for a new, the legitimate autonomy respecting, holistic and theonomic humanism. This way will not be the broad and easy road on which the masses move. It is the small and steep path the Gospel shows us (Mt. 7.13f.). Yet, it is in fact from here that new radiance and appeal can emanate.

This can be individual families, small communities, spiritual centres and monasteries. Already in the past, monasteries were, during critical transition periods, important bearers of culture and cells from which new Christian life sprang forth. They can be this again today, not by secularizing, but by living out vocations in radical and simultaneously holistic ways. The Church can make its contribution to a renewal of culture especially by inspiring and encouraging such oases and biotopes, and by providing them space in which the Christian alternative can be lived invitingly and where it can be convincingly experienced. In this it makes a contribution for the continuation and renewal of a positive human culture and for a new humanism that emerges from out of the spirit of the Gospel.

The testimony of the martyrs

Concerning the dialogue of the Church with the world, one should not have too many illusions, as if there could ever be a more or less perfect harmony between Church and world and Church and culture. Any attempt at a cultural synthesis and a reconciliation between Church and any culture founders because of the reality of sin and the structures of sin in the world and in the Church. Any such attempt will sooner or later be impeded by the reality of the cross. The Church remains within history the Church on the way. It proceeds on the path of Passover which again and again should lead through the cross to the splendour of Easter and the new creation. The final reconciliation and transfiguration of the world can only be effected by God when in the end he will be all in all (1 Cor. 15.28).

The apocalyptic message of the Bible even expects a dramatic apocalyptic intensification of the conflict between God's kingdom and the kingdom of 'this world' (understood in the sense of John's gospel). Our present time is also characterized by this. Thus, unlike any other century, the twentieth century was a century of martyrs, especially in Mexico, Spain, under National Socialism, Communism, in China and many other countries of the Third World. So far this history of martyrs has continued in the twenty-first century. At present Christians are the most persecuted or suppressed group worldwide. It has to suffice just to mention a few famous names out of the uncountable host of martyrs: Maximilian Kolbe, Edith Stein, Alfred Delp, Dietrich Bonhoeffer, Paul Schneider, Metropolitan Serafim, Oscar Romero.[173]

The martyrs resisted those systems that despised the togetherness of God and humanity on the bases of race, class and state and the will to destroy the Church and Christianity. Because of their Christian faith, they were witnesses of Christian freedom and hope for the victory of life over death, of truth over lie, and of love over brutal violence. If the blood of martyrs is the seed for new Christians,[174] then the blood of so many martyrs in the last century can be a reason to hope for a renewed Church in the new twenty-first century.

7

Whither the way of the Church?

After looking back through the course of the history of the Church and the theology of the last century and the beginning of the new one, and after exploring the nature and the mission of the Church, we must finally ask: how can it and how will it go on with the Church? *Whither* the Church?[1]

A complex and multi-layered crisis

In view of the undeniable crisis and numerical decline in church membership in Western Europe, many Christians are worried and ask about the future of the Church. The answer to this question is only possible if one asks first about the causes of this situation, which are multi-layered. Obviously there is accumulated anger about individual incidents and decisions as well as about lacking communication and involvement in decisions. Above all, there is a confidence crisis caused by the terrible abuse scandals that have recently become public. All this must be taken very seriously. Yet, all these are occasions in which worries and anger are articulated and feelings about deeper and often unspoken causes are vented.

The underlying cause is that an epoch of church history is coming to an end, while new perspectives are emerging concerning how and toward what end the Church will move forward.[2] Not surprisingly, fears abound. The milieu-supported *Volkskirche* as it developed at the beginning of the nineteenth century and after the end of the imperial church is coming to an end. These days, being Christian and church membership are no longer supported by the milieu and no longer practically self-evident, but are a matter of personal decision. This leads to a decrease in the number of practising faithful and, almost inevitably, to a decrease in spiritual vocations, in particular vocations to the priesthood. Together, the declining number of faithful and the resulting lack of priests cause problems for the system of parishes and pastoral care as it grew in the time of the *Volkskirche*.[3] The parish is no longer the spiritual home. Many therefore feel neglected and homeless in the Church and ask how it is to go on. This question makes laypeople and priests worry about the future. The ecclesiastical ministry has yet to succeed in developing a convincing perspective for the future.

If one looks even deeper, then one has to speak of a darkening of God in our time and of a crisis of faith and God which very generally reflects the crisis of our Western civilization and which, among others, has led to the church crisis. That this is not only the opinion of theologians is highlighted, besides many others, by Friedrich Nietzsche's word of the death of God, Martin Heidegger's hint of an absence of God and Martin Buber speaking of an eclipse of God.[4] Errors and misbehaviour in the Church have undoubtedly contributed to the fact that it could have come this far. Yet, the roots for the crisis of faith and God are deeper and reach further back into the European history of ideas.[5] From the perspective of human history, Europe has thereby gone its own special way, and it is by no means clear if it will end well.

Courage for the future

Obviously, no one can predict the future. No individual or group, influential and powerful as they may be at the moment, can determine the course of events in the long run. For people of faith, the future lies in God's hand, while, from a human perspective, the future results from many, unpredictable free decisions. Each generation looks at the world with different eyes and develops its own lifestyle. Thus not only external conditions of life change, but also mentalities and attitudes often change quickly – for good or bad. Hence, the future is never just the continuation of that which was and which is and it does not merely result from an extrapolation of often short-lived present trends. Predictions about the future often have a short expiry date.

This applies in a double sense when we look at concrete prognoses about the future of the Church. It is promised to the Church that the powers of darkness will not overpower it and that it will exist until the end of time (Mt. 16.18; 24.20). The Holy Spirit is promised to the Church; it is the Spirit that guides and leads it (Jn 14.26; 15.26; 16.13). As Christians we have the irrevocable certainty that the Church will be and it will be until the end of time; the Church will always be one and the same Church of Jesus Christ as it has existed throughout all centuries. Finally, since the creation the question about God is written into the hearts of man (Rom. 1.19f.). Humans can keep it down or suppress it, but it will make itself felt again and again, even though unfortunately often in a distorted form.[6] For those who believe, there is no reason for pessimism, resignation and panic. Even though no one can predict the concrete future of the Church, for Christians it is basically not uncertain.

Like the Christian faith in general, this confidence cannot be proven. It is a matter of faith. There are good reasons for it, yet they can be completely convincing only in the light of faith and in a global personal decision. Thus, the Church would be hopelessly overtaxed if it intended to prove itself by a shining renewed form. This would be nothing but triumphalism in a new style. Under the sign of the Cross, the Church will always remain a cause for umbrage, a *scandalum*. Still, the scandal of the Cross, written into the nature of the Church and essential to its nature, must not become an excuse for self-inflicted, unnecessary scandals or obstacles to faith. Instead, the Church must time and time again go the way of renewal and reform.[7] In today's critical transition situation this is even more urgent and necessary. It is only through renewal and reform that the Church can radiate courage for the future to people of good will.

Partings and departures

The courage of the Church for the future is not based on battalions, financial power or political influence. All this pertains to times past which, in this respect, we do not have to mourn. On the contrary, the loss of secular power which came with the end of the Constantine era is a liberation from a lot of ballast. There is probably still rather too much of this ballast in Germany. After the end of the imperial church and the subsequent separation of Church and State, from a universal Church perspective the church in Germany set out a special way that had many things supporting it and which brought many advantages for both sides. Yet, in view of decreasing numbers of church members on the one hand and, on the other, considering the increased religio-ideological pluralism in society, we cannot expect realistically that everything will continue as before. The rich endowment of the church in Germany is not only a good thing, but also brings the danger of institutional, personal, bureaucratic and lordly behaviour and procedures that accord to those of the secular world but not to the image of the Church of the future as the Second Vatican Council outlined it.

In the future, we will thus have to leave behind many things we are used to and which are dear to us. Outwardly, the Church of the future will be poorer. As in the beginning it will be a diaspora church, and, if we are not completely mistaken, will be smaller in numbers in Europe, in a world which has become pluralistic. There are many reasons to believe that it will become a – hopefully – qualitative and creative minority. Many of the new churches built during the years of plenty will be too big. Yet, was this not also true for the medieval cathedrals? Some churches will be closed and used for other purposes. The structure of our parishes will change. Many of the great and beneficial charitable and social institutions will have to be rededicated. This parting and this change have long since begun.

Every parting is difficult. Yet, parting is only hopeless if it does not become a new departure. Announced as the century of the Church, the twentieth century was not only a century of collapses and destruction but, with the liturgical, biblical, patristic and pastoral renewal movements, it was also a century of important and further leading departures. Through this we have rediscovered many hidden treasures of Tradition: Holy Scripture, liturgy, the Church Fathers. The Second Vatican Council adopted the insights given to us by God's Spirit and initiated a renewal from the origin. It rediscovered the Church as people of God and as *communio* and highlighted anew the co-responsibility of the laity. It broke open some historically conditioned narrowness and led it back to the original catholic breadth. Therefore we could build new bridges to the Oriental-Orthodox, the Orthodox and the Protestant churches and communities and to all people of good will. Finally, the Council consciously accepted the end of the Constantine era. It renounced secular privileges[8] and, in an unfortunately too little-recognized and notably little-quoted passage of the constitution on the Church, it established the model of a poor church for and with the poor.[9]

Out of the spirit of a two-thousand-year-old Tradition, the documents of the Council have given us a compass for the way into the future of the new century and millennium. Some of the seed has already grown and bears good fruit in parishes, and in old and new communities. In addition there are manifold post-conciliar beginnings. The Church after the Council is not the spiritual desert as some would like to depict it, but is young and vibrant, more alive than its critics and detractors think.

The rich treasures and the many inspirations of the Council are far from being exhausted. Many insights of the Council have been only too hesitatingly realized by the post-conciliar reception, whereas others have been buried, misinterpreted and abused. Some great ideas have been reduced to a few slogans and standard demands. They have become campaign slogans in the disputes between the different groups within the Church. As a result, the conciliar dynamic has slackened and has largely become lost. Besides renewal, the twentieth century, which had been announced as the century of the Church, also led to crises and distortions in the awareness and life of the Church. A certain paralysis and stagnation have appeared. There is a need for a new departure.

This departure is necessary in a situation that has substantially changed since the immediate post-conciliar period of the 1970s. The institutional reform issues often raised since then will not do justice on their own to the new social and cultural problem situation and in particular not to the faith and God crisis manifested since then. We will have to go deeper. A new beginning is only possible if, similar to the movements leading to Vatican II, three things come together: a spiritual renewal nourished from the sources, solid theological reflection, and an ecclesial spirit.

The Church – 'black, but beautiful'

Does the Church have the power for such a departure? On the face of the Church there are many stains and wrinkles mirroring the trouble and toil, and also some failure in the two thousand years of its history. The Church also suffers today from scandals, inner crises and weaknesses. The Church acknowledges this and confesses the guilt it has heaped on itself. It does this not only in an individual public *Mea culpa*; it does it every day hundreds of thousands of times at the beginning of each celebration of the Eucharist. It can do that because it believes in forgiveness and the grace of a new beginning. It knows that from the supposedly dead root new life can and will awaken (Isa. 11.1).

Thus the Church has weathered many storms in its history. It has often been cruelly persecuted, but it survived all its persecutors from Nero to Stalin, Hitler and Mao and all seemingly powerful, hostile regimes. Neither is today the first time that it has experienced an inner crisis. It has often been declared dead and the death bell has been rung for it. Time and again it has renewed itself and then shown new life and new energy. It has often been despised, but its cultural achievements are also admired until today by its greatest despisers. It has often suffered inner crises and substantial scandals, but it has renewed itself again and up to the present it has produced uncountable holy men and women, many who let themselves be consumed in the ministry for the poorest of the poor. The Church is black, but beautiful (Song 1.5).

Not least, power and strength, which are also present in today's Church, become obvious in the number of martyrs, countable only in thousands, of the past and the beginning of this century.[10] They did not bend their knees in front of tyrants or new idols. They put up resistance and for their faith they accepted prison and camps, humiliation and torture and finally death. At present, Christians are the most persecuted group of people in the world. As always before, the blood of martyrs has proven to be the seed of new Christians. So, finally, the countless martyrs of the past as well as of the current century are the reason for the hope that their rich seed will grow in the new century and millennium.

The lasting relevance of Christianity and the Church

At the beginning of the new century and millennium, the challenges faced not only by Christianity but also by mankind are enormous and they are global. Rapid scientific and technological developments increasingly invade the mystery of life and make it manipulable; mankind becoming one in the process of globalization contains many open and even more hidden conflicts of a clash of ethnic groups, cultures and religions. The question of peace and security depends on whether we reach a relatively just and solidary distribution of the goods of this world belonging to all people and to a universal respect for the basic human rights. In addition, there are problems of the environment and the natural balance of the earth, in other words of keeping the creation as an environment worth living in for humans. Finally, because of the modern information and communication media, there is the flood of information that no one can cope with sensibly, in which reality and its medial representation become blurred and which is thereby exposed to manifold manipulations. The list of upcoming problems could easily be extended.

The drama of the situation is even bigger as we live in a spiritually poor time lacking great ideas, ideals and vision which are necessary for meeting the challenges. The ideologies and utopias of the nineteenth and first half of the twentieth centuries are exhausted. They discredited themselves in the catastrophes of the twentieth century. Any attempt to get them back out of the junk room of the history of ideas, as attempted by some versions of the new atheism, can be nothing more than a final gasp of past and overcome powers and can only lead us deeper into the catastrophe again. Wherever one looks, the spiritual and moral resources which are necessary for coping with the enormous problems and challenges have become scarce, so resignation and scepticism are spreading.

According to attentive observers outside the Church,[11] at least in our cultural sphere, but also because of the global interconnection of the problems far beyond that, the Church is the only instance that knows how to proclaim a message of the kingdom of God begun in Jesus Christ which can be light of the world (*Lumen gentium*) and which can radiate joy and hope (*Gaudium et spes*). It is a message of hope which today has become a scarce commodity. This message is not averse to reason; it is not merely a dream or a sheer utopia. It searches for and desires understanding. This message can be rationally deciphered and lifted up into understanding. From it perspectives result for building a just, solidary and peaceful world and a future for all. It may not have specific technological, economic and political answers to offer, but it shows us the direction where such answers are possible and it gives us simultaneously confidence and courage to search for solutions in this direction and also to find them. It provides power which pushes and motivates to cope with the upcoming problems. Therefore the Church has become anything but superfluous and irrelevant.

The Church as eschatological sign

Ultimately, however, the future of the Church cannot be explained and justified by the relevance of a solution to the upcoming problems of humanity. Relevance comes only through identity. A church that perceived and justified itself only as a political icebreaker, as a social service agency or even responsible for holistic human wellness as 'feel-good' church, such a church would be exchangeable and replaceable. The Church cannot borrow its identity from somewhere else. It cannot base itself on other movements, conform or live on credit. If the Church tested such options it would become a reed shaken by the wind, which is driven to and from and eventually toppled over by each gush of opinions and the appearance of new fashion.

The Church can only have relevance and future if it is distinctive, if it has identity in itself and knows who and what it is as Church. The Church has received such identity only as the Church of Jesus Christ, that is, only from God who reveals himself to the Church through Jesus Christ in the Holy Spirit. This is expressed in the images of the people of God, body of Christ, house of the Holy Spirit and other metaphors. The Church has its identity as an eschatological sign, as a quasi-sacramental representation of the eschaton, of that which itself is the final ground and goal of all reality. For this reason, ecclesiology is only possible as theology, which means, in the horizon of the question of God. This question is the problem and also the promise which is, not only today, the linchpin of everything.

'Eschatological sign' means that the Church is not itself the eschaton. It is not God's kingdom on earth. Yet, it is also not just a hidden church, which is only present in events here and there. It is institution and event and, as such, sign and instrument of God's kingdom already breaking into the present. Despite all weakness and sometimes also sluggishness, as *sacramentum futuri* something even now shines in its earthly form, especially in its liturgy, of the splendour and beauty of God who in the end will be all in all (1 Cor. 15.28).

As eschatological sign the Church becomes necessarily a sign of contradiction, and if I am not completely mistaken, the controversy between the kingdom of God and the realm of this world enters today into a new dramatic phase. We should have no illusions about this. The powers of godlessness and evil also storm today against the Church and are also partly at work within the Church. The Church of the future can do nothing but stand beneath the sign of the Cross.

In our situation, the Church becomes a prophetic-critical sign against the inner-worldly secularism that thinks it can cope with life out of personal insights and achievements and that believes it can plan for and forge the fortune of life on its own. The Church becomes a prophetic-critical sign against egoism, individualism and hedonism seeking only its own advantage and the satisfaction of momentary needs and no longer having any sense of solidarity and the common good of all. Finally, it becomes the prophetic-critical sign against the spreading banalization of human existence which, like Nietzsche's last man, is satisfied lowbrow with small happiness and no longer sees a star shining above life.[12] The challenges of this humanism without God and of the life as if God did not exist, as well as the conflicts resulting therefrom, whether welcome or unwelcome (2 Tim. 4.2), must be faced. The Church must prove itself in these controversies as a sign and a safeguard of the transcendence of the human person.[13]

Three priorities

So, what should and can we do? Some external aesthetic surgery, a mere face-lifting, will not suffice. Likewise, useful as they may be, it will not be enough simply to adopt modern methods of communication. It helps little to paint over the façade if the fundaments have become fragile, and improved methods of communication do not help much if the content has become unclear and devoid of substance. We must have no illusions: institutional reforms alone and without spiritual renewal are of little use. All that is often demanded in this respect has long since been realized by other churches. Nevertheless, with respect to the basic question 'how can the Church be today and witness the message of God today?' they are by no means better off. We must start deeper – not more liberal, but more radical.

I restrict myself to three priorities:

First, in a situation in which God seems to be dead for many and in which many believe that they can live without God, the Church needs the courage to speak again of God and to witness him as the foundation and goal of all reality and as fulfilment of human striving and longing and as the true happiness of life.[14] The God crisis or, as one might say as well, the darkness or eclipse of God, is the fundamental crisis of the present time. It is this crisis that the Church must address first. After all, the Church is not to witness to itself and to continuously speak only of itself. It is not that interesting, and it can never truly be interesting for outsiders. It is only the sign and instrument of God's presence amidst our lives whoever is not interested in God will be uninterested in the Church as well. God holds and carries all. Without him everything falls back into nothingness. Without the living God everything else is in the air, and starts to crumble and collapse.

The message of God is not a message of fear. From the very beginning of God's history with humanity there has been a promise of blessing for all generations of the earth (Gen. 12.2f.), a promise that God is there, i.e. that he is with us and among us (Exod. 3.14), and that he is this finally and unsurpassably in Jesus Christ. So, the message of God is one of hope and life, a message that lets us breathe and gives courage, but only if we do not belittle it, play it down or trivialize it. The beginning of wisdom is the fear of the Lord (Ps. 111.10; Prov. 1.7; 9.10). Fear in this context does not mean fright but reverence, reverence before God as the holy one, the one beyond all that is merely temporal. God is also the one who resists all injustice, violence and lies, and who takes an account of each person in such a way that all masks are removed and everyone is viewed equally. Finally, he is the one who ultimately establishes justice, truth, life and love. Only the one who knows of the holiness of God and of his judgement over all injustice, lies and hard-heartedness can comprehend the message of infinite mercy, grace and love in all its inscrutability and incomprehensibility as the message of hope for a different and new life.

So we must again reflect and consider the first commandment (Exod. 20.2–6; Deut. 5.6–10) and liberate ourselves from the dead tin gods and idols, which we created to suit ourselves, from the ideologies and utopias, from our hubris, self-delusion and falsehoods, and we must convert to the true and living God (1 Thess. 1.9). We must take seriously the main commandment of Jesus and love God with all our heart and mind and all our strength (Mk 12.29f. par). It is only to him that we can give undivided love, and in this love, become free within ourselves from all other claims to absoluteness, free also from ourselves and from others. It is only in this way that we as Church can be not only a people but the people of God. We need new joy in God and new enthusiasm for him. In our largely secularized world we need to make a theocentric turn.

There is a second point. The message of God is not about some vague feeling, some highest being, a vague transcendence or a mixed potpourri drawn from out of all religions. It is about the God of Abraham, Isaac and Jacob, the God who appeared concretely on the human countenance of Jesus Christ, and who, in Jesus Christ, became man among us humans. As Pope John Paul II said in his programme for the third millennium, we must begin anew from Jesus Christ.[15] This has been the programme of all renewal and reform movements in the course of church history, not least that of Francis of Assisi. There can be no other programme today. For no one can lay down any other foundation than the one which is there already, namely Jesus Christ (1 Cor. 3.11).

The opening words of Vatican II's constitution on the Church highlight this all-decisive point. They are: '*lumen gentium cum sit Christus*', 'Christ is the light of the nations.' It is not the Church that is the light of the nations. The Church is not in the centre. It must not desire to shine. Instead, Christ is to shine and radiate through it. The Church is like the moon that only reflects the light it receives from the sun. Hence, the Church can only have a future if it radiates Jesus Christ and his message of the coming kingdom of God.

To bring Jesus close to today's people, it does not help to tailor him according to our human standards or even to utilize him for our personal or political goals. We must not turn Jesus into a good man, a rabbi or wisdom teacher, or depict him as an idealist or social revolutionary, or make him one founder of religions among others. Even though he had something of all of them, in this we are far from grasping the centre of his being, his unique relationship to the one whom he called his father. It is only in this way that Jesus is a novelty. He exceeds all of our bounds and, precisely in this, he liberates us from the dictatorship of that which determines today's zeitgeist and is considered as politically correct. The beatitudes of the sermon on the mount are the true revolution. We must hear Jesus' demand to the full and must not leave out what was objectionable already for Jesus' contemporaries. We can weather the passion stories of our time only if we join with him in the night of his passion in order to go with him on the path to the resurrection to a new life. We must let ourselves be newly invited to the way of following him in order to live out of his friendship. The theocentric turn thus leads us to the Christological concentration.

Thirdly and finally. Jesus Christ did not simply live two thousand years ago and then depart from us. He lives and continues to work through the

Holy Spirit in the Church and in the world. So the Church is more than an institution; it is as institution time and again a new event in the Holy Spirit.[16] It becomes new each time the word of God is proclaimed as the light of life and when it is accepted in faith, when the liturgy is celebrated and the sacraments are administered and the service of the Samaritan is performed for the sick and the dying, for helpless, searching and frightened people and for people living on the edge of our society. Church is where two or three come together in the name of Jesus. Church occurs daily in thousands and thousands of different ways.

As the creation of the Holy Spirit, the Church needs today first and foremost a spiritual renewal. The apostle admonishes: 'do not stifle the Spirit' (1 Thess. 5.19).

Spiritual renewal does not mean some pseudo-charismatic excitement involving constantly new events, causing momentary emotional enthusiasm, but which are in fact nothing but a flash in the pan and quickly die away. As long as the fire does not burn deep down in the quiet of the heart and become embers, the spectacle and bustle of large events are of no use. It needs saintly Christians. For this is God's will: our sanctification (1 Thess. 4.3). This means that the Church should strive to do exceptional things, but to do normal things with exceptional dedication and faithfulness. It is about greater love which is the fulfilment of the whole law (Rom. 13.10) and the bond of perfection (Col. 3.14). Where this love is absent, everything else is of no use and simply a gong booming or a cymbal clashing (1 Cor. 13.1).

The Church of tomorrow cannot be a church as liberal as possible. Instead it is to be, in the original sense of the word, radical – that is, a church renewed from its roots (*radix*) which lives out of the word of God and the sacraments, out of prayer, out of the spirit of repentance and penance, in the service of others and which orientates itself at the beatitudes of the sermon on the mount. Thank God that today there are not only signs of crisis but also signs of spiritual renewal and encouraging evidence of spiritual departures and selfless commitment for the poorest of the poor. In this way, the theocentric turn and the Christological concentration should become fruitful in a spiritual deepening.

The programmatic slogan 'new evangelization'

The new evangelization is about this threefold vision. It is the decisive slogan for the renewal of the Church. In this we are on solid ground because Gospel and evangelization are foundational words of Jesus' message and of the New Testament. The new evangelization, initiated by Pope John Paul II and adopted by Pope Benedict XVI, therefore takes up an old and originally biblical basic concern in a new way.[17]

In a new way – that means it is not about re-evangelization, nor a return to a previous epoch or a Reconquista, a militant reconquering. The long era of the unity between spiritual and temporal order, as it existed in antiquity, the Middle Ages and far into modern times, is irretrievably over. We must face the modern and postmodern situation. Taking the modern situation seriously does not mean to assimilate to it uncritically but to engage with it in a critical-constructive way. The Second Vatican Council did this when it took up basic modern concerns in an independent, critical and further leading way. So it acknowledged the freedom of religion as a basic, universal human right and with the independence of the secular departments it acknowledged the legitimate issues of modern secularity. In other words, secular affairs must be dealt with in a secular way according to their factual immanent laws.[18]

The Council could not acknowledge the legitimate concerns of modern secularity through weak assimilation, but only by proceeding from the innermost centre of the Christian message. This speaks of God who is not part of this world but infinitely beyond all worldly things and different from them and who, as the transcendent one, is present in his creation and so does not abolish the independent being of the creational reality but rather gives and leaves humans freedom. In Jesus Christ he became man without confusion and without separation. In other words, God united himself in a unique personal (hypostatic) way with human nature and in a way of grace with each human being, yet in a way that the divine does not absorb the human and also does not mix, but which sets it free in its independence.

Thus the Council could acknowledge the worldliness of the world and its legitimate independence. Yet, as soon as this detaches itself from its foundational basis and secularity turns into secularism, a spiritual vacuum develops in which everything becomes devoid of foundation and meaning. We experience such a vacuum at present in our Western world. New religious trends or an intolerant and thereby absolutizing secularism – a contradiction in terms – try to enter this vacuum, to implant themselves there and to fill it. From this, new challenges arise for the Church. In contrast to the eighteenth or nineteenth centuries, in the twenty-first century the problem is no longer integralism, in other words the Christian and ecclesial total claim combined with clericalism, but secularism wanting to privatize, marginalize and ultimately eliminate everything religious. This challenge is at the same time the chance for the Church today, through the new evangelization, to fill in a Christian way the vacuum and desire of the human heart for something more and for all, ultimately for God. Many people, more than we think, wait for this.

Of course, new evangelization does not mean a new gospel. It wants to express the one and same Gospel of Jesus Christ in this new situation in a new way. It takes up the basic message of Scripture and of the Fathers' Tradition which says that God is a god of humans who wants to live among us, with us and in us and that this being with, at and in God is the ultimate fulfilment and true happiness of man. The basic message expresses itself, as already shown, in the idea of the *communio* of God and man, in the idea of the 'divinization of man' and in the indwelling of the Holy Spirit in us, and finally in the patristic doctrine of the birth of God in man, found again in the mysticism of Meister Eckhart.[19] This message of the fullness of life and hope for eternity can fill the void and, at the same time, the longing of man.

Such new evangelization is not a quickly completed programme of action. It rather initiates a long and laborious process of rethinking and conversion and renewal out of the depth and centre of the Gospel. It leads into a paschal event of the dying of the old life and the resurrection into new life. It is only in this way that there can be a renewal of Europe and a new form of its culture. With this we are only at the beginning of a new beginning.

The new evangelization presupposes self-evangelization. The blind cannot lead the blind (Mt. 15.14). Only inspired people can inspire. Whoever wants to renew the Church must renew themselves and let themselves be excited by the message of God who appeared to us in Jesus Christ and works through the Holy Spirit in the Church and in us. They must let themselves be inspired by a truly catholic vision of the Church as we find it in Holy Scripture, the Church Fathers and at the last Council. Reduced, sociologically narrowed images of the Church will get us nowhere. Finally, nobody can convince, even less inspire others with a know-it-all critique and lamenting suffering at the Church. One has to love the Church with all its spots and wrinkles, just as Christ loved the Church and gave himself up for it (Eph. 5.25).

New joy in faith and in the Church leads by itself to a renewal of missionary consciousness. This is the basic precondition for the new evangelization. There is the saying that the mouth speaks out of the abundance of the heart. We can go even one step further and say: that which fills the heart radiates into the whole life. Who is convinced in faith also becomes a witness of faith, not only through the word but also a witness of action and of life. They speak not only with their mouth but with their whole existence. Such missionary drive has nothing to do with the intrusive making of proselytes. The Church meets every honest conviction with respect. It has every reason to appear self-critical, humble and modest, but it has no reason to become defeatist or to hide. On the contrary, it must get out of the defensive and give witness of its message as a message of life, otherwise it would not be the Church of Jesus Christ. Whoever loses the will to live and grow, decreases and dies in the end. The rediscovery of missionary consciousness is a basic precondition that the Church has a future in the world.

Finally, the new evangelization requires a renewed theology. It must be deeply rooted in Holy Scripture and in the Tradition of the Church. At the same time it must make its 'object' effective and translate it into the present reality of life and culture. The three basic principles with which, at the beginning of the nineteenth century, the Tübingen School helped to overcome the spirit of the Enlightenment and to initiate an ecclesial renewal, remain valid under the new conditions at the beginning of the twenty-first century: scholarly rigour, ecclesial faithfulness, and critical constructive contemporaneousness.[20]

Martyria, leiturgia, diakonia

What we need in the new evangelization are not all various kinds of new pastoral special programmes, nor must we get distracted and concentrate on minor or peripheral questions. We should concentrate our powers on the essential and fundamental and undertake with new energy what happens anyway; we should build the Church into the future through *martyria, leiturgia, diakonia.*

As for Jesus and the apostles, the first accent is on *martyria*, the missionary proclamation. For this the sermon is still decisive. Here the Church still has a chance that no other social group has: Sunday after Sunday it can reach millions of people and witness to them the good news of the Gospel – not as an abstract doctrine, but as a message of life and for life. This does not require any rhetorical gems such as funny ideas and introductions. Rather, what people need is the substantial brown bread of the Gospel, which, if interpreted exegetically and profoundly and close to life, is always interesting, surprising, new and relevant.

Admittedly, today we reach only the smaller part of the population to which Sunday morning sermons are directed. But if those whom we reach are 'infected' thereby, they will transmit this message and bring God anew into the conversation in the family and their environment. Thus, evangelization occurs by way of the snowball effect and in concentric circles, face to face, from person to person. The use and utilization of modern media as well as public manifestations can and must be involved as well, but cannot replace personal witnessing.

Such witnessing requires those who stand for the faith not only with their mouth but with their whole existence. Only witnesses can convince. Convincing, however, requires linguistic competence in the faith and solid knowledge about the faith. Hence, since biblical times, catechesis has pertained to missionary proclamation, understood as initiation, as holistic introduction into the faith and into the life of the Church. For how is one to give account of one's hope (1 Pet. 3.15) if one no longer knows the alphabet of faith or if one has become a religious dyslexic? Thus, catechesis has always been a basic task of the Church and it is a basic duty of the ecclesiastical ministry to introduce each new generation and older seeking Christians into the faith and the life of the Church.[21]

Here we have many things that leave a lot to be desired. Religious knowledge and the ability of the majority of Christians to speak and witness has reached a low point. This is no reproach to the many catechists who often do their best. Yet, considering the present state of affairs in most of our parishes and dioceses regarding catechesis for baptism, confession, communion and confirmation, it cannot go on like this if we wish to be responsible. A catechetic renewal in the sense of an introduction into the faith and the life of the Church not only for children but also for adolescents and adults is urgently necessary. Yet, a substantial renewal of the Christian initiation still lies before us.

In addition to *martyria* there is *leiturgia*.[22] Just as the Word becomes incarnate once and for all in Jesus Christ, so it wants to condense again and again in the Church in sacramental signs. The Centre and climax of the life of the Church is the celebration of the liturgy, in particular the Eucharist.[23] Thus, for the new evangelization, what Saint Benedict told his monks in his rule applies: nothing is to be put before the work of God.[24] There may have been external circumstances behind the fact that the Second Vatican Council commenced with the discussion and adoption of the constitution on the liturgy, yet there was also a theological necessity.

The leitmotif of the conciliar liturgical renewal, the full, conscious and active participation of the whole people of God has become the leitmotif for the whole conciliar ecclesial renewal. Post-conciliar liturgical reform has borne much good fruit. The table of the Word is set richer than before and the conscious participation of the people of God in the liturgical celebration has been made easier through a greater transparency of the rites and use of the vernacular. Unfortunately, the implementation of the reforms also caused a certain impoverishment in the symbolic acts and often banalizations too, through which the Eucharist has become reduced to a celebration of the meal and the understanding that liturgy is the presentation of Christ's cross and resurrection and the pre-celebration of the eschatological glorification and adoration of God has become lost. Here, rethinking and further, substantial reforms are necessary. Full, conscious and active participation cannot primarily consist of the broadest possible distribution of liturgical roles. Active and celebratory participation means first of all inner taking part out of the spirit of reverence and adoration.

If liturgy is beautifully celebrated utilizing all available human arts, then it does not require additional explanations or constantly new, original ideas. Liturgy, rather, becomes in itself a source of fascination which attracts and appeals. Augustine gives us a telling example. He describes as he listened in Milan during the liturgy to the hymns and songs: 'The voices flowed into mine ears, and the truth was poured forth into my heart.'[25] The liturgy is therefore not simply an extension of our daily world into the space of the Church. It should, rather, point beyond the grey everyday life, keep at least a glimpse open into the other world of God and give us thus a foretaste of the glory of his kingdom. Where liturgy is celebrated in this way, it becomes evangelization through its language of symbols.

Diakonia is the third aspect of a new evangelization. This was emphasized by two great witnesses of faith of the twentieth century, Dietrich Bonhoeffer and Alfred Delp. They have impressed upon the Church of the twenty-first century that the Church following Jesus does not exist for itself, but instead it must be the Church for others and that it can only have a future as the Church for others.[26] The Church must open up its often bourgeois milieu and in following Jesus it must be Church for others, especially the Church for the poor, the persecuted and all suffering. More precisely, it must be the Church with the poor, with the persecuted and with the suffering. It must be the Church that is compassionate and sensitive to suffering.

This does not mean that the Church should become a kind of social agency and a globally acting relief organization. Obviously, as ecclesial relief organizations do with commitment and success, the Church should work in its own country and globally to its best ability for relieving emergency situations, for a new civilization of sharing and for a globalization not only of economic interest but of solidarity – in a nutshell, for freedom, justice and peace in the world and for protecting Creation. Yet, all these laudable initiatives and activities must radiate the fact that the Church primarily has a spiritual commission. The *diakonia* applies not only to bodily works of mercy, but also to spiritual works of mercy: teaching the unknowing, counselling the doubting, comforting the mourning, admonishing the sinners, forgiving willingly those who insult, tolerating the unpleasant ones, praying for all.[27] Love is purposeless and must not be utilized in a missionary or even proselytic way, but as testimony of action to every such encounter with which it can become evangelization.

In all material support, personal attention must be given preference over structural measures. This also entails that people in difficult situations of life who do not fit into the pattern of the ecclesial order, such as remarried divorcees, can reconcile themselves with the Church in justified individual cases. This presupposes a new order of penance and reconciliation in the Church beyond rigorism and laxism. This is the only way that, for people in difficult situations, the countenance of the merciful God can shine again in the Church.

Diakonia concerns also one's personal lifestyle, not least that of the clergy. The days of a feudal, rich and lordly church are over. They also do not accord with Jesus' own example, who became poor for our sake (2 Cor. 8.9). The representatives of the Church should therefore avoid any impression of wealth and power, following the example of Jesus and for the sake of the Church's credibility. Unfortunately, we have had so far too little reception of what the Second Vatican Council says about this issue of a poor church with the poor. Clearly, poverty is a relative term; it results from a comparison with that which is perceived in each social situation as an adequate standard of living. Considering our situation it is thus more honest to speak of a simple, evangelical-apostolic lifestyle which nevertheless should have form and dignity and should not be confused with formlessness and wastefulness. The simple life in the style of the Gospel as lived by Francis of Assisi and as he gave his brothers in his rule, saved the powerful church at that time from decay. In today's world where there is so much poverty, such testimony of an apostolic lifestyle is again necessary.

The fraternal, dialogical and communicative Church

Martyria, leiturgia and *diakonia* happen in the *communio* of the Church and are expressions of the *communio* of the Church. This brings us back to institutional problems. It would indeed be naive and would contradict the incarnatory nature of Christianity to think spiritual renewal was possible without institutional reforms. Already a look into the history of religious orders highlights that in each case the charisma of the founder of the order, as it were, was placed into the institution of the order to give the charisma lasting permanence. Likewise renewed *communio* ecclesiology must take on institutional form and at the same time keep in mind that institutional reforms without spiritual renewal remain soulless, ultimately dead structures.

To understand the Church as *communio* leads to a communicative, dialogical and fraternal style in the Church which is just as distinct from older imperial, feudal and authoritarian stately patterns of behaviour as from a pseudo-modern bureaucratic style. Both have led to an alienation of many faithful from the Church. Such a social form does not spring from a democratization of the Church, but of a realization of the people of God reality and *communio* reality pertaining to the Church. In this sense the life of the Church today and in future internally and externally should be influenced by a communicative, participatory and dialogical style of fraternity, friendship and trust and by a dialogue culture willing to listen and learn.

To this pertain the reviving and strengthening of synodal institutions in the Church, on the level of the local as well as the universal Church.[28] In this we are only at the beginning of a new way to give the Church a young, fresh face and a renewed form. This renewal is anything but a novelty. It has nothing to do with an occasionally invoked counsel church. As repeatedly demonstrated, it is rather in line with oldest Tradition that must be taken up under today's new conditions in order to overcome in the spirit of the *communio* a one-sided, authoritative-hierarchical style stemming from social patterns that have become obsolete.

Ecclesial *communio* is not, however, the *Fraternité* of the French Revolution. It knows about the constitutive importance of the ecclesiastical office. For *communio* does not produce itself nor come into existence alone through fraternal dialogue. It presupposes reconciliation which is ultimately a gift of the redemption liberating from sinful entanglements. In its opposition to the community the ecclesiastical ministry represents this inner-worldly, not derivable, graceful opposite. It is, therefore, a constitutive service in and for the ecclesial *communio*. Fraternity in the Church cannot exist without spiritual fatherhood. To it *auctoritas* pertains in the original sense of the word, *augere* to grow, and *auctor* which actually means 'multiplier'. So, authority is not to supress life, but to create and increase life, to let life grow and to further life. Today we urgently need such authority, which is derived not only from its official position but also from the power of the personality.

This intertwining and opposition of ministry and community of the Church is necessary at all levels of ecclesial life. On the 'lowest level' of the parish, such communicative and participatory style requires manageable pastoral units. A parish, particularly if in future it covers a larger area, must be a community of communities.[29] This includes house and base communities which are biotopes of faith in which Christian life is experienced and lived and where active participation in ecclesial life can be concretely practised. They can then radiate the light and warmth of faith into the environment.

Such small communities must not assume separate existences and isolate themselves. They must be open for life in the respective community and open to the global Church. In particular, in a networked world, parishes and communities must go beyond the often limited perspective of their own church tower and be truly catholic and open themselves for the greater Church in the diocese and in the worldwide Church. Despite all necessary rooting in their own respective cultures and histories, the time of national churches that characterized modern times since the Middle Ages and which witnessed, among other difficulties, unfortunate schisms and conflicts is irrevocably over. Being Christian and Church in the twenty-first century should be characterized, above all, by worldwide solidarity with sisters and brothers in need, especially with persecuted and suppressed Christians in many countries of the world. This also includes the old biblical and primal Christian virtue of hospitality towards those who come to us driven by need and persecution.

In an increasingly globalized and yet internally torn world, on the universal level the Church needs, for the sake of the unity in diversity of individual churches, both a strong centre which keeps the Church together in the one faith of Peter and a strengthening of its collegiate/synodal structures. The two do not contradict each other. Instead the stronger integration of both aspects as intended by the Second Vatican Council could contribute to the overcoming of the still-existing, unity-weakening and disturbing anti-Roman affect[30] and the strengthening of the Church's inner. Thus it will be inevitable in the future to resist a centralism which wants to rule and control everything and to give the local churches, the church in a country, a culture or also the church of a continent, more direct responsibility. By consequence, the importance of the vocation given to the Petrine office to strengthen the sisters and brothers will not decrease but increase. Peter is with his faith the rock upon which the Church is built. In difficult times such as ours, we must gather round Peter.

In addition to inward dialogue, there is outward dialogue as the Second Vatican Council initiated it, that is, dialogue with God's people of the old covenant, ecumenical dialogue as well as dialogue with other religions, with today's culture and with all people of good will. With these dialogues, the Council indicated the way from a closed Church perceiving itself as a castle or fortress towards a communicatively and dialogically open Church. Dialogue does not imply giving up one's own identity but rather a growing in one's own identity, for it is essential for Christian identity to exist for others and with others. This rules out both assimilation and a fearsome siege mentality. In all dialogues the basic rule should prevail: 'test everything and hold on to what is good' (1 Thess. 5.21).

Nobody can say already today where the ecumenical dialogue will lead us, what it will mean for the future form of the Church, how the greater unity in an equally greater diversity will one day concretely appear. To reach this greater unity in truth and love, a way lies ahead which is long and arduous. We only know that this dialogue and this way are the vocation of Jesus and a work of the Holy Spirit. This way is therefore irreversible and irrevocable. It is a crucial building block for the Church of the future. We must therefore do what we can do today in truth and love. Nevertheless, we cannot 'make' the unity. The most important thing is to pray incessantly for unity and to prepare ourselves through inner conversion. Finally, the inter-religious dialogue is a way into an open future. It is the only possible alternative to violence and a clash of cultures, ethnic groups and religions. Through this dialogue in truth and love the Church, as eschatological people of God, can be, amidst the conflicts of our world, the anticipatory image and instrument of the eschatological peace (*shalom*).

Hope for a renewed Pentecost – joy in God and joy in the Church

With these inward and outward dialogues, the Second Vatican Council initiated developments that present us with challenges, which, however, we cannot programme. The Council showed us the direction for the present historical hour of our departure from the slowly but inexorably disappearing forms of the *Volkskirche* and to a new kind of being Church. It has given us light for the way, but not one that illuminates, like floodlights, a whole track into the future. Rather, it has placed in our hands a lantern, which, like every lantern, shines ahead only a little way. It provides light only for each next step, which then can and must be followed by further steps.

So the renewal of the Church cannot be predetermined by an elaborate programme. Ultimately, the renewal is only possible through a renewed Pentecost, of which the blessed Pope John XXIII spoke at the convocation and then at the opening of the Second Vatican Council on 11 October

1962. If we are convinced that ultimately only the Spirit of Pentecost can give renewal, then we must, above all, do what the first disciples did before Pentecost. At that time, the apostles, the women who had accompanied Jesus, together with Mary, the mother of Jesus, gathered and with one heart they joined constantly in prayer (Acts 1.12–14). Also today, the future of the Church will be determined in the first line by those who pray and the Church of the future will be, above anything, a church of those who pray.

As at the first Pentecost, the Spirit can come with storm and fire (Acts 2.2f.), with the storm that blows some things away and with the fire that burns some of those things we consider important today. Yet, as with the prophet Elijah, the Spirit can also come in the light murmuring of the wind (1 Kings 19.12f.), and cleanse us and the world with its glow from inside and change us. He can make us newly aware that we do not need to worry, that, rather, the joy in God is our strength (Neh. 8.10). If we have out of this joy as people of God joy in the Church, the Church will also live tomorrow and have future the day after tomorrow. As anticipation of the coming kingdom of God, the Church will then attract the seeking and the asking, young and older people, and it will be again the spiritual home for many.

If the chapters above have contributed just a little to such joy of God and the Church, then they were not written in vain. They did not seek and have not sought to be.

NOTES

I. My journey in and with the Church

1 For more detailed commentary, see W. Kasper and D. Deckers, *Wo das Herz des Glaubens schlägt. Die Erfahrung eines Lebens*, Freiburg i. Br. 2008.

2 Cf. WKGS 11.

3 R. Guardini, *Vom Sinn der Kirche* (1922; *The Church and the Catholic*, New York: Sheed & Ward, 1940), Mainz 1955, 19. At about the same time, the Protestant bishop Otto Dibelius published his volume *Das Jahrhundert der Kirche*, Berlin 1927.

4 It is quite telling that, in the changed situation after the Second World War, R. Guardini, who had done much to promote a Christian culture in the spirit of the contemporaneous youth movement, came rather quickly to a largely critical view of modern times. See Guardini, *The End of the Modern World* (1950), Wilmington, DE: ISI Books 2001; and *Power and Responsibility* (1951), Chicago: H. Regnery 1961. On this, see also A. Knoll, *Glaube und Kultur bei Romano Guardini*, Paderborn 1993.

5 W. Solowjew, *Kurze Erzählung vom Antichrist* (= V. Solovyov, *A Short Story of the Anti-Christ*) (1900), Munich 1968, 33, 37–40. Solovyov was probably thinking of the younger Protestant Tübingen School of Ferdinand Christian Baur and David Friedrich Strauß and their historical-critical interpretation of the Bible and the history of dogma. Yet, the Catholic Tübingen School took a critical approach towards the issue. As a consequence, it is necessary to distinguish the two schools from one another.

6 On the history of ecclesiology in the nineteenth and twentieth centuries: R. Aubert, 'La géographie ecclésiologique au XIXe siècle', in: *L'ecclésiologie au XIXe siècle*, Paris 1960, 11–55; Y. Congar, 'Die Lehre von der Kirche', in: HDG III/3d (1971); G. McCool, *Catholic Theology in the Nineteenth Century*, New York 1977; M. Kehl, 'Ekklesiologie', in: LThK[3] 3, 571–3. Recent research reports: ThQ 181 (2001) 238–46; 184 (2004) 287–303; 187 (2007) 234–45.

7 See the overview of the history and theology of the Tübingen School in M. Seckler, 'Tübinger Schule', in: LThK[3] 10, 287–90 (Lit.); M. Kessler/ O. Fuchs (eds), *Theologie als Instanz der Moderne, Beiträge und Studien zu Johann Sebastian Drey und zur Katholischen Tübinger Schule*, Tübingen 2005.

8 On this issue, see K.-H. Menke, *Vernunft und Offenbarung nach A. Rosmini*, Innsbruck – Vienna – Munich 1980.

9 On this issue, see WKGS 10, 15–83.

10 On this topic, see the following articles and essays by W. Kasper: 'Verständnis der Theologie damals und heute', in: *Theologie im Wandel. Festschrift zum 150 jährigen Bestehen der katholisch-theologischen Fakultät der Universität Tübingen*, edited by the Faculty of Catholic Theology at the university of Tübingen, Munich – Freiburg 1967, 90–115; 'Johann Adam Möhler –Wegbereiter des modernen Katholizismus', in: IKaZ 17 (1988) 433–3; '"Vom Geist und Wesen des Katholizismus": Bedeutung, Wirkungsgeschichte und Aktualität von Johann Sebastian Dreys und Johann Adam Möhlers Wesensbestimmung des Katholizismus', in: ThQ 183 (2003) 196–212; 'Die Einheit der Kirche im Licht der Tübinger Schule', in: M. Kessler/O. Fuchs (eds), *Theologie als Instanz der Moderne. Beiträge und Studien zu Johann Sebastian Drey und zur Katholischen Tübinger Schule*, Tübingen 2005, 189–206.

11 W. Kasper, *Das Absolute in der Geschichte. Philosophie und Theologie der Geschichte in der Spätphilosophie Schellings* (1965): WKGS 2; Kasper, 'Freiheit als philosophisches und theologisches Problem in der Philosophie Schellings', in: *Glaube und Geschichte*, Mainz 1990, 33–47.

12 W. Schulz, *Die Vollendung des deutschen Idealismus in der Spätphilosophie Schellings*, Stuttgart 1955.

13 From an ecclesiological perspective, see especially W. Kasper, 'Steuermann mitten im Sturm. Das Bischofsamt nach Thomas von Aquin', in: ThQ 179 (1999) 1–23.

14 W. Kasper, 'Ermutigung zum Denken. Von der Unerlässlichkeit der Metaphysik für die Sache der Theologie', in: ThQ 169 (1989) 257–71.

15 F. X. Arnold, *Seelsorge aus der Mitte der Heilsgeschichte*, Freiburg i. Br. 1956, 178–94, following A. Graf, *Kritische Darstellung des gegenwärtigen Zustands der praktischen Theologie*, Tübingen 1841.

16 Basic works include G. Alberigo, *A History of Vatican II (1959–65)*, 5 vols, Maryknoll: Orbis Books 1996–2006; P. Hünermann et al. (eds), *Herders Theologischer Kommentar zum Zweiten Vatikanischen Konzil* (= HThK. Vat II; 5 vols), Freiburg i. Br., 2004–5; C. Theobald, *La réception du concile Vatican II*, Paris 2009 (only vol. 1 has been published at the time of writing). Additionally, see H. J. Pottmeyer, 'Kontinuität und Innovation in der Ekklesiologie des II. Vaticanums', in: G. Alberigo et al. (eds), *Kirche im Wandel. Eine kritische Zwischenbilanz nach dem Zweiten Vatikanum*, Düsseldorf 1982, 89–110; H. J. Pottmeyer et al., *Die Rezeption des Zweiten Vatikanischen Konzils*, Düsseldorf 1986; W. Kasper, 'The Continuing Challenge of the Second Vatican Council: The Hermeneutics of the Conciliar Statements', in: *Theology and Church*, New York: Crossroad, 166–76. O. H. Pesch, *Das Zweite Vatikanische Konzil. Vorgeschichte, Verlauf, Ergebnisse, Nachgeschichte*, Würzburg 1993; P. Hünermann (ed.), *Das II. Vatikanum – Christlicher Glaube im Horizont globaler Modernisierung*, Paderborn 1998; K. Lehmann, 'Hermeneutik für einen künftigen Umgang mit dem Konzil', in: G. Wassilowsky (ed.) *Zweites Vatikanum – vergessene Anstöße, gegenwärtige Fortschreibungen* (QD 207), Freiburg i. Br. 2004, 71–89. A. Marchetto, *Il Concilio ecumenico Vaticano II*, Città del Vaticano 2005. O. Rush, *Still*

Interpreting Vatican II. Some Hermeneutical Principles, New York 2004; J.W. O'Malley, *What happened at Vatican II*, Cambridge, MA 2008; G. Martelet, *N'oublions pas Vatican II*, Paris 2010.

17 See AAS 56 (1964), 1009f.

18 See H. G. Gadamer, *Wahrheit und Methode*, Tübingen 1960.

19 The pastoral intention is officially defined in this sense in a note in the pastoral constitution *Gaudium et spes* 1. On this problem, see F. Kolfhaus, *Pastorale Lehrverkündigung – Grundmotiv des Zweiten Vatikanischen Konzils*, Berlin 2010;W. Beinert, 'Nur pastoral oder dogmatisch verpflichtend?', in: StdZ 135 (2010) 3–15.

20 On the term 'reception,' see Y. Congar, 'La 'réception' comme réalité ecclésiologique' (1972), in: *Église et Papauté*, Paris 1994, 229–66; A. Grillmeier, 'Konzil und Rezeption', in: *Mit ihm und in ihm*, Freiburg i. Br. 1995, 303–34; G. Routhier, *La réception d'un concile*, Paris 1993; W. Beinert, 'Die Rezeption und ihre Bedeutung für Leben und Lehre der Kirche', in: W. Pannenberg/T. Schneider (eds), *Verbindliches Zeugnis*, vol. 2, Freiburg i. Br. – Göttingen 1995, 193–218.

21 On this, see M. Seckler, 'Über den Kompromiss in Sachen der Lehre', in: *Im Spannungsfeld von Wissenschaft und Kirche*, Freiburg i. Br. 1980, 99–109.

22 A critical view not only of the post-conciliar development but also of important individual statements from the Council, such as those on ecumenism and freedom of religion, can be observed clearly in the work of the priestly Society of St Pius X (SSPX), which was founded by archbishop Marcel Lefebvre. Behind the work of this group lies a static understanding of Tradition which basically stops with the post-Tridentine tradition and rejects its further development in the spirit of the biblical and patristic Tradition. On this issue, see Y. Congar, *Challenge to the Church: the Case of Archbishop Lefebvre,* London 1977; F. Michel/B. Sesboüé, *De Mgr Lefebvre à Mgr Williamson. Anatomie d'un schisme*, Paris 2009; A. Schifferle, *Die Piusbruderschaft. Informationen – Positionen – Perspektiven*, Kevelaer 2009.

23 So Pope Benedict XVI in his Christmas address to the cardinals and the members of the Roman Curia (22 December 2005). Already the Extraordinary Synod of Bishops in 1985 had argued along the same lines. See *Zukunft aus der Kraft des Konzils. Die außerordentliche Bischofssynode '85. Die Dokumente mit einem Kommentar von W. Kasper*, Freiburg i. Br. 1986, 22f.

24 DH 802; 875; 1381.

25 LG 16; GS 10; 22.

26 J. H. Newman, *Essay on the Development of Christian Doctrine* (1845), Baltimore: Penguin 1974.

27 See Y. Congar, *La tradition et les traditions*, 2 vols, Paris 1960–63. This distinction between the *one* Tradition and traditions was also embraced by the Fourth World Conference on Faith and Order in Montreal (1963).

28 J. Behm, 'καιρός', in ThWNT 3, 451f.

29 Irenaeus of Lyons, *adversus haereses* III, 4, 2.

30 John XXIII, Apostolic Constitution on the convocation of the Council, *Humanae salutis* (December 25, 1961), 23.

31 Controversies followed, on the one hand, with the traditionalistic Society of St Pius X, founded by archbishop Marcel Lefevbre, and, on the other, with individual theologians such as H. Küng, E. Schillebeeckx, L. Boff, etc. In the following, I shall refrain from a controversial discussion of these and other positions. Instead, I will try to present the doctrine of the Church positively. On the reception of the conciliar ecclesiology, see B. Stubenrauch and M. Seewald, 'Das Konzil und die Kirche. Zur Rezeption einer vielschichtigen Ekklesiologie', in: IKaZ 39 (2010), 600–16.

32 *Zukunft aus der Kraft des Konzils.*

33 Regarding this expansion of the horizon, see sections I.5; II.2.2.

34 For additional commentary on this point, see sections II.3.3 and II.5.8.

35 Now together in two massive volumes, titled *Kirche – Zeichen unter den Völkern* (*Gesammelte Schriften* vol. 8/1 and 2), Freiburg i. Br. 2010.

36 On this, see my two early publications: W. Kasper, *Dogma unter dem Wort Gottes*, Mainz 1965, and *The Methods of Dogmatic Theology* (1967), Shannon: Ecclesia Press 1969. For both publications, I found help from the hermeneutics of H.-G. Gadamer, for instance, in *Wahrheit und Methode*, Tübingen 1960. K. Lehmann came to a similar point of view in the essay titled, 'Die dogmatische Denkform als hermeneutisches Problem', in: *Gegenwart des Glaubens*, Mainz 1974, 35–53.

37 *A New Catechism: Catholic Faith for Adults, Authorized Edition of the Dutch Catechism with Supplement* (1966), New York: Crossroad, 1988.

38 The English edition is published as *Introduction to the Christian Faith* (1972), London: Burns & Oates 1980.

39 See *Gemeinsame Synode der Bistümer der Bundesrepublik Deutschland. Offizielle Gesamtausgabe*, Freiburg i. Br. 1976, 84–111.

40 Thomas Aquinas, *Summa theologiae* II/II q. 120 a. 2.

41 See W. Kasper, 'Gerechtigkeit und Barmherzigkeit. Überlegungen zu einer Applikationstheorie kirchenrechtlicher Normen', in: *Kirche und Theologie*, vol. 2, Mainz 1999, 183–91. On the relation between *epikeia* and Orthodox economy (*oikonomia*), see Y. Congar, 'Kat'oikonomian', in: *Diversités et communion*, Paris 1982, 80–94. It was already J. H. Newman who rightly warned of an abuse of the principle of *oikonomia* leading to arbitrariness. See *Apologia pro vita sua*, Oxford: Clarendon Press 1967, 299–301.

42 On the nature of the virtue of prudence in Thomas Aquinas, see J. Pieper, *Das Viergespann*, Munich 1964, 13–64. One could also mention *discretion* (spiritual discernment), which, according to the Rule of St Benedict, should govern the decisions of the abbot (c. 2, 24; 37; 64, 17–19).

43 This concept formed the background for the initiative which I undertook together with the former Archbishop O. Sailer (Freiburg i. Br.) and the then bishop, now Cardinal, Karl Lehmann (Mainz), in 1993, concerning pastoral care for remarried divorcees. We did not question the indissolubility of marriage, quite the contrary. Likewise, we did not present a general solution.

Rather we stressed the differences and complexities of the individual situations which make a consideration seem appropriate. We did not think everything through to the end at that time. In the meantime, though, then the pastoral problem has become even more pressing.

44 See. B. Häring, *Frei in Christus*, vol. 1, Freiburg i. Br. 1979, 65f. One can also point to Franz Xaver von Linsenmann († 1898), moral theologian at Tübingen and bishop elect of Rottenburg.

45 J. B. Metz, *Glaube in Geschichte und Gesellschaft. Studien zu einer praktischen Fundamentaltheologie*, Mainz 1977; and, *Zum Begriff der neuen Politischen Theologie 1967–97*, Mainz 1997.

46 On the theology of liberation, see the two documents by the Sacred Congregation for the Doctrine of Faith: *Instruction on Certain Aspects of the 'Theology of Liberation'* (6 August 1984); *Instruction on Christian Freedom and Liberation* (22 March 1986).

47 G. Gutiérrez, *A Theology of Liberation* (1971), London: SCM Press 1988 (revised translation with new introduction).

48 WKGS 3, 38f., 59., 76–78.289f., 336f. See also the essay titled 'Zur Theologie der Befreiung: Die Theologie der Befreiung aus europäischer Perspektive', in: J. B. Metz (ed.), *Die Theologie der Befreiung. Hoffnung oder Gefahr für die Kirche?*, Düsseldorf 1986, 77–98.

49 London: Collins 1971 (extended new ed. New York: Continuum 1994); H. Küng et al., *Fehlbar? Eine Bilanz*, Zurich 1973; W. Jens (ed.), *Um nichts als die Wahrheit. Eine Dokumentation*, Munich 1978; N. Greinacher/H. Haag (eds), *Der Fall Küng*, Munich1980.

50 *Declaration regarding certain aspects of the theological doctrine of Professor Hans Küng – Christi Ecclesia* (December 15, 1979). This had been preceded by the *Declaration in Defence of the Catholic Doctrine on the Church Against Certain Errors of the Present Day – Mysterium Ecclesiae* (24 June 1973). For a critical discussion of H. Küng's position, see K. Rahner (ed.), *Zum Problem Unfehlbarkeit. Antworten auf die Anfrage von Hans Küng* (QD 54), Freiburg i. Br. 1971, and below, sections II.5.4, note 275.

51 H. Küng has presented his view of those events in: *Umstrittene Wahrheit. Erinnerungen*, Munich 2007. I do not wish to comment here on this and his partly disparaging assessments.

52 See 'Freiheit des Evangeliums und dogmatische Bindung in der katholischen Theologie. Grundlagenüberlegungen zur Unfehlbarkeitsdebatte', in: W. Kern, *Die Theologie und das Lehramt*, Freiburg i. Br. 1982, 201–33.

53 Newman, *Apologia pro vita sua*, 54f.; W. Kasper, 'Erneuerung des dogmatischen Prinzips', in: A. Ziegenaus (ed.), *Veritati Catholicae.* (Festschrift L. Scheffczyk), Aschaffenburg 1985, 43–62. In a similar vein, see K. Lehmann, 'Die dogmatische Denkform', in: *Gegenwart des Glaubens*, Mainz 1974, 35–53.

54 See W. Kasper (ed.), *Logik der Liebe und der Herrlichkeit Gottes. Hans Urs von Balthasar im Gespräch* (Festschrift K. Lehmann), Ostfildern 2006.

55 See the articles by W. Kasper, 'Kirche als Sakrament des Geistes', in:

W. Kasper/G. Sauter (eds), *Die Kirche – Ort des Geistes*, Freiburg i. Br. 1976, 13–55; and, 'Die Lehre vom Hl. Geist und die Annäherung zwischen Ost und West', in: *Wege der Einheit*, Freiburg i. Br. 2005, 132–61. For similar accounts, see J. Ratzinger, H. Mühlen, M. Kehl and, especially, Y. Congar, *I believe in the Holy Spirit*, London: Chapman 1983. For additional details, see section II.3.3.

56 LG 7.

57 H. Küng, *The Church*, New York: Sheed & Ward 1968; J. Moltmann, *The Church in the Power of the Spirit*, New York: Harper & Row 1977.

58 See section II.4.8.

59 See *Zukunft aus der Kraft des Konzils*. See additionally the post-synodal apostolic exhortation by John Paul II, *Christifideles laici* (1988), 18–20.

60 The foundational work was done by H. de Lubac, *Corpus mysticum*, Paris 1944; *L'Eucharistie e l'Église au Moyen Âge*, Paris 1949 (English: *Corpus Mysticum: The Eucharist and the Church in the Middle Ages*, Notre Dame, Ind, 2007); Méditation sur l'Église, Paris 1953 (English: *The Splendour of the Church*, New York: Sheed & Ward 1956). In addition, see L. Hertling, *Communio und Primat*, Rome 1943. The term became programmatic through H. U. von Balthasar, 'Communio. Ein Programm', in: IKaZ 1 (1972) 4–17.

61 LG 3, 7, 9, 11, 48; etc.

62 This was worked out by W. Thönissen, in *Gemeinschaft durch Teilhabe an Jesus Christus. Ein katholisches Modell für die Einheit der Kirchen*, Freiburg i. Br. 1996.

63 LG 4; UR 2. For the relation between '*communio* ecclesiology' and the ecclesiology of the People of God, the latter of which is generally seen as the basic ecclesiology of the Council, see below, section II.3.1.

64 See B. Forte, *La Chiesa della Trinità*, Cinisello-Balsamo 1995.

65 On this, see W. Kasper, 'Church as Communio', in: Comm 13 (1986), 100–17; and, *Sacrament of Unity – The Eucharist and the Church*, New York 2004; and, 'Communio: The Guiding Concept of Catholic Ecumenical Theology', in: *That they all may be one*, London: Burns & Oates 2004, 50–74. Concerning a Eucharistic ecclesiology, see sections II.2.2 and II.3.2.

66 Important representatives include J. Hamer, Y. Congar, A. Piolanti, H. U. von Balthasar, J. Ratzinger, J.-M. Tillard, O. Saier, E. Corecco, B. Forte, W. Breuning, G. Greshake, M. Kehl, P. J. Cordes, H. Döring, B. J. Hilberath, J. Werbick, etc. See J. Drumm, 'communio', in: $LThK^3$ 2, 1280–3; J. Rigal, *L'Ecclésiologie de communion. Son évolution et ses fondements*, Paris 2000; J. Rahner, 'Communio – communio ecclesiarum – communio hierarchica', in: IKaZ 39 (2010) 665–79.

67 A. Afanassieff, A. Schmemann, Zizioulas, etc., are representatives from Orthodox theology.

68 P. Althaus, D. Bonhoeffer, W. Elert, C. Schwöbel. Cf. R. Schäfer, 'communio', in: RGG^4 4, 435–7. The Fifth World Conference on Faith and Order in Santiago de Compostela (1993) has also become important on this point.

69 See J. C. Scannone et al., *Comunión: ¿Un nuevo Paradigma?*, San Benito 2006.

70 I adopted this idea from Schelling, first in *Das Absolute in der Geschichte* (1965): WKGS 2; and later in *Der Gott Jesu Christi* (1982; *The God of Jesus Christ*): WKGS 4, 37f, 428, 445, 471f. M. Heidegger treated this idea extensively in *Schellings Abhandlung über das Wesen der menschlichen Freiheit* (1809), Tübingen 1971, 107, 154, 211, 223–5. Among others in a similar vein, see J. Ratzinger, *Einführung in das Christentum* (*Introduction to Christianity*), Munich 1968, 142–50; K. Hemmerle, *Thesen zu einer trinitarischen Ontologie*, Einsiedeln 1976; G. Greshake, *Der dreieine Gott*, Freiburg i. Br. 1997, 457–60. One finds similar approaches to Trinitarian ontology in recent Orthodox theology (V. Solovyov, N. Berdyaev, S. Bulgakow, J. Zizioulas, et al.), as well as in the more recent trend in Anglican theology commonly referred to as Radical Orthodoxy (R. Williams, J. Milbank, etc.). On the history of this concept, see 'Relation', in: HWPh. 8, 578–611.

71 See sections II.1.2 and II.6.2.

72 Those who invoke the reproachful invective 'relativism' are correct and justified insofar as they wish to secure the uniqueness and distinctiveness of the Christian message and to prevent this message from losing ground to the attitude, widely held today, that Christianity possesses an 'indifferent, equal validity' vis-a-vis other religions and world views. And yet, this legitimate concern must not become a mere Shibboleth. Undoubtedly, while not everything is relative, much still is, even in the Church. It is therefore necessary to clarify and so to differentiate the term relativism. In the history of philosophy, this term appears rather late and as a collective name for very different phenomena. One has to distinguish between logical, ethical, sckeptical, epistemological, and linguistic-philosophical forms of relativism. See G. Koenig, 'Relativismus', in: HWPh. 8, 613–22.

73 See M. Kehl, *Die Kirche*, Würzburg 1992, passim; J. Hilberath, 'Kirche als communio. Beschwörung oder Projektbeschreibung', in: ThQ 174 (1994) 45–65; J. Werbick, *Kirche*, Freiburg i. Br. 1994, 317–71.

74 See sections II.5.5, II.7.

75 On this, see section II.5.6.

76 The reflections below on this topic go back to my time as diocesan bishop. See 'Neue Evangelisierung als theologische, pastorale und geistliche Herausforderung', in: WKGS 5, 245–317.

77 On ecumenical theology, see sections II.4.1 and II.6.2.2. My own contributions to this discussion include *That they may all be one. The Call to Unity*, London – New York: Burns & Oates 2004; *A Handbook of Spiritual Ecumenism*, New York: New City Press 2006; *The Petrine Ministry. Catholics and Orthodox in Dialogue*, New York: Newman Press 2006; *Harvesting the Fruits. Basic Aspects of Christian Faith in Ecumenical Dialogue*, London: Continuum 2009.

78 John Paul II, *Encyclical Ut unum sint* (1995), 28.

79 ΤΟΜΟΣ ΑΓΑΠΗΣ, Vatican – Phanar (1958–70), Rome – Istanbul 1971, particularly 284–94.

80 Common Declaration of Pope Paul VI and of the Pope of Alexandria

Shenouda III (Coptic Orthodox Church, 1973), of Pope John Paul II and his Holiness Mar Ignatius Zakka I Iwas (Syrian Orthodox Church, 1984), of Pope John Paul II and the Supreme Patriarch of all Armenians Karekin I (Armenian Apostolic Church of Etchmiadzine, 1996) and of Pope John Paul II and the Catholicos Patriarch of Mar Dinkha IV (Assyrian Church of the East, 1994). Because of the consensus over Christology with the Assyrian Church, this led, in 2001, to an agreement between the Pontifical Council for Promoting Christian Unity, the Congregation for the Doctrine of Faith and the Congregation for the Oriental Churches to guidelines for admission to the Eucharist between the Chaldean Church and the Assyrian Church and with this to the recognition of the anaphora of Addai and Mari.

81 See sections II.2.2, II.4.2, II.6.2.2.

82 *Kirchengemeinschaft nach evangelischem Verständnis. Ein Votum zum geordneten Miteinander, Bekenntnis verschiedener Kirchen* (2001). On this issue see section II.4.2.

83 W. Kasper, *Harvesting the Fruits. Basic Aspects of Christian Faith in Ecumenical Dialogue*, London: Continuum 2009.

84 Since E. Troeltsch, *Die Soziallehren der christlichen Kirchen und Gruppen* (1912), repr. Aalen 1965, one must also recognize the positive significance of such groups for the implementation of the idea of tolerance, the emergence of modern individualism and the freedom of the Church from the State.

85 On the theological questions, see section II.6.2.1.

86 For this, see the document *We Remember: a Reflection on the Shoah* (1998).

87 See W. Kasper, 'La preghiera del Venerdì Santo per gli ebrei', in: *OR*, 10 April 2008, 4.

88 John Paul II, *Address to the Jewish Community of Rome* (during his visit to the Great Synagogue, 13 April 1986). See section II.6.2.1.

89 See W. Kasper, 'Neue Evangelisierung als theologische, pastorale und geistliche Herausforderung', in: WKGS 5, 245–317. See section II.7.

90 Foundational texts include Y. Congar, *True and False Reform in the Church* (1950), Collegeville, Minn.; Liturgical Press 2011; Groupe des Dombes, *For the Conversion of the Churches*, Geneva: WCC Publications 1993.

91 GS 1.

92 GS 4–10.

93 See J.-F. Lyotard, *The Postmodern Condition: a Report on Knowledge*, Minneapolis: University of Minnesota Press 1984;W. Welsch, *Unsere postmoderne Moderne*, Weinheim 1987; P. Koslowski, et al. (eds), *Moderne oder Postmoderne?*, Weinheim 1986; W. Kasper, 'Die Kirche angesichts der Herausforderungen der Postmoderne', in: *Theologie und Kirche*, vol. 2, Mainz 1999, 249–64. For a constructive discussion, see C. Theobald, *Le christianisme comme style. Une manière de faire de la théologie en postmodernité*, 2 vols, Paris 2007–8.

94 F. Nietzsche, *Die fröhliche Wissenschaft* (*The Gay Science*), in: *Gesamtausgabe Werke* (ed. Schlechta), vol. 2, 126–8, 205f.

95 F. Nietzsche, 'Aus dem Nachlass', in: ibid. vol. 3, 634f, 675, 678, and others.

96 A. Delp, *Im Angesicht des Todes*, Frankfurt a.M. 1961, especially 131–7; D. Bonhoeffer, *Letters and Papers from Prison*, edited by C. Gremmels, et al., Minneapolis 2010.

97 This is the description of the situation by C. Taylor in his standard work, *A Secular Age*, Cambridge, MA – London 2007. Taylor rightly observes again that the theory of secularization, which presumes a necessary connection between modernization and secularization, has become obsolete. On the previous debate, see W. Kasper, 'Säkularisierung', in: StL^7 4, 993–8.

98 Thus the famous formulation of M. Weber, 'Wissenschaft als Beruf' (1919), in: *Gesammelte Aufsätze zur Wissenschaftslehre*, Tübingen 1973, 594.

99 Concerning this, at least ambivalent, thesis, see WKGS 4, 20–2.

100 As fascinatingly described in R. Safranski, *Romantik. Eine deutsche Affäre*, Munich 2007.

101 This has been demonstrated by J. Habermas in *Glauben und Wissen* (Frankfurt a. M.2001), and in other more recent writings. On this subject, see W. Kasper, 'Glaube, der nach seinem Verstehen fragt', in: StdZ 134 (2009) 507–19.

102 T.W. Adorno, *Minima Moralia. Reflexionen aus dem beschädigten Leben* (= *Minima Moralia: Reflections from damaged life*, London: Verso 2005), Frankfurt a.M. 1970, 333.

103 J.-L. Marion, *Le croire pour le voir. Réflexions sur la rationalité de la révélation et l'irrationalité de quelques croyants*, Paris 2010, 115–25.

104 H. U. von Balthasar, *The God Question and Modern Man* (1956), Eugene, Or.: 2000; J. B. Metz, 'Gotteskrise. Versuch zur "geistigen Situation der Zeit"', in: *Diagnosen zur Zeit*, Düsseldorf 1994, 86–92;W. Kasper, 'Es ist Zeit, von Gott zu reden', in: G. Augustin (ed.), *Die Gottesfrage heute* (ThiD 1), Freiburg i. Br. 2009, 13–31; and, 'Die Gottesfrage als Zukunftsfrage', in: *Die Politische Meinung*, 470/2009, 42–8; G. Augustin/K. Krämer (eds), *Gott denken und bezeugen* (Festschrift W. Kasper), Freiburg i. Br. 2008. See also section II.6.2.4.

105 This theory has been taken up repeatedly. See Kehl, *Die Kirche*, 173–210; and, *Wohin geht die Kirche?*, Freiburg 1996; Werbick, *Kirche*, 127–34; J. Ratzinger in: M. Pera/J. Ratzinger, *Ohne Wurzeln. Der Relativismus und die Krise der europäischen Kultur*, Augsburg 2005, 129–35. Pope Benedict XVI has expressed himself on various occasions in much the same way. See section II.6.2.4.

II. Outlines of Catholic ecclesiology

1. Preliminary considerations from the perspective of fundamental theology

1 *Smalcald Articles* III, 12, in: *Book of Concord*, edited by T. G. Tappert, Philadelphia: Fortress Press 1959, 315.

2 See section II.2.2.

3 The conflict culminates in the question if and to what extent it is possible to speak of the non-Catholic churches as churches, that is, as churches in the actual theological sense. The question will be addressed in detail below, in Chapter II.4.1. In the following parts we take it as given that these non-Catholic, other communities call themselves churches and that the public also calls them as such. Their self-description and the public description are thus to be respected. Still, one needs to bear in mind that the word 'church' is understood and used in a different theological sense.

4 Classic works on the sociology of religion and of churches include those by E. Durkheim, M. Weber, T. Luckmann, N. Luhmann, P. L. Berger, etc. From a Catholic perspective, see F. X. Kaufmann, K. Gabriel, M. Ebertz, A. Greeley, etc. From a theological point of view, see M. Kehl, *Kirche als Institution. Zur theologischen Begründung des institutionellen Charakters der Kirche*, Frankfurt a.M. 1976.

5 DH 1ff.; 150. The theological questions of method can be adumbrated in this context. Regarding the question of method in dogmatic theology, see W. Kasper, *The Methods of Dogmatic Theology* (1967), Shannon 1969. These issues are dealt with extensively in WKGS 7.

6 Cf. J. N. D. Kelly, *Early Christian Creeds*, London 1972.

7 Thomas Aquinas, *Summa theologiae* II/II q. 1 a. 9.

8 DV 5.

9 Already the Church Fathers, especially Augustine, laid down the foundations for the axiom '*fides quaerens intellectum*'. It was substantially developed by Anselm of Canterbury (*Proslogion, prooem.*). On this point, see John Paul II, Encyclical *Fides et ratio* (1998); Benedict XVI, *Glaube und Vernunft. Die Regensburger Rede*, Freiburg i. Br. 2006; M. Seckler, 'Theologie als Glaubenswissenschaft', in: HFThess. 4, Freiburg i. Br. 1988, 180–241; W. Kasper, 'Wissenschaftspraxis der Theologie', in: ibid., 242–77; and, 'Zustimmung zum Denken. Von der Unerlässlichkeit der Metaphysik für die Sache der Theologie', in: ThQ 169 (1989) 257–71; WKGS 4, 16–22; and, 'Glaube, der nach seinem Verstehen fragt. Ein Beitrag zur Diskussion um ein aktuelles Thema', in: StdZ 134 (2009) 507–19.

10 For the arts, see H.-G. Gadamer, *Wahrheit und Methode*, Tübingen 1960. The philosophy of communication will be dealt with in the following section. Regarding sciences, we can point to the theory of the paradigm shift as found in T. Kuhn, *The Structure of Scientific Revolutions*, Chicago 1982.

11 LG 8. See also my detailed commentary on this issue below, in sections II.2.2 and II.3.2 and II.4.1.

12 Thomas Aquinas, *Summa theologiae* I q.1 a.7 c. a.: '*Omnia autem pertractantur in sacra doctrina sub ratione Dei vel quia sunt ipse Deus; vel quia habent ordinem ad Deum, ut ad principium et finem.*' (But in sacred doctrine, all things are treated of under the aspect of God: either because they are God Himself or because they refer to God as their beginning and end.)

13 J. Ratzinger, 'Identifikation mit der Kirche', in: JRGS 8/1, 178–92.

14 On the biblical meaning of 'euangelion' (gospel): G. Friedrich, 'εὐαγγέλιον', in: ThWNT 2, 718–34; W. Kasper, *Dogma unter dem Wort Gottes*, Mainz 1965, 84–98; and, 'Was heißt Evangelium und Evangelisierung?', in: WKGS 5, 254–65.

15 Irenaeus of Lyons, *adversus haereses* III, 4, 2.

16 Cf. D. van den Eynde, *Les normes de l'enseignement chrétien dans la littérature patristique des trois premiers siècles*, Gembloux 1933; B. Häggelund, 'Die Bedeutung der "regula fidei" als Grundlage theologischer Aussagen', in: *Studia theologica* 12 (1958) 1–44. A summary of this can be found in W. Beinert, 'Regula fidei', in: $LThK^3$ 8, 876f.

17 An important study is H. de Lubac, *History and Spirit*, (1950), San Francisco 2007; cf. Kasper, *Dogma unter dem Wort Gottes*, 86–92.

18 See WA 2, 430, etc. See also Martin Luther's famous quote: 'euangelion (gospel) is nothing but a sermon and proclamation of the grace and mercy of God, which is earned and given through the Lord Jesus Christ. It is in the actual sense not so much what has been written in books and with letters but rather an oral sermon and a living word and voice that sounds throughout all the world and that cries publicly that it can be heard everywhere ...' (WA 10 I, 1,13). On this, see Kasper, *Dogma unter dem Wort Gottes*, 16f.

19 For detailed commentary, see sections II.2.2.

20 F. Schleiermacher, *The Christian Faith* (1821/22), London: T & T Clark 2008.

21 ThQ 1 (1819) 3–24; 193–210, 559–75. Reprinted in: J. R. Geiselmann (ed.), *Geist des Christentums und des Katholizismus*, Mainz 1940, 193–234. Regarding its significance, see M. Seckler, 'Johann Sebastian Dreys Programmschrift *Vom Geist und Wesen des Katholizismus* neu gelesen, oder Die kultisch-liturgische Dimension in der theologischen Architektur des Christentums', in: P. Walter et al. (eds), *Kirche in ökumenischer Perspektive* (Festschrift W. Kasper), Freiburg i. Br. 2003, 115–32.

22 Edited and introduced by M. Seckler, Johann Sebastian Drey, *Nachgelassene Schriften*, vol. 3, Tübingen 2007. English: *Brief Introduction to the Study of Theology*, Notre Dame, Ind.: University of Notre Dame Press 1994.

23 J. A. Möhler, *Die Einheit in der Kirche oder das Prinzip des Katholizismus* (with introduction and commentary, edited by J. R. Geiselmann), Darmstadt 1957. English: *Unity in the Church or the Principle of Catholicism*, Washington: Catholic University of America Press 1996.

24 J. A. Möhler, *Symbolik oder Darstellung der dogmatischen Gegensätze der Katholiken und Protestanten nach ihren öffentlichen Bekenntnisschriften* (with introduction and commentary, edited by J. R. Geiselmann), Darmstadt 1958. English: *Symbolism: Exposition of the Doctrinal Differences between Catholics and Protestants as Evidenced in their Symbolical Writings*, New York: Crossroad Publishing 1997.

25 Möhler, *Unity in the Church*, 113. (*Die Einheit in der Kirche*, 44.48; cf. 380.)

26 Möhler, *Symbolik* 389. K. Barth took offence at this formulation. On the one hand, he clearly saw the importance of the Tübingen School (*Church Dogmatics* I/2, 560ff.), and he called Möhler the father of modern Catholicism (ibid., 561). On the other, he also made the Tübingen School responsible for 'the heresy of neo-Protestantism in Catholicism' (ibid. 546) because, in his view, the Tübingen School had embraced Schleiermacher's teaching of community spirit, which identifies the Church with revelation. M. Seckler has clearly refuted for Drey this widespread misjudgment (Johann Sebastian Dreys Programmschrift [as in note 21], 73*–106*). Regarding Möhler, Barth overlooks that Möhler distanced himself early on, in *Unity*, from Schleiermacher's teaching of community spirit and that he understood the spirit as the Holy Spirit dwelling in the Church, that is, he understood the Spirit as a divine person. It is with good reason that Möhler speaks in the above-quoted passage from *Symbolik* of 'presentation', and elsewhere of 'image-ness' (ibid., 353). So there can be no talk of identifying Christ with the Church. See also below, sections II.2.1 and II.3.2.

27 Augustine, *Contra epist. Manichaei* 5.

28 J. Lortz, *Die Reformation in Deutschland*, vol. 1, Freiburg i. Br. 1949, 162. It is the achievement of Lortz to have initiated, on the Catholic side and over against the then predominantly polemic treatment of Martin Luther's person and theology (Cochläus, Deinfle, Grisar, etc.), an objective, historical assessment of Luther. He nevertheless reaches the conclusion that Luther was never, in the full sense of the word, a 'listener', but that, 'from his roots, he was subjectivisticly disposed'. So also E. Iserloh, *Reformation, Katholische Reform und Gegenreformation* (*Handbuch der Kirchengeschichte* 4), Freiburg i. Br. 1967, 23. The subjectivism thesis was pointedly accentuated by P. Hacker, *Das Ich im Glauben bei Luther* (1966), repr. Bonn 2002 (with a preface by J. Ratzinger). For a different reading, see O. H. Pesch, *Die Theologie der Rechtfertigung bei Martin Luther und Thomas von Aquin*, Mainz 1967. Pesch argues that the existential theology of Luther and the sapiential theology of Thomas Aquinas must be recognized as two possible basic modes of expression. For additional commentary on the Catholic side, see Y. Congar, *Martin Luther. Sa vie, sa foi, sa réforme*, Paris 1983; J. Wicks, *Luther's Reform*, Mainz 1992. See also sections II.2.2, II.4.1 and 4; II.5.1 and 3.

29 So claims the Lutheran theologian W. Trillhaas, *Dogmatik*, Berlin 1962, 510, 519. Trillhaas forcefully illustrates the resulting 'Protestant problem' (ibid., 511–22).

30 WA DB 7, 384.

31 Cf. *Formula of Concord*, in: *Book of Concord*, 465. Similarly, see J. Calvin, *Institutio* IV, 8, 4–8 and the confessions of the Reformed tradition; cf. W. Niesel (ed.), *Bekenntnisschriften und Kirchenordnungen der nach Gottes Wort reformierten Kirche*, Zollikon – Zürich 1938, 43, 13, 64, 23, 67, 18ff.

32 See ibid., 67; 123, 238.

33 G. Ebeling, 'Die Bedeutung der historisch-kritischen Methode für die protestantische Theologie und Kirche', in: *Wort und Glaube* (*Word and*

Faith), vol. 1, Tübingen, 1960, 1–49; and, '"Sola scriptura" und das Problem der Tradition', in: *Wort Gottes und Tradition* (*The Word of God and Tradition*), Göttingen 1964, 91–143; W. Pannenberg, 'The Crisis of the Scripture Principle', in: *Basic Questions in Theology* (1967), vol. 1, London: SCM Press 1970, 1–14.

34 A critical examination of this term, which was introduced by E. Troeltsch, is found in E. Herms, *Kirche, Geschöpf und Werkzeug des Evangeliums*, Tübingen 2010, 1–32.

35 E. Peterson made this very clear in his correspondence with A. von Harnack, the influential representative of Neoprotestantism. See *Theologische Traktate*, Munich, 1951, 295–321.

36 A particularly important early study is W. von Löwenich, *Luthers theologia crucis*, Munich 1929. One must also mention studies by W. Elert, E. Sommerlath, P. Althaus, P. Brunner, E. Schlink, W. Trillhaas, etc. For contemporary expressions, see those by U. Kühn, G. Wenz, W. Härle, E. Herms, etc. Also fundamental here is the hermeneutical theology by G. Ebeling, etc., and the more recent conceptions after K. Barth by such theologians as J. Moltmann, E. Jüngel and others. Pannenberg has presented his own, historical-theological approach, summarized in *Systematic Theology*, vol. 3, Grand Rapids, Mich.: Eerdmans 1998.

37 K. Barth, *Der Römerbrief* (1919; *The Epistle to the Romans*), in *Karl Barth Gesamtausgabe* II/16, Zürich 1985, 3. For the placement and development of Barth's theology. See H. U. von Balthasar, *The Theology of Karl Barth*, New York: Holt, Rinehart and Winston 1971. On the Catholic reception in general, see B. Dahlke, *Die katholische Rezeption Karl Barths. Theologische Erneuerung im Vorfeld des Zweiten Vatikanischen Konzils*, Tübingen 2010.

38 See T. Schneider/W. Pannenberg (eds), *Verbindliches Zeugnis*, vol. 3: *Schriftverständnis und Schriftgebrauch*, Freiburg i. Br. – Göttingen 1998.

39 K. Barth, *CD* I/1 §1.

40 Ibid., 10.

41 *CD* I/2, 890.

42 See the exchange of letters between K. Barth and R. Bultmann, collected in Bernd Jaspert, *Karl Barth – Rudolf Bultmann Letters, 1922–66*, Grand Rapids, Mich.: 1981.

43 On this, see E. Käsemann (ed.), *Das Neue Testament als Kanon. Dokumentation und kritische Analyse zur gegenwärtigen Diskussion*, Göttingen 1970.

44 E. Peterson, 'Was ist Theologie?', in ibid., 11–43. Here: 32.

45 DH 1501/1504.

46 J. R. Geiselmann, 'Das Konzil von Trient und das Verhältnis der Heiligen Schrift und den nichtgeschriebenen Traditionen', in M. Schmaus (ed.), *Die mündliche Überlieferung*, Munich 1957, 168–93; *Die Heilige Schrift und die Tradition* (QD 18), Freiburg i. Br. 1962. J. Ratzinger agreed to this point, but comes to a different overall interpretation of the Council. See 'Offenbarung und Überlieferung', in: K. Rahner/J. Ratzinger, *Offenbarung und Überlieferung* (QD 25, *Revelation and Tradition*), Freiburg i. Br. 1964, 50–69.

47 So J. S. Drey, *Die Apologetik als wissenschaftliche Nachweisung der Göttlichkeit des Christentums in seiner Erscheinung*, vol. 1, Mainz ^{2}1844, 373–8.

48 The extent to which Geiselmann represented the material sufficiency of Scripture not along but rather in contradiction to Lutheran orthodoxy becomes obvious in his book *Die lebendige Überlieferung als Norm des christlichen Glaubens dargestellt im Geist der Traditionslehre Johannes Ev. Kuhns*, Freiburg i. Br. 1959. Already the title speaks for itself. In *Die Heilige Schrift und die Tradition* (= *The Meaning of Tradition*), he concludes that Holy Scripture needs the living Tradition as its interpreter. 'There is no sufficiency of Holy Scripture as such' (ibid., 272).

49 See B. Decker, 'Sola Scriptura bei Thomas von Aquin', in: L. Lennart (ed.), *Universitas* (Festschrift A. Stohr), vol. 1, Mainz 1960, 117–29; Y. Congar, '"Traditio" und "Sacra doctrina" bei Thomas von Aquin', in: J. Betz/H. Fries, *Kirche und Überlieferung* (Festschrift J. R. Geiselmann), Freiburg i. Br. 1960, 170–210.

50 See W. Kasper, *Die Lehre von der Tradition in der Römischen Schule*, Freiburg i. Br. 1962, 163ff, 205ff, 353ff, 399f.

51 The controversy is objectively and differentiatedly presented in J. Ratzinger, *Aus meinem Leben*, Stuttgart 1998, 106–32. However, regarding this point, earlier texts, which have become accessible only recently, contain unfounded criticisms of Geiselmann. An extensive presentation is found in R. Vorderholzer, 'Offenbarung, Schrift und Kirche. Eine Relecture von *Dei Verbum*', in: IKaZ 39 (2010) 287–303.

52 DV 9f. Pope Benedict XVI unfolds this context in detail in the post-synodal apostolic exhortation *Verbum Domini. On the Word of God in the Life and Mission of the Church* (2010). Meanwhile, the ecumenical discussion of the last few decades has made considerable progress on this question. However, no consensus has been reached so far concerning the question of who is to decide upon the proper interpretation of Scripture. On the present state of the debate: cf. W. Kasper, *Harvesting the Fruits*, London 2009, 87–99, 150f, 197f, 202f. On the understanding of Tradition, see above, sections I.4 and II.4.4.

53 O. Cullmann, *Die ersten christlichen Glaubensbekenntnisse*, Zollikon – Zürich 1949; H. Schlier, 'Kerygma und Sophia. Zur neutestamentlichen Grundlegung des Dogmas', in: *Die Zeit der Kirche*, Freiburg i. Br. 1955, 206–32; V. H. Neufeld, *The Earliest Christian Confessions*, Leiden 1963; K. Lehmann, *Auferweckt am dritten Tag nach der Schrift* (QD 38), Freiburg i. Br. 1968; H. Schlier, 'Die Anfänge des christologischen Credos', in: B. Welte (ed.), *Zur Frühgeschichte der Christologie* (QD 51), Freiburg i. Br. 1970, 13–58; J. N. D. Kelly, *Early Christian Creeds* (1950), London: Continuum 2006.

54 On this, see Kasper, *Dogma unter dem Wort Gottes*, 25–57. See also section I.5 note 52. On the question of infallibility, see section II.5.4.

55 See U. Wilckens, *Standpunkte. Grundlegende Themen biblischer Theologie*, Neukirchen-Vluyn 2010, Introduction 7–9.

56 DV 21.

57 H. Strathmann, 'Die Krisis des Kanons der Kirche', in: Käsemann, *Das Neue Testament als Kanon*, 41.

58 J. E. Kuhn, *Einleitung in die katholische Dogmatik*, Tübingen [2]1859, 87.91; and, 'Die formalen Prinzipien des Katholicismus und Protestantismus', in: ThQ 40 (1858) 3.62.185–251.385–442.

59 Quoted from Kasper, *Die Lehre von der Tradition*, 206.

60 DH 246.

61 For the interpretation of this axiom, see DH 3792.3828.

62 LG 12; 35.

63 DH 1501.

64 DV 8.

65 Foundational texts include H. de Lubac, *L'Écriture dans la Tradition*, Paris 1966; and, *Exégèse médiévale. Les quatre sens de l'écriture* (1959–64), Paris 1993 (English: *Medieval Exegesis. The Four Senses of Scripture*, Edinburgh: T & T Clark Ltd. 2001); *Histoire et Esprit. L'intelligence de l'Écriture d'après Origène*, Paris 2002 (English: *History and Spirit: the Understanding of Scripture according to Origen*, San Francisco: Ignatius Press 2007); and, *Der geistige Sinn der Schrift*, Einsiedeln 1952.

66 J. de Ghellinck, *'Pagina' et 'Sacra doctrina'. Histoire d'un mot et transformation de l'objet primitivement désigné* (Mélanges A. Pelzer), Louvain 1947, 23–59.

67 Thomas Aquinas, *Summa theologiae* I q. 1 a. 1. The topological methodology of Melchior Cano has been repeatedly researched in recent time. In addition to older interpretations (A. Lang, A. Gardeil, etc.), we must refer especially to the works by E. Klinger, B. Körner, K. Lehmann. I follow M. Seckler: 'Die ekklesiologische Bedeutung des Systems der "loci theologici". Erkenntnistheoretische Katholizität und strukturale Weisheit', in: *Die schiefen Wände des Lehrhauses. Katholizität als Herausforderung*, Freiburg i. Br. 1988, 79–104.

68 See M. Seckler's criticism of a theology with a one sided orientation towards the magisterium: *Theologie und kirchliche Wissenschaft – ein römisches Modell im Spannungsfeld von Wissenschaft und Kirche*, Freiburg i. Br. 1980, 62–84; and, 'Kirchliches Lehramt und theologische Wissenschaft', in: *Die schiefen Wände des Lehrhauses* (as in note 67), 105–35; and, 'Kirchlichkeit und Freiheit der Theologie', in: ibid., 136–55.

69 At the Council and during the preparation of the pastoral constitution *Gaudium et spes*, a controversy occurred regarding the theological significance of the signs of the times between German (K. Rahner, J. Ratzinger, etc.) and French theologians (M. D. Chenu, etc.). See section II.6.4. After Vatican II, this question became, once again, acute, this time in the debate about the theology of liberation and its introduction of Marxist social analysis into the theological argumentation. See section I.5. Within theology, there emerged the discussion of the methodological and normative relevance of those instances which, following Thomas Aquinas, M. Cano identified as '*loci alieni*' (reason, philosophy and history).

70 See DH 3016. On this, see W. Kasper, 'Kirche ins Denken erheben. Überlegungen zum Thema Glauben und Verstehen in der Ekklesiologie', in: H. A. Mooney et al. (eds), *Theologie aus dem Geist des Humanismus* (Festschrift P. Walter), Freiburg i. Br. 2010, 156–64.

71 Thomas Aquinas, *Summa theologiae* I q. 1 a. 8.

72 UR 11. Understood correctly, the axiom of the *hierarchia veritatum* is a principle of interpretation, rather than a principle of reduction that would authorize the exclusion of so-called secondary truths as adiaphora. See U. Valeske, *Hierarchia veritatum*, Munich 1968; Y. Congar, 'The Hierarchy of Truths', in: *Diversity and Communion*, Mystic: Twenty-Third Publications 1985, 126–33.

73 In this context it is interesting that, according to some versions, the original form of the creed was not 'We believe in the Church' but 'We believe the Church'. This is to say, we do not believe in the Church as we believe 'in God', 'in Jesus Christ' and 'in the Holy Spirit'. On the contrary: because we 'believe in God', we also believe God 'the Church'. Thomas Aquinas also prefers the formula '*credo ecclesiam*' to the formula '*credo in ecclesiam*' (*Summa theologiae* II/II q. 1 a. 9 ad 5). For this distinction, see J. B. Metz, 'Credo Deum, Deo, in Deum', in: LThK^{2} 3, 86–8.

74 Bonaventura, *Sent. prooemium* q. 3.

75 Bonaventura, *Sent.* III dist. 35, q. 1.

76 Meister Eckhart, *Sermo di Augustini*, 6. Further evidence can be found in B. Hallersleben, 'Weisheit III', in LThK^{3} 3, 86–8.

77 Although I cannot discuss this in detail within the present context, I refer to the teaching of faith and assent by J. H. Newman, *An Essay in Aid of a Grammar of Assent*, Garden City, NY, 1955. From a Thomistic perspective, see P. Rousselot, 'Les yeux de la foi', in: RechScRel 1 (1910) 241–59, 444–75. For the symbolism and metaphor of light in philosophy and theology, see J. Ratzinger, 'Licht', in: HThG 2, 44–54. An extensive analysis of the act of faith would go beyond the space available here. For this, see W. Kasper, 'Was alles Erkennen übersteigt. Besinnung auf den christlichen Glauben' (1987), in: WKGS 5, 175–241.

78 B. Pascal, *Thoughts On Religion* (Pensées), Oxford: University Press 1995, 158 (Fragment 277).

79 See W. Kasper, 'Ermutigung zum Denken. Von der Unerlässlichkeit der Metaphysik für die Sache der Theologie', in: ThQ 169 (1989) 257–71.

80 See J. Heinrichs, 'Dialog, dialogisch', in: HWPh. 2, 226–9; B. Langemeyer, *Der dialogische Personalismus in der evangelischen und katholischen Theologie*, Paderborn 1963; B. Casper, *Das dialogische Denken*, Freiburg i. Br. 1967; J. Heinrichs/G. Sauter, 'Dialogik', in: TRE 8, 687–709; E. Levinas, 'Dialog', in: *Christl. Glaube in moderner Gesellschaft*, vol. 1, Freiburg i. Br. 1981, 61–85; J.-C Basset, *Le dialogue interreligieux*, Paris 1996, 11–29.

81 The term 'dialogue' appears in the documents of the Council in a number of very different contexts: e.g., dialogue of God with man (DV 2, 8, 25), dialogue with God (GS 19); dialogue with the world (GS 3; 28, 40, 43; CD 13; OT 19; AG 11; AA 14; PO 19), inter-religious dialogue (NA 2, 4; GS 21,

28, 92; AG 11, 16, 38, 41, 92), ecumenical dialogue (UR 4, 9, 11, 14, 18f., 21ff.; GE 11), dialogue in the Church (GS 4; AG 20; AA 12), dialogue and development of man (GS 25; IM 1). Also important is the encyclical dedicated particularly to the dialogue by Pope Paul VI, *Ecclesiam suam* (1964).

82 John Paul II, Encyclical *Ut unum sint* (1995), 28.

83 Aristotle, *politeia* 1253a, 3f.

84 See M. Pohlenz, *Die Stoa. Geschichte einer geistigen Bewegung*, 2 vols, Göttingen [4]1970.

85 Plato, *theaitetos* 155d; Aristotle, *metaphysica* 982b.

86 J. Habermas, *Zeitdiagnosen*, Frankfurt a. M. 2003, 22–49. On this, see W. Kasper, 'Die Zusage von Heil. Religion und die Zukunft des Menschen', in: L. Honnefelder/M. C. Schmidt (eds), *Die Zukunft des Menschen. Perspektiven und Orientierungen*, Paderborn 2007, 87–104.

87 I. Kant, *Kritik der reinen Vernunft* (= *Critique of Pure Reason*), B 834.

88 For a discussion of the theory of communicative action of J. Habermas, K.-O. Apel, etc., see H. Peukert, *Science, Action, and Fundamental Theology: Toward a Theology of Communicative Action*, Cambridge, MA: MIT Press 1984; H. J. Höhn, *Kirche und kommunikatives Handeln. Studien zur Theologie und Praxis der Kirche in der Auseinandersetzung mit den Sozialtheorien Niklas Luhmanns und Jürgen Habermas'*, Frankfurt a.M. 1985; M. Kehl, *Die Kirche*, Würzburg 1992, 132–47.

89 On this point and in more detail, see section II.2.1. See also H. U. von Balthasar's extensive commentary in *Theo-logic*, vol. 1, San Francisco: Ignatius Press 2000, especially the last chapter 'Truth as Participation', 227–70.

90 J. Habermas, *Glauben und Wissen*, Frankfurt a. M.2001, as well as in other more recent publications. See W. Kasper, 'Glaube, der nach seinem Verstehen fragt. Ein Beitrag zur Diskussion um ein aktuelles Thema', in: StdZ 134 (2009) 507–19.

91 T. W. Adorno, *Minima Moralia. Reflexionen aus dem beschädigten Leben* (*Minima Moralia: Reflections from a Damaged Life*), Frankfurt a.M. 1970, 333 (the full quotation is found above in section I.8, note 102).

92 Pascal, *Thoughts on Religion*, 120–26 (Fragment 233).

93 It was, in particular, W. Pannenberg who demonstrated this anticipatory structure of faith and who made it systematically productive. See his comprehensive remarks in *Systematische Theologie* (*Systematic Theology*), vol. 1, Göttingen 1988, 249ff.

94 This is presented impressively in the document (which was decisively shaped by J. B. Metz) of the Joint Synod of the German dioceses (Gemeinsame Synode der Bistümer Deutschlands), titled 'Unsere Hoffnung', in: *Gemeinsame Synode der Bistümer der Bundesrepublik Deutschlands*, Freiburg i. Br. 1976, 84–111. A similar approach concerning the idea of God's kingdom is found in W. Pannenberg, *Thesen zur Theologie der Kirche*, Munich 1970; and *Systematic Theology*, vol. 3, Grand Rapids, MI. 1998.

2. The horizons of universal and salvation history

1 The best and most extensive presentation of the history of ecclesiology is found in P. V. Dias/P.-T Camelot/Y. Congar (eds), HDG III/3a–d (1970–4). In addition, see H. Fries, 'Wandel des Kirchenbilds und dogmengeschichtliche Entfaltung', in: MySal IV/1, Einsiedeln 1972, 223–85; B. Sesboüé, *La théologie au XXe siècle et l'avenir de la foi. Entretiens avec Marc Leboucher*, Paris 2007; K. Berger/G. May/J. Finkenzeller/U. Kühn, 'Kirche', in: TRE 18, 198–252, 262–77; W. Kasper/J. Drumm, 'Kirche II', in: LThK[3] 5, 1458–64, as well as the respective articles in the RGG, EKL, NHThG and others.

2 General presentations include R. Schnackenburg, *The Church in the New Testament*, London 1965; H. Schlier, 'Die Ekklesiologie des Neuen Testaments', in: MySal IV/1, Einsiedeln 1972, 101–221. See also the aforementioned articles in various encyclopaedias and summary presentations of New Testament theology.

3 This rich material was collected by H. Rahner in *Symbole der Kirche. Die Ekklesiologie der Väter*, Salzburg 1964. See also H.-J. Vogt, *Bilder der frühen Kirche*, Munich 1993.

4 Ambrose, *Commentary on Luke's Gospel* II, 38.

5 See section II.3.2.

6 See section II.5.3.

7 On Luther, see section II.1.2, notes 28–31, and sections II.4.1 and 4; II.5.1 and 3.

8 See the similar expression of this in the *Heidelberg Catechism* (1563), in: *Creeds and Confessions of Faith in the Christian Tradition*, vol. 2: *Creeds and Confessions of the Reformation Era* (ed. J. Pelikan/V. Hotchkiss), New Haven: Yale University Press, 2003, 439ff.

9 On the development of the Reformation understanding of church from Luther to Melanchthon and Calvin and on up to Lutheran orthodoxy, see U. Kühn, 'Kirche VI/1', in: TRE 18, 262–7.

10 W. Pannenberg, 'Einheit der Kirche als Glaubenswirklichkeit und als ökumenisches Ziel', in: *Ethik und Ekklesiologie*, Göttingen 1977, 205; and, 'Reformation und Einheit der Kirche', in: ibid., 255f.

11 A number of Protestant interpreters maintain that the '*satis est*' is, in fact, not satis (sufficient), and thus that the formula should be complemented with passages from Articles V, XIV and XXVIII, which speak about the ministry in the Church. See, for examples, E. Schlink, *Theologie der lutherischen Bekenntnisschriften*, Munich 1948, 275f.; Pannenberg, 'Reformation und Einheit', 266; G. Wenz, *Theologie der Bekenntnisschriften der evangelisch-lutherischen Kirche*, vol. 2, Berlin 1998, 143; H. Meyer, 'Simul satis est et non satis est? Die "satis est" – Aussage von *Confessio Augustana* VII im ökumenischen Dialog', in: *Versöhnte Verschiedenheit. Aufsätze zur ökumenischen Theologie*, vol. 3, Frankfurt a.M. – Paderborn 2009, 63–77.

12 See *Augsburg Confession*, Art. V; XIV; XXVIII.

13 See ibid., Art. V.

14 See ibid., Art. XIV.

15 See ibid., Art. XXVIII. On these issues, see sections II.4.1 and 4, II.5.1 and 3.

16 See section II.1.2.

17 WA 18, 652.

18 R. Bellarmine, *Controversiae* IV, 2, 3.

19 See section II.5.4.

20 See section I.3 and II.1, notes 21–6.

21 For this, see J. R. Geiselmann, *Die katholische Tübinger Schule. Ihre theologische Eigenart*, Freiburg i. Br. 1864, 191–279; J. Rief, *Reich Gottes und Gesellschaft nach J. S. Drey und J. B. Hirscher*, Paderborn 1965; E. Klinger, *Ekklesiologie der Neuzeit. Grundlegung bei Melchior Cano und Entwicklung bis zum Zweiten Vatikanischen Konzil*, Freiburg i. Br. 1978, 118–202; W. Fürst, *Wahrheit im Interesse der Freiheit*, Mainz 1979; M. Seckler, 'Das Reich-Gottes-Motiv in den Anfängen der Tübinger Schule', in ThQ 168 (1988), 257–88; L. Hell, *Reich Gottes als Systemidee der Theologie*, Mainz 1993.

22 For a summary, see W. Pannenberg, *Systematic Theology*, vol. 3, Edinburgh: T&T Clark, 1998.

23 For examples: Georges Florovsky, Sergei Bulgakov, Vladimir Lossky, Alexander Schmemann, John Meyendorff, Paul Evdokimov, John Zizioulas, etc.

24 Emil Brunner, Eduard Thurneysen, Friedrich Gogarten, Rudolf Bultmann, etc.

25 Dietrich Bonhoeffer, Hans Asmussen, Werner Elert, Paul Althaus, Peter Brunner, Ernst Sommerlath, Ernst Kinder, Edmund Schlink, Ulrich Kühn, etc.

26 See section I.4.

27 See section II.2.7.

28 See section II.1, note 26.

29 The question is still unresolved whether ecclesiology is to be placed *after* the doctrine of grace or justification (the traditional view) or *before* it (so goes the view proposed in more recent systematic presentations such as those of M. Schmaus, MySal, etc.). For my part, the most convincing solution is the one suggested by W. Pannenberg (*Systematische Theologie*, vol. 3 [*Systematic Theology*], 93), who incorporates the doctrine of election and grace into ecclesiology, which in turn, has its place within the horizon of the eschatological message of God's kingdom.

30 Thomas Aquinas, *Summa theologiae* I q. 1. a. 3 ad 1.

31 Thomas Aquinas, *Summa theologiae* II/II q. 1 ad 1.

32 Ibid., a. 2 ad 2.

33 Ibid., a. 6 s.c.

34 Bonaventura, I Sent. prooemium q. 1.

35 F. Holböck/T. Sartory (eds), *Mysterium Kirche*, 2 vols, Salzburg 1962; G. Baraúna (ed.), *De Ecclesia. 'Beiträge zur Konstitution über die Kirche' des*

Zweiten Vatikanischen Konzils, vol. 1, Freiburg i. Br. – Frankfurt a.M. 1966; J. Ratzinger, 'Die Kirche als Heilssakrament', in: JRGS 8/1, 244–57; and, 'Die Ekklesiologie des Zweiten Vatikanischen Konzils', in: ibid. 258–82.

36 LG 1.

37 Irenaeus of Lyons, *adversus haereses* IV, 20, 7.

38 See H. Rahner, *Symbole der Kirche. Die Ekklesiologie der Väter*, Salzburg 1964, 91–139; and, *Griechische Mythen in christlicher Deutung* (*Greek Myths and Christian Mystery*, London: Burns & Oates 1963) Basel 1966, 89–158.

39 See section II.1.2.

40 K. Rahner, 'The Concept of Mystery in Catholic Theology', in: *Theological Investigations*, vol. 4, Baltimore: Helicon Press 1966, 36–73; G. Ebeling, 'Profanität und Geheimnis', in: *Wort und Glaube*, vol. 2, Tübingen 1969, 184–208; WKGS 4, 216–25; E. Jüngel, *Gott als Geheimnis der Welt. Zur Begründung der Theologie des Gekreuzigten im Streit zwischen Theismus und Atheismus* (*God as the Mystery of the World*, Grand Rapids: Eerdmans, 1983), Tübingen 1977, 307–408.

41 This in fact well-meaning attempt is found in H. Lübbe, *Religion nach der Aufklärung*, Graz: Styra 1986.

42 D. Bonhoeffer, *Widerstand und Ergebung. Briefe und Aufzeichnungen aus der Haft* (*Letters and Papers from Prison*, Minneapolis: Fortress Press 2010), edited by E. Bethge, Munich 1977, 341, etc.

43 The task of unpacking and demonstrating this belongs to the field of fundamental theology. Moreover, the doctrine of God and cannot be addressed here. On this, see WKGS 4, 183–97.

44 Thomas Aquinas, *Summa theologiae* I q. 2 a. 3; *Summa contra gentiles* I 13; 15; 16; 44.

45 So H. U. von Balthasar, *Theologik* (*Theo-logic*, vol. 2, San Francisco: Ignatius Press 2004), vol. 2, Einsiedeln 1985, 91–8; also A. M. Haas, *Wind des Absoluten: Mystische Weisheit der Postmoderne*, Einsiedeln 2009. This book is a continuation of H. U. von Balthasar, *The God Question and Modern Man* (1956), New York: Seabury Press 1967.

46 J. Hochstaffl, *Negative Theologie. Ein Versuch zur Vermittlung des patristischen Begriffs*, Munich 1976; and, 'Negative Theologie', in: LThK3 7, 723–5; W. Oelmüller, *Negative Theologie heute. Die Lage der Menschen vor Gott*, Munich 1999.

47 WKGS 2, 181–98, 216–19.

48 WKGS 206–16; M. Seckler, 'Der Begriff der Offenbarung', in: HFThess. 2, 62f.

49 NA 2. On this, see sections II.2.5 and III.5.3.

50 DV 2.

51 On this, see M. Seckler, 'Der Begriff der Offenbarung', 64–7. For an overview, see A. Dulles, *Models of Revelation*, Garden City, NY: Doubleday 1983.

52 See section I.4; and section II.2.1. In addition, see H. U. von Balthasar, *Die Gottesfrage des heutigen Menschen* (1956), new extended ed., Einsiedeln 2009, 27–32, 61–79.

53 Schelling addressed this failure and its reversal in his negative and positive philosophy. Admittedly, he tried to reflect upon positive philosophy via the model of negative philosophy and failed in this attempt. In this respect, the Bible is both more radical and more consequent. It perceives the reversal as radical and underivable from God. On this, see WKGS 2, 181–234, 598–604.

54 On this determination of dialectic, see J. E. Kuhn, *Einleitung in die katholische Dogmatik*, Tübingen [2]1859, 240f.

55 W. Löser, '"Universale concretum" als Grundgesetz der oeconomia revelationis', in: HFThess. 2, 108–21.

56 Ignatius of Antioch, *ad Polycarpum* III, 2: Irenaeus of Lyons, *adversus haereses* IV, 20, 4. See von Balthasar, *Die Gottesfrage des heutigen Menschen*, 63f, 98–113.

57 G. Bornkamm, 'μυστήριον', in: ThWNT 4, 820–31.

58 G. Bornkamm, 'μυστήριον', in: ThWNT 4, 825. For Jesus' message of the kingdom of God, see section II.2.2.

59 For the interpretation, see WKGS 4, 304–16.

60 See the interpretation of H. Schlier, *Brief an die Epheser*, Düsseldorf, 1957, 74–99. Whereas Schlier assumes a Hellenistic background, F. Manns (*Le Judéo-christianisme. Mémoire ou Prophétie?*, Paris 2000) has shown that such views can also be understood against the background of the Judaism of that time.

61 See LG 2–4.

62 For this problem, see E. Jüngel, *Gott als Geheimnis der Welt. Zur Begründung der Theologie des Gekreuzigten im Streit zwischen Theismus und Atheismus* (*God as the Mystery*), Tübingen 1977, 55–138.

63 This is based in parts on Schelling, 'Philosophie der Kunst', in Samtlche Werke V, 424f.; 'Philosophie der Offenbarung', in: Samtlche Werke XIV, 174. Cf. WKGS 2, 521–30. At this point we can also make positive use of the basic intentions of Martin Luther's theology of the Cross. On this, see W. Kasper, 'Das Kreuz als Offenbarung der Liebe Gottes', in: Cath(M) 61 (2007) 1–14.

64 LG 4. See Cyprian, *de oratione Domini*, 23. in a similar vein, see Augustine, *sermones* 71, 20, 33; and John of Damascus, *liber adversus Iconoclastas* 12. In the light of such explicit statements by the Council and its reference to Cyprian and other important Church Fathers, the critique in the otherwise instructive article 'Das Konzil und die Kirche' (in: IKaZ 39 (2010), 607f., 612) by B. Stubenrauch and M. Seewald concerning the Trinitarian analogy of the Church is incomprehensible.

65 UR 2.

66 N. A. Nissiotis, *Die Theologie der Ostkirche im ökumenischen Dialog. Kirche und Welt in orthodoxer Sicht*, Stuttgart 1968, 52–7; J. Zizioulas, *L'être ecclésiale*, Geneva 1981; B. Bobrinskoy, *Le mystère de l'Église*, Paris 2003, 130–34.

67 C. Journet, *L'Église du Verbe incarné*, vol. 3, Paris 1969; B. Forte, *La Chiesa icona della Trinità. Breve ecclesiologia*, Brescia 1984; B. Forte, *La Chiesa della Trinità. Saggio sul mistero della Chiesa comunione e missione*, Cinisello-Balsamo, 1995; J. M. Tillard, *L'Église des églises. L'ecclésiologie de communion*, Paris 1987; M. Kehl, *Die Kirche. Eine katholische Ekklesiologie*, Würzburg 1992, 63–103. For an overview, see M. Naro, 'Trinità e Chiesa', in: *Dizionario di ecclesiologia*, Roma 2010, 1465–75. See also J. Moltmann, *The Church in the Power of the Spirit*, New York: Harper & Row, 1977.

68 Regarding this point, see WKGS 4, 31–3, 383–5, 463–77.

69 On this dialectic of determination, see J.E. Kuhn, *Katholische Dogmatik*, vol. 2, Tübingen 1857, 498ff, 545ff.; WKGS 4, 449f.

70 See H.J. Klauck, *Der erste Johannesbrief* (EKK XXIII/1), Neukirchen 1991, 73f.

71 See R. Schnackenburg, *Die Johannesbriefe* (*The Johannine Epistles: Introduction and Commentary*, New York: Crossroad 1992), Freiburg i. Br. 1953, 57–62.

72 See K. H. Schelkle, *Die Petrusbriefe. Der Judasbrief* (HThK XII/2), Freiburg i. Br. 1961, 188f.; A. Vögtle, *Der Judasbrief. Der zweite Petrusbrief* (EKK XXII), Neukirchen 1994, 140f. Concerning its vast reception history, see Vögtle, ibid. 145–8.

73 See I.4.

74 See E. Peterson, 'Monotheism as a Political Problem: a Contribution to the History of Political Theology in the Roman Empire' (1935), in: *Theological Tractates*, Stanford: University Press 2011, 68–105.

75 On the monastic tradition, see S. Chialà et al. (eds), *La Paternità spirituale nella tradizione ortodossa*, Bose 2009; G. Bunge, *Geistliche Vaterschaft* (Eremos, 1), Münster 2010.

76 See Benedictine Rule, cap 2f., 64.

77 Such is Kant's criticism in *Der Streit der Fakultäten* (*The Conflict of the Faculties*, New York: Abaris Books 1979) A 49f.

78 This construction is first found in African Bible translations. Tertullian uses it and transmits it further. See *ad martyres* 3, 3,1; *de spectaculis* 24, 4; *adversus Marcionem* IV, 34, 5; V, 8, 3.

79 See Cyprian of Carthage, *de ecclesiae unitate* 7; ep. 66, 8.

80 See G. Philips, *L'église et son mystère*, vol. 1, Paris 1967, 72–4; Ratzinger, 'Die Kirche als Heilssakrament', 244–7.

81 See O. Semmelroth, *Die Kirche als Ursakrament*, Frankfurt a.M. 1953; K. Rahner, *The Church and the Sacraments* (QD 10), Freiburg i. Br. 1963; E. Schillebeeckx, *Christ the Sacrament of the Encounter with God*, London: Sheed & Ward 1963; L. Boff, *Die Kirche als Sakrament im Horizont der Welterfahrung*, Paderborn 1972; Y. Congar, *Un peuple messianique. L'Église sacrement du salut. Salut et libération*, Paris 1975.W. Beinert, 'Die Sakramentalität der Kirche im theologischen Gespräch', in: J. Pfammater/F.

Furger (eds), *Theologische Berichte* 9, Zürich 1980, 13–66; W. Kasper, 'Die Kirche als universales Sakrament des Heils' (1984), in: WKGS 11, 306–27; J. Meyer zu Schlochtern, *Sakrament Kirche. Wirken Gottes im Handeln der Menschen*, Freiburg i. Br. 1992; *Die sakramentale Struktur der Kirche in der ökumenischen Diskussion*, ed. by Johann-Adam-Möhler Institut, Paderborn 1983; P. Hünermann, 'Die Kirche: Sakrament des Heils', in: HThK.Vat II 2, 324–36.

82 LG 1.

83 See LG 9; 48; also SC 5, 26; GS 42, 45; AG 1, 5 and others.

84 See Augustine, ep. 69, 6.

85 See Augustine, *enarrationes in Psalmos* 138, 2.

86 It was already in 1520 that Luther, basically in line with Augustine, said that we should reserve the term 'sacrament' for Jesus Christ, and that the sacramental actions of the Church should rather be called sacramentals (WA 6, 501, 37f.). K. Barth argues similarly in *Church Dogmatics* (1955), vol. IV/2 §64, London: T. & T. Clark 2009, 55. Concerning this question, G. Ebeling perceived a basic difference between the Catholic and Lutheran understanding of Church, cf. *Dogmatik des christlichen Glaubens*, Tübingen, 1979, 314f. Following Luther and Barth, E. Jüngel also initially formulated a harsh criticism, yet, in the end, built an intellectual bridge towards a sacramental understandings of the Church, in 'The Church as Sacrament', in: *Theological Essays*, vol. I, Edinburgh: T & T Clark 1989, 189–213. G. Wenz ('Sakramente', in: TRE 29, 663–95) and W. Pannenberg (*Systematische Theologie*, vol. 3, 52–5) strive even more explicitly to mediate. Meanwhile, regarding this question, we can notice an ecclesiological basic consensus. The term 'sacrament' was taken up by the plenary meeting of the World Council of Churches in Uppsala (1968), the Faith and Order Commission in Accra (1974), Bangalore (1978) and Leuven (1971). It was also used in bilateral dialogues, cf. W. Kasper, *Harvesting the Fruits. Aspects of Christian Faith in Ecumenical Dialogue*, London/New York 2009, 68–71. Hence, the term 'sacrament' has lost its significance for distinguishing between Catholic and Protestant ecclesiologies.

87 LG 8. The expression 'coalesce' is occasionally criticized because it can suggest a union of natures. This would contradict Christological dogma. For the union in Christ is not a union of natures but a hypostatic union. The union in the Church is neither a union of natures nor a hypostatic union. According to the Church Fathers it is not a hypostatic union (καθ' ὑπόστασιν) but a relational union (κατὰ σχέσιν).

88 Critical opposition to this on the part of Protestant theology typically consists of an application of arguments made against the the notion of cooperation of Man in the *act* of salvation to the problem of the cooperation of the Church in the *mediation* of salvation. The latter, however, has a biblical foundation (cf. 1 Cor. 3.9; 2 Cor. 6.1). Luther himself rejected an enthusiastic view of the mediation of salvation which disregards the Word and sacrament. Instead he spoke of *cooperatores* (WA 18, 695). Cf. E. Herms, *Kirche – Geschöpf und Werkzeug des Evangeliums*, Tübingen 2010, XIVf.; 50. See section II 3.3.

89 Leo the Great, *sermones* 74, 2.

90 Thomas Aquinas, *Summa theologiae* III q 65 a. 1; cf. q 60 a. 6.

91 Thomas Aquinas, *Summa theologiae* III q 60 a. 2: *signum rei sacrae inquantum est sanctificans homines. Suppl.* q. 29 a. 2: *significando causat.*

92 For the term 'symbolic reality' (Realsymbol), see Rahner, 'The Theology of the Symbol', in: *Theological Investigations*, vol. 4, 221–52.

93 LG 8; cf. Augustine, *de civitate Dei* XVIII, 51, 2.

94 LG 48.

95 Cf. II 2.1.

96 Cf. II 4.1.

97 Thomas Aquinas, *IV Sent* d. 4 q. 1 a. 1 q. 1a 1 ad 4; *Summa theologiae* III q. 60 a. 3.

98 LG 3.

99 For example, see Thomas Aquinas, *Summa theologiae* II/II q. 183 a. 2 and 3; *Suppl.* q. 34 a. 1.

100 Schelling, *Philosophie der Kunst*, in *Samtliche Werke* V, 455f.

101 On J. M Sailer, see R. Geiselmann, *Von lebendiger Religiosität zum Leben der Kirche*, Stuttgart 1952, 191–8.

102 J. S. Drey, see Geiselmann, *Geist des Christentums und des Katholizismus. Ausgewählte Schriften katholischer Theologie im Zeitalter des deutschen Idealismus und der Romantik*, Mainz 1940, 213–25, also: J. S. Drey, *Kurze Einleitung in das Studium der Theologie* (*Brief Introduction to the Study of Theology*, Notre Dame, Ind.: University of Notre Dame Press 1994) Tübingen 1819, §278.

103 J. A. Möhler, *Symbolism*, §37. (*Symbolik*, §37, 393–5).

104 Einsiedeln 1961–4. For remarks of particular importance for ecclesiology, see vol. 1, 535–81. Reference to Schiller, Fichte, Schelling, Hegel and others are found in vol. 3/1, 848–921.

105 *Gotteslob* [German Hymnal, T.H.] 639.

106 Origen, *in Ezechielem* 9, 1.

107 K. Kuhn, 'βασιλεύς, βασιλεία', in: ThWNT I, 563–9; J. Jeremias, *Das Königtum Gottes in den Psalmen. Israels Begegnung mit dem kanaanäischen Mythos in den Jahwe-König-Psalmen*, Göttingen 1987.

108 K. L. Schmidt, 'βασιλεία', in: ThWNT I, 579–92; R. Schnackenburg, *Gottes Herrschaft und Reich. Eine bibeltheologische Studie*, Freiburg i. Br. 1959; H. Schürmann, *Gottes Reich – Jesu Geschick*, Freiburg i. Br. 1983; WKGS 3, 83–139; H. Merklein, *Jesu Botschaft von der Gottesherrschaft*, Stuttgart 1983; J. Gnilka, *Jesus von Nazareth* (*Jesus of Nazareth: Message and history*), Freiburg i. Br. 1990; U. Wilckens, *Theologie des Neuen Testaments*, vol. I/1, Neukirchen-Vluyn 2002; F. Hahn, *Theologie des Neuen Testaments*, vol. 1, Tübingen 2002.

109 J. Jeremias, *Jesu Verheißung für die Völker*, Göttingen 1959. G. Lohfink, *Die Sammlung Israels*, Munich 1975.

110 Origen, *Commentatorium in Mt. XIV*, 7.

111 For the still-classic presentation of the first quest, which is, at the same time, its funeral address, see A. Schweitzer, *Geschichte der Leben-Jesu-Forschung*, Tübingen 1913.

112 A. von Harnack, *Das Wesen des Christentums* (1900), Munich (reprint) 1964, 45.

113 Ibid., 117–67; here 156.

114 A. von Harnack, *Lehrbuch der Dogmengeschichte*, vol. 1, (1885), Darmstadt (reprint) 1964, 20. M. Werner (*Die Entstehung des christlichen Dogmas*, Bern – Tübingen 1941) developed Harnack's theory of Hellenization further with the thesis that the de-eschatologization was a prerequisite for the Hellenization of Christianity. For an overview of the Hellenization debate, see J. Drumm, 'Hellenisierung', in: $LThK^3$ 4, 1407–9.

115 A. Loisy, *L'Évangile et l'Église* (1902). This thesis, directed against A. Harnack, was apologetic insofar as Loisy understood it in the sense of a development. In 1904, M. Blondel wrote against such a historicist perspective in his famous essay, 'Geschichte und Dogma', Mainz 1963, which is still worth reading.

116 E. Peterson, 'The Church' (1929), in: *Theological Tractates*, Stanford: University Press 2011, 30–40.

117 R. Bultmann, *Das Verhältnis der urchristlichen Christusbotschaft zum historischen Jesus*, Heidelberg 1960; Bultmann, *Theology of the New Testament*, Waco, TX: Baylor University Press 2007, §§1–4.

118 WKGS 3, 156–62.

119 In particular, see W. Trilling, 'Implizite Ekklesiologie', in: *Die Botschaft Jesu*, Freiburg i. Br. 1978, 57–72. For a summary, see G. Lohfink, *Wie hat Jesus Gemeinde gewollt?*, Freiburg i. Br. 1982; Lohfink, 'Jesus und die Kirche', in: HFThess. 3, 27–64; Lohfink, *Braucht Gott die Kirche?*, Freiburg i. Br. 1998. Very detailed: K. Berger, 'Kirche II', in: TRE 18, 201–18.

120 The handbooks of apologetics usually base the foundation of the Church on the word to Peter: 'You are Peter and on this rock I will build my church.' (Mt. 16:18) For Catholic ecclesiology there is no question concerning the significance of this statement and of the special vocation of Peter. Yet, in its present version, the statement attributed to Peter is hardly an authentic logia (see section II.5.4). In addition, the statement must be seen in a wider ecclesiological context. An isolated approach regarding this sentence leads to a one-sidedly institutional view of the Church. The second passage in the synoptic gospels in which we find the word 'church' is the community rule in Mt. 18.17f., which also has to be regarded as a later logia attributed to Jesus.

121 H. Schürmann emphasized the continuity – of faith as well as in sociological terms – which, in spite of all interruptions, exists, through the cross, between the time before and after Easter. See, for example, 'Die vorösterlichen Anfänge der Logientradition', in: H. Ristow/K. Matthiae (eds), *Der historische Jesus und der kerygmatische Christus*, Berlin 1960, 342–70.

122 K. H Rengstorf, 'ἑπτά', in: ThWNT 2, 630f.

123 Concerning the extensive discussion in H. Lietzmann, J. Jeremias, H. Schürmann, F. Hahn, H. J. Klauck, R. Pesch, H. Merklein, etc., see WKGS 3, 184, 240–2, 390; WKGS 10, 43–5. On the issue of dating, see Benedict XVI., *Jesus von Nazareth* (*Jesus of Nazareth*, vol. 2, San Francisco: Ignatius Press 2011), vol. 2, Freiburg i. Br. 2011, 126–34.

124 WKGS 3, 219–21.

125 Vielhauer/G. Strecker, 'Apokalyptik des Urchristentums, Einleitung', in: W. Schneemelcher (ed.), *Neutestamentliche Apokryphen in deutscher Übersetzung*, vol. 2, Tübingen [5]1989, 491–547. F. Hahn, *Frühjüdische und urchristliche Apokalyptik. Eine Einführung*, Neukirchen-Vluyn 1998.

126 E. Peterson, 'The Church' (1929), in: *Theological Tractates*, Stanford: University Press 2011, 30–40. Peterson put forward the hypothesis that the Church is only possible on the basis of the precondition of the unbelief of the Jews, and, in connection to this, to the non-appearance of God's kingdom. However, today the separation between the Church and Judaism is considered in a more differentiated way and in the context of a longer historical process. Cf. H. U. Weidemann, in his reflections following Erik Peterson, in: Erik Peterson, *Ekklesia. Studien zum christlichen Kirchenbegriff*, Würzburg 2010, 158–64. Along similar lines, H. Schlier regards Pentecost as the origin of the Church: 'Ekklesiologie des Neuen Testaments', in: MySal IV/1, Einsiedeln 1972, 101–221.

127 See Berger, 'Kirche II', 213.

128 See ibid 203f. For more detailed commentary, see section II.3.2.

129 See LG 5, 9.

130 LG 3.

131 LG 48.

132 AG 9.

133 On the original meaning of the word, see K. L. Schmidt, 'ἐκκλησία', in: ThWNT 3, 516–20, 530–5. In further detail, see W. Schrage, '"Ekklesia" und "Synagoge". Zum Ursprung des christlichen Kirchenbegriffs', in: ZThK 60 (1963) 178–202, K. Berger, 'Volksversammlung und Gemeinde Gottes. Zu den Anfängen der christlichen Verwendung von "ekklesia"', in: ZThK 73 (1976) 167–207; also Berger, 'Kirche II', 201, 214f.

134 E. Peterson had already suggested this in 'Synagoge und Ekklesia. Bedeutung und Verhältnis beider Begriffe', in: *Ausgewählte Schriften*. Sonderband, Würzburg 2010, 11–26. In line with the then accepted, yet now superseded state of research, Peterson began from the premise of the distinction of the Church from the Jewish synagogue. Yet, it was his achievement to be the first to point out the Hellenistic background of ecclesia.

135 For the extensive debate, see J. Ernst/J. Kremsmaier/D. Sattler, 'Binden und Lösen', in: LThK[3] 2, 463–5. See section II.5.4.

136 A detailed description of the Hellenistic culture in Palestine of that time is presented in M. Hengel, *Judentum und Hellenismus*, Tübingen 1969. For the importance of the Hellenistic Christians in Jerusalem, see U. Wilckens, *Theologie des Neuen Testaments*, vols 1/2, Neukirchen 2003, 230–39.

137 So also K. Holl, *Der Kirchenbegriff des Paulus in seinem Verhältnis zu dem der Urgemeinde*, Berlin 1921; H. Campenhausen, *Kirchliches Amt und geistliche Vollmacht in den ersten drei Jahrhunderten*, Tübingen 1953.

138 See section II.3.2.

139 For an extensive discussion of this see section II.5.5.

140 WA 50, 625.

141 *Book of Concord*, 417.

142 M. Luther, *The Smalcald Articles*, in: *Book of Concord*, 315; see also 614.

143 M. Luther, *Small Catechism*, in: *Book of Concord*, 345.

144 G. Gloege, 'Gemeinde I', in: RGG^3 2, 1328f.

145 On the debate concerning the Early Catholicism initiated by A. Harnack, R. Sohm, and then later again by E. Käsemann, see section II.4.3.

146 E. Brunner, *Das Missverständnis der Kirche*, Stuttgart 1951.

147 K. Barth, *CD* IV/1, §67, 653ff.; IV/2 §67, especially 676ff.

148 E. Peterson highlighted this concrete formal gestalt in his correspondence with A. Harnack (*Theologische Traktate*, Munich 1955, 293–322), in the light of new descriptions of the problem. See H. Schlier (*Das bleibend Katholische. Ein Versuch über ein Prinzip des Katholischen*, Münster 1970), H. U. von Balthasar (*Katholisch. Aspekte des Mysteriums*, Einsiedeln 1975) and L. Scheffczyk (*Katholische Glaubenswelt. Wahrheit und Gestalt*, Aschaffenburg 1977).

149 J. L. Leuba, *Institution und Ereignis*, Göttingen 1957, became decisive for the discussion. On the Catholic side, see the critical works: H. Fries, *Kirche als Ereignis*, Düsseldorf 1958; Y. Congar, *Christus – Maria – Kirche* (*Christ, Our Lady and the Church: a Study in Eirenic Theology*, London: Longmans, Green & Co. 1957), Mainz 1965, 13f.; A. Dulles, *Models of the Church*, Garden City, NY 1987, 81–93; from the Orthodox side P. Evdokimov, *L'ortodossia*, Bologna 1981, 177–80; from the Protestant side Moltmann, *Kirche in der Kraft des Geistes* (*Church in the Power of the Spirit*), 359f.; Pannenberg, *Systematische Theologie* (*Systematic Theology*), 50.

150 See the respective articles in: *Dictionary of the Ecumenical Movement*, Geneva 2002; 'Anglican Communion' (21–4); 'Lutheran World Federation' (722–4); 'World Alliance of Reformed Churches' (1217f.); 'World Methodist Council' (1244f.); 'World Evangelical Alliance' (1249f.).

151 *Agreement of the Churches of the Reformation in Europe* (Leuenberg Agreement, 1973); *The Church of Jesus Christ. The Contribution of the Reformation towards Ecumenical Dialogue on Church Unity* (Leuenberg Documents 1). For its history, see E. Schieffer, *Von Schauenburg nach Leuenberg. Entstehung und Bedeutung der Konkordie reformatorischer Kirchen in Europa*, Paderborn 1983. The most extensive rationale for the Leuenberg concept is found in E. Herms, *Kirche – Geschöpf und Werkzeug des Evangeliums*, Tübingen 2010.

152 W.-D. Hauschild, 'Evangelische Kirche Deutschland I', in: RGG^4 2, 1713–17.

153 For more detailed commentary, see section II.5.4.

154 This aspect, too, was already pointed out by Peterson in: 'Ekklesia und Himmelstadt', in: *Synagoge und Ekklesia* (as in note 134), 26–52; idem, 'The Book on the Angels: Their Place and Meaning in the Liturgy', in: *Theological Tractates*, Stanford: University Press 2011, 106–42. On the basis of recent research, it has become necessary to reconsider and differentiate individual aspects of his position here. In particular one needs to point not to the Hellenistic-Platonic, but, rather, to the rabbinic background for the idea of the heavenly city. Cf. Weidemann, *Überlegungen*, 164–71.

155 E. Käsemann, *Das wandernde Gottesvolk. Eine Untersuchung zum Hebräerbrief*, Göttingen [2]1957.

156 Irenaeus of Lyons, *adversus haereses* III, 16:6, 22:1–3.

157 Irenaeus of Lyons, *adversus haereses* III, 17:2.

158 Hrabanus Maurus, *De Universo*, lib. 22 c. 3.

159 Ambrose, *explanatio super Psalmos* 118, 2, 33; 118, 22, 41.

160 John Chrysostom, *in Johannem homeliea*, 65, 1. (On John 11.49.50).

161 Hilary of Poitiers, *tractatus super Psalmos* 121, 4.

162 Augustine, *enarrationes in Psalmos* 147, 19.

163 Augustine, *de civitate Dei* IX, 17; cf. *sermones* 175; 266–9; *in Johannis evangelium* VI, 10.

164 O. Cullmann, *Christus und die Zeit. Die urchristliche Zeit- und Geschichtsauffassung*, Zürich 1948; H. Conzelmann, *Die Mitte der Zeit. Studien zur Theologie des Lukas*, Tübingen [5]1964.

165 On serving the coming kingdom of God, see sections II.6.1; II.6.2.3 and 4.

166 On this, see W. Nigg, *Das ewige Reich*, Zürich 1954; E. Gilson, Les *métamorphoses de la cite de Dieu*, Vrin 1952; A. Dempf, *Sacrum Imperium*, Darmstadt 1962.

167 R. Bultmann; *Geschichte und Eschatologie* (*The Presence of Eternity: History and Eschatology*, New York: Harper 1957), Tübingen 1958, 183f.

168 Concerning other forms, see section II.3.1.

169 See section II.5.8.

170 See section II.4.4.

171 Augustine, *de civitate Dei* III, 30; XVIII 22, 46.

172 Ibid. XIV, 28.

173 Ibid. I, 36; *de doctrina christiana* III 323, 45.

174 This must be taken into account when interpreting passages which suggest an identification of the Church with the kingdom of God, such as *de civitate Dei* XX, 9, 1f.

175 Ibid. XVIII, 51, 2.

176 Ibid. XXII, 30.

177 On this point, I refer to the last section of Peterson, *Der Monotheismus als politisches Problem*, 103f.

178 M. Seckler, *Das Heil in der Geschichte. Geschichtstheologisches Denken bei Thomas von Aquin*, Munich 1964.

179 Thomas Aquinas, *IV Sent.* q. 18, a. 1, ad 1 sol 1; *Summa theologiae* I q. 64 a. 2 ad 3; II/II q. 99 a. 1 ad 2 and others.

180 Thomas Aquinas, *Summa theologiae* II/II q. 105 a. 1–2.

181 Thomas Aquinas, *Summa theologiae* II/I q. 106 a. 4 ad 4.

182 Bonaventura was by far more benevolent towards the movement started by Joachim of Fiore. As this cannot be discussed here, we direct the reader to the detailed comments in J. Ratzinger, *The Theology of History in St. Bonaventure* (1959), Chicago: Franciscan Herald Press 1989. A substantially extended edition is found in idem, *Das Offenbarungsverständnis und die Geschichtstheologie Bonaventuras* (JRGS 2), Freiburg i.Br. 2009.

183 K. Löwith, *Weltgeschichte als Heilsgeschehen*, Stuttgart 1953.

184 J. B. Metz, *Glaube in Geschichte und Gesellschaft*, Mainz 1977; also, *Zum Begriff der neuen politischen Theologie. 1967–97*, Mainz 1997; H. Peukert (ed.), *Diskussion zur 'politischen Theologie'*, Mainz – Munich 1969; R. Strunk, *Politische Ekklesiologie im Zeitalter der Revolution*, Mainz 1971; J. Ratzinger, *Church, Ecumenism and Politics*, New York: Crossroad 1988. In this context, see also J. Moltmann, *The Church in the Power of the Spirit*, New York: Harper & Row 1977. In North America, R. Niebuhr became especially influential. See *Christ and Culture*, New York: Harper 1951.

185 N. Lohfink, *Die messianische Alternative*, Freiburg i. Br. 1961; and, *Kirchenträume*, Freiburg i. Br. 1982; G. Lohfink, *Wie hat Jesus Gemeinde gewollt?*, Freiburg i. Br. 1982; and, *Gottes Taten weiter geben*, Freiburg i. Br. 1985. See section II.6.2.4.

186 See section II.2.4.

187 LG 3.

188 See sections II.6.4, II.7.

189 1 *Clement* 14, 1; 2 *Clement* 14, 1; *Shepherd of Hermas*, visiones 2, 4, 1; Epiphanius, *panarion* I, 1, 5; Cyprian, *de ecclesiae unitate*, 7; Augustine, *retractationes* 1, 12, 13.

190 G. von Rad, *Wisdom in Israel* (1970), London: SCM 1993; M. Hengel, *Judentum und Hellenismus* (*Judaism and Hellenism*, London: SCM 1981), Tübingen 1973, 291–318; H. Gese, *Zur biblischen Theologie* (*Essays on Biblical Theology*, Minneapolis: Augsburg Publ. House 1981), Munich 1977, 152–201. On the 'manifold wisdom of God', see H. Schlier, *Der Brief an die Epheser*, Düsseldorf 1957, particularly 158–67. Instead of the Hellenistic background emphasised by Schlier, today the Judaeo-Christian background is stressed. Cf. Manns, *Le Judéo-Christianisme* (cf. note 60), 225–36; W. Kasper, 'Gottes Gegenwart in Jesus Christus. Vorüberlegungen zu einer weisheitlichen Christologie', in: W. Baier et al. (eds), *Weisheit Gottes – Weisheit der Welt* (Festschrift J. Ratzinger), vol. 2, St. Ottilien 1987, 311–28; and, 'Jesus Christus – das Licht der Welt. Die Weisheitschristologie als Auslegungsschlüssel der Weltweisheit', in: G. Augustin et al. (eds), *Christus Gottes schöpferisches Wort* (Festschrift C. Schönborn), Freiburg i. Br. 2010, 293–9.

191 Justin, *apologia* I, 46; *apologia* II, 7, 10, 13.

192 Justin, *apologia* II, 10.

193 Justin, *apologia* I, 5.

194 Justin, *apologia* I, 46.

195 Clement of Alexandria, *stromata* I, 15.

196 Similarly, we find a perspective of universal history in the Tübingen theologians J. S. Drey, J. A. Möhler, and F. X. Staudenmaier. In addition, one must mention the Russian sophiology (V. Solovyev, S. Bulgakov, etc.), to which we are not able to pay sufficient attention.

197 AG 9, 11, 15; NA 2; GS 92; OT 16.

198 LG 13.

199 See J. Gnilka, *Das Evangelium nach Markus* (EKK II/2), Neukirchen 1979, 153f. See therein especially the comments on reception history (*Wirkungsgeschichte*) (154f.).

200 I cannot discuss here the question of the right to resistance in connection with the interpretation of Romans 13:1–7. On the reception history (*Wirkungsgeschichte*) of Romans, see U. Wilckens, *Der Brief an die Römer* (EKK VI/3), Neukirchen 1982, 43–66.

201 GS 36, 41, 56, 76.

202 GS 76.

203 Cf. Y. Congar, *The Mystery of the Temple*, London: Burns & Oates 1962; E. Peterson, 'Ekklesia und Himmelstadt', in: *Ekklesia*, 26–52; G. Schrenk, 'ἱερόν', in: ThWNT 3, 230–47; O. Michel, 'ναός', in: ThWNT 4, 884–95; 'οἶκος', in: ThWNT 5, 122–33. On Augustine's metaphor of the house, see J. Ratzinger, *Volk und Haus Gottes in Augustins Lehre von der Kirche* (1954), St. Ottilien 1992.

204 See section II.4.2.

205 Ignatius of Antioch, *ad Magnesios* 7, 2.

206 On this, see J. Werbick, *Kirche*, Freiburg i. Br. 1994, 217–22.

207 Thomas Aquinas, *Summa theologiae* II/II q. 99 a. 1 ad 2; III q. 64 a. 2 ad 3 and others.

208 DV 26. This word originates from a tradition of the Fathers that reaches as far back as Thomas a Kempis, *De imitatione Christi* IV, 11, 21f. See also J. Ratzinger, 'Kommentar', in: LThK.E 2, 572.

209 DV 2. My own writings on the theology of the Word will be published in WKGS 7. I owe particular thanks to my teacher of New Testament exegesis, K. H. Schelkle, and also L. Scheffczyk, H. Volk, M. Seckler and the recently published book by P. W. Scheele, *Wort des Lebens. Eine Theologie des Wortes*, Würzburg 2007.

210 K. L. Schmidt, 'ἐκκλησία', in: ThWNT 3, 505f, 530–2; U. Wilckens, *Theologie des Neuen Testaments*, vol. 2/2, Neukirchen 2009, 86–91.

211 Luther asserted this emphatically (WA 2, 430; etc.). Yet, it is no longer a matter of denominational difference.

212 So Cyril of Jerusalem, *Mystagogic Catechetical Lectures* XVIII, 24–6; Augustine, *de fide et symbolo* 9, 21; ep. 93, 1, 3; 98, 5; *in Johannis evangelium* 26, 17. The definition by Isidore of Seville became important for the Middle Ages: '*ecclesia vocatur proprie, propter quod omnes ad se vocet et in unum congreget*' (*de origine officiorum ecclesiasticorum* I, 1). On this definition, see Thomas Aquinas, *Summa theologiae* III q. 8 a. 4 ad 2; *Summa contra gentiles* IV, 78 among others as well as the *Catechismus Tridentinus* 10, 2. Cf. Lubac, *Glauben aus der Liebe* (*Catholicism: Christ and the common destiny of man*, San Francisco: Ignatius Press 1988), Einsiedeln 1970, 57f.

213 M. Luther, WA 50, 629.

214 DV 1. See also the commentary by Ratzinger in 'Kommentar,' 504f. See also Benedict XVI, Post-synodal apostolic exhortation on the Word of God in the life and mission of the Church, *Verbum Domini* (2010).

215 AG 2.

216 Pope Paul VI, Apostolic Exhortation on Evangelisation in the Modern World, *Evangelii Nuntiandi* (1975), 14.

217 Thomas Aquinas, *Compendium theologiae* 1.

218 On this analogy, see section II.2.2.

219 Leo the Great, *sermones* 74, 2.

220 On the theology of the sacraments and the liturgy, see WKGS 10. See section I.2.2.

221 Cyril of Jerusalem, *mystagogiae* VI, 3.

222 Cyril of Alexandria, *commentarium in evangelium Joannis* XI, 18, 11.

223 This was highlighted by F. Kattenbusch, in *Der Quellort der Kirchenidee* (Festschrift A. Harnack), Tübingen, 1921, 143–72; and, more recently, by Wilckens, in *Theologie des Neuen Testaments*, 91–5.

224 On the history and understanding of communio sanctorum, see J. N. D. Kelly, *Altchristliche Glaubensbekenntnisse* (*Early Christian Creeds*, London 1972), Göttingen 1972, 381–90. For a good overview of the different meanings, see K. B. Osborne, 'Communion of Saints', in: J. Komanchak et al. (eds), *The New Dictionary of Theology*, Dublin 1987, 213–6. On the importance of J. A. Möhler for the rediscovery of the original meaning of the communio sanctorum, see J. R. Geiselmann, *Die theologische Anthropologie Johann Adam Möhlers*, Freiburg i. Br. 1955, 56–106.

225 N. Baumert, *KOINONEIN und METECHEIN – synonym?*, Stuttgart 2003.

226 Augustine, *in Johannis evangelium* 26, 6, 13. For further statements on this by Augustine, see section II.3.2.

227 DH 802; 1635.

228 SC 47.

229 Bonaventura, *Sent.* IV d. 8 p. 2 a. 2 q. 1.

230 Thomas Aquinas, *Summa theologiae* III q. 73 a. 6.

231 Benedict XVI, Post-synodal apostolic exhortation on the Eucharist as the source and summit of the Church's life and mission, *Sacramentum Caritatis* (2007), 14.

232 On this, see W. Kasper, *Sakrament der Einheit. Eucharistie und Kirche* (*Sacrament of Unity – the Eucharist and the Church*, New York: Crossroad 2004), Freiburg i. Br. 2004, particularly 115–46; B. Forte, *La Chiesa nell'Eucaristia*, Napoli 1975.

233 M. Luther, WA 2, 743. Cf. W. Elert, *Eucharist and Church Fellowship in the First Four Centuries* (1954), St. Louis: Concordia Publishing House 1966.

234 See W. Kasper, *Harvesting the Fruits. Basic Aspects of Christian Faith in Ecumenical Dialogue*, London: Continuum 2009, Chapter 4.

235 This image is already found in Tertullian, in *de oratione* 2; *de anima* 43, 10; *de baptismo* 20, also in Ambrose, *expositio evangelii secundum Lucam* III, 23; *de virginibus* V, 22, 31 and others.

236 Cyprian, *de ecclesiae unitate*, 6; ep. 74, 7; cf. ep. 15, 2.

237 Tertullian, *de paenitentia* VI, 16; Augustine, ep. 98, 9.

238 Augustine, *In Johannis evangelium* 80, 3. The connection between the word of God in Scripture, in the Eucharist and in the Church is impressively presented by Origen. On this, see H. de Lubac, *Geist aus der Geschichte. Das Schriftverständnis des Origenes* (*History and Spirit: the Understanding of Scripture according to Origen*, San Francisco: Ignatius Press, 2007), Einsiedeln 1968, 393–436.

239 Thomas Aquinas, *Summa theologiae* III q. 60 a. 6–8.

240 M. Luther, *Large Catechism*, in: *Book of Concord*, 438, 447.

241 SC 56.

242 LG 11; cf. 26; CD 30; PO 5.

243 DH 246.

244 Thomas Aquinas, *Summa theologiae* III q. 60, a. 3.

245 See section II.2.2.

246 On Maximus the Confessor, see H. U. von Balthasar, *Kosmische Liturgie* (*Cosmic Liturgy: the Universe according to Maximus the Confessor*, San Francisco: Ignatius Press 2003), Einsiedeln 1961, 314–25.

247 On this, see section II.4.2.

248 De Lubac, *Geist aus der Geschichte* (*History and Spirit*), 23–61, demonstrated that the condemnation of this teaching does not, in fact, apply to that of Origen.

249 On this, see Y. Congar, *The Wide World my Parish: Salvation and its Problems*, London: Darton, Longman & Todd 1961; F. Ricken, 'Ecclesia ... universale salutis sacramentum', in: Schol 40 (1965) 352–88; J. Ratzinger, 'Kein Heil außerhalb der Kirche?', in: *Das neue Volk Gottes*, Düsseldorf 1969, 339–61; W. Kern, *Außerhalb der Kirche kein Heil?*, Freiburg i. Br. 1979; and, 'Heilsnotwendigkeit', in: LThK[3] 4, 1346–8; B. Sesboüé, *Hors de l'Église pas de salut. Histoire d'une formule et problèmes d'interprétation*, Paris 2004.

250 H. Rahner, *Symbole der Kirche*, Salzburg 1964, 504–47.

251 Origen, *in Jesu nave* 3, 5; *in Iosuam homeliae* III, 5.

252 Cyprian of Carthage, *ep.* 73, 21; *de ecclesiae unitate* 6, 14, 17.

253 DH 802.

254 DH 875.

255 DH 1351.

256 DH 2005.

257 DH 2429.

258 Thomas Aquinas, *Summa theologiae* III q. 68 a 2.

259 DH 1524.

260 R. Bellarmine, *Disputationes de controversiis*, IV, 3, 3.

261 DH 3821.

262 DH 3866–73. K. Rahner, 'Membership of the Church according to the Teaching of Pius XII's Encyclical *Mystici Corporis Christi*', in: *Man in the Church* (*Theological Investigations* II), London: Darton, Longman & Todd, 1963, 1–88.

263 LG 16; cf. GS 22.

264 See section II.2.3.

265 Athanasius, *contra Arianos* I, 42; II, 61, 74.

266 Augustine, *sermones* 341, 9, 11; *enarrationes in Psalmos* 90, 1; *de civitate Dei* XVIII, 51.

267 See Y. Congar, 'Ecclesia ab Abel', in: M. Reding (ed.), *Abhandlungen über Theologie und Kirche* (Festschrift K. Adam), Düsseldorf 1952, 79–108. The frequently repeated statement by Augustine – that many who are inside are outside, and those who are outside are, in fact, inside – is also important here. This statement is quoted in LG 14, note 26.

268 Thomas Aquinas, *Summa theologiae* III q. 8, a. 3. On this, see M. Seckler, 'Das Haupt aller Menschen', in: *Die schiefen Wände des Lehrhauses*, Freiburg i. Br. 1988, 26–39. Further references for Thomas' universal perspective on the Church are found in Seckler, *Das Heil in der Geschichte*, 220 note 17. On the foundation of this doctrine by the Church Fathers, see de Lubac, *Geist aus der Geschichte* (*History and Spirit*), 34–6.

269 Thomas Aquinas, *Summa theologiae* III q. 68 a. 2.

270 GS 10, 45.

271 AG 9, 11, 15; NA 2 and others. See section II.2.3.

272 GS 22.

273 GS 10.

274 John Paul II, Encyclical on the permanent validity of the Church's missionary mandate, *Redemptoris missio* (1990), 28. On this, see section II.6.1.

275 Rahner's theory of the anonymous Christian is basically a speculative elaboration of the theory of subjective choice with the help of Rahner's transcendental-existential approach. It can be understood correctly within ecclesiology. Nevertheless, it has caused a number of misunderstandings. In addition, it seems to restrict the meaning of mission more or less to 'making

explicit' and 'enlightening' the so-called anonymous Christians about that which they already are. Just so, it does not sufficiently take into account the reality of other religions and their negative, idolatrous and partly inhumane aspects. Therefore, it is in danger of diminishing the meaning of mission and of explicit Christianity. Cf. K. Rahner, *Theological Investigations* (London: Darton, Longman & Todd): 'The Christian among Unbelieving Relations' (vol. 3, 355–72), 'Anonymous Christians' (vol. 6, 390–8), 'Anonymous Christianity and the Missionary Task of the Church' (vol. 12/I, 161–78), 'Observations on the Problem of the "Anonymous Christian"' (vol. 14, 280–94, there also further literature on this topic). In a different way, P. Tillich speaks of a latent Christendom (*Systematische Theologie*, (*Systematic Theology*, vol. 3, London: SCM 1978), vol. 3, Stuttgart 1966, 171–82), and T. Rendtorff of a Christianity outside the Church (*Christentum außerhalb der Kirche*, [Stundenbücher vol. 89] Hamburg 1969).

276 On this, see Congregation for the Doctrine of Faith, Declaration on the Unicity and Salvific Universality of Jesus Christ and the Church, *Dominus Jesus* (2000).

277 LG 14; AG 1–9. For further details on the issue of mission, see section II.6.1.

278 See additional comments on the inter-religious dialogue below, section II.6.2.3.

3. Defining the nature of the Church

1 LG 6.

2 In particular, it was M. D. Koster, in *Volk Gottes im Werden* (1940), new edition. Mainz 1971, who highlighted the importance of the 'people of God-ecclesiology', contributed to its renewal and also placed it against the 'body of Christ-ecclesiology'.

3 H. U. von Balthasar, 'Preface' to the new German translation of H. de Lubac, Die Kirche (*The Splendour of the Church*, New York: Sheed & Ward 1956), Einsiedeln 1968, 9; J. Ratzinger, 'Vom Ursprung und Wesen der Kirche', in: JRGS 8/1, 150f.; and, 'Die Ekklesiologie des Zweiten Vatikanischen Konzils', ibid. 269–82; and, *Volk und Haus Gottes in Augustins Lehre von der Kirche* (1954), repr. St. Ottilien 1992.

4 Y. Congar provides a thoroughly-researched, detailed demonstration of this in 'The Church: The People of God', in: *Concilium* 1 (1965) 7–19; '"Ecclesia" et "populus (fidelis)" dans l'ecclésiologie de Saint Thomas', in: *Église et Papauté*, Paris 2002, 211–27.

5 On this, see N. A. Dahl, *Das Volk Gottes*, Darmstadt 1963; F. Mussner, 'Volk Gottes im Neuen Testament', in: *Praesentia salutis*, Düsseldorf 1967, 244–54; G. Lohfink, *Die Sammlung Israels*, Munich 1975; N. Lohfink, 'Beobachtungen zur Geschichte des Ausdrucks "am Jhwh"', in: *Studien zur biblischen Theologie*, Stuttgart 1999, 98–132. In the background here is the influential study of E. Käsemann, *The Wandering People of God* (1939), Minneapolis: Augsburg Publishing House 1984.

6 In the history of religions and the Christian theology of scripture, the name Yahweh – or the Tetragrammaton, JHWH, which is holy and unutterable for Jews – has raised many questions and given way to many different interpretations. It seems certain that it cannot be translated in the sense of Greek metaphysics as the 'being one' (ὁ ὢν or τό ὄν), which is the translation of the LXX and, subsequently, its usage in the Tradition. It is more the Semitic 'being' as event, as current and dynamic presence in the sense of 'being here present' and 'being with it'. See A. Deissler, *Die Grundbotschaft des Alten Testaments*, Freiburg i. Br. 1972, 48–52; M. Rose, 'Jahwe', in: TRE 16, 438–41. On the reception history (*Wirkungsgeschichte*), see WKGS 4, 248–55.

7 See *Catechismus Romanus*, Nr. 81.

8 M. Luther, *Book of Concord*, 416; WA 5, 293; 50, 625.

9 On Vatican II, see O. Semmelroth, 'Die Kirche, das neue Gottesvolk', in: G. Baraúna (ed.), *De Ecclesia*, vol. 1, Freiburg i. Br. – Frankfurt a.M. 1966, 365–79; Ratzinger, 'Vom Ursprung und Wesen der Kirche', 269–75.

10 LG 9.

11 Particularly LG 9–17. See section II.4.1.

12 On this issue, see section II.5.2.

13 *Epistle of Barnabas* 5, 7; 7, 5; 13, 1. See additional comments below, section II.6.2.1.

14 Augustine, *sermones* 341, 9, 11; *enarrationes in Psalmos* 90, 1; *de civitate Dei* XVIII, 51.

15 LG 2; Y. Congar, 'Ecclesia ab Abel', in: M. Reding (ed.), *Abhandlungen über Theologie und Kirche* (Festschrift K. Adam), Düsseldorf 1952, 79–108. See section II.2.4.

16 LG 9.

17 H. Rahner, *Symbole der Kirche. Die Ekklesiologie der Väter*, Salzburg 1964, 272–303; H.-J. Vogt, *Bilder der frühen Kirche*, Munich 1993, 24–36; F. Manns, *Le Judéo-christianisme. Mémoire ou prophétie?*, Paris 2000, 236–8. Basil impressively compares the state of the Church with a sea battle, see Basil of Caesarea, *de spiritu sancto*, 30, 64e–67e.

18 Augustine, *de civitate Dei* XVIII, 51, 2.

19 Following E. von Ivanka (*Rhomäerreich und Gottesvolk*, Freiburg i. Br. – Munich 1968), Ratzinger rightly opposes this equation. However, one cannot blame Orthodox ecclesiology in general for this identification. It is with good reason that the Ecumenical Patriarch of Constantinople calls himself ecumenical. In addition, famous and influential Russian-Orthodox theologians in exile, such as N. Afansjev, G. Florovskij, P. Evdokimov and J. Meyendorff have consciously opposed the so-called phyletism (identifying the Church with a phyle, i.e. a tribe or a culture). Over against this they posit a Eucharistic *communio* ecclesiology. This has also become important for Greek Orthodox theology, for instance, for J. Ziziloulas.

20 E. Schlink, 'Die Struktur der dogmatischen Aussage als dogmatisches Problem', in: KuD 3 (1957) 231–306; W. Pannenberg, 'Analogy and

Doxology', in: *Basic Questions in Theology*, vol. 1, London: SCM Press 1970, 212–38; G. Wainwright, *Doxology*, London 1980; A. Kallis, 'Theologie als Doxologie', in: K. Richter (ed.), *Liturgie – ein vergessenes Thema der Theologie*, Freiburg i. Br. 1986, 45–53; J. Drumm, *Doxologie und Dogma. Die Bedeutung der Doxologie für die Wiedergewinnung theologischer Rede in der evangelischen Theologie*, Paderborn 1991; and, 'Doxologie II–III', in: LThK[3] 3, 355–7.

21 The German original is 'Gott loben, ist unser Amt' [T.H.] *Gotteslob* [the German Catholic Hymnal, T.H.] 474, 5. In the same direction, see also K. Koch, *Die Kirche Gottes. Gemeinschaft im Geheimnis des Glaubens*, Augsburg 2007.

22 Thomas Aquinas, *Summa theologiae* II/II q. 1 a. 1.

23 Thomas Aquinas, *Summa theologiae* II/II q. 1 a. 2.

24 Thomas Aquinas, *Summa theologiae* II/II q. 1 a. 6.

25 Thomas Aquinas, *Summa theologiae* II/II q. 1 a. 6 and 8.

26 Along these lines, see also Schleiermacher's famous, though, as he himself put it, preliminary formula, according to which the difference between Protestantism and Catholicism boils down to the fact that, 'for the former the relation of the individual to the Church depends on his relation to Christ whereas for the latter, in contrast, the relation of the individual to Christ depends on his relation to the Church' (*Der christliche Glaube* [*The Christian Faith*, London: T.&T. Clark, 2003], §24).

27 J. H. Newman, *Apologia pro vita sua*, 216–18.

28 J. H. Newman, *A Letter Addressed to his Grace the Duke of Norfolk on the Occasion of Mr Gladstone's Recent expostulation*, London: Pickering 1875.

29 E. Käsemann, *Leib und Leib Christi*, Tübingen 1933; A. Wikenhauser, *Die Kirche als der mystische Leib Christi*, Münster 1937; L. Cerfaux, *The Church in the Theology of St. Paul* (1948), New York: Herder & Herder 1959; E. Mersch, *The Whole Christ*, London: Dobson 1949; J. A. T. Robinson, *The Body. A Study in Pauline Theology*, London: SCM 1952; H. Merklein, 'Entstehung und Gehalt des paulinischen Leib-Christi-Gedankens', in: M. Böhnke/H. Heinz (eds), *Im Gespräch mit dem dreieinen Gott*, Düsseldorf 1985, 115–40; T. Söding, 'Ihr aber seid Christi Leib', in: *Das Wort vom Kreuz*, Tübingen 1997, 272–99. Special attention should be paid to the systematic perspective offered by C. Journet in, *The Church of the Word Incarnate* (1941), London: Sheed & Ward 1954.

30 Plato, *Protagoras* 322d.

31 H. W. Robinson, *Corporate Personality in Ancient Israel*, Philadelphia: Fortress 1964.

32 K.-H. Menke, *Stellvertretung. Schlüsselbegriff christlichen Lebens und theologische Grundkategorie*, Freiburg – Einsiedeln 1997.

33 What was once a widely held interpretation, namely, that this should be understood against the backdrop of its Hellenistic context in the sense of the Gnostic mythology of primordial man, has been superseded in favor of Hebrew-Jewish images. See Manns, *Le Judéo-christianisme*.

34 On this, see the interpretation, still dominated by the question of the Hellenistic background, by H. Schlier, *Der Brief an die Epheser*, Düsseldorf 1957, 84–99.

35 On patristic exegesis, see H. Rahner, *Symbole der Kirche* (cf. note 17), 177–235.

36 Origen, *hexaemeron* 9.

37 Augustine, *tractatus in evangelium Iohannis* 15, 8; cf. Tertullian, *de anima* 43; Ambrose, *expositio evangelii secundum Lucam* II, 86; Thomas Aquinas, *Summa theologiae* I q. 92, a. 3.

38 Augustine, *enarrationes in Psalmos* 90, 1.

39 F. Hofmann, *Der Kirchenbegriff des hl. Augustinus*, Munich 1933, 148, 152–68.

40 Augustine, *sermones* 341, 11.

41 Augustine, *sermones* 137, 1.

42 Augustine, *de dono perseverantia* 7, 14.

43 Augustine, *enarrationes in Psalmos* 17, 4.

44 Augustine, *enarrationes in Psalmos* 30, 2, 4; *de doctrina christiana* 3, 37, 55.

45 Augustine, *sermones* 133, 8.

46 Augustine, *tractatus in evangelium Iohannis* 111, 6.

47 Augustine, *sermones* 137, 2; cf. *tractatus in evangelium Iohannis* 21, 7.

48 Augustine, *tractatus in evangelium Iohannis* 26, 13.

49 Augustine, *enarrationes in Psalmos* 30, 1, 3.

50 Hofmann, *Der Kirchenbegriff des hl. Augustinus* (cf. note 39), 390–413.

51 Augustine, *tractatus in evangelium Iohannis* 26, 13.

52 Augustine, *enarrationes in Psalmos* 33, 1, 6.

53 Augustine, *sermones* 227.

54 Augustine, *sermones* 272.

55 Augustine, *tractatus in evangelium Iohannis* 26, 17 and others.

56 It was particularly H. de Lubac, in *Corpus Mysticum: the Eucharist and the Church in the Middle Ages* (1949), London: SCM 2006, who showed this radical change. See the detailed summary in J. Ratzinger, 'Leib Christi II', in: $LThK^2$ 6, 9, 10–12.

57 Augustine, *tractatus in evangelium Iohannis* 26, 6, 13.

58 Thomas Aquinas, *Summa theologiae* III q. 73 a. 2 and 6.

59 Möhler's ecclesiology cannot simply be understood in the sense of Romanticism as organologic. It is profoundly pneumatologically and Christologically conceived. In particular, his statement that the Church is Christ living on (*Symbolism* §36) must be interpreted within its context. Möhler obviously proceeds from Jesus Christ as the subject efficacious in the Church and only from this perspective moves to the statement that can be perceived as an identification or continuation of the Incarnation. Elsewhere the Church is, for him, understood in the sense of a real symbol, even an image of the archetype, Jesus Christ (*Symbolism* §34). See section II.1.2 notes 23–6 above.

60 In addition to the above-mentioned volume by de Lubac, *Corpus Mysticum*, are his important books *Catholicism: Christ and the Common Destiny of Man* (1938), San Francisco: Ignatius Press 1988, and *Méditations sur l'Église*, Paris 1952.

61 LG 7.

62 SC 59; LG 11.

63 On the problem of the relation between universal Church and individual church, see section II.5.5.

64 LG 8.

65 LG 6, 9, 39.

66 On this, see D. Valentini, 'La donna e la Chiesa alla luce della simbolica dell'alleanza nuziale', in: *Lo Spirito e la sposa*, Vatican City 2009, 113–45. On the issue of women in the Church, see section II.4.2.

67 This topic was already profoundly explored, in the spirit of the Church Fathers, by M. J. Scheeben, in *Mysterien des Christentums* (1865; *The Mysteries of Christianity*, London: Herder 1958), Freiburg i. Br. 1951, 445–52. More recent treatises include H. U. von Balthasar, *The Spouse of the Word* (1961), San Francisco: Ignatius Press 1991; G. Mazzanti, *Teologia sponsale e sacramento delle nozze*, Bologna 2004; A. Scola, *Das hochzeitliche Geheimnis*, Einsiedeln 2006.; M. Ouellet, *Mistero e sacramento dell'amore. Teologia del matrimonio e della famiglia per la nuova evangelizzazione*, Siena 2007, 163–8; F. Pilloni, *Immagine viva di Cristo Sposo. Ministero e diakonia della Chiesa sposa*, Cantalupa 2009. Closely related to this is the Marian dimension of the Church. On this, see section II.3.4.

68 This aspect was beautifully worked out by C. Journet in *L'Église sainte mais non sans pécheurs*, Saint-Maur 1999. He distinguishes between the Holy Spirit as the uncreated soul of the Church and love as the created soul of the Church.

69 J. Jeremias, 'νύμφη', in: ThWNT 4, 1092–9.

70 Cf. E. Stauffer, 'γάμος', in: ThWNT 1, 651–5. This article demonstrates that the New Testament concepts are rooted in Old Testament and rabbinic sources and cannot be deduced from the idea, which was widespread in the mystery cults, of a ἱερὸς γάμος.

71 Ephrem the Syrian, *Hymns de Ecclesia* (*Lobgesang aus der Wüste*, Sophia 7), Freiburg i. Br. 1967, 59–67; Selected writings of the Syrian poets are found in *Bibliothek der Kirchenväter*, vol. 6, Munich 1913, 329–32, 347–50.

72 Y. Congar, 'Die Lehre von der Kirche von Augustinus bis zum abendländischen Schisma', in: HDG III/3c, 77f.

73 P. Dinzelbacher/D. R. Bauer (ed.), *Frauenmystik des Mittelalters*, Ostfildern 1985.

74 On this, and from a feminist perspective, see E. Schüssler Fiorenza, *In Memory of Her: A Feminist Theological Reconstruction of Christian Origins* (New York: Crossroad 1984). See also the beautiful interpretation of John 8:1–11 in K. Rahner, 'The Church of Sinners', in: *Theological Investigations*, vol. 6, Baltimore: Helicon Press 1969, 253–69.

75 All of this material is collected in H. U. von Balthasar, 'Casta meretrix', in: *Spouse of the Word*, (Explorations in Theology II; 1960), San Francisco: Ignatius Press 1991, 193–288. On this point, see section II.4.2.

76 M. Luther, WA VI, 487–573.

77 Hildegard of Bingen, *Letter* 52.

78 Thomas Aquinas, *Summa theologiae* III q. 8 a. 3 ad 2.

79 J. A. Möhler characterizes this deistic understanding mockingly like this: '(In the beginning) God created the hierarchy and so the Church is now provided for more than enough until the end of the world' (ThQ 5 [1823] 497).

80 See the old wording of the Creed in DH 10ff. and the Nicene-Constantinopolitan Creed, DH 150.

81 See the most comprehensive presentations in Y. Congar, *I believe in the Holy Spirit*, London: Chapman 1983; H. U. von Balthasar, *Creator Spirit* (1967), San Francisco: Ignatius Press 1993; H. Mühlen, *Una mystica Persona*, Munich 1968; J. Moltmann, *The Spirit of Life: a Universal Affirmation*, Minneapolis: Fortress Press 1992; M. Welker, *God the Spirit*, Minneapolis: Fortress Press 1994; B. J. Hilberath, *Pneumatologie*, Düsseldorf 1994. My own contributions on this: W. Kasper/G. Sauter (eds), *Kirche – Ort des Geistes*, Freiburg i. Br. 1976;W. Kasper (ed.), *Gegenwart des Geistes, Aspekte der Pneumatologie* (QD 85), Freiburg i. Br. 1979; 'The Renewal of Pneumatology in Contemporary Catholic Life and Theology: Toward a Rapprochement between East and West', in: *That They All may Be One*, London: Burns & Oates 2004, 122–35. More generally, on this chapter, see WKGS 4, 317–59.

82 Irenaeus of Lyons, *adversus haereses* III, 24, 1.

83 Hippolytus of Rome, *traditio apostolica* 31, 35.

84 Chrysostom, *homilia de sancta pentecoste* I, 4.

85 Augustine, *tractatus in evangelium Iohannis* 32, 8.

86 Augustine, *sermones* 267, 4.

87 There have been various different interpretations of this passage in patristic exegesis, see H. Rahner, *Symbole der Kirche*, 177–235; R. Schnackenburg, *Das Johannesevangelium* (*The Gospel according to John*, New York Seabury Press 1980), vol. 2, Freiburg i. Br. 1971, 210–17.

88 Irenaeus of Lyons, *epideixis* 89; cf. *adversus haereses* IV, 33, 13; V, 18, 2.

89 I must mention especially V. Lossky, and also S. Bulgakow, N. Afanasiew, P. Evdokimov, O. Clément, B. Bobrinskoy, and N. A. Nissiotis. This critique is based on the Orthodox refutation of the Latin-western addition of the filioque to the creed which says that the spirit proceeds from the Father and from the Son. Many Orthodox theologians consider this a one-sided linking of the Spirit and his saving work to that of the Son. This cannot be discussed further in the present context. See, rather, WKGS 4, 264–73.

90 Y. Congar, *Der Heilige Geist* (*I believe in …*), Freiburg i. Br. 1982, 140–7.

91 J. A. Möhler, *Symbolism*, §37.

92 LG 7.

93 LG 4, 7, 9, 21, 48; DV 8, 21, 23; AG 2, 4, 15, etc.

94 John Paul II, *Tertio millennio adveniente* (1994), 45–7.

95 Irenaeus of Lyons, *adversus haereses* III, 24, 1.

96 Thomas Aquinas, *Summa theologiae* I/II q. 106 a. 1.

97 Thomas Aquinas, *Summa theologiae* I/II q. 108 a. 1.

98 SC 43; UR 1; PO 22.

99 LG 12, which was a matter of controversy at the Council, is of particular importance. In addition, see LG 4, 7, 30, 50; AG 4, 23, 28; PO 4, 9.

100 So, in particular, since Gregory the Great, *in Ezechielem homiliae* 29, 4.

101 P. J. Cordes, *Born of the Spirit*, South Bend: Greenlawn Press 1995; and, *Nicht immer das alte Lied*, Paderborn 1999; J. Ratzinger, *Kirchliche Bewegungen und neue Gemeinschaften – Unterscheidungen und Kriterien*, Munich 2007; H. Gasper, 'Charismatische Bewegung', in: *Lexikon der Ökumene und Konfessionskunde*, Freiburg i. Br. 2007, 210–18; M. Tigges/ J. Halkenhäuser, 'Geistliche Gemeinschaften und Bewegungen', in: ibid., 451–7; F. P. Tebartz-van Elst, 'Pfingstbewegung', in: ibid., 1045–50; J. Ratzinger, 'The Theological Locus of Ecclesial Movements', in: *Communio* 25 (1998), 29–41.

102 K. Rahner, *The Dynamic Element in the Church*, London: Burns & Oates 1964; H. Küng, Die Kirche (*The Church*, London: Search Press 1967) Freiburg i. Br. 1967, 181–244; G. Hasenhüttl, *Charisma – Ordnungsprinzip der Kirche*, Freiburg i. Br. 1969; L. Boff, *Church, Charism and Power*, New York: Crossroad 1985; J. Ratzinger, 'Bemerkungen zur Frage der Charismen in der Kirche' (1970), in: JRGS 8/1, 345–62.

103 M. Weber, *Wirtschaft und Gesellschaft* (*Economy and Society: an Outline of Interpretive Sociology*, New York: Bedminster Press 1968), Tübingen 1922, 140.

104 See the influential piece by E. Käsemann, 'Amt und Charisma im NT', in: *Exegetische Versuche und Besinnungen*, Göttingen 1964, 109–34. A more balanced account is that of H. Schürmann, 'Die geistlichen Gnadengaben', in: Baraúna (ed.), *De Ecclesia*, vol. 1, 494–519. A good overview is found in H. Conzelmann, 'χάρισμα', in: ThWNT 9, 393–7.

105 The *New Jerusalem Bible renders this* as much as your faith; the *English Standard Version* as in proportion to your faith, which is found only in this passage in the New Testament, has triggered a significant effective history (*Wirkungsgeschichte*) that has its foundations in this New Testament passage, only in the sense that it signifies a unity in the diversity of the different charismas. On the history of the interpretation of this phrase, see K.-H. Menke, 'Analogia fidei', in: LThK[3] 1, 574–7.

106 Thomas Aquinas, *Summa theologiae* I/II q. 106 a. 4.

107 E. Benz, *Ecclesia spiritualis. Kirchenidee und Geschichtstheologie der franziskanischen Reform*, Stuttgart 1934; K. Löwith, *Weltgeschichte und Heilsgeschehen. Die theologischen Voraussetzungen der Geschichtsphilosophie*, Stuttgart 1953; J. Ratzinger, *The Theology of History*

in St. Bonaventure (1959), Chicago: Franciscan Herald Press 1989; H. de Lubac, *La postérité spirituelle Joachim de Fiore*, Paris – Namur 1979; Y. Congar, *Je crois en l'Esprit saint* (*I believe in* ..., cf. note 81), vol. 1, Paris 1979, 175–89. See section II.2.2.

108 R. A. Knox, *Enthusiasm*, New York: Oxford University Press 1961.

109 W. Hollenweger, *The Pentecostals: the Charismatic Movement in the Churches*, Minneapolis: Augsburg Publishing House 1972; H. Cox, *Fire from Heaven: The Rise of Pentecostal Spirituality and the Reshaping of Religion in the 21st Century*, Cambridge (MA) 2001; P. Jenkins, *The Next Christendom. The Coming of Global Christianity*, Oxford – New York 2002; K. McDonell, *The Holy Spirit and Power*, New York 1975; K. McDonnell, *Presence, Power, Praise*, 3 vols, Collegeville MN 1980; M. Robeck, *Azusa Street. Mission and Revival. The Birth of the Global Pentecostal Movement*, Nashville 2006.

110 Ignatius of Antioch, *ad Ephesios* 2, 2; *ad Magnesios* 6, 2, etc.

111 Cyprian of Carthage, ep. 68, 8; cf. 58, 4.

112 Basil of Caesarea, *de spiritu sancto* 9, 19d; 16, 31b; 34a.

113 So R. Sohm, *Das altkatholische Kirchenrecht und das Dekret Gratians*, Munich – Leipzig 1918. See section II.2.2.

114 So K. Barth, *CD* IV/1 §62, 644ff., which consists of a heavy criticism of ecclesiological docetism (653ff.). See also *CD* IV/2, 614ff., debating R. Sohm (679ff.).

115 Taking his cues from the doctrine of the 'theological loci' of Melchior Cano, M. Seckler comes to the same result. See 'Die ekklesiologische Bedeutung des Systems der "loci theogici". Erkenntnistheoretische Katholizität und strukturale Weisheit', in: *Die schiefen Wände des Lehrhauses. Katholizität als Herausforderung*, Freiburg i. Br. 1988, 79–104.

116 J. A. Möhler, *Symbolism*, §37. See also the often quoted passages from Möhler, in *Unity*, 6f.

117 John Paul II, *Novo millennio ineunte* (2001), 46.

118 Augustine, *de trinitate* 5, 11.14f.; 6, 10f.; 15, 17–21. cf. WKGS 4, 273–82.

119 See section I.6.

120 AG 4.

121 GS 22; cf. NA 2.

122 John Paul II, *Redemptoris missio* (1990), 28.

123 Ibid., 26.

124 Ibid., 29; cf. 55–7. On the possibility of salvation outside the visible church, see above II.2.5; on the inter-religious dialogue, see section II.6.2.3.

125 NA 2.

126 LG 8, 15; UR 2f.

127 See section II.6.2.

128 DThC 4, 1374–415; *Dictionnaire de Spiritualité* 3, 1222–91. H. Wulf, 'Unterscheidung der Geister', in: $LThK^2$ 10, 533–5.

129 GS 4, 11; AA 14.

130 LG 12.

131 M. Seckler, 'Glaubenssinn', in: LThK^{2} 4, 945–8.

132 Eusebius of Caesarea, *historia ecclesiastica* V, 27.

133 Origen, *homilia in canticum canticorum* 1, 10.

134 Ignatius of Loyola, *The Spiritual Exercises of St. Ignatius*, Gardener Books 2007, 352–68. See M. Kehl, *Die Kirche*, Würzburg 1992, 19–23; E.-M. Faber, 'Sentire cum ecclesia', in: LThK^{3} 9, 471f.

135 J. A. Möhler, *Symbolism* §38.

136 Ignatius of Loyola, *Exercises* 315–21.

137 My inspiration on this point is due to the following works: Semmelroth, *Mary, Archetype of the Church* (1954), Dublin: Gill & Son 1964; K. Rahner, *Mary, Mother of the Lord* (1956), New York: Herder & Herder 1963; Y. Congar, *Christ, Our Lady and the Church*, London: Longmans, Green & Cor. 1957; J. Ratzinger, *Daughter Zion*, San Francisco: Ignatius Press 1983; W. Beinert, (ed.) *Maria heute ehren*, Freiburg i. Br. 1977; W. Beinert/ H. Petri (eds), *Handbuch der Marienkunde*, 2 vols, Regensburg 1996–7; L. Scheffczyk, *Maria, Mutter und Gefährtin Christi*, Augsburg 2003; G. Lohfink/L. Weimer, *Maria – nicht ohne Israel*, Freiburg i. Br. 2008. See also my own volume: W. Kasper, *Meditazione su Maria*, Saronno (VA) 2001.

138 LG 58.

139 DH 252.

140 H. Schürmann, 'Jesu letzte Weisung', in: *Ursprung und Gestalt*, Düsseldorf 1970, 13–28. See also U. Wilckens, *Das Evangelium nach Johannes*, Göttingen ^{17}1998, 296f.

141 The substance of the title 'Mother of the Church' is clearly expounded in LG 53. As a Marian title, 'Mother of the Church', it was solemnly proclaimed by Pope Paul VI on November 21, 1964.

142 *Das Magnifikat. Verdeutscht und ausgelegt durch D. Martin Luther* (with an introduction by H. Riedlinger), Freiburg i. Br. 1982. Luther's interpretation of the Magnificat is by no means isolated; rather it is confirmed by many other statements of the Reformers. See W. Tappolet/A. Ebneter, *Das Marienlob der Reformatoren*, Tübingen 1962.

143 DH 2802.

144 The manifold problems associated with the virgin birth – both exegetical in nature and otherwise – are beyond the scope of the present volume. For commentary on some of these, see WKGS 3, 326, 374.

145 K. Barth, *CD* IV/1, 207.

146 LG 56.

147 LG 60.

148 LG 61f.

149 John of Damascus, *de fide orthodoxa* 26.

150 LG 53.

151 Ambrose of Milan, *expositio evangelii secundum Lucam* II, 7.

152 LG 53.

153 H. U. von Balthasar, 'The Marian Principle', in: *Elucidations*, London: SPCK 1975, 72.

154 Justin, *dialogus cum Tryphone Iudaeo* C 1; Irenaeus of Lyons, *adversus haereses* III, 22, 4; V, 19, 1f.; and, *demonstratio praedicationis apostolicae* 32f.

155 Thomas Aquinas, *Summa theologiae* III q. 30 a. 1.

156 DH 3900–94.

157 LG 65.

4. The marks of the Church of Jesus Christ

1 DH 150. On the problem, see G. Thils, *Les notes de l'église dans l'apologétique catholique depuis la réforme*, Gembloux 1937; Y. Congar, 'Die Wesenseigenschaften der katholischen Kirche', in: MySal IV/1, Einsiedeln 1972, 357–67; H. J. Pottmeyer, 'Die Frage nach der wahren Kirche', in: HFThess. 3, 212–41.

2 See CA VII; *Book of Concord*, 169; M. Luther, 'On the Councils and the Church' (1539), in: WA 50, 628–44; 'Against Hanswurst' (1541), in: WA 51, 480–5. Hereto: On this point, see W. Härle, 'Kirche VII', in: TRE 8, 289–93.

3 J. Calvin, *Insitutio religionis christianae* IV, 1, 5.8f.; 2, 1.

4 Y. Congar, 'Romanité et catholicité', in: *Église et papauté*, Paris 2002, 31–64.

5 DH 3014.

6 See above, section II.2.1.

7 DH 5, 42, 44, 48, 54.

8 DH 150. Y. Congar, 'Die eine Kirche', in: MySal IV/1, 368–457.

9 See E. Stauffer, 'εἷς', in: ThWNT 2, 432–40; H. Schlier, 'Über das Prinzip der kirchlichen Einheit im Neuen Testament', in: *Der Hl. Geist und die Kirche*, Freiburg i. Br. 1980, 179–200; F. Hahn/K. Kertelge/ R. Schnackenburg, *Einheit der Kirche* (QD 84), Freiburg i. Br. 1979; K. Kertelge, 'Koinonia und Einheit nach dem NT', in: J. Schreiner, et al. (eds), *Communio Sanctorum* (Festschrift P. W. Scheele), Würzburg 1988, 53–67; H. J. Klauck, 'Gespaltene Gemeinde', in: *Gemeinde – Amt – Sakrament*, Würzburg 1989, 59–68.

10 The Trinitarian aspect is of particular importance for Orthodox theology. See B. Bobrinskoy, *Le mystère de l'Église. Cours de théologie dogmatique*, Paris 2003, 130f. See section II.2.2.

11 Cyprian of Carthage, *de oratione Domini* 23; ep. 75, 3.

12 See section II.5.5.

13 This thesis is found in E. Käsemann, 'Begründet der neutestamentliche Kanon

die Einheit der Kirche?', in: *Exegetische Besinnungen und Versuche* (*Essays on New Testament Themes*, London: SCM 1964), Göttingen 1960, 214–23; and, 'Zum Thema der Nichtobektivierbarkeit', in: ibid. 224–36. On this, see G. Ebeling, 'Das Neue Testament und die Vielzahl der Konfessionen', in: *Wort Gottes und Tradition* (*The Word of God and Tradition*, London: Collins 1968), Göttingen 1964, 144–54; Y. Congar, 'Diversity and Unity according to the New Testament', in *Diversity and Communion*, Mystic: Twenty-Third Publ. 1985, 9–14.

14 H. Schlier, 'αἵρεσις', in: ThWNT 1, 181–3.

15 This was shown particularly by J. A. Möhler, *Unity in the Church or the Principle of Catholicism* (1825), Washington, DC: Catholic University Press of America 1996.

16 R. Bellarmine, *Disputationes de controversiis* IV, 3, 2.

17 LG 14; UR 2.

18 Aristotle, *metaphysica* 14, 1: 1088 a.

19 LG 4; UR 2.

20 Irenaeus of Lyons, in: Eusebius of Caesarea, *historia ecclesiastica* V, 24, 13.

21 Augustine, *in Ioannis evangelium* tractatus VI, 10.

22 Individual references in F. Hofmann, *Der Kirchenbegriff des hl. Augustinus*, Munich 1933, 168–70.

23 LG 23.

24 LG 13.

25 UR 14.

26 P. Hadot, 'Eine (das), Einheit', in: HWPh. 2, 361–7.

27 References are found in Hofmann, *Der Kirchenbegriff des hl. Augustinus*, 150f.

28 Thomas Aquinas, *de veritate* q. 1 a. 1. See E. Heintel, 'Eine (das), Einheit', in: HWPh. 2, 373f.

29 See section II.2.2.

30 1 Clement 46, 6 and Irenaeus of Lyons, *adversus haereses* IV, 6, 7 and 9, 3; V, 18, 2f. Further evidence is found in H. de Lubac, *Glauben aus der Liebe* (*Catholicism: Christ and the Common Destiny of Man*, San Francisco: Ignatius Press 1988), Einsiedeln 1970, 23–43.

31 GS 23.

32 GS 32.

33 GS 29.

34 GS 4.

35 LG 1 and others.

36 LG 9.

37 GS 42.

38 E. Peterson, 'Monotheism as a Political Problem: A Contribution to the History of Political Theology in the Roman Empire', in: *Theological Tractates* (1951),

Stanford: Stanford University Press 2011, 68–105, E. Peterson presents a thesis on the end of political theology that is opposite to the dogma of Nicaea.

39 There were serious controversies concerning this aspect at the plenary assembly of the Faith and Order Commission of the World Council of Churches in Louvain in 1971, the topic of which was the issue of the unity of the Church and the unity of humanity. See the commentary by W. Pannenberg in 'Einheit der Kirche und Einheit der Menschheit', in: W. Pannenberg, *Ethik und Ekklesiologie*, Göttingen 1977, 318–33, and the report on the assembly by J. Ratzinger in: JRGS 8/2, 695–703.

40 H. Schlier, 'αἵρεσις', in: ThWNT 1, 181–3.

41 W. Grundmann, 'δεῖ', in: ThWNT 2, 21–5.

42 H. Schlier, 'αἵρεσις', 182. Following Cullmann, J. Ratzinger points out the ecumenical significance of this statement by Paul: JRGS 8/2, 734.

43 On the conceptual history, see Y. Congar, 'Wesenseigenschaften der Kirche', in: MySal IV/1, 411–15.

44 See section II.6.2.2.

45 UR 1, 3.

46 UR 1, 4.

47 UR 7f.

48 This was the ingenious concept of J. A. Möhler, *Die Einheit in der Kirche*, §46. See W. Kasper, 'Situation und Zukunft der Ökumene', in: ThQ 181 (2001) 175–90; and, '"Vom Geist und Wesen des Katholizismus"'. Bedeutung, Wirkungsgeschichte und Aktualität von Johann Sebastian Dreys und Johann Adam Möhlers Wesensbestimmung des Katholizismus', in: ThQ 183 (2003), 196–212.

49 LG 8, 14.

50 M. Luther, *Apol.* VII; *Book of Concord*, 171.

51 M. Luther, WA 18, 652.

52 On this problem, see W. Härle, 'Kirche VII', in: TRE 18, 286–9.

53 K. Barth, *CD* IV/1, 660f.

54 D. Bonhoeffer, *Sanctorum Communio* (1930; English edn, Minneapolis: Fortress Press 1998), repr. Munich 1954, 80.

55 CA Art. VII. Cf. On this issue, see section II.2.2.

56 See sections II.5.3 and 4.

57 W. Härle ('Kirche', 280f. 293) has highlighted the fundamental difference. He ascribes 'essential unity' to the hidden Church. But it remains for the visible church a critical target, such that, as the Leuenberg Agreement puts it, we must strive for a variety of independent ecclesial institutions which share a common understanding of the Gospel. See section II.2.2.

58 LG 8; UR 4; DH 1.

59 G. Philips, *L'Église et son mystère au deuxième Concile du Vatican. Histoire, texte et commentaire de la Constitution* Lumen gentium, vol. 1, Paris 1967, 119.

60 *Declaration on the unicity and salvific universality of Jesus Christ and the Church – Dominus Jesus* (2000); *Responses to Some Questions Regarding Certain Aspects of the Doctrine on the Church* (2007).

61 On the meaning of 'subsistit in', see A. Grillmeier, 'Dogmatische Konstitution über die Kirche', in: LThK.E 1, 170–6, 200–5; M. Kehl, 'Die eine Kirche und die vielen Kirchen', in: StdZ 219 (2001) 3–16; A. von Teuffenbach, *Die Bedeutung des subsistit in* (LG 8), Munich 2002; W. Kasper, 'Il Decreto sull'ecumenismo. Una nuova lettura dopo 40 anni', in: *OR* (12 November 2004), 8–9; K. J. Becker, 'Subsistit in', in: *OR* (5/6 December 2005), 6–7; F. A. Sullivan, 'Quaestio diputata. A Response to Karl Becker on the Meaning of "subsistit in"', in: *ThSt* 67 (2006) 395–409; and, 'Further Thoughts on the Meaning of subsistit in', in: ibid. 71 (2010) 133–47. E. Jüngel, 'Kirche im eigentlichen Sinn', in: NZZ (October 12, 2009); D. Valentini, 'Subsistit in', in: *Dizionario di ecclesiologia*, Roma 2010, 1383–408.

62 The meaning of 'subsistit in' cannot be derived from the (in no way uniform) scholastic usage of subsistence, as this knows the term 'subsistit', but not the phrase 'subsistit in'. The debates of the Council presupposed that 'est' and 'subsistit in' factually mean the same. This terminological change, therefore, does not imply a break but rather a development, clarification and deepening of the previous doctrine.

63 This intention becomes obvious in the *Relatio* of the Council's Commissio doctrinalis. See G. Alberigo/F. Magistretti (eds), *Synopsis historica*, Bologna 1975, 440.

64 John Paul II, Encyclical *Ut unum sint* 13.

65 One wonders whether the word 'elements' was an unfortunate choice. It can give the impression of something quantifiable which, as we are dealing with spiritual matters here, cannot be the intention. In terms of content the expression goes back to Calvin's 'vestigia Ecclesia', with which he however means only sad remainders (*Institutio* IV, 2, 11). The 'elements' received a positive definition from the first general secretary of the World Council of Churches (WCC), Visser t'Hooft, and in the Toronto *Statement* of the WCC Central Committee (1950). On this issue, see W. Thönissen, 'Vestigia aut elementa Ecclesiae? Zur ökumenischen Rezeption eines kontroverstheologisch umstrittenen ekklesiologischen Lehrstücks', in: H. A. Mooney et al. (eds), *Theologie aus dem Geist des Humanismus* (Festschrift P. Walter), Freiburg i. Br. 2010, 395–415.

66 UR 3; *Ut unum sint* 10.

67 UR 3.

68 *Ut unum sint* 11.

69 UR 4; *Ut unum sint* 11.

70 *Ut unum sint* 28, 56.

71 This basically rejects again the so-called 'branch theory', which is particularly widespread in Anglicanism. Accordingly, the Catholic, Orthodox and Protestant churches are, in their respective ways, each branches of the one trunk of the Church.

72 UR 15.

73 On the meaning of the term 'defectus ordinis', see P. Walter, '"Sacramentum Ordinis defectus" (UR 22, 3). Die Aussage des II. Vaticanums im Licht des ökumenischen Dialogs', in: D. Sattler/C. Axt-Piscalar (eds) *Das kirchliche Amt in apostolischer Nachfolge*, vol. 3 (*Dialog der Kirchen* 14), Freiburg i. Br. 2008, 86–101.

74 See section II.2.2.

75 Council of the Evangelical Church in Germany (EKD), *A Protestant Understanding of Ecclesial Communion* (2001) (EKD Texte 69).

76 Y. Congar, 'Die Heilige Kirche', in: MySal IV/1, 458–77; C. Journet, *L'Église sainte mais non sans pécheurs*, Saint-Maur 1999; T. Hainthaler et al. (eds), *Heiligkeit und Apostolizität der Kirche* (Pro Oriente 35), Innsbruck – Vienna 2010.

77 Ignatius of Antioch, *ad Trallianos*, prooemium.

78 DH 1–5; 10–36; and others.

79 DH 10.

80 DH 150.

81 P. Nautin, *Je crois à l'Esprit Saint dans la Sainte Église pour la Résurrection de la chair*, Paris 1947.

82 This expression goes back to the description of 'the holy' by R. Otto, who speaks of the experience of the holy as a paradoxical experience of the 'mysterium tremendum fascinosum', that is, as the mystery that frightens and at the same time attracts.

83 O. Proksch/K. G. Kuhn, 'ἅγιος', in: ThWNT 1, 87–112.

84 F. Hauck, 'ἁγνός', in: ThWNT 1, 123f.

85 See sections II.2.3 and II.3.3.

86 This statement has to be seen together with those passages in the fourth Gospel and in 1 John that speak of 'remaining': Jn 6.57; 14.16f.; 15.4ff.; 10.16.

87 DH 33, 46, 48. Later magisterial statements at the Council of Trent (DH 1678), of Leo XIII, *Divinum illud* (1897, DH 3329ff.) and Pius XII, *Mystici corporis* (1943, DH 3807f., 3814f.).

88 J. A. Möhler, *Unity*, Addenda 1 and 2, 269–73. Note here also the respective references to the Church Fathers.

89 H. Schauf, *Die Einwohnung des Hl. Geistes. Die Lehre von der nichtappropriierten Einwohnung des Hl. Geistes als Beitrag zur Theologiegeschichte des 19. Jahrhunderts unter besonderer Berücksichtigung der beiden Theologen Carl Passaglia und Clemens Schrader*, Freiburg i. Br. 1941.

90 Fundamental theology and dogmatic principles deal in detail with the inerrancy and infallibility of the Church. On this point, see W. Kasper, 'Freiheit des Evangeliums und dogmatische Bindung', in: *Theologie und Kirche* (*Theology and Church*, London: SCM 1989), Mainz 1987, 43–72; and, 'Zum Verständnis unfehlbarer Ex-cathedra-Entscheidungen', in: WKGS 12, 648–52. See also section II.5.4.

91 This question is addressed in detail beneath the heading of sacramental theology under the keywords '*opus operatum*' and '*opus operantis*'. Unfortunately, we cannot give this issue its due attention here.

92 On the controversialist problem of '*cooperatio*', see section II.2, note 108.

93 LG 39–42.

94 Mt. 5.3-12; Lk. 6.20–6.

95 C. Journet, *L'Église sainte mais non sans pécheurs*, Saint-Maur 1999.

96 The interpretation, repeated often since the Enlightenment, of the Lord's Prayer as an un-Jewish prayer expressing the novelty of the gospel is probably obsolete by now. The same is true of a purely eschatological interpretation that understands it as a prayer for the eschatological self-revelation of God. One should rather understand this prayer from a Jewish context, such as the Aramaic qaddish prayer. Today we can follow again the teaching of the Church Fathers and of the whole Tradition up to the nineteenth century, according to which the Lord's Prayer is both a summary of Jesus' message and an instruction for a Christian life. See U. Luz, *Das Evangelium nach Matthäus* (EKK I/1; *Matthew: a Commentary*, Minneapolis: Augsburg 1989–2005), Neukirchen 1985, 332–9. For the Jewish parallels, see H. Strack/P. Billerbeck, *Kommentar zum Neuen Testament aus Talmud und Midrash*, vol. 1: *Das Evangelium nach Matthäus*, Munich 1961, 406–24.

97 Elaborating this in detail touches upon the doctrine of grace, usually by way of the use of the three divine virtues of faith, hope and love. Unfortunately, in academic theology the disciplines of asceticism and mysticism have become detached, so that today those two disciplines are unduly neglected.

98 LG 43–7. On the spiritual movements, see section II.5.8.

99 John Paul II, Post-synodal Apostolic Exhortation, *Christifideles laici* (1988). See section II.5.2.

100 *Epistle to Diognetus*, chapter 5.

101 On the exegesis of this, see section II.2.2, and section II.5.4.

102 D. Bonhoeffer, 'Costly Grace', in: *The Cost of Discipleship* (1937), New York: Touchstone 1959, 43f.; and, 'The Church of Christ and the Life of Discipleship', in: ibid., 223–304.

103 I cannot, in the present context, deal with the history, theology and practice of the sacrament of penance. I refer to the research by B. Poschmann, K. Rahner and others, as well as to my own contributions in WKGS 10, 337–422.

104 LG 11.

105 GS 43.

106 UR 4, 6.

107 GS 19.

108 Augustine, *de civitate Dei* I, 36; *de doctrina christiana* III, 323, 45.

109 See the rich material in H. U. von Balthasar, 'Casta meretrix', in: *Spouse of the Word* (1961), San Francisco: Ignatius Press 1991, 193–288. Admittedly, one might hold reservations against the title of this meritorious and

extremely valuable collection of material. The formula '*casta meretrix*' appears in only one place in the patristic literature in Ambrose of Milan (*expositio evangelii secundum Lucam* VI, 23). There it can be found in a complicated passage which deals with the typological interpretation of the Old Testament prostitute Rahab (Joshua 2). D. Tettamanzi has shown in an in-depth analysis of Ambrose's use of language that the expression 'casta meretrix' does not mean that the Church was 'simul iusta et peccatrix'. Rather, the Church, which was once a sinful prostitute, is now sanctified and thus holy. See D. Tettamanzi, *La Chiesa risplende della luce di Cristo. Il Mistero della Chiesa e i sui Ministeri nel pensiero di sant'Ambrogio*, Milan 2007, 38–40.

110 On this see the study by the International Theological Commission, *Memory and Reconciliation: the Church and the Faults of the Past* (1999); J. Ratzinger, 'Die Schuld der Kirche', in: JRGS 8/2, 495–502.

111 John Paul II, Apostolic Exhortation, *Reconciliatio et Paenitentia* (1984), 16; *Ut unum sint* 34.

112 M. Luther, Sermon on Easter Sunday 9 April 1531 (WA 34/1, 276, 7f.). On this point, see A. Birmelé, 'La peccabilité de l'Église comme enjeu oecuménique', in: RHPhR 67 (1987) 399–419; E. Jüngel, 'The Church as Sacrament', in: *Theological Essays*, vol. I, Edinburgh: T & T Clark 1989, 189–213; H. Meyer, 'Sündige Kirche? Zum ekklesiologischen Aspekt der Debatte um eine katholisch/evangelisch "Grunddifferenz"', in: *Versöhnte Verschiedenheit*, vol. 2, Frankfurt a. M.– Paderborn 2000, 251–65.

113 T. Schneider/G. Wenz (eds), *Gerecht und Sünder zugleich?* (*Dialog der Kirchen* 11), Freiburg i. Br. – Göttingen 2001.

114 H. de Lubac, *Die Kirche. Eine Betrachtung* (*The Splendor of the Church*, San Francisco: Ignatius Press 1999), Einsiedeln 1968, 89–104; also Y. Congar, 'Wesenseigenschaften der Kirche', in: MySal IV/1, 463.

115 K. Rahner, 'The Church of Sinners', in: *Theological Investigations*, vol. 6, Baltimore: Helicon Press 1969, 253–69; 'The Sinful Church in the Decrees of Vatican II', in ibid., 270–94.

116 Ambrose of Milan, *expositio evangelii secundum Lucam* VI, 21.

117 J. A. Möhler, *Symbolism*, §37.

118 Thomas Aquinas, *Summa theologiae* III q. 8 a. 3 ad 2.

119 On this, see Y. Congar, *Vraie et fausse réforme dans l'Église*, Paris 1950. K. Rahner, *The Shape of the Church to Come*, New York: Seabury 1974; Groupe de Dombes, *For the Conversion of the Churches*, Geneva: WCC Publications 1993; J. Ratzinger, 'Was heißt Erneuerung der Kirche?' (1966), in: JRGS 8/2, 1186–202; and, 'Eine Gemeinschaft auf dem Weg. Von der Kirche und ihrer immerwährenden Erneuerung', in: ibid., 1216–30.

120 LG 8; cf. UR 6–8. Even though it happens repeatedly, the statement must not be confused with the (not Luther's own, but rather Post-Reformation) formula of the 'ecclesia semper reformanda'. The latter encapsulates the danger that it 'reforms itself away' from its own reformatory basis of being Church and that it thus falls into a kind of self-secularization. See T. Mahlmann, 'Reformation', in: HWPh. 8, 420f.

121 UR 7.

122 W. Beinert, *Um das dritte Kirchenattribut*, 2 vols, Essen 1964; and, 'Katholisch, Katholizität', in: HWPh. 4, 787–9; Y. Congar, 'Die katholische Kirche', in: MySal, Bd. IV/1, Einsiedeln 1972, 478–502; H. U. von Balthasar, *In the Fullness of Faith: on the Centrality of the Distinctively Catholic* (1975), San Francisco: Ignatius Press 1988; A. Dulles, *The Catholicity of the Church*, Oxford 1985; and, *The Reshaping of Catholicism*, San Francisco 1988; M. Seckler, 'Katholisch als Konfessionsbezeichnung', in: *Die schiefen Wände des Lehrhauses. Katholizität als Herausforderung*, Freiburg i. Br. 1988, 178–97; P. Steinacker, 'Katholizität', in: TRE 18, 72–80; S. Hell (ed.), *Katholizität. Konfessionalismus oder Weltweite?*, Innsbruck 2007.

123 DH 2–5.

124 DH 127f.

125 DH 150.

126 See K. Wenzel, 'Katholisch', in: $LThK^3$ 5, 1345f.

127 Ignatius of Antioch, *ad Smyrnaeos* 8, 2.

128 See Ignatius of Antioch, *ad Ephesios* 6, 2.

129 Polycarp, *ep. circularis*, praescriptum.

130 Ibid. 8, 1.

131 Ibid. 19, 2.

132 Ibid. 16, 2.

133 Augustine, ep. 93, 23.

134 Augustine, *contra litteras Petiliani* II, 38, 91.

135 Cyril of Jerusalem, *mystagogiae* 18, 23.

136 *Commonitorium* c.2. These criteria of *universitas*, *antiquitas* and *consensus* do not apply cumulatively but consecutively, so that in case of insufficient universality the older age decides. In addition, Vincent explains in Chapter 23 that the principle of *antiquitas* does not exclude an organic dogmatic development in history '*eodem sensu eademque sententia*'. This principle was taken up by Vatican I (DH 3020). However, as will be shown directly, below, it can be differently interpreted and applied.

137 Thomas Aquinas, *Sent.* IV d. 13 q. 13 sol 1; *Expositio super Symbolum apostolicum*, a. 9. See M. Seckler, 'Geist der Katholizität. Thomas von Aquin und die Theologie', in: *Im Spannungsfeld von Wissenschaft und Theologie*, Freiburg i. Br. 1980, 163–77.

138 DH 870–2. See Seckler, 'Katholisch als Konfessionsbezeichnung', 184–7.

139 J. Meyendorff, *Orthodoxy and Catholicity*, New York 1965; J. Zizioulas, *L'Être ecclésiale*, Geneva 1981, 116f.; Bobrinskoy, *Le mystère de l'Église*, 151–8.

140 Luther held fast to the declared belief in the catholic Church (WA 50, 624; 51, 479), but accused the pope of abandoning the 'catholica' in favour of 'romana' and thus turning the Church into a sect (WA 7, 753; 50, 626).

Whereas, for Luther, the true and false churches are in conflict with one another within the one Church, Melanchthon shows tendencies towards an independent visible denominational church. See Elert, *Morphologie des Luthertums* (*The Structure of Lutheranism*, St. Louis: Concordia 1962), vol. 1, Munich 1931, 240–55; Steinacker, 'Katholizität', 76f. For Calvin 'catholic' is an attribute of the invisible Church (*Genevan Catechism* of 1542, question 93), similar today for example the Lutheran W. Härle ('Kirche', 293).

141 DH 1868.

142 J. S. Drey, 'Vom Geist und Wesen des Katholizismus', in: ThQ 1 (1819) 3– 24, 193–210, 369–92, 559–75; J. A. Möhler, *Unity in the Church or the Principle of Catholicism*. For other theologians of that milieu, see J. R. Geiselmann (ed.), *Geist des Christentums und des Katholizismus*, Mainz 1940.

143 K. Adam, *The Spirit of Catholicism* (1924), London: Sheed & Ward 1929; H. de Lubac, *Catholicism: Christ and Common Destiny of Man* (1938), San Francisco: Ignatius Press 1988; Y. Congar, 'Katholizität', in: *Heilige Kirche*, Stuttgart 1966, 159–65; H. Schlier, 'Das bleibend Katholische. Ein Versuch über ein Prinzip des Katholischen', in: *Das Ende der Zeit. Exegetische Aufsätze und Vorträge* III, Freiburg i. Br. 1971, 297–320; H. U. von Balthasar, *In the Fullness of Faith: on the Centrality of the Distinctively Catholic* (1975), San Francisco: Ignatius Press 1988.

144 So stated in R. Guardini, *Vom Wesen katholischer Weltanschauung* (afterword by H. Fries), Basel 1953.

145 LG 13.

146 LG 8; UR 3.

147 COD 499.

148 UR 17.

149 See note 39.

150 In the CA jubilee year of 1980, some mulled over the possibility of recognizing the catholicity of the Confessio Augustana. Among others, see H. Meyer, et al. (eds), *Confessio Augustana. Bekenntnis des einen Glaubens*, Paderborn – Frankfurt a.M. 1980; also: *Um die eine Kirche. evangelische Katholizität* (Festschrift H. J. Mund), ed. by the Hochkirchlichen Vereinigung Augsburgischen Bekenntnisses, Munich – Gräfelfing 1984.

151 In the English language the Creed was left intact. Native English speakers tend to distinguish theologically between 'Catholic Church' (Capital C) in the sense of a denomination and 'catholic Church' pertaining to the nature of the Church.

152 W. Pannenberg, 'Die Bedeutung der Eschatologie für das Verständnis der Apostolizität und Katholizität', in: *Ethik und Ekklesiologie*, Göttingen 1977, 219–40; J. Moltmann, *Kirche in der Kraft des Geistes* (*The Church in the Power of the Spirit*, London: SCM Press 1981), Munich 1975, 373–8.

153 See section II.2, note 172.

154 LG 8. See section II.2.1.

155 H. Küng, *Die Kirche* (*The Church*, London 1967), Freiburg i. Br. 1967, 370. In a different sense, E. Przywara spoke of catholic ecumenicity, in: *Ringen der Gegenwart. Gesammelte Aufsätze*, vol. 2, Augsburg 1929, 609–23.

156 One must mention Melanchthon and Erasmus, then Johannes Piscator, Valentin Andreae, Molanus, and especially Georg Calixt and Comenius from the Unity of Brethern. See C. Böttigheimer, *Zwischen Polemik und Irenik. Die Theologie der einen Kirche bei Georg Calixt*, Münster 1996; M. Richter, 'Comenius als ökumenischer Denker', in: *Comenius-Jahrbuch* 16/17 (2008/09) 45–61.

157 Regarding the content, this programme on the basis of the *Book of Common Prayer* (1662) is contained in the still-authoritative Chicago-Lambeth-Quadrilateral (1886) of the Anglican Communion, which states, as the basis of its unity, Holy Scripture, the Creeds, the sacraments (baptism and the Eucharist) and the historical episcopate. During his time as an Anglican, J. H. Newman advocated this concept in 'On the Prophetical Office of the Church' (1837), where he envisaged a via media between Protestantism and Rome. Later he realized the impossibility of this middle way and, in time, joined the path leading toward the Catholic Church. See *Apologia pro vita sua* (1864). See also section II.4.4.

158 *Together in Mission and Ministry. The Porvoo Common Statement (Conversations between the British and Irish Anglican Churches and the Nordic and Baltic Lutheran Churches)*, 1992.

159 *Agreement of the Churches of the Reformation in Europe* (Leuenberg Agreement). See H. Meyer., '"Einheit in versöhnter Verschiedenheit". Hintergrund, Entstehung und Bedeutung des Gedankens', in: *Versöhnte Verschiedenheit*, vol. 1, Frankfurt a.M. – Paderborn 1998, 101–19. On this point, see section II.2.2, and section II.6.2.2.

160 On this classicistic understanding of Tradition, see J. R. Geiselmann, *Die katholische Tübinger Schule. Ihre theologische Eigenart*, Freiburg i. Br. 1964, 162–75.

161 See section II.5.4.

162 UR 2–4.

163 LG 8, 15; UR 3f.; *Ut unum sint* 10f.

164 See sections II.4.1 and II.6.2.2.

165 J. H. Newman, *Essay on the Development of Christian Doctrine* (1845), Baltimore: Penguin 1974.

166 J. H. Newman, *Apologia pro vita sua*, 179f.; and, *Essay on the Development of Christian Doctrine* (1845), 137; and, *An Essay in Aid of a Grammar of Assent* (1870), Notre Dame: University of Notre Dame Press 1979, 382–9 and others.

167 See here the letters and diaries of J. H. Newman from his Catholic period in: *The Letters and Diaries of John Henry Newman* (ed. by J. Ker and T. Gornall), Oxford: Claredon Press 1978.

168 UR 5–8; *Ut unum sint* 15f.

169 Congar, 'Apostolizität', in: *Heilige Kirche*, Stuttgart 1966, 186–90; and, 'Apostolicité de ministère et apostolicité de doctrine', in: *Ministères et communion ecclésiale*, Paris 1971, 51–94; and, 'Die Apostolizität der Kirche', in: MySal III/1, 534–98; T. Schneider/G. Wenz (eds), *Das kirchliche Amt in apostolischer Nachfolge*, vol. 1, Freiburg i. Br. – Göttingen 2004; T. Hainthaler et al. (eds), *Heiligkeit und Apostolizität der Kirche*, (*Pro Oriente* 35), Innsbruck – Vienna 2010. An extensive bibliography is presented by W. Beinert, in 'Apostolisch. Anatomie eines Begriffs', in: D. Sattler/G.Wenz (eds), *Das kirchliche Amt in apostolischer Nachfolge*, vol. 2, Freiburg i. Br. – Göttingen 2006, 301–3.

170 Ignatius of Antioch, *ad Trallianos*, praescriptum. This translation is contentious. Others translate the phrase 'ἐν ἀποστολικῷ χαρακτῆρι' as 'in an apostolic way'.

171 Polycarp, *ep. circularis* 16.

172 DH 3, 42, 44, 46f., 48, 50.

173 DH 150.

174 Strack/Billerbeck, *Kommentar zum Neuen Testament*, vol. 1 (cf. note 96), 590.

175 K. H. Rengstorf, 'ἀπόστολος', in: ThWNT 1, 406–46; R. Schnackenburg, 'Apostolizität. Stand der Forschung, in: Katholizität und Apostolizität in der Forschung', in: R. Groscurth (ed.), *Katholizität und Apostolizität*, Göttingen 1971, 51–73; K. Kertelge, 'Das Apostel-Amt des Paulus, sein Ursprung und seine Bedeutung', in: BZ NF 14 (1970), 161–81; F. Hahn, 'Der Apostolat im Urchristentum', in: KuD 20 (1974) 54–77; J. Roloff, 'Apostel, Apostolat, Apostolizität I. Neues Testament', in: TRE 3, 430–45.

176 This eschatological dimension was pointed out, in particular, by W. Pannenberg, 'Die Bedeutung der Eschatologie für das Verständnis der Apostolizität und der Katholizität der Kirche', in: *Ethik und Ekklesiologie*, Göttingen 1977, 219–40. This aspect is applied with emphasis especially on the Orthodox side. See P. Evdokimov, *L'Ortodossia*, Bologna 1981, 231–5; J. Zizioulas, *Being as Communion*, New York 1985, 171–208.

177 So the concise wording by Evdokimov, *L'Ortodossia*, 231.

178 See sections II.2.1 and II.2.2.

179 Y. Congar repeatedly stressed this point. See 'Die Lehre von der Kirche von Augustinus bis zum abendländischen Schisma', in: HDG III 3 c, Freiburg i. Br, 1971, 96f, 106f.

180 Bobrinskoy, *Le mystère de l'Église*, 164–6. As an example for this type of 'mission through presence' Bobrinskoy refers to the testimony of Charles de Foucauld.

181 Irenaeus of Lyons, *adversus haereses* III, 4, 2.

182 Y. Congar, *Tradition and Traditions*, 2 vols, New York: Macmillan 1966, 1967. See section I, note 27.

183 Among the latter, there is a Junias who received special attention (Rom. 16.7). According to some readings, the original name was not Junias but Junia. From this people often deduce that, in the apostolic period, a woman can be called apostle. Yet, besides the hypothetical nature of this thesis (it is worth noting that Nestle-Aland still prefers Junias), it says nothing more than the fact that a woman was the delegate of a community but not that she was an apostle in the proper meaning of the word.

184 A detailed collection of the various meanings can be found in Beinert, 'Apostolisch', 275f.

185 G. G. Blum, 'Apostel, Apostolat, Apostolizität II', in: TRE 3, 445–66.

186 H. Schürmann, 'Das Testament des Paulus für die Kirche Apg 20, 18–35', in: O. Schilling (ed.), *Unio Christianorum* (Festschrift L. Jäger), Paderborn 1962, 108–46.

187 1 Clement 42.1–4; cf. 44.2.

188 Ignatius of Antioch, *ad Magnesios* 6, 1; *ad Trallianos* 3, 1.

189 Irenaeus of Lyons, *adversus haereses* III, Praescript.

190 Ibid. III, 1, 1.

191 Ibid. III, 2, 2.

192 Ibid. III, 3, 1.

193 Ibid. III, 4, 1.

194 Ibid. III, 2, 2.

195 Ibid. III, 3, 3.

196 Ibid. IV, 33, 8.

197 Ibid. III, 1, 1.

198 Ibid. IV, 26, 2.

199 Ibid. III, 24, 1.

200 Ibid. III, 4, 2.

201 Tertullian, *de praescriptione haereticorum* 20; 21, 4; 32, 1.3.

202 Eusebius of Caesarea, *historia ecclesiastica* IV, 1, 4f.

203 Ibid. IV, 22, 3.

204 Ibid. IV, 22, 2f.; 7f.

205 Ibid. IV, 26, 2.

206 Similar Basil, *de Spiritu Sancto* 9, 20d.

207 This holistic view is of particular importance in Orthodox theology. See J. Zizioulas, *Being as Communion*, New York 1985, 171–208; Bobrinskoy, *Le mystère de l'Église*, 161–4.

208 J. Ratzinger, 'Primacy, Episcopate, and Apostolic Succession', in: K. Rahner/J. Ratzinger, *The Episcopate and Primacy* (QD 11), London: Burns & Oates 1962, 37–63.

209 See K. Lehmann, 'Das theologische Verständnis der Ordination nach dem liturgischen Zeugnis der Priesterweihe', in: R. Mumm (ed.), *Ordination und kirchliches Amt*, Paderborn – Bielefeld 1976, 19–52.

210 See W. Kasper, 'Die apostolische Sukzession als ökumenisches Problem', in: W. Pannenberg (ed.), *Lehrverurteilungen – kirchentrennend?*, vol. 3,

Freiburg – Göttingen 1990, 329–49; M. Kehl, *Die Kirche. Eine katholische Ekklesiologie*, Würzburg 1994, 343–6; W. Beinert, 'Apostolisch. Anatomie eines Begriffs', in: Sattler/Wenz, *Das kirchliche Amt* (cf. note 169), 298f.

211 R. Sohm, *Wesen und Ursprung des Katholizismus*, Leipzig 1909; and, *Das altkatholische Kirchenrecht und das Dekret Gratians* (1918), repr. Darmstadt 1967.

212 A. von Harnack, *Entstehung und Entwicklung der Kirchenverfassung und des Kirchrechts in den ersten zwei Jahrhunderten*, Leipzig 1910, 121–86.

213 E. Peterson, 'Heiliges Recht und Kirchenrecht', in: *Ekklesia*, Würzburg 2010, 52–83. On this, see section II.2.2.

214 E. Käsemann, 'The Canon of the New Testament and the Unity of the Church', in: *Essays on New Testament Themes*, London: SCM Press 1964, 95–107; and, 'Paul and Early Catholicism', in: *New Testament Questions of Today*, London: SCM Press 1969, 236–51; and, 'Unity and Multiplicity and the New Testament Doctrine of the Church', in: ibid., 252–9. Summary of the discussion in K. Kertelge/K. H. Neufeld, 'Frühkatholizismus', in: LThK[3] 4, 201–4. See sections II.2.1; II.4.1.

215 B. S. Childs, *Die Theologie der einen Bibel*, 2 vols, Freiburg i. Br. 1994, 1996.

216 So already K. Holl, *Der Kirchenbegriff des Paulus in seinem Verhältnis zu dem der Urgemeinde*, Berlin 1921; H. Campenhausen, *Ecclesiastical Authority and Spiritual Power in the Church of the First Three Centuries* (1953), London: Black 1969. See section II.5.3.

217 Origen, *commentaria in evamgelium secundum Matthaeum* XV, 24.

218 K. S. Frank, 'Vita apostolica und dominus apostolicus. Zur altkirchlichen Apostelnachfolge', in: G. Schwaiger (ed.), *Konzil und Papst. Historische Beiträge zur Frage der höchsten Gewalt in der Kirche* (Festschrift H. Tüchle), Munich 1975, 19–41; P. Segl, 'Armutsbewegung', in: LThK[3] 1, 1012–14.

219 M. Luther, 'Tischreden' ('Table Discourse', October 1533), in: *Luthers Werke in Auswahl* (O. Clemen), vol. 8, 79 (624).

220 On this, see E. Iserloh, 'Reformation, Katholische Reform und Gegenreformation', in: HKG 4, Freiburg i. Br. 1967, 56–60; V. Leppin, *Martin Luther*, Darmstadt 2006, 138–41.

221 On this, see section II.1.2.

222 Iserloh, 'Reformation', 65; O. H. Pesch, *Hinführung zu Luther*, Mainz 1982, 103–15; Leppin, *Martin Luther*, 144–51.

223 M. Luther, 'The Papacy in Rome: an Answer to the Celebrated Romanist at Leipzig' in: WA 5, 296f.

224 M. Luther, 'On the Councils and the Church' (1539), in: WA 50, 628–44; 'Against Hanswurst' (1541), in: WA 51, 479–87.

225 See section II.5.2.

226 G. Kretschmar, 'Die Wiederentdeckung des Konzepts der "Apostolischen Sukzession" im Umkreis der Reformation', in: B. Hägglund (ed.), *Kirche in der Schule Luthers* (Festschrift J. Heubach), Erlangen 1995, 231–79.

227 On the criticism of a theology that is one-sidedly oriented to the Magisterium, see section II.1.2.

228 See Eusebius, *historia ecclesiastica* V, 28, 6. See the commentary by A. Grillmeier, in: LThK.E 1, 189–91 and F. Klostermann in: ibid., 273–6. Also important in this context is J. H. Newman, *On Consulting the Faithful in Matters of Doctrine*, London: Collins 1961.

229 LG 12; cf. 35.

230 Cf. II.1.2.

231 See the commentary by J. Ratzinger, which remains important for this issue, in LThK.E 2, 498–528; H. de Lubac, *Die göttliche Offenbarung. Kommentar zum Vorwort und zum ersten Kapitel der Dogmatischen Konstitution* Dei Verbum *des Zweiten Vatikanischen Konzils*, Einsiedeln 2001. For a critical assessment, see O. H. Pesch, *Das Zweite Vatikanische Konzil. Vorgeschichte – Verlauf – Nachgeschichte*, Würzburg 1993, 271–90. By contrast, many positive voices are found in H. Hoping, in: HThK.Vat II 3, 697–831. Unfortunately, the constitution has been insufficiently received for a long time. One can only hope that the post-synodal document, *Verbum Domini* (2010), will bring a change.

232 DV 1.

233 So Ratzinger, 'Kommentar', 504f.

234 DV 7. See Irenaeus of Lyons, *adversus haereses* III, 3, 1.

235 DV 8.

236 On the distinction between '*traditio*' and '*traditiones*', see section I.4, note 27.

237 DV 8.

238 DV 9.

239 DV 10.

240 On this, see section II.1.2, note 67.

241 LG 8; cf. GS 1; 21.

242 I can only mention the most important documents and publications: WCC-Roman Catholic Church Joint Working Group, *Study document on catholicity and apostolicity*, Geneva 1970; Faith and Order Commission of the World Council of Churches, *Baptism, Eucharist and Ministry*, Geneva 1982, part 3, no. 35–8 (43f.). *Confessing the One Faith: an Ecumenical Explication of the Apostolic Faith as it is Confessed in the Nicene-Constantinopolitan Creed (381)*, Geneva: WCC Publications 1996, 9–11; *Das kirchliche Amt in apostolischer Nachfolge*, 3 vols (*Dialog der Kirchen* 12–14), Freiburg i. Br. – Göttingen 2004–8; *Die Apostolizität der Kirche* (Study document of the German Lutheran/Roman Catholic Commission for unity), Paderborn – Frankfurt a. M.2009; W. Kasper, *Harvesting the Fruits*, London 2009, 83–6.107f, 151f. An overview of the discussion can be found in H. Meyer, 'Apostolische Kontinuität – Kirchliches Amt – Apostolische Sukzession', in: *Versöhnte Verschiedenheit. Aufsätze zur ökumenischen Theologie*, vol. 2, Frankfurt a.M. – Paderborn 2000, 298–316; P. Staples, 'Apostolicity', in: *Dictionary of the Ecumenical Movement*, Geneva 2002, 49–53; W. Beinert, 'Apostolizität der Kirche', in: *Lexikon der Ökumene*

und Konfessionskunde, Freiburg i. Br. 2007, 93–5. On the dialogue with the Orthodox churches, see J. Oeldemann, *Die Apostolizität der Kirche im ökumenischen Gespräch mit der Orthodoxie*, Paderborn 2000.

243 On this, see II.5.3.

244 So argues W. Härle, in 'Kirche', in: TRE 8, 292.

245 On this basic problem, see section II.2.2.

246 See note 157.

247 *Together in Mission and Ministry. The Porvoo Common Statement (Conversations between the British and Irish Anglican Churches and the Nordic and Baltic Lutheran Churches)*, 1992.

248 UR 13.

249 DH 3315–9.

250 On this, see section II.5.3.

251 On this, see sections II.5.1 and 3.

5. The concrete form of the Church as *communio*

1 Aristotle, *metaphysica* V, 2, 1013a. See also Thomas Aquinas, *Summa contra gentiles* 1, 1; *Summa theologiae* I q. 5 a. 2, and elsewhere.

2 On the interpretation, see K. H. Schelkle, *Die Petrusbriefe* (HThK.NT XIII/2), Freiburg i. Br. 1961, 57–72; N. Brox, *Der erste Petrusbrief* (EKK XXI), Zürich – Neukirchen 1979, 94–110.

3 Origen, *contra Celsum* VIII, 73–5.

4 Origen, *homilia in Leviticum* IX, 1, 2, 8.

5 Augustine, *de civitate Dei* X, 3.

6 Leo the Great, *sermones* IV, 1.

7 Bonaventura, *Sermo de sancte Laurentio*, 1.

8 Augustine, *de civitate Dei* XX, 10; cf. Ambrose, de sacramentis IV, 3.

9 Leo the Great, *sermones* III, 1.

10 See Brox, *Der erste Petrusbrief*, 108f., which, in note 362, references further sources. In addition, a broad collection of literature is found in H. de Lubac, *Die Kirche* (*The Splendour of the Church*, San Francisco: Ignatius Press 1999), Einsiedeln 1968, 118–27; R. Hanson, 'Amt/Ämter/ Ämterverständnis', in: TRE 2, 543–9.

11 Thomas Aquinas, *Summa theologiae* Suppl. q. 22 a. 6 ad 1.

12 Ibid., III q. 63 a. 2–6.

13 Ibid., III q. 80 a. 12 ad 3; q. 82 a. 2 ad 2; a. 8; Suppl. q. 34 a. 2 ad 1–3.

14 Ibid., Suppl. q. 31 a. 1 ad 1; *Summa contra gentiles* IV, 73.

15 WA 6, 408.

16 WA 6, 564.

17 WA 7, 27.

18 WA 11, 408–16.

19 WA 50, 632f.

20 CA Art. 5; cf. 14; 28.

21 See the overview in W. Pannenberg, 'Das kirchliche Amt in der Sicht der lutherischen Lehre', in: Lehrverurteilungen – kirchentrennend? (Dialog der Kirchen 6; *The Condemnations of the Reformation Era: Do They Still Divide?*), Freiburg i. Br. – Göttingen 1990, 286–305; and, *Systematische Theologie* (*Systematic Theology*), vol. 3, Göttingen 1993, 410f, 417–19. There also find a unique interpretation of CA 5.

22 See the joint Lutheran/Roman Catholic Commission, *The Ministry in the Church* (1981) and K. Lehmann/W. Pannenberg, *Lehrverurteilungen – kirchentrennend?*, vol. 1–3, (*The Condemnations of the Reformation Era: Do They Still Divide?*), Freiburg i. Br. – Göttingen 1986–90.

23 See the United Evangelical Lutheran Church of Germany (VELKD) Document, *Allgemeines Priestertum. Ordination und Beauftragung nach evangelischem Verständnis* (2004) and *Ordnungsgemäß berufen: Eine Empfehlung der Bischofskonferenz der VELKD zur Berufung zu Wortverkündigung und Sakramentsverwaltung nach evangelischem Verständnis* (2006). On this, see the critical commentary of W. Dietz, in 'Systematisch-theologische Aspekte von Ordination und Ordinationsvollmacht im Licht evangelischer Theologie', in D. Sattler/G. Wenz (eds), *Das kirchliche Amt in apostolischer Nachfolge*, vol. 2, Freiburg i. Br. – Göttingen, 2006, 97–144; U. Wilckens, 'Kirchliches Amt und gemeinsames Priestertum aller Getauften im Blick auf die Kirchenverfassungen der Lutherischen Kirchen', in ibid., 241–73.

24 See W. Elert, *Morphologie des Luthertums* (*The Structure of Lutheranism*, vol. 1, St Louis, MI: Concordia, 1962), vol. 1, Munich 1931, 327–31.

25 See P. Brunner, *Vom Amt des Bischofs*, Berlin 1955, 46.

26 How little Luther had in common with the modern idea of freedom becomes evident also in the debate with Erasmus of Rotterdam in the work *Vom unfreien Willen* (1523; *On the Bondage of the Will*), as well as in his statements concerning the Peasants' War.

27 W. Maurer, *Das synodale Bischofsamt. seit 1918*, Berlin 1955; C. Dinkel, 'Synode III', in TRE 22, 571–5; F. Nüssel, 'Zum Verständnis des evangelischen Bischofsamtes in der Neuzeit', in: Sattler/Wenz (eds), *Das kirchliche Amt in apostolischer Nachfolge*, 145–89.

28 So already in the Geneva *Confession de foy. Discipline ecclésiastique* of 1559. Cf. J. Mehlhausen, 'Presbyteral-synodale Kirchenverfassung', in: TRE 27, 331– 40.

29 LG 9–13, 32–7. See the commentaries by A. Grillmeier, in: LThK.E 1, 176–209 and F. Klostermann, in: ibid., 260–83; also P. Hünermann, in: HThK.Vat II 2, 371–93, 466–82.

30 SC 14.

31 LG 19, 34; AA 3; PO 2.

32 See section II.5.3.

33 Foundational for a renewed theology of the laity is the work by Y. Congar titled, *Laypeople in the Church: a Study for a Theology of the Laity*, London: Chapman 1957. The post-conciliar literature on the theology, ministry, spirituality, apostolate, congregations and councils of the laypeople is endless. For examples, see K. Rahner, 'Notes on the Lay Apostolate', in: *Theological Investigations*, vol. 2, Baltimore: Helicon Press 1963, 319–52; H. U. von Balthasar, 'The Layman and the Church', in: *Spouse of the word* (1969), San Francisco: Ignatius Press 1991, 315–32; E. Schillebeeckx, *Gesammelte Schriften*, vol. 2, Mainz 1970, 140–72; M. Keller, 'Theologie des Laientums', in: MySal IV/2, 393–421; W. Kasper, 'The Mission of the Laity', in: *Theological Digest* (1988) 133–8; B. Forte, *Laie sein*, Munich 1987; P. Neuner, *Der Laie und das Gottesvolk*, Frankfurt a.M. 1988; M. Kehl, *Die Kirche. Eine katholische Ekklesiologie*, Würzburg 1992, 117–25; J.Werbick, 'Laie', in: LThK[3] 6, 589–94; B. Kranemann/M. Wijlens (eds), *Gesendet in den Weinberg des Herrn. Laien in der katholischen Kirche heute und morgen*, Würzburg 2010.

34 Y. Congar, *Der Laie*, Stuttgart 1957, 21f.; J. B. Bauer, 'Die Wortgeschichte von "laicus"', in: ZkThess. 81 (1959) 224–8; I. de la Potterie, "L'origine et le sens primitif du mot 'laic'", in: I. de la Potterie/S. Lyonnet, *La vie selon l'esprit*, Paris 1965, 13–29.

35 1 *Clement* 40, 5.

36 J. Ratzinger, *Christliche Brüderlichkeit* (1958; *The Meaning of Christian Brotherhood*, San Francisco: Ignatius Press 1993), in: JRGS 8/1, 65f.

37 A detailed presentation of the material is found in Congar, *Der Laie*, 387–431.

38 *Decretum Gratiani*, C. VII, C. XII q. 1.

39 See Congar, *Der Laie*, 34–43.

40 See section II.5.1.

41 DH 1763–78. See also section II.5.3.

42 See section II.5.8.

43 SC 11, 14.

44 H. Godin/Y. Daniel, 'France a Missionary Land?' (1943) in: Maisie Ward, *France Pagan?: The Mission of Abbé Godin*, New York Sheed & Ward 1949, 63–191. On this, see also the prophetic pastoral letter by Cardinal Emmanuel Suhard of Paris, *Essor ou déclin de l'Église* (1947). This call was heard and taken up very early in Germany by A. Delp. Cf. R. Bleistein, *Alfred Delp. Geschichte eines Zeugen*, Frankfurt a.M. 1989, 432.

45 LG 30–8; AA 1–8. See the commentaries by F. Klostermann, in LThK.E 1, 260–83; 2, 602–33; by P. Hünermann, in: HThK.Vat II 2, 460–82; G. Bausenhart, in: ibid. 4, 38–68.

46 LG 31.

47 AA 3.

48 LG 31.

49 Commentary by Klostermann, 264ff.

50 AA 2.

51 GS 36, 41, 56, 76, AA 7.

52 LG 31, 33f., 37; AA 1, 17.

53 See below, section II.5.3.

54 LG 37.

55 LG 12, 35. There are several misconceptions concerning the term '*sensus fidei*'. It means a sense for the faith given through grace by the *lumen fidei*. This sense comes not from abstract theological reflection but from the lived experience of faith. Therefore one must distinguish the *sensus fidei* from the resulting *consensus fidelium* which is also empirically ascertainable. Still, the *consensus fidelium* is not simply a matter of demographic research, it requires an informed and, as well and above all, a formed faith, thus a life of faith and in the faith. See M. Seckler, 'Glaubenssinn', in $LThK^2$ 4, 945–8.

56 LG 39–42.

57 *Christifideles laici*, 10.

58 *Christifideles laici*, 15.

59 On the discussion: J. Ratzinger/H. Maier, *Demokratie in der Kirche*, Limburg 1970. See section II.3.1.

60 F. Hafner, *Kirche im Kontext der Grund- und Menschenrechte*, Fribourg 1992; W. Kasper, *Wahrheit und Freiheit. Die Erklärung des II. Vatikanischen Konzils über die Religionsfreiheit*, Heidelberg 1988.

61 See CIC can. 208–23, 224–30.

62 There is an ongoing and particularly acrimonious debate concerning the question of the entitlement to the Eucharist. Obviously, just like all sacraments, the Eucharist is grace from God and not a right that can be claimed. However, the Eucharist has been entrusted to the Church with the mandate to administer it to those faithful who are disposed for it. Thus the ecclesiastical ministry has the duty, especially on Sundays and feast days, to make the Eucharist appropriately accessible to the faithful as is physically possible. This, however, does not entail the right to receive the Eucharist in a specific parish or at a specific time. In addition, in cases where the norms of the law for the proper disposition are not fulfilled, the Church has the right to exclude someone from the Eucharist. On the question of celibacy which is often raised in this context, see section II.5.3.

63 AA 26. See W. Kasper, 'Kollegiale Strukturen in der Kirche – der theologische Ort der Räte des gemeinsamen Apostolats' (1969), in: WKGS 12, 19–37. See section II.5.5.

64 Cyprian, ep. 14, 1, 4; cf. 19, 2.

65 *Rule of St Benedict* 3.

66 J. H. Newman, *On Consulting the Faithful in Matters of Doctrine*, London: Collins 1961.

67 From a sociological perspective, see M. Ebertz, 'Laisierung der Kirche? Aspekte ihrer funktionalen Demokratisierung in der modernen Gesellschaft',

in: Kranemann/Wijlens, *Gesendet in den Weinberg des Herrn* (cf. note 33), 53–76.

68 On this, see W. Kasper, 'Die pastoralen Dienste in der Gemeinde' (1976), in: WKGS 12, 69–95; G. Greshake, 'Amt IX', in: LThK^3 1, 554f.; and, *Priester sein in dieser Zeit*, (= new edn of *The Meaning of Priesthood*, Westminster, Md: Christian Classics, 1989) Freiburg i. Br. 2000, 147–54; P. Neuner, 'Laien im Spannungsfeld von dogmatischen Vorgaben und kirchlichen Aufgaben', in: Kranemann/Wijlens, *Gesendet in den Weinberg des Herrn*, 26–9.

69 M. Wijlens, 'Die Kooperation von Laien mit kirchlichem Seelsorgeauftrag und Klerikern', in: Kranemann/Wijlens, *Gesendet in den Weinberg des Herrn* (cf. note 33), 31–47, here: 32.

70 LG 23; AA 17; CIC can. 517 §2. The Synod on the Laity (1988) paid special attention to the office of readers and acolytes with the wish that the Motu Proprio of Paul VI, *Ministeria quaedam* (1972), ought to be examined against the practices that have developed in particular churches and especially with regard to the definition of criteria with which candidates for each office should selected. See *Christifideles laici*, 23.

71 See section II.5.3.

72 Such was also the recommendation after a long deliberation by the Würzburger Synode (Joint Synod of the German Dioceses 1971–5), 'Die pastoralen Dienste in der Gemeinde', in: *Gemeinsame Synode der Bistümer in der Bundesrepublik Deutschland. Offizielle Gesamtausgabe* I, Freiburg i. Br. 1976, 612f.

73 LG 11; cf. AA 1; John Paul II, *Christifideles laici*, 40; Apostolic Exhortation *Familiaris consortio*, on the Christian family in the modern world (1981), 15, 21, 42–8, 49f., 51–64, 73–6. Cf. W. Kasper, *Theology of Christian Marriage*, London: Burns & Oates 1980. In this context it is not possible to discuss numerous material, economical-social and especially ethical problems of today which arise in the context of marriage and family.

74 On a moral theological assessment, see *Catechism of the Catholic Church*, no. 2357–9.

75 A collection of relevant literature by D. Sattler can be found in: T. Schneider, *Mann und Frau – Grundproblem theologischer Anthropologie* (QD 121), Freiburg i. Br. 1989, 201–13. G. Dautzenberg et al. (eds), *Die Frau im Urchristentum* (QD 95), Freiburg i. Br. 1983. H. U. von Balthasar et al. (eds), The *Church and Women*, San Francisco: Ignatius Press 1988; G. L. Müller, *Frauen in der Kirche. Eigensein und Mitverantwortung*, Würzburg 1999. From the perspective of feminist theology, among others: A. Jensen, *God's Self-confident Daughters: Early Christianity and the Liberation of Women*, Louisville, KY: John Knox Press 1996; E. Schüssler-Fiorenza, *In Memory of Her*, New York: Crossroad 1990.

76 See John XXIII, Encyclical, *Pacem in terris*, on establishing universal peace (1963), 22.

77 GS 9, 29, 52, 59f.

78 AA 9.

79 See John Paul II, *Mulieris dignitatem*, on the dignity and vocation of women (1988). On this, see D. Valentini, *La donna e la Chiesa alla luce della simbolica dell'alleanza nuziale: lo Spirito e la sposa*, Vatican City 2009, 113–45; many references on this topic there in note 1.

80 John Paul II, *Christifideles laici* (1988), 49–51. In addition, see Congregation for the Doctrine of Faith, *Letter to the Bishops on the Collaboration of Men and Women in the Church and in the World* (2004).

81 See section II.3.4.

82 On the problem of Junia/Junias in Romans 16.7, see section II.4.4.

83 The passage concerning women keeping silent in the assembly (1 Cor. 14.34) is one of the most controversial statements in 1 Cor. Many consider it to be an interpolation from 1 Tim. 2.11f. In any case, it conflicts with many other statements of the Apostle in 1 Cor. 11.11 and Gal. 3.28. Hence, one must not consider this passage individually and, by consequence, attempt to derive a theology of women therefrom. It must be interpreted within the entire context of Paul's theological thinking. It appears that, in 1 Cor. 14, Paul calls to mind a custom in the assemblies which does not intend to claim universal validity for all times. After all, Paul knows women who are gifted with prophecy (1 Cor. 11.5). Further to this, he knew of the household of Philip, one of the seven, whose daughters were prophetically gifted virgins (Acts 21.9). In the course of the history of the Church there have been many holy women who spoke up in the Church, such as Catherine of Siena, Leoba and Thecla, Hildegard of Bingen and others. On the exegetical problem of 1 Cor. 14.34, see W. Schrage, *Der erste Brief an die Korinther* (EKK VII/3), Zürich – Neukirchen 1999, 477–502.

84 W. Kasper, 'The Position of Woman as a Problem of Theological Anthropology', in: H. Moll (ed.), *The Church and Women. A Compendium*, San Francisco 1988, 51–64; and, 'Die Frau als Person – von der Kirche ernst genommen? Systematisch-theologische Überlegungen', in: *Zur Zeit* 50 (1981) 2–31; T. Schneider (ed.), *Mann und Frau – Grundproblem theologischer Anthropologie* (QD 121), Freiburg i. Br. 1989.

85 L. Bouyer, *Women in the Church*, San Francisco: Ignatius Press 1979; H. U. von Balthasar, *Theodramatik* (*Theo-drama: Theological Dramatic Theory*, San Francisco: Ignatius Press 1988–98), vol. II/2, Einsiedeln 1978, 260–330. See section II.3.2, on the theme of the Church as bride.

86 On the issue of the ordination of women, see II.5.3.

87 I. Wetter, *Mary Ward*, Aschaffenburg 1985; W. Nigg, *Mary Ward – Eine Frau gibt nicht auf*, Zürich 2009.

88 The term 'office' (λειτουργία) first appears in Clement of Rome (1 Clement 40, 2.5; 41, 1; 44, 2.3.6; cf. Didache 15, 1). It is also there that we find for the first time a distinction between office holders and laypeople (40, 5).

89 H. W. Beyer, 'διακοεῖν, διακονία', in: ThWNT 2, 81–8.

90 See K.-H. Rengstorf, 'μαθητής', in: ThWNT 4, 447–60; K.-H. Schelkle, *Discipleship and Priesthood* (1957), London: Sheed & Ward 1966; M. Hengel, *The Charismatic Leader and his Followers* (1968), New York: Crossroad 1981; U. Wilckens, *Theologie des Neuen Testaments*, vol. I/1, Neukirchen 2002, 304–14.

91 On this, see section II.2.2.

92 On this, see sections II.2.2, II.4.4.

93 E. Schweizer, *Church Order in the New Testament*, London: SCM Press 1961; H. von Campenhausen, *Ecclesiastical Authority and Spiritual Power in the Church of the First Three Centuries*, London: Black 1969; H. Schlier, 'Die neutestamentlichen Grundlagen des Priesteramtes', in: *Der priesterliche Dienst*, vol. 1 (QD 46), Freiburg i. Br. 1970, 81–114; J. Martin, 'Die Genese des Amtspriestertums in der frühen Kirche', in: *Der priesterliche Dienst*, Bd. 3 (QD 48), Freiburg i. Br. 1972; H. Merklein, *Das kirchliche Amt im Epheserbrief*, Munich 1973; K. Kertelge, *Gemeinde und Amt im Neuen Testament*, Munich 1972; and (ed.), *Das kirchliche Amt im Neuen Testament*, Darmstadt 1977; F. Hahn, 'Neutestamentliche Grundlagen für eine Lehre vom kirchlichen Amt', in: *Dienst und Amt*, Regensburg 1973, 7–40; J. Roloff, 'Amt/ Ämter/Ämterverständnis IV', in: TRE 2, 509–33; and, *Der erste Brief an Timotheus*, Zürich – Neukirchen 1988, Excursus 169–89; A. Vögtle, *Die Dynamik des Anfangs, Leben und Fragen der jungen Kirche*, Freiburg i. Br. 1988; H. J. Klauck, *Gemeinde – Amt – Sakrament*, Würzburg 1989; F. Hahn, *Theologie des Neuen Testaments*, vol. 2, Tübingen 2002, 606–24.

94 On this issue, see section II.5.4.

95 C. Maurer, 'ἐπίθεσις', in: ThWNT 8, 160–62.

96 *1 Clement*, *Shepherd of Hermas*.

97 On this, see Hahn, *Theologie des Neuen Testaments*, 618–24. See sections II.2.2 and II.3.3.

98 See sections II.4.1 and 4.4.

99 On the history and theology of the episcopal offices, see K. Rahner/ J. Ratzinger, *The Episcopate and the Primacy* (QD 11), London: Nelson 1962; J. Colson, *L'Épiscopat catholique*, Paris 1963; G. Baraúna (ed.), *De Ecclesia*, vol. 2 (chapter 3), Freiburg i. Br. – Frankfurt a.M. 1966; L. Ott, *Das Weihesakrament* (HDG IV/5), Freiburg i. Br. 1969; Y. Congar, *Ministères et communion ecclésiale*, Paris 1971; R. Hanson, 'Amt/Ämter/ Ämterverständnis V', in: TRE 1, 533–52; G. Martelet, *Théologie du sacerdoce*, 3 vols, Paris 1984–90; H. J. Pottmeyer, 'Bischof II, III', in: $LThK^3$ 2, 484–8; E. Dassmann, *Ämter und Dienste in den frühchristlichen Gemeinden*, Bonn 1994; T. Schumacher, *Bischof – Presbyter – Diakon. Geschichte und Theologie des Amtes im Überblick*, Munich 2010.

100 Ignatius of Antioch, *ad Magnesios* 6, 1.

101 Ignatius of Antioch, *ad Ephesios* 2, 2; cf. 20, 2.

102 Ibid. 4, 1f.

103 On this point, see section II.4.4.

104 B. Botte (ed.), *La Tradition apostolique de Saint Hippolyte* (LQF 39), Münster 1963, 6–10.

105 On this point, see P. Walter 'Das Verhältnis von Episkopat und Presbyterat von der Alten Kirche bis zum Reformationsjahrhundert', in: Sattler/Wenz (eds), *Das kirchliche Amt in apostolischer Nachfolge*, 45f.

106 Cyprian of Carthage, ep. 45, 2; 63.

107 Cyprian of Carthage, *de unitate ecclesiae* 5; cf. ep. 55, 1, 1; 21, 1.

108 Cyprian of Carthage, ep. 66 8, 3.

109 *La Tradition apostolique*, 4–7.

110 Canon 4, in COD 6f. (G. Alberigo et al., *Decrees of the Ecumenical Councils* [English edn by N. Tanner], London: Sheed & Ward 1990).

111 P. T. Camelot, *Die Lehre von der Kirche* (HDG III/3b), Freiburg i. Br. 1970, 5f, 9, 39–41.

112 On this point, see E. Dassmann, 'Entstehung und theologische Begründung der kirchlichen Ämter in der Alten Kirche', in: IKaZ 22 (1993) 350–62.

113 DH 1776.

114 LG 28.

115 A. M. Landgraf, 'Die Lehre vom Episkopat als ordo', in: *Dogmengeschichte der Frühscholastik*, vol. 3/2, Regensburg 1955, 277–302; Ott, *Das Weihesakrament*, 40–51; Walter, 'Das Verhältnis von Episkopat und Presbyterat', 39–96.

116 Hieronymus, *in epistulam ad Titum* 146.

117 On this, see W. Aymans, 'Kirchengewalt II', in: $LThK^3$ 6, 10f.

118 Peter Lombard, *Sent.* IV d. 24 c.15.

119 See J. Lécuyer, 'Les étapes de l'enseignement thomiste sur l'épiscopat', in: *Revue Thomiste* 57 (1957) 29–52; W. Kasper, 'Steuermann mitten im Sturm. Das Bischofsamt nach Thomas von Aquin' (1999), in: WKGS 12, 451–81.

120 Thomas Aquinas, *Summa theologiae* III q. 73 a. 2 and 6. See section II.3.2.

121 See DH 1145, 1290, 1435. On this, see F. Gillmann, *Zur Lehre der Scholastik vom Spender der Firmung und des Weihesakraments*, Paderborn 1920; Ott, *Das Weihesakrament*, 105f.

122 See Smalcald Article II (*Book of Concord*, 293). Similarly, see the *Heidelberg Catechism*, Question 80, in: *Creeds and Confessions of Faith in the Christian Tradition*, vol. 2: *Creeds and Confessions of the Reformation Era* (ed. J. Pelikan/V. Hotchkiss), New Haven: Yale University Press, 2003, 445.

123 WA 6, 560–67. For individual evidence for the position of the later Luther and the confessional writings (particularly the *Confessio Augustana*), see section II.5.1.

124 See CA V; Geneva Church Order (1561), 4 (*Creeds and Confessions of Faith in the Christian Tradition*, vol. 2: *Creeds and Confessions of the Reformation Era*, 313f.); Confessio Belgica (1561), 30 (*Creeds and Confessions*, 420f.).

125 In contrast to Luther, Calvin emphasized the structuring of the ministry into pastors, teachers, elders and deacons (*Institutio christianae religionis* IV, 3, 1 and 8f.). See A. Ganoczy, *Ecclesia ministrans. Dienende Kirche und kirchlicher Dienst bei Calvin*, Freiburg i. Br. 1968.

126 P. Melanchthon, *Apologia* 13 (*Book of Concord*, 212).

127 J. Calvin, *Institutio christianae religionis* IV, 3, 16.

128 *Smalcald Article* X (*Book of Concord*, 314).

129 WA 12, 191–4.

130 *Tractatus de poetstate papae* 66–72 (Treatise on the Power and Primacy of the Pope, in: *Book of Concord*, 331f). See also *Formula of Concord, Solida declaratio* X, 19 (*Book of Concord*, 619).

131 DH 1764; 1771. For the history and interpretation of the Tridentine Decree, see H. Jedin, *Geschichte des Konzils von Trient*, vol. IV/1 and IV/2, Freiburg i. Br. 1975; Ott, *Das Weihesakrament*, 119–27; K. L. Becker, 'Der Unterschied von Bischof und Priester im Weihedekret des Konzils von Trient und nach der Kirchenkonstitution des II. Vatikanischen Konzils', in: K. Rahner (ed.), *Zum Problem der Unfehlbarkeit* (QD 54), Freiburg i. Br. 1971, 289–308; H. Müller, *Zum Verhältnis von Episkopat und Presbyterat im 2. Vatikanischen Konzil*, Vienna 1971; J. Freitag, *Sacramentum ordinis auf dem Konzil von Trient*, Innsbruck – Vienna 1990.

132 DH 1766, 1773.

133 DH 1767, 1774.

134 Ibid.

135 DH 1768, 1777.

136 In opposition to K. L. Becker, J.Freitag (*Sacramentum ordinis auf dem Konzil von Trient* [cf. note 131], 312–15) wants to show that, in can. 6, the council divested itself of the purely sacerdotal perspective and, thereafter, no longer made the priest, but rather the bishop, the centre of the *ordo*.

137 See Walter, 'Das Verhältnis von Episkopat und Presbyterat', 77–84.

138 On this point, see section II.5.4.

139 DH 1769, 1777.

140 DH 1769, 1777f.

141 See *Decreta super reformatione* in: COD 720–9. On this, see H. Jedin, 'Das Bischofsideal der Katholischen Reformation. Eine Studie über die Bischofsspiegel vornehmlich des 16. Jahrhunderts', in: *Kirche des Glaubens – Kirche der Geschichte*, Freiburg i. Br. 1966, 75–117. On this, see II.5.4.

142 The development emerged already in the run-up to the council. See Y. Congar (ed.), *L'Épiscopat et l'Église universelle*, Paris 1962. For the council, see the commentaries to *Lumen Gentium* by K. Rahner in: LThK.E 1, 210–47 and J. Ratzinger, in: ibid., 348–59; P. Hünermann, in: HThK.Vat II 2, 263–582. W. Breuning, 'Das Verständnis des katholischen Bischofsamtes nach dem Zweiten Vatikanischen Konzil', in: W. Sanders (ed.), *Bischofsamt. – Amt der Einheit*, Munich 1983, 9–30; L. Hell, '"Fülle des Priestertums". Probleme und Chancen der Wesensbestimmung des Bischofsamt durch das Zweite Vatikanische Konzil', in: TThZ 12 (2003) 90–101; W. Thönissen, 'Dienst am Wort Gottes. Das Amt der Bischöfe nach dem Zweiten

Vatikanischen Konzil', in: Sattler/Wenz, *Das kirchliche Amt in apostolischer Nachfolge*, 190–215.

143 LG 20.

144 LG 21, 26. There remains an ambiguity of no small significance concerning the understanding of the priesthood. Is the episcopal ordination the top (*apex*) of a hierarchical order and one degree of ordination beyond the ordination to the priesthood, which would basically follow the understanding of the medieval theories? Or is priestly ordination a graded participation in the fullness (*plenitudo*) of the episcopal ordination which, as a consequence of abandoning a thousand-year-old theory, necessitates urgently the question concerning the properties of the priest? The documents of the Council use the term '*apex*' as well as the term '*plenitudo*'.

145 With the theory of determination, the question of jurisdiction returns through the back door. On the problem of the *notae previae*, see the article by J. Ratzinger in: LThK.E 1, 357f.

146 LG 22f. On this, see Y. Congar, *La collégialité épiscopale*, Paris 1963; J. Ratzinger, 'Die bischöfliche Kollegialität nach der Lehre des Zweiten Vatikanischen Konzils', in: *Das neue Volk Gottes*, Düsseldorf 1969, 171–200; and, 'Die pastoralen Implikationen der Lehre von der Kollegialität der Bischöfe', in: ibid. 201–24.

147 LG 21; cf. CD 2.

148 The way the *communio hierarchica* is placed directly next to the sacramental *communio* based on ordination creates, of course, the impression that the patristic-sacramental and the medieval juridical ecclesiology have not completely been brought into harmony with each other, and that the new approach has not, by consequence, been thought through to the end. See A. Acerbi, *Due ecclesiologie. Ecclesiologia giuridica ed ecclesiologia di comunione nella* Lumen gentium, Bologna 1975. See sections II.4 and 5.4.

149 On the significance of the local or individual churches, see section II.5.6.

150 CD 11–18.

151 CD 20; cf. GS 76.

152 The teaching of the Council on the priesthood is found mainly in LG 28 and PO 2–6. Cf. In addition, see SC 7, 33; LG 10, 17, 20f., 28; CD 15, 28f.; DV 25; PO, OT and AG passim.

153 SC 7; PO 1f.

154 SC 7; LG 10, 28; PO 2, 13.

155 On this decree, see the commentary in LThK.E 3, 170–98; P. J. Cordes, *Sendung zum Dienst. Exegetisch-historische und systematische Studien zum Konzilsdekret* Vom Dienst und Leben der Priester, Frankfurt a.M. 1972; P. Hünermann/O. Fuchs, in: HThK.Vat II 4, 339–580.

156 J. Ratzinger, *Priestly Ministry: a Search for its Meaning* (1968), New York: Sentinel Press 1971, and also the newly published contributions in JRGS 12, 350–419; K. Lehmann, 'Das dogmatische Problem des theologischen Ansatzes zum Verständnis des Amtspriesters', in: F. Henrich, *Existenzprobleme des Priesters*, Munich 1969, 135–50; H. Schlier,

'Grundelemente des priesterlichen Amtes im NT', in: ThPh. 44 (1969) 161–80 as well as QD 46–51; E. Schillebeeckx, *Christliche Identität und kirchliches Amt*, Düsseldorf 1985; J. Freitag, *Sakramentale Sendung*, Freiburg i. Br. 1990; Greshake, *Priester sein in dieser Zeit* (cf. note 68); Kehl, *Die Kirche*, 430–59. My own contributions are republished in WKGS 12, 153–423.

157 To name just a few titles from the enormous amount of literature: J. Ratzinger, *Ministers of Your Joy* (1988), New York: Crossroad: 1989; W. Kasper, *Diener der Freude* (2007), in: WKGS 12, 325–423; G. Augustin, *Zur Freude berufen. Ermutigung zum Priesterseins*, Freiburg i. Br. 2010.

158 There is an immense amount of literature on this problem. I will avoid literature critical of celibacy (such as G. Denzler, *Die Geschichte des Zölibats*, Freiburg i. Br. 2002) and restrict myself to a few volumes that try to give a positive rationale. Still worth reading are J. A. Möhler, *The Spirit of Celibacy* (1828), Chicago: Hillenbrand Books, 2007. J. Bours/F. Kamphaus, *Leidenschaft für Gott. Ehelosigkeit, Armut, Gehorsam*. Freiburg i. Br. 1991; A. M. Stickler, *The Case for Clerical Celibacy*, San Francisco: Ignatius Press 1995; S. Heid, *Celibacy in the Early Church*, San Francisco: Ignatius Press 2000; K. Berger, *Zölibat. Eine theologische Begründung*, Leipzig 2009.

159 See section II.3.2.

160 Recently and in particular, I de la Potterie. So already Tertullian, *de monogamia* 12. On the overall problem, see B. Kötting, 'Digamus', in: RAC 3, 1017–24. For the different, mainly Protestant interpretations, see R. Roloff, *Der erste Brief an Timotheus*, Zürich – Neukirchen 1988, 155f.

161 DH 118f., cf. 185.

162 Canon 3, in COD 7.

163 Canon 6 and 7, in COD 198.

164 DH 1809.

165 PO 16.

166 Paul VI, Encyclical, *Sacerdotalis coelibatus* (1967); John Paul II, Post-Synodal Apostolic Exhortation, *Pastores dabo vobis* (1992), 29; Benedict XVI, Post-Synodal Apostolic Exhortation, *Sacramentum caritatis* (2007), 24. See also, *Catechism of the Catholic Church* (1993), 1579f.

167 LG 29.

168 J. Daniélou, 'Le ministère des femmes dans l'église', in: *Maison-Dieu* 61 (1960) 70–96; H. van der Meer, *Women Priests in the Catholic Church* (QD 42), Philadelphia: Temple University Press 1973; G. Dautzenberg (ed.), *Die Frau im Urchristentum* (QD 95), Freiburg i. Br. 1983; E. Dassmann, 'Kirchliche Ämter für Frauen in frühchristlicher Zeit', in: Pastoralblatt 41 (1989) 257–65; I. Riedel-Spangenberger/A. Schavan, 'Amt XII', in: $LThK^3$ 1, 557–61; M. Hauke, *Women in the Priesthood? A Systematic Analysis in the Light of the Order of Creation and Redemption*, San Francisco: Ignatius Press 1988; W. Gross (ed.), *Frauenordination*, Munich 1996; S. Demel, *Frauen und kirchliches Amt. Vom Ende eines Tabus in der katholischen Kirche*, Freiburg i. Br. 2004. G. L. Müller, *Der Empfänger* *des Weihesakraments. Quellen zur Lehre und Praxis der Kirche, nur Männern das Weiheamt zu spenden*, Würzburg 1999; and, *Priesthood and Diaconate: the Recipient of the Sacrament of Holy Orders from the Perspective of Creation Theology and Christology*, San Francisco: Ignatius Press 2002. The older theological literature has been compiled by D. Sattler, in: Schneider (ed.), *Mann und Frau*, 209f. A good summary of the debate is found in Greshake, *Priester sein in dieser Zeit*, 154–67. See section II.5.2.

169 See section II.5.1.

170 So the declaration by the Congregation for the Doctrine of Faith, *Inter insigniores* (October 15, 1976); John Paul II, Apostolic Letter, *Ordinatio sacerdotalis* (May 22, 1994) and the *Responsum* of the Congregation for the Doctrine of Faith (October 28, 1995). On the issue of the diaconate for women, see section II.5.3. For the Orthodox position, see B. Bobrinskoy, *Le mystère de l'Église*, Paris 2003, 256–308; here 238–48.

171 See section II.4.2.

172 On this, see section II.5.2.

173 On the history and theology of the diaconate, see K. Rahner/H. Vorgrimler, *Diaconia in Christo* (QD 15/16), Freiburg i. Br. 1962; Y. Congar (ed.) *Le diacre dans l'Église et le monde d'aujourd'hui*, Paris 1966; J. G. Plöger/ H. J. Weber (eds), *Der Diakon. Wiederentdeckung und Erneuerung seines Dienstes*, Freiburg i. Br. 1980; G. L. Müller, 'Theologische Überlegungen zur Weiterentwicklung des Diakonats', in: MThZ 40 (1989) 129–43; A. Weiß, *Der ständige Diakon*, Würzburg 1991; S. Zardoni, *I diaconi nella Chiesa*, Bologna 1991; M. Hauke, 'Das spezifische Profil des Diakonates', in: *Forum kath. Theol.* 17 (2001) 81–127; W. Kasper, 'Der Diakon in ekklesiologischer Sicht' (1997), in: WKGS 12, 127–49; and, 'Diaconato', in: G. Calabrese (ed.), *Dizionario di ecclesiologia*, Rome 2010, 409–21.

174 Sessio XXIII, Decr. super reformatione, can. 17, in: COD 726.

175 See LG 29; SC 86: DV 25; OE 17; CD 15; AG 15f. Post-conciliar documents: Paul VI, *Sacrum diaconatus* (1967); *Ad pascendum* (1972); CIC 1992 and 1997; Congregation for Catholic Education, *Ratio fundamentalis* (2003); International Theological Commission, *The Diaconate* (2002).

176 LG 29.

177 On the open questions, see G. Greshake, 'Diakon V', in: $LThK^3$ 3, 183f.

178 Didascalia 9; 11; Hippolytus, *traditio apostolica* 4, 8, 21, 24; Thomas Aquinas, *Summa theologiae* III q. 82 a. 3 ad 1.

179 A positive vote, see P. Hünermann et al. (eds), *Diakonat. Ein Amt für Frauen in der Kirche – ein frauengerechtes Amt?*, Ostfildern 1997.

180 See A. G. Martimort, *Deaconesses: a Historical Study*, San Francisco: Ignatius Press 1986; L. Scheffczyk (ed.), *Diakonat und Diakonissen*, St. Ottilien 2002.

181 Synod of Nîmes (396) and Synod of Orange (441).

182 On this, see section II.5.2.

183 See A. Grillmeier, in: LThK.E 1, 176–8.

184 LG 10.

185 See F. Klostermann, in: LThK.E 1, 181–3.

186 So also the *Catechism of the Catholic Church* (1993), 1547.

187 See W. Kasper, 'Amt und Gemeinde' (1970), in: WKGS 12, 38–68.

188 LG 37.

189 SC 7, 33; LG 10, 21, 28; PO 2.

190 See SC 33 and LG 10. Thomas Aquinas knows this double representation of the office. See *Summa theologiae* Suppl. q. 31 a.1 ad 1; *Summa contra gentiles* IV, 73. On this in detail, see Greshake, *Priester sein in dieser Zeit*, 126–9.

191 On the multilateral level, one must name in particular the third part of the *Lima Documents* (1982). The conversations with the Anglican Communion and the Lutheran World Foundation have progressed far. All documents are found in H. Meyer et al. (eds), *Growth in Agreement*, 3 vols, Geneva: WCC Publications, 1984–2007. Also important are the conversations of the 'Ökumenische Arbeitskreis evangelischer und katholischer Theologen' (ÖAK, Ecumenical Working Group of Evangelical and Catholic Theologians): K. Lehmann/W. Pannenberg (eds), *Condemnations of the Reformation Era: Do They still Divide?*, vol. 1, Minneapolis: Fortress 1990; T. Schneider (eds), *Das kirchliche Amt in apostolischer Nachfolge*, 3 vols, Freiburg i. Br. – Göttingen 2004–8; H. Meyer, 'Das kirchliche Amt im Horizont des evangelisch-lutherischen Verständnisses der Kirche', in: *Versöhnte Verschiedenheit. Aufsätze zur ökumenischen Theologie*, vol. 3, Frankfurt a. M. – Paderborn 2009, 79–93; and, 'Differenzierte Partizipation. Möglichkeiten einer evangelischen Teilhabe am historischen Bischofsamt', in: ibid. 94–108. A general overview of the bilateral dialogues is found in W. Kasper, *Harvesting the Fruits*, London: Continuum 2009, 108–11, 117–19, 151–3.

192 See ibid., 170f, 178ff.

193 International: *Episcopé and Episcopate in Ecumenical Perspective*, Geneva 1980; *Episkopé and Episcopacy and the Quest of Visible Unity* (1999); Community of Protestant Churches in Europe (CPCE): *Neudettelsauer Theses* (1982–6), *Tampere Theses* (1986), *The Church of Jesus Christ* (1994), Consultation Ministry Ordination and Episcope; Lutheran World Federation: *The Episcopal Ministry within the Apostolicity of the Church* (2002). Theological statements: D. Wendebourg (ed.), *Das bischöfliche Amt. Kirchengeschichtliche und ökumenische Studien zur Frage des kirchlichen Amtes*, Göttingen 1999; and, 'Das Amt und die Ämter', in: ZEvKR 45 (2000) 5–37; F. Nüssel, 'Zum Verständnis des evangelischen Bischofsamtes in der Neuzeit', in: Sattler/Wenz, *Das kirchliche Amt in apostolischer Nachfolge*, 145–89; current debate: *The Episcopal Ministry within the Apostolicity of the Church. A Lutheran Statement*, Geneva 2002; Report by G. Wenz, in: Sattler/Wenz, *Das kirchliche Amt in apostolischer Nachfolge*, 384 note 5. Cf. Kasper, *Harvesting the Fruits*, 199ff.

194 See section II.4.4.

195 Leo XIII, *Epistula Apostolicae curae et caritatis* (1896, DH 3315–19).

196 UR 22. On this, see P. Walter, '"Sacramentum Ordinis defectus" (UR 22, 3). Die Aussage des II. Vaticanums im Licht des ökumenischen Dialogs', in: T. Schneider (ed.), *Das kirchliche Amt in apostolischer Nachfolge*, vol. 3 (*Dialog der Kirchen* 14), Freiburg i. Br. 2008, 86–101.

197 For an example of an early phase, see the *Ämtermemorandum der ökumenischen Universitätsinstitute*, Mainz 1972; H. Fries/K. Rahner, *Unity of the Churches: an Actual Possibility* (QD 100), New York: Paulist Press 1985, Theses V, VII, VIII; O. H. Pesch, 'Auf den Weg zu einer "Gemeinsamen Erklärung zum kirchlichen Amt in apostolischer Nachfolge"', in: Sattler/Wenz, *Das kirchliche Amt in apostolischer Nachfolge*, 155–66; the study document of the Lutheran/Roman Catholic Commission on Unity, *The Apostolicity of the Church* (2006), chapter 3.6. See Kasper, *Harvesting the Fruits*, 80ff.

198 So W. Beinert, 'Apostolisch. Anatomie eines Begriffs', in: Sattler/Wenz, *Das kirchliche Amt in apostolischer Nachfolge*, 274–303 and by O. H. Pesch, 'Hermeneutik des Ämterwandels?' and 'Thesen zu einem ökumenischen Verständnis vom kirchlichen Amt', in: ibid. 304–27 and 328–55.

199 This is precisely why the appeal to a presbyterial succession is not really helpful. What might be called presbyterial succession was, in the late medieval period, only possible in consensus within the *ecclesia catholica*, which, at that time (and, in retrospect, in a problematic way), found its expression through papal dispensation.

200 See section II.5.1.

201 On synodal government and the imprecise principle of 'led by bishops' and governed by synods', see G. Gassmann, 'Synode III/3', in: TRE 32, 582.

202 See section II.5.2. For the different understanding of synods, see section II.5.5.

203 DH 1611.

204 DH 3318.

205 Pope John Paul II, Encyclical, *Ut unum sint* (1995) 88. Pope Benedict XVI, during his visit in the Phanar (November 30, 2006).

206 'Petrine office' is more recent nomenclature than the traditional 'primacy of the Bishop of Rome'. Both terms must be distinguished from the term 'papacy' as a specific historical embodiment.

207 The exegetical literature pertinent here is endless. I can name only a few: O. Cullmann, Peter: *Disciple, Apostle, Martyr*, Philadelphia: Westminster Press 1953; and, 'Πέτρος, Κηφᾶς', in: ThWNT 4, 99–112; A. Vögtle, 'Messiasbekenntnis und Petrusverheißung', in: *Das Evangelium und die Evangelien*, Düsseldorf 1971, 137–70; R. Brown/K. P. Donfried/J. Reumann, *Peter in the New Testament*, Minneapolis, Augsburg 1973; J. Gnilka, *Matthäusevangelium II* (HThK.NT 2), Freiburg i. Br. 1988, 46–80; U. Luz, *Das Evangelium nach Matthäus* (EKK I/2, *Matthew: a Commentary*, Minneapolis: Augsburg 1989–2005), Zürich – Neukirchen 1990, 450–83; J. Roloff, *Die Kirche im Neuen Testament* (NTD suppl. vol. 10), Göttingen 1993,

162–5; O. Böcher, 'Petrus I', in: TRE 26, 263–73; L. Wehr, 'Petrus', in: LThK[3] 8, 90–5; R. Pesch, *Die biblischen Grundlagen des Primats* (QD 187), Freiburg i. Br. 2001; M. Hengel, *Saint Peter: the Underestimated Apostle*, Grand Rapids: Eerdmans 2010. For biblical as well as historical considerations, see G. L. Müller (ed.), *Der Primat des Nachfolgers Petri im Geheimnis der Kirche. Studien der Kongregation für die Glaubenslehre*, Würzburg 2010.

208 By and large, opinions diverge between, on one hand, most of the Eastern Church Fathers (who, typically following Origen, though some borrowing the insight from Augustine, see the Church as being based upon the faith of Peter), and, on the other, Western Fathers such as Hieronymus, Hilary and Leo the Great, who were occasionally joined by a handful from the East, most notably Maximus the Confessor (who, in a tradition dating back to the thrid century, apply Matthew 16.18f. also to the *successors* of Peter). To a third group belong, among others, John Chrysostom, Theodoret, Theodore of Mopsuestia, and John of Damascus. Augustine, who, like most Eastern Fathers, identified the faith of Peter as a 'type of the church', left the question unanswered in his *retractationes*. (I, 21, 1). See J. Ludwig, *Die Primatworte Mt. 16, 18–19 in der altkirchlichen Exegese*, Münster 1952; J.-M. R. Tillard, *L'évêque de Rome*, Paris 1982, 142–6.

209 Strack-Billerbeck, *Kommentar zum Neuen Testament aus Talmud und Midrasch*, vol. 1, Munich 1961, 737–47; J. Ernst, 'Binden und Lösen', in: LThK[3] 2, 463f.

210 An enormous amount of literature exists on the history of the papacy. In addition to the well-known histories of the papacy by Pastor, Caspar, Haller, Seppelt, etc. See Y. Congar, 'Die Lehre von der Kirche', in: HDG III/3 c and d, Freiburg i. Br. 1971; G. Schwaiger, *Päpstlicher Primat und Autorität der allgemeinen Konzilien im Spiegel der Geschichte*, Paderborn 1977; K. Schatz, *Papal Primacy: from its Origins to the Present*, Collegeville, Minn.: Liturgical Press 1996; and, *Allgemeine Konzilien – Brennpunkt der Kirchengeschichte*, Paderborn 2008; M. Maccarone, 'Sedes Apostolica – Vicarius Petri. La perpetuità del primato di Pietro nella sede e nel vescovo di Roma', in: *Il primato del vescovo di Roma nel primo millennio*, Vatican City 1991; W. Kasper, 'Petrusdienst und Petrusamt', in: WKGS 12, 580–635.

211 So J. H. Newman, *An Essay on the Development of Christian Doctrine* (1845), Harmondsworth: Penguin 1974.

212 K. Froehlich, 'Petrus II', in: TRE 26, 273–8; A. Angenendt, 'Petrus III', in: LThK[3] 8, 95f.

213 Ignatius of Antioch, *ad Romanos*, praescriptum.

214 Irenaeus of Lyons, *adversus haereses* III, 3, 2.

215 Tertullian, *de praescriptione haereticorum* 21; cf. 36.

216 DH 133–5. See H. J. Sieben, 'Sanctissimi Petri apostoli memoriam honoremus. Die Sardicinischen Appelationskanones im Wandel der Geschichte', in: ThPh. 58 (1983) 501–34.

217 Canon VI, in: COD 8f.

218 Canon III, in: COD 32.

219 Jerome, ep. 15, 2.

220 DH 181f.

221 DH 217f.

222 See Y. Congar in: HDG III/3 c, 11f.

223 Leo the Great, *sermones* 4, 3f.; 5; cf. ep. 9; *sermones* 96, 3.

224 Leo the Great, ep. 14,1.

225 Canon XXVIII, in COD 100.

226 DH 350f. As was Ambrose before him, Gelasius made important contributions to the defence of the independence of the Church against the emperor (DH 347).

227 Cyprian of Carthage, *de unitate ecclesiae* 5.

228 Cyprian of Carthage, ibid. 4.

229 Cyprian of Carthage, ep. 48, 3.

230 Cyprian of Carthage, ep. 59, 14.

231 Augustine, *sermones* 131, 10.

232 Augustine, *sermones* 270, 2; *in Ioannis evangelium* 50, 12; 124, 5.

233 Augustine, *de baptismo* 2, 1, 2; 3, 17, 22; *sermones* 71, 2, 7; 1, 31, 10; 295, 4, 4; ep. 43, 3, 7.

234 Thomas Aquinas, *Super evangelium Matthaei*, 16, lc 2; cf. F. Gillmann, 'Zur scholastischen Auslegung von Mt. 16,18', in: AKathKR 104 (1924) 89–122; K. Froehlich, *Formen der Auslegung von Matthäus 19, 23–18 im lateinischen Mittelalter*, Tübingen 1963.

235 P. T. Camelot, *Ephesus und Chalkedon*, Mainz 1963, 141–3, 146–52, 155–69, 192–6; S. Horn, *Petrou Cathedra. Der Bischof von Rom und die Synoden von Ephesus und Chalkedon*, Paderborn 1982, 248–50.

236 See Y. Congar, HDG III/3 c, 13f.

237 Gregory the Great, ep. 5, 20.

238 Gregory the Great, ep. 2, 31.

239 Gregory the Great, ep. 18; 43 and others.

240 V. Peri, *La Pentarchia. Istituzione ecclesiale e teoria canonico-teologica*, Spoleto 1988; F. R. Gahbauer, *Die Pentarchietheorie*, Frankfurt a.M. 1993; E. Morini, *Roma nella Pentarchia*, Spoleto 2001.

241 DH 363–5.

242 DH 542–8.The weak pope Honorius (625–38) was condemned at this council (DH 552; cf. 562).

243 J.-C. Larchet, *Maxime le Confesseur, médiateur entre l'Orient e l'Occident*, Paris 1998.

244 DH 638–42.

245 DH 661–4.

246 Since the *Decretum Gratiani* (1140), the West has accepted as the eighth ecumenical council only the council of 869/870, but not the synod of 879/880. Additionally, Catholic researchers have urged the Church either to revise the former decision or to regard both synods in unison. Such

recognition would also be helpful from an ecumenical perspective. See LThK³ 6, 316.

247 On this, see Y. Congar, *After Nine Hundred Years: the Background of the Schism between the Eastern and Western Churches* (1959), Westport, Conn: Greenwood, 1978; H. Chadwick, *East and West: The Making of a Rift in the Church. From Apostolic Times until the Council of Florence*, Oxford: Oxford University Press 2003.

248 Y. Congar, 'Der Platz des Papsttums in der Kirchenfrömmigkeit der Reformer des 11. Jahrhunderts', in: J. Daniélou et al. (eds), *Sentire ecclesiam* (Festschrift H. Rahner), Freiburg 1961, 196–217.

249 DH 774f. On the history of the title 'vicarius Christi', see Y. Congar, in: HDG III/3c, 119f.; and, 'Titel, welche für den Papst verwendet werden', in: Conc(D) 11 (1975) 538–44.

250 DH 811.

251 On the occasion of the 700th anniversary of the Second Council of Lyons, Pope Paul VI spoke of a universal council and thereby indicated the difference between East and West regarding the councils of the Old Church which are recognized by both.

252 DH 871.

253 DH 875.

254 Y. Congar, 'L'ecclésiologie de Saint Bernhard', in: *Eglise et Papauté*, Paris 1994, 115–85.

255 Y. Congar, in: HDG III/3c, 82–89, 127–38.

256 B. Tierney, *Foundations of the Conciliar Theory*, Cambridge: Cambridge University Press 1968.

257 COD 408f.; J. Gill, *Konstanz und Florenz*, Mainz 1967.

258 So already Juan de Torquemada who otherwise has a totally papalist attitude; in contemporary theology: J. Ratzinger, 'Primat und Episkopat', in: *Das neue Volk Gottes*, Düsseldorf 1969, 139.

259 DH 1307f.

260 G. Seebass, 'Antichrist III', in: TRE 3, 24–43; K. H. Müller/M. Häusler/B. Claret, 'Antichrist', in: LThK³ 1, 744–7.

261 The accusation, which Luther voiced initially only with hesitation, eventually entered the Reformation confessions, see particularly *Smalcald Article* Part II / Art. IV (*Book of Concord*, 300f.); Formula of Concord (*Book of Concord*, 614f.). On the present problem, see, below, the excursus on the contemporary ecumenical debate.

262 COD 681f.; 736–41. Cf. H. Jedin, *Geschichte des Konzils von Trient* (= *A History of the Council of Trent*), vol. IV/1, Freiburg i. Br. 1975, 116–37, 237–63; vol. IV/2, 50–79; K. Ganzer, 'Gallikanische und römische Primatsauffassung im Widerstreit. Zu den ekklesiologischen Auseinandersetzungen auf dem Konzil von Trient', in: HJ 109 (1989) 109–63.

263 R. Aubert, *Vaticanum I*, Mainz 1965; H. J. Pottmeyer, *Unfehlbarkeit und*

Souveränität, Mainz 1975, 427–9; and, J. Zizioulas, 'Recent discussion on Primacy in Relation to Vatican I', in: W. Kasper (ed.), *The Petrine Ministry. Catholics and Orthodox in Dialogue*, New York: Newman Press 2006, 210–29; M. O'Gara, *Triumph and Defeat. Infallibility, Vatican I and the French Minority Bishops*, Washington DC: Catholic University of America Press 1988; and, especially, the basic work by K. Schatz, *Vaticanum I. 1869–70*, 3 vols, Paderborn 1992–6.

264 DH 3057; 3060.

265 DH 3056f.; 3059; 3070f.

266 DH 3050–2.

267 DH 3055.

268 DH 3058.

269 DH 3959–64.

270 DH 3065–75.

271 DH 3059.

272 DH 3060–4.

273 DH 3061.

274 DH 3112–17.

275 On the origin of the term 'infallible' during the mendicant controversy in the thirteenth and fourteenth centuries, see B. Tierney, *Origins of Papal Infallibility 1150–1350*, Leiden 1974; Y. Congar, in: HDG III/3c, 159–61. H. Küng, *Infallible? An Unresolved Enquiry* (1970), (new expanded edn, New York: Continuum, 1994) has changed the question insofar as he focuses on the possibility or impossibility of infallible statements. In contrast, the council speaks of infallible magisterial acts which result, under clearly defined conditions, in irreformable statements. That the Christian faith is expressed in binding statements accords with the formation of the faith which has its foundations in the New Testament and runs through the whole of Tradition. Luther also expressly maintained the assertory character of the faith: '*Tolle assertiones et christianismum tulisti*' (WA 18, 603). Without binding statements of faith, a common confession and thus a community of faith would be impossible. However, the idea of the irreformability of such statements does not exclude a deepening and complementary development of dogma (cf. DH 3020; DV 8). It also does not rule out that such statements need to be interpreted and that recognized criteria for this reinterpretation exist. Such statements, as irreformable, remain worth thinking about and reflecting upon (H. Schlier). For the discussion of Küng's position, see section I.5, notes 49–53.

276 DH 3065.

277 DH 3070.

278 Using the term '*tenendum*' instead of '*credendum*' helps to clarify that even derived truths are infallibly presented; derived truths, that is, which are not directly ingredient to divine revelation, but are historically or logically entailed in such a way that, without them, faith cannot be correctly retained, represented, or even believed above.

279 DH 3075.

280 DH 3069.

281 On this in addition to the commentaries in LThK.E 1 and HThK.Vat II 2: J. Ratzinger (ed.), 'Dienst an der Einheit und Freiheit der Kirche', in: *Dienst an der Einheit*, Düsseldorf 1978, 81–104; and, 'Das Petrusamt als Dienst an der Einheit. Die Lehre des I. und II. Vatikanischen Konzils und die gegenwärtige Diskussion', in: V. von Aristi et al. (eds), *Das Papstamt. Dienst oder Hindernis für die Ökumene*, Regensburg 1985, 113–38; H. J. Pottmeyer, *Die Rolle des Papsttums im dritten Jahrtausend* (QD 179), Freiburg i. Br. 1999; J.-G. Boeglin, *Pierre dans la communion des Églises. Le ministère pétrinien dans la perspective de l'Église-Communion et de la communion des Églises*, Paris 2004; J. Zizioulas, 'Recent Discussions on Primacy in Relation to Vatican I', in: Kasper (ed.), *The Petrine Ministry*, 210–30; D. Valentini, *Identità e storicità nella Chiesa*, Rome 2007, 139–256.

282 LG 18, 22, 25.

283 LG 20.

284 LG 22f.

285 On this and the following, see II.5.3.

286 LG 22f.; Nota praevia 2.

287 LG 22, 25.

288 Of course, the title 'Bishop of the Catholic Church', with which Paul VI signed the documents of the Council, is ambiguous. See H. Marot, 'Note sur l'expression Episcopus catholicae Ecclesiae', in: Irén 37 (1964) 221–6.

289 Council of Nicaea, can. 4, in: COD 7.

290 Cyprian, *de unitate ecclesiae* 5.

291 Mansi 52, 1109f.1201f. On this, see W. Kasper, 'Primat und Episkopat nach dem Vaticanum I' (1962), in: WKGS 12, 499–531.

292 LG 22.

293 The statement is interpreted by *Nota praevia* 4 and is exacerbated through the unfortunate wording that states that the pope is able to use his power at his discretion (*ad placitum*) at any time. The Council's text expresses less provocatively than what is, in fact, factually meant. It speaks of a free exercise (*libere*) (LG 22) with which the pope decides in his own judgement, (*secundum propriam discretionem*), what is best for the Church in light of the changing conditions. It is also along similar lines that the theological commission of the Council rejected the wording, suggested by Paul VI, that the pope is '*uni Domino devinctus*'. The commission considered this to be an oversimplification, for the pope is also bound by revelation, the fundamental structures of the Church, the sacraments and the decisions of previous councils, etc. See LThK.E 1, 227. On the interpretation, see J. Ratzinger, ibid., 190–7.

294 On this, see section II.5.5.

295 See W. Kasper, 'Petrine Ministry and Synodality', in: *The Jurist* 66 (2006),

298–300; and, 'Canon law and ecumenism', in: *The Jurist* 69 (2009) 171–89. See other contributions in: *The Jurist* 1999, 2004, 2008f. A quite critical study that addresses the reception of the Council through the CIC 1983 is G. Bier, *Die Rechtsstellung des Diözesanbischofs nach dem Codex Iuris Canonici von 1983,* Würzburg 2001.

296 *Il primato del successore di Pietro nel ministero della Chiesa. Considerazioni della Congregazione per la Dottrina della Fede*, Vatican City 2002, 12 (German: G. L. Müller [ed.], *Der Primat des Nachfolgers Petri*, Würzburg 2010, 24).

297 DH 1307f.

298 See K. Ganzer, 'Bischofswahl, Bischofsernennung', in: LThK[3] 2, 504–6.

299 Ignatius of Antioch, *ad Romanos*, *prooemium* (also quoted in LG 1 and AG 22).

300 See the correspondence between Metropolitan Damaskinos and Cardinal J. Ratzinger, collected in JRGS 8/2, 784–6.

301 On the infallibility debate instigated by H. Küng, see section I.5, notes 49–51; W. Kasper, 'Freiheit des Evangeliums und dogmatische Bindung in der katholischen Theologie. Grundlagenüberlegungen zur Unfehlbarkeitsdebatte', in: *Theologie und Kirche* (*Theology and Church*, New York: Crossroads 1989), Mainz 1987, 43–71.

302 On this, see section 1.

303 See B. Tierney, *Origins of Papal Infallibility 1150–1350*, Leiden 1974. A short summary of the history as well as systematic-theological account can be found in W. Beinert, 'Unfehlbarkeit', in: LThK[3] 10, 389–91. See note 275 above.

304 On the biblical concept of truth, see W. Kasper, *Dogma unter dem Wort Gottes*, Mainz 1965.

305 DH 3008.

306 See the declaration of the Congregation for the Doctrine of Faith *Mysterium Ecclesiae* (1973), 5. Luther writes: 'Christus cum Ecclesia sua manet usque ad consummationem mundi. Et Ecclesia Dei est firmamentum et columna veritatis. Haec inquam novimus, nam sic habet symbolum omnium nostrum: Credo Ecclesiam sanctam catholicam, ut impossibile sit, illam errare etiam in minimo articulo' ('De servo arbitrio' [1525], in: WA 18, 649f.). The *Confessio Augustana* states: 'una sancta ecclesia perpetuo mansura' (Art. 7).

307 LG 12, 35.

308 See notes 231–3 above.

309 LG 25. The wording 'must be' is intended to leave open the possibility of presenting infallible truths which are not directly contained in revelation but which, however, are historically or logically necessarily entailed in truths of faith (cf. above note 278). Cf. *Mysterium Ecclesiae* 3; *Professio fidei et iurisiurandum fidelitatis* (1989); Motu proprio *Ad tuendam fidem* (1998).

310 J. A. Möhler, *Symbolik* (*Symbolism*; 1832), Darmstadt 1958, 454.

311 DH 3074.

312 See section I.4, note 20.

313 On this, see the declaration of the Congregation for the Doctrine of Faith, *Mysterium Ecclesiae* (1973), chapter 5.

314 DH 3020.

315 DV 8.

316 See the elucidating contribution by H. Schlier, 'Das bleibend Katholische. Ein Versuch über ein Prinzip des Katholischen', in: *Das Ende der Zeit. Exegetische Aufsätze und Vorträge III*, Freiburg i. Br. 1971, 297–320. In this context we do well to recall the word of Luther: 'Tolle assertiones et Christianismum tulisti' (WA 18, 603).

317 DH 3016.

318 DV 11.

319 LG 12, 35.

320 DH 246. For the interpretation, see DH 3792, 3828. Also on this point, see A. Schilson, 'Gedachte Liturgie als Mystagogie', in: E. Schockenhoff/P. Walter (eds), *Dogma und Glaube* (Festschrift W. Kasper), Mainz 1993, 213–34.

321 On this, see J. Drumm, *Doxologie und Dogma. Die Bedeutung der Doxologie für die Wiedergewinnung theologischer Rede in der evangelischen Theologie*, Paderborn 1991.

322 Thomas Aquinas, *Summa theologiae* II/II q. 1 a 1: God is, as the *prima veritas*, the formal object of faith. In this sense: '*Actus autem credentis non terminatur ad enuntiabile sed ad rem*' (ibid., q. 1 a. 2).

323 DH 3016.

324 On this, see G. Greshake, 'Die Geburt der Dogmatik aus der Spiritualität', in: Schockenhoff/Walter (eds), *Dogma und Glaube*, 237–52.

325 DH 3015.

326 DH 3016.

327 On this, see section II.1.2.

328 An overview of this is found in H. Leipold, 'Papsttum II', in: TRE 25, 676–95; A. Acerbi (ed.), *Il ministero del Papa in prospettiva ecumenica*, Milan 1999; W. Kasper, 'Das Petrusamt in ökumenischer Perspektive', in: S. Hell/L. Lies (eds), *Papstamt. Hoffnung, Chance, Ärgernis*, Innsbruck – Vienna 2000, 211–23; J.-M. R. Tillard, 'Primacy', in: *Dictionary of the Ecumenical Movement*, Geneva 2002, 931–4; N. Bux, 'Die Lehre vom Primat des Petrus im Kontext des Ökumenismus', in: G. L. Müller (ed.), *Der Primat des Nachfolgers Petrus im Geheimnis der Kirche. Studien der Kongregation für die Glaubenslehre*, Würzburg 2010, 167–205. It should be noted that Müller wholly disregards the dialogue documents.

329 Encyclical *Ut unum sint*, 95. Summary and analysis of the reactions of the Pontifical Council for Christian Unity, in: *Information Service* 109 (2002/ I-II) 33–47.

330 A text that is particularly foundational for the position of the ecumenical dialogue is the Ravenna document by the Joint International Orthodox-Roman Catholic Commission *Ecclesiological and Canonical Consequences of the Sacramental Nature of the Church. Ecclesial Communion, Conciliarity*

and Authority (2007); in addition, the North American Orthodox-Roman Catholic Consultation, *Steps toward a reunited Church. A Sketch of an Orthodox-Catholic Vision for the Future* (2010).

331 For this point commentators frequently refer to the thesis by J. Ratzinger from 1976: 'Rome must not require from the East with respect to the doctrine of primacy than had been formulated and was lived in the first millennium' *Theologische Prinzipienlehre* (1982; *Principles of Catholic Theology*, San Francisco 1987, 199), in: JRGS 8/2, 724. Ratzinger later rightly qualified this thesis in *Kirche, Ökumene und Politik* (1987; *Church, Ecumenism and Politics. New Essays in Ecclesiology*, Middlegreen 1988), in: JRGS 8/2, 996f, 1000ff.

332 OE 25; UR 14–18.

333 On the contemporary Orthodox view, see J. Meyendorff et al., *The Primacy of Peter in the Orthodox Church*, London 1963; J. Meyendorff, *Orthodoxy and Catholicity*, New York 1965; O. Clément, *You are Peter: an Orthodox Theologian's Reflection on the Exercise of Papal Primacy*, New York: New City Press 2003; B. Bobrinskoy, *Le mystère de l'Église*, Paris 2003, 256–308; Zizioulas, 'Recent Discussions on Primacy in Orthodox Theology', 231–48.

334 DH 1307f.

335 So also Ratzinger, 'Primat', in: LThK[2] 6, 761–3.

336 DH 3061; cf. 3112–7.

337 The canon law applicable for those Oriental churches in full communion with Rome already moves in that direction, insofar as it does not require the bishops of those churches to be appointed by the pope. Instead, they are elected by the respective synods, whereupon the pope grants the elected bishop the *communio*. In addition, the apostolic constitution, *Sacri canones* (1990), which implemented the Oriental canon law, stipulates that these regulations of the present Oriental canon law are only preliminary and that they do not yet claim the capacity to enforce what the final regulations will be like in case of a full *communio* with the separated Oriental churches.

338 See the overview in H. Meyer, 'Der päpstliche Primat im katholisch/lutherischen Dialog', in: *Versöhnte Verschiedenheit*, vol. 2, Frankfurt a. M.– Paderborn, 2000, 339 note 3.

339 Sympathetic interpretations can be found in W. Pannenberg, 'Evangelische Überlegungen zum Petrusdienst des römischen Bischofs' (1998), in: *Kirche und Ökumene*, Göttingen 2000, 366–77; and, 'Die lutherische Tradition und die Frage eines Petrusdienstes an der Einheit der Christen' (1996), in: ibid., 386–8; H. Meyer, 'Der päpstliche Primat im katholisch/lutherischen Dialog', in: *Versöhnte Verschiedenheit*, vol. 2, Frankfurt a.M.– Paderborn 2000, 339–66; G. Wenz, 'Das Petrusamt aus lutherischer Sicht', in: Hell/ Lies, *Papstamt*. 67–95; U. Wilckens, *Standpunkte. Grundlegende Themen biblischer Theologie*, Neukirchen-Vluyn, 2010, 110f, 199f.; as well as the collaborators of the volume by J. Puglisi. For critical alternatives, see J. Moltmann, 'Has the Papacy an Ecumenical Future?', in: *Concilium* (5/1995) 135–7; L. Vischer, 'Das Amt der Einheit und das gemeinsame Zeugnis der

Kirchen heute', in: ÖR 47 (1998) 188–201; U. H. J. Körtner, 'Braucht die Kirche ein Amt der Einheit? Das Papsttum aus reformierter Sicht', in: Hell/ Lies, *Papstamt*, 97–114.

340 WA 38, 181. On this, see H. Meyer, 'Das Papsttum bei Luther und in den Bekenntnisschriften', in: *Versöhnte Verschiedenheit*, 317–38. Cf. W. Klausnitzer, *Das Papstamt im Disput zwischen Lutheranern und Katholiken*, Innsbruck 1987.

341 *Book of Concord*, 316f.

342 *Final Report* (1981) (in: *Growth in Agreement* [= GiA] I, 62–7); *Authority in the Church I* (1976) (GiA I, 88–99); *Authority in the Church II* (1981) (GiA I, 106–18); The Gift of Authority III (GiA III, 60–81).

343 *Das geistliche Amt in der Kirche*, Paderborn – Frankfurt a.M. 1981, 50. This had been preceded by the Catholic/Lutheran dialogue in the USA, *Papal Primacy and the Universal Church* (Minneapolis, MN 1974). Already the Malta Report, *The Gospel and the Church* (1972) (GiA I, 167–89) built upon this with similar formulations. This was followed by *Facing Unity* (1984) (GiA II, 443–84) and *Church and Justification* (1993) (GiA II, 485–565).

344 Groupe de Dombes, *The Ministry of Communion in the Universal Church*, 1985.

345 *Communio Sanctorum. Die Kirche als Gemeinschaft der Heiligen*, Paderborn – Frankfurt a. M. 2000, 77–99.

346 Group of Farfa Sabina, *Gemeinschaft der Kirchen und Petrusamt. Lutherisch-katholische Annäherungen*, Frankfurt a.M. 2010. Whereas the many positive suggestions of the document are commendable, unfortunately it does not discuss the fundamental problems concerning the understanding of Church and ministry and the different ecumenical objectives. The presentations preceding the final report are found in J. Puglisi (ed.), *How Can the Petrine Ministry Be a Service to the Unity of the Universal Church?*, Grand Rapids (Mich.): Eerdmans 2010.

347 Eusebius, *Church History* V, 16, 10; VII, 7, 5. H. J. Sieben, *Die Konzilsidee der Alten Kirche*, Paderborn 1979; *Die Konzilsidee des lateinischen Mittelalters*, Paderborn 1984; *Die katholische Konzilsidee von der Reformation bis zur Aufklärung*, Paderborn 1988; *Die katholische Konzilsidee im 19. und 20. Jahrhundert*, Paderborn 1993; 'Konzil I', in: LThK[3] 6, 345–8. See the overview in F. R. Gahbauer, 'Synode I & II', in: TRE 32, 559–71.

348 On the respective canon of Vincent of Lérins, see section II.4.3.

349 Augustine, *de baptismo*, II, 4, 5; II, 7, 12; V, 17, 23.

350 See H. J. Sieben, 'Definitionen und Kriterien ökumenischer Konzilien vor der morgenländischen Kirchenspaltung (1054)', in: *Studien zum Ökumenischen Konzil*, Paderborn 2010, 69–106. See section II.5.4.

351 Thus Pope Julius I. (337–52) rejected the Arian decisions of the Synod of Tyre (335) and its condemnation of Athanasius. The Synod of Sardica (342/343) then fundamentally stated the possibility of appealing to Rome. On this, see section II.5.4.

352 A bridge to ecumenical understanding has recently opened up through the famous canon 34 of the Apostolic Canones (Les constitutions apostoliques, vol. III, livre 8 [SC 336], Paris 1987, 285), which dates back to the third or fourth century. This canon states that, at a level above all others, there must be a first one (πρώτος, primas) among the bishops, without whom the others cannot decide on important questions and who, in turn, can do nothing himself without the consent of the others. J. Zizioulas and others are prepared to accept this principle, at least in an analogical sense, at the universal level, insofar as they perceive in it a pristine path toward an agreement on the primacy of the Bishop of Rome. Obviously, the extent to which such an approach is sustainable requires further substantial discussions and depends upon its specific interpretation in relation to the universal level.

353 See section II.5.1.

354 See C. Dinkel/R. Preul/H. Gassmann, 'Synode III', in: TRE 32, 571–84.

355 H. J. Pottmeyer, 'Theologie der synodalen Strukturen', in: A. Exeler (ed.), *Fragen der Kirche heute*, Würzburg 1971, 164–72; E. Corecco, 'Sinodalità', in: *Nuovo Dizionario di Teologia* 1982, 1466–95; Kehl, *Die Kirche* (cf. note 33), 103–17; D. Valentini, 'Per una sinodalità della Chiesa e nella Chiesa', in: M. Sodi (ed.), *'Ubi Petrus ibi Ecclesia' (Misc. Benedetto XVI)*, Rom 2007, 157–78; G. Alberigo, 'Sinodo come liturgia', in: *Il Regno* 13 (2007) 443–56.

356 On the appropriate understanding, see section II.5.4.

357 LG 22f.

358 CD 36; CIC can. 439–46; 460–8.

359 CD 27; PO 7; AA 26.

360 CD 37f.

361 CD 5.

362 R. M. Schmitz, 'Kardinal', in: LThK[3] 5, 1230–1; J. Ritter, 'Kongregationen, römische', in: LThK[3] 6, 249–52; H. Kalb, 'Konsistorium I', in: LThK[3] 6, 293.

363 John Paul II, Encyclical, *Ut unum sint* (1995), 95.

364 H. Maier (in: 'Braucht Rom eine Regierung?', in: StdZ 126 [2001] 147–60) demonstrated that, for the Curia as well, greater synodal and collaborative spirit is desirable, and, indeed, indispensable.

365 Mt. 16.18; 1 Cor. 10.32; 12.2; Eph. 1.22; 5.23; Col. 1.18, etc.

366 Acts 16.5; Rom. 16.4.16; 1 Cor. 11.16; 15.9; 2 Cor. 8.1.18.23f.; 11.8.28; Gal. 1.2.22.

367 Many passages on this point are found in H. de Lubac, *Quellen kirchlicher Einheit*, Einsiedeln 1974, 49. The problem was dealt with very early from a non-Catholic perspective by F. Heiler, *Altkirchliche Autonomie und päpstlicher Zentralismus*, Munich 1941.

368 LG 26.

369 Tertullian, *de praescriptione haereticoum* 20, 7f. The understanding of the

Old Church was worked out well by L. Hertling, *Communio: Church and Papacy in Early Christianity* (1943), Chicago: Loyola Press 1972.

370 Cyprian, *de ecclesiae unitate*, 4; ep. 25, 24, 66, 8.

371 Basil, ep. 26f., 34, 36, 76, 80, etc.

372 DH 3112–17.

373 LG 13.

374 LG 23.

375 LG 26.

376 LG 26, 23.

377 *Communionis notio* 9.

378 W. Kasper, 'Zur Theologie und Praxis des bischöflichen Amtes' (1988), in: WKGS 12, 482–96; 'Das Verhältnis von Universalkirche und Ortskirche' (2000), in: WKGS 11, 509–22. On this, see J. Ratzinger, 'Die Ekklesiologie der Konstitution Lumen gentium' (2000), in: JRGS 8/1, 573–96; 'Ortskirche und Universalkirche. Antwort an Walter Kasper' (2001), in: ibid., 597–604. My reply to Ratzinger is found in *America* 185 (2001), 28f. A detailed account of the controversy is found in M. Kehl, 'Zum jüngsten Disput um das Verhältnis von Universalkirche und Ortskirche', in: *Kirche in ökumenischer Perspektive* (Festschrift W. Kasper), Freiburg i. Br. 2003, 81–101. Systematic considerations are discussed in D. Valentini, *Identità e storicità nella Chiesa*, Rome 2007, 93–136. Many further aspects are covered in A. Buckenmaier, *Universale Kirche vor Ort. Zum Verhältnis von Universalkirche und Ortskirche*, Regensburg 2009.

379 H. de Lubac, 'Einzelkirche und Ortskirche', in: *Quellen kirchlicher Einheit*, Einsiedeln 1974, 52f.

380 Paul VI, Apostolic Exhortation *Evangelii nuntiandi* (1975), 61f.

381 LG 2, 23, 25.

382 P. McPartlan, 'Local Church and the Universal Church', in: *IJSCC* 4 (2004) 21–33.

383 Aristotle, *metaphysica* 1088 a 6.

384 Thomas Aquinas, *Quodlibet* X q. 1 a. 1. On the philosophically and theologically fundamental topic of unity and diversity, see P. Hadot/K. Flasch/E. Heintel, 'Das Eine, Einheit', in: HWPh. 2, 361–84.

385 LG 8.

386 UR 18.

387 See F. König (ed.), *Zentralismus statt Kollegialität? Kirche im Spannungsfeld*, Düsseldorf 1990; R. Quinn, *The Reform of the Papacy. The Costly Call to Christian Unity*, New York: Crossroad 1999.

388 J. A. Möhler, *Unity* (1825), §70.

389 For an overview of the history, see H. Paarhammer, 'Pfarrei I', in: TRE 26, 337–47; P. Krämer, 'Pfarrei I', in: LThK^3 8, 162–4.

390 E. Gatz (ed.), *Pfarr- und Gemeindeorganisation. Studien zu ihrer historischen Entwicklung in Deutschland, Österreich und der Schweiz seit dem Ende des*

18. Jahrhunderts, Paderborn 1987; and, *Geschichte des kirchlichen Lebens in den deutschsprachigen Ländern seit dem Ende des 18. Jahrhunderts*, Freiburg i. Br. 1991.

391 H. Rahner (ed.), *The Parish, from Theology to Practice* (1956), Westminster, Md.: Newman Press 1958; P. Wess, *Gemeindekirche – Zukunft der Volkskirche*, Vienna 1976; H. Wieh, *Konzil und Gemeinde*, Freiburg i. Br. 1978; H. Fischer/N. Greinacher/F. Klostermann, *Die Gemeinde*, Mainz 1970; F. Klostermann, *Gemeinde – Kirche der Zukunft*, Freiburg i. Br. 1974; W. Kasper, 'Zur Theologie der Gemeinde' (1971), in: WKGS 11, 477–88; K. Lehmann, *Gemeinde* (CGG 29), Freiburg i. Br. 1982, 5–6.

392 LG 29; cf. SC 42.

393 John Paul II, *Christifideles laici* (1988), 26.

394 CIC can. 515 §1.

395 On this, see F. X. Arnold/K. Rahner (eds), *Handbuch der Pastoraltheologie*, 5 vols, Freiburg i. Br. 1964–72; K. Rahner, *The Shape of the Church to Come*, New York: Seabury Press 1974. From a pastoral-sociological perspective, see K. Gabriel, *Christentum zwischen Tradition und Postmoderne*, Freiburg i. Br. 1995; M. Ebertz, *Erosion der Gnadenanstalt? Zum Wandel der Sozialgestalt von Kirche*, Frankfurt a.M. 1998; W. Huber, *Kirche in der Zeitenwende. Gesellschaftlicher Wandel und Erneuerung der Kirche*, Göttingen 1998; P. M. Zulehner, *Kirche umbauen – nicht totsparen*, Ostfildern 2009.

396 I fully agree with the analysis and resulting conclusion by M. Kehl and G. Greshake (*Priester sein in dieser Zeit*, 216–34).

397 On this, see Kehl, *Die Kirche*, 173–210; and, *Wohin geht die Kirche?*, Freiburg 1996; J. Werbick, *Kirche*, Freiburg i. Br. 1994, 127–34; J. Ratzinger in: M. Pera/J. Ratzinger, *Ohne Wurzeln. Der Relativismus und die Krise der europäischen Kultur*, Augsburg 2005, 129–35. See above, section I.8.

398 GS 1.

399 On this, see W. Kasper, *Diener der Freude*, in: WKGS 12, 325–423, here 413–18.

400 Acts 2.46; 10.2; 21.8; Rom. 16.5.10f.; 1 Cor. 16.19; Col. 4.15; Phlm 2. On the early Christian house churches, which were already known in the Judaeo-Christian period and which are found in the New Testament, see J. Klauck, *Hausgemeinde und Hauskirche im frühen Christentum*, Stuttgart 1981; E. Dassmann, 'Haus', in: RAC 13, 849–90.

401 Many are suspicious of the term 'basic community'. Pope Paul VI, *Evangelii nuntiandi* (1975, 58) and Pope John Paul II, *Redemptoris missio* (1990, 51), but demonstrated that, if appropriately understood, this term and what it stands for are justified and serves as a hope for the universal Church.

402 Philip Neri († 1585), the second apostle of Rome, began founding oratories during the time of upheaval throughout Europe in the sixteenth century. The same idea was later taken up again by John Henry Newman († 1890) with his oratory in Birmingham.

403 LG 44.

404 A foundational source on this point is the chapter dedicated to people in religious orders of the Constitution on the Church, LG 43–7, the decree on the adaptation and renewal of religious life, *Perfectae caritatis,* as well as, following the Bishops' Synod on the religious orders, the post-synodal apostolic exhortation by Pope John Paul II, *Vita consecrata* (1996), on the consecrated life and its mission in the Church and in the world. An excellent first overview of the history and theology of religious orders, especially for readers unfamiliar with the topic, is found in K. S. Frank, 'Orden, Ordensstand I–III', in: LThK[3] 1998, 1090–6; L. Holtz, *Geschichte des christlichen Ordenslebens*, Einsiedeln [2]1991.

405 LG 43.

406 LG 44; PC 5.

407 PC 1; cf. LG 44.

408 John Paul II, Post-synodal exhortation, *Vita consecrata* (1996), 3.

409 So asserts, among others, the fourth Lateran council (1215), can. 12f. (COD 240–2); can. 52 (COD 259); can. 57 (COD 262); the 2. Council of Lyons (1274) can. 23 (COD 326f.), the Council of Trent (1545–63) (COD 776–84) and again the Second Vatican Council II (1962–5).

410 J. B. Metz, *Followers of Christ. The Religious Life and the Church*, New York: Paulist Press 1978.

411 A research overview is found in K. S. Frank, *With Greater Liberty: A Short History of Christian Monasticism and Religious Orders*, Kalamazoo, Mich.: Cistercian Publ. 1993; F. von Lilienfeld, 'Mönchtum II', in: TRE 33, 150–93. Still interesting, the volume by M. Viller/K. Rahner, *Aszese und Mystik in der Väterzeit* (1939), Freiburg i. Br. 1989; new: B. McGinn et al. (eds), *Christian Spirituality*, 3 vols, New York: Crossroad 1985–9. Among the many historical studies work reading, see especially W. Dirks, *Die Antwort der Mönche*, Frankfurt a.M. 1982; W. Nigg, *Warriors of God: the Great Religious Orders and their Founders*, New York: Knopf 1959.

412 Athanasius, *Vita Antonii.*

413 H. U. von Balthasar, *Die großen Ordensregeln*, Einsiedeln 1974. In the Middle Ages, the Rule of St Augustine became particularly decisive for the Augustinian Canon Regulars and especially for the Premonstratensians founded by St Norbert of Xanten († 1134).

414 Sulpicius Severus, *The Life of St Martin*, London: Sands & Cor. 1928.

415 *The Writings of Francis of Assisi: Letters and Prayer*, St Bonaventure, NY: Franciscan Institute Publication 2010.

416 *A Pilgrim's Testament: the Memoirs of St Ignatius of Loyola*, Saint Louis: Institute of Jesuit Sources, 1995; *The Spiritual Exercises of St. Ignatius*, Gardener Books 2007.

417 PC 2.

418 In a certain sense, the predecessors of this phenomenon are the secular institutes which were canonically ordered in the Apostolic Constitution by Pius XII, *Provida mater ecclesia* (1947). Examples of recent spiritual movements and communities include Cursillo, Work of Mary (Focolare Movement),

Charismatic Movement, Comunione e Liberazione, Schoenstatt Movement, Emmanuel Community, Community of the Beatitudes, Chemin Neuf, Shalom, etc. Similar movements and communities exist in other churches.

419 On this, see John Paul II, Post-synodal Exhortation, *Christifideles laici* (1988), 29; Encyclical *Redemptoris missio* 72; *Message for the World Congress of Ecclesial Movements and New Communities* (St Peter's Square, 30 May 1998); Benedict XVI, *Message to the Participants of the Second World Congress on Ecclesial Movements and New Communities* (22 May 2006). J. Ratzinger, 'Die kirchlichen Bewegungen und ihr theologischer Ort', in: JRGS 8/1, 363–90; 'Bewegungen, die Kirche, die Welt', in: ibid., 391–422.

420 This point was elaborated by Pius X and by Pius XI, Inaugural Encyclical, *Ubi arcano* (1922).

6. The missionary and dialogical Church

1 LG 3.

2 LG 9.

3 More recent publications, see J. Schütte (ed.), *Mission nach dem Konzil*, Mainz 1967; L. Rütti, *Zur Theologie der Mission. Kritische Analysen und neue Orientierung*, Mainz – Munich 1972; H. W. Gensichen, *Glaube für die Welt. Theologische Aspekte der Mission*, Gütersloh 1971; W. Kasper, 'Überlegungen zu Theologie der Mission' (1976) in: WKGS 11, 370–93; H. Bürkle, *Missionstheologie*, Stuttgart 1979; and, *Die Mission der Kirche*, Paderborn 2002; and, *Erkennen und Bekennen. Schriften zum missionarischen Dialog*, St. Ottilien 2010; G. Collet, *Das Missionsverständnis der Kirche in der gegenwärtigen Diskussion*, Mainz 1984; P. Beyerhaus, *Er sandte sein Wort. Theologie der Mission*, Wuppertal 1996; M. Sievernich, *Die christliche Mission. Geschichte und Gegenwart*, Darmstadt 2009; G. Colzani, 'Missione', in: *Dizionario di ecclesiologia*, Rome 2010, 866–88; G. Augustin/K. Krämer (eds), *Mission als Herausforderung. Impulse zur Neuevangelisierung* (ThiD 6), Freiburg i. Br. 2011.

4 AG 2.

5 F. Hahn, *Mission in the New Testament*, London: SCM Press, 1965; K. Kertelge (ed.), *Mission im NT* (QD 93), Freiburg i. Br. 1982.

6 S. Neill, *A History of Christian Missions*, London ^{2}1990.

7 Summarised in G. Collet, 'Missionskritik', in: LThK^{3} 7, 316f.

8 So the world conference on World Mission and Evangelism of the World Council of Churches in Bangkok 1973.

9 See section II.2.5.

10 See section II.6.2.3.

11 As far as I know this thesis was first put forward by H. Halbfas, in *Fundamentalkatechetik. Sprache und Erfahrung im Religionsunterricht*, Düsseldorf 1968. On the proper understanding of the possibility of salvation outside the Church, see section II.2.5.

12 So Rütti, *Zur Theologie der Mission.*

13 LG 2–4; AG 2–4.

14 AG 2.

15 AG 2–4.

16 AG 5.

17 LG 1.

18 AG 9.

19 AG 2.

20 See John Paul II, Encyclical, *Redemptoris missio* (1990) on the permanent validity of the Church's missionary mandate.

21 Starting with K. Barth, this idea has been developed particularly in Protestant theology. Cf. G. F. Vicedom, *The Mission of God. An Introduction to a Theology of Mission* (1958), St Louis: Concordia Publishing House, 1965; and, *Actio Dei. Mission und Reich Gottes*, Munich 1975. Catholic theology can take up this idea, but, it must complement it with the emphasis on the sacramental character of the Church as sign and instrument of mission. Also important from a Protestant perspective is H. W. Gensichen, *Glaube für die Welt*, Gütersloh 1971.

22 LG 9.

23 J. Moltmann, *The Church in the Power of the Spirit* (1975), New York: Harper & Row, 1977, 10.

24 See section II.2.2.

25 Tertullian, *apologeticum* 50, 13.

26 W. Kasper, 'Neue Evangelisierung als theologische, pastorale und geistliche Herausforderung', in: WKGS 5, 245–317.

27 Conference on Mission, Mexico City, 1963.

28 AG 6; 19–22.

29 AG 11.

30 AG 16. See section II.6.2.3.

31 See II 6.2.4.

32 AG 15. See section II.6.2.2.

33 On this, see John Paul II, Encyclical *Redemptoris missio* (1990), 55–7; Pontifical Council for Inter-religious Dialogue, *Dialogue and Proclamation* (1991); Congregation for the Doctrine of Faith, *Doctrinal Note on Some Aspects of Evangelization* (2007).

34 See section II.1.3.

35 DV 2f.

36 GS 1.

37 John Paul II, Encyclical *Ut unum sint* (1995), 28; cf. 57.

38 On this point, I am indebted to A. Bea, J. Österreicher, H. U. von Balthasar, J. Ratzinger, J. M. Lustiger, C. Thoma and F. Mussner; on the Protestant side D. Bonhoeffer and K. Barth; on the Jewish side M. Buber, F. Rosenzweig,

E. L. Ehrlich, and to many Jewish friends with whom I have been acquainted in recent years. On this, see W. Kasper, 'Die Reichsprogromnacht und die Gleichgültigkeit', in: *Freiburger Rundbrief* NF 1 (1993/94) 95–100; and, 'Juden und Christen – Schulter an Schulter', in: ibid. 9 (2002) 250–6; and, *Non ho perduto nessuno. Comunione, dialogo ecumenico, evangelizzazione*, Bologna 2005, 75–119; and, 'Juden und Christen – das eine Volk Gottes', in: IKaZ 39 (2010) 418–27 (see also the complete edition of this journal, which continues this dialogue) and the extensive preface to P. A. Cunningham/J. Sievers/M. Boys (eds), *Christ Jesus and the Jewish People Today. New Explorations of Theological Interrelationships*, Grand Rapids, MI – Rome 2011.

39 On this, see document by the Pontifical Biblical Commission: *The Jewish People and their Sacred Scriptures in the Christian Bible* (2001).

40 This appears for the first time in the *Epistle of Barnabas* 5,7; 7,5; 13,1.

41 See the many declarations and documents in H. H. Henrix et al. (eds), *Die Kirche und das Judentum*, 2 vols, Paderborn – Munich – Gütersloh 1988, 2001.

42 On the history and interpretation, see J. Oesterreicher, in: LThK.E 2, 406–78, 490–4; R. Siebenrock, in: HThK.Vat II 3, 618–26, 661–4.

43 LG 16; cf. DV 14f.

44 Hebrews 8:13, which refers to the first covenant as old and obsolete, is often cited against this thesis, itself based upon Romans 9–11. However, Hebrews does not speak about the covenant of Abraham as such, but about the abolition of the Levitical temple cult and of the cultic sacrifices through the one sacrifice of Jesus Christ.

45 See note 41 above.

46 The foundations for the more recent Jewish research of Jesus were laid by J. Klausner. We note, in particular, the studies of D. Flussner and Schalom ben Chorin. An essential source here is J. Neusner, *Ein Rabbi spricht mit Jesus*, Freiburg i. Br. 2007.

47 A pioneering, though, in many parts, obsolete study is J. Daniélou, *The Theology of Jewish Christianity* (1954), London: Darton, Longman & Todd 1964; and, *Das Judenchristentum und die Anfänge der Kirche*, Cologne 1964. See the more recent discussion in G. Strecker, 'Judenchristentum', in: TRE 17, 310–25; F. Manns, *Le Judéo-Christianisme. Mémoire ou prophétie?*, Paris 2000.

48 H. Frankenmölle/J. Wohlmuth (eds), *Das Heil der Anderen. Problemfeld 'Judenmission'* (QD 238), Freiburg i. Br. 2010.

49 On the discussion of one and two parallel covenants, see J. T. Pawlikowski, 'Judentum und Christentum', in: TRE 18, 386–403; by the same author in far more detail: 'Reflections on Covenant and Mission', in: E. Kessler/ M. J. Wright (eds), *Themes in Jewish-Christian Relations*, Cambridge: Orchard Academic 2005, 273–99.

50 On this question, see W. Kasper/H. Heinz, 'Theologische Schwerpunkte im christlich- jüdischen Dialog', in: *Freiburg Rundbrief NF* 14 (2007) 18–25.

51 On the relation of the two consecutive covenants, see G. von Rad, *Theologie*

des Alten Testaments (*Old Testament Theology*, Peabody, MA: Prince Press 2005), vol. 2, Munich [6]1975, 339–447.

52 On this, see W. Kasper, 'La preghiera del Venerdì Santo per gli ebrei', in: *OR* (April 10, 2008), 4, A shorter version is published as 'Das Wann und Wie entscheidet Gott', in: FAZ (March 20, 2008), 39. On this point and partly critical, see Frankenmölle/Wohlmuth (eds), *Das Heil der Anderen* (as in note 48).

53 See section II.4.1.

54 On the history of the ecumenical movement, see R. Rouse/S. C. Neill, *Geschichte der ökumenischen Bewegung 1517–948*, 2 vols, Göttingen 1957–8, and continued by H. E. Frey Göttingen 1974; G. Thils, *Histoire doctrinale du mouvement œcuménique*, Paris 1962; G. Tavard, *Geschichte der ökumenischen Bewegung*, Mainz 1964; H. J. Urban/H. Wagner (eds), *Handbuch der Ökumenik*, vol. 1–2, Paderborn 1985–6; R. Frieling, *Der Weg des ökumenischen Gedankens*, Göttingen 1992.

55 On this, see J. R. Geiselmann, *Einführung zur Symbolik von J. A. Möhler*, Darmstadt 1958, [15]–[148].

56 Pope Leo XIII recommended the prayer for unity in 1895, Pius X endorsed the prayer week for unity in 1908, Benedict XV established it permanently in 1916, and John Paul II once again expressly underlined its importance (*Ut unum sint*, 24).

57 A first impetus came from the two encyclicals (1902 and 1920) by the Ecumenical Patriarch Joachim III, later from the Ecumenical Patriarch Athenagoras in the correspondence with Pope Paul VI (*Tomos agapis*, 1971), the theologians of Saint Serge in Paris and Saint Vladimir's Seminary in New York (G. Florovsky, S. Bulgakov, V. Lossky, P. Evdokimov, J. Meyendorff, A. Schmemann, O. Clément, V. Borovoj), as well as N. Nissiotis, D. Staniloae, and others were all influential here. Also significant was the Orthodox Centre of the Ecumenical Patriarchate in Chambésy-Geneva with the Metropolitan Damaskinos.

58 The foundation was laid by the Oxford Movement in the nineteenth century, and in the twentieth century, archbishops, bishops and theologians such as W. Temple, C. H. Brent, A. M. Ramsey, E. W. Scott, S. Neill, L. Newbigin, etc. Also important was the Anglican Centre in Rome.

59 N. Söderblom, F. Heiler, J. Mott,W. A. Visser 't Hooft, R. Niebuhr, D. Bonhoeffer, W. Stählin, H. Asmussen, E. Schlink, etc. Important here are the ecumenical Institutes Bossey near Geneva and the Ecumenical Institute of the Lutheran World Federation in Strasbourg. Ecumenically important Protestant spiritual communities and fraternities include, in particular, Taizé with its founder R. Schutz, Grandchamps, Communität Casteller Ring (CCR), Evangelical Sisterhood of Mary, Communität Christusbruderschaft Selbitz (CCB), Michaelsbruderschaft (Evangelical Brotherhood of St Michael), Bund für evangelisch-katholische Einheit (League for Evangelical-Catholic Unity), Brotherhood of St James and others. On this, see J. Halkenhäuser, *Kirche und Kommunität. Ein Beitrag zur Geschichte und zum Auftrag der kommunitären Bewegung in den Kirchen der Reformation*, Paderborn [2]1985.

60 See especially the grand old master of ecumenical theology, Y. Congar, in *Divided Christendom: a Catholic study of the Problem of Reunion* (1937), London: G. Bles, 1939; and, *Vraie et fausse réforme dans l'Église*, Paris 1950. From the German-speaking areas of Europe, special mention goes to R. Grosche, K. Adam, O. Karrer, P. Simon, J. Höfer, T. Sartory, H. U. von Balthasar, K. Rahner, H. Fries, etc. Also important were the later cardinals A. Bea, L. Jaeger, and J. Willebrands. Ecumenically important monasteries include Chevetogne in Belgium, Niederaltaich in Germany, St. Johns Collegeville, Bose. And more recent spiritual movements and communities include the Focolare Movement (founded by Chiara Lubich), the Community of Sant'Egidio, the Chemin Neuf Community, L'Arche (founded by Jean Vanier) and others. Ecumenical institutes: Johann-Adam-Möhler-Institut in Paderborn, Pro Oriente in Vienna.

61 See W. Thönissen, 'Päpstlicher Rat zur Förderung der Einheit der Christen', in: *Lexikon der Ökumene und Konfessionskunde*, Freiburg i. Br. 2007, 1031f.

62 UR 1. See the first document of Vatican II, SC 1.

63 UR 1, 4.

64 UR 2–4.

65 Listing all of the many documents would be beyond the scope of this volume. For this I refer to the following sources: for the international dialogues: H. Meyer et al. (eds), *Growth in Agreement*, 3 vols, Geneva: WCC Publications, 1984–2007. For the dialogue with Orthodox and the Oriental-Orthodox churches: T. Bremer et al. (eds), *Orthodoxie im Dialog*, Trier 1999 as well as J. Borelli/J. E. Erickson, *The Quest for Unity. Orthodox and Catholics in Dialogue*, New York – Washington, DC 1996. Rich information is found in the respective articles in: N. Lossky et al. (eds). *Dictionary of the Ecumenical Movement*, Geneva [2]2002; W. Thönissen et al. (eds), *Lexikon der Ökumene und Konfessionskunde*, Freiburg i. Br. 2007; in addition W. Kasper, *Harvesting the Fruits*, London: Continuum 2009.

66 *Ut unum sint*, 3.

67 *Ut unum sint*, 20, 25.

68 *Ut unum sint*, 9.

69 Benedict XVI, *Address to the Cardinals at the End of the Conclave*, 20 April 2005.

70 Benedict XVI, *Homily at the End of the Week of Prayer for Christian Unity*, 2010.

71 UR 2–4.

72 UR 3; cf. LG 14f.

73 UR 3; cf. LG 15; *Ut unum sint*, 11f.

74 LG 8; cf. UR 3, 11. See section II.4.1.

75 *Ut unum sint*, 13.

76 UR 22. For a more precise interpretation of this, especially for Protestant Christians, difficult statement, see sections II.4.1 and II.5.3.

77 UR 3; *Ut unum sint*, 2, 14.

78 UR 4.

79 Contributions to ecumenical theology include Y. Congar, *Diversity and Communion* (1982), Mystic, Conn: Twenty-Third Publications 1985; P. Neuner, *Ökumenische Theologie*, Darmstadt 1997; Lossky, 'Theology, ecumenical', in: *Dictionary of the Ecumenical Movement*, 1109–11; F. Nüssel/D. Sattler, *Einführung in die ökumenische Theologie*, Darmstadt 2008. My own contributions include W. Kasper, 'Situation und Zukunft der Ökumene', in: ThQ 181 (2001) 175–90; and, *That They All Be One: the Call to Unity*, London: Burns & Oates, 2004; and, 'Was heißt Theologie zu treiben?' (Speech of acceptance on receiving the theological prize of the Salzburger Hochschulwochen), in: *Gott im Kommen. Salzburger Hochschulwochen 2006*, Innsbruck – Wien 2006, 250–8.

80 UR 11.

81 P. D. Murray (ed.), *Receptive Ecumenism and the Call to Catholic Learning. Exploring a Way for Contemporary Ecumenism*, Oxford: Oxford University Press 2008.

82 Important events were the 'World Conference on Church and Society' (1966) and the plenary assembly of the World Council of Churches in Uppsala (1968). The question was controversially discussed by the Faith and Order Commission in Louvain in 1971. The programme was precisely formulated by K. Raiser, *Ecumenism in Transition*, Geneva: WCC Publications 1991; J. B. Metz, *Reform und Gegenreformation heute*, Mainz 1969. J. Ratzinger, 'Zur Lage der Ökumene', in: JRGS 8/2, 744–7.

83 In H. Fries/K. Rahner, *Unity of the Churches – an Actual Possibility* (QD 100), New York: Paulist Press 1985, the question of truth (especially in the essential second thesis) is pushed too much into the background behind a pragmatic argumentation. This is why the ecumenical optimism expressed therein that the unity would be reached easily and fast has not stood the test.

84 See J. Ratzinger, 'Zum Fortgang der Ökumene' (1986) in: JRGS 8/2, 731–8.

85 See note 65, and above I.7. On the bilateral Catholic-Protestant dialogues, see Kasper, *Harvesting the Fruits* (as in note 65).

86 Many additional, extensive contributions are found in P. Walter/K. Krämer/G. Augustin (eds), *Kirche in ökumenischer Perspektive* (Festschrift W. Kasper), Freiburg i. Br. 2003.

87 H. Meyer, *That All May Be One: Perceptions and Models of Ecumenicity*, Grand Rapids, Mich.: Eerdmans, 1999; Neuner, *Ökumenische Theologie*, 281–96; Best, 'Unity, models', in: *Dictionary of the Ecumenical Movement*, 1173–5.

88 For the interpretation, see sections II.2.2 and II.4.2.1.

89 H. Meyer et al. (eds), *Dokumente wachsender Übereinstimmung*, vol. 3, 724–31. This volume also contains a number of similar declarations concerning entrance into church communion.

90 Ibid., 749–77. Not quite consequent is the *Meissen Agreement* (1988), ibid., 732–48.

91 See section II.4.2.3.

92 See section II.2.2.

93 See section II.5.4.

94 John Paul II, Encyclical *Slavorum Apostoli* (1985), 27.

95 *Ut unum sint*, 28; 57.

96 O. Cullmann, *Unity through Diversity: its Foundation, and a Contribution to the Discussion Concerning the Possibilities of its Actualization*, Philadelphia: Fortress Press, 1988.

97 J. Ratzinger, 'Die Kirche und die Kirchen', in: *Reformatio* 13 (1964) 85–108, here 105.

98 J. A. Möhler, *Die Einheit in der Kirche* (*Unity in the Church*) §46, 153. On Möhler's cultural and theological historical background, see J. R. Geiselmann in his introduction to the new edition of *Einheit*, [63]–[85]; W. Kasper, '"Vom Geist und Wesen des Katholizismus": Bedeutung, Wirkungsgeschichte und Aktualität von Johann Sebastian Dreys und Johann Adam Möhlers Wesensbestimmung des Katholizismus', in: ThQ 183 (2003) 196–212. A wording similar to Möhler's is found in K. Koch, *Gelähmte Ökumene*, Freiburg i. Br. 1991, 37.

99 On the overall concern, see W. Kasper, 'Ökumene des Lebens und Eucharistiegemeinschaft: Perspektiven für die Zukunft' (2004), in: WKGS 10, 251–66; and, *A Handbook of Spiritual Ecumenism*, Hyde Park, NY: New City Press 2007; Augustin, 'Ökumene als geistlicher Prozess', 522–50.

100 UR 8; *Ut unum sint* 15f., 21f., 33–5. Important here is the document of the Groupe des Dombes, *For the Conversion of the Churches*, Geneva: WCC Publications, 1993.

101 *Ut unum sint*, 27.

102 *Ut unum sint*, 57; Apostolic Letter *Orientale Lumen* (1995), 20–7.

103 NA 1.

104 NA 4. See section II.6.2.1.

105 NA 3.

106 The most important documents on the Catholic side, see Paul VI, Apostolic Exhortation *Evangelii nuntiandi* on evangelization in the modern world (1975); Pontifical Council for Inter-religious Dialogue: *The Church and other Religions – Dialogue and Mission* (1984); John Paul II, Encyclical *Redemptoris missio* on the permanent validity of the Church's missionary mandate (1990); International Theological Commission: *Christianity and the World Religions* (1997); Congregation for the Doctrine of Faith: Declaration *Dominus Jesus* (2000); *Doctrinal Note on some Aspects of Evangelization* (2007). Collection of all documents: Pontifical Council for Inter-religious Dialogue: *Interreligious Dialogue*, F. Gioia, Boston (ed.) 2006; E. Fürlinger (ed.), *Der Dialog muss weitergehen. Ausgewählte Dokumente zum interreligiösen Dialog*, Freiburg i. Br. 2009.

107 I must restrict my references to important German Catholic literature:

K. Rahner, 'Christianity and the Non-Christian Religions', in: *Theological Investigations* 5, London: Darton, Longman & Todd 1966, 115–34; W. Kasper (ed.), *Absolutheit des Christentums* (QD 79), Freiburg i. Br. 1977; H. Waldenfels, *Begegnung der Religionen*, Bonn 1990; M. von Brück/J. Werbick (eds), *Der einzige Weg zum Heil?* (QD 143), Freiburg i. Br. 1993; G. Augustin, *Gott eint – trennt Christus?*, Paderborn 1993; B. Stubenrauch, *Dialogisches Dogma. Der christliche Auftrag zur interreligiösen Begegnung* (QD 158), Freiburg i. Br. 1995; H. Bürkle, *Der Mensch auf der Suche nach Gott. Die Frage der Religionen*, Paderborn 1996; R. Schwager (ed.), *Relativierung der Wahrheit? Die Herausforderung des christlichen Absolutheitsanspruchs durch pluralistische Religionstheologien* (QD 170), Freiburg i. Br. 1998; H. Küng, *Spurensuche. Die Weltreligionen auf dem Weg*, Munich 1999; G. Müller/M. Serretti (eds), *Einzigkeit und Universalität Jesu Christi*, Einsiedeln 2001; J. Ratzinger, *Glaube – Wahrheit – Toleranz. Das Christentum und die Weltreligionen*, Freiburg i. Br. 2003; K. Lehmann (ed.), *Weltreligionen. Verstehen – Verständigung – Verantwortung*, Frankfurt a.M. – Leipzig 2009; J. Dupuis, *Unterwegs zu einer christlichen Theologie des religiösen Pluralismus*, Innsbruck 2010.

108 S. P. Huntington, *The Clash of Civilizations and the Remaking of World Order*, London: Simon & Schuster, 1997. The topic of religion and violence has taken on a central role in the international dialogue. See, for examples, J. Assmann, *Moses der Ägypter*, Munich 1998; *The Price of Monotheism*, Stanford: Stanford University Press 2010; *Monotheismus und die Sprache der Gewalt*, Vienna 2006; I. Beck, *A God of One's Own: Religion's Capacity for Peace and Potential for Violence*, Cambridge: Polity 2010.

109 The 'Projekt Weltethos' (Project for a Global Ethic) belongs to this context: H. Küng, *Global Responsibility: in Search of a New World Ethic* (1990), Eugene, OR: Wipf & Stock Publishers 2004; and, *A Global Ethic for Global Politics and Economics*, New York: Oxford University Press 1998; and, *Dokumentation zum Weltethos*, Munich 2002; and, *Weltethos christlich verstanden. Positionen – Erfahrungen – Impulse*, Freiburg i. Br. 2005; and, *Wozu Weltethos? Religion und Ethik in Zeiten der Globalisierung. Im Gespräch mit Jürgen Hoeren*, Freiburg i. Br. [2]2006. On this, see note 113 below.

110 See C. H. Ratschow, 'Religion I & II', in: HWPh. 8, 632–7.

111 See W. Foerster, 'εὐσέβεια', in: ThWNT 7, 175–8.

112 On the term 'religion', see Lehmann (ed.), *Weltreligionen*.

113 For my part, the limits of the project of a global ethic seem to fall into this abstraction (cf. above note 109). On this problem, see the fundamental criticism by R. Spaemann, 'Weltethos als "Projekt"', in *Merkur* 50 (1996), 891–904.

114 J. H. Leuba, *A Psychological Study of Religion*, London 1912, Appendix.

115 Previous names and terms are found in WKGS 4, 27 note 31.

116 On this, ibid., 78–108.

117 R. Otto, *The Idea of the Holy: an Inquiry into the Non-rational Factor in the Idea of the Divine and its Relation to the Rational* (1936), London: Oxford University Press 1970.

118 See the Declaration on Religious Freedom of the Second Vatican Council, *Dignitatis humanae.*

119 See Justin, *apologia* I, 46; *apologia* II, 7, 10, 13, etc. See section II.2.3.

120 See M. Seckler, *Das Heil in der Geschichte. Geschichtstheologisches Denken bei Thomas von Aquin*, Munich 1964, 220f.

121 LG 16; GS 22; AA 7; cf. DV 3; GS 57. See section II.4.

122 AG 7.

123 John Paul II, Encyclical, *Redemptoris missio* (1990), 28f., 55–7.

124 See J. Ratzinger, 'Der Dialog der Religionen und das jüdisch-christliche Verhältnis', in: JRGS 8/1, 1128f. A basic discussion from a Christological perspective of the theory of religious pluralism is found in K.-H. Menke, *Jesus ist Gottes Sohn. Denkformen und Brennpunkte der Christologie*, Regensburg ^{2}2011.

125 On this, see W. Kasper, 'Absoluteness of Christianity', in: *Sacramentum Mundi*, vol. 1, London: Burns & Oates 1968, 311–13; K. Lehmann, 'Absolutheit des Christentums als philosophisches und theologisches Problem', in: W. Kasper, *Absolutheit des Christentums* (QD 79), Freiburg i. Br. 1977, 13–38; H. Waldenfels, 'Absolutheit des Christentums', in: LThK^{3} 1, 80–2.

126 E. Troeltsch, *The Absoluteness of Christianity and the History of Religions* (1929), Richmond: John Knox Press, 1971.

127 On the correct understanding of the inerrancy and infallibility of the Church, see section II.5.4.

128 The first World's Parliament of Religions (founded in Chicago in 1893) based its programme for unification on the Golden Rule. The second Parliament of World Religions included the rule in its declaration on a global ethic. See 'Goldene Regel', in: TRE 13, 570–83. However, see note 113 above.

129 Cf. G. Stählin, 'ξένος', in: ThWNT 5, 1–36; O. Hiltbrunner et al., 'Gastfreundschaft', in: RAC 8, 1061–123.

130 J. Ratzinger has repeatedly stressed the concept of representation for the dialogue with the religions. See 'Kirche – Zeichen unter den Völkern', in: JRGS 8/1, 1032–4; 'Kein Heil außerhalb der Kirche?', in: ibid., 1073–7 and others.

131 See the commentary by C. Moeller, in: LThK.E 3, 280–2 and by J. Ratzinger, in: ibid., 313–54; H. J. Sander, 'Theologischer Kommentar zur Pastoralkonstitution über die Kirche in der Welt von heute *Gaudium et spes*', in: HThK.Vat II 4 (this document details not only the genesis of the document, but also its history of reception). On the meaning of 'pastoral', see above, sections I.4 and I.5.

132 GS 1.

133 The idea of the 'signs of the times' incorporates Mt. 16.3 and Lk. 12.56. Yet those passages speak about the beginning of God's kingdom. In contrast, in GS, the locution 'signs of the times' refers to inner-historical phenomena that need to be interpreted in the light of the Gospel (GS 4, 10f., 22, 40, 42f., etc.) and which, conversely, shine their light upon the Gospel (GS 42; 44; 62). It remains unclear how the 'signs of the times' are to be defined and classified

methodologically and theologically. See K. Rahner, 'On the Theological Problems Entailed in the Idea of a "Pastoral Constitution"', in *Theological Investigations* 10 (1967), New York: Seabury Press 1977, 293–317.

134 GS 10, 22, 45, 93.

135 On one side there were mostly the French theologians, above all, M. D. Chenu, who wanted to positively emphasize the theological meaning of the 'signs of the times'. See M. D. Chenu, 'Les signes des temps', in: Y. Congar/ M. Peuchmaurd (eds), *L'Église dans le monde de ce temps. Constitution Pastorale* Gaudium et Spes, vol. 2, Paris 1967, 205–25. On the other side were the German theologians, in particular K. Rahner and J. Ratzinger, who favoured a Christological point of departure and who kept themselves rather detached, especially from the prepared drafts for GS. Later, John Paul II took up in particular the Christological approach of GS 22. See on this Sander, 'Theologischer Kommentar', 835–64. However, Sander's own, bipolar, topological approach seems problematic to me. It gives way to the danger that theology will fall into the clutches of a purely secularized diagnosis of history and society, as indeed was the case in some forms of liberation theology.

136 On this, see sections II.2.4 and II.3.3.

137 See section II.3.3.

138 GS 2.

139 GS 3.

140 The particular chapter on the 'Proper Development of Culture' (GS 53–62) was tackled relatively late during the Council. See the introduction and commentary by R. Tucci in: LThK.E 3, 447–84; Sander, 'Theologischer Kommentar', 780–8. Even though this chapter has its weaknesses, its topic is of fundamental importance far beyond the questions it deals with.

141 See the overview in 'Kultur, Kulturphilosophie', in HWPh. 4, 1309–24; 'Kultur', in: TRE 20, 176–209, as well as in: LThK[3] 6, 514–16. I prefer the term 'culture' in the sense of 'culture of life' to the nowadays usually used term 'society'. While society looks mainly at the coexistence and communication of humans, culture takes up the relation of humanity and of human communities to the world. It thus focuses upon the social construction of reality (P. L. Berger/T. Luckmann).

142 See P. Koslowski/R. Spaemann/R. Löw, *Moderne oder Postmoderne?*, Weinheim 1986. cf. I.3.

143 On this, see H. Wolf (ed.), *Antimodernismus und Modernismus in der katholischen Kirche. Beiträge zum theologiegeschichtlichen Vorfeld des II. Vatikanums*, Paderborn 1998. Anti-modernism is addressed mainly in the encyclical *Mirari vos* by Gregory XVI (1832, DH 2730–2), in the *Syllabus* of Pius IX. (1864, DH 2901–80) and in the *Syllabus* of Pius X (1907, DH 3401–66) as well as in his encyclical *Pascendi dominici gregis* (1907, DH 3475–500). GS is no anti-syllabus. The liberal freedom of conscience and religion denounced in the *Syllabus* is not the same as the positive freedom of conscience and religion which is orientated towards the truth and which Vatican II taught in a completely different context. Between the *Syllabus* and Gs, there is an evolution of knowledge, but no contradiction or discontinuity.

144 DH 1.

145 GS 26f., 29, 41, 59, 66, 73, 76; DH 6.

146 GS 9, 29, 60.

147 GS 36, 41, 56; AA7.

148 GS 76.

149 See for example GS 9, 37, 43, 54, 56f., etc.

150 GS 4–8.

151 GS 19.

152 GS 7, 56.

153 John Paul II, Encyclical *Evangelium vitae* (1995), 12, 17, 21, 24, 28, 95.

154 One should name among others J. J. Rousseau, S. Kierkegaard, K. Marx, F. Nietzsche, L. N. Tolstoy, S. Freud, M. Weber, O. Spengler, M. Heidegger, K. Jaspers, E. Jüngel, R. Guardini, R. Spaemann.

155 M. Horkheimer/T. W. Adorno, *Dialectic of Enlightenment* (1969), New York: Continuum 1972.

156 J. Habermas/J. Ratzinger, *Dialectics of Secularization: on Reason and Religion*, San Francisco: Ignatius Press 2006.

157 J. Habermas, *Glauben und Wissen*, Frankfurt a.M. 2001; and, *Zwischen Naturalismus und Religion*, Frankfurt a.M. 2005.

158 On the secularisation thesis, see section I.7.

159 Paul VI, Apostolic Exhortation *Evangelii nuntiandi* (1975), 20.

160 John Paul II, Encyclical *Redemptoris missio* (1990), 37.

161 Benedict XVI, *Glaube und Vernunft. Die Regensburger Vorlesung. Kommentiert von G. Schwan, A. T. Khoury, Kardinal K. Lehmann*, Freiburg i. Br. 2007.

162 On the basic problem, see W. Kasper, 'Nature, Grace and Culture: on the Meaning of Secularization', in: D. Schindler/L. Bouyer (eds), *Catholicism and Secularization in America Essays on Nature, Grace, and Culture*, Huntington, Ind., 1990, 31–51; and 'Kirche und Kultur', in: *Begegnung: Hefte der Künstlerseelsorge der Erzdiözese München und Freising für den Dialog zwischen Kirche und Kunst* 3/1991, 4–11; and, 'Kirche und Kultur: Evangelisierung und Inkulturation', in: B. Fraling/H. Hoping et al. (eds), *Kirche und Theologie im kulturellen Dialog* (Festschrift P. Hünermann), Freiburg i. Br. 1994, 157–62.

163 H. U. von Balthasar, *The God Question and Modern Man* (also the extended new German edition *Die Gottesfrage des heutigen Menschen*, Einsiedeln 2009), New York: Seabury Press, 1967; J. B. Metz, 'Gotteskrise. Versuch zur "geistigen Situation der Zeit"', in: *Diagnosen zur Zeit*, Düsseldorf 1994, 86–92; W. Kasper, *The God of Jesus Christ*, London: Continuum 2012; and, 'Es ist Zeit, von Gott zu reden', in: G. Augustin (ed.), *Die Gottesfrage heute* (ThiD 1), Freiburg i. Br. 2009, 13–31; and, 'Die Gottesfrage als Zukunftsfrage', in: *Die Politische Meinung* 470/2009, 42–8. K. Lehmann, *Es ist Zeit, an Gott zu denken. Ein Gespräch mit Jürgen Hoeren*, Freiburg i. Br. 2000; J. Ratzinger, *The God of Jesus Christ: Meditations on the Triune*

God, San Francisco: Ignatius Press 2008; A. Franz/C. Maaß, *Diesseits des Schweigens. Heute von Gott sprechen* (QD 240), Freiburg i. Br. 2011. Further contributions are found in G. Augustin/K. Krämer (eds), *Gott denken und bezeugen* (Festschrift W. Kasper), Freiburg i. Br. 2008.

164 See W. Kasper, 'Autonomie und Theonomie', in: *Theologie und Kirche*, Mainz 1987, 140–75.

165 Concerning this formulation, I am indebted to a comment by R. Spaemann, cf. P. Koslowski et al. (eds), *Moderne oder Postmoderne*, Weinheim 1986, 60.

166 See 'Inkulturation', in: LThK[3] 5, 504–10.

167 SC 38, 40, 119; GS 40–5; AG 10–12, 19–22; Paul VI, *Evangelii nuntiandi* (1975), 18–20; 31–5; John Paul II, *Catechesi tradendae* (1979), 53; *Familiaris consortio* (1981), 10; *Slavorum Apostolorum* (1985), 21f.; *Redemptoris missio* (1990), 52–4, etc.

168 See sections II. 2.2 and II.2.3. The basic problem concerning the historicity and trans-historicity of statements of faith, which is briefly, and, in terms of hermeneutics, insufficiently addressed in GS 62, cannot be discussed here. Cf. II.5.4.

169 W. Kasper, 'Neue Evangelisierung als theologische, pastorale und geistliche Herausforderung', in: WKGS 5, 235–317. See section II.7.

170 So the Hochland-circle (founded by Carl Muth). Important representative of this circle are F. X. Kraus, A. Ehrhard, P. Funk, K. Bernhart, J. Wittig, H. Schell, E. Przywara, T. Haecker, etc. On this, see G. Schwaiger, *Aufbruch ins 20. Jahrhundert. Zum Streit um Reformkatholizismus und Modernismus*, Göttingen 1976. There have been similar movements in France (Le Sillon) and Italy (Bishop G. Bonomelli, the journal *Il Rinnovamento*, etc.).

171 See section I.2.

172 See section I.7 and II.5.7.

173 Pope John Paul II, Apostolic Letter *Tertio millennio adveniente* (1994), 37; Homily on the occasion of the commemoration of witnesses to the faith of the twentieth century (at the Colosseum, May 7, 2000). K.-J. Hummel/ C. Strohm (eds), *Zeugen einer besseren Welt. Christliche Märtyrer des 20. Jahrhunderts*, Leipzig 2000; A. Riccardi, *Salz der Erde, Licht der Welt. Glaubenszeugnis und Christenverfolgung im 20. Jahrhundert*, Freiburg i. Br. 2002; H. Moll (ed.), *Zeugen für Christus. Das deutsche Martyrologium des 20. Jahrhunderts*, 2 vols, Paderborn [5]2010.

174 Tertullian, *apologeticum* 50, 30.

7. Whither the way of the Church?

1 There is no shortage of literature on the future of the Church. To name only a few: J. Ratzinger, 'Wie wird die Kirche im Jahr 2000 aussehen?', in: *Glaube und Zukunft der Kirche*, Munich 1970 (reprinted in JRGS 8/2), 107–25, 130–1; and 'The Church on the threshold of the Third Millennium',

in: *Pilgrim Fellowship of Faith: the Church as Communion*, San Francisco: Ignatius Press, 2005; W. Kasper, *Faith and the Future* (1978), New York: Crossroad 1982; 'Kirche – wohin gehst du?' (1987), in: WKGS 11, 212–37; K. Rahner, 'The Future of the Church and the Church of the Future', in: *Theological Investigations* 20, New York: Crossroad 1981, 103–14 (as well as many other texts in vols 22 and 23); K. Lehmann, *Neuer Mut zum Kirchesein*, Freiburg i. Br. 1982; K. Koch, *Kirche ohne Zukunft? Plädoyer für neue Wege der Glaubensvermittlung*, Freiburg i. Br. 1993; M. Kehl, *Wohin geht die Kirche?*, Freiburg i. Br. 1996; C. M. Martini (ed.), *Un tempo di grazia. Quale futuro per la Chiesa?*, Milan 2000; H. Küng, *Ist die Kirche noch zu retten?*, Munich 2011. From the perspective of social science, see F. X. Kaufmann, *Kirchenkrise. Wie überlebt das Christentum?*, Freiburg i. Br. 2011.

2 See section I.8.

3 See section II.5.7.

4 F. Nietzsche, *Die fröhliche Wissenschaft*, (*The Gay Science*, Mineola, NY: Dover Publ. 2006) in: *Werke. Kritische Gesamtausgabe* (ed. Schlechta) vol. 2, Munich 1955, 126–8.205f.; M. Heidegger, *Erläuterungen zu Hölderlins Dichtung* (*Elucidations of Hölderlin's Poetry*, Amherst, NY: Humanity Books, 2000), Frankfurt a.M. 1951, 27; M. Buber, *Gottesfinsternis. Betrachtungen über die Beziehungen zwischen Religion und Philosophie* (WW 1; *Eclipse of God: Studies in the Relation between Religion and Philosophy*), Munich 1962, 503–603. See section II.6.2.4, note 163.

5 On this detail, see W. Kasper, *The God of Jesus Christ* (1982), London: Continuum 2012.

6 On the ambivalent topic of the return of religion, see ibid., 7–12.

7 LG 8. See sections I.8; II.4.2.2.

8 GS 76.

9 LG 8, 3.

10 See section II.6.2.4.

11 See section I.8.

12 F. Nietzsche, *Also sprach Zarathustra* (*Thus spoke Zarathustra*), in: *Werke. Kritische Gesamtausgabe* (ed. Schlechta), vol. 2, Munich 1955, 284f.

13 GS 76.

14 See note 4 above, and section II.6.2.4, note 163.

15 Pope John Paul II, Apostolic Letter *Novo millennio ineunte* (2001), 29. Benedict XVI has taken up this impulse in his two published volumes on Jesus Christ: *Jesus of Nazareth*, 2 vols, San Francisco: Ignatius Press 2008/2011. On Christology: W. Kasper, *Jesus the Christ* (1974), London: Burns & Oates, 1976.

16 W. Kasper (ed.), *Gegenwart des Geistes. Aspekte der Pneumatologie*, Freiburg i.Br. 1980; and, 'Kirche – Werk des Heiligen Geistes', in: M. Lutz-Bachmann/B. Schlegelberger (eds), *Krise und Erneuerung der Kirche: Theologische Ortsbestimmungen*, Berlin – Hildesheim 1989, 26–43.

17 W. Kasper, 'Neue Evangelisierung als theologische, pastorale und geistliche Herausforderung', in: WKGS 5, 235–317.

18 DH; GS 36, 41, 56, 76. See section II 6.2.4. On this, see W. Kasper, 'Autonomie und Theonomie. Zur Ortsbestimmung des Christentums in der modernen Welt', in: *Theologie und Kirche*, Mainz 1987, 140–75.

19 On the topic of the birth of God, see H. Rahner, *Symbole der Kirche. Die Ekklesiologie der Väter*, Salzburg 1964, 13–87.

20 See section I.3, note 7.

21 This was pointed out quite early by J. Ratzinger, *Die Krise der Katechese und ihre Überwindung. Rede in Frankreich. Mit Reden von D. J. Ryan; G. Danneels; F. Macharski*, Einsiedeln 1983; W. Kasper (ed.), *Einführung in den Katholischen Erwachsenenkatechismus*, Düsseldorf 1985; and, 'Das Glaubensbekenntnis der Kirche: Zum Entwurf eines neuen katholischen Erwachsenenkatechismus', in: IKaZ 3 (1984) 255–71; and, 'Der neue Katholische Erwachsenenkatechismus', in: KatBl 110 (1985) 363–70.

22 J. Ratzinger, *The Spirit of the Liturgy*, San Francisco: Ignatius Press 2000; W. Kasper, 'Aspekte einer Theologie der Liturgie. Liturgie angesichts der Krise der Moderne – Für eine neue liturgische Kultur', in: WKGS 10, 15–83.

23 SC 10; LG 11.

24 *Rule of Saint Benedict* 43, 3.

25 Augustine, *confessiones* IX, 6, 14.

26 D. Bonhoeffer, *Widerstand und Ergebung* (*Letters and Papers from Prison*, London: SCM 1981), new ed., Munich 1970, 413–16; A. Delp, *Mit gefesselten Händen. Aufzeichnungen aus dem Gefängnis*, Freiburg i. Br. 2007, 127–38.

27 *Catechism of the Catholic Church*, No. 2447.

28 See section II.5.5.

29 See section II.5.7.

30 On this, see H. U. von Balthasar, *Der antirömische Affekt. Wie lässt sich das Papsttum in die Gesamtkirche integrieren?*, Einsiedeln [2]1989.

ABBREVIATIONS

The abbreviations are taken from the lists of abbreviations in the *Lexikon für Theologie und Kirche*[3] (LThK), vol. 11, 692*–746*; and *The SBL Handbook of Style*, 89–152.

In addition:

HThK.Vat II	*Herders theologischer Kommentar zum Zweiten Vatikanischen Konzil*, 5 vol., ed. by P. Hünermann and B.J. Hilberath, Freiburg i.Br.: Herder, 2004–6.
JRGS	*Joseph Ratzinger Gesammelte Schriften*, ed. by G.L. Müller, Freiburg i.Br.: Herder, 2008ff.
ThiD	*Theologie im Dialog*, ed. by G. Augustin, K. Krämer and M. Schulze, Freiburg i.Br.: Herder, 2009ff.
WKGS	*Walter Kasper Gesammelte Schriften*, ed. by G. Augustin and K. Krämer, Freiburg i.Br.: Herder, 2007ff.
WKGS 2	W. Kasper, *Das Absolute in der Geschichte* (2010).
WKGS 3	W. Kasper, *Jesus der Christus* (2007). (= *Jesus the Christ*, London: T&T Clark 2011).
WKGS 4	W. Kasper, *Der Gott Jesus Christi* (2008). (= *The God of Jesus Christ*, London: Continuum 2012).
WKGS 5	W. Kasper, *Das Evangelium Jesu Christi* (2009).
WKGS 10	W. Kasper, *Die Liturgie der Kirche* (2010).
WKGS 11	W. Kasper, *Die Kirche Jesu Christi* (2008).
WKGS 12	W. Kasper, *Die Kirche und ihre Ämter* (2009).

INDEX